T5-ASQ-343

Melanesians and Missionaries

MELANESIANS AND MISSIONARIES

An Ethnohistorical Study of Social and Religious Change in the Southwest Pacific

Darrell L. Whiteman

LIBRARY OF CONGRESS CATALOGING IN PUBLICATION DATA

Whiteman, Darrell L. 1947–
Melanesians and Missionaries

Bibliography: p
Includes index.
1. Missions—New Hebrides. 2.Missions—Solomon Islands. 3. Culture conflict—New Hebrides. 4. Culture conflict—Solomon Islands. 5. New Hebrides—Social conditions. 6. Solomon Islands—Social conditions. 7. Melanesians—Cultural assimilation. I. Title.
BV3675.W48 1983 306'.6'0993'4 83-1192
ISBN 0–87808–334–0

PUBLISHED BY
WILLIAM CAREY LIBRARY
P.O. Box 40129, Pasadena, CA 91114
1705 N. Sierra Bonita, Pasadena, CA 91104
(818) 798-0819

TYPESET BY BOZOTRONICS, SEATTLE
PRINTED BY McNAUGHTON AND GUNN LITHOGRAPHERS, ANN ARBOR

Printed in the United States of America.

To Laurie
my friend

Go to the people, live among them,
learn from them, love them.
Start with what they know
build on what they have.

— *old Chinese poem*

Contents

The Contact Period — 1850-1900

The Period of Penetration — 1900-1942

The Period of Absorption — 1942-1975

The Period of Autonomy — 1975-Present

Conclusion

Illustrations

FIGURES

MAPS

Tables

Abbreviations

A.J.C.P.	Australian Joint Copying Project (microfilm)
B.S.I.P.	British Solomon Islands Protectorate
C.O.	Colonial Office, London
COM	Church of Melanesia
LMS	London Missionary Society
M.M.R.	Melanesian Mission, *Annual Report*
N.L.A.	National Library of Australia, Canberra
P.I.M.	*Pacific Islands Monthly*
S.C.L.	*Southern Cross Log,* Australian and New Zealand edition
S.C.L.E.	*Southern Cross Log,* English edition
SDA	Seventh Day Adventists
SPCK	The Society for Promoting Christian Knowledge
SPG	Society for the Propogation of the Gospel
SSEC	South Sea Evangelical Church
SSEM	South Sea Evangelical Mission
W.P.A.	Western Pacific Archives, Suva
W.P.H.C.	Western Pacific High Commission: Inward Correspondence

Preface

This book is a positive but critical description and analysis of social and cultural changes that have resulted from the interaction of Melanesians with European Anglican missionaries. It is a book for anthropologists, historians and missiologists and should be of value to anyone interested in the missionary enterprise. For many years I have had a keen interest in understanding how missionaries function as agents of change. This interest was probably kindled initially during a two-year stint as a mission volunteer in Central Africa where I observed missionaries first hand and began asking some probing questions about their impact, their effectiveness, and the Africans' perception and understanding of their work, etc. But this book is about Melanesia, not Africa.

The primary stimulus that led me to study the Anglicans in Melanesia was Alan Tippett's seminal work, *Solomon Islands Christianity*. In trying to understand the factors that led up to Silas Eto's breakaway movement from the Methodist Mission, he compared the Methodists over and against the Anglican Melanesian Mission. When Tippett suggested one day that the Melanesian Mission would make an exciting, in-depth, ethnohistorical study, I was hooked. The Anglicans had compiled an impressive record when compared to the other missions in the area, and the documents they left behind were rich in ethnographic data and demonstrated a cultural empathy and sensitivity for Melanesians and their culture. My task was a herculean one, but it has also been a very enjoyable one.

I want to note briefly how this book is organized and make some suggestions which may be helpful as a guide to the reader. Chapter 1 is primarily anthropological. Those readers interested in the theoretical foundation of this study will find culture change theory, ethnohistorical method, analytical framework, and hypotheses discussed in this opening chapter. Chapter 2 is once again primarily anthropological in scope and will interest those readers who want to understand in some depth various aspects of traditional Melanesian society and culture. These first two chapters lay the theoretical and ethnographic foundation for the next three chapters, which are primarily historical and focus on the 125-year period of the Melanesian Mission. Nevertheless, as you will discover, there is a lot of anthropology and missiology woven through these chapters.

With the previous chapters serving as a foundation, Chapter 6 is primarily the result of my fieldwork in the Solomon Islands. It describes and analyzes the Church of Melanesia today, and pursues the question, "What does it mean to a Melanesian to be a Christian within the Anglican tradition that was introduced by missionaries over a 125-year period?"

Foreword

What a pleasure to be asked to write a Foreword for this kind of missiological book which clearly belongs to the new age of mission! When I went out to the mission field before World War II it was certainly still the heyday of Colonialism. Missionaries of my day and generation were trained in theology, but not in anthropology. We had to learn that the hard way in the field situation. The most exciting thing of those days was to experience the transition from foreign mission to indigenous church. For seventeen years I was engaged in that process after I had reacted against the colonial paternalism for an introductory term. I learned to serve as a subordinate under an island Superintendent, and found it a mind-stretching experience.

Now Colonialism has gone and my generation of the transition has gone with it. But I was to enter still another phase of missionary change. I was teamed with Dr. Donald McGavran in developing a theory of mission appropriate to a new era, trying to give it an anthropological undergirding which was not available during my years of training. When the sending churches in America, after a long battle, accepted the fact that the discipline of anthropology could be Christian, we suddenly found ourselves in demand at consultations and seminars all over the country and we were asked to do research in field mission situations around the Third World. In Pasadena, the School of World Mission became a significant research centre for national leaders and mid-term missionaries who were confronting a new era of mission. We denied that the day of mission was dead, and I think we proved our point.

It was at one of those conferences in Florida where missionaries and anthropologists were confronting each other that I first met Darrell Whiteman face to face. We developed a warm friendship and in time we might well have claimed the Pauline designation of "fellow-labourers" in Christ. We have attended anthropological conferences together, each presenting papers, often in the same symposium, and have shared our joys and problems. We differed at one point. My vision was one of current transition from the old to the new. He stood in the transition with his vision in the new day. Now with my allotted three score years and ten behind me my travelling days are done, and I am content to lay aside my armour. A new day has come and a new generation has been born.

My young comrade will carry on hopefully for many years after I have crossed the river. And now he has written a book — and what a book! How my heart warms that he should want me to write the Foreword! Quite beyond my personal pleasure at this, I can honestly say that this book, *Melanesians and Missionaries*, is a truly significant piece of work. It is a revised and updated version of a doctoral dissertation in ethnohistory, which means that it is far more than a piece of popular journalism.

His perceptions of what actually happened in the periods of contact and Colonialism are remarkable. As a missionary case study both his historical and anthropological contexts are, I believe, accurately depicted. His evaluations are fair and far more objective than those of many historians and anthropologists who have written purely from the slant of their own disciplines regardless of the methodology of the other. Darrell Whiteman stands between the disciplines. The book is a good model on historiography for the anthropologist, and a good model on anthropological research methods for the historian.

Melanesians and Missionaries opens up a whole new world of important resource material in missionary letters and journals as a "data base" for research. It challenges the superficial view that all missionaries have been foreign destroyers of culture, and demonstrates that if some have been culturally ethnocentric, others have revealed remarkable anthropological perception long before the contours of a discipline of anthropology had taken shape. The adequate recognition of this fact has been long overdue.

In this book Dr. Whiteman stands back and surveys the history of a Mission in Melanesia through the Pre-contact, Contact and Colonial Periods quite objectively, and this he can do because he himself belongs to the Post-Colonial Period. The same fact makes the book so essential for this New Age. He is sufficiently detached from Colonialism, but not too far-distant from it. He can consider both documentary material and indigenous informants with a kindly, yet critical objectivity. He writes with a forward vision with respect to his own missionary paradigm; but without the defensiveness that writers of my generation (maybe with the same paradigm) would feel obliged to make in their evaluations, especially if they had first to convince their own generation that the day for change had arrived.

Many key missiological issues are discussed in depth, such as nativistic reactions to the Colonial Order, and the precise dynamics of the transition from Mission to Church. These are not really new issues but are viewed from a close, but not too close, distance, such as should benefit missionary trainees of the new era. As an analysis of the phenomenology of religious change (conversion), and the formal institutionalizing of new religious structures, the volume is a rich mine of information, both in its description of phenomena and its extensive documentation. It is a great bibliographical card index for every Professor of Missions, or to change the metaphor, a road map for every scholar in missiology.

As a study of socioreligious change, which must have a diachronic dimension, Dr. Whiteman shows how the strategy of mission under different bishops varied within clear-cut periods. He discloses the effects of these policy changes on the emerging church structures. He is using the model of the cultural continuum from ethnohistory which is a dynamic treatment of history as over and against the formal listing of events and dates.

The book is a beautiful case study in missiography for missionary historians as well as the general reader. One confronts Bishop Patteson's concept of "the Melanesian ethos," for example, and observes its effect in his day, and again how this is later threatened by the paternalism of one of his successors. One sees the growing Melanesian reaction against Colonialism, and a wide sweep of nativism. Whiteman includes a survey of "Marching Rule" as an example of this nativistic reaction, which is better documented than any other survey of which I know.

Any one of these issues might have claimed a book in itself, a synchronic study at a point in time; but Darrell Whiteman, with anthropological holism, places these units of change in a developing chronology, a continuing stream of innovative activity that reveals the emerging Christian community in a cultural continuum. It makes a fine case study.

This kind of dynamic writing fills a crying need in our church and mission histories. Dr. Whiteman is a good ethnohistorian and he has used his method well, bringing together his documentary resources and his field research in village situations in Melanesia. Theory grows out of field situations and, after being related to documents in archives and libraries, is tested again back in the field, and thereafter can be used as a model for collecting, classifying and interpreting data. Once again, the book is a good case study in missionary historiography. In the same way, the opening chapter is a good survey of the theory of applied anthropology relating to "directed change" and offers the reader a set of conceptual models for pulling together the kind of data one collects in studying a Melanesian religious community in a continuum of change.

Although *Melanesians and Missionaries* is a book of and for the Post-Colonial Age, it draws a great many insights from the missionary anthropology of the transitional period. For example, the missionary is portrayed as the innovative advocate, but not the innovator. It is the islander who, in accepting the innovation (new religion), becomes the innovator, and, in point of fact, gives it its meaning. Or again, rather than depicting the islander as a passive, dominated figure in a "culture clash" event, the islander is seen as a creative actor in a drama of "culture contact," giving the meaning to any accepted innovation.

These are only two of many links with the missionary anthropology of my generation. This book is not new in the sense of being entirely different, but only in that it proceeds from the transitional period into the new, retaining much that is surely worth preserving, and reaching out beyond into Tomorrow. As an historical study it draws from the Past and interprets the Past for the good of the Future.

Darrell Whiteman's book is thus itself part of a continuum — a missiological continuum. All stages from the beginning of Christian Mission have shared a common paradigm in the Great Commission which has given us our goals, and our criteria for testing; but there have been many differences in the time units of the sequence. Twenty years ago my generation of missiologists was confronting such *cliches* as "Missionary, Go Home," and "The day of the mission is dead," and we had our battles to fight. We know that the Christian Mission began with the first coming of Christ and goes on until His coming again.

Through this continuum there are many phases. The day of Colonialism has gone. I began in it and saw it die. I belong to a liminal period between Colonial and Post-Colonial times. I think our work is done now. Our battles of transition have been fought. The new era belongs to younger men.

I put this book in the new period rather than the liminal one, because it could not have been written in the days of my training, and it can only be written now because the battles of the transition have been won. The findings of the book are important for Christian Mission today and tomorrow; but so, too, are its methodology of research, its mastery of anthropological theory, its superb documentation, and the way it presents a cultural continuum as a dynamic process.

It is certainly not a promotional missionary book, but a missiological textbook, which I trust missionary educators, administrators and field missionaries will come to grips with. How I wish there had been this kind of case study for young missionaries in my training days fifty years ago! But that could not have been. Anthropology and ethnohistory had to be explored and applied, and missiology had to emerge before this kind of book either could be written or be acceptable as missionary literature.

But now as the obstructions of Colonialism have been removed, the resources for research have been explored, and the anthropological criteria for evaluations have been articulated (the major issues faced in our transitional years), a "New Era" has now begun and a "great and effectual door is open to us." So, although this book reflects on the Past, it belongs in the new age, and I gladly recommend it to all thoughtful people with missionary concern. Grappling with issues raised in this book will bring the insights needed for the New Age of Post-Colonial Mission. It will help the new generation to be obedient to the mandate set before it still —the Great Commission.

A. R. Tippett
Research Fellow
St. Mark's Library
Canberra, Australia.

MARIANA ISLANDS
NORTH P
PHILIPPINES
GUAM
MICRONESIA
CAROLINE ISLANDS
INDONESIA
MELANESIA
NAURU
Manus
New Ireland
New Britain
SOLOMON ISLANDS
Bougainville
Choiseul
NEW GUINEA
Santa Isabel
New Georgia
Malaita
Guadalcanal
Santa Cr
San Cristobal
Banks'
Espiritu Santo
Pentec
Malekula
Tana
VANUAT
(New Hebrid
NEW CALEDONIA
AUSTRALIA
Norfo
Sydney
NEW ZEALAND

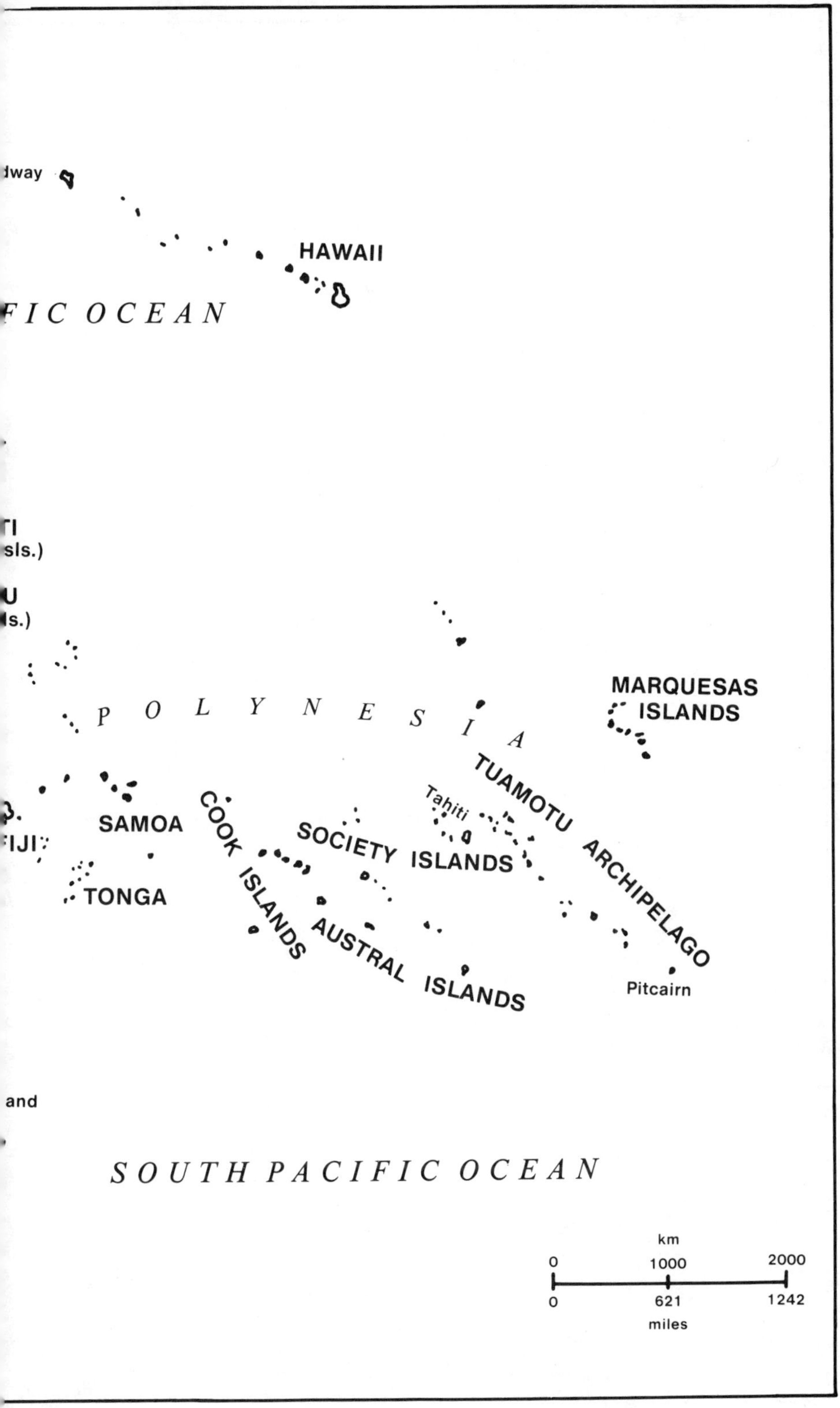

dway

HAWAII

FIC OCEAN

TI
sls.)

U
ls.)

MARQUESAS ISLANDS

P O L Y N E S I A

TUAMOTU ARCHIPELAGO

Tahiti

SAMOA

FIJI

COOK ISLANDS

SOCIETY ISLANDS

TONGA

AUSTRAL ISLANDS

Pitcairn

and

SOUTH PACIFIC OCEAN

km
0 1000 2000
0 621 1242
miles

Chapter 1

Missionaries and Culture Change

At mid-day on the 20th of September, 1871, Bishop John Coleridge Patteson went ashore on the small coral atoll of Nukapu in the Reef Islands. These Polynesian-speaking inhabitants knew him from five previous visits, and he felt he had nothing to fear. He had visited the island the previous year and had exchanged names with Moto, one of the island's chiefs. It was low tide when the ship's boat, with Patteson and a crew of four, reached the outlying reef nearly two miles from shore. The water was too shallow for the boat to cross the reef and enter the lagoon, so only Patteson transferred into a waiting canoe belonging to Moto and went ashore.

Reaching the island he entered a palm-leaf canoe house to rest while Moto went to procure food for his guest. As Patteson lay down on a mat reserved for guests, an islander named Teandule came in from behind and dealt him a fatal blow, crushing the right side of his skull with a heavy wooden mallet used for beating tapa cloth.

Meanwhile, the ship's boat, lying beyond the reef, had been surrounded by four canoes at about ten yards distance. Nearly three-quarters of an hour after Patteson had gone ashore, the men in the canoes began shouting and shooting arrows at those in the boat, injuring three of them. They managed, however, to raise the boat's sail and row back to the ship where they were lifted on board to have the bone-tipped arrows removed.

The men then went back in the boat to search for Patteson on shore. By 4:00 p.m. the tide was sufficiently high to allow the boat to cross the reef and enter the lagoon. As the crew drew near the shore they observed a woman paddling out in a canoe and pulling what appeared to be an empty one behind her. As the boat came closer she let the canoe go adrift. Inside was the body of Patteson, prepared for burial and wrapped in a mat. All his clothes, except his shoes and socks, had been removed and on his chest lay a sago palm frond tied in five knots.[1]

The murder of Bishop Patteson at Nukapu became an important historic event in Melanesia. It was a catalyst in bringing stronger regulations to bear on the labor trade, for there had been increasing abuses in the practice of securing islanders to work the sugar plantations of Queensland and Fiji, and the blame for Patteson's death was laid at this door.[2]

In addition to its historical significance, Patteson's death is an important anthropological event, for in microcosm it focuses our attention on the complex problems of culture contact in Melanesia during the last half of the nineteenth century. The interaction of diverse types of Europeans with Melanesians set in motion different kinds of indigenous responses and subsequent cultural changes. What is the cultural significance of the attack made on Patteson and his companions? What did the periodic visits of the mission ship, *Southern Cross*, mean to the residents of Nukapu and the many other islands in Melanesia where it called? How did they interpret Patteson's purpose and presence in the islands? What kinds of culture change resulted from the Melanesian Mission's contact with the islanders?

These are some of the important questions I will attempt to answer in this study, for I am interested in the changing culture of Melanesia and the role of European Christian missionaries in that change process. Because much of this study is organized chronologically, it may appear that this is a history of the Melanesian Mission, but it is more than that.[3] It is in fact a study of culture change, concerned with the broader and more theoretical question of what kinds of changes missionaries introduce, and how potential indigenous converts respond. The study takes place in the cultural-geographical area of Melanesia in the Southwest Pacific. The principal protagonists in the unfolding drama are Anglican missionaries with the Melanesian Mission, and Melanesian islanders. This study will look at what happened when these two groups interacted with one another.

However, it is important to realize that the Melanesian Mission was not an isolated agent of change in this part of the Pacific. Explorers, whalers, sandalwood traders, labor recruiters, and later, colonial administrators and other missions, all brought their own interests and subsequent demands on the islanders with whom they interacted.[4] Each of these alien contacts brought ideas and materials that set in motion changes in Melanesian society and culture.

Most people, when they stop to think about it, would agree that missionaries bring about cultural changes, but there is a fair amount of heated debate about whether or not they should be doing so. Those antagonistic toward missionaries believe they have no right to be meddling in natives' lives, destroying their cultures. Those who are sympathetic toward missionaries often believe that the missionary's "higher calling" gives him license, if not a mandate, to introduce as many changes as possible to native people and their culture. In this debate there is often a conspicuous absence of attention given to an objective analysis of specific case studies of missionaries. Unfortunately, people's preconceived notions arising from their philosophical presuppositions frequently preclude them from looking at missionary work in an objective manner. Instead, they look for anecdotal material to support their assumptions, and of course there is plenty to be found, on both sides of the debate.

Is there some way out of this subjective woods? I think there is. I believe that the clearest path will be found when we objectively study missionaries as agents of change. This will require an objective analysis of the facts, but also a sensitive and sympathetic understanding of the experiential dimension. We need to analyze missionaries as agents of change instead of anecdotally writing them off as pompous proselytizers. We need to understand indigenous converts as active, creative innovators instead of assuming they are simply dupes, passively acquiescing to missionary manipulation. When one takes this approach to this controversial discussion, it soon becomes clear that traditional stereotypes are woefully inadequate to describe what happens when missionaries and potential converts interact. This is what I have attempted to do in this book in hopes that it will shed some empirical light on this heated debate.

The Study of Culture Change

Before we get into the topic of missionaries as agents of change, it will be helpful to see where this kind of study fits into the general pattern of anthropological research and the study of culture change. The subject of change has attracted anthropologists from the inception of their discipline. Granted, early anthropology developed within the paradigm of unilinear evolution and its preoccupation was in assimilating ethnographic data to develop the "stages" of man's evolutionary progress. These nineteenth century arm-chair theorists were concerned with culture change in the sense that they were interested in plotting man's "progress" up the evolutionary ladder from the stage of "savagery" to "civilization."[5]

By the turn of the century these grand evolutionary schemes were beginning to crumble for want of supporting ethnographic data. The anthropological pendulum began swinging away from evolution toward diffusion. English, German and American schools of thought developed distinctly different theories and methodological approaches to the study of diffusion.[6] However, their common concern with culture change was related to the problem of how cultural elements and complexes move through time and space. The diversity of cultures was no longer explained in terms of their place in an evolutionary sequence, but by the degree to which they had borrowed items and ideas from other cultures.

In the 1920's and 1930's a surge of American anthropological interest in culture change took the form of acculturation studies, focusing primarily on American Indians. Simultaneously in Britain, anthropologists began turning their attention to the changing African societies under the impact of colonialism, in what was subsequently termed the study of culture contact.[7] This shift in emphasis was important. It signaled a change in interest from salvage anthropology which was concerned primarily with reconstructing the pre-contact cultures of a given society, to an interest in indigenous societies undergoing rapid culture change as a result of the impact of Western dominance and influence.

Some scholars such as Kroeber (1948: 426) viewed the new emphasis as a mere fad, noting there had been "a sudden interest, almost excitement, beginning about 1920-25 and culminating perhaps in 1935-40." From his perspective of 1948 he believed the phase would soon pass. However, it has not passed, as a cursory review of recent Ph.D. dissertation research in this field demonstrates.[8]

The study of acculturation reached new levels of rigor and systematic analysis in the 1936 "Memorandum" authored by Redfield, Linton and Herskovits.[9] It brought an important codification of the numerous variables involved in this type of culture change, and was instrumental in ushering in a decade or more of systematic structured acculturation studies.[10]

Central to the concept and study of acculturation is the person(s) who as a carrier of one cultural tradition comes into contact with another culture and actively advocates changes in its members. These people are engaged in what Linton (1940: 502) calls "directed culture change." As noted above, the agents of change making their impact on Melanesia have been both numerous and diversified. The first were explorers in the region,[11] followed later by whalers and then sandalwood and *beche-de-mer* traders for the lucrative Chinese market. Missionaries, labor recruiters and finally government officials followed in suit. These have all been significant agents of change as acculturative forces from the West.

By studying how indigenes and Europeans interact through time, we can further our understanding of how and why people in a given cultural context choose to change their behavior and cultural traditions. Moreover, we also learn a great deal about the complement to change such as cultural stability, persistence and continuity. In studying the dynamics of culture one learns about the stability of culture.[12]

To date there have been very few field studies focusing on the missionary as an agent of culture change.[13] However, the recent (1975) symposium on "Missionary Activity in Oceania" organized by the Association for Social Anthropology in Oceania, and the symposium on "Missionaries, Anthropologists and Culture Change" at the XIth International Congress of Anthropological and Ethnological Sciences (1983), indicates a growing interest in dealing with this vast body of data.[14] One of the aims of this study is to help fill that lacuna in anthropological research by analyzing the process of change that occurs when an indigenous population encounters Christian missionaries.

In addition to focusing on the missionary as an agent of culture change, this study will consider the indigene's own innovative role in responding creatively and dynamically to the proposals advocated by the missionary.

Too much of our anthropological research has portrayed indigenes as passive recipients and ignored their dynamic and innovative activity in the change process. This study will explore what the missionaries did to the Melanesians. But, perhaps more importantly, it will seek to understand what the Melanesians did, that is, how they interpreted the missionaries' messages, why they choose to become converts, and what it means to a Melanesian convert to be a Christian in his own society. The models of culture change that I have used to do this study will be briefly explained in the following section.

Some Models of Culture Change

I want to make explicit the models that have served as the foundation for investigating the culture change resulting from missionary-islander interaction in Melanesia. I have found the combination of three approaches to the study of culture change to be the most salient framework for study and investigation. The first of these approaches is the model of innovation developed by anthropologist Homer G. Barnett. The second one is inspired by Arthur Niehoff's (1966) discussion of the relationship between the people advocating change and those accepting it. The third approach from F. E. Williams (1935), looks at how directed culture change, such as we have with Anglican missionaries in Melanesia, results in the blending of cultures. A brief discussion of each of these approaches will now follow.

Innovation.

The Melanesians did not passively acquiesce to missionary proposals for change, but rather, they actively responded by either rejection of the proposed change, or innovative acceptance and modification. H. G. Barnett (1940, 1941, 1942a, 1942b, 1953, 1961, 1965) has made a major contribution to our understanding of culture change by focusing on what the innovator does in the process of culture change. Barnett deals with advocacy, innovation, acceptance, rejection, and modification — all important elements in any theory of culture change. The essence of his theory is that all culture change, whether from within the society or advocated from without, involves the fundamental socio-psychological process of individual innovation.

What does this mean in terms of our present study? It means that social and religious changes were advocated by the missionaries, who in this study, are called advocates of cultural change. But the new ideas of the missionaries, introduced from outside the culture, were understood and interpreted by Melanesians in terms of the ideas already existing in their culture. The Melanesians, not the missionaries, were the innovators. Barnett (1953: 7) defines an innovation as "any thought, behavior, or thing that is new because it is qualitatively different from existing forms." The emphasis in this model is on the reorganization of ideas rather than on quantitative variation. Culture change takes place **not** when there is just more or less of the same thing, but when an idea, a behavior pattern or a material object is qualitatively different from existing forms. Barnett (1953: 9) puts it this way: "Innovation does not result from the addition or subtraction of parts. It takes place only when there is a recombination of them." The culture change introduced into Melanesia by Anglican missionaries occurred when Melanesians recombined the ideas introduced from outside with the pre-existing ideas already in their culture. There are of course an infinite number of possible recombinations of cultural elements, but the basic processes are limited to a set few.[15] In **Appendix 2**, this model of culture change is further elaborated and applied to this study, showing how ideas introduced into Melanesia by missionaries were recombined with the ideas already existing in the minds of the Melanesians.

What is important for our purposes is to see how Barnett's model of innovation is especially useful for understanding the process of acculturation.[16] His model draws our attention to the fact that the locus of culture change is the individual innovator and not some grand mechanistic scheme of cultural determinism whereby culture change inevitably follows a set pattern. This now leads us to the second model.

The Arena of Advocate-Innovator Interaction.

In this study attention is focused on the cultural arena of Melanesia where islanders and missionaries came into direct contact with each other for extended periods of time. The missionary as an advocate of change and the indigene as a potential receptor (innovator) form the dynamic relationship in the change process.

Niehoff (1966) has made a significant contribution in furthering our understanding of this process. Drawing on Barnett, he developed a model specific to the advocate-innovator relationship. He states (1966: 40) that directed socio-cultural change "is a process that begins with an idea on the part of a change agent and ends in its adoption or rejection by the potential recipients." Niehoff envisions the process as one of action on the part of the agent of change (advocate) and reaction on the part of the recipients (innovators). He notes that:

> . . . action is basically the body of techniques and strategies that are employed to convince the recipients to adopt the idea, whereas the reaction is the attitudes and behavior that stem from the recipients' perception of the value of the innovation and their motivations, which are products of how the idea was presented and of the ways in which the new idea will affect their traditional customs (1966: 40).

change process? Neihoff (1966: 12-41) lists eight sets of characteristics of the change agent which will determine what kind of role he plays in the interaction setting, and nine characteristics of the recipients which will determine whether they accept, reject, or modify the proposed idea.[20]

Niehoff (1966: 40-41) reduced his list of seventeen characteristics to six which he calls the "primary process variables." The first three relate to the role of the agent of change:

1. The methods of communication used by the agent of change,
2. The kind of participation he obtains from the recipients, and
3. The manner in which he utilizes and adapts the change he advocates into the existing cultural patterns.

The last three "primary process variables" relate to the role of the recipient or indigenous innovator:

4. The degree to which the potential recipients experience a felt need for that which is advocated,
5. The degree to which their traditional leaders are brought into the planning and implementation of the process,
6. Whether the recipients perceive any practical benefit in adopting the proposed change.

Although their terminology is different, Barnett and Niehoff are in agreement as to the fundamental process of culture change. While Barnett emphasizes the process of innovation in the mind of the innovator, Niehoff puts greater emphasis on the role of the agent of change, stressing that his "performance" is frequently the most critical variable in determining whether his proposed change will be accepted or not. Too often we shift the "blame" for rejection of the proposed change onto the traditional societies which we assume are inherently conservative. In point of fact it is often our blundering lack of cross-cultural awareness that causes our proposed change to be rejected.

In this study I will be focusing on these primary process variables in an attempt to arrive at an explanation of why Melanesians perceived and responded to the change advocated by missionaries in the way that they did. Why, for example, did Melanesians reject some of the changes advocated by missionaries? Why were some accepted without alteration while others were greatly modified in the process of reintegration into the indigenous cultural context?

This brings into focus a primary problem — that of meaning. As Boas (1903) pointed out years ago, meaning is not tied intrinsically to form.[21] This is especially true when cultural forms or ideas are introduced cross-culturally. The meaning that a particular cultural form may have for the advocate is seldom the same meaning that the recipients will give to it. This is because the meaning of a cultural form is tied to a specific cultural context. If a form is removed from one culture and reinstated in another, the meaning it has for people in the first context will nearly always be different from the meaning people will give it in another context. The problem of meaning is probably the most difficult area with which an agent of change must deal. It is one of the main problems missionaries face in their communication of the Gospel.

In terms of Barnett's model, the introduced cultural form or idea (novelty) must connect with a configuration in the mind of the potential recipient if it is to have meaning. He notes (1953: 334-35) that,

> Meaning is the insight which comes when the idea of the presented thing is referable to the idea of some past experience. It is an evidence of contact, the idea of the one thing being understood in terms of its mental associates.

Unless some kind of meaning can be assigned to an introduced novelty it will not survive in the new cultural context. It will be rejected by the potential recipients. If some meaning is assigned to it, it is very unlikely to be identical with the meaning given to it by the agent of change. This problem is underscored by Barnett (1953: 338) who notes that,

> The significance of a novelty must be understood to be the meaning it has for the acceptor. This is not necessarily the meaning that it has for its introducer. The identifications of an introducer or of an observer need not, and often do not coincide with the equations made by individuals who are the acceptors or rejectors.

This problem is particularly relevant in an analysis of missionary contact. In advocating the adoption of Christianity by Melanesians, missionaries, like administrators, teachers, and doctors in cross-cultural situations, frequently assumed that it would have the same meaning for the islanders in their context as it did for the missionaries in theirs.[22]

The Blending of Cultures.

A third model I want to consider is one developed by F. E. Williams who worked for two decades in Papua New Guinea as a government anthropologist. He was of course concerned with applied anthropology and so he attempted to relate his anthropological research to the problems of colonial administration and acculturation. Out of this context came an important essay on, *The Blending of Cultures* (1935). In this essay Williams developed a model to demonstrate how the interaction of indigenous Melanesian cultures and Western agents of change produced a blending of cultures in a new form that was neither wholly Melanesian nor European, but a blending of elements from each.[23]

Whereas Barnett deals with the process of innovation and change, and Niehoff directs our attention to the factors that inhibit or promote the adoption of proposed change, Williams' contribution is oriented from the perspective of the advocate of directed change. It is a model for the change agent to follow if his proposals are to be meaningfully integrated and not disruptive to the indigenous society.

In the culture contact situation there are two diametrically opposed views regarding change in indigenous societies. One position calls for total noninterference on the part of Western agents of change, and the other calls for a complete change in the indigenous society. Not infrequently anthropologists have been accused of promoting the former position and missionaries the latter.[24] Williams rejects both. He suggests that the ideal should lie somewhere in between them — in the blending of cultures.

This ideal blend will retain the best of the indigenous cultures (from an anthropological perspective) while removing some features that are disruptive in the indigenous culture, or are clearly incompatible with the ideal envisaged or no longer relevant to the changing situation. A cultural void is not created by the removal of certain elements, for in their place, the agent of change advocates functional substitutes. Moreover, Williams' model does not call for only replacing indigenous features with European-inspired substitutes; he goes a step further in suggesting that positive borrowing from European culture be advocated, "such as will make the new blend something richer and fuller than the native has hitherto known." The result of this blending of cultures should be a substantial increase in cultural content, "for the necessary subtractions will be much less than the possible addition" (1935: 7).

There are three steps taken by the advocate in this process of directed cultural change:

1. Maintaining and encouraging those positive elements of indigenous culture which will comprise most of the culture. This is the task of **Maintenance.**
2. Removing from the indigenous culture those negative elements that will be incompatible with the projected new blend and thus likely to hinder its functioning. This step is the task of **Expurgation.**
3. Making positive contributions from European culture that will be functionally integrated into the new blend and thus expand the indigenes' cultural horizons. This is the task of **Expansion.**

While holding to a functional view of culture, Williams does not subscribe to a rigid mechanical model which suggests that every element is in harmony with all others, so much so that breakdown or dysfunction in one leads to dysfunction and collapse of the whole culture. He boldly states, (1935: 15)

> I venture to put forward the heterodox suggestion that the view of culture as an integrated, organized system has been carried too far. Culture is after all only the work of human minds and has been put together in a strangely haphazard manner. It would indeed be surprising then if we found it completely organized; nor,

> I think, do the facts justify such an assumption. The most that can be said of culture is that it is partially-organized, semi-integrated.

Williams (1935: 31) points out that the ultimate aim of culture is the preservation of society and thus in any program of directed cultural change, the "real task is to fit the culture to the man, rather than the man to the culture."[25] Society and culture are inseparable and yet, they arc analytically distinct entities, each subject to change, but change in different directions and at different rates.[26] Thus, a society can continue to exist irrespective of changes in its cultural content, for its existence is not dependent on a static cultural inventory.

Each culture has areas of imperfect fit — points where strains and stresses, abuses and maladjustments exist. Cultural imperfections thus open the door for change, and provide an appropriate avenue whereby the agent of change can advocate positive contributions of cultural borrowing and substitution.

Williams' model is a useful tool for analyzing the role of the Melanesian Mission in advocating change in Melanesian societies. At what points did the missionaries maintain and encourage the indigenous culture or advocate removal of certain elements they deemed inappropriate? At what point on the axis of non-interference versus complete change, did they advocate a "blending of cultures?" It will be interesting to observe how the "blending of cultures" changed over time and how the missionaries defined success and failure in their work accordingly.

Toward an Eclectic Model of Change.

I have briefly reviewed three models of culture change developed by Barnett, Niehoff and Williams in an attempt to develop a model for analyzing the interaction of Melanesians and missionaries. Barnett writing on advocacy, innovation, acceptance, rejection and the modification of ideas, has given us the fundamental process of culture change. Building on Barnett's concept of innovation, Niehoff has developed a model showing how an introduced idea eventually becomes integrated into the new cultural context or rejected altogether. He suggests a set of "primary process variables" that impinge on the contact situation and promote acceptance or rejection of the proposed change. He lays special emphasis on the change agent's role in influencing the response the recipients will make. Williams' model of the blending of cultures gives us a useful analytical tool for evaluating the cultural impact of an agent of change.

In reviewing the anthropological literature I have selected the writings of the above scholars whose theoretical contributions I believe are useful in building an eclectic model of culture change to account for the phenomenon of acculturation in Melanesian societies. I will use this model in analyzing the change which has transpired in Melanesia and the role of the Melanesian Mission in that process. The model that emerges is based on the following premises:

1. Although all cultures are functionally integrated, their integration is neither static nor rigid. It is an integration that strives for dynamic equilibrium.
2. Every culture is an adaptive system designed to meet the needs of a society's members. As such, it is open to change and demonstrates tremendous plasticity in its ability to adjust to a changing physical, social and ideological environment.
3. The role that an advocate of change may play is important in the process of innovation; however, in the final analysis, the decision to innovate and accept, modify or reject the proposed change, is determined by individual members of the recipient society.
4. Innovation is a socio-psychological process in which the final outcome of change is a product of both the configuration of the introduced ideas and its relationship to indigenous configurations existing in the minds of members of the recipient society.
5. The net result of indigenous societies under the impact of Western cultural influence is a blending of cultures, where the emerging form is a functioning combination of both indigenous and introduced elements.
6. The composition of this blending of cultures is a product of those changes advocated from outside the society, the methods employed by the agent of change in advocating change, and the indigenes' perception and subsequent response to that proposed change.

Methodology

Now that we have laid the theoretical foundation for this study I will turn my attention to the methodology employed. I believe any valid study of culture change must be based not only on synchronic (a single time dimension), but also on diachronic analysis, which analyzes change through time. To exclude the time dimension from a study of change is to deny the very context in which change takes place. Both Herskovits and Linton throughout their writings on cultural dynamics emphasize the importance of the historical dimension in any study of change. In Herskovits' study of acculturation (1938: 25), he cogently remarks that,

> It must be emphasized that the study of cultural change—or, for that matter, the study of culture as a whole—cannot be attempted without a vivid sense of the historically dynamic nature of the phenomenon. Hence, the more background that is available, the better the treatment; or, conversely, and even more importantly, the less the sense of history, the more sterile the results.

Anthropologists are now recovering from the ahistorical bias which once dominated social anthropology.[27] In this study I have employed ethnohistorical methods to develop a diachronic approach to the study of socio-cultural change.[28]

Ethnohistory is not a separate discipline with a set of theories independent of other theories in socio-cultural anthropology. As Carmack (1972: 232) notes,

> Ethnohistory is a special set of techniques and methods for studying culture through the use of written and oral traditions. As methodology it is complementary not only to archaeology, but also to historical linguistics, ethnography and paleobiology.[29]

In this study I use an ethnohistorical approach to understand how different cultural systems such as religion have functioned and changed over time. I am interested in the problem of how these systems have enabled Melanesian societies to maintain dynamic equilibrium even though they have undergone change.[30] Ethnohistorical methods have been used successfully by others interested in analyzing missionary influence in culture change.[31] If an ethnohistorical approach is followed, then there is,

1. A focus on the past conditions of cultures,
2. A utilization of either oral or written traditions and documentation as primary sources of data, and
3. An analysis of change over time in those cultures under study (Sturtevant 1966).

The Cultural Continuum and Ethnohistorical Research.

An ethnohistorical approach used in this study is one articulated by Dark (1957) in which he combines synchronic and diachronic analysis[32] in what he terms the "cultural continuum" approach or scheme.[33] By using the cultural continuum, an even balance is maintained between synchronic and diachronic analysis as

> . . . the culture of an ethnic group is shown developing over time, expanding or contracting spatially, its content and structure, altering and readjusting as it changes. Synthesis is spatial and temporal (Dark 1957: 243).

In studying culture change I am interested in structure and process, and therefore, the cultural continuum approach is suited ideally. It combines the analysis of both structural (synchronic) and developmental (diachronic) aspects of culture change, as illustrated in Figure 1.3. The direction of the arrows indicates that diachronic analysis is from one period to the next, but that synchronic analysis is also done within each period. The cultural continuum combines both methods in the study of culture change.

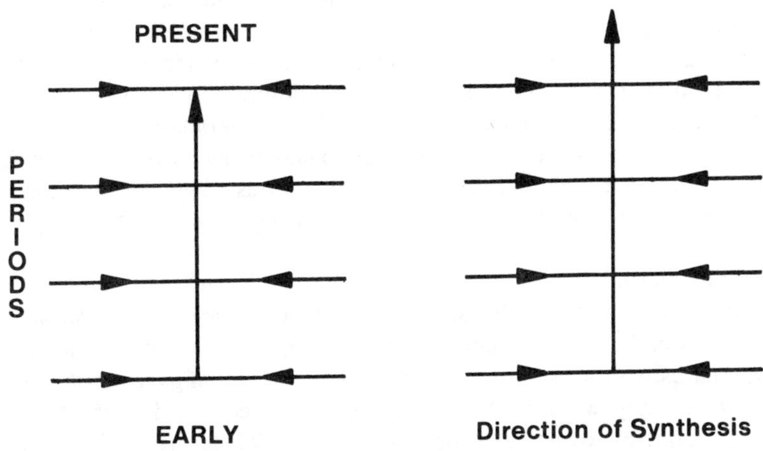

Fig. 3. The Cultural Continuum (after Dark 1957: 268).

If one uses a synchronic approach in analysis, attention is drawn to increasing one's understanding of the institutions within a given culture and their functional relationship to the whole at a single point in time. A sense of development is created by drawing arbitrary periods of time and giving a full synchronic analysis within each period. Since emphasis is on the synchronic analysis, the diachronic analysis is left in the background. Periods are juxtaposed in chronological order and thus development is only implied.

A contrasting approach emphasizes the diachronic dimension to the neglect of the synchronic. Emphasis is on the developmental aspects of particular institutions through time. Thus a study may emphasize the change in religion over time, but ignore the way in which religion may relate to other aspects of the culture within each period. This is particularly pertinent to the present study, for if there is one thing we have learned from studying the cultural impact of missions, it is that the introduction of religious change into a society seldom stops with religious change. It brings ramifications that reverberate throughout the culture.

The culture continuum uses both the synchronic (structural) and diachronic (developmental) approaches. This is why it has such value for an ethnohistorical study such as the present one dealing with the cultural impact of missionaries as agents of change through time. We are interested in how and why Melanesians converted to Christianity at different points in time. But we are also interested in how this religious change was related to other areas of Melanesian society and culture.

Using the cultural continuum scheme this study will focus on five synchronic levels. I have called these levels the pre-contact and contact periods, and the periods of penetration, absorption and autonomy.[34] An attempt will be made to give as full a cultural description as possible for each period. Hopefully the analysis will not be a compilation of disjointed synchronic studies. An effort will be made to understand how each synchronic level is related developmentally to other periods. This will be done by analyzing changes in particular institutions through time.[35]

The Data Base.

The primary data for this study come from two sources: (1) missionary documents in the form of reports, journals, diaries, letters, etc. written by the missionaries who lived in the islands and spoke the language of the people with whom they worked; (2) ethnographic data collected in the Solomon Islands during my own twelve months of fieldwork from April 1977, to April 1978. In doing an ethnohistorical study in which archival research is combined with fieldwork, I have attempted to present a holistic and diachronic view of culture change. By combining two distinct yet complementary research strategies, I believe I have arrived at a more comprehensive understanding of the missionary's role as an agent of change in Melanesia. Either method in isolation would not have yielded the holistic approach I have attempted to achieve.

Having discussed the theoretical foundation of culture change and the ethnohistorical methodology which has guided this study, we now need to briefly consider the analytical framework that has been used to organize it.

An Analytical Framework.

Spicer (1961) has developed an analytical framework for analyzing culture change in six American Indian societies. The approach adopted sought to discover the relationship between changes in Indian cultures and the conditions of contact under which those changes took place. The concept of a "contact community" was developed to define the social relationships that existed between Europeans and Indians at any given point in time. The nature of the contact community was a decisive factor in the kinds of culture change that transpired. The contact history for each culture was divided into periods based on the following criteria:

1. What was the nature of the structural linkage between the indigenous society and European intruders? That is, was it primarily ecclesiastical, political, economic, etc.? And, what was the nature of the combination of these different institutional linkages?
2. What kinds of roles and accompanying sanctions were assumed by Europeans in the contact situation and what was the kind and degree of power they had to enforce these sanctions?

3. How stable was the societal structure of the indigenous society in the contact situation? Were new types of communities already in the process of formation or decline before intensive contact?

Following Spicer's model, I will divide the contact history of Melanesia into different periods for analysis, employing the criteria outlined above. Periods are essentially characterized by differences in the reaction of Melanesians to European contact.

The Melanesian Mission began its contact with islanders in 1849 and ended its formal activity in 1975, when it became the autonomous Church of Melanesia. To understand the processes of change that occurred during this time, this era of mission contact, plus the pre-contact period, will be divided into the following five sequences:

Period I	**Pre-contact**	**prior to 1850**
Period II	**Contact**	**ca. 1850–1900**
Period III	**Penetration**	**ca. 1900–1942**
Period IV	**Absorption**	**ca. 1942–1975**
Period V	**Autonomy**	**ca. 1975 to present**

For each period, I will discuss the important historical events, the nature of the contact communities, and finally, the predominant type of change occurring in the period.[36] Chapters 2–6 in this book correspond with Periods I–V.

In this study attention is focused on the Melanesian Mission as the primary European component in the contact community. The nature and function of this community changed considerably during its 125-year history. For each period delineated within this study, the contact community will be analyzed in an attempt to discover answers to the following questions.[37] In what social structures did the participants in the different social systems interact, and in what social structures did they not jointly participate? What elements of the indigenous culture were the intruding Europeans interested in changing and how did they go about it? How did indigenes respond to such programs of change?

Hypotheses and Questions to Be Pursued

Spicer (1961: 519) notes that, "Essentially . . . what we are concerned with in the study of culture contact are processes of social and cultural integration which the coming-together of members of different societies sets in motion." He goes on to note that,

> . . . what has been most interesting about contact situations has been the wide variety in the results of contact. Every contact involves some degree of social and cultural integration, but there is a wide range in what become more or less stabilized situations with varying degrees of integration (1961: 519).

If this is so, then we need to investigate the degree to which change advocated by the Melanesian Mission became integrated into Melanesian societies.

Acknowledging the role indigenes play in innovation and missionaries play in advocacy, this study will attempt to answer the following questions: To what degree did introduced cultural elements become adopted and integrated into the recipients' culture? Was this integration a function of the way in which the advocate of change presented his ideas in culturally meaningful terms and/or was it dependent on the degree to which these ideas met the needs of individual members in the recipient society?

In the case of missionaries introducing Christianity, the adoption of the new religion by an indigenous population may take on a formal expression midway between polar positions: foreign or Western at one end, and indigenous or local at the other. At one end of the continuum the acceptor perceives the meaning of Christianity in totally foreign forms and thus copies the cultural modes of the missionary. At the other end of the continuum, the adoption of Christianity may be expressed through indigenous patterns and forms. The data from Melanesia demonstrate this in numerous ways. For example, at the level of material culture one is struck by the high degree of indigenous art-forms used in church architecture and decor, whereas the worship pattern has very little indigenous resemblance, borrowing formal prayers and singing from the Church of England in England, rather than developing an Anglican Melanesian pattern.

One of the problems this study explores is to understand why some Christian converts express their faith in familiar, local ways, whereas others use only foreign forms borrowed from the missionary.

A corollary to the problem articulated above is the notion that the degree to which the indigenous population formally expresses its adopted Christianity at either end of this foreign-indigenous axis, is dependent on ways in which the missionary introduces the new religion. If for example, he is paternalistic and fosters a posture of adherent dependence on himself, it is hypothesized that the formal expression of the adherent's religion will be similar to the missionary's in outward expression, and thus have a Western or foreign character. In such cases I would question the degree to which the new religion will become an integrated part of society. More than likely, it will remain obtrusive and foreign, not an integral part of the indigene's worldview and could even be an irritant.

If on the other hand, the missionary advocate is empathetic, non-paternalistic, and consciously encourages the expression of faith in indigenous rather than in Western forms, I would hypothesize that the adopted religion will integrate more readily into the indigenous society as a dynamic and functioning element.[38]

This points to two related problems in this study—one of felt needs, and the other of functional substitutes.

An incentive to innovate must be present if an innovation is to occur. The term "felt need" has come into usage to cover that set of psychological factors that motivate people to change their behavior and/or cultural inventory. Barnett uses the term "subliminal wants" to cover the same phenomenon. He notes that, "A need must be inwardly sensed by the individual, which is to say that it cannot be imputed to him by an observer on the basis of the latter's experience" (1953: 98).

This is indeed a crucial factor in many "aid programs" designed to improve the quality of life for people in the Third World. For example, what an American AID official might believe people need, may not, in any way, be perceived by them to be a need, and so his advocacy for change "falls on deaf ears."

This problem is encountered in the present study of missionary advocates. Regardless of how much a missionary believes that a pagan needs Christianity, a change in the indigene's religious system will not ensue unless the native perceives that by adopting the new religion his needs will be adequately met, or that the net gain in doing so will be greater than the net loss. Moreover, an indigene may choose to adopt "Christianity" because of the material goods that he perceives to be an inherent part of the introduced culture complex. Indeed, the data indicate that initially many islanders responded to the missionaries by accepting the material goods they offered, while rejecting the theology and ethical imperatives they advocated for the islanders to adopt. European material culture, not religion, or ethics, met the Melanesians' felt needs.[39]

The problem of functional substitutes will also be dealt with in this study. Rivers (1922) drew attention to the need for functional substitutes (although the term is not his) in his study of depopulation in Melanesia. He believed that the rapid decline of Melanesian populations was due primarily to their lack of interest in life—a psychological state of lethargy. This had developed, he reasoned, because Europeans prohibited behavior which was offensive to themselves, without replacing it with something that could fulfill the same or similar functions. Europeans simply did not realize how tightly integrated were the various Melanesian behavior patterns. Consequently serious cultural vacuums were created, when, for example, behavior such as headhunting was abolished by the government, and nothing replaced it that was functionally equivalent.

In the movement from animism to Christianity which has occurred in many parts of Melanesia, there have been many functional substitutes for the old religious system — innovative substitutes fulfilling time-honored functions. In this study I will examine the different functional substitutes the missionaries advocated, as well as discuss those which they could have, but did not, introduce.[40]

Another anthropological problem we will face in this study is the problem of communication. We will discover the significant linguistic difficulties encountered by the missionaries amidst the legion of Melanesian languages.

But cross-cultural communication is not just a linguistic problem; it is a philosophical and cultural one as well. When members of two diverse cultures interact they come to that situation with different worldviews, values, and presuppositions. It is difficult at best, if not impossible, for complete and accurate communication to occur between a pagan Melanesian and a European missionary, each operating with such different mental maps. And yet, this is the foundation on which directed culture change must proceed. Luzbetak (1963: 17) underscores the difficulties of cross-cultural communication by noting that,

> Whenever a message is sent from "outside" the culture, the message is necessarily clothed in the terms of that culture unless a positive effort is made to the contrary. Although in intercultural communication it may happen that at times the receiving society will try to interpret the message in terms of the sending society's way of life, such is generally not the case in regard to the missionary's message, which is interpreted (and misinterpreted) almost exclusively in terms of the receiving society's cultural experience. The communication that takes the receptor's cultural background into account has the best chance of remaining substantially unaltered and of being properly understood.[41]

Summary

This opening chapter has set the stage, so to speak, for the material to follow. In rather simplified terms I have spelled out how this study of Melanesian and missionary interaction is a study of culture change. Drawing on the seminal ideas of Barnett, Niehoff and Williams, I have developed a theoretical model that will help us understand the data that emerges. I have made explicit the ethnohistorical methodology used in this study and the analytical framework around which it is organized.

The major problem I have researched in this study is that of the role of missionaries as agents of culture change in Melanesia. This is accompanied by several related anthropological problems briefly mentioned above: the problem of meaning, felt needs, functional substitutes, and communication. I suggest that this research is relevant to anthropology because its extensive data base has been too long ignored, although it might well have contributed significantly to a better understanding of culture change in general and agents of change in particular. I believe this research is also relevant to historians because it emphasizes the active participation of the Melanesians instead of simply chronicling the names, dates and important events of the missionaries. And finally, I believe the case study as presented here is useful for missiologists who can examine their theoretical principles in light of actual events over a significant span of time.

CHAPTER 1 NOTES

1. Log book for the Melanesian Mission vessel *Southern Cross*, entry for Wednesday, September 20, 1871, Melanesian Mission Museum, Mission Bay, Auckland, New Zealand. For further discussion concerning the murder and surrounding events of Patteson's death see page 162, footnote 125. For published accounts of Patteson's death, cf. Yonge (1874, II: 566-569), Armstrong (1900: 120-122), Fox (1958: 25-27), Gutch (1971: 206-209), and Hilliard (1978: 66-71).

2. In her speech at the opening of Parliament in 1872, Queen Victoria mentioned the murder of Patteson in connection with the labor trade. In February of that year, the Pacific Islands Protection Bill was introduced into Parliament, and in the ensuing debate, Patteson's death was frequently mentioned and explicitly connected to abuses in the labor trade. The Bill was passed as the "Pacific Islands' Protection Act" in June, 1872, and came to be known as the Kidnapping Act. Cf. Great Britain, *Hansard's Parliamentary Debates*, 3rd series, 211 (1872: 184-189), Great Britain, *Parliamentary Papers*, Vol. 43, C.496, (1872: 97-107), Vol. 50, 244 (1873), Great Britain and Colonial Office (1873), Parnaby (1964: 3-7), Gutch (1971: 212-213), Hilliard (1978: 67-72).

   R. H. Codrington, writing in the Hobart *Mercury*, November 18, 1871, articulated the view of the Melanesian Mission concerning the incident:

   > There is very little doubt but that the slave trade which is desolating these islands was the cause of this attack . . . Bishop Patteson was known throughout the islands as a friend, and now even he is killed to revenge the outrages of his countrymen. The guilt surely does not lie upon the savages who executed, but on the traders who provoked the deed (quoted in Hilliard, 1978: 68).

   Another anthropologically-minded missionary, Lorimer Fison, wrote a carefully reasoned, but impassioned Letter to the Editor of the *Sydney Morning Herald*, November 18, 1871, in which he connected Patteson's death with the labor trade, noting that,

   > Bishop Patteson's murderers killed him as they would a great chief against whom they had no personal animosity, nay for whom they had even a great respect, but whom, for tribal reasons, it was necessary to put to death.

   For additional newspaper articles, cf. *New Zealand Herald*, November 1, 1871; *Sydney Morning Herald*, November 7, 1871.

3. For histories of the Melanesian Mission cf. Armstrong (1900), and Fox (1958); both of these are uncritical studies written by mission protagonists. For an excellent critical study, cf. Hilliard (1966, 1978).
4. For studies of these various European acculturative influences, cf. Davidson (1942), Parsonson (1949), Belshaw (1954), Shineberg (1967, 1971), Corris (1973a, 1973b), Hilliard (1966, 1978), and Laracy (1976). For discussion concerning explorers in Melanesia, cf. Amherst and Thompson (1901), Beaglehole (1966), and Jack-Hinton (1969). Excellent general mission/church histories in Oceania are found in Forman (1982) and Garrett (1982).
5. Studies within the unilinear evolutionary paradigm analyzed change in terms of progressive movement from lower to higher states. For example, Frazer (1890) stated that progressive movement in the evolution of religion went from magic to religion to science. Years earlier, Auguste Compte (1830-1842) had postulated the intellectual development of man in the following evolutionary sequence: theological — metaphysical — positivist systems. Westermark (1906-1908) and Hobhouse (1908) each wrote on the evolution of morals.

   The evolution of marriage from primitive promiscuity to paternity and monogamy was the subject of great debate and discussion with differing opinions offered by Bachofen (1861), Maine (1861), McLennan (1865), and Morgan (1877) to name a few.

   Scholars like Tylor (1865, 1871) and Lubbock (1865, 1870) in Great Britain, and Morgan (1877) in America, mapped out large schemes of evolutionary development in numerous aspects of society and culture, with varying degrees of scientific acumen. One of the most ambitious and prolific writers of this era was the social-philosopher Herbert Spencer, whose evolutionary brush was applied to many canvases. Articulating the principle that evolution is from simple to complex, from homogeneous to heterogeneous forms in the inorganic, organic, and super-organic realms, he voraciously applied his scheme to biology, psychology, sociology, education and ethics.

   It is important to note that while socio-cultural evolution flourished in the contemporary intellectual climate of biological evolution, it is a misjudgment to credit Darwinian evolution as the catalytic model that stimulated studies of man and culture within this paradigm. Granted, evolutionary thinking was in the air, but the antecedents to socio-cultural evolution predated Darwin, reaching back at least as far as the Scottish historian Robertson (1777), cf. Teggart (1925: 105-123), Lowie (1937: 41) and Hoebel (1972: 59-61).

6. The English school was the last to come and the first to go on the anthropological scene, owing to its extreme theories as expressed in the work of G. Elliot Smith (1928, 1929, 1933) and especially his disciple, W. J. Perry (1923). In essence, they believed that Egypt had been the cultural center of the world from whence civilization had diffused, becoming more diluted the further it traveled from the Egyptian center. Emphasizing the uninventiveness of man (except for Egypt, of course), they denied independent development elsewhere in the world.

   A more tempered, but nevertheless ambitious theory of cultural development is found in the German-Austrian school which flourished from 1910 to 1940. The principal architect of this theory and method was Fritz Graebner (1911), followed by Wilhelm Schmidt (1931, 1939). Schmidt and colleagues founded the journal *Anthropos* in 1906, which served as an organ for diffusion studies. Their Kulturkreise model held that intensive development of culture had occurred not just in Egypt, but in several regional centers. From here culture complexes (which they assembled frequently from disparate cultural elements) were said to diffuse *en bloc*. Cultural borrowing was emphasized in their theory to the neglect of independent invention. For a critique of Graebner, cf. Boas (1911), and further evaluations of the Kulturekreise school are found in Kluckhohn (1936) and Heine-Geldern (1964).

   In the United States reaction to Unilinear Evolution led to the development of the culture-historical "school" pioneered by Franz Boas and his students and others. In contrast to the English and German theorists who attempted to develop broad, regional, continental and worldwide culture histories, the Americans worked with smaller, relatively homogeneous, environmental and cultural regions, in which they attempted to demonstrate that cultures were related historically. Boas' students and others did not operate with a consensus of theory and method that could be defined as a school of thought. Diversity in theory and method characterized the studies of this period which dominated American anthropology from ca. 1900-1935. For representative studies of this era, cf. Wissler (1914, 1917, 1923), Lowie (1916), Sapir (1916), and Waterman (1927). Cf. Spier (1921).

7. For American acculturation studies, cf. Radin (1913), Redfield (1930), Mead (1932), E. Parsons (1936), Herskovits (1937b), Linton (1940), Lewis (1942) and F. Keesing (1953). For a review of theory and method and a critique of thirty-nine monographs and fifty-five articles dealing with North American Indian acculturation, see Siegel (1955).

For African studies of culture contact, cf. Westermann (1934), Thurnwald (1935), Hunter (1936) and Schapera (1936). Considerable discussion was devoted to methodology in studying culture contact in Africa, cf. Mair (1934, 1938), Hunter (1934), Culwick (1935), Richards (1935), Schapera (1935, 1938), Fortes (1936, 1938), Wagner (1936), and Malinowski (1938, 1939).

The term culture-clash had been used earlier in studies describing the impact of European cultures on indigenous societies, cf. Pitt-Rivers (1927). By the 1930's the "culture-clash" term had been replaced with the concept of culture-contact, implying that the contact of cultures did not always and automatically lead to conflict.

An increasing interest in acculturation in Oceania is also evident during this period with most of the students trained in the British tradition, cf. Rivers (1922), Gifford (1924), Pitt-Rivers (1927), Mead (1928), Piddington (1932), Deacon (1934), Hogbin (1934, 1939), Keesing (1934), F. E. Williams (1935), H. W. Williams (1935), Elkin (1936), and Groves (1936).

8. For example, thirty-four dissertations dealing specifically with acculturation are listed in Dissertation Abstracts International, *Retrospective Index*, Vol. 5:1, 1970.

9. See Appendix I for the complete text of "A Memorandum for the Study of Acculturation." *American Anthropologist* 38: 149-152.

10. Cf. Linton (1940) and Herskovits (1938) in which Herskovits reviews the history of the term beginning with J. W. Powell in 1880. Herskovits then reviews recent acculturation studies, and ends by recommending areas for further acculturation research.

11. The Solomon Islands were first "discovered" in 1568 by Mendana. He then made a return voyage to Santa Cruz in 1595 with plans to establish a Spanish colony, but it failed after only two months. Again in 1605 Quiros made another attempt to establish a colony, this time in the New Hebrides, but it also was unsuccessful. The Solomon Islands were to become lost to European navigators for two hundred years, owing primarily to the fact that they were located outside the main routes of transpacific voyages, but also due to the fact that the Spanish had consistently underestimated the distance between Peru and the Solomon Islands.

In 1767 Carteret sailed through the Solomons and in 1768 Bougainville sailed through the New Hebrides and the Solomon Islands. De'Surville in 1769, Cook in 1774, LePerouse in 1787, and Shortland in 1788 followed in succession in this part of Melanesia. From 1790 to 1838, navigation through Melanesia increased considerably, as evidenced by the following explorers in the area: 1790—Ball, 1791—Edwards, 1792—Manning, 1793—D'Entrecasteaux, 1794—Wilkinson and Page, 1796—Hogan, 1797—Wilson, 1798—Cameron, 1802—Simpson, 1813—Dillon, 1822—Kroutcheff, 1823—Duperrey, 1826—Dillon, 1827—Dillon, 1828—Dumont d'Urville, 1829—de Tromelin, 1831—Morrell, 1838—Dumont d'Urville. For further discussion on the early navigators, cf. Beaglehole (1966), K. Green (1974).

12. Cf. Herskovits (1937a).

13. Elkin (1953: 158) in a review of anthropological research in Melanesia notes that studies of missionary impact on culture change should have high priority. Beidelman (1974) notes that studies of missionary activity in Africa have been seriously lacking. Some notable exceptions to this general rule of a lack of anthropological interest in studying missionaries are found in the work of Holmes (Samoa), Salamone (Nigeria), Tippett (Fiji, Solomon Islands), and Ubanowicz (Tonga). The most recent anthropological study of missionaries is Beidelman's *Colonial Evangelism* (1982) in which he focuses on the work of the Church Missionary Society among the Ukaguru in Tanzania.

    For a study of Christian missions among the Navaho see Rapoport (1954). Stipe (1968) has written on agents of change, including missionaries, and their role in the acculturation of the Eastern Dakota.

    Although anthropologists have not turned their attention to the study of missionaries with any great enthusiasm, modern missiologists have compiled a significant number of studies which are of value to anthropology and the study of culture change, cf. Mylene (1908), Pickett (1933), Oliver (1952), Taylor (1958), Taylor and Lehmann (1961), Hayward (1966), R. Lee (1967), Tippett (1967), Andersson (1968), Luke and Carman (1968), Lalive d'Epiney (1969), Van Akkern (1970), Conley (1976).

14. This Oceania symposium was published in 1978, and edited by J. Boutilier, D. Hughes, and S. Tiffany. See also *Journal de la Societe des Oceanistes*, Vol. 25 (December) 1969, which is given entirely to a discussion of missionary activity in Oceania. Further evidence of this growing anthropological interest in missionaries is the symposium on "Theoretical and Ethnographic Attention on Missionaries" at the 1979 Annual Meeting of the American Anthropological Association. Also the excellent article by Stipe (1980) and comments by critics in *Current Anthropology* (Vol. 21: 165-179) followed by Delfendahl's (1981) remarks, demonstrate increasing interest in this topic.

15. For a full discussion of the processes involved in innovation, see Barnett (1953: 181-224). For a recent attempt to integrate Barnett's theory of innovation with general systems theory, see Collins (1977). Conley (1976) has used Barnett's model in relating it to Opler's model of cultural themes in an analysis of conversion among the Kalamantan Kenyah. Tippett (1973b) uses the model to demonstrate St. Paul's conversion from Judaism to Christianity, in line with the point I have made above — an innovation is a recombination, not something emerging from nothing.

16. Cf. Wallace (1961: 120-163), and Tippett (1971: 198-220, especially p. 210).

17. Cf. Foster (1973: 82-147) for a discussion of cultural, social and psychological barriers to change.

18. For example, Pitt-Rivers (1927) and Hunter (1936) exemplify this approach to culture change.

19. Cf. Barger (1977) for an interesting discussion of different levels and kinds of integration in the process of culture change. He distinguishes between behavioral integration and material integration, and notes that, "culture change can simultaneously but independently occur on different levels" (1977: 480). See also my discussion of integration below, pp. 372–392.

20. For a complete list of these characteristics and a detailed discussion of how they relate to the advocate and innovator in the process of acceptance of introduced ideas and/or material items, see Niehoff (1966: 12-41).

    Naylor (1974: 217-230) develops Niehoff's model further by shifting emphasis to the "interaction situation," the dynamic arena in which the advocate and recipient interact.

21. Cf. Malinowski (1949) for a discussion of meaning and language. Malinowski holds that nuances in meaning are context-specific, and thus the formal word conveys mixed meaning.

22. Cf. Herskovits (1955: 492-496) for a discussion of reinterpretation which is essentially a problem of meaning.

23. This model is similar to Malinowski's (1945: 73-83) "three column approach" to the study of culture change. Cf. Tippett (1967: 128-129).

24. Cf. Salamone (1977, 1979), Burridge (1978), Hiebert (1978b), Hughes (1978).

25. Goldschmidt (1966) has written a theoretical essay from this point of view, namely, culture must bend to meet the needs of the individuals in society, cf. Goldschmidt (1956).

26. I hold to a primarily mentalistic view of culture change and define culture as the complex array of ideas that man carries in his head, which are expressed in the form of material artifacts and observable behavior. On the other hand, a society is composed of a group of individuals who in living and working together hold certain cultural elements in common, which enables them to organize and define themselves as a social unit, with well-defined limits.

27. Cf. Barnes (1954), Gluckman (1958), M. G. Smith (1960, 1962), Fallers (1965), and Southall (1965).

28. Cf. Valentine (1958) and his discussion of the use of ethnohistorical methods in that study. See also Valentine (1960) for an example of ethnohistory used in a study of culture change in Melanesia. Some other examples of studies relying on ethnohistorical methods in the study of culture change are, F. Keesing (1939) and O. Lewis (1942). This use of ethnohistory in the study of culture change is in agreement with what Evans-Pritchard (1964: 152) regarded to be the proper task of social anthropology.

29. Cf. Sturtevant (1966). For further definition and subsequent discussion of the concept of ethnohistory, cf. "Symposium on the Concept of Ethnohistory," and comments, *Ethnohistory* 8: 12-92, 256-280. See also Fenton (1962).

30. Cf. Evans-Pritchard (1962: 46-65).

31. Cf. Berkhofer (1963, 1965a, 1965b), Harris (1967), Stipe (1968), Welbourn (1971), Ubanowicz (1972), Tippett (1973a), Beidelman (1974, 1982).

32. The distinction between diachronic and synchronic analysis came into anthropology from linguistics, cf. Nadel (1951: 100-101) for a discussion of these two different modes of inquiry.

33. Although Dark does not acknowledge any specific antecedents, we meet the concept of a "culture continuum" in Linton (1936: 294-298). He notes that any synchronic level which is arbitrarily drawn, represents only a partial, incomplete and perhaps even distorted picture of the culture in its processual and developmental aspects. His analogy to a film clip is most pertinent:

> The cross-section of the culture continuum which it is possible for the anthropologist to study thus bears much the same relation to the whole that a short section of motion-picture film, clipped out at random, bears to the entire picture. It is a part of a continuous movement which has been artificially caught and fixed. Such a section of film will give only hints of the total action and will show some of the actors in strange and grotesque attitudes, perhaps poised in the air in the middle of a leap. Similarly, the section of culture cuts across and artificially fixes a series of changes which are in all stages of completion and makes conditions which are really transitory appear permanent (1936: 296).

34. Synchronic levels are always arbitrary, the degree of time depth within each level being determined by the data available. Most standard ethnographies written from data collected in a twelve month period encompass one synchronic level, with data obtainable from usually two or three generations. The synchronic levels in this study are based on five different periods of the pre-contact and contact history.
35. Firth (1929) employs the cultural continuum model most successfully. He divides the period of Maori transformation into four phases: (1) initial impact, (2) enthusiastic adoption of cultural forms, (3) reaction, and (4) acceptance of European standards. His emphasis was on the change in economic structure which he demonstrated conclusively by using historical data; however, he did not limit himself to a discussion of change in the economic structure of Maori culture, but related change in economic life to change throughout the society.
36. This scheme is presented for the entire study in a chart below, p. 426.
37. Cf. Spicer (1961: 525).
38. Cf. Belshaw (1964: 14).
39. For further discussion on the relationship of "felt needs" to missionary communication, see Kraft (1979: 77-79).
40. Cf. Tippett (1967: 269-272).
41. For a detailed discussion of the problems of cross-cultural communication of Christianity, see Kraft (1979, especially, pp. 147-166). See also Nida (1960), Hesselgrave (1978) and Nida and Reyburn (1981).

Chapter 2

Pre-Contact Melanesian Society and Culture

This chapter focuses on the pre-contact period and is divided into three sections. The first section discusses some methodological problems encountered in this chapter. This is followed by a brief discussion of the Spanish voyage of discovery to the Solomon Islands in 1568. This section has been included here because the situation in which the Spanish and Melanesians interacted was clearly in the pre-contact period. That is, there is no evidence that the Solomon Islands had ever been visited before by Europeans. The Spanish accounts of their interaction with the islanders, although written from an ethnocentric bias and based on limited observations, are nevertheless valuable sources of ethnographic information. They give us the first glimpse of Solomon Islanders before they came under the influence of European contact. Moreover, the Spanish accounts are unique historically because they describe island life that went undisturbed and unnoticed for over two hundred years after the observations were initially made. It is for this reason that this data has been presented here; however, it is acknowledged that the Spanish interaction with Melanesians in the sixteenth century had no relevance to later missionary policies in relating to the islanders in the nineteenth century.

The third section of this chapter presents a pre-contact base-line for Melanesia. I begin by discussing the pre-history and linguistic situation in Melanesia, then the Melanesian habitat and cultural adaptation, social organization, and conclude the chapter with a section on traditional religion and magic.

Methodological Considerations

In this chapter, more than any other in this study, I am confronted by a peculiar problem of ethnohistorical reconstruction, namely that of projecting beyond the documentary sources into the pre-contact period. I ask the question—"What was Melanesia like before the Europeans disturbed it?" Such an exercise is only possible within certain limits. My sources are limited, for they are (especially the early Spanish sources) charged with foreign values of their own day, which have to be eliminated to get at the ethnographically valid data within them. I must concede this weakness of the study. However, I am fortunate to have a very fine source in the writings of R. H. Codrington, W. G. Ivens, A. I. Hopkins, C. E. Fox and a few others whose observations were made in non-Christian and non-contact situations. These missionary-scholars were extremely perceptive, spoke the languages and lived in the native setting. Even so, the problem of projection is a major one.

The second problem is the theoretical construct of Melanesia as an entity and within Melanesia, the Solomon Islands and northern New Hebrides as part of this construct. Anthropology has forced us into the former, and politico-social events into the latter. Both are artificial, one for classificatory reasons, the other as a result of colonial history. When analysis is projected back to the pre-contact period, one finds that neither has much, if any, factual reality. The boundaries of Melanesia are extremely difficult to delineate and its internal diversity is considerable.[1] It is very difficult to universalize for such a large complex of humanity. Nor were the Solomon Islands or northern New Hebrides an entity. The ethnic validity of this is one of the current problems of the new political structure. In the projection of this study into the pre-contact period, as far as the indigenes were concerned, there was no such thing as Melanesia, the Solomon Islands or Banks' Islands. Their very names are contact categories and concepts.

The problem today is to delineate how the Malaita man and the Shortland Islander come to be known as Solomon Islanders. As we go back, even only as far as the days of Marching Rule, the problem was the entity of Malaita itself, where, for example, the salt-water and mountain peoples saw themselves as quite distinct, "us and them," and as enemies.

The third methodological problem faced in this chapter is the literary integration of the chapter itself. By its very nature it is analytical. Analytical categories are a descriptive device which suggests an artificial compartmentalization. Therefore, in arranging the data as linguistic, economic, religious and so on as the case may be, one must state at the outset that this is no more than an artificial mechanism, a heuristic device for reporting or describing data. In reality there are no such compartments. Life is a whole and lived as a whole. The language has its religious dimensions, the religion is dependent on linguistic articulation, the economic has its religious rituals, and all, as a total integrated unit, relate *en masse* to the daily life of the people within very small homogeneous territorial domestic units. The people are aware of their entity and their belongingness within the group and are not conscious of this or that as religious, economic, political, etc.

These three methodological problems of (1) projection into the past, (2) entity, and (3) analytical categories, need to be faced before analysis of the subject matter for the pre-contact period proceeds.

The Pre-contact Baseline.

In concluding this section on methodology, it is important to consider the problems in developing a pre-contact baseline, where one is forced to rely primarily on European accounts of Melanesian society and culture. In other words, a pre-contact period cannot be reconstructed without recourse to documents recorded in the contact period. In the case of Melanesia, the sixteenth century Spanish records give us a view of the culture before any contact with Europeans had been made, and a view of the islanders two hundred years before they would be encountered and reported on again by Europeans. So it is indeed a unique opportunity that is seldom available to the student of culture change.

Observations recorded in the twentieth century are also of value in helping to reconstruct the pre-contact period, for in some parts of Melanesia, there was still very little culture change occurring as late as the beginning of this century. Documents useful for such an endeavor are those created by individuals encountering islanders who have remained isolated from the main streams of European influence in the island world.

From about 1850 onward, this isolation was increasingly exposed to European influence, so that by the beginning of the twentieth century there were very few places in our area of study where islanders were living a completely traditional way of life.[2]

In discussing the pre-contact period in Melanesia it is important to avoid the fallacy of assuming that the pre-contact period is static and only becomes dynamic after contact with Western culture has begun. Such a popular view, as expressed in the comments by Amherst and Thompson below, suffers from an ethnocentric bias which erroneously assumes that social and cultural change begins only after European contact has been made. It is true that in some areas of the society the rate of culture change is frequently accelerated after European contact, but it is erroneous to assume a static period before this time. The history of Melanesia prior to European contact was not a static period, as archaeological and linguistic evidence demonstrates. It was one in which there was a great deal of culture contact and change between different groups of people which we have come to lump into one large category called Melanesian.[3]

The Iberian Intrusion

The first written accounts of Melanesians in the Southwest Pacific come from the Spanish expedition to the Solomon Islands in 1568. A collection of six documents including journals, papers and letters, translated and edited by Amherst and Thompson (1901) gives a vivid ethnographic account which is most useful as a starting point in determining the pre-contact cultural baseline.[4] Amherst and Thompson (1901: lxxvi) in their introduction draw attention to the value these documents have for the anthropologist. They note:

> For the student of ethnology these manuscripts are full of suggestion for they reveal to us an isolated island race which is even now very little affected by intercourse with strangers, as they were nearly three hundred and fifty years ago. By all the laws of evolution, they should have been either progressing or deteriorating in the interval. They have done neither. As they are now, so were they then, head-hunting, eating the bodies of the slain, using the same arms, building the same vessels, wearing the same ornaments.

The Spanish encounter with the Solomon Islanders needs to be understood in terms of its historical context, for this was the era when Spain was in her glory, and expeditions of discovery were motivated by the conquest for souls, land and gold.

In 1567 the Governor of Peru, Lope Garcia de Castro, selected his nephew, 25-year old Alvaro de Mendana de Neyra, to lead the expedition. Two ships, the *Los Reyes* (200 tons) and the *Todos Santos* (140 tons), were quickly prepared and renamed the *Capitana* and *Almiranta*. An expeditionary force was assembled, consisting of 150 men, including four Franciscan friars and seventy soldiers, together with sailors and negro slaves.

What was the purpose of the expedition? It is certain there was no one single purpose, but rather several motivating factors, objectives, and goals behind the expedition. Gallego, in the prologue of his journal, says that it was "to enlighten and convert to Christianity all infidels and to lead them as labourers into the vineyard of the Lord" (Amherst and Thompson 1901: 3). Although it is difficult to comprehend from the vantage point of the twentieth century, the importance of this religious motive in any sixteenth century Iberian exploration cannot be underestimated. In reading the manuscripts of those who took part in the discovery of the Solomon Islands, it is clear that the conversion of the islanders was foremost in the minds of the leaders. Madariaga (1955: 106-107) depicts the importance of this religious element in Spanish thinking of the time:

> . . . how can we understand that age in which faith was like air and light, one of the very conditions of existence, the very breath with which people spoke? . . . All men, whatever their colour and nation, were either Christians, infidels, or liable to being enlightened and brought into Christianity. The service of God meant one or another of these two simple things: to bring into the fold the unconverted, ignorant peoples still outside the faith; or to make war against the infidels who refused to be converted and were the enemies of God and His Church . . . This service to God was also a service to the King-Emperor. After all, was not the Emperor the minister of God on earth? This was a central idea in Spanish

> political philosophy . . . the King was to be obeyed not as king but as the minister of God . . . State and religion, faith and civilisation were one in those days, so that the service of God and the service of the King were but one in yet this other sense that conversion was, in the eyes of the century, less a religious-individual than a political-collective act. *Cujus rex eius religio* was the principle of the era.

But of course, there were other goals for the expedition as well. The discovery of new lands, and the subsequent expansion of the Spanish empire and the search for wealth and trade, must certainly be counted among them. This was the era of searching for the biblical Ophir of King Solomon, for it was commonly held that the source of his gold had come from a vast austral continent, yet to be found. The Incas were also reputed to have known of islands in the South Pacific that were rich with deposits of gold. Thus, the incentives for the expedition, while not internally inconsistent in their time, were nevertheless certainly quite varied, providing strong motivation for its undertaking. If one believes the primary goals of the expedition were the conversion of islanders to Christianity, the discovery of gold, and the exploration of the vast austral continent, then the Spanish came home empty-handed, having failed on all three counts.[5]

It is against this background that Mendana left Callao, the port city of Lima, Peru, at 4:00 p.m. on Wednesday, the 19th of November — St. Ysabel Day, in the year 1567. He believed the rich islands to be discovered were in the vicinity of 15° South, 600 Iberian leagues (1920 nautical miles) west of Peru. Eighty days and over 8,000 miles later, a large island, presumably a continent, was finally sighted, but they could not get up to it until the evening of the next day, Sunday, the 8th of February, 1568. The following morning as Mendana proceeded to enter a harbor to protect the ships from the northwest winds, a bright star (Venus) appeared to them over the main topsail. Unaware that this was a common occurrence in these parts, and believing it to be a special sign sent to them as a good omen, they named the harbor Bahia de la Estrella. To the island they gave the name Santa Ysabel, after the patron saint of the voyage, on whose day they had departed from Peru.

The islanders' reaction to this strange intrusion was one of caution and friendliness.[6] The initial contact of Europeans has frequently been interpreted by Melanesians as the coming of supernatural beings, either in the form of incarnate spirits or as ghosts of their ancestors.[7] Whether this mode of interpretation was initially given to the Spanish is unknown, but subsequent intercourse with these strangers would soon convince the islanders that these beings were definitely human, exhibiting both the strengths and weaknesses of their humanity.[8]

Many canoes described as "long and pointed at the ends in the shape of a crescent moon" (Amherst and Thompson 1901: 227), came out to inspect the strangers as they anchored in the harbor.[9] The islanders were well-equipped for warfare, carrying bows and arrows, clubs and lances, but they would not come alongside the vessels until Mendana threw them a colored cap, which they quickly gave to their "chief," putting it on his head. This gesture must have eased their fear somewhat, for they then came alongside the vessels asking for more caps and inquiring who was the "chief" of the Spanish force. When Mendana was pointed out as the "chief," "about two dozen of them came up to the ship and the General embraced some of them and showed them kindness, and he ordered bread and wine to be given to them, and they ate preserves and meat" (Amherst and Thompson 1901: 227). The islanders quickly made themselves at home on the ships, receiving gladly beads, caps, jingling bells, and other items Mendana gave them, as well as helping themselves to any loose items about the ship and then throwing them overboard to their comrades waiting in canoes below.[10] The leader of the group, called Billebanarra, took away a silver goblet which Mendana had given him full of wine. The legend of that goblet survives today on Santa Isabel, and it is reputed to be hidden in a cave along with many other artifacts from the former days of headhunting and warfare.

The Spanish took possession of the land in the name of their King, Don Phillip II, and erected a cross to commemorate the occasion. A convenient place was then chosen for the ship's carpenters to begin building a brigantine, which would subsequently be used for most of the exploration of the Solomon Islands.

The local Big Man, Billebanarra, exchanged names with Mendana as a token of friendship, common in many parts of the Pacific. But the cordial reception given the Spanish by the Isabel Islanders was not to last long. Despite the fact Mendana was intent on ensuring that the Spanish initiate no hostility, conflict with the islanders was inevitable. The expedition needed fresh food, which was occasionally given freely in the form of taro, coconuts, fish and pork. The sudden, unannounced invasion of 150 men demanding food, however, would have placed severe demands on any local subsistence economy. When food failed to come by the good will of the islanders, the Spanish felt they had no options open to them except to use force to obtain what they needed.

The Spanish conducted two expeditions into the interior of Santa Isabel in hopes of procuring food and exploring the land. On the first trip they soon encountered opposition from the inhabitants in the interior who threatened them and demanded they go away. The Spanish grabbed an islander as a hostage in a futile attempt to ward off an attack. When it came, they responded to the islanders' arrows and spears with their arquebuses and swords, wounding several indigenes as they fought their way back to the beach. Mendana was incensed by the behavior of his men, and ordered the hostage returned to his people.

The skirmish, however, proved to be the model for subsequent encounters. When the Spanish could not get what they felt they needed by bartering, they then took food by force, or frequently took people as hostages or canoes to hold in ransom until their demands were met. On every island the Spanish contacted, a skirmish between themselves and the islanders ensued. Nevertheless, their intentions were not to plunder or steal provisions at will, for they frequently left some trade beads, or other items, in exchange for food they had taken from a village.

Their cultural impact could not have been very significant or lasting. Materially they left behind a few trade items such as glass beads, jingling bells, shirts and caps. The use of firearms for weapons would certainly have left a lasting impression on the islanders, for it is estimated conservatively that at least one hundred islanders died in their encounter with the Spanish.[11]

After six months the Spanish were in a desperate situation. The islanders were on to this marauding monster and so they not only ceased to come out and gather around the vessels in curiosity, but they fled to the hills taking their food with them and leaving behind an empty village.[12] The pattern of ransoming people and canoes for food no longer worked. The ships were in bad repair, their stores were dangerously low and there was no longer any hope of getting food from the islanders. Their ammunition was running low, as was the morale of the expeditionary force. It was imperative to leave immediately for Peru if they hoped to make it back alive. A discussion was held regarding the advisability of attempting to establish a colony in the islands. Although the land was fertile and beautiful, they had discovered neither gold nor silver, and to establish a colony they would have had to rely on arms and ammunition, which by this time had dwindled to almost nothing.

They chose to leave. After six months of constant vigilance against attack and without having discovered any valuable minerals, there was little incentive to stay.[13]

Throughout their time in the Solomons the Spanish had taken islanders, occasionally by force, to act as interpreters.[14] By the time their six-month long exploration had come to an end, however, the kidnapped islanders had all escaped. To make sure that they had a few native specimens, six islanders from San Cristobal were kidnapped just as they were leaving the Solomons and were taken back to Peru, where three died shortly after they arrived.

On August 11, 1568, the Spanish intruders set sail for Peru, beating along the coast of San Cristobal for seven days until they cleared Santa Ana and Santa Catalina, whence they headed northeast. The homeward journey was long and desperate, as food supplies ran low, and they encountered a terrible hurricane which separated the two ships from each other. Finally, they arrived along the coast of Lower California by December 20th, 1568. Calling at different places for supplies and repairs, they finally returned to anchor at Callao, Peru, on Sunday the 26th of July, 1569. One third of the original 150 men who had set out for Callao twenty months earlier had died during the voyage. There was no Ophir of Solomon to report — only a group of islands overgrown with dense tropical vegetation and thickly populated by a savage race of naked and hostile cannibals. The official view of the discoveries written by the Licentiate Juan de Crosco to the king is most revealing:

> In my opinion, according to the report that I have received, they were of little importance, although they say that they heard of better lands; for in the course of these discoveries they found no specimens of spices, nor of gold and silver, nor of merchandise, nor of any other source of profit, and all the people were naked savages . . . The advantage that might be derived from exploring these islands would be to make slaves of the people, or to found a settlement in some port in one of them, where provisions could be collected for the discovery of the mainland, where it is reported that there is gold and silver, and that the people are clothed (Amherst and Thompson 1901: lviii).

The behavior of the Spanish has been assessed by several writers from various points of view. Guppy (1887) is extremely critical of their behavior. While making allowance for the spirit of the age, he believes they were most inhumane in their interaction with the islanders. A. H. Markham (1873: 8) on the other hand, believes they handled their intercourse with the islanders in a most humane fashion. Amherst and Thompson (1901: lxiv-lxv) do not pass severe judgment, but acknowledge that the Spanish seemed to have had little option as they were in need of food in a land of plenty, with hosts who refused to give them any. Regardless of what judgment we may wish to pass on the expedition today, the fact remains, the result of the Spanish expedition was destruction and loss of life.[15] It can fairly be said that the Solomon Islanders gained little from their first interaction with Europeans. Unfortunately, this first encounter was only a harbinger of things to come when three hundred years later intercourse with Europeans would intensify.

Some Spanish Observations of the Melanesians.

Mendana spent six months in the Solomons and with the aid of the brigantine constructed on Santa Isabel, the Spanish visited ten major islands — Santa Isabel, Nggela, Guadalcanal, Malaita, Ulawa, Three Sisters, Ugi, San Cristobal, Santa Catalina and Santa Ana. Their observations, although based on superficial intercourse with the islanders, are most intriguing and of course very valuable in piecing together a pre-contact picture of Melanesian society. Although the primary objectives of the voyage were not fulfilled and the discovery was believed to be of little importance, the record left behind by the expedition is invaluable and gives us a picture of Melanesian society and culture before European contact.

The hallmark of Melanesia, namely cultural and linguistic diversity, was as evident to the Spanish in 1568 as it would be to visitors three hundred years later. This diversity was expressed in a multitude of small, local autonomous political entities, taking the form of coastal villages of perhaps several hundred people, and dispersed hamlets of several families in the interior of the larger islands. The rugged mountainous terrain contributed to political segmentation, as isolation prompted an evolution toward linguistic and cultural diversity rather than an amalgamation of societies.[16]

This high degree of sectionalism was manifest in several ways. For example, when the brigantine was on the opposite side of Santa Isabel from Estrella Bay where the Spanish had anchored, they were surprised to discover that news of their arrival had not yet penetrated this area. Catoira in his journal wrote:

> The people of this island are very bold. They have no friendship the one with the other; and this is a well ascertained fact, for although we had been two months and a half on this Island of Santa Ysabel, the whole island did not know of our arrival, but only here and there (Amherst and Thompson 1901: 296).

The Spanish observed that these autonomous political entities were in a state of continual hostility and warfare with each other.[17] Any stranger was by definition a potential enemy, and the Spanish were treated as such by the Melanesians for they were always approached cautiously. Unfortunately, the conduct of the Spanish did little to assuage the Melanesians' fears that these new and enigmatic strangers were indeed their enemies and to be feared greatly.

On two occasions, in Santa Isabel and Guadalcanal, the Spanish were requested to participate in partnership with the islanders in internal island hostility by raiding a neighboring enemy. On Santa Isabel, Mendana agreed to the request and sent a small force against an enemy of the Estrella Bay Big Man as a demonstration of his friendship and alliance with him.

The cunning and treachery of the islanders, which Europeans would later come to understand as the Melanesians' basic mode of fighting, were soon discovered by the Spanish, as evidenced by Catoira's remarks regarding the islanders of Guadalcanal on May 14, 1568:

> . . . and as we anchored, some canoes with chiefs in them came out, and they came on board, and made great friends with the General, and he gave them some beads and they showed us friendship, although it was feigned; but it was always so with them, for beneath their friendship they practise much treachery (Amherst and Thompson 1901: 303).

The sectionalism of the population expressed itself in distinct bush and coastal dwellers, comprising many small politically autonomous social groups, each with a "chief" as the Spanish called them. There was generally an absence of any supra-local powers capable of controlling large segments of the population. Although the Spanish did not encounter any "chiefs" who had power over an entire island, they did however, discover the Big Man Ponemonefa, who resided on San Jorge island, which was densely populated at the time. He was said to have power and influence over a great deal of Santa Isabel, to the degree that those on the northeast side of the island at Estrella Bay acknowledged his suzerainty. In writing about this powerful leader, Catoira noted:

> This Ponemonefa also holds lands in the island of Santa Ysabel, and is more powerful than any other *taurigui* (the local name for a Big Man, according to the Spanish). They call him *Caybaco*, that is to say, "Great Lord" and all fear him (Amherst and Thompson 1901: 293).[18]

In contrast to what Europeans observed in the nineteenth century, the Spanish reported that all the islands were densely populated. There are frequent references to gatherings of more than one thousand islanders meeting the Spanish on the beach. The interior was also heavily populated, for as Catoira observed of Guadalcanal, "We saw so many villages on the hill-tops that it was marvelous, for more than thirty villages of ten and twenty houses and more, could be counted within a league and a half of the road" (Amherst and Thompson 1901: 308-309). Looking down on the Guadalcanal plains, which today are used for commercial production of rice and palm oil, Catoira continues, "We saw much smoke in the plains, which was not surprising as the land is so densely populated" (Amherst and Thompson 1901: 309). The richness of the land, full of people and produce, was overwhelming, for as Catoira notes, "It seemed to be the most delightful land that there is in the world. The abundance which the people appear to possess cannot be expressed" (Amherst and Thompson 1901: 379).[19]

This abundance was not limited to Guadalcanal. As the Spanish approached San Cristobal from Ugi they were amazed at the number of villages along the coast. Catoira's journal reports, "As far as our people could see, all the shore was full of houses, and there were so many (houses) and so many people in that land, that they were astonished" (Amherst and Thompson 1901: 359).

This was a land of plenty — rich in people and produce to feed them. In fact, this is precisely what made the Spaniards' situation so trying, for they were in need of food in a land of plenty, but were unable to obtain what they needed. They observed taro growing on terraced hillsides where it was artificially irrigated. Yams and pana were the other principal root crops, supplemented by coconuts, plantains, and "sweet almonds" or the canarium nut.[20] The Spanish do not report seeing any *kumara* or sweet potato (*Ipomoea batatas*) which today is the main staple in the Solomons. Of the domesticated animals, dogs and "hens and cocks of Castille of all colours" (Amherst and Thompson 1901: 319) were observed, and although pigs seemed to be an important part of the Melanesian ecology, the Spanish frequently had difficulty in acquiring as many as they wanted. This could have been because they were difficult to capture upon request if allowed to run freely, or due to a small number of pigs available, or because of the high value placed on them, which made the islanders reticent to part with them at any price. Fishing was also a part of the islanders' subsistence economy and on at least one occasion the Spanish were given a turtle to eat.

The material culture of the Solomon Islanders favorably impressed them, to the point where several recorded that these savages must have a fair amount of intelligence to be able to construct such elegant, large and swift canoes, and such well-built houses. According to Catoira, the best canoes, which were highly decorative, were encountered on San Cristobal.[21] The largest canoes they saw were sixty feet long and seven feet wide, and were capable of carrying forty to fifty men. Canoes on Malaita were discovered to have store rooms, from which the Spanish inferred that they were used for trading with other islands.

The focus of the islanders' material culture seemed to the Spaniards to be their weapons and articles used in warfare. The weapons of Malaita were reported to be the most numerous and advanced of all those encountered. However, bow and arrows, spears and clubs, comprised the basic inventory throughout the Solomons. This formidable arsenal, however, was no match for the Spanish arquebuses and cannon. When the Spaniards fired on the islanders, a more deadly weapon had never before been witnessed by them, and they quickly fled in retreat. Warfare seemed to be the cultural focus of these islanders and thus they were prepared to meet the Spanish on these terms, but the firearms of the latter, made the encounter heavily one-sided. But there was more to the material culture than weapons. Small reed pipes (pan pipes) were used as the principal musical instruments. Conch shells were also employed. The traditional Melanesian valuables and personal ornaments were clearly evident to the Spanish — strings of shell money, arm bands carved from shell, necklaces of porpoise or dog's teeth, etc.

The Spanish journals are also full of reports on Melanesian customs, and although they are very ethnocentric, they are nevertheless valuable sources of information. Many of the customs which they observed then are still practiced today, while others have completely disappeared.

The custom of exchanging names as a sign of friendship and alliance, which is found in many parts of Oceania, was entered into with the Spanish. Most of the Spanish-islander interaction was hostile, however, and so there is more information regarding their animosity than other kinds of behavior. For example, a sign of peace which the Spanish observed in several of the islands, was for the indigene to sit down. To stand up was a sign of hostility and impending confrontation. This "peace sign" was still practiced during this century.[22] Wild gesticulations, grimaces and distortions of the face and body were signs of hostility and designed to intimidate one's foe. Mendana's men soon learned to decode this signal as a sign of imminent attack. Off the coast of Guadalcanal, two canoes came out with seven boys rowing an adult man. Catoira reports, "He made two hostile attacks on our men giving great shouts, and dancing in his canoe, brandishing his club, making grimaces and contortions like a devil" (Amherst and Thompson 1901: 339-340). Another hostile gesture shown by the islanders toward their enemies was to turn an exposed buttocks toward the enemy, which they did on several occasions to the Spanish. They would then turn and spit on their enemies.

A great deal of comment was given to native dress, or non-dress, as the case may be. The Big Men encountered by the Spanish were always considerably decked out in their finery of ornaments which differentiated them from the commoners. A Big Man could appear as a very impressive person, as evidenced by the Big Man of Estrella Bay. Catoira reports of a meeting between Mendana and him:

> And he sent to say that he would come presently; and he assembled eight canoes of Indians and after a little time he came very grandly, with many white armlets, made of bone, upon his arms, a large plate of the same hanging from his neck, and bracelets of very small deer's (sic) teeth, and very small stones like coral, which he wore on his arms and legs; and although he was a savage, we marvelled at the dignity and gravity with which he came, for he was seated in his canoe (Amherst and Thompson 1901: 268).[23]

Although many of the islanders wore pubic aprons of some form as their only clothing, most of those encountered on south Malaita, Ulawa and San Cristobal (which also forms a cultural area) wore nothing at all. This complete nakedness of both men and women astounded the Spaniards. Although their bodies were not clothed, it does not follow that islanders paid no attention to their personal appearance, for elaborate measures were taken to color the hair or fix it in one way or another. White and blue wigs were reported to be worn by islanders on Ulawa and Malaita. The women of Ulawa were said to go naked with flowers in their hair, like nymphs, while others were observed to wear "their hair well arranged and of two or three colours, the sides in some cases being blue, and the middle of the head white and fair, and red and green, and others all white and fair, for they bleach it so" (Amherst and Thompson 1901: 353). While I did not observe hair colored red, blue, or green, the custom of bleaching hair with lime is found beyond the confines of Melanesia in many parts of Oceania, and is still practiced today in the Solomons.

Two customs in particular, which the Spaniards found revolting to their sense of propriety were, (1) the attempt to sell three Santa Isabel women to them, and (2) the practice of cannibalism which they encountered on nearly every island they visited. The most disturbing scene occurred on Santa Isabel when Mendana was offered a piece of human flesh. This was a very gracious and respectful Melanesian act. Perhaps he was unaware of the high tribute paid to him when he was offered the upper quarter of a young boy, for in his "acceptance speech" he ordered the portion of flesh to be buried, so that all could see that the practice of cannibalism was evil (Amherst and Thompson 1901: 258).[24] Although human skulls were seen in several places, it is unknown whether headhunting was carried on to even a fraction of the degree that it was practiced in the nineteenth century.

The Spanish documents make several references to Solomon Island religious ritual, but nothing, except their own imputations, regarding religious beliefs.[25] On Santa Isabel, during an expedition into the interior of the island, the Spanish encountered "temples" dedicated to the worship of snakes, toads, lizards, scorpions, and insects, to which they quickly set fire. Also on Santa Isabel, mention is made of seeing a *mochadero*, which upon closer inspection, contained items for working magic and sorcery. The islanders on Nggela appeared to lack the "temples" found on Santa Isabel, and thus Catoira concluded that, "It would be easy to implant in them our Holy Catholic Faith, for they have no temples nor *mochaderos*, as in other islands" (Amherst and Thompson 1901: 289).[26] On Guadalcanal, after an important Big Man had been killed by the Spanish, they observed the islanders stripping the coconuts from trees belonging to the deceased, and marking the trees with taboo signs.

On the island of Ulawa they discovered what they believed to be a "very large and broad temple, wherein were painted many figures of devils with horns like those of goats" (Amherst and Thompson 1901: 335). Amherst and Thompson (1901: 335) remark that these were canoe houses or public halls and that the paintings and carvings of sea-ghosts which are very remarkable in this district, might easily have been mistaken for devils with horns.[27] They suggest that, "Though offerings are made to the spirits represented by the carvings, the figures are not idols, nor are the buildings temples in the English sense of the word" (1901: 335).

On Guadalcanal the Spaniards found a human skull which was being roasted by a fire. Amherst and Thompson (1901: 368) comment that,

> This was no doubt a *mangite*, or sacred relic of a dead relation exhumed from the grave to be suspended in the house. The *mangite* is the instrument by which the help of the *lio'a* or ghost, can be invoked.[28]

On San Cristobal the Spanish encountered what they interpreted to be devil possession. Catoira notes:

> Some Indians appeared who seemed to be invoking the Devil by spells, for one, having drawn a circle, entered into it, and began to speak very fast in his own language, walking up and down without quitting it. And the Devil, as we supposed, entered into two of them for the two made grimaces, and a violent shuddering shook them all over, and they were disfigured, making diabolical grimaces and performing other strange antics, which struck us with amazement (Amherst and Thompson 1901: 391).

Reporting on the same incident, Gallego's account (in Guppy 1887: 228) notes that as the Spanish were preparing to enter a village to take it in order to procure food and provisions, the islanders held a consultation in which:

> One of the headmen was seen to make incantations and invocations to the devil, which caused real terror, because it seemed as though his body was possessed by a devil. There were two other Indians, who, whilst making great contortions with their faces and violently shaking themselves, scraped up the sand with their feet and hands and threw it into the air. They made toward the boats with loud shouting and yells of rage and tossed the water in the air.[29]

Despite the obvious cultural lens through which these observations were made and recorded, they are still very informative. When Europeans described Solomon Islanders' behavior three hundred years later very similar incidents as these were recorded. Amherst and Thompson writing at the beginning of this century express it in the following manner:

> In the history of travel there is probably no other instance of the veil being lifted for a brief moment to afford a glimpse of the life of an isolated island race, and then dropped again for nigh three centuries, during which no ripple from the outer world came to disturb the silent backwater. If a solitary example could be held to prove anything, these documents would show that human progress is dependent upon constant impulses from other races of mankind; and that, left to itself, a people will stop at the point it had reached when it was cut off, and thereafter remain stagnant (1901: lxxvii).

This concludes the brief discussion of the Spanish encounter with the Solomon Islanders. Attention will now shift to the third section of this chapter as I will attempt to develop a pre-contact socio-cultural baseline. In studying socio-cultural change and the impact of agents of change, it is important to have as full and accurate a picture as possible of what the traditional society and culture were like before intensive European contact was made. With this end in mind, I will begin with a discussion of Melanesian prehistory.

Melanesian Prehistory

Given the diversity of languages and cultures found in Melanesia today, and the rich phenotypic mosaic of the people themselves, one would expect the prehistory of the region to be complicated and complex. Although most of the archaeological investigations have been undertaken since the 1960's, the available evidence, thus far, points to a very complicated history of Melanesian settlement with many migrations of people from different places at different times.

In reviewing the prehistory of Melanesia, one usually starts with New Guinea[30] which is assumed to be the first part of Melanesia to be inhabited by man. Those who first came must have come via the sea, for there is no evidence of a land bridge ever existing between New Guinea and the islands of Indonesia.[31] However, a land bridge is believed to have existed between Tasmania, Australia and New Guinea up until 8,000 years ago. Since there is evidence for man in Australia by at least 32,000 years ago,[32] it is assumed that man would have been in New Guinea by that date as well.

We are not surprised then, to discover evidence for man in the New Guinea Highlands by 28,000 B.C.[33] These early inhabitants were hunters and gatherers, and the ecology of New Guinea would have been sufficiently diversified to support them. Hunters and gatherers, however, were not restricted to New Guinea alone, for there is evidence of a pre-pottery, pre-agricultural stage in some of the larger islands in which the ecosystem would have been capable of supporting a hunting and gathering population. According to Shutler and Shutler (1975: 97):

> This evidence comes from New Britain, where undated but primitive stone tools similar to some reported from early Highland New Guinea sites have been found, from New Ireland, and from New Caledonia where radiocarbon dates on the order of 10,000 B.P. (before the present) have been obtained.

To date, no similar evidence for hunters and gatherers has been found in the Western Solomons, although Green (1977: 9) believes that such a discovery would not be surprising. As one moves further east into Oceania, however, the ecology of the islands is not as varied as in New Guinea and thus would be less likely to support a hunting and gathering population. In addition, the distance between the islands increases and navigation in large expanses of open sea would have required considerable skill and appropriate technology. Moreover, an interesting navigational note is that from San Cristobal, at the southeastern end of the Solomon Islands chain, it would be possible to sail all the way back to Indonesia from one island to another, with the distant island nearly always in view.[34] It is conceivable that hunters and gatherers could have occupied some of the islands in the Solomon group, but to date there is no evidence for such an occupation.

The present-day descendants of these original inhabitants cannot be clearly determined, although some effort has been made to combine physical-anthropological and linguistic data to distinguish Papuans, speaking non-Austronesian languages, from Melanesians, speaking Austronesian languages, and to assume the former to be descended from earlier inhabitants, and the latter to have migrated into Melanesia thousands of years later. The facts, however, do not always fall so neatly into such a simplified schema.[35]

The cultural evolution from a hunting and gathering economy to the beginning of domestication of plants and animals took place in the New Guinea Highlands by at least 4,000 B.C. as the evidence of pig bones would seem to indicate. Pigs are not indigenous to New Guinea or elsewhere in Melanesia, and so must have been brought to the island by man. This means that they were probably domesticated rather than feral pigs that were introduced. Since domesticated pigs would require some form of domesticated roots or vegetables, it is more than likely that those who introduced the pig also possessed the knowledge of domesticating plants.[36] At present it is unknown whether the introduction of agriculture into the Melanesian economy occurred independently in New Guinea, or was introduced from outside by a people migrating into the area who also introduced the art of pottery making.[37]

What is known, however, is that there was a significant expansion of Neolithic seafarers moving eastward from Indonesia and/or the Asian Mainland, into Island Melanesia 3,000 to 4,000 years ago. This was not a single expansion of one group, coming from one place at one time, but rather, several groups with diverse origins, migrating at different times. Domesticated taro, yam, breadfruit, banana and coconut, pigs and chickens, and the outrigger canoe were all introduced into the Oceanic world, presumably by Austronesian speakers who began migrating into Melanesia at this time.[38]

In the work of reconstructing Melanesian prehistory, pottery is a most useful diagnostic element.[39] Golson (1968) has identified three ceramic traditions in Melanesia: (1) Lapita-Watom, (2) paddle impressed, and (3) incised and applied pottery.

The earliest, well-dated, culture of island Melanesia is the highly developed and elaborately decorated Lapita pottery tradition.[40] Named for a site on the west coast of New Caledonia, Lapita pottery seems likely to be attributed to a mobile group of Austronesian Neolithic seafarers and traders who were expanding in central and eastern Melanesia after 1300 B.C.[41] Although the period for Lapita pottery lasted only nine hundred years, it nevertheless obtained a wide geographical distribution from the Admiralty Islands off New Guinea, down through Melanesia, and eastward as far as Tonga and Samoa.[42] Many prehistorians, as Green notes, believe that "the Lapita materials represent a group of closely-related communities which moved from Eastern Melanesia into Polynesia, and there became the ancestors of all Polynesians" (1977: 19-21). One of the outstanding features of the people associated with Lapita pottery was their superb seamanship, enabling the establishment of elaborate inter-island exchange networks which of course characterize many of the later trade systems found throughout Melanesia. For example, obsidian associated with Lapita sites of the Main Reef and Santa Cruz Islands was imported from volcanic sources in the Banks' Islands, and as far away as the Talasea Peninsula in New Britain and from sources in the Admirality Islands, a distance of over one thousand miles.[43]

Contemporary with Lapita were other groups in Melanesia. For example, Green (1977: 13) notes that in the Solomon Islands there were at least three culturally distinct populations inhabiting the region more than 3,000 years ago. One of these groups is identified by non-ceramic evidence from Fotoruma Cave on Guadalcanal. Archaeological investigations have revealed a group of people occupying the cave prior to the first dated occupational layer whose age is established between 1000 and 1300 B.C.[44]

In the New Hebrides (Vanuatu), Jose Garanger (1971, 1972) has pioneered archaeological investigations and reports that four distinct ceramic traditions have been found. The earliest tradition is incised and applied pottery and appears in the central New Hebrides by 645 B.C. This pottery tradition, Garanger calls Mangaasi, and notes that it is the main type of pottery for nearly two thousand years in the central New Hebridean cultures. A second tradition is paddle-impressed pottery, uncovered on the island of Efate. While no exact date has been determined, its introduction is prior to 1600 A.D. A third tradition, found at Eureti, is a Lapita type pottery in shape, but is a non-decorated ware. Its date (350 B.C.) is at least contemporary with Lapita, if not earlier. The fourth tradition, outlined by Garanger for the New Hebrides, is pottery with internal incisions from Tongoa, and dated at 1000 A.D.

By 1400 A.D. pottery was abandoned and Garanger speculates that this was due to the arrival of a new people coming by canoe from the south. The migration of these people is known from oral tradition and legends about a great chief named Roymata. Garanger's excavation of his elaborate burial with human sacrifices at Retoka, on Hat Island near Efate, has been dated at 1265 A.D.[45]

Moving now to a third area, in the Western Solomons, the work of Specht (1969) on Buka, has identified a ceramic tradition that began ca. 500 B.C., and runs to the present, with, of course, stylistic changes. Specht has identified two styles within this tradition as Buka and Sohano.

Bellwood (1975: 15) believes that the non-Lapita pottery in Melanesia, represented by Sohano (Western Solomons), Mangaasi (central New Hebrides), and later incised wares from New Caledonia and Fiji, may all belong to a single important series which may be contrasted with Lapita pottery. He speculates:

> Throughout eastern Melanesia it is tempting to recognize an early Lapitoid series whose makers were ancestral to the Polynesians, contemporary with and eventually replaced by a parallel paddle-impressed, incised and applique series whose makers have contributed substantially to present Melanesian culture and phenotype (1975: 15).

As can be seen from the brief discussion above, there are many unresolved problems in Melanesian prehistory. For example, despite the numerous Lapita sites and the recognized importance of this cultural tradition, it is not yet known from where the original Lapita potters came. Shutler and Shutler note some of the problems that confront the prehistorian in his attempt to sort out the origin and dispersal of the Lapita potters:

> Various questions surround the role of Lapita pottery in Melanesia. It is not clear whether it represents a type of pottery spread widely throughout Melanesia by migration, diffusion, trade or all three, or whether it represents a whole culture (1975: 73).

Nevertheless, a few things are certain with regard to Lapita pottery, for in both western and eastern Melanesia, the coastal orientation of Lapita sites is consistently maintained. In addition, the long-range trading associated with the Lapita cultures is also clearly established. Shutler and Shutler present a reasonable hypothesis regarding the identity of the Lapita peoples. They note:

> It is tempting to view Lapita and similar pottery as evidence of the rapid spread of Austronesian-speaking seagoing farmers. However, there is no conclusive evidence that the Lapita people were farmers. The fate of this kind of pottery in Melanesia is quite unknown. It may have been replaced by new kinds of pottery brought by new people or simply altered into types. The evidence from Buka, from the New Hebrides and from Fiji suggests that both processes took place (1975: 73-74).

The correlation of material culture, gene pools, and language is indeed a monumental task yet to be completed in Melanesia. A complicated Melanesian prehistory is to be expected, given the cultural diversity that Europeans discovered upon contact, and which continues to exist today. What I have attempted to demonstrate in this brief review is the diachronic dimension of this Melanesian diversity. The above evidence also underscores the point that the pre-contact period was dynamic and not static. In conclusion, Shutler and Shutler summarize the pre-history of Melanesia and note the complexities of the problem:

> The people of Melanesia are the result of an extremely old and continuing flow of people from the Asiatic mainland into the islands of the southwest Pacific. During the later part of their history they have, in addition, maintained sporadic contact with

> people inhabiting island groups to the north and east. From time to time and from many places, new movements of people have brought changes to the gene pools, to the languages and customs, and to the subsistence patterns of the people of the Melanesian islands (1975: 75-77).

The Linguistic Situation in Melanesia

The following discussion on language has been included in this pre-contact chapter for the purpose of reviewing the linguistic evidence to see if it lends support to my suggestion that the pre-contact period was a dynamic and **not** a static one. The data demonstrate that there was a great deal of non-European culture contact through migration of different peoples into the Pacific Basin. The same data also demonstrate that the impressive **cultural** diversity of the area is related to, and has its roots in, a significant linguistic diversity.

The value of linguistic data for prehistoric reconstruction has been firmly established, especially since the advent of glottochronology and lexicostatistics.[46] In this brief review of the linguistic situation in Melanesia one discovers that much of the data accords with the sketchy outlines of prehistory now being developed by culture historians. Indeed, it is an integral part of the culture historians' emerging picture of the settlement patterns in Oceania.

Melanesia is one of the most linguistically diverse areas of the world. The causes for such diversity cannot simply be explained by the laws of linguistic change, for there does not seem to be sufficient time depth to account for the divergence of so many languages in a relatively small geographical area. Other factors must be considered to account for this tremendous diversity, including the geography and topography of the island world, the high degree of social and political fragmentation and the relative frequency of bilingualism in an area as ethnically diverse as Melanesia.[47] Melanesian speech communities are very small, comprising only a few hundred to a few thousand speakers for each language. The languages of Melanesia are truly legion, for Wurm (1971) has suggested as many as one thousand for the New Guinea area alone.

As one moves eastward from New Guinea into Island Melanesia and then into Polynesia, the linguistic diversity decreases.[48] In contrast to Melanesia, Polynesia appears linguistically to be very homogeneous. This is in agreement with present broad outlines of prehistory, which suggest that man entered Oceania from the west, migrating in a southeasterly direction to occupy the island world. One would expect to find the greatest diversity where there is the longest time-depth for man's occupation of the islands, but as noted above, the time-depth alone cannot account for such Melanesian linguistic diversity.

The languages of Melanesia fall into two large categories. About three hundred languages are included in the Austronesian family and the remaining seven hundred or more are grouped into different phyla and collectively called Papuan, or non-Austronesian. Most of these are found in the New Guinea area, with some in the Western Solomons.[49] The eastern geographical extension of non-Austronesian languages has now been established in the Santa Cruz Islands.[50] The relationship between many of these languages is unclear, and for this reason many linguists have preferred the term non-Austronesian rather than Papuan, to convey the notion that these languages are negatively classified together. What they have in common is that they are not Austronesian languages. Nevertheless, investigators are now beginning to bring some order out of this linguistic chaos.[51]

Most of the languages in Island Melanesia, with which this study is concerned belong to a sub-group of the large (spatially and numerically) Austronesian family, which is divided into Western Austronesian (Indonesian) and Eastern Austronesian (Oceanic). The languages of the Western branch comprise at least two hundred languages, widely dispersed geographically from Madagascar to Taiwan, with a few languages in Vietnam, Cambodia and Malaysia, but most of them spoken in the region of Indonesia and the Philippines.[52] There is greater linguistic affinity among the languages of the Oceanic sub-group of the Austronesian family, than between the languages in the Indonesian sub-group. The Oceanic branch, containing at least three hundred languages, is dispersed east of 135° East Longitude, into the islands of Melanesia, Micronesia and Polynesia.

Since the non-Austronesian languages cluster in western Melanesia, in New Guinea, New Britain, and the Western Solomons, most scholars associate these languages with the earliest inhabitants of Melanesia coming from the Asiatic mainland.[53] Within this interpretive framework, the non-Austronesian languages in the Santa Cruz-Main Reef Islands group appear to be an anomaly, since they are found so far east of the main cluster, and separated by a wide expanse of open sea between Santa Cruz and the southeast end of the Solomon Islands chain, which would have required a considerable navigational feat for the non-Austronesian speakers to make a land-fall. As noted above, pottery associated with the Lapita tradition has been uncovered in this area. All other Lapita sites, however, are assumed to be associated with Austronesian speakers; thus a notable exception has been found to the presumed pattern established elsewhere in the Pacific. How do we account for this anomaly? Roger Green (1963, 1976: 51-55) argues that the non-Austronesian speakers of Island Melanesia were not the original inhabitants of this area, and that in Santa Cruz and the Main Reef group, they followed Austronesians who preceded them in settling the area.[54]

There has been considerable debate regarding the origin and routes of dispersal of the Austronesian languages in Melanesia.[55] I will very briefly review the arguments of three different scholars, each offering a different interpretation of the data.

1. **Capell** (1962) holds the view that Austronesian languages were derived from the Asiatic mainland, and that a series of migrations of Austronesian speakers took place at different times. Melanesian languages, according to Capell, are a form of pidginization, resulting from the mixing of Austronesian with non-Austronesian speakers. Capell believes the Polynesian languages do not show any evidence of a mixing with a non-Austronesian sub-stratum and are the result of a separate migration of people moving from the Asian mainland, through Melanesia and out into the islands of Polynesia. Contrary to many scholars who hold that the Polynesian outliers in Melanesia are the result of a westward migration of people from western Polynesia, Capell believes that they demonstrate his thesis of a later migration of Austronesian speakers moving eastward to Polynesia, and are colonies that were left behind.

2. **Isidore Dyen** (1965) offers a very different interpretation of the data and suggests an alternative pattern of migration of Pacific languages. Beginning with the assumption that the geographical area of greatest diversity would be the homeland of Austronesian languages, he assigns the origin of Austronesian languages to western Melanesia.[56] From here he postulates a series of migrations distributing the Austronesian languages to Micronesia, Polynesia, Indonesia and beyond. However, as Bellwood (1975: 11) notes, this view does not agree with the available archaeological and physical anthropological evidence. The tremendous linguistic diversity found in western Melanesia is far better explained by long-term borrowing from non-Austronesian languages, the high degree of social and political fragmentation aided by geographical isolation, and the relative frequency of bilingualism in an area as culturally diverse as western Melanesia.

3. **George Grace** (1964, 1968) gives us a third interpretation, and one with which I am inclined to be more in agreement. He establishes the original homeland of the Austronesian languages in Southeast Asia where they split from the Kadai languages. A differentiation between Eastern and Western Austronesian followed, with considerable migration of Austronesian speakers, so that by 1500 B.C., Austronesian languages were distributed throughout Indonesia, the Philippines, Taiwan and Melanesia.

This debate on the origin and dispersal of Oceanic languages demonstrates the complexity of the problem. Chowning warns us against any simplified interpretation. She cautions:

> My own belief is that the history of Austronesian languages in Melanesia has been long and complicated, and that the greatest mistake is to over-simplify it, among other things by trying to explain everything in terms of unidirectional movements of people (1977: 13).

Nevertheless, tentative conclusions can be drawn and a general picture, as outlined below, begins to emerge.

Approximately four to five thousand years ago, the major groups of islands in Melanesia were settled by Austronesian (Oceanic) speakers.[57] An Oceanic language, either in the Southeast Solomons or Northern New Hebrides, began spreading over the entire Southeast Solomons, the Banks', and northern and central New Hebrides islands about four thousand years ago. As the speakers of this Oceanic language dispersed, their language began differentiating, thus giving rise to the tremendous linguistic diversity found in this area today. The result of this dispersal of Oceanic speakers was a splitting of the language into two groups: (1) Southeast Solomon, and (2) Eastern Oceanic.

The Eastern Oceanic group then divided into a Northern New Hebrides language group and a Central Pacific group, whose speakers migrated eastward to Fiji. Around 1000 B.C., this Central Pacific language group began breaking up into the Fijian and Polynesian groups which are ancestral to the languages spoken today.[58] To this general scheme must be added the westward migration of Polynesian speakers, in the last two thousand years or less, back into Melanesia and settling the outliers such as Anuta, Tikopia, the Duff Islands, etc.

The Classification of Melanesian Languages.

1. The Solomon Islands. In the Western Solomons the relationship of languages to each other is not as clearly understood as it is for the Central and Southeastern Solomon Islands. Hackman (1968) identifies 74 speech communities in the Solomons (excluding Bougainville and islands politically incorporated into Papua New Guinea).[59] With such linguistic diversity as we find in Melanesia the question is often asked if all of these languages are distinct languages or just dialects. The question of "language" versus "dialect" is a complicated problem. Many of the islands have a series of speech communities that form dialect-chains running from one end of the island to the other. In a dialect-chain one speech community can understand the language of an adjacent speech community, but it cannot understand the language of another community that is separated from it by one or more different speech communities.[60] In other words, people in the middle of the dialect chain can communicate with speech communities on either side of them. But people at one end of the island, or dialect chain, will not be able to communicate with people at the other end.

Of these 74 "languages," 62 are Austronesian and the remaining 12 are non-Austronesian. Of the 62 Austronesian languages, 5 are Polynesian, spoken on the outlying islands, and 57 are the Melanesian languages spoken in the major islands. These languages are then divided, according to Hackman, into Western, Central and Eastern Solomonese. Pawley (1972: 99-110) proposes a classification of Southeast Solomonic, in which two large subgroups are fairly well marked: (1) Guadalcanal-Nggellalic, and (2) Cristobal-Malaitan.

2. The New Hebrides. In the New Hebrides the classification of languages has been attempted by Tryon (1972). He identifies 110 languages, including 3 Polynesian languages, spoken in the New Hebrides. These languages he divides into 10 different groups. A higher order classification is then established in terms of two types of languages: (1) an Oceanic type (45 languages), and (2) a Melanesian type. Tryon states that the Oceanic type appears to be closely related to the languages of the South Solomons and Fiji.

The reconstruction of the dispersal of Melanesian languages and their classification show clearly that the linguistic picture is very complex, and that Melanesians have experienced a long history of culture contact with other island peoples. In this sense, the linguistic data is in agreement with the archaeological evidence, both suggesting a significant diachronic dimension to the diversity one finds in Melanesia today.

Traditional Melanesian Habitat and Cultural Adaptation

The above discussion of prehistory and language provides a foundation for considering other traditional cultural elements in Melanesia. In this section different modes of cultural adaptation to the Melanesian ecosystem will be discussed. Attention will focus on the subsistence economy, trade networks, forms of indigenous wealth, and various items of traditional Melanesian material culture.

The Subsistence Economy.

The economic life of Melanesia is fairly uniform. Swidden agriculture and pig-raising comprise the subsistence economy by which the islanders live. In the larger islands, where the distinction is found between coastal dwellers and bushmen, there is also a difference in diet. Those on the coast engage in fishing activities while those in the interior hunt feral pigs to supplement their diet. Traditional Melanesian diet was comprised almost entirely of root crops, taro and yam being the principal staples before the introduction of the sweet potato.[61] Sago in swampy areas was sometimes an important substitute. Breadfruit was a more important supplement in the New Hebrides than in the Solomon Islands. Bananas and other fruit, as well as the canarium nut (almond), were also used for food, and as supplements to a fairly uniform and bland diet.[62] The majority of root crops, unlike cereals, were not suitable for storing for long periods of time. Although Polynesians developed methods for preserving some foods, this skill was not highly developed in Melanesia, thus necessitating the procurement of fresh food nearly every day. This activity was the responsibility of every family in the local group.

Swidden agriculture requires large blocks of land, since garden plots become depleted of their nutrients after a short time, and must lie fallow to regain their fertility. To Melanesians, access to the use of land constitutes their birthright, for land is their most valuable possession. The relationship between people and the land is a very close one, and all groups that are politically significant have their roots in land. Individuals seldom owned land personally, for it was generally held in trust by the corporate group. Membership in a group was normally determined by descent or residence, or some combination of the two.[63] A great variety of systems of land tenure exists in Melanesia, and the only universal seems to be that of the closeness, both ecologically and culturally, of man-land relationships. However, the only known incidents of warfare over land occur in the New Guinea Highlands where there is considerably more pressure on the land due to higher population densities than exist in Island Melanesia.[64] In discussing the variety in systems of land tenure in Melanesia, Chowning observes that:

> The details of the systems of land tenure differ greatly from society to society. Some permit permanent alienation and individual ownership; others do not. It is not uncommon to find distinctions made between gardening land, village land or house sites, and bush land, with different systems of rights applied to each, not to mention the rights that relate to sacred places, grave sites, paths, water supplies, sago swamps, and fishing areas. Trees often constitute a special category of real property and are treated differently both from gardening land and from temporary gardens (1977: 39).[65]

The basis of subsistence economies in traditional Melanesia consisted of gardening, hunting and fishing. Unlike commercial economies in the West where there is emphasis on economic development through progressively expanding capital formation, Melanesian economies employed simple and nondurable material equipment and expressed the prime values of kinship-based cooperation and reciprosity.[66]

Trade Networks.

On the whole, traditional Melanesian communities were self-sufficient. Trade between communities did occur, however, and in many areas fairly elaborate exchange networks were developed. Trade was primarily in exchange for scarce raw materials, such as stone for axes and adzes, pigments, shell for making valuables and ornaments, and also for manufactured items such as pottery, salt, and canoes. Exchange of food products also occurred, as for example salt-water people exchanging fish for vegetables grown by their bitter enemies in the bush, or as in the Banks' Islands, where food on one island was exchanged for shell money and fish on another.[67]

The partly ceremonial *kula* trade ring,[68] made anthropologically famous by Malinowski's (1922) excellent analysis and description, is not representative of the widespread and elaborate systems found elsewhere in Melanesia which were usually utilitarian.[69]

Although traditional Melanesian societies are characteristically egalitarian, this does not mean there were no specialists within each community. While everyone was involved in some way with obtaining sufficient food, in addition, some individuals specialized in providing goods and services, such as the manufacture of utilitarian items or elaborate ornaments, or performance of magic ritual. Such individuals were paid, but they were not full-time specialists, freed from normal garden activities.[70]

Indigenous Wealth.

There were primarily two kinds of indigenous wealth in traditional Melanesian society: (1) pigs, and (2) portable valuables, frequently made from shell. Porpoise teeth, dogs' teeth, curved boars' tusks, and pierced stone discs, comprised other forms of personal wealth.

In addition, there were non-material forms of indigenous wealth; such items as labor, magical charms, and specialist knowledge were saleable commodities. For example, a man renowned for his *mana* could acquire material property in exchange for offering his powers and prestige to some particular end.

There were also indigenous forms of "money" which in some societies approached the Western use of the term, allowing individuals to purchase goods and services in exchange for the currency, or as in the Banks' Islands, where individuals loaned shell money at interest rates of up to 100 percent.

In the Northern New Hebrides, specially made woven mats were used as money, primarily to buy steps in the graded men's society. Shell money was used in the Banks' Islands and the Solomon Islands. Each small round disc was made from certain shells, which were broken and rubbed into shape. A small hole was drilled in the center and then the discs were strung on to a string usually a fathom in length.[71] Another type of money found only in Santa Cruz, is known as red feather money. The red breast-feathers of a small honey-eater (*Myzomela cardinalis*) are plucked and then glued on to a prepared belt which measures about 15 feet in length. It is then coiled up and stored.[72]

The uses of indigenous wealth were primarily for major transactions such as compensation for death and marriage payments. In some societies individuals stored valuables as an index of their importance and prestige in the community, but frequently the accumulation was followed by an ostentatious display and its redistribution. An important aspect of the traditional socio-economic system was the exchange and distribution of wealth, both in the form of pigs and other food, as well as valuables. This was one of the principal avenues by which a potential Big Man emerged and established his role as a community leader. Thus a great deal of wealth was distributed by competitive reciprocity commonly involving leading men in lavish displays of wealth and "gifts" of valuables to rivals, who were then placed in the person's debt, and thus obliged to make a return display.[73] There are many obvious similarities between the Melanesian economic system of exchange and the well-known potlach of the American Indians in the Pacific Northwest.[74]

Material Culture.

The topic of traditional Melanesian material culture is indeed complex, but must nevertheless be briefly considered in this section. There is no uniform artistic style in decorative arts, or in utilitarian objects, or in major works such as house and canoe building. The most characteristic feature of Melanesian material culture is its variety and diversity of form.

One important focus of traditional material culture was on weapons. Spears, clubs, shields, and bows and arrows were the principal items and these were frequently elaborately decorated. As there was no knowledge, throughout the area, of the use of metals, most weapons were made completely from wood, although in some areas projectile points were tipped with flint, or with human or animal bone. In the Solomon Islands, protective shields were made from tightly woven cane as well as from solid wood.[75]

The principal Neolithic tools were digging sticks and the adze and axe. The latter two employed either shell or polished stone for the cutting blade. At the time of European contact, the use of pottery was not widespread in Melanesia. Cooking was done with hot stones in pits covered with leaves, so that food was steamed rather than boiled in pots.

There was not a wide variety of musical instruments in Melanesia. The slit-gong, conch shell, castanets, bamboo flutes and pan-pipes, comprised the main inventory. In the New Hebrides, slit-gongs were elaborately carved, but there were none in Santa Cruz or Nggela in the Solomon Islands.[76]

The majority of decorative artwork was related to paraphernalia used on ceremonial occasions, and was frequently ingenious and often highly decorated. Noteworthy in this category are the elaborate costumes associated with the secret societies.[77] An outstanding development of Melanesian material culture is that used for religious and ceremonial purposes. Ceremonial ornamentation and the many ritual props combined with it, produced elaborate materials in the form of wood carvings, tapa cloth with intricate designs, masks, head-dresses and other items. In some of the islands this elaborate religious paraphernalia was immediately destroyed after its use on ceremonial occasions. In other places it was kept as a family heirloom and brought out only on appropriate occasions.

Decorative art, however, was not just ceremonial, but was applied to many utilitarian objects as well. In the Solomon Islands house posts were elaborately carved with figures of men, crocodiles, and sharks.[78] Wooden bowls used in making puddings and mixing food were generally carved with elaborate artistic motifs. Lime "boxes" containing lime used in chewing areca nut, were often sketched with ornate designs on the outside of the container.[79] One of the outstanding techniques used in the Solomon Islands was inlaid work using mother-of-pearl shell. Nearly all utilitarian objects were potential sources for decorative art and in many cases there was no religious significance associated with it.[80]

Among larger enterprises such as canoe and house building, there was also great variety in skill and deployment of available natural resources. This variety is seen in the number of different house types that existed in traditional Melanesian society. As in canoe building, the simplest and crudest houses were found in the Banks' and northern New Hebrides, while the best built and most developed styles were in the coastal villages of the Solomon Islands, with perhaps the best of these appearing on Santa Isabel where they were constructed on piles. Also on Santa Isabel there were tree houses, built 90-100 feet up in the limbs of tall trees and entered by way of a rope ladder. These houses appear to have been built in response to the heavy headhunting raids in the nineteenth century, and were primarily used as a means for protection in attack instead of a permanent dwelling place.[81]

The art of canoe building reached high development in some parts of Melanesia. Perhaps the most impressive Melanesian canoes were the large deep sea canoes built in Fiji.[82] In our geographical area of consideration, a notable difference in construction existed between canoes built in the Banks' and New Hebrides and those in the Solomon Islands.[83]

Canoes in the Banks' and New Hebrides were dugout canoes with an attached outrigger. Although a clumsy creation compared to the elegant canoes in the Solomon Islands, these outriggered craft employed sails, whereas those in the Solomons were propelled by men paddling. The outrigger canoe is more characteristic of Melanesia, with the Solomon Islands' canoes being the exception.

Intermediary between the Banks' and Solomons was the Santa Cruz canoe, which while attaching the outrigger to a hollowed-out tree trunk, was a better canoe in workmanship and construction than those found to the south of the area. It employed a large sail and was capable of long sea voyages.[84]

The elegant plank canoes of the Solomons are one of the outstanding achievements of traditional Melanesian material culture. Canoes varied in size from small ones for children, to the large war canoes (*tomako*) measuring up to 60 feet long by 6 feet wide, and capable of carrying 100 men.[85] These canoes were built from planks hewn out from specially selected trees. The planks were fitted and sewn together with the seams caulked with a resin produced from a local tree. The art of inlay with pearl shell was frequently applied to these canoes. Thus, the Solomon Island canoes were not only among the fastest paddled in the Pacific, but also the most beautifully decorated.[86]

There are of course other areas of Melanesian material culture that could be discussed, but the brief treatment given here must suffice for this study. In later sections when I discuss specific areas of culture change, greater detail will be given to those areas of material culture that changed through time.[87]

In summarizing this brief section on the traditional cultural adaptation to Melanesian habitat, I want to emphasize the importance of the integration that was obtained. This integration occurred at many levels in the society. For example, although most communities were essentially self-sufficient, symbiotic trade networks were developed which, while serving primarily utilitarian ends, occasionally had ceremonial dimensions to them. One community would provide one resource in exchange for another in a reciprocal arrangement that frequently involved many communities in an elaborately organized, highly efficient and dynamic system. Melanesian people were one with their natural surroundings, employing the resources of their environment harmoniously with their social and religious concerns. This interweaving of horticulture, religion, social organization, technology and economics into a unified system in equilibrium is one of the most characteristic features of traditional Melanesian society.[88] It is not surprising then to discover that as change occurred in some areas of the society and culture, it quickly ramified throughout, affecting the ecological balance between man and nature. Since the focus of this study is on socio-religious change, this area will be discussed in greater depth, but it cannot be discussed independently of changes that have occurred in the overall ecological adaptation of Melanesians.

Social Organization in Traditional Melanesian Society

The concept of social organization is broad and inclusive of many domains that relate to how people organize their social relations. However, in this section only a select few will be briefly discussed. These include, kinship, leadership, residence, and warfare as they relate to traditional Melanesian societies.

Kinship.

Melanesian societies, like those throughout Oceania, are all kinship-based, as opposed to market-dominated societies.[89] They are all stateless and lack any centralized authority. In contrast to Polynesia, Melanesian societies are minute in scale. Thus, for example, in Island Melanesia the largest social unit possessing a coherent system for the maintenance of internal order is normally a group consisting of no more than seventy to three hundred people. In the New Guinea Highlands, this may exceed to a thousand or more, but this is still small when compared to eastern Polynesia, where the number would range in the tens of thousands. As the group is small, so is its clearly defined geographical area, which seldom extends beyond a few square miles.[90]

In Melanesia the formation of local groups is based primarily on kinship and descent. Given the great diversity of other cultural domains, one is not surprised to discover a variety of social systems and types of kinship nomenclature within Melanesia. Descent is both unilinear and double, and is reckoned patrilineally, matrilineally and cognatically. The Iroquois type of kinship nomenclature is the most common, but the Omaha, Choctaw, and Hawaiian types are found as well.

In Rivers' classic survey of Melanesian social organization he identified four kinds of social systems in traditional Melanesian society (1914 II: 70):

1. A dual organization with a matrilineal descent.
2. Social organization based on totemic clans, following primarily matrilineal, but also patrilineal descent.
3. Local groupings based on non-totemic exogamous clans which are primarily matrilineal, but also patrilineal.
4. Social organization in which exogamous clans are absent and marriage is regulated only geneologically, with either matrilineal or patrilineal descent.

He determined that the earliest form of social structure in Island Melanesia was a dual organization with matrilineal descent.[91] In this belief, he is supported by Codrington (1891: 21) who acknowledged that, "Nothing seems more fundamental than the divisions of the people into two or more classes, which are exogamous, and in which descent is counted through the mother." In Island Melanesia therefore, local groups organized into exogamous matrilineal clans, are, according to Codrington (1891: 21), "the foundation on which the fabric of native society is built."

At the time of contact, the dual organization in its most fundamental form of matrilineal moieties, was found in the Banks' Islands and the northern New Hebrides. The distribution of matrilineal descent systems is confined primarily to the New Hebrides, the Solomons, New Ireland, the eastern half of New Britain and the Massim district of New Guinea. In the Solomon Islands, Nggela, Santa Isabel, Savo, and part of Guadalcanal form a distinctively matrilineal area. The strict moiety system is absent however, for on Nggela there are six exogamous clans, and on Santa Isabel there are three.[92] The Shortland Islands and Buin district of Bougainville in the Western Solomons are matrilineal, but Choiseul is distinguished by cognatic descent.[93]

Rivers (1914 II: 79) found exogamous totemic clans in the Santa Cruz Group, the Shortlands and in the Buin district of Bougainville, and on Efate in the New Hebrides. A modified form of totemism existed in the matrilineal region of the Solomons, namely, Nggela, Guadalcanal, Savo, and Santa Isabel.

In the southeastern Solomons, in an area comprised of linguistically related societies (Ulawa, Ugi, and parts of Malaita, Guadalcanal, and San Cristobal), patrilineal descent without exogamous clans is the dominant social system, thus forming an interesting exception to the pattern of exogamous matrilineal clans found in most other parts of Island Melanesia.[94]

The local group (70-300 people) based on different patterns of kinship and social organization and residentially defined, was the primary political entity in traditional Melanesian society. The small size of these political entities is one of the most characteristic features of Melanesian social organization.[95]

Leadership Within the Local Group.

In such small, kinship-based societies as we find in Melanesia, there is seldom any institutionalized social stratification. With notable exceptions, the general pattern is one of egalitarian societies. Granting the universal qualifications affecting status, such as age, sex and personal characteristics, traditional Melanesian societies were essentially egalitarian in the sense that everyone had equal access to resources. The whole population carried out the same kind of tasks.[96] Some interesting exceptions to this Melanesian egalitarianism were found in the Western Solomons where a slavery complex existed primarily for use in religious ritual and human sacrifice.[97] In Sa'a, south Malaita, there existed an institutionalized distinction between a chiefly class and commoners. In the southern New Hebrides, where there is more Polynesian influence, minor chiefs existed, and in New Caledonia, a more elaborate and highly structured chieftainship was present in the pre-contact period. In Fiji, at the eastern border of Melanesia, an institutionalized chieftainship was even more developed.[98]

Elaborately ranked secret societies were found on Nggela in the Solomons, and in the Banks' and northern New Hebrides. An index of a man's status in these cultures was the grade he achieved in the secret society. The top grades were open to all, but because of the expensive price involved, only a select few reached the highest positions. A man in the top grade had tremendous prestige and consequent influence in community affairs.[99]

Leadership in these egalitarian Melanesian societies was primarily achieved, and not ascribed, as was common in Polynesia. A person's position and prestige was not governed by a hereditary rank. It was related to his seniority within a kin group, and to the grade he achieved in areas where there were secret societies.

One of the primary mechanisms, whereby one became recognized as a leader and gained personal influence in the community, was the accumulation and distribution of indigenous wealth, such as shell-money, pigs, and vegetables. In communities organized around exogamous clans, frequently the "heads" of each clan, would be recognized as the "chiefs" of a village, but in many societies, one man in particular emerged as the leader of the local group. In Melanesia, indigenous terms describing this person have often been translated into the English gloss, "Big Man." The model of the Melanesian Big Man as the socio-political leader of a local group is well known for its remarkable contrast with leadership roles in traditional societies found elsewhere in the world.[100]

Reflecting the socio-political minuteness of the local group in Melanesia, the characteristic Big Man may have true command ability within his own group, but outside it, he has no authority, and so he must settle for only fame and indirect influence. Sahlins, in characterizing this general model of leadership in Melanesia, says:

> The indicative quality of big-man authority is everywhere the same; it is personal power. Big men do not come to office; they do not succeed to, nor are they installed in, existing positions of leadership over political groups. The attainment of big-man status is rather the outcome of a series of acts which elevate a person above the common herd and attract about him a coterie of loyal, lesser men. It is not accurate to speak of "big-man" as a political title, for it is but an acknowledged standing in interpersonal relations — a "prince among men" so to speak as opposed to "the Prince of the Danes" (1970: 206).

In Polynesia, an institutionalized position of leadership exists and a man is nominated by virtue of his hereditary rank to fill that position as a chief. In contrast, a Melanesian Big Man emerges as a leader in a local group primarily because of his personal attributes. The position of his father, or his mother's brother before him, can certainly help him in obtaining Big Man status for himself, but in no way does it guarantee it. In Polynesia leadership is based on institutionalized position (office); in Melanesia, it is based on individual personality.[101]

What are the important personal attributes that enable a Melanesian to emerge from the group as a central leader? Valentine's characterization of a Melanesian Big Man articulates clearly the necessary personal attributes and the *modus operandi* of a potential leader:

> The typical traditional Melanesian headman or "big man" achieves prestige and power through hard work in the gardens, prowess in

> warfare, a reputation as a magician, shrewdness in trading, a commanding personality, or skill in attracting and organizing followers. He must constantly validate his status and humble his rivals by financing and organizing feasts and ceremonies within a context of complex mutual obligations. He has no official hierarchy or sanctified office on which to base his claims of social ascendancy. His control of the economic activities of others is far less than of Polynesian and Micronesian chiefs. He is not exempt from subsistence tasks, and he does not work within a system of graded occupational specialities. He achieves little or nothing in the way of privileged consumption, and any surplus which he controls must be expended in further competitive activities if he is to maintain his position. (1970: 342).

In Island Melanesia particularly, the authority and power of a Big Man rested on the belief that his supernatural power was derived from spirits and ghosts with whom he communicated. Thus, the personal attributes of an individual Big Man which enabled him to rise to a position of leadership were supplemented by belief that he also had access to supernatural power (*mana*) and possessed it. By virtue of his access to such power, lesser men often feared him and were in subjugation to him. The importance that supernatural power was believed to have in the rise and maintenance of a man's authority as a leader, cannot be over emphasized. Thus, in many Melanesian societies it was not uncommon to find a local Big Man also engaged as the chief sacrificer or "priest" for a particular ghost or spirit whom the community venerated. Secular and sacred power were welded together in the person of the Melanesian Big Man — one known to have *mana.*[102]

Residence Patterns in Melanesian Societies.

The local group in Melanesia is in many ways a self-contained unit. Mechanisms for social control are confined within this local group, and as its members survive on a subsistence economy, they are self-sufficient politically as well as economically.

The residential pattern for local groups in Melanesia takes on one of three different forms: (1) a nucleated village, (2) a cluster of hamlets, or (3) a series of neighboring homesteads.[103]

In these communities (especially in the nucleated villages) traditionally there were commonly two foci of residence: (1) single or multiple-family household dwellings, and (2) a men's club house, which was frequently the focal point of a village and was surrounded by an aura of sanctity which made it particularly dangerous for women and children to enter.[104]

In the larger Melanesian islands the residence pattern frequently demonstrated a distinction between those dwelling on or near the coast and those living in the mountainous interior.[105] Generally the "salt-water people" on the coast lived in nucleated villages, where the size of the local group reached the upper limits of the Melanesian pattern (300 people). In the interior the "bush people" frequently lived in dispersed hamlets and the size of the local group was generally smaller than its counterpart on the coast (perhaps 20 people, and all related through kinship and/or descent).[106]

The distinction between bushmen and salt-water people is one of the most striking features of traditional Melanesian culture. Noting the difference between these two groups, Hopkins says:

> They are hereditary foes and live in a state of perpetual hostility tempered by truces necessitated by their mutual need of each other. The bush man requires fish and access to the sea; the coast man wants vegetable food and access to the bush tracks (1928: 151).

Frequently salt-water people viewed those in the bush as "country bumpkins" and as poor specimens of humanity at best. However, on San Cristobal, it was believed that bushmen had more *mana* than coastal peoples.

This distinction between coastal people and bushmen was more pronounced in the Soloman Islands than in the New Hebrides, reaching its most definite expression on Malaita. On many parts of Malaita, coastal dwellers went one step further in segregating themselves from the bushmen, by living on small islets off the coast, or constructing artificial islands in the lagoon, which were crowded with as many as four hundred inhabitants.[107]

In the larger Melanesian islands such as Malaita, Rivers (1914 II: 305) noted that:

> The two peoples are not merely different in physical appearance, in language and in many elements of culture, but they are sometimes in a state of continual warfare, tempered only by trade relations.

Moreover, Hopkins (1928: 140) noted that the general pattern of hostility between groups on the island was such that villages or hamlets on the same elevation level in one district would be allies, but those above or below the line would be hostile enemies.

Traditional Melanesian Warfare.

This section will deal with another characteristic of traditional Melanesian societies, namely the internecine hostility that existed between local groups. Given the small scale of Melanesian socio-political entities, it is not surprising to find local groups in competition with each other, but the amount of fighting that existed in Melanesia cannot be explained in terms of competition for scarce resources. Motivations for aggravating hostility varied from one area to another. Hopkins, writing about the Solomon Islands says the main cause of the chronic state of hostility between local groups was the firm belief in sorcery. He reasons:

> Death to the Solomon Island philosophy is unnatural, caused by spirits. These spirits may be those of their own tribe, neglected and angry; but far more probably it is some spirit of another tribe who has caused the death. If so, it is because that spirit has been invoked by an enemy. And so tribe lived suspicious of tribe, with but little intercourse, and that little always heavy with fear of possible evil machinations under a guise of friendship (1928: 169).

Other causes of warfare were the stealing of pigs or canoes, and the abduction of women. The need to avenge any previous killings was also a compelling motive for such activity. If a Big Man or his property were cursed, this frequently led to warfare. If a man cursed another, or if two men quarreled, or if a wife cursed her husband, then the man would have to go out seeking a victim to kill in order to restore his *mana*.[108] Adultery with the wife of a Big Man or illicit sexual intercourse with his daughter also brought on a state of hostility and warfare.[109]

If the above incidents were direct causes for warfare, then it must be added that the ideology of warfare was supported by cultural assumptions about the behavior of warriors. Courageous and skillful warriors were held up as the Melanesian masculine ideal, and successful raiding brought prestige to the group. In Herskovits' term (1955: 485) warfare was a cultural focus of traditional Melanesian society.[110]

Several methods of warfare existed, including occasional participation on an established battleground where both sides would fight until one or the other had had enough. In these battles there was seldom any wholesale slaughter, since warriors were content to kill only one or two of the enemy. The more frequent methods, however, involved surprise raids, frequently in the hours just before dawn, or stalking and killing individuals in order to earn blood money.[111] Numerous references are found in the early contact literature describing the "treachery and cowardice" of the Melanesians. Such ethnocentric evaluations, however, fail to appreciate the strategy of guerrilla warfare in which the islanders were so adept. Seldom were large-scale numbers slaughtered in battle, for normally a sportive surprise attack, in which only several victims were taken, would suffice.[112]

Headhunting was an aggressive act compelled by motives different from that of mere raiding. Codrington (1891: 345) says that the headhunting complex in Melanesia was limited to Santa Isabel and westward. That is, islanders did not make expeditions for the sole purpose of obtaining heads. However, in other parts of the Solomons the heads of the fallen enemy were kept and displayed as trophies. The center of headhunting was in the Roviana Lagoon in New Georgia, and from here organized raids, up to one hundred miles away, were carried out for the sole purpose of obtaining heads, and carrying them back in their canoes to their villages. Here they were preserved on display as visible signs of the headhunters' power and success. Headhunting was integrally interwoven into the islanders' religious system, for in gaining a human head, one acquired *mana*, since heads were one of the most potent repositories of *mana*.[113]

Related to headhunting was a slavery complex. Slaves were, however, not taken and maintained for the purpose of service and servitude, but were kept to ensure a supply for human sacrifices which were frequently required in the islanders' religious ritual. The building of a men's house, the launching of a war canoe, etc. were all occasions for such sacrifices.[114]

Cannibalism was a cultural element in many traditional Melanesian societies, with its distribution spread from Fiji to New Guinea. In Fiji and among the Tolai in New Britain at the time of European contact, cannibalism was practiced primarily for gustatory rather than ceremonial and religious reasons. In both these areas, human flesh was sold in open markets. It is questionable whether the gustatory motivation for cannibalism went far back into the pre-contact period. For example, in Fiji, cannibalism was initially ceremonial and not the secular activity that it became when it reached its peak in the early nineteenth century after the introduction of firearms to the islanders. Cannibalism in the Solomon Islands was primarily for reasons other than the craving for human flesh. Hopkins notes that:

> It was the triumphal sacrifice of a victim; it marked the extremity of revenge and contempt. Further, perhaps the main *raison d'etre* was this: The eaters absorbed the *mana* not only of the victim, but of his tribe, from whom he was inseparable in thought (1928: 201).

It is unlikely that cannibalism was a universal practice in Melanesia, and where it did occur, it was probably occasional and sporadic. Codrington (1891: 343) says it did not exist in the Banks' Islands and the Santa Cruz Group, although it was practiced in the northern New Hebrides.[115]

In summarizing this section on social organization, it should be emphasized that there are numerous ethnographic vetoes that can be raised in objection to any generalized statement about Melanesia. This is the nature of this area of study, and thus one must always be alert to the exception to the pattern that exists. Nevertheless, there is a general Melanesian model that emerges from the ethnographic data, and it includes the following factors.

The socio-political entity in traditional Melanesian society was a minute local grouping of 70-300 individuals. Kinship and residence were the primary criteria by which local groups were formed. Leadership was generally achieved rather than ascribed, and the values of Melanesian leadership were expressed in the model of the Big Man. With few exceptions, there were no hereditary political authorities, or hereditary ranks and status. It was an egalitarian society, and personal advancement was given to anyone who worked hard and/or was skillful in organizing others. Political and legal security depended on support from relatives and kinsmen and protection under a local Big Man.[116] Outside this local group, hostility with other groups was endemic with various causes leading to open warfare or stealthy attacks by individuals. Cannibalism, headhunting, and the capture of slaves was practiced by some, but certainly not all Melanesian communities.

Traditional Melanesian Religion and Magic

Since the focus of this study is on socio-religious change introduced by Anglican missionaries, it is important to have a good understanding of the traditional religious system before the missionaries arrived in Melanesia. For this reason, this section is necessarily lengthy. Discussion will first center on Melanesian epistemology and worldview. The role of ghosts and spirits in the traditional religious system will be discussed, as well as the important concept of *mana.* The section will conclude by looking at traditional Melanesian magico-religious ritual.

Melanesian Epistemology and Worldview.

In Melanesia there is as much diversity of religious beliefs and practices as there is a diversity of languages and other cultural domains. Nevertheless, some generalized statements are possible. Lawrence and Meggitt (1965: 1-26) have drawn some analytical distinctions between religion in the New Guinea Highlands and that of coastal New Guinea and Island Melanesia. The geographical limits of this study are confined to Island Melanesia, and thus generalizations are not intended to necessarily apply to the Highlands area.[117] The discussion to follow will be concerned with traditional Melanesian belief systems and magico-religious practices which in some areas may show considerable continuity from the traditional to the contemporary, but the discussion of the present day beliefs and practices will be reserved for Chapter Six.[118]

Melanesian epistemology is essentially religious. What I define analytically as "religious knowledge" is to the Melanesian, the most important. Melanesians, however, do not live in a compartmentalized world of secular and spiritual domains, but have an integrated worldview, in which physical and spiritual realities dovetail. Melanesians are a very religious people, and traditional religion played a dominant role in the affairs of men and permeated the life of the community. Any anthropological analysis of traditional Melanesian religion is bound to be artificial in the sense that the etic categories I use to describe their religious experience are not equivalent with the emic realities of Melanesian life. Etic categories are scientific, "objective" categories derived from the anthropologist's worldview, and applied to a specific event, an experience, or a system of beliefs, etc. in order to understand it. In contrast, an emic analysis tries to understand an indigene's subjective experience in terms of his own worldview, rather than using analytical tools that are created by the anthropological observer. An emic analysis is an insider's view, an etic analysis is an outsider's view. For example, we encounter this problem with the anthropological concept of "religion." It may be a useful analytical tool for purposes of investigation, but in the synthesis of Melanesian life, it is difficult to delimit such a category as distinct from other realities, and it is doubtful that a Melanesian would do so.

The traditional Melanesian worldview, in contrast to that of Western man's, has an entirely different understanding of man's place in the cosmos, and his relationship to it. Mantovani cogently articulates one of these differences:

> In Theism, we have God as the creator and Lord. Man, created in his image participates in his Lordship over other creatures. An abyss divides the creator from the creature and the Lord of all creatures—man—from nature. This attitude is completely lacking in traditional culture. Man feels himself part, not Lord, of creation and as a consequence he cannot exploit nature as a Theist can do (1977: 163).

This integration of the cosmos, like an animistic continuum of living and dead men, animals, plants and spirits, is the basis of Melanesian worldview. It is basic to understanding how religious beliefs and rituals function in Melanesian society.[119]

The central value of Melanesian culture is the continuation, protection, maintenance and celebration of Life. Time, energy, and attention are given to pursuing this value.[120] By maintenance of Life as a central value, I do not mean merely human biological existence. I mean cosmic life and renewal.[121] The Hebrew concept of Shalom — physical and spiritual well-being, reconciliation, justice — comes close to capturing the essence of this central Melanesian value. Human beings are the central focus of this cosmic life — the center of the Melanesian universe — but it is inclusive of plants, animals, inorganic matter and spirit beings, all belonging to an integrated universe pulsating with energy. Ancestors are perceived as the living dead, playing an active role in this cosmic life. The categories of life and death, sacred and secular, animate and inanimate, do not have the same definite features for a Melanesian as Western man would give them.[122]

This cosmic life, as a central Melanesian value, is maintained principally through right relationships with both human and spirit beings, and by the accumulation of indigenous wealth. Commenting on the traditional religion of the islanders of South Pentecost in Vanuatu, Lane says that:

> The ultimate purpose is to create and perpetuate satisfactory relations within the inner circle of kin, to cope with dangers from

> outside, and to ensure successful existence for the group, and within the framework of the group, for the individual (1965: 276).

It is around this central value of celebrating Life and the attending activities that accompany it, that one discovers the richness of Melanesian spirituality and ritual.

Cosmic renewal is the concern of Melanesian religion, and it is through an essentially religious epistemology and existential experience that life "makes sense." A religious system concerned with metaphysical absolutes and buttressed by dogma is totally alien to Melanesian belief and practice. Melanesian religion is more experiential than it is cerebral. It is a religious experience that people feel more in their livers or their stomachs, than in their heads. Traditional Melanesians are concerned with the question, "Does it work, is it effective, etc.?" The question, "Is it true?" which is important for Westerners, would not be an important element in Melanesian belief. If answered in the affirmative, the question, "Is it true?" would elicit the response, "Sure, **because** it works, it is effective, etc." A true god is one which is effective. A lying god is one who claims to be a god but is impotent. In this sense Melanesian religion is pragmatic. That is, performance of ritual brings results that are empirically verified. For example, if results are not forthcoming, then a change of religious allegiance or practice is easily made to more powerful spirit-beings, or to more effective ritual. The critical issue is one of Power, which to the Melanesian is the manifestation of Truth.[123]

Undoubtedly this aspect of Melanesian religion was one of the contributing factors in indigenes' motivation to adopt Christianity when missionary contact was first made. From the islanders' perspective, many of the traditional festivals and rituals were changed in favor of more powerful ones that would ensure life and cosmic renewal. Missionaries did not have to wage a campaign to convince islanders of the superiority of their rituals. It was plain to the observer — Europeans had **Life** in a way unimagined before. Surely their rituals must be more powerful than Melanesian ones. Mantovani, in speaking of the Chimbu, notes that:

> The old rituals were only used to get life, and facts proved them insufficient, so, logically, people discarded them. It denotes utter superficiality to blame "the mission" for the loss of traditional celebrations (1977: 164).

If one distinguishes between internal religious attitudes and external celebrations, it becomes clear that in many areas of missionary encounter, the traditional religious beliefs were seldom discarded. The rituals were simply updated, because, empirically, Christian ritual appeared to be more effective than traditional ritual in bringing to pass those things which celebrated life. In this kind of situation the traditional religious beliefs have remained fundamentally unchanged, although the ritual has been significantly altered.

Religious beliefs of Melanesians are not held as a separate domain and compartmentalized from the rest of life. Thus, when one speaks of religious beliefs, one is taking an etic category and imposing it on the Melanesian situation. Through analysis one is able to systematically order beliefs into what appears to be a coherent system of Melanesian theology. But this is an etic grid applied to the data, and not an emic domain that inherently emerges. The multitude of Melanesian beliefs relate to the central value of maintaining cosmic life, and this is expressed in the Melanesian worldview. But these beliefs are seldom developed into any precise and systematic detail or woven into an over-all scheme which we could call a religious system. Thus, from our point of view, there are contradictions in their beliefs and ideas that are logically incoherent and inconsistent. This is of little concern, however, for as Lane (1965: 253) notes for islanders of South Pentecost, "Only when belief is translated into rituals and ceremony do organization and precision predominate." Although some Melanesian societies would be more adept in intellectualizing their beliefs, what is true of South Pentecost would hold generally throughout Melanesia. The abstract and cognitive take second place to the pragmatic and experiential.

Melanesian religion has often been characterized as materialistic. The fecundity of women, the health of children, and the strength of men, are its universal concerns and express the underlying philosophical concern for cosmic renewal. Melanesian religion is materialistic in that it attempts to assure for its adherents the visible signs of life — health, abundance of food and wealth, and amicable relationships between the living and the dead. Melanesian belief and ritual focus on man's control of the cosmos for his own material well-being. They are concerned with economic and socio-political elements, which in Melanesia, are characteristically unstable and fluid, and are thus cause for anxiety and tension.

Melanesians believe that the most valuable knowledge is that which allows them to hold control of the cosmos, and thus the prevailing attitude toward religion is essentially pragmatic and materialistic. Belief and ritual must be productive, assuring the believer of an overt manifestation of material well-being, which in turn affirms the central value of Melanesian culture—the celebration of Life. Commenting on this pragmatic and materialistic tendency, Lawrence and Meggitt (1965: 18) note that in Melanesia, "Religion is a technology rather than a spiritual force for human salvation." In essence, religion in Melanesia is a technical means to a materialistic end, the end being the welfare of the individual within the group, ensuring protection from dangers without and successful existence of members within. This is the clearest sign of the successful celebration of Life and cosmic renewal.

The above discussion delineates the general philosophical background underlying Melanesian religion. From this foundation arises a diversity of beliefs and practices. In the following discussion I will focus on some of the important elements within the Melanesian religious paradigm: (1) the role of ghosts and spirits in Melanesian belief, (2) the concept of *mana* and its central role in the religious system, and (3) the practice of ritual techniques whereby man attempts to control the cosmos and gain for himself material advantage.

Melanesian Ghosts.

In Melanesia the primary focus of worship is on ghosts who are perceived as the disembodied souls of ancestors, and on spirit beings who are believed never to have been in human form. Codrington (1881: 311, 1891: 122-123) draws our attention to a pattern that distinguishes the Solomon Islands in western Melanesia from the Banks' and New Hebrides in eastern Melanesia.[124] In the Solomons, religious belief and practice emphasize the importance of ghosts rather than spirits. Concomitantly, there is a more highly developed sacrificial system in the Solomon Islands than in the Banks' and New Hebrides where emphasis is on spirits rather than ghosts. Codrington notes:

> It may be said, then, that Melanesian religion divides the people into two groups; one, where, with an accompanying belief in spirits never men, worship is directed to the ghosts of the dead, as in the Solomon Islands; the other, where both ghosts and spirits have an important place, but the spirits have more worship than the ghosts, as is the case in the New Hebrides and Banks' Islands (1891: 123).

In the Solomon Islands the *tindalo* of Nggela, *tidatho* of Bugotu district in Santa Isabel, the *tinda'o* of Guadalcanal, the *lio'a* of Sa'a, South Malaita, and the *'ataro* of San Cristobal, are all indigenous terms for disembodied spirits of the dead, which in this discussion we will call ghosts. When a man dies, his soul goes to an abode where ghosts are said to reside. There are many different beliefs as to where this abode may be. Not infrequently it is a nearby island, as in the case of Santa Isabel, where islanders believe San Jorge to be the abode of the spirits of their ancestors, and call the island *momolu nai'itu* — island of spirits.[125]

Once a person dies his soul does not automatically become an important ghost which is worshipped by the living, for this is dependent on whether or not the person was important before death. If a woman, a child, or a common man dies, the soul will unlikely become an important ghost which will be feared, invoked, and propitiated. To have power and importance as a ghost, a man must have been important when he was alive, demonstrating his power, which he received from the dead who had gone before him. Codrington (1891: 125) notes that, "The supernatural power abiding in the powerful living man abides in his ghost after death, with increased vigour and more ease of movement." Thus, a Big Man in life can become an even bigger man in death. He becomes a ghost. In death there is no barrier to his activity and influence. If ghosts appear to be the alpha and omega of traditional religion in western Melanesia, it is because Melanesians believe that ghosts are as preoccupied as the living with cosmic renewal and the celebration of Life. The concept of the "living dead" expresses the belief that cosmic Life reaches beyond the grave, and so death is no obstacle to continued existence. It is the form and manner of existence that changes, not existence itself.

Thus, although every person has a soul which has a continued existence beyond death, every ghost does not become an object of worship. In the chauvinistic Melanesian societies, it is not surprising to find that the ghosts of women were seldom worshipped. Only those of men, and only men of importance, or men who had demonstrated particular skill in some avenue of life were worshipped. For example, if a man were unusually skillful in hunting, fishing, fighting, or sorcery, when he died, his ghost would be called upon to help the living in these same activities. On Nggela, the ghost (*tindalo*) of one renowned for fighting was called a *keramo*, and was venerated when islanders prepared for fighting.[126]

After the death of a Big Man, someone comes forth and claims particular acquaintance with his ghost. He then proceeds to communicate with the ghost through sacrifice and ritual, requesting that his power be demonstrated. If his power is convincingly manifest, then he will become a ghost who is worthy of veneration by the living through ritual invocation and by making offerings to him. The sacrificer, then, becomes in a sense, a priest whose function is to make sacrifices and call on the ghost of this particular individual. His status as an important ghost, worthy of veneration, will continue as long as there is empirically validated proof that he is active and productive, or until a more powerful and important man dies and a new cult is formed around his ghost. Thus, by natural attrition, a ghost slowly fades in importance. Traditionally in Melanesia there were no written languages, and so no written history. Thus by the fourth generation after the death of a Big Man, when there are no longer any living who knew him when he was alive, his ghost becomes forgotten. The life of a ghost, therefore, is dependent on his activity and competition with more recent ghosts. Ghosts are not believed to die, they simply sink into oblivion. Thus, there is a tendency in Melanesian religion for the living to concentrate their interest more on the recent dead than upon remote ancestors.[127]

In the New Guinea Highlands, where a sharp distinction is drawn between remote and recent dead, Melanesians believe that the ancestral spirits of recent dead punish their descendants for wrongdoing, while economic benefits are believed to come from the ancestral spirits of the remote dead.[128] This punitive exercise attributed to the recent dead, gives the Highlanders' religion more of a moralistic and ethical content than is normally found in most of the religions in Island Melanesia.[129]

Melanesian Spirits.

A familiar characteristic of many animistic religions does **not** exist in Melanesia, namely a belief in a spirit which animates natural objects such as trees, streams, waterfalls, rocks, etc., so that the spirit is to the natural phenomenon as the soul is believed to be to the body of man.[130] Moreover, spirits are personal, not impersonal, and occasionally are manifest in observable form. For example, traditionally in the Solomon Islands some indigenes believed that spirits took the form of snakes, and so on several islands, snakes were venerated. In similar fashion, the spirits of disembodied men (ghosts) frequently became incarnate in the form of sharks, crocodiles, fish, birds, fireflies and also snakes.[131]

Solomon Islanders distinguish between spirits and ghosts, believing that the former were never men. On Nggela, spirit-beings known as *vigona*, who exercised their power in storms, calms, rain, drought and other environmental phenomena, are believed by the islanders to be different from ghosts, and yet, it is difficult for them not to believe that the *vigona* spirits were once men.

In the Banks' Islands and northern New Hebrides where spirits play a more important role in the religion of the islanders, spirit-beings are mainly incorporeal (but occasionally corporeal), numerous and often unnamed. In the Banks' Islands a spirit is called a *vui*; in the northern New Hebrides it is *wui*. These spirits are frequently associated with sacred stones and haunt places that are believed to be sacred. They are frequently associated with certain snakes, sharks, owls and other animals, which act as mediums of communication between human beings and spirits. These spirits are believed to be powerful in helping those who know how to approach them. Since they are not believed to be evil spirits, they are not feared, although they are known to have the capacity for injuring men. Spirits are believed to be like men in essence, but not in form. Since they are not bound by human limitations and frailties, they are considerably more powerful than human beings.

In the Banks' Islands and New Hebrides, Qat and Tagaro respectively, represent corporeal spirits who have become culture heroes. Many legends and myths have grown up around them. There is an interesting similarity between these myths and legends and those found in other parts of Oceania. As Codrington notes:

> The legends of the Banks' Islanders concerning Qat will be found to correspond to those which prevail among the Maoris and other Polynesian people, concerning Maui and Tangaroa (1881:268).[132]

An example of two spirits with the status of culture-heroes in the Solomon Islands are Koevasi on Nggela and Kohausibware on San Cristobal. These were female creator spirits from whom the human race came. While both are subjects of myths and stories, neither was an object of worship.[133]

Another class of spirits (*vui*) is considerably less important than the culture heroes Qat and Tagaro. Codrington (1891: 152) has compared them with dwarfs and trolls in European stories. They are believed to be full of mystical magic power. People claiming to have a relationship with them will receive money from their neighbors on behalf of the spirit which enables the donor to procure a share of good-will and fortune from the spirit. These spirits may be identified as either male or female and occasionally they take on human form.[134] Codrington (1891: 153) notes that in the islanders' minds there seems to be some confusion between these spirits and the ghosts of the deceased human beings.

Corporeal spirits such as Qat are invoked in prayers. It is believed that the forces of nature are ordinarily controlled by incorporeal spirits.[135] Incorporeal spirits have a more important role in the religious beliefs of Banks' Islanders than do the corporeal ones such as Qat. Codrington (1881: 275) says, "They have no names, and no stories are told of them and they have no shape, but they are numerous and they are present and powerful to assist men who can communicate with them." The mediums through which one communicates with these spirits are principally stones, followed by snakes, and then various other creatures — owls, sharks, lizards, eels, crabs, etc.

Communication with the spirits is not available to everyone, but only to those certain people who have the gift. A man will use a particular stone or snake through which he communicates to the spirit and obtains favors from it. If one sacrifices upon a sacred stone, it is believed that the spirit will bring a man strength in fighting, abundant crops, a multitude of pigs and all the good things of life.[136] A person who has demonstrated ability to communicate with a spirit will often receive money from others who wish to sacrifice to it, in order to obtain some of the resulting benefits.

In the Banks' Islands only shell money is offered in sacrificing to the spirits. No food is offered as in the Solomon Islands. In eastern Melanesia the spirits are generally beneficent rather than malevolent and are not propitiated out of fear. The spirits that bring harm, spite, or mischief are the ghosts of the dead (*tamate*). In this Melanesian theological system, it is men, not spirits, who practice cruelty and hatred, and this is reflected in an indigenous distinction between ghosts of men (*tamate*) who are harmful, and spirits (*vui*) who were never human, but come to the aid of those who call on them. It is through the *vui* that man attempts to control rain or sunshine, and produce abundant crops of yams and breadfruit. Prayers are not made to these incorporeal spirits, but to ghosts and to the culture-heroes such as Qat.

Creator Spirits.

Brief mention should be made of the role of creator gods or spirits in Melanesia. Unlike the Judeo-Christian God, who creates the world from nothing, many Melanesians believe the universe has always existed and no one entity is credited for having brought it into existence. Qat in the Banks' Islands and Tagaro in the New Hebrides are male deities who are represented as creating men and animals, but they were born into a world already created. Further to the south at Eromanga, islanders believe in a creator god called Nobu, who after making men at Eromanga, went off to another island and has since been inactive in the affairs of men. In the Solomon Islands we find a similar pattern. On San Cristobal, a female deity named Kohausibware, who lived on the mountain at Bauro, is credited with having made men, pigs, fruit trees, yams and animals. This spirit frequently took the form of a snake and thus, says Codrington (1881: 299), snakes on the mountain at Bauro are venerated as being the descendants or representatives of Kohausibware, who has since left the island and now resides at Marau on the southeast end of Guadalcanal. On Nggela and Guadalcanal, another female deity named Koevasi was credited with creating many things, including another woman who gave rise to the inhabitants of the island. From New Georgia, Goldie (1908: 30) reports the existence of a Great and Good Spirit, who is invested with omnipotence and omniscience, and is responsible for the existence of everything.

The pattern that emerges in Melanesia is that these spirit-beings responsible for the creation of mankind have become the object of legend and myth, but not the object of worship. They are not active in the everyday life of human beings. They are unapproachable by mere mortals. The memory of their existence is perpetuated by myth and legend. It is ghosts and spirits who are active in the affairs of men, and so it is to them that Melanesians turn in worship and propitiation. Tippett notes the significance that this belief pattern had for Solomon Islanders in their encounter with Christianity:

> We see, then, that Solomon Island religion was more the worship of ghosts and spirits than of the almost-forgotten creator. When Christianity arrived the religious encounter was not between a pagan deity and the Christian God, Creator and Ruler of the Universe and Father of Mankind. The encounter had to take place on the level of daily life against those powers which dealt with the relevant problems of gardening, fishing, war, security, food supply and the personal life crises (1967: 5).

The Concept of *Mana* in Melanesian Religion.

Ghosts and spirits are familiar entities in many religious systems, but a more unusual concept that pervades Melanesian religion is that of *mana*. *Mana* is of central importance in understanding Melanesian life and worldview. If we suggest that ghosts and spirits are the prime-movers of Melanesian religion, it is *mana*, then, that sustains them as entities, providing them with power for their activities.

The concept of *mana* was first introduced into the anthropological literature by R. H. Codrington in 1881 and 1891. Codrington was a member of the Melanesian Mission, and from 1867 to 1887, was headmaster of the Norfolk Island school. It was here that he had access to so many Melanesian "scholars" who, coming directly from the islands, provided him with first-hand information regarding their beliefs and practices. It was R. R. Marett (1914: 99-121) who picked up on the notion of *mana* and brought it into prominence as a religious concept among anthropologists and comparative religionists.[137] Since then, a tremendous volume of literature has emerged around the idea of *mana*, and it has served as an important element in many theorists' constructs of the evolution of religion.[138]

In the Hibbert Lecture of 1878, Max Muller quoted from a letter he had received from Codrington, in describing this intriguing concept.[139]

> It is a power or influence, not physical, and in a way supernatural; but it shews itself in physical force, or in any kind of power or excellence which a man possesses. This Mana is not fixed in anything, and can be conveyed in almost anything; but spirits, whether disembodied souls or supernatural beings, have it and can impart it; and it essentially belongs to personal beings to originate it, though it may act through the medium of water, or a stone, or a bone. All Melanesian religion consists, in fact, in getting this Mana for one's self, or getting it used for one's benefit — all religion, that is, as far as religious practices go, prayers and sacrifice.

In the introduction of this section I noted that a central Melanesian value was the celebration of Life through maintaining right relations with kinsmen and by accumulating material wealth. It should now be clear that the concept of *mana* is central to this celebration of Life, and cosmic renewal. *Mana* is power that makes Life and cosmic renewal possible. Without it, there is only existence. With *mana* there is Life in all its fullness. The presence or absence of *mana* is ascertained by empirical proof, and it is this dimension of religious experience that characterizes Melanesians as hard-nosed empirical pragmatists. For example, if a man happens on to a stone of unusual shape which clearly distinguishes it from a mere common stone, he assumes there must be *mana* in it. So he puts the stone to the test to prove whether or not it is possessed with *mana*. He buries it at the foot of a tree if it happens to resemble the fruit in shape and size, or perhaps he buries it in the ground when he plants his garden. If there is a high yield on the tree or abundant crops in the garden, then he knows the stone has *mana*.[140]

Success in any field of endeavor, whether it be fighting, hunting, gardening, fishing, carving, etc., is proof to the Melanesian that a man has *mana*. A man becomes a leader of people, not because he automatically inherits the role, but because he has demonstrated conclusively and empirically to his fellows, that he has *mana*. He could not have been successful without it, and so because he is successful, he must have *mana*!

We can see then that the concept *mana* emerges from Melanesian speculation about a kind of metaphysical source, which, if tapped correctly, will provide a full participation in the abundance of Life. Codrington (1891: 120) emphasizes this point when he states:

> Of course, a yam naturally grows when planted, that is well known, but it will not be very large unless *mana* come in play; a canoe will not be swift unless *mana* be brought to bear upon it, similarly a net will not catch many fish, nor an arrow inflict a mortal wound.

To make a crude paraphrase, "without *mana* there is no salvation;" salvation, of course, being an abundance and success in all the possibilities of human life (Knight n.d.: 6).

Although all spirits and ghosts and some men possess *mana*, it is an accumulating, quantitative entity for which material objects frequently act as repositories. In the Western Solomons particularly, human skulls were perceived as one of the greatest repositories of *mana*.[141] *Mana* is also believed to exist in certain word patterns and formulae. These formulae may be passed from father to son, or from mother's brother to sister's son, or sold for a consideration.

The most important thing about understanding *mana* is that to Melanesians it is not a highly abstract or philosophical concept. Western scholars, including Codrington, have made far more of it philosophically and intellectually than would Melanesians. To Melanesians, *mana* is related to results obtained, and not to an abstract concept upon which is hung a philosophical argument. In his study of *mana* on Tikopia, Firth (1940: 498) noted that, "The Tikopian is content with concrete description of the results of activity and does not pursue the intellectual problem as to the nature of that activity." Although this Tikopian attitude comes from a Polynesian outlier in Melanesia, I believe it is representative of the area.

To conclude this brief discussion of *mana*, we will turn to Codrington who articulates the fundamental position this concept holds in Melanesian thought:

> By whatever name it is called, it is the belief in this supernatural power, and in the efficacy of the various means by which spirits and ghosts can be induced to exercise it for the benefit of men, that is the foundation of the rites and practices which can be called religious; and it is from the same belief that everything which may be called Magic and Witchcraft draws its origin. Wizards, doctors, weather-mongers, prophets, diviners, dreamers, all alike, everywhere in the islands, work by this power (1891: 192).

With this background, I will now proceed to discuss the actual practice of Melanesian religion, focusing now on the role of magico-religious ritual in the islanders' religious system.

Melanesian Magico-religious Ritual.

Many scholars of Melanesian culture have articulated the difficulty in drawing a distinction between religion and magic. For example, Lawrence and Meggitt (1965: 6) note that, "In Melanesia it is impossible to make any convincing distinctions between religion and magic." None of the classical distinctions between religion and magic developed by Tylor, Frazer, and Durkheim appear to hold up, and it is clear that there are no **indigenous** distinctions made between the two.[142] For this reason I have chosen to refer to ritual as magico-religious phenomena rather than pitting one over against the other.

A distinction, however, between belief and ritual is useful, and so in this section I will discuss traditional magico-religious ritual employed by Melanesians. The primary focus of Melanesian ritual is to obtain *mana* from spirits and ghosts who have it. This motive force is, of course, expressed in many different ways and so one discovers a variety of ritual acts. Discussion will first center on eastern Melanesia, followed by focusing on the western area.

Magico-religious Ritual in Eastern Melanesia. In eastern Melanesia where spirits are emphasized more than ghosts, islanders make offerings of money to the spirits. Sacred stones, which we find throughout Melanesia, are the primary medium for this activity. It is believed that the spirits are present at the stone, not in the stone. In no way could the stone be called an idol. In this part of Melanesia where graded men's societies play such an important role in the culture, spirits are invoked in order to gain worldly advancement in the form of shell-money and pigs.

In the Banks' Islands one can receive *mana* by scattering shell-money into a deep pool among the coral rocks, calling on the ghosts of one's immediate ancestors. Then one dives to the bottom of the pool and by sitting there for a moment he will obtain *mana* from the ghosts of his ancestors.

In understanding Melanesian ritual, it is important to realize that Melanesian religious experience is very personal and private. Public display of piety is quite alien. Codrington notes of the Banks' Islands:

> There are no sacred buildings and no priests; there is no public worship; and those who have communication with *Vuis* (spirits) apply to them for their own benefit, and for those who pay them for their intercession (1881: 286).

Sacrifice to a spirit is not done by everyone, but only by those who claim to have access to a spirit, and have been taught the proper ritual procedure whereby communication is held.

Ghosts are also important in eastern Melanesia, but are second to spirits. Ghosts have a different role and communication with them is somewhat different than that with spirits. On the whole, one does not pray to spirits, but ghosts are propitiated. While spirits are believed to be beneficent, ghosts are perceived to be malevolent and thus the cause of sickness and misfortune. It is to ghosts that one turns when desiring to inflict injury on a neighbor or enemy. A human bone is the primary medium for communication with a ghost. In the New Hebrides and Banks' Islands there are three methods whereby the power of a ghost can be brought to bear to do harm:[143]

1. **Garata**. This is a form of sorcery which is performed by taking some food, hair, nail clippings, excrement, or anything closely connected with the individual one desires to harm. It is through the medium of these materials that the *mana* of the ghost causes sickness to take place in the individual. This form of sorcery is common throughout Melanesia.
2. **Talamatai**. This is another form of sorcery using a different technique. An individual takes a bit of bone and stone, and certain leaves, as well as any other substance believed to have *mana*, and puts them all into a piece of bamboo. This magical bundle, now enriched with *mana*, is set in a path. The first unfortunate person to come along and step over it is soon smitten with some disease.
3. **Tamatetiqa**. This is a very interesting form of inflicting injury on another, and is known as a "ghost shooter." It is believed to work by putting bones, leaves and other substances with *mana* into a piece of hollow bamboo. It is also believed that the person using the instrument increases its potency and effectiveness by fasting beforehand. When he is ready to employ it, he takes the piece of bamboo filled with mana-enriched substances, and holds his thumb over the open end to prevent the dangerous power from escaping. When his intended victim is in sight, he then takes aim, lifts his thumb and lets go all the dreadful magical power inside. Whoever is hit, dies.

In summary, eastern Melanesia emphasizes the role of spirits over ghosts in their belief and ritual. Spirits are not believed to be malevolent but are helpful to those who know how to communicate with them. Communication is normally held through a sacrificial offering of shell-money performed at a sacred stone, either for one's own benefit or on behalf of a client from whom the sacrificer has received a payment in pigs and/or mats. The object of the ritual is to receive *mana* from the beneficent spirits.

Ghosts (*Tamate*) are believed to be malevolent spirits causing human suffering, sickness and disease. Communication with them is frequently through the medium of human bone and by the use of ritual charms. Ghosts are feared and propitiated. The burial places of important men are believed to be sacred and here sacrifices of mats, food, and pigs are occasionally made.

Magico-religious Ritual in Western Melanesia. In the Solomon Islands of western Melanesia, we meet a somewhat different pattern; however, the objective of ritual is the same — the acquisition of *mana* which is manifest in power and material well-being, empirically verified by the corporate group to which one belongs.

A universal pattern in the Solomon Islands was the sacrifice of pigs to ghosts, and not infrequently human beings were sacrificed as well. While ritual acts performed on behalf of the dead were nearly always done with economic ends in view, ghosts were also petitioned to cause or remove sickness. The acquisition of *mana*, which because of its association with ghosts tends to be more personal than impersonal, was gained principally through prayer and sacrifice to the ghosts.

An example of this sacrifice comes from San Cristobal, where, when the people prepared for war with an enemy, the help of a powerful ghost (*'ataro*) was obtained by sacrificing a pig. The pig was strangled near the sacred place where the offering was to be made, and was then dismembered. The chief sacrificer then took a piece of the pig, dipped it in blood, and entered the sacred house, calling to the *'ataro* for his help in the war about to be fought. As he entered, he did so with awe, for this was a most sacred place. The piece of pig was burned in a fire built on a stone, and then blood was poured over the fire. As the flames leapt up to the roof, and the aroma of the burnt pig filled the room, those present were assured that the *'ataro* had heard their plea.[144]

Traditionally people called on ghosts not only when they were preparing for battle, but as a regular daily practice and for help in every area of human need. Even today in curing sickness, producing abundant crops, assuring successful hunting or fishing, and in dealing with all the crises of life, the ghosts of the dead are invoked for their assistance and protection. Prayers to the ghosts are private property and considered to be a most valuable commodity. The words (often very different from those in the lexicon of the local language) are believed to contain *mana*, and are handed down from one generation to the next, or taught for a consideration. The control of rain, sunshine, wind and calm is believed to be effected by charms which have *mana* from the dead. It is the most recent dead whose ghosts are believed to be the most powerful in these matters.

Ghosts are believed to become incarnate in the form of sharks, crocodiles, and other creatures of land and water. On Ulawa, a boy must catch a bonito fish to demonstrate that he is entering manhood. Such a difficult task is believed to require much *mana* in order to be successful, and so sharks, which are believed to be incarnate ghosts and full of *mana*, are thought to be helpful in catching the fish.

On Nggela, where islanders claimed it had been introduced from the Western Solomons, human flesh was eaten in sacrifice to ghosts. However, the belief that *mana* is obtained from eating human flesh probably prevailed throughout the Solomon Islands.[145] Prayer and sacrifice, common elsewhere, were the primary ritual activities whereby Nggela islanders obtained assistance from ghosts (*tindalo*), and from the spirits of famous warriors (*keramo*) long deceased. Certain leaves, ginger, bark or roots through which *mana* is conveyed, were used to obtain *mana* by eating and chewing them, and by tying them as amulets about the person.

Human skulls were believed to be particularly potent repositories of *mana*. Thus on Santa Isabel, the death of a Big Man occasioned an expedition for heads which would add *mana* to the new *tidatho* (ghost). An expedition like this would assure that a Big Man in life would be powerful in death as a ghost. Sacrificing human beings added much *mana* to a *tidatho*, and in return, *mana* was received from him. The religious complex of headhunting was so integrated with the acquisition of *mana* that it formed a built-in system. Self-perpetuation of headhunting was assured by a continuous cycle. By acquiring human heads one gained *mana*, which then gave one greater confidence and strength for acquiring even more heads. Heads were obtained for the purpose of honoring a living or deceased Big Man, or for the inauguration of a new war canoe (*tomako*), or the building of a Men's House, etc.[146] The object in mind was that the new canoe, or Big Man or his ghost, would be invested with *mana*. Acquisition of *mana* was the compelling motivation for such activity. At the time of European contact in the nineteenth century, the center of this headhunting complex in the Solomons was in the Roviana Lagoon of New Georgia in the Western Solomons.[147]

In summary, religious belief and practice in the Solomon Islands was similar to that found in eastern Melanesia, in the sense that the acquisition of *mana* was the driving force behind all ritual. Solomon Islanders emphasized the worship of ghosts more than spirits, and an elaborate sacrificial system was developed which included the ubiquitous sacrificing of pigs, and occasionally human beings, to the ghosts of their ancestors. Human sacrifice was practiced with the belief that such an offering gave even more *mana* to the ghost, for human sacrifice had a much higher *mana* value than the sacrifice of a pig. The ghost in return, gave *mana* to those who participated in the sacrifice. Offerings of food made to ghosts were consumed by fire as well as eaten by the participants.

Although an organized priesthood did not exist,[148] there were those who were the recognized authorities to offer sacrifices to the ghosts of particular men. However, every man had the right to call on his father's ghost, and on the ghosts of his ancestors, asking for help and protection. Knowledge of correct ritual was valuable and private, and was passed on from one generation to the next. This knowledge could also be purchased, but it was not **public** knowledge; it was private.

The acquisition of *mana* was used for both positive and negative purposes. The practice of sorcery was found throughout the Solomons, as indeed, throughout the whole of Melanesia, and islanders had ambivalent attitudes toward it. Fear of sorcery was great, and yet, it was recognized as a valuable social control. On the other hand, numerous magico-religious rituals were employed positively to gain *mana* for protection, for curing disease, ensuring abundant crops, or success in hunting and fishing, as well as for "love magic" employed to gain the favor of the opposite sex.

In this chapter the discussion of traditional Melanesian religion and magic has of necessity been brief.[149] Perhaps no better summary of the topic can be found than that which comes from Codrington, an ethnographer and missionary, who had such profound insight into and an understanding of Melanesian religion:

> . . . in all the islands, it is plainly believed that power of a spiritual character belongs to the dead, and may be obtained from them by living men. Whatever power of this kind a man possesses in his lifetime, though it may show itself in bodily excellence, is conceived of as supernatural, and attaching to that part of his nature, his soul, by whatever name it may be called, which not only survives the dissolution of the body, but is even enabled to act more effectively by death. . . . A Melanesian, therefore, whether it be in the islands where spiritual beings, not the ghosts of men, are much regarded, or in those where the lately dead have almost the worship that is given, moves always in a world of which great part is invisible; his body is not all himself; the grave does not close altogether the future for him. By one means or another, by stones or leaves, he can put himself into communication with the unseen powers; he can please them by sacrifices and he can gain their help by prayers (1881: 311-312).

Summary of the Pre-contact Period

Although this has been a lengthy chapter, the discussion of the different areas of the pre-contact situation in Melanesian society and culture has necessarily been brief. However, I believe a sufficient foundation has now been laid to provide an understanding of the culture change that ensued after intensive European contact began.

Above I analyzed traditional Melanesian society on a grid of theoretical categories which are artificial and critical rather than Melanesian or real. However, by organizing the data in terms of these theoretical categories such as social organization, ecological adaptation, and religion, it will be easier to understand how change in each of them occurred under European culture contact. Nevertheless, it is important to remember that to the Melanesians living in the pre-contact period, their society and culture were an integrated whole, not a bunch of analytical categories.

In this chapter we have viewed traditional Solomon Islands society and culture through the eyes of Iberian intruders in the sixteenth century. Many of the observations of the Spanish accord with those of European observers two and three hundred years later. The Spanish encounter was also a harbinger of intercultural relationships between Melanesians and Europeans in the nineteenth and twentieth centuries, when considerable misunderstanding and exploitation of the islanders occurred.

In discussing the prehistory and linguistic situation in Melanesia, I have attempted to demonstrate the lengthy time dimension of the tremendous linguistic and cultural diversity that Europeans encountered upon intitial contact. The prehistory has shown that the islands of Melanesia were populated by diverse people from different origins, in successive waves of migration. The legion of languages, discussed in this chapter, proved to be one of the most difficult obstacles for missionaries to overcome, since learning one language would give a missionary access to a speech community of only several thousand speakers at the most, and not infrequently, only several hundred people.

The topography of Melanesia consists of mountainous islands covered with dense tropical vegetation from the summit to the coast. From these islands and the lagoons adjacent to them, Melanesians lived on a subsistence economy, developed elaborate intra- and inter-island trade networks, and created some magnificent items of material culture, using only local materials of the island world. Melanesian Man was tied closely to the land, and lived in harmony with the ecological niche in which he found himself.

The Melanesian societies adapting to this tropical island environment were small, kinship-based, politically autonomous entities in which groups were organized by a variety of residential and genealogical patterns. Leadership in these small groups was based primarily on a person's abilities and achievements, rather than on inherited rank. The model of the Melanesian Big Man symbolized the predominant mode of leadership, in which a man gathers around himself a cadre of followers and supporters.

At the time of contact one of the predominant themes in Melanesian society was warfare in which raiding, headhunting, and cannibalism were important activities in many of the societies. This internecine hostility between groups created difficulties for missionaries in the contact period, but it also helped to create a climate in which islanders were more open to accepting and adopting the missionaries' message when Christianity was presented as the way of peace.

The primary focus of religion in traditional Melanesia was on the acquisition of *mana* or supernatural power. Islanders were concerned with the efficacy of ritual techniques for gaining supernatural assistance in promoting their own well-being. Whether islanders called on the ghosts of their ancestors, or on the numerous spirits, they nevertheless believed that these supernatural beings were capable of intervening in the affairs of this world and in assisting islanders in their daily activities. Thus, traditional Melanesian religion was essentially pragmatic and materialistic, concerned with life here and now. It was with this Melanesian worldview that islanders understood and interpreted the missionaries' message and activities.

The preceding two chapters have set the theoretical and ethnographic stage for what is to follow. We now enter the contact period. Our objective will be to understand what happened when Anglican missionaries and pagan Melanesians encountered one another.

CHAPTER 2 NOTES

1. Cf. Brookfield and Hart (1971: xliii-liv), and Chowning (1977: 1-3).
2. Cf. Sayes (1976) whose thesis on the Ethnohistory of San Cristobal concludes that by the time Fox (1924) began his study of Arosi society in 1915, the traditional way of life had all but vanished due to the intensity of European contact.
3. Before any European contact there was a series of migrations occurring in Melanesia. The precise dates and migratory routes are unknown to us; however, archaeological evidence and the diffusion of myths, proves that their actual occurrence is beyond speculation.

   This migration thesis is the principal line of argument in Rivers' (1914) two volume history of Melanesian society in which he hypothesizes an original indigenous dual organization culture, followed by a kava-making people, and then later by a betel-chewing people. Rivers' hypothesis of kava and betel cultures is based on evidence of spacial distribution of the plants themselves and the social customs associated with them. It is this mix of different peoples migrating into the area that has given Melanesia its distinctive cultural diversity. Thus, this was a dynamic, not a static, cultural arena, with bush and coastal interaction, interisland trade and communication networks, internecine warfare and migrating populations.
4. The two most important manuscripts are by Gallego and Catoira.

   (1) The *Relacion* of Hernan Gallego. This is the logbook of the Chief Pilot, and is the most informative regarding navigational information, especially because Gallego went with the brigantine on its excursions

within the Solomons. Four editions of this manuscript (all hand copied) are known to exist. I examined the one from which Amherst made his translations, which is now housed in the Alexander Turnbull Library, Wellington, New Zealand. English translations of Gallego are found in Amherst and Thompson (1901: 1-80) and Guppy (1887: 192-245).

(2) The *Relacion* of the Chief Purser, Gomez Hernandez Catoira (dated, La Plata, June 4, 1573). Ethnographically this is the most valuable account of all the manuscripts and I have relied upon it extensively. Although it is second to Gallego's *Relacion* in terms of the navigational information supplied, it surpasses his in terms of its detailed and literary description of the voyage. There is more information regarding the personalities of the leaders and the internal politics of the expedition, the islands and their inhabitants, including descriptions of their appearance, material culture and social customs. In addition, Catoira gives us the most detail on the nature of the Spanish-Melanesian interaction. This manuscript has been translated (except for a few passages which Amherst must have found objectionable) and is found in Amherst and Thompson (1901: 217-462).

Ivens (1926) has amplified and corrected the text which accompanies the translation of the original Spanish documents, prepared by Amherst and Thompson. For additional primary sources, see Conway (1946) and Fleurieu (1791: 4-16) who, relying on a confusing account by Figueroa, published in Madrid in 1613, describes the 1567 voyage of Mendana. For additional discussion relevant to the Spanish expedition, see Woodford (1888, 1890b). For a broader frame of reference with which to understand the Spanish attitude regarding the Christianization of indigenes in other areas of the world during this period, see S. F. Cook's *Ibero-American Studies Series*, (1976) and Hanke's (1970) *Aristotle and the American Indian.*

5. For a scholarly and detailed treatment of the 1567 expedition, cf. Jack-Hinton (1969: 28-67). This important work deals with the history of the discovery of the Solomon Islands, and thus emphasizes navigational rather than ethnographic data.

6. For nearly identical reactions of the islanders to European visitors two hundred years later, see Fleurieu's account (1791: 106-163) of Surville's visit to the Solomon Islands in 1769, when he had brief intercourse with the islanders of Santa Isabel and Ulawa. See also Bougainville's account (1772: 318-322) of his 1768 voyage through the Solomon Islands where he encountered indigenes on Choiseul and Buka. Bougainville is the one who has given us the names of the islands. Cf. Dunmore (1969: 61-74), and Jack-Hinton (1969: 255-266).

7. Cf Codrington (1891: 11).
8. Cf. L. Rohorua (1898: 6-7). An interesting question is whether the memory of the Spanish visit was kept alive through indigenous legends. Three hundred years later there seemed to have been little evidence of the Spanish visit. However, on Santa Ana, the islanders annually acted out the legend of a company of Europeans arriving at their island, of an ensuing battle, and then of the absorption of the intruders into the indigenous population. This could be a reference to the Spanish expedition of 1595 in which a settlement was briefly established at Pamua on San Cristobal, cf. J. Allen (1976), R. Green (1973). For further reference to this interesting legend and related folklore, cf. Kuper (1924), S. Mead (1973a, 1973b), Sayes (1976: 25).
9. Cf. Woodford (1909).
10. The following description from Surville's 1769 voyage appears as a carbon copy of the Spanish experience:

    > Though nothing was neglected to conciliate the friendship of these Indians, it was evident that they were not wholly free from apprehension; their manner, their looks, and the signs they made to each other, all bespoke distrust; and, on the least movement made in the vessel, they jumped into their canoes, or even into the sea. They had a wonderful adroitness in stealing whatever was within their reach, and it was not easy to persuade them to restore it (Fleurieu 1791: 117).

11. Shineberg (1971), has discussed in some detail the role of firearms in the Spanish encounter with the Solomon Islanders, and to a lesser extent, the importance of firearms in the nineteenth century trade relations between Europeans and Melanesians.
12. The last island to be visited by the Spanish was San Cristobal when they were in their worst condition and in desperate need of food and provisions. For a brief summary of Melanesian-Spaniard interaction, particularly as it relates to San Cristobal, cf. Sayes (1976: 34-37).
13. The establishment of a colony in the Solomons remained the life dream of Mendana, but it was not until 1595 that he was able to attempt it again. The story of this misadventure is most intriguing. Until recently it was thought that the Spanish had missed the original Solomon Islands altogether and had only made contact at Santa Cruz where they established a colony that lasted only two months before it was abandoned. Now archaelogical investigation at Pamua, San Cristobal, indicates that the Spanish were there as well. For details see Jack-Hinton (1969: 113-132), R. Green (1973), Allen and Green (1972), and Allen (1976). Primary sources are found in Fleurieu

(1791: 17-27) and C. R. Markham (1904).

14. Surville during his 1769 voyage of discovery also captured a Solomon Islander to use an an interpreter. He soon discovered that the indigene's linguistic knowledge was limited to a small geographical area as he was unable to communicate with indigenes from other islands. He refused to go ashore at Ulawa when the offer was made, preferring to stay with the French who had kidnapped him from Santa Isabel. This indigene did however learn French and was able to communicate a great deal about island life. Cf. Fleurieu (1791: 102, 134-144), Dunmore (1969: 66-68).

15. For a brief discussion and evaluation of the Spanish visit, cf. Woodford (1890b: 1-7). A Catholic missionary evaluation of the Spanish encounter, which emphasizes the religious aspects and barely mentions the hostile relations, is found in Raucaz (1928: 11-28).

16. Tippett (1967), reporting from observation made as late as 1964, notes that this segmentation was still evident not only for the Solomons as a political creation, but that even islands like Malaita were not yet perceived as entities.

17. Guppy (1887: 18) reports of perhaps an extreme example of this endemic hostility which he found on Santa Ana, an island 2½ miles in length with two villages which were interconnected through marriage, but which were frequently at war with each other.

18. Cf. Gallego's report of this San Jorge Big Man in Guppy (1887: 210).

19. Cf. Gallego's observations of the population density on the coast of Guadalcanal in Guppy (1887: 216).

20. Cf. Yen (1973).

21. In comparing the canoes of Ulawa, which is in the same culture area as San Cristobal, with those of Santa Isabel, Surville's 1769 voyage through the Solomons concluded that,

    > Their canoes, which, like those of Port Praslin (Santa Isabel), are without sails or out-rigger, are nearly of the same construction, but worked more skillfully; that of the chief, particularly, was a masterpiece for the finishing of the work, and the design, and polish of the inlaying, which was composed of various coloured woods, and pieces of mother-of-pearl adjusted and incrusted with much art (Fleurieu 1791: 154).

22. In the 1930's a District Officer on Santa Isabel became irate over the "disrespect" shown him by the islanders. His complaint was that whenever he entered a village all the men would immediately sit down instead of standing to recognize his authority and importance. It was

only later that he learned the cultural importance of islanders sitting in his presence.

23. Catoira has probably made a mistake in inferring the original material from which the ornaments were made. The armlets and breast-plate were probably made from a clam shell, and the "deer's" teeth are probably the teeth of a porpoise since deer do not exist in this habitat.

24. Cf. Gallego's report of this incident in Guppy (1887: 203).

25. In contrast to the Spanish experience, Surville in 1769 was able to learn of the role of ancestors in Solomon Islands religious belief from the islander captured from Santa Isabel:

    > Concerning the religion of his country, the young savage could give no satisfactory intelligence; he only said it is believed that after death men go to heaven, but that they return from time to time to converse with their friends. Endeavors were made to persuade him, that it is absurd to believe in these apparitions of the dead, but he insisted upon it that they do appear, and always at night; they mark out the place where fish may be caught in great abundance, and they never fail to announce good and bad news (Fluerieu 1791: 140-141).

26. An interesting post-script to this comment of Catoira's is that Nggela was in fact the first island in the Solomons where a substantial response was made toward accepting Christianity, cf. Penny (1887: 174-232). On this movement toward Christianity, see discussion below, pp. 137-142.

27. See the native drawings of these sea-ghosts from this area in Codrington (1891: 197, 259), and Fox (1924: 125-128). An interesting note is that the 10¢ piece in the new Solomon Island currency issued in 1977, has a rendition of a traditional sea-ghost on the "tail" side of the coin.

28. Cf. Codrington (1891: 254, 262).

29. Evidently the Spanish were observing a not uncommon phenomena—*'ataro* or ghost possession, cf. Codrington (1891: 218-220), and Fox (1924: 117-118).

30. Cf. J. Peter White (1971), Swadling (1981: 2, 12-13). Given the parameters of this study the discussion of Melanesian prehistory is not central to the topic and therefore must necessarily be brief. For an excellent and more detailed review of Melanesian prehistory, see Bellwood (1979: 233-279).

31. This is the area of the hypothetical Wallace Line, in which the naturalist Alfred R. Wallace (1869) drew attention to the demarcation of the flora and fauna, distinguishing the Asian mainland and some of

the Indonesian islands from the remainder of the island world to the east. Cf. Golson (1972).

32. Barbetti and Allen (1972); Bowler, Thorne and Polach (1972).
33. J. Peter White (1971). The oldest known site in New Guinea is at Kosipe (near Mt. Albert Edward) where stone tools have been uncovered and dated to be 26,000 years old (Swadling 1981: 12-13). However it is likely that human beings have inhabited New Guinea for 50,000 years (Swadling 1981: 2).
34. R. Green (1977: 12).
35. For a review of the physical anthropology of Melanesia, cf. Swindler (1968). Also, Shutler and Shutler (1967) discuss the origins of the Melanesians, reviewing the interdisciplinary data relevant to this question.
36. For a discussion of the development of agriculture in Melanesia, cf. Yen (1971: 7-10).
37. Cf. Bulmer and Bulmer (1964).
38. Bellwood (1975: 11).
39. An important consideration in dealing with pottery in Oceania is the notion that if pottery making is going to diffuse as a technology, it is limited to volcanic islands where there is clay. Coral atolls lack the requisite soil composition for its manufacture. On the different island types in Oceania, see William Thomas (1968: 12).
40. Cf. Golson (1971), R. Green (1977: 17-22), and Bellwood (1979: 244-255).
41. Bellwood (1975: 13).
42. Cf. Shutler and Shutler (1975: 57-63).
43. R. Green (1977: 21-22).
44. *Ibid.*, pp. 16-17. Since the beginning of the Southeast Solomons Culture History Program, directed by Roger Green and Douglas Yen in 1970, and continuing to the present, a great deal of interdisciplinary data is being gathered, and filling what was a major gap in the prehistory of Melanesia. All the findings and conclusions have yet to be published; however, a preliminary report has been issued—Green and Cresswell (1976).
45. Cf. Bellwood (1979: 270-272).
46. Cf. Grace (1961, 1964), Capell (1962), Wurm (1967), Pawley (1972), R. Green (1976).
47. Bellwood (1975: 11).

48. The exception to this pattern is in the northern New Hebrides and southeast Solomons where there is considerable linguistic diversity.
49. Capell (1969).
50. Davenport (1962), R. Green (1976).
51. Cf. Wurm (1971).
52. Pawley (1972: 1).
53. Shutler and Shutler (1967: 92).
54. There is no unanimous agreement among scholars regarding the status of the Santa Cruz—Reef Islands Group as non-Austronesian languages. Although Davenport (1962), Wurm (1970) and R. Green (1976) hold to the view that these are non-Austronesian languages, Lincoln (1975) in his mapping of all the Austronesian languages of Melanesia, has included the group in the Austronesian family. Greenberg (1971: 816-818) has argued that the languages, as a sub-group, belong to a higher order grouping he calls Central Melanesian, which ranks as one of the fourteen major groups comprising his non-Austronesian, Indo-Pacific family.
55. For various discussions dealing with the migration of Austronesian speakers, cf. Grace (1961, 1964), Capell (1962), and Wurm (1967).
56. Murdock (1964) picked up on Dyen's hypothesis and developed a scheme for Oceanic culture history. Although Murdock heralded Dyen's argument as a revolutionary breakthrough, culture historians today give little weight to his argument.
57. R. Green (1976: 55-60) believes a sub-group of these original speakers still survives in Utupua and Vanikolo islands in the Southeast Solomons.
58. For this review I have relied heavily on R. Green (1976, 1977).
59. The Ninth Edition of *Ethnologue* (Grimes, 1978), notes that there are presently 77 languages listed for the Solomon Islands.
60. For an example of a dialect chain on Santa Isabel, cf. Whiteman and Simons (1978). Cf. Simons (1978) for a discussion of "dialects" vs. "languages" in the Solomon Islands, and their relationship to linguistic intelligibility in intra-island communication.
61. For an interesting discussion regarding the effect of the sweet potato on Highland New Guinea, cf. Watson (1965). While the sweet potato was introduced into New Guinea prior to European contact, it was absent from the Solomon Islands and the New Hebrides until the contact period, when it was apparently introduced into the area by Melanesian scholars returning from the Melanesian Mission school,

first in New Zealand, and then later on Norfolk Island. Cf. Yen (1974), and Brookfield and Hart (1971: 83-84).

62. For further discussion on food crops and their use in Melanesia, cf. Guppy (1887: 81-97), Codrington (1891: 303-304), Ivens (1927: 355-374, 379-382; 1930: 266-275), Hopkins (1928: 229-233), Barrau (1958), and Brookfield and Hart (1971: 80-83).

63. Hogbin and Wedgewood (1952-3: 241).

64. For a brief survey of land use in Melanesia, cf. Chowning (1977: 24-40). See also the articles related to Melanesia in Crocombe (1971). For a discussion of land tenure in the Solomon Islands, cf. Allan (1957), Heath (1980).

65. Trees are a special category because they are frequently owned by the person who planted them, while the land they are grown on may belong to another person or group.

66. Valentine (1958: 53).

67. Codrington (1891: 298).

68. The kula ring represented a double cycle — one ceremonial, the other market exchange, but each with a different market value system. For an interesting discussion of a pre-contact trade network in the Western Solomon Islands, cf. Tippett (1967: 186-187).

69. For additional information on trade networks in Melanesia, cf. Davenport (1964), and Harding (1967).

70. Chowning (1977: 52).

71. Cf. Woodford (1908).

72. Cf. Davenport (1962). For further discussion on types of traditional "money" in Melanesia, cf. Penny (1887: 85-88), Codrington (1891: 323-328), Woodford (1908), Rivers (1914 II: 384-393), Ivens (1927: 390-392; 1930: 276-278), and Hopkins (1928: 66).

73. Valentine (1958: 53).

74. Cf. Belshaw (1950a, 1954) and Tippett (1967: 171-189), for a discussion on the relationship of the indigenous economic system to subsequent culture change.

75. For a photo of a Solomon Island shield, see Williamson (1914: 32, 60). Engravings of a shield and other weapons from Melanesia are found in Brenchley (1873: 222, 281), Markham (1873: 198), Penny (1887: 201).

76. For additional information on music and musical instruments, cf. Guppy (1887: 130-145), Codrington (1891: 304-313), Rivers (1914

II: 446-450), Ivens (1927: 294-299), Hopkins (1928: 55-56, 176-177), Suri (1976: 36-47).

77. See drawings of these costumes in Codrington (1891: 70, 73, 78-79, 91).

78. See drawing in Brenchley (1873: 262, and frontispiece) for an example from the island of Ugi.

79. For examples of ornamentation on utilitarian objects, cf. Codrington (1891: 328-331). Drawings of elaborately carved pudding bowls are found in Fox (1924: 11-12), Ivens (1927: 163-164, 166). For a detailed study of Solomon Island sculpture, cf. Waite (1969).

80. For further discussion of decorative art and particularly shell inlaid work, cf. Ivens (1927: 153-155, 392-395), and Hopkins (1928: 58). See also Waite (1969).

81. In 1866 Bishop Patteson of the Melanesian Mission observed these tree-houses on Santa Isabel. I quote at length from the description of them:

> The Bishop slept on shore last night at one place, which he describes as a most extraordinary habitation. A site for the village has been chosen on a hill surmounted by steep, almost perpendicular, coral rocks; the forest has been cleared for some space all around, so as to prevent any enemy from approaching unperceived; there is a wall of stones of considerable height on that side of the village where the rock is less precipitous, with one narrow entrance, approached only by a smooth slippery trunk of a tree, laid at a somewhat steep inclination over a hollow below; but the tree-houses with which we made acquaintance of old at this island, are at this place on a scale almost incredible. Tall trees, rising out of the steep slippery sides of the hill, are chosen for these great bamboo nests, of which there are six at this one village. From the wall of the fort — for so the village may fairly be called — or from the base, ladders are carried up to these tree-houses. It is surprising to see men, women, and children passing up and down these ladders. The Bishop confessed that he was afraid to make the attempt in the dusk of the evening. It was his intention to sleep in one of these curious houses, but he says that he had no idea of their real character at this particular place. A day or two afterwards, however, he went up into the highest tree-house, and, with Mr. Atkin, made careful measurements. The house in which the people wished him to sleep is built on the top of a tree, which rises up from the hollow before mentioned, near the fort. The top of the stone wall is on a level with the trunk, at a height of thirty-four feet from the ground. The ladder reaching from the fort to the tree-house had forty-two rowels, at an

> average distance of eighteen inches from one another. The whole height of the house from the ground is ninety-four feet; its length is eighteen feet; breadth, ten feet; height, eight feet; — all being inside measurement. Some of the trees were at a much greater distance from the fort, and the ladders at a proportionately greater angle. One woman, carrying a load, walked up one of these ladders without touching anything with her hand, with no balancing pole, after the fashion of our civilised performers, and without exciting the least remark or notice from the people standing about. On the naked branches of these trees, one man was walking about, hanging out his fishing net, without grasping anything with his hand, where one slip would have sent him down on to stones and stumps of trees, ninety or one hundred feet below. Accustomed from childhood to these feats, they seem wholly unconscious of any danger, or indifferent to it. No accident occurred whilst they were making these houses, though to us it seemed an almost impossible undertaking to accomplish without the help of "wings."
>
> All this has been rendered necessary by their continued quarrels. They never heard of another mode of living. Insecurity of life and property causes no questioning and little uneasiness; it is simply the necessary condition of human life. They fear no attack when once safely lodged in their houses in the clouds. They say that no one would dare to attempt to burn or cut down the tree, for they keep a large stock of stones and spears aloft, and say that they could crush any men who attempted to come near their tree. (*Journal of the Mission Voyage to the Melanesian Islands of the Schooner "Southern Cross" . . . May-October, 1866.* Melanesian Mission, Auckland 1866, pp. 10-11).

For further discussion on house types in Melanesia, cf. Brenchley (1873: 292-293), Penny (1887: 80-83), Codrington (1891: 298-303), Rivers (1914 II: 254-258), Ivens (1927: 375-379), Hopkins (1928: 182-191).

82. Cf. Tippett (1968: 31-34, 81-116).

83. Cf. Haddon and Hornell (1936-1938, Vol. 2).

84. Cf. Davenport (1964).

85. Canoes of larger size were probably built during the pre-contact period. Hopkins (1928: 192) reports that the largest canoe he ever saw was one launched in 1906. It measured 120 ft. long, and 7 ft. wide, and seated 120 men. This canoe was built by people from one of the artificial islands of Malaita. It proved, however, to be too big and cumbersome and was never put to significant use.

86. Cf. Ivens (1927) frontispiece, for a colored native drawing of an Ulawa canoe, and Hopkins (1928: 56) for a photo of a San Cristobal canoe. For further detail on canoes in Melanesia, cf. Guppy (1887: 146ff), Penny (1887: 77-80), Woodford (1890b: 157-159, 1909), Codrington (1891: 290-298), Rivers (1914 II: 450-454), Ivens (1927: 149-154), Hopkins (1928: 192-200), and Haddon and Hornell (1936-1938, Vol. 2).

87. For additional discussion of Melanesian material culture, cf. Guppy (1887: 57-80), Woodford (1890b: 148, 152, 157-160), Codrington (1891: 290-331), Rivers (1914 II: 439-463), Fox (1924: 281-295), Ivens (1927: 375-395), and Hopkins (1928: 54-66, 182-200).

88. For an example of the complexity and integration of the ecology in the Buka-Bougainville area of the Western Solomons, see Blackwood (1935: 439-461). For an excellent discussion on the relationship of social organization to ecological adaptation among the Baegu of Malaita, see Ross (1973).

89. Sahlins (1958: 2-3).

90. Hogbin and Wedgewood (1952-53: 242). In addition to the excellent survey of Melanesian socio-political organization by Hogbin and Wedgewood (1952-53), see also, Codrington (1891: 46-58), Rivers (1914 II: 70-80), Belshaw (1950b: 23-26). For an interesting comparison of New Britain with Samoa, cf. Brown (1910: 23-49). Two classic articles comparing Melanesia with Polynesia and Micronesia are, Sahlins (1970), and Valentine 1970).

91. Rivers (1914 II: 83). I am distinguishing Island Melanesia from Melanesia as a whole, for in the New Guinea Highlands social organization is almost entirely patrilineal.

92. Cf. Bogesi (1948: 213-214), and G. White (1978: 57-63).

93. Cf. Scheffler (1963, 1965).

94. For further discussion of the social organization of this area of the Southeast Solomons, and its relationship to the more general pattern of culture found elsewhere in Melanesia, see Fox (1924: 7-77, 204-209), Ivens (1927: 462-482).

95. Chowning (1977: 41).

96. Hogbin (1958: 84-85).

97. Cf. Guppy (1887: 33-35), Woodford (1890b: 154, 181), and Tippett (1967: 147-159).

98. The Fijian Chieftainship had a time depth of approximately four hundred years, going back as far as the Nakanvadra migration (A. R.

Tippett, personal communication).

99. For greater detail on secret societies in Melanesia, cf. Penny (1887: 70-73), Codrington (1891: 69-115), Rivers (1914 II: 205-233).

100. Although leadership in traditional Melanesia was very heavily male dominated, there were occasional women who rose to positions of considerable influence and leadership, equal to that of a Big Man. For example, on the matrilineal island of Santa Isabel, oral history tells of a "Queen" Sumana among the Zabana (Kia) people.

101. At the time of European contact in Fiji, the pattern of leadership was closer to that of Polynesia than what I have generalized in Melanesia. Hereditary chieftainships did exist, going back eight to twelve generations, or approximately four hundred years.

102. For further discussion of Melanesian Big Men, cf. Codrington (1891: 46-54), Fox (1924: 296-300), Scheffler (1964b). Characterizations of Melanesian Big Men can be found in Oliver (1955: 422-439), and Keesing (1978a). Goldie (1908: 24) notes three types of leaders in New Georgia, where the most important leader had sway over a large area and obtained his position through heredity. The famous Ingava of Roviana was such a chief. For a description of him, see Edge-Partington (1907). Other nineteenth century Big Men were Gorai of the Shortlands described in Guppy (1887: 13-40), and Kwaisulia of the Lau Lagoon, Malaita, portrayed by Corris (1970).

On the island of Santa Isabel, Dudley Tuti was, until his retirement as Bishop in 1981, not only the Bishop of the only church on the island, but also the Paramount Chief, which carries secular authority. Because of his high position in both Church and State, islanders frequently would speak of him as having more *mana* than any other man on the island. For further discussion of Dudley Tuti as Bishop and Paramount Chief, see G. White (1978: 261-272). See also White's (1978: 66-129) discussion of the Big Man model.

103. Hogbin and Wedgewood (1952-53: 242).

104. As far as village structures are concerned, the family households and the club house are two clear types. Another form which was not universal in Melanesia, but did exist in some societies, was a separate dwelling place for young men who had not yet graduated to the married state and obtained adult status.

105. On the island of Malaita, the bush/salt-water distinction is obvious because residence, occupation and lifestyles are clearly distinguishable as either bush or salt water. However, in some parts of Melanesia, the distinction is between mountain people and coastal people. For

example, in Viti Levu, the coastal people have up to a ten-mile territorial domain, which makes them agricultural as well as salt-water. In terms of time-depth analysis, the intriguing question in Melanesia is when and how did two peoples' lifestyles emerge? Are the coastal people a later migration which forced the aboriginal people into the interior? This is a common interpretation, but a conclusive study has yet to be done.

106. For an excellent study of a Malaita bush-people, which focuses on the relationship between social organization and ecological adaptation, see Ross (1973).

107. Cf. Woodford (1908), and Ivens (1930). Fox (1924: 141-142) disputes the claim that a significant difference existed between bush and coastal people in the Arosi district of San Cristobal, and attributes the notion to Europeans' exaggerated estimate of the bush men.

108. Ivens (1927: 259), Hopkins (1928: 172-173).

109. Cf. Ivens (1927: 299).

110. W. R. Geddes (1948) in his study of culture change in Fiji, described the pre-contact society as "war oriented." His study is a good example of the war focus in Melanesia. See also T. Williams (1858: 43-59) for his discussion of Fijian war.

111. Ivens (1927: 299). Cf. Hopkins (1928: 171-172).

112. For additional material on the role of warfare in traditional Melanesian society, cf. Fox (1924: 305-313), Ivens (1927: 294-303, 1930: 178-201), Hopkins (1928: 168-181), Hocart (1931), A. Lewis (1932: 83-92). For a discussion of Fijian warfare, cf. Fison (1907: xviii-xxx), and Tippett (1954, 1968: 53-79, 1973a: 39-80). For the New Guinea Highlands, cf. Meggitt (1977), P. Brown (1978: 207-215).

113. For an excellent analysis and diagram of the role of headhunting in the cycle of village life in Roviana, cf. Tippett (1967: 147-151). See McKinnon (1972: 58-69, 1975) for an interesting discussion on the relationship between raiding and trading in the Western Solomons in the pre-contact period. See also, Woodford (1890a: 152-153), and Jackson (1972, 1975).

114. Cf. Guppy (1887: 33-35), Woodford (1890a: 154, 181), Fox (1924: 36), and Tippett (1967: 147-159).

115. For a discussion of Fijian cannibalism, cf. Fison (1907: xxxvi-xlv). Tippett (1973a: 5-6) in demonstrating the ethnohistorical method of upstreaming, shows how cannibalism in Fiji evolved from a sacred to a secular event and experience. For a discussion of cannibalism in

Melanesia in general, cf. Codrington (1891: 343-344). For the Solomon Islands, cf. Ivens (1927: 25) and Hopkins (1928: 201-204).

116. Worsley (1957: 15-16).

117. Since the geographical boundaries of this study are confined primarily to that area in which the Melanesian Mission was an agent of change, namely the Solomon Islands, Banks' Islands, and Northern New Hebrides, generalizations for this area will not necessarily apply to New Guinea in the west and Fiji in the east, or the Southern New Hebrides and New Caledonia in the south.

118. See below, pp. 330-358.

119. For an interesting study of Enga worldview in the New Guinea Highlands, cf. R. Lacey (1973).

120. Gibbs (1977: 167).

121. On the relationship of "cargo-cults" to cosmic regeneration in Melanesian religion, cf. Eliade (1970).

122. For example, islanders on South Pentecost in the New Hebrides divide their world into two primary categories—animate and inanimate, but their defining qualities for these categories are different from mine. Thus, an unusual looking stone, though conceded to be inanimate at present, is considered to have been animate at one time. It was perhaps a spirit-being and moved to its present location. Another example is a ghost which may be perceived as animate or inanimate, depending on human recognition. As long as the memory of the dead person is kept alive, then his ghost will be recognized and remembered, and as an animated spirit-being, it will participate in the affairs of human beings. Ghosts do not die, they simply fade away, fade from the memory of the living community, and become inanimate, while their importance is replaced by ghosts of the more recent dead (Lane 1965: 253-254).

123. For an excellent discussion of the concept of power in traditional Melanesian cosmology in relationship to Christianity, see Ahrens (1977).

124. In this discussion I will use the terms Eastern and Western Melanesia, but I am referring to the eastern and western parts of the area under study. Thus, Western Melanesia refers to the Santa Cruz and Solomon Islands, Eastern Melanesia to the Banks' Islands and Northern New Hebrides—not to Fiji at the eastern-most end of Melanesia.

125. Cf. Bogesi (1948: 209).

126. Codrington (1891: 126).

127. This is very different from Fijian ancestor worship where there is a deification of both recent and remote dead, coexisting together. The remote ancestors, known by name for twelve to fifteen generations, were associated with all things — fertility, prosperity, etc. Fijians applied to the recent dead for aid in warfare. Cf. Hocart (1922a).

128. Lawrence and Meggitt (1965: 11).

129. In many of the New Guinea Highlands religions there is a clear connection with moral and ethical domains. For example, the principal "god" of the Huli in the Southern Highlands, is a guardian of ethics. The prevailing attitude of Highlanders is that ghosts will respond to ritual only if the laws of clanship and kinship are scrupulously observed, and thus their religion is very concerned with ethical behavior (Lawrence and Meggitt 1965: 16).

130. Codrington (1891: 123).

131. Ivens (1936: 17).

132. For stories about the culture-hero Qat, cf. Codrington (1881: 271-274, 1891: 154-167). The legend of Qat is that he and his brothers left the islands after their work of creation had been completed. When they left, they took everything good with them, and so it was believed that some day they would return, bringing with them paradise again. When Selwyn and Patteson of the Melanesian Mission first arrived in 1854, the islanders thought they were the returning brothers of Qat. In similar fashion, Captain Cook was received as the returning Rono in the Hawaiian Islands.

133. Codrington (1891: 150). For stories of Kohausibware, or Kahausipwari in Bauro, or Hatuibwari, a male serpent deity in Arosi, cf. Fox (1924: 236-240).

134. The Kakamora of San Cristobal is an example of this type of being. For a description and stories about this mischievous being, cf. Fox (1924: 138-147).

135. Codrington (1881: 267).

136. *Ibid.* pp. 275-276.

137. In his discussion of *mana*, Marett (1914: 99-121) argues that *tabu* is the counterpart to *mana* in the indigenous religious system, being the negative mode of the supernatural, to which *mana* corresponds as the positive mode. This pattern is found in Melanesia. However, *tabu* in Melanesia, does not appear to have played such an important role in the culture as it did in Polynesia, where there was greater fear of the supernatural power connected with it, cf. G. Brown (1910: 273-282).

Codrington (1891: 215-216) gives us an example of how *tabu* functioned in the Solomon Islands:

> . . . in Florida (Nggela) a chief will forbid something to be done or touched under a penalty; he has said, for example, *tambu hangalatu*, any one who violates his prohibition must pay him a hundred strings of money; it seems to the European a proof of the power of the chief; but to the native the power of the chief, in this and everything else, rests on the persuasion that the chief has his *tindalo* at his back. The sense of this in the particular case is remote, the apprehension of angering the chief is present and effective, but the ultimate sanction is the power of the *tindalo*.

For additional references to *tabu* in Melanesia, cf. Guppy (1887: 32), Williamson (1914: 51-53), Fox (1924: 297, 303), Ivens (1927: 253-276, 1930: 237-239), and Hopkins (1928: 124-136).

138. Codrington's description of *mana* is still the classic definition used today. For further and more recent studies of this concept, cf. Hogbin (1936) and Firth (1940). Capell (1940) has done an interesting study of *mana*, focusing on the linguistic distribution of the concept throughout Oceania. See also Hocart's (1914, 1922b, 1932) discussion of *mana*.

139. Quoted from footnote in Codrington (1891: 118-119).

140. Codrington (1891: 119). Cf. *S.C.L.*, Jan., 1927, pp. 25-27.

141. Cf. Tippett (1967: 7-8) for an illuminating discussion on the relationship of *mana* to human skulls and other material objects, and the significance this had for islanders in their encounter with Christianity.

142. However, there are two different ways in which men obtain *mana*: (1) through sacrifice or prayer (appeal to the supernatural), and (2) by chant or manipulation. These are different techniques, but there is a blending of religious and magical attitudes toward the acquisition of *mana*.

143. Sorcery in Melanesia is widespread, and the local diversity of form and function is considerable. See, for example, the list of forms of sorcery in the Solomon Islands compiled by Tippett (1967: 15). The cure for sorcery frequently involves the encounter of two sources of *mana*; the **antidote** must be more powerful than the **poison**, if a cure is effective. For an excellent theoretical study and ethnographic survey of sorcery and witchcraft in Melanesia, cf. Patterson (1974-1975). See also M. MacDonald (1981) and Osborne (1982).

144. Codrington (1881: 300-301).

145. *Ibid.* p. 305.

146. For a graphic portrayal of human sacrifice in New Georgia, Solomon

Islands, cf. Woodford (1890a: 155-157).

147. Cf. Tippett (1967: 147-159) for a discussion of the dynamics of the Western Solomons headhunting and slavery complex, and its relationship to the introduction of Christianity by the Methodist Mission. See also Jackson (1972, 1975) for a study of the role of headhunting in the conversion of the islanders on Santa Isabel. See also discussion below, pp. 359-364.

148. In some societies, however, there was a hierarchy of indigenous priests, with each ascending grade having more power and prestige. For example, among the Lau in Malaita, an informant told me there were traditionally three grades: (1) *Foaniewou*, (2) *Foakali*, and (3) *Fata-abu*. My informant, an old Anglican priest, and son of a powerful pagan priest, informed me that in the minds of the islanders, the traditional graded system of the priesthood, corresponded to that introduced by the Anglicans, namely, bishops, priests, and deacons.

149. This has been a brief overview of a very complex subject. The principal sources on which I have relied are Codrington (1881, 1891). For further discussion, cf. Guppy (1887: 53-56), Penny (1887: 53-73), G. Brown (1910: 190-250), Rivers (1914 II: 258-291, 404-422), Williamson (1914: 71-85), Hocart (1922a, 1925), Fox (1924: 78-137, 236-269), Ivens (1927: 178-207, 277-293; 1930: 218-230), Hopkins (1928: 205-215), Raucaz (1928: 63-65), Layard (1942: 205-683), Guiart (1962) and R. Keesing (1982).

Other materials that are very helpful in the study of Melanesian religion are found in Lawrence and Meggitt (1965), Lawrence (1973), Parratt (1976), Knight (1978), Habel (1979), Leenhardt (1979), Trompf, Loeliger and Kadiba (1980).

Chapter 3

Missionary Contact and Melanesian Response

With this chapter we enter the period of initial contact between Melanesians and missionaries. We will discuss the beginning of the Melanesian Mission and the founding principles on which it developed its philosophy and strategy of evangelization. The period covers the last half of the nineteenth century.

I will begin by discussing the work and missionary philosophy of George Augustus Selwyn, first Bishop of New Zealand, who laid down the principles on which the foundation of the Melanesian Mission was established. This will be followed by a brief discussion of the cultural context in which the first missionaries operated. Attention will focus next on the person of John Coleridge Patteson, first Bishop of Melanesia, who left an indelible mark on the Melanesian Mission, shaping mission policy and philosophy for decades to follow.

The second part of the chapter will consider the role of the Central School in the training of Melanesians, and will conclude with a brief discussion of two movements toward Christianity that occurred in the Banks' Islands and on Nggela in the Solomons.

G. A. Selwyn: Founder of the Melanesian Mission

In an anthropological study of missionaries as agents of culture change it is necessary to have a thorough understanding of the important personalities that shaped the structure and nature of the cross-cultural relationships in this dynamic arena of Melanesian and missionary interaction. Therefore, in this chapter, attention will focus on two personalities, George A. Selwyn, and John Coleridge Patteson, whose philosophies of culture contact did much to direct the course of the mission's activities.

The origin of the Anglican Melanesian Mission is traced back to George Augustus Selwyn, who at the age of 32, was consecrated the first Bishop of New Zealand in 1841.[1] Due to a clerical error in the Letters Patent of October 14, 1841, his New Zealand Diocese extended from 47° south latitude to 34° **north** latitude instead of south latitude, thus placing under his episcopal care a wedge of the globe extending nearly from Antarctica up into the North Pacific Ocean.[2] However, Selwyn's personal charge came less from the legality of his Letters Patent, than from the inspiration and sense of spiritual responsibility he received from the commission of the Archbishop of Canterbury, Bishop Howley, who exhorted him to regard the New Zealand Church as a "fountain diffusing the streams of salvation over the islands and coasts of the Pacific."[3] Selwyn never waivered from this commission. Writing to his friend Edward Coleridgc in 1852, he declared, "If the Archbishop had told me to go to Japan or Borneo, I should have endeavored to go; the wisdom or possibility of the Mission not depending on my judgments, but the simple duty of obedience."[4]

On the outward journey to New Zealand, he spent the months aboard ship learning the Maori language and mastering it sufficiently to enable him to address the native New Zealanders in their own language when he stepped ashore.[5] The first six years of Selwyn's activity were spent in New Zealand, organizing the Anglican Church, establishing and coordinating missionary work among the Maoris, and touring throughout his diocese. His unbounded energy enabled him to travel relentlessly through North and South Island, and he quickly gained a reputation for his long treks across land, covering hundreds of miles a year on foot. Selwyn was a brilliant organizer and administrator as well as a visionary. He was a man whose personal attributes made him eminently suited for such pioneering work. He has been called, "The missionary bishop *par excellence*, combining zeal and energy with vision and a genius for organization."[6]

In 1843 Selwyn inaugurated St. John's College, presumably named after St. John's College, Cambridge, where he studied (1827-1830) and was elected a fellow.[7] He established his headquarters here in Auckland, with the objective of having a center where both European and Maori students would receive theological training, interspersed with training in "useful industry" such as agriculture, animal husbandry, and trades such as carpentry and printing. His philosophy of education is succinctly expressed in a prayer he wrote for the college, that "true religion, sound learning, and useful industry may here forever flourish and abound."[8] Selwyn also hoped that through the non-academic program the school would become self-supporting.[9]

In December 1847, Selwyn left New Zealand for a ten-week tour of Tonga, Samoa, the New Hebrides and New Caledonia, as temporary chaplain aboard HMS *Dido*. In Tonga, he met with the Wesleyan missionaries and in Samoa with members of the London Missionary Society. Although their ecclesiastical perspectives differed from his, he nevertheless paid close attention to the methods they had used in their approach to missionary work. They appeared to have been successful in Polynesia, for by 1848 a second generation of Christian converts was emerging. From the Polynesian islands he sailed to Melanesia, visiting islands in the New Hebrides and New Caledonia. The Melanesian contrast was imposing, for although European contact had been made since the 1820's through whalers, traders, and from

1841, by men in search of sandalwood for the lucrative China market, missionary contact and influence had been negligible. Selwyn quickly felt that the evangelizing methods employed in Polynesia would not be suitable for conditions in Melanesia. The islanders had earned a reputation as bloodthirsty savages and the popular opinion held that a European could not land on the shores of these islands without great risk of losing his life.

However, an incident at the Isle of Pines influenced Selwyn considerably in his later interaction with Melanesians. Here he encountered the veteran sandalwood trader, James Paddon, sitting on his ship, leisurely smoking his pipe, while islanders loaded his vessel with sandalwood. This peaceful image did not square with the notorious reputation of the island and so Selwyn inquired as to the "secret" of his successful operation. Captain Paddon explained that, "By kindness and fair dealing I have traded with these people for many years. I never cheated them, I never treated them badly, we thoroughly understand each other."[10] Selwyn would later refer to Paddon as "My Tutor" for his instructive lesson in intercultural relationships.[11]

This brief but informative reconnaissance in 1848 helped Selwyn to solidify his "plan of attack" for the evangelization of the Melanesian islands under his episcopal charge. However, the whole of Melanesia was not simply a *tabula rasa* on which Selwyn could conduct his missionary enterprises, for there were already others in the "field." The London Missionary Society had sent Samoan and Rarotongan teachers to different places in the Loyalty Group, New Caledonia and the southern New Hebrides. Although their presence was not formidable nor their efforts very successful,[12] they had nevertheless established a beginning. The French Marist Fathers, who after their unsuccessful attempt in 1845 to establish work in the Solomons, tried once again by opening up work on the Isle of Pines and Aneiteum. The Presbyterians from Nova Scotia, whom Selwyn had met in Samoa while the former were on their way to Melanesia, were just beginning to establish a base at Aneiteum in the southern New Hebrides. The remainder of the field north to New Guinea was virgin territory for the young bishop of New Zealand. Selwyn had set as one of his founding principles to follow the code of comity whereby he would "never interfere with any Christianization already undertaken by any religious body or sect whatever."[13] He wanted to clearly avoid the scramble for souls and a "Divided Christianity" which he felt characterized much of the missionary work elsewhere in the Pacific.

Anthropological Problems and Missiological Principles

Selwyn was convinced that the evangelization of Melanesia called for a strategy far different from the well-established practice used in other parts of Oceania. His argument for an innovative approach was based on the following three considerations relative to Melanesia as a uniquely different mission field from that of Polynesia, or for that matter, different even from other parts of the world.

1. The Diversity of Languages. As noted above in Chapter 2 (pp. 47–48), because of the small populations of socially and geographically isolated speech communities, if a missionary were to be stationed permanently on an island and learn the "local" language, he might soon discover that the maximum number of people with whom he could communicate might not exceed three hundred. Selwyn experienced this frustration, and writing to a friend exclaimed,

> Here I have been for a fortnight working away, as I supposed, at the language of New Caledonia, by aid of a little translation of portions of Scripture made by a native teacher, sent by the London Mission from Rarotonga, and just when I have begun to see my way, and to be able to communicate a little with an Isle of Pines boy, whom I found here, I learn that this is only a dialect used in the southern extremity of the island, and not understood in the parts which I wished to attack first.[14]

To appoint a missionary for each speech community in Melanesia was impossible with the available resources and personnel. Thus, in a resolution passed by the Anglican bishops meeting in Sydney in 1850, it was declared that, "The multiplicity of languages makes it necessary to conduct instruction in some one language common to all, which must be English."[15] An interesting oversight in this resolution is that English was common to none of the Melanesians, only to the missionaries who wished to convert them.

2. Climate. It was believed that the climate, particularly in the islands of central and northern Melanesia, was too unhealthful for Europeans to establish permanent residence there. The death of over seventy Samoan and Rarotongan missionaries was frequently cited as justification for this decision.[16] The deadly malaria was feared, and for good reason, as prophylactic drugs had not yet been discovered for the prevention of malarial attacks.

3. Indigenous Melanesian Social Structure. As noted in Chapter 2 (pp. 56–64) Melanesian social structure is significantly different from that of Polynesia, where, given a hierarchical structure and ascribed status, missionaries found that once a paramount chief was converted, frequently large groups of islanders followed suit. In contrast, the fragmented and egalitarian social structure of Melanesian society meant that if a Big Man converted, his influence would frequently be limited to no more than several hundred "followers," and his conversion in no way assured that others would follow his lead. In addition, the state of endemic hostility between social groups mitigated against a missionary being able to move around freely from one area of an island to another.[17]

Selwyn also believed that the most effective method of evangelism would be to remove potential converts from the confines of their culture, for it might prove too much of a cross to bear for the young Christians if initially they had to follow a new ethical system in an old social context of warfare, traditional religious practices, and customs. The meeting of bishops in 1850, for the founding of the Australian Board of Missions, concluded in a resolution that, "The low state of barbarism in which these races now are seems to require that a select number should be brought under the most careful training at a distance from their own tribes."[18]

These three areas of consideration, language, climate and social structure, led Selwyn to conclude that sending missionaries out to the islands on a permanent basis would be impractical and ineffective. The alternative then, was to bring potential converts to where the missionaries were headquartered — at St. John's College in Auckland. He wrote to his father in 1849, outlining the scheme he envisioned would work:

> I have already written Edward Coleridge from Aneiteum on the course which seems to be open to us to obtain at once a decisive influence over the natives of these islands. It is not to establish Mission Stations at first, which would involve a great cost, require a great number of missionaries, and risk a great loss of life in the first instance; but to have one Floating Mission House; with Bishop, Teachers, School, Portable Printing Press, etc. on board; to hover round the islands; and invite the young men on board, to let them see the inhabitants of other islands, whom they have known only as enemies, seated at the same table, and joining in the same classes with themselves; if they seem to be afraid or unwilling to leave their own shore, to land them at home to tell what they have seen; the more adventurous will be willing to try their wings by a short flight to the next island, and will easily be trained like Carrier Pigeons to undertake the longer voyage to the Central College in New Zealand. The select youths, of whose disposition we have good hope, will be induced to stay with us; the others may be gratified with a few presents and returned to their own places.[19]

Selwyn's plan for returning the Melanesian "scholars"[20] to their home islands coincided with seasonal changes in New Zealand, as he explains in the same letter to his father:

> While the weather is most unfavourable for visitation in New Zealand, it is safe and pleasant among the tropical Islands. On the contrary, during our Summer which is fine and favourable for navigation, the hurricanes prevail within the tropical regions of the Pacific.[21]

Whether obliged by the peculiar circumstances of Melanesia or determined on the basis of missiological principles, Selwyn chose to develop a system whereby the evangelizing of Melanesia would rely primarily on the islanders themselves. His ultimate goal, articulated in the beginning, was an independent island church, "with its own staff of clergy, its own laws, its own bishop."[22]

To implement this strategy he set as his mission headquarters, St. John's College, located in a rural setting five miles from Auckland.[23] Selwyn had established St. John's shortly after arriving in New Zealand for the purpose of combining cathedral and collegiate functions in educating English, Maori and Melanesian students. However, this amalgamation of ethnic groups was difficult to achieve, as Selwyn noted in writing to a friend in England in 1849:

> We are succeeding at last, I hope, in amalgamating the two races on an equality of privileges and position; but it was uphill work; it seemed so natural to every English boy and man to have a Maori for his fag. I think that by God's blessing we shall succeed at last, and if we do, it will be a glorious measure of success; for our College will be a Propaganda of 20 or 30 languages, sending out Missionaries and Native Teachers to places whose names are not in the charts, and the languages of whose people is unknown even to Hawtrey and Latham.[24]

During the New Zealand winter months, he proposed to cruise throughout Melanesia, visiting the various island groups, and opening up friendly relations with as many people as possible. Upon gaining the islanders' confidence he hoped to persuade them to entrust some of their most promising young men to go with him to St. John's for the summer months.[25] Here the islanders would be taught English, the arts of civilization and the rudiments of Christianity. At the outset of the New Zealand winter, the scholars would be returned to their islands, where it was hoped they would disseminate among their fellows all they had learned at St. John's. After their first year, if it was felt that they would benefit from further training, they would be implored to return the following year. If not, they were left in their villages and others were sought to take their places. This process would continue for several years until the young Melanesians were baptized and sufficiently instructed so as to enable them to return permanently to their homes and embark on evangelizing their own people.[26]

This, in principle, was Selwyn's scheme, which he began to put into practice in 1849. Although the designation "Melanesian Mission" did not come into use until the early 1850's, the founding date for the mission has always been considered to be 1849, the year Selwyn set sail from New Zealand on a 3,000 mile voyage to Melanesia. Navigating the small 21-ton schooner *Undine*, Selwyn visited the Loyalty Islands, New Caledonia, and the southern New Hebrides, bringing back with him five young men to begin his missionary endeavors. Shortly after midnight on October 1st, 1849, Selwyn arrived back at St. John's and exuberantly announced to his wife, "I've got them."[27]

The following May, in 1850, Selwyn returned the first group of scholars to their homes, and in the same year Captain Erskine of HMS *Havannah*, delivered to Selwyn three New Hebrideans and one Solomon Islander from San Cristobal who had requested to join Erskine's ship during its tour of the islands. Selwyn had played an important role in the October, 1850, formation of the Australian Board of Missions, and was thus given a larger ship, the 100 ton *Border Maid*, in which to conduct his tours of the islands. In July, 1851, Selwyn, accompanied by William Tyrrell, Bishop of Newcastle, sailed in the *Border Maid* as far north as Malekula in the New Hebrides. On this tour they returned with thirteen Melanesians from six islands, including five who had been to St. John's previously.[28]

In 1852 the Mission contact was expanded further to include the Banks' Islands, Santa Cruz and San Cristobal in the Solomons. On this tour Selwyn brought back twenty-seven scholars from eight different islands, and baptized nineteen islanders on the voyage. The following year, 1853, with some difficulty due to shipping, the Melanesians were returned to their home islands. However, because of Selwyn's visit to England in 1854-1855, another tour of the islands was not made until 1856. In that year thirteen scholars were brought to New Zealand, including seven from Marau Sound on Guadalcanal and several others from the northwest end of San Cristobal.

In 1857, an expansive tour of sixty-six islands netted thirty-four scholars from nine different islands.[29] In the following year forty-five Melanesians came from twelve different islands, and in 1859, fifteen islands were represented by thirty-eight scholars.

YEAR	No. of Islanders brought to N.Z.	No. of Islands represented
1849	5	n/a
1851	13	6
1852	27	8
1856	13	n/a
1857	34	9
1858	45	12
1859	38	15

Table 3.1. Islanders Taken to New Zealand by the Melanesian Mission.

Thus in the first decade of the Mission's activity, there was an increasing number of scholars coming from an increasing number of islands visited. From 1849 to 1860, eighty-one different islands were contacted and 152 Melanesians from twenty-six islands were brought to New Zealand for training at the Central School. Of this total, the Loyalty Islands had provided thirty-six, and these had come primarily in the early stages of missionary contact. From Guadalcanal twenty-two had come, but only once; eighteen had come from San Cristobal, and eleven from Mota in the Banks' Group.[30]

These are the statistics for this early period, but what is their significance? Given the large number of islands visited, the Mission was attracting young people away from less than one third of them, and of those who did come, only thirty-nine returned for one or more seasons in New Zealand — a little over twenty-five percent of the total.

To understand the cultural dynamics of this period, and to evaluate whether the proposed scheme was working as Selwyn had designed it, three interrelated questions must be considered: (1) What was the socio-cultural milieu in which missionary-islander interaction occurred? (2) What were the missionaries' attitudes toward and perceptions of the Melanesians? (3) What were the motivating factors that compelled young Melanesians to leave their homes and sail away with the missionaries to New Zealand? I will now proceed to discuss each of these questions as part of a larger framework for evaluating the Melanesian Mission's unique scheme of evangelization.

The Socio-Cultural Context of Missionary-Islander Interaction

It should be self-evident in this study that generalizations intended for the whole of Melanesia seldom stand the test of careful scrutiny. This is certainly the case in considering the cultural context in which the Melanesian Mission first encountered the islanders.

For example, in many of the islands the missionaries had been preceded by other European agents who had interacted with the islanders for a variety of purposes and from a mixed set of motives. Selwyn frequently bemoaned the fact that Christian missionaries had arrived so late on the scene. In writing to a friend, during the first voyage of the *Undine* in 1849, he lamented:

> While I have been sleeping in my bed in New Zealand, these islands, the Isle of Pines, New Caledonia, New Hebrides, New Ireland, New Britain, New Guinea, the Loyalty Islands, the Kingsmills, etc. etc. have been riddled through and through, by the Whale fishers, and Traders of the South Sea. That odious black slug, the beche-la-mer, has been dragged out of its hole in every coral reef, to make black broth for Chinese Mandarins, by the unconquerable daring of English traders, while I, like a worse black slug as I am, have left the world all its field of mischief to itself. The same daring men have robbed every one of these islands of its Sandalwood, to furnish incense for the idolatrous worship of these Chinese temples, before I have taught a single Islander to offer up his sacrifice of prayer to the true and only God. Even a mere Sydney speculator could induce nearly a

> hundred men from some of the wildest islands in the Pacific, to sail in his ships to Sydney, to keep his flocks and herds, before I to whom the "Chief Shepherd" has given his commandment to seek out His sheep that are scattered over a thousand isles, have sought out, or found so much as one of these which have strayed and are lost.[31]

On the other hand, there were islands where there was little or no evidence of previous European contact, the islanders appearing just as Captain Cook had described them seventy-five years earlier, or as Mendana and Quiros had encountered them over two centuries prior to Cook.[32] In some of the islands these Anglican missionaries were the first known contacts of Europeans with Melanesians. Thus, for example, in the Banks' Islands, the missionaries were believed to be ancestral spirits who had returned from the dead; a substantial body of Melanesian mythology and folklore supported this initial belief. George Sarawia, the first Melanesian to be ordained to the priesthood in 1868, wrote several years later of his initial encounter with the missionaries, and I quote at length from his interesting perception:

> When I was still a little boy, I had not yet seen a white man or a big ship, but I saw them for the first time the year the bishops first came to us at Vanua Lava, when they dropped anchor at Nawano, which was the harbour where I lived, and which they had just discovered. My being taken by the bishops started like this: they anchored in the evening, and next morning I paddled out to the side of the ship to buy something for myself from them. But when I reached the ship, I saw Bishop Selwyn standing at the side, and I was afraid of him, because he was wearing black clothes, but his face was very white. So I drifted far away from the ship, because I was afraid, but he beckoned to me to climb up on to the ship. But I was still afraid because it was the first time I had seen a white man, so I paddled off, but he still beckoned me (as he could not yet speak the Mota language). But he called me by just beckoning with his hand, but I was still shy; I had not made up my mind to climb on board, but he still called me.
>
> Then Bishop Patteson came too, and both of them went on calling me to come on board, but I was still afraid and thought to myself, "Those two want me to go to them, but I don't know them yet," for I was still a heathen, but I thought that they were like the people of my land, ready to deceive someone in order to kill him. I thought like that because I did not know the Bishop; I thought I had better beware lest they deceived me on the ship and killed me, and I was still afraid, but the ship was now close. Then I made up my mind to go with them, so I paddled up to the ship, and Bishop Selwyn threw me a line, and I tied up my canoe with it; then he took my hand and pulled me up on board, so that I should see that

> they welcomed me kindly. So we three went to the stern and sat down, and they asked me the name of the island, and the names of the people. I told them and they wrote them down in a book, but I did not know then what a book was. And I looked at the feet of all the people on the ship, and thought it was really their feet, but it was only leather shoes they were wearing. I said to myself that these men were made partly of clamshell, and my bones quaked.
>
> We used to have wrong ideas about the white men; we thought they were some of our own people who had died long ago and had come to life again in the land that they had sailed from.[33]

Thus, for some islanders, their contact with the Melanesian Mission was their first encounter with Europeans, but for many others, they knew all too well who the white man was, for they had encountered him in several capacities.

After Port Jackson was established in Australia in 1788, it soon became the commercial center of the Southwest Pacific, from whence ships sailed in search of Pacific wealth, and through the islands enroute to China, delivering resources from the area and returning with tea. Initially the commercial ventures were in search of seal skins, beginning in 1729, with the "sealing rush" to Bass Strait between Australia and Tasmania coming in 1802. A decade later the great days of sealing had come and almost gone.[34]

Whaling was the next great enterprise to enter the Pacific, beginning in the 1820's and flourishing through to the 1860's. It was dominated by Americans until the advent of the Civil War. Then the discovery of petroleum as a substitute for whale oil used in lighting lamps soon brought the industry into decline.

The islanders' intercourse with sealers and whalers was primarily concerned with exchanging food (pigs, root crops, and coconuts) for material goods such as fish-hooks, metal tools, firearms and ammunition, cloth, glass beads, tobacco, pipes, and matches. Whalers also introduced alcohol and venereal disease into some island populations, but the incidents of this were undoubtedly higher in Polynesia than in Melanesia. Whalers have been severely criticized for their lax moral conduct with islanders, leading to the popular conception that they "hung their consciences on Cape Horn" as they entered the Pacific.[35] For many islanders their first European contact was with the whalers.[36]

Following the whalers came the traders in search of sandalwood (in southern Melanesia), *beche-de-mer* (trepang), tortoise and pearl shell.[37] The very nature of their activity led to a closer relationship between themselves and the islanders than the whalers had had. Those in search of *beche-de-mer*, shell, sandalwood and other island products, required the direct participation and cooperation of islanders if their business enterprises were to prosper. It is true as Grattan (1963a: 192) has noted that, "The early white traders were not under any discipline but their own, and it was simply the discipline of cupidity." It must be remembered, however, that the trader needed the help and cooperation of the islanders, and so to blatantly abuse them would have been counterproductive.[38] In exchange for services and products, the traders, like the whalers, introduced a considerable amount of "trade goods" into the Melanesian economy, and also participated in the complex exchange network in some of the islands. Thus, for example, the tortoise shell in the Western Solomons was purchased to exchange for pigs at Tana in the New Hebrides, which in turn were traded for sandalwood on the island of Espiritu Santo.[39]

A third category of Europeans whose intercourse with Melanesians predated missionary contact includes beachcombers, deserters and castaways. Unlike the previous Europeans discussed above, beachcombers tended to become more integrated into their host society, provided they were not immediately killed. Maude (1968: 161) has noted that the most striking characteristic of the beachcomber was his "conformity to the social patterns of his hosts, in marked contrast to the attitudes of dominant superiority affected by his successors."

The source for this population was not only convicts escaped from English and French penal colonies established in Australia and New Caledonia, but also men working the whaling and trading vessels as well, who either chose to stay behind, or who were deliberately abandoned in the islands. In his interesting discussion of beachcombers and castaways, Maude (1968: 134-177) notes that because of the reputation for its hostile and cannibal natives, "Melanesia and New Guinea were scarcely propitious homes for beachcombers during the earlier part of the century, and even the convicts apparently by-passed the area" (1968: 146). It is true that Polynesia was by far the preferred haven of rest for these wanderlust men, but there were more in Melanesia than Maude acknowledges. For example, in the Solomon Islands, San Cristobal was a favorite spot, and Sayes (1976: 45) has unearthed references to fourteen residing on this island between 1820 and 1870. One man in particular, Fredrick Bradford, was a resident on San Cristobal for nearly two months in 1860, and he has left a valuable ethnographic record of his stay.[40]

For analytical convenience I have lumped Europeans into categories by profession and arranged these categories chronologically, except for the beachcombers who were products of every period of commercial enterprise. Nevertheless, there was a significant variety of personalities within each category; not every beachcomber was as notorious as John Bow or Jack Jones, nor did every trader deal as fairly with the islanders as did Andrew Cheyne.[41] With some notable exceptions, Grattan's summary of the period is true, in that:

> Most of the people who come to gather natural resources, such as sandalwood, beche-de-mer, and coconut oil, seemed to regard the islands much as shoplifters regard a rich, unguarded shop: the stuff was there for no other reason than to be "lifted" (1963a: 192-193).

I believe the greatest impact these Europeans had on the islanders was in the introduction of Western material objects into Melanesian society.[42] Many islanders became so desirous of items such as tobacco that their want soon became a need, a need that could only be satisfied through exchange with Europeans. Shineberg (1967: 151) cogently depicts this web of economic exchange in the Southwest Pacific when she notes that, "Traders sold tobacco for Pacific Islanders to smoke in order that the Chinese might burn sandalwood in order that Australians might drink tea, proving that human frailty knows no race."[43] From the missionaries' point of view, the traders' influence on the islanders was far more than just the addition of material culture. They also introduced customs odious to the missionary. Selwyn wrote to his father in 1848, concerning the negative effect of the European traders' contact with the islanders of Rotuma which he briefly visited aboard HMS *Dido*:

> Already the effects of their intercourse with foreigners is seen, in the scanty numbers of their children. How many ministers of evil there are in all parts of the world, for one preacher of righteousness. The same instruments by which you buy oil for your lamps have shut up the Pacific Ocean in spiritual darkness.[44]

Selwyn noted throughout a journal letter written to his sons in 1857 the significant differences between those islands visited by traders and whalers and those that were not. In the former case, the demeanor of the islanders was always more brash and cocksure and unpleasant to deal with. He lamented time and again the pity that these islanders' first experience with Europeans had been with the class of sailors from whaling and trading vessels rather than with the missionary.[45] Like many "salvage anthropologists" the missionaries soon gained a preference for the "untouched" natives, who had not yet been "spoiled" by contact with disreputable Europeans. For example, at Ulawa in the Solomon Islands, which had had considerable contact with Europeans, the mission ship put in anchor, and was soon greeted by an islander asking in broken English whether or not he could provide the missionary and his crew with women for the night. This was too much to take, and the would-be entrepreneur was quickly put overboard.[46]

Because of this prior European contact, the missionaries were necessarily forced into a mold of having to "trade" with the islanders. Selwyn refused to trade tobacco, but fish-hooks, metal tools, cloth, and "trinkets" were a part of the manifest for every voyage through the islands. Critics of the Melanesian Mission accused the missionaries of buying their potential converts, but given the cultural context in which they first contacted the islanders, they seem to have had little alternative than continuing a practice initiated by traders and later followed by the more scrupulous labor recruiters.[47] However, this system of establishing markets led to islanders' identifying the visit of the mission vessel more with an opportunity to buy and sell, than with the Mission's objective of evangelization. Later the acceptance of Christianity by some islanders was conditioned upon receiving gifts and supplies. For example, on San Cristobal after five years of missionary contact, it was becoming abundantly clear to the missionaries that what they perceived as a necessary means (trade) to an end (evangelization), was an end in itself for the islanders. Patteson in his exasperation with the San Cristobal islanders' perception of the Mission's purpose, gathered a group of 60-70 men together and explained to them that:

> It is not our intention to be always coming hither merely to give you fish hooks and a few hatchets, and to give some of your young men an opportunity of seeing other lands. Our object is to teach you the knowledge of the great Father in Heaven and of His Son Jesus Christ, and the Holy Spirit of God.[48]

Dead silence followed his presentation.

Missionary Attitudes Toward and Perceptions of the Melanesians

The second topic to consider in attempting to understand the cultural dynamics of this period of early missionary contact is the nature of the missionary-islander relationships that were established. Popular opinion at the time held that Melanesians were one of the lowest specimens of humanity ever encountered by the "civilized" world, but an investigation of missionaries' diaries, letters, and journals, reveals that their attitudes ran counter to this popular notion.[49] During Selwyn's first voyage in the *Undine*, he wrote to his father saying:

> I have long been looking for a "Savage" in the English sense of the word, and have never yet met with one. As I come to understand the languages of these Islanders, or to converse with those who know them, I find them to be men of like feelings with ourselves; influenced mainly by the same arguments, guided by a sense of right and wrong; deliberate in council even more than ourselves; clear in defining and tenacious in maintaining their right; often wrong in their premises, but generally reasoning rightly upon such grounds as they have. Ferocity is no more part of the nature of a "Savage" than it was natural for the French people in the highest pitch of civilization to shed blood like water.[50]

Although Selwyn was intent on changing the religious allegiance of Melanesians, unlike some of his colleagues in other missions in the Pacific, he did not feel the islanders were "utterly depraved."[51] If anything, he would have used this term to describe some of his fellow countrymen involved in commercial enterprises, but he would not have used it in describing a Melanesian. Selwyn held strongly to the notion that any hostility shown by Melanesians toward Europeans was the result of provocation by the latter rather than inherent in every potential Melanesian-European encounter. This philosophy held him in good stead with the islanders, for he went cautiously but fearlessly among them, swimming ashore from the ship's boat, always unarmed. On only one occasion, on an initial visit to Malekula, did he run into danger, but his calm presence of mind enabled the mission party to leave the island before being attacked.[52] Bishop Tyrrell of Newcastle, who accompanied Selwyn on this tour in the *Border Maid*, wrote a detailed account of this event, and articulated the theory of retaliation held by the Mission:

> Revenge or retaliation is with them a principle or point of honour, and as they can draw no distinction between one white man and another, however different they may be in calling or even in country, when they have received any injury from a ship or boat they will always retaliate if they can, upon the next white men who come to their Island, and it is of course quite impossible to know what ship or boat may have visited an Island some few days or weeks or months before you visit it, or how they may have treated the natives. In many cases we know, that the poor natives have been treated barbarously.[53]

This theory of Melanesian retaliation for previous wrong-doing by Europeans appears time and again in the Melanesian Mission literature. It would be forged forever in the history of the Mission twenty years later with the death of Bishop Patteson, murdered at Nukapu, in assumed retaliation for a previous atrocity committed against the indigenes of that island.

The initial contact with an island was always the most dangerous, for regardless of whether or not the islanders had had previous contact with Europeans, the Melanesian Mission was unknown to them, and hence a potential enemy against whom they must be on guard. In writing to his two sons during the expansive and successful voyage of 1857, Selwyn outlined the procedure for initiating contact with the islanders. The preferred tactic was to keep the mission ship out to sea where it could easily be moving on its way again in case of danger. However, that was never necessary since they were always received without hostility and in most cases in open and warm friendship. If they were visiting an island for the first time, Selwyn would swim ashore alone, with presents stowed in his bishop's top hat.[54] The party would row ashore in a whale boat, and if possible would have an island guide in their company to act as interpreter in explaining their friendly intentions and their purpose for coming. Whenever possible, they always dealt with the local "chief" of the island, and Selwyn's letters speak very highly of these men, noting that they conducted themselves in a most civil manner and usually acted as mediators between the missionaries and the mass of islanders who wanted to trade. The missionaries preferred small crowds, for they were easier to communicate with, since larger groups of people were usually given to greater excitement.

On the tour in 1857, the Mission encountered several Polynesian-speaking islands such as Tikopia and Rennell, whose language was sufficiently cognate to Maori to allow the missionaries to communicate with ease. It is interesting to note in the letter to his sons the frequent comments Selwyn makes about the advantages of an aristocracy in dealing with these people.[55] Since these were Polynesians, not Melanesians, their social structure was less egalitarian and more stratified, and the Chief had more power and influence than did the Melanesian Big Man.

However, Selwyn was in Melanesia, not Polynesia, and so upon discovering who was the local Big Man, he would exchange an axe for a bow and arrows, and would then start collecting the names of people, the name of the island, the names of different objects, and definitions of local flora and fauna. Yams would be purchased with calico, for the goal of these initial encounters was only to establish friendly contact. On subsequent visits to the island, the missionary would utilize the vocabulary compiled previously, and addressing individuals by name, would explain their purpose in coming and try to acquire a boy or young man for the school in New Zealand. In brief, this was the method employed, founded on the attitude of deep respect for the Melanesian as a person, if not always in agreement with every aspect of his culture.

Melanesian Perception of Missionaries

The third area of inquiry into the cultural dynamics of the early contact period presents us with an important theoretical problem, the solution to which involves us in a severe methodological problem. Unfortunately for the ethnohistorian, documentation of missionary-islander contact is primarily on the side of the missionaries who wrote freely in their journals and letters about their experiences and their perceptions of Melanesians. Unfortunately there are very few documents identifying the islanders' perceptions of the mission or articulating their motivations for joining; thus, we are forced to rely more on inference than on direct evidence in reconstructing the Melanesians' side of the missionary-islander relationship.[56]

In the case of the Melanesian Mission we are fortunate to have several documents left by islanders who describe their initial motivation for going away with the mission ship. George Sarawia, after gaining trust in the missionaries, wrote several years later of his motivation for going with the ship in 1858:

> I had made up my mind at the beginning to go with the Bishops for this reason: I wanted to go myself to the real source of things, and get for myself an axe and a knife, and fish hooks and calico, and plenty of other things. I thought they were just there to be picked up, and I wanted to get plenty for myself. I did not go for any other reason but only because I had seen lots of these things on the ship, and wanted to go and get plenty for myself. Also I wanted to see where the white people's country was, and what it was like. But I did not realise that the Bishop wanted to take me with another end in view, a better one, one which would not end or decay, as material things do.[57]

Similarly, a decade later, Clement Marau from Merlav in the Banks' was motivated to go with the mission ship: "I thought I would get fish-hooks and axes and clothes, and then go home."[58]

The very personalities of Selwyn and Patteson[59] were clearly magnetic forces in drawing islanders away, and cannot be dismissed in discussing Melanesian motivation for leaving the islands on the mission ship. Mrs. William Martin, wife of the Chief Justice in New Zealand, wrote in 1851, of the islanders who had come to St. John's for the year:

> . . . I think the Bishop was pleased and satisfied with their progress, and encouraged by it. They all think and talk much of him, and with pleasure of his going to the Islands, and how their friends will welcome him; and they laugh about "Picopo *oui-oui*" as they call the French bishop, coming in "large ship, guns here, guns there — go **bomb bomb**. He no land. Our Bishop come little ship, no guns: he land, everybody say, 'Come here.' " They think the Bishop can do everything; (which is pretty near the truth), that he wrote all the books they see.[60]

The desire for adventure, to see the white man's country and bring back some of his material products, and the attractiveness of the missionaries' winsome personalities, are all factors in a complex of mixed motives which forms the basis for understanding why islanders wanted to come away from the security of their homes and entrust themselves to these Europeans. It is unlikely that any came away understanding the Mission's main purpose in inviting them, or if they did, it probably was of secondary importance.[61] There seems to have been little difficulty in attracting young people to come away for one season, but to obtain re-enlistments was far more difficult. Thus, for example, a report ca. 1858, of the voyage to the islands notes that the Mission visit to Mwaata, San Cristobal, was successful in getting only one of the five previous scholars to return with them for a second year. However, many others wanted to come for their first visit and the problem was one of selecting from the many, not of inducing a few.[62]

In the first ten years, Selwyn's initial scheme was put into action, and considerable contact was made with the Melanesians. But the nature of the contact was limited primarily to initiating friendly relations with the islanders, rather than seeing any large group conversions to Christianity.[63] However, there were converts out of this period such as George Sarawia of Vanua Lava and Mano Wadrokal of Mare, who would eventually emerge as future Melanesian leaders. Although the vast majority of those who came away to spend a season in the school had no interest in returning and did little if any teaching of Christianity to their fellows upon their return home, this did not seem to dismay the missionaries. They were convinced their approach was right for the circumstances, and that it would necessarily take a long time to see the conversion of large numbers of Melanesians to Christianity. Patteson wrote in the Report of the Melanesian Mission for the years 1859 and 1860:

> To anyone who has hitherto followed the history of the Mission it will be evident that we are not to expect that the progress can be other than gradual. A great change must pass upon a native of the Melanesian islands as we see him, destitute of any kind of clothing, with bow and arrows tipped with human bone, waving his spear and club, or standing with painted face and girdle of human teeth watching the cautious approach of our boat, or it may be with wild gesticulations and noisy cries beckoning us to the shore, or dashing through the surf to meet the boat — a great change indeed must pass upon such a one, before he can be brought by the grace of God to sit "clothed and in his right mind" at the feet of Christ.[64]

In evaluating the beginning period of the Melanesian Mission it is evident that Selwyn's scheme was not very successful. But given the cultural context in which he attempted to convince Melanesians of the superiority of his religion, this lack of success is not surprising. There were numerous obstacles that hindered successful advocacy, and at this point in the history of missionary contact, it is obvious that few Melanesians felt the urgency or desire to innovate and adopt Christianity as their own belief system.

After several years of operation it became increasingly clear to Selwyn that he could not administrate the "Northern Mission" as it was initially called, and adequately handle the running of his diocese in New Zealand. He came under increasing criticism for neglecting the "home front" in New Zealand in pursuit of evangelization in the islands.[65] Selwyn therefore went to England in 1854 with three goals in mind: (1) to arrange for the subdivision of his diocese by establishing bishoprics at Wellington and Canterbury (Christchurch), (2) to secure legal authority for the Church of New Zealand to manage its own affairs by a General Synod composed of bishops, presbyters and laity, and (3) to establish an endowment fund of £10,000 for a Missionary Bishop and full recognition of the Melanesian Mission, as well as the selection of a chaplain to aid him in his work in the islands.[66] His trip was successful, and in addition to raising the endowment, he gathered enough support (£1,800) from friends interested in his missionary endeavors in Melanesia to build a 65-ton schooner in which to conduct his island visitation. It was christened *Southern Cross*, the first of nine subsequent ships by that name to ply the waters of Melanesia.

Bishop John Coleridge Patteson's Philosophy of Culture Contact

In this study I am considering missionaries as models of change agents. However, contrary to popular opinion, and James Michener's book *Hawaii*, there is no accurate stereotypic model of nineteenth century Pacific missionaries, for there was a wide variety of types. John Colderidge Patteson, the first Bishop of Melanesia, is a most interesting example of a missionary advocate in Oceania. In this section attention will focus on Patteson's personality and his philosophy of mission, in an attempt to understand more clearly the role of missionaries in advocating religious change.

To help him in his work Selwyn was looking for "men of a right stamp," by which he meant well-educated, aristocratic, Victorian gentlemen who were not afraid to get their hands dirty, were willing to do any menial task and play the role of a humble servant. This was a tall order, but Selwyn found his man in the person of John Coleridge Patteson, who answered to all these requirements and more. Well-educated at Eton and Oxford, and a member of a prominent English family, Patteson brought a good pedigree and the right credentials to the Melanesian Mission still in its infancy.[67]

Patteson was eminently suited for work in Melanesia. His constitution preferred the climate of the tropics to the cold and wet weather of England. He had an attractive and winsome personality and a capacity for friendship, leading Fox (1958: 12) to call him a, "Friend and Interpreter of Melanesians."

Patteson's foremost skill was his linguistic ability and capacity for language acquisition which was never equaled in the history of the Mission. Like Selwyn before him, he learned the Maori language sufficiently well on the voyage out from England to enable him to converse freely with the native New Zealanders as soon as he arrived. During the first several years Patteson learned a number of Melanesian languages, and eventually spoke twenty-four during his sixteen years of work in the islands.[68]

Selwyn continued making voyages to the islands until 1859, but he steadily handed over responsibility for the running of the Mission to Patteson. By 1860, Selwyn had successfully removed the legal and ecclesiastical obstacles to establishing a Melanesian Missionary Bishopric, and the mantle of leadership fell to Patteson, who at the age of 33, was consecrated the first Bishop of Melanesia on February 24th, 1861.

Patteson brought a personal style and philosophy to his work that would influence the history of the Melanesian Mission more than any other single personality.[69] Even today, throughout Anglican communities in Vanuatu and the Solomon Islands, the anniversary of his death, September 20th, is commemorated by church services, dramas reenacting the scene of his murder, and large feasts. Hundreds of Melanesians have taken the name Patteson as their Christian names. To many Anglican Melanesians today, Patteson is a saint, a man who died on their behalf.[70] It is therefore important in this study that we consider, although briefly, the nature of his thought and personality, and the influence he has had on the islanders.

From an anthropological point of view, the most interesting thing about Patteson was his commitment to the idea that Melanesia must be evangelized by the Melanesians, and the notion that Christianity was a "universal religion" and as such, was not culture-bound. He believed that its basic doctrines were applicable to all cultures, but that the formal application of these doctrines would vary from one cultural context to another. To force an "English Christianity" upon Melanesians, he asserted, was "a great mistake."

It is important to realize that Patteson was developing his views at a time when the implicit assumption of the nineteenth century missionary ethos was that Christianity and Civilization were part and parcel of the "new way of life."[71] Although Patteson was not the only voice in the nineteenth century calling for a culturally sensitive approach to missionary work, he nevertheless represented a minority position. In commenting on the missionary enterprise of his day, he noted:

> We seek to denationalize these races, as far as I can see, whereas we ought to change as little as possible — only what is clearly incompatible with the simplest form of Christian teaching and practice. I don't mean we are to compromise truth, but to study the native character, and not present the truth in an unnecessarily unattractive form. Don't we overlay it a good deal with human traditions, and still more often take it for granted that what suits us must be necessary for them, and *vice versa*?
>
> So many of our missionaries are not accustomed, not taught to think of these things. They grow up with certain modes of thought, hereditary notions, and they seek to reproduce these, no respect being had to the utterly dissimilar character and circumstances of the heathen.[72]

Unlike many of his contemporaries, Patteson did not view Melanesian religion as an expression of total depravity. To the contrary, he believed there was an "element of faith" in the pagan religion which should be preserved. He wrote:

> We must fasten on that, and not rudely destroy the superstition, lest with it we destroy the principle of faith in things and beings unseen. I often think that to shake man's faith in his old belief, however wrong it may be, before one can substitute something true and right, is, to say the least a dangerous experiment.[73]

Contemporary scholars have commented on the secularizing effect that many Christian missionaries have had on their host societies.[74] In an attempt to win a hearing for their religion, their approach has often been one of confrontation and competition instead of compatibility. Some have attempted to undermine belief in the pagan religion in order to create a religious void which Christianity will presumably fill. What these missionaries have failed to realize is that the very act of eroding faith in the indigenous religion can also destroy the foundation on which the innovator must erect a new belief structure if he is to accept Christianity as a meaningful and functional element in his own cultural framework. Patteson's understanding of the importance of a functional substitute for the traditional religious system, places him squarely in the theory of culture change as innovation. As a missionary with cross-cultural sensitivity, he realized the importance of building cognitive bridges if islanders were to accept Christianity as a meaningful substitute for their traditional beliefs.

However, Patteson was aware of the difficulties of putting the principle of indigenous Christianity into practice. For example, he wrote that:

> It is not always easy to be patient and to remember the position which the heathen man occupies and the point of view from which he must needs regard everything brought to him.[75]

Concomitant with the possibility of an indigenous Melanesian Christianity, about which Patteson thought and wrote a great deal, was the notion that any social and behavioral change commensurate with conversion to Christianity, must come from the islanders of their own accord and then only after they understood the reasons for making such changes. He was critical, for example, of other missionaries in the Pacific who insisted on an external conformity to the Ten Commandments, before its significance and meaning were understood. He believed that this was likely to generate formalism and hypocrisy in converts, and disdainfully wrote:

> I notice continually the tendency of the very men who denounce "forms" to produce formation.
>
> It is nearest to the native mind; it generates hypocrisy and mere outward observance of certain rules, which during the few years that the people remain docile on their first acceptance of the new teaching, they are content to submit to.[76]

Patteson believed the missionary's role must be that of an educator, and that given the requisite understanding of Christian principles, islanders would themselves initiate changes in their traditional customs and culture. He detested, for example, the London Missionary Society missionaries in the Loyalty Islands meddling in indigenous political affairs. In a letter to Selwyn, Patteson wrote in 1859 of dissatisfaction among the Loyalty Islanders with the missionaries in residence there:

> They are dissatisfied for two reasons mainly. The better sort, because they get so little teaching, and because they are told that it is sinful not to obey the missionary in matters not affecting his missionary character, e.g. on one occasion, people refusing to work gratis, he (the missionary Mr. Creagh) said, "Then I shan't explain God's word to you," and accordingly on Sunday narrated to them all their enormities, specifying their refusal to make a stone fence, and gave them no word of Prayer or Exposition. They — the better sort — can't believe this to be scriptural nor their neglect of the sick, nor its general character of their way of going on — neglect of heathen, etc. — The worser sort dislike them, because they assume the position of chiefs and order them about.[77]

Patteson's commitment to the principle that converts should initiate their own social and behavioral changes, rather than the missionary enforcing changes, came not only from his cross-cultural sensitivity, but from his belief in the Melanesian capacity for thoroughly understanding the basic tenets of Christianity. He had a great respect for Melanesians' intellect and never believed them to be, nor treated them as if they were, inferior to Europeans. His full and ready acceptance of Melanesians as persons with human dignity, with whom he interacted on a level of equality, was certainly a rare model of the white man's behavior during this era of European contact in Melanesia.

It was Patteson's firm belief in the educability of Melanesians that led him to see the Central School as having such an important role in the evangelization scheme for Melanesia. It was here, in sessions of interaction between teacher and pupil, that Melanesians could come to understand fully the principles of Christianity and internalize them sufficiently to explain to their fellows at home the ways of the New Teaching. Patteson saw conversion as an internalization of Christianity rather than a blind conformity to social norms imposed by the missionary from outside the culture.

In summarizing Patteson and his work, there are several points of interest to us in this study, for they bear on his relationship with the 565 young men who came under his direct influence[78] and they help us understand his philosophy of culture contact which not only determined policies during his time, but set the tone of the Mission for decades to follow:

1. He had a kind and gentle nature, a tremendous capacity for friendship, and a winsome personality, all of which contributed positively to his role as an advocate of religious change, and attracted Melanesians to the Mission.
2. He had a unique ability for language acquisition and analysis, enabling him to reduce to writing many of the twenty-four languages he spoke.
3. He distinguished between what he believed to be the fundamental elements of Christianity and the secondary application of those elements in creating a Christian lifeway in every cultural context, including

Melanesia. In short, he believed in the possibility of a Melanesian Christianity as distinct from English Christianity.

4. He viewed the missionary's role in evangelization as one of teaching Melanesians to understand and internalize the principles of Christianity, and then leaving to their own discretion the social and behavioral changes that should follow.
5. He held firmly to the notion that Melanesians were equal, as human beings, in every respect to Europeans, including their capacity to understand and internalize Christianity.
6. Finally, Patteson, although not trained as an ethnologist, had a deep respect for Melanesian languages and culture.

The essence of Patteson's philosophy of culture contact and his methodology of missionary work is summarized in the following address he delivered in Sydney in 1864:

> I do testify to you that if you go the right way to work in dealing with the native races, if you treat them with entire confidence — assume the existence in them of those instincts which belong to them as human beings, and seek to elicit from them all their latent yearnings and cravings after something better than what they at present possess, — recognizing in them a sense and a power of appreciating truth, — not troubling yourself with arguments about their superstitious practices, but stating the positive truth, and trusting to that truth to win a power in their hearts — being careful of everything you do in your intercourse with them, — never taking any step beyond the correctly ascertained knowledge of subjects you speak about, — and being content to proceed cautiously rather than aiming to produce speedy results — you may, under God's blessing, lay the sure foundations upon which native churches may be built in Melanesia to last forever.[79]

The focal point of Patteson's missionary work was the Central School to which we now turn for discussion.

Patteson's Methods of Advocating Religious Change

Thus far in this chapter we have considered two of the more important missionary personalities in this early contact period, namely, Selwyn and Patteson. Although a missionary's personal philosophy and working procedures influence his role as an agent of change, there is another dimension, equally important. This is the entire realm of institutional structures in which the missionary functions and which shape the nature of his interaction with potential converts. In other words, in the dynamic cultural arena of Melanesian-missionary interaction, personalities **plus** institutional structures impinge on the interaction setting. Therefore, in this section attention will now shift away from missionary personalities and focus on the formation of the Melanesian Mission's institutional structures. I will begin by discussing the role of the Central School, including the missionaries' educational philosophy and their methods of training. Next I will consider the emergence of a Mission *lingua franca*, and then I will conclude this section with a discussion of the cultural significance of the Mission's training school for those Melanesians who were trained there.

The Central School.

An element of the Melanesian Mission that is critical in understanding the role of the Mission as an agent of culture change is that of the Central School to which young people from many different islands were taken for training.

Patteson once called the Central School "the real work" of the Mission.[80] The importance he placed on the role of education in the total Melanesian Mission scheme is underscored in a letter written in 1862:

> I am fully persuaded that no abiding work would be done by hastily placing imperfectly educated men on heathen islands. The quickest way to occupy the islands of Melanesia is to secure, **from these islands** a supply of really competent and earnest men, speaking their own languages, accustomed to the climate, conversant with the habits and modes of thought of the islanders; you may depend on it that the true nursery of Missionaries for the islands is the Central School at Kohimarama.[81]

The Central School was initially at St. John's where training was combined for Melanesians, Maoris, and Europeans. However, its location, atop a windy hill, proved to be too bleak and cold for the delicate constitutions of the Melanesian scholars, and so they moved to their own site in 1859. This was Kohimarama,[82] situated a few miles from St. John's, on the south shore of Auckland Bay, in a sheltered area that provided a more agreeable climate for the young men from the tropics. On a 157 acre site, St. Andrew's College was erected through gifts of £600 from Patteson's father, Sir John Patteson, and £1,600 from his cousin, Charlotte Yonge, who donated the royalties from her popular novel, *The Daisy Chain.*

St. Andrew's College functioned at Kohimarama for only eight years, for after two consecutive summers (1863-1864) of a fatal dysentery epidemic, earlier doubts were revived about the suitability of New Zealand as a base for the Melanesian Mission. In addition to the cold climate, New Zealand presented other problems, not least of which was the long and arduous voyage necessitated by being so far removed from the islands. The distance from the Central Solomons was no less than 2,000 miles, requiring six weeks to travel on rough open seas. With the idea in mind of moving the school closer to the islands, negotiations had been underway for several years to settle the Mission headquarters on Norfolk Island. The island had been abandoned as an English penal colony in 1855. The following year the Pitcairn Islanders, descendants from the *Bounty* mutineers of 1789, had relocated here, and in the judgment of Governor John Young of New South Wales, the presence of the Melanesian Mission would be a positive influence for the good of the Pitcairn Islanders. Therefore, 1,000 acres, or 1/9 of the total island, was sold to the Mission and the headquarters moved there in 1867.[83]

Norfolk Island, being 600 miles closer to Melanesia, had many advantages over New Zealand. The Island of "Eternal Spring" was suitable for the European staff and required only light clothing for the Melanesians. In addition, nearly all the tropical food, with the exception of breadfruit and coconuts, could be grown in its fertile soil. Patteson had come to believe that the contrast of Colonial life in New Zealand was too great with that of the scholars' life in their own islands, and thus Norfolk Island would reduce the culture shock experienced by the Melanesians when they first came from their island villages. In addition, he had become increasingly irritated with all the "extra-curricular" duties in New Zealand that took him away from his Melanesian work, and so by removing the school to Norfolk Island, he could devote himself entirely to things wholly Melanesian.[84]

The Melanesian Mission's Educational Philosophy and Training Methods.

The model for the Central School was that of the English public schools, especially Eton from whence Selwyn and Patteson had obtained their early education. The Arnoldian[85] system brought an orderly and disciplined routine to the school life.[86] At Norfolk Island the entire company of Melanesian young men was divided into four houses, based on the region of Melanesia from whence they came. A European missionary was in charge of each house and during the winter months he would frequently accompany some of his group back to their islands and establish residence with them for several months. Also on the mission grounds, each island group built for themselves a *natima* (Mota for a small men's house), and it was here that scholars would congregate in their free time to smoke and chat among themselves, occasionally cooking some island food. In addition, all the Melanesian scholars were divided into sets of 8-10 islanders from different places, whose responsibility it was to attend to the cooking for one week on a rotating basis. While not cooking, each set occupied a table in the common hall. C. E. Fox, missionary-anthropologist and historian, elaborates on the method whereby the sets were selected:

> The cook sets were chosen twice a year when the ship arrived from the islands with perhaps 100 new boys and others returning from holiday. The "captain" and "mate" from different islands, were chosen by the Headmaster, and these chose their "sailors"

> from the crowd assembled in the hall, lazy boys being chosen last and feeling uncomfortable as they waited for their names to be called (1958: 218).

There was a great emphasis placed on corporate spirit, and all activities from picnics and singing to playing cricket and soccer, were designed to achieve this end. Visitors to the school were impressed with the orderliness of daily operations, given the "raw material" of the school.[87] Nevertheless, the traditional inter-island hostilities were not completely suppressed within the confines of Norfolk Island, as Coombe relates:

> House matches are very popular when no outside team is available; or those who are going down to the ship will challenge those who are staying up. A thing we never venture to do is to pit the northern and southern islanders against one another. There is a strange deep-rooted suspicion and enmity between the groups, probably of centuries standing: and the reflection of it is too often visible even among the Christian lads at Norfolk Island. Our aim, therefore, in school, and games, and kuk-sets, and everything else is to mix up North and South together — to merge in friendly effort, shoulder to shoulder, the hostile feeling which is born in the natives of the two divisions of our Diocese (1909: 48-49).

In reminiscing about his early days with the Melanesian Mission, Fox recalls with dramatic flare an incident that erupted, demonstrating that while Norfolk Island may have been one of "the happiest of schools," fierce quarrels between Solomon Islanders and New Hebrideans did occur occasionally:

> One Christmas Eve a little New Hebridean stabbed a little Mala (Malaita) boy during a quarrel and blood flowed. In less than five minutes some one hundred and fifty Solomon Islanders had thrown off all their clothes and, stark naked, seized axes, knives, spears, anything that came to hand, and were in full cry after some sixty New Hebrideans, who for their part were going all out for the sea coast. It was an exciting time for housemasters. Below the school grounds were a number of small houses, one belonging to each island, where the boys used to cook the fish they caught, and smoke and enjoy themselves. The armed and naked Solomon Islanders rushed for those owned by the New Hebrideans to slaughter anyone they could find in them—but they were all quickly empty except for one in which a quiet New Hebridean "head cook" sat smoking. As the Solomon Islanders rushed down to it they shouted, "Anyone in there?" and the New Hebridean very wisely shouted "No!" and the Solomon Islanders rushed on past it, to the relief of the housemaster who felt helpless to do anything. These riots were not common but they did occur from time to time (1962: 15-16).

Given the occasional ruckus between Melanesians, it was nevertheless an orderly and peaceful life that predominated. For many scholars such a peaceful coexistence between islanders and between Melanesian scholars and European missionaries was in marked contrast to life in their home islands. Clement Marau from the Banks' Islands, recalled his reaction to the life at Norfolk Island:

> When I had been here some little time I saw that there was nothing but peace in the place; I never heard of fighting or quarrelling or bad conduct . . . And I heard continually the sound of the bell ringing to call people together, and I saw everything done regularly and in good order: and then I thought quietly within myself that this was a different way of living, and a thoroughly good one.[88]

In New Zealand, young scholars continually commented to Patteson about how they enjoyed their peaceful outings with him, never having to fear falling prey to some enemy attack. For most, it was a different world altogether.

The thrust of the mission education was clearly the acquisition and understanding of religious knowledge, but this instruction was supplemented with singing, using the sol-fa system, and training in "practical skills" by working in the gardens, on the farm, and at the printing press. Above all, the concern was for "building character" in the young Melanesian scholars. In writing to his sister and describing the ideal type of men he wanted to join the mission and work with him, Patteson declared, "The real thing is to train a certain number of lads in habits of attention, punctuality, tidiness, etc."[89]

At Kohimarama in New Zealand, the school owed "all the punctuality, order, and method, etc." to Lonsdale Pritt,[90] a harsh disciplinarian whose quick temper was a menace to Melanesian and European alike. When it became clear to Patteson that Pritt's behavior was the reason given by some scholars for refusing to return to the school, Patteson asked him to leave, conveniently at the same time the Mission moved its headquarters to Norfolk Island.[91]

Robert H. Codrington: Missionary-Anthropologist.

Despite the often purported notion of the Melanesian Mission as a crack regiment of English gentlemen and scholars, there were in fact very few who joined the Mission answering to this description. An exception, however, was the headmaster of St. Barnabas College at Norfolk Island from 1867 to 1887. This was Robert Henry Codrington, a name well known in Pacific anthropology for his contributions to Melanesian ethnology and linguistics. Contrary to Hays (1958: 141), Rosenstiel (1959: 110), Lessa and Vogt (1965: 255) and other writers, Codrington was never a bishop, declining the offer to succeed Bishop Patteson in 1872. Hilliard (1978: 36) says of Codrington, "His combination of remarkable erudition with personal geniality gave him a crucial role among the English staff as the one person who could talk on equal terms with both the bishop and the younger clergy." Not only was he an admirable companion and colleague to Patteson, but his friendship with Melanesians has made him a legendary figure in the Melanesian Mission tradition. Patteson wrote of him, "He is so bright, so sociable, so pleasant and such an element of usefulness, and such a bond of union for us all."[92]

It was his unique position as head of a multi-cultural, polyglot training center that enabled Codrington to collect materials for his two classic studies: *The Melanesian Languages* (1885), and *The Melanesians: Studies in Their Anthropology and Folk-lore* (1891).

The scholarly Codrington was also an avid gardener and his influence was seen throughout St. Barnabas from the neat English-style garden to his decorations of the chapel on festive occasions. Drawing on his wide reading and expansive knowledge, Codrington taught an evening class with the advanced scholars called "Things of this World," in which he would discuss everything from topics on natural history to things from the white man's world. Fox comments on his role as a teacher and headmaster:

> He was not a great disciplinarian like Pritt, yet he was so great a teacher, so wise and patient, so loved by the boys, that he held them in the hollow of his hand. His lessons on the parables and miracles, written in the Mota language, are magnificent teaching. They show deep understanding of the Melanesian mind and the power of a born teacher (1958: 220).[93]

The Emergence of a *Lingua Franca*.

With the diversity of languages represented at the Central School, the problem of instruction had to be overcome. Initially Patteson held separate classes for scholars in six or seven languages, but the burden of such a time-consuming system eventually became too great. Selwyn urged the adoption of English, but Patteson did not feel this to be a wise choice.[94] The grammar was unfamiliar, it was difficult to learn English pronunciation, and it was difficult to read and write it.

During this same period in the mid 1860's, there was an increasing percentage of scholars from the Banks' Islands who spoke Mota, and with Pritt's linguistic limitations this was the only language he learned to speak. Thus, more by chance than by design, Mota became the *lingua franca* of the school. It has since been hailed by many as a fortunate choice — "The best Melanesian language for the purpose," wrote Fox (1958: 216), a language full and rich in nuances, one easily learned by other Melanesians, and one that did not prove too difficult for Europeans to acquire. After its unofficial adoption, Mota became the official language of the Melanesian Mission for the next sixty years.[95]

The Cultural Significance of Norfolk Island.

In line with the English approach to public education, traditions were an important part of the corporate life of the school. The Mission adopted the Mota word *lingai* (traditions) to capture the meaning of the distinctive customs and folkways which emerged in the life of the Mission and were expressed in the culture of Norfolk Island living. One of the dominant structures, embodying this *lingai* was the Memorial Chapel to Bishop Patteson, built from 1875-1880 under Codrington's supervision, and described by Fox (1962: 11) as "the most beautiful school chapel in the southern hemisphere." It has served to ensure the lasting memory of Patteson, enshrining his name in the hall-of-fame of Melanesian Mission personalities.[96]

The physical layout of St. Barnabas College resembled a Victorian school with its quadrangular pattern and this was set in the picturesque scene of Norfolk Island with its famous pine trees, "dotted about in clumps, making the scene very like a well-kept English park."[97] Without question, a little bit of England had been transplanted to Norfolk Island.

The inner life of the community, while professed to be egalitarian, was more like a well-run family with the Bishop and Headmaster in authority.[98] A visitor to Norfolk Island in 1872, described it in the following terms:

> No one of them is kept by Mr. Codrington at arm's length; but all are encouraged to treat him as sons should treat a father, with confidence and respect. As in a well-commanded regiment of soldiers (where threatening and scolding are not needed), or in a well brought up family, perfect discipline is maintained, and all kept in their places, by the uniform administration of the "unwritten law of love."[99]

It was within this familial context that the daily routine functioned: beginning and ending with prayers in the chapel which were in the High Church Anglican tradition of reverence and order in liturgical worship. The daily timetable, punctuated regularly by ringing bells, is reproduced below:[100]

6:00 a.m.	Wake to a bell.
7:00 a.m.	Prayers in the chapel.
7:20 a.m.	Breakfast in the common hall.
8:15 a.m.	School—New Testament and Prayerbook.
9:45 a.m.	School—English or Arithmetic.
11:00 a.m.	Work in gardens.
1:00 p.m.	Dinner in the common hall.
2:00 p.m.	School—writing.
3:00 p.m.	Free time—usually games and sports.
6:00 p.m.	Evening tea in the common hall.
6:45 p.m.	Prayers in the chapel.
7:00 p.m.	School—Old Testament, general information and music.

8:00 p.m.	**Quiet time—preparation for next day's lessons, followed by compline.**
10:00 p.m.	**Lights out.**

This timetable demonstrates how regimented and orderly was the life at Norfolk Island for the Melanesian scholars. It is hard to imagine a greater cultural contrast to their traditional village life, where, although daily activity had its own rhythms, it was not constrained by clocks or punctuated by ringing bells. However, this orderly system underscored the missionaries' philosophy of education and evangelism. They perceived that teaching Melanesians to function in such an orderly manner would make them better teachers for their own people. Order was seen as part and parcel of the Christian way of life.

There were generally 150-200 or more scholars in residence, including a few young women, going through a course of training that generally lasted eight years. A small number of young women had first been brought to the Central School in New Zealand in 1859, for the purpose of preparing them to become suitable Christian wives for the prospective Melanesian teachers. They were taught separately from the young men, and much of their time and training was spent in making and mending shirts and trousers for the young men in attendance.[101]

It should be apparent by now that the life and culture at Norfolk Island was distinctly different from that in the villages of the islanders.[102] Although the expressed ideology of the Melanesian Mission was that in the process of evangelizing islanders, their objective was to produce Christians, not Englishmen, the external and internal environment of Norfolk Island seems to suggest that both were equally important. The emphasis on didactical instruction and the cultivation of habits of discipline, punctuality, tidiness, and orderliness were all good Victorian virtues. Even the self-proclaimed "equality of races" was couched in more of a benevolent paternalism, modeling the nineteenth century upper-middle class family, than a truly egalitarian community.[103] Throughout the fifty-year period when the Mission headquarters was established on Norfolk Island, the community became increasingly more English and less egalitarian.[104] Perhaps Codrington's own words best express the changes that were transpiring. In a letter to his like-minded, fellow missionary-anthropologist, Lorimer Fison of Fiji, he lamented:

> They call me the "old man" and it doesn't come natural to them to come and sit and talk with me as in older days. I have to send for them, and keep them in confinement with questions till I have done with them. I don't think there is any change of affection between us, but a change of relation. It belongs to a general change which has gone on here of late years, and by reason of circumstances. There are so many more white people about, and they tend to get together separate from the natives. There is not

> the same common life I fancy as there used to be. If I go out for a walk with a lot of boys, some white young man joins. He walks alongside of me and talks English — the boys get together by themselves. I struggle in vain against it, but it is the natural result I suppose of changed circumstances. It is a certain satisfaction to me to feel thus dissatisfied. I am getting too old and it is getting time for me to get out of the way.[105]

Norfolk Island, with its own set of traditions (*lingai*), became so entrenched as the center of operations, that a missionary's time spent away in the islands was viewed as an incidental break in the regular routine of duties at the Central School. In other words, the institutional structures came to have such a tenacious hold on the missionaries living at Norfolk Island, that they tended to lose touch with the realities of Melanesian village life — the place where Christianity would have its most important and significant encounter. W. G. Ivens, one of the few outspoken critics of the system, questioned this policy, and observed that:

> The native teachers of the Melanesian Mission trained in a fairly cool climate at Norfolk Island and surrounded by the things of civilization, have certainly not proved any more useful as propagandist than the native teachers of other Missionary bodies in the Pacific, who were trained in or near their own homes (1918: 203-204).

The consequences of this extractionist approach will be discussed below, pp. 147-148.

Thus far in this chapter I have discussed the principles and operating procedures on which the Melanesian Mission was founded, some of the dominant personalities of the period, and the Mission's institutional structures. As noted above, the missionaries did not anticipate immediate and overwhelming success in their work. While acknowledging that their unique method of evangelism might not yield quick results, they believed it would nevertheless have a more effective and long-lasting impact. In the following two sections I briefly examine the Melanesians' response on Mota in the Banks' Islands, and Nggela in the Solomons. In these areas, particularly, missionaries encountered a positive response to their message of "Good News."

Socio-Religious Change in Mota and the Banks' Islands

The island of Mota in the Banks' Group provides a good case study in which to examine the dynamic cultural arena of Melanesian-missionary interaction. This section briefly reviews the religious change advocated by Anglican missionaries, and the innovative response by Banks' Islanders, who adopted Christianity and then went as indigenous missionaries to other islands in the group. The ensuing socio-religious change resulting from conversion will also be examined briefly in this section.

The Early Phase of Culture Contact.

Selwyn and Patteson first made contact with Mota during their voyage through the Banks' Islands in 1857. Although they did not land, they were successful in inducing a few boys to come aboard the *Southern Cross*. Presents were given and contact made, with the promise that they would return in eight months, which they did in 1858. They were successful at this time in taking two lads with them to the "winter school" held on Lifu in the Loyalty Islands which was superintended by Patteson. The following year in 1859, Patteson went ashore at Mota and slept in a village, which in turn had a decided effect on inducing several other scholars to come away in the *Southern Cross* for school in New Zealand. The same year the Mota language was reduced to writing by Patteson. In 1860, he and another missionary, Benjamin Dudley, spent the "winter school" season on Mota, in company with other scholars from different Melanesian islands, including the Solomons.[106]

Here, for the first time, the missionaries' eyes were opened to the reality of the Melanesian cultural context, in which, it was hoped, their scholars would introduce Christianity to their own people. Initially the Mota islanders' perception of the missionaries did not match the role the missionaries perceived for themselves. An example of this is portrayed in Dudley's diary, written on May 24th, 1860. He notes that after landing:

> . . . we bathed, and had a talk with a few people about, who were principally anxious to know how many hatchets we had brought, etc. Even now they seem scarcely able to comprehend that one should come for any other purpose than that of trading for yams, etc.[107]

The period of the winter school coincided with a two-month initiation into one of the grades of the *Suqe* graded society.[108] This, of course, isolated some of the population from all other activities, and understandably distracted some of the returned scholars away from the daily routine of the school. Dudley penned his disappointment on many occasions, of which the following is a good example. He recorded on July 2nd, 1860:

> This morning I saw Wonpas, two years a scholar of ours, without any clothes, engaged in purchasing himself up in some mysterious rites in the "suqe" or custom of eating apart from the women. Rovemal also, another scholar, made his appearance without clothes, having apparently forgotten, or at any rate given up what he had learnt in New Zealand.[109]

The progress of the missionaries was impaired, however, not only by the distractions of the *Suqe* initiation ceremonies, but also by the cognitive indifference of the islanders to what the missionaries **said**. Dudley's diary for June 22nd, 1860, articulates the frustration he felt with the situation:

> In talking with them they always allow that their old superstitions are wrong and that the new religion is the good one, but there they end. They go on just as ever with the "*ogeara*" (*sic — salagoro*[110]) and heathen feasts. There is nothing for it but patient waiting until it pleases God's Holy Spirit to shine in their hearts, and then their whole religious system will fall together.[111]

Although the islanders appeared indifferent to the missionaries' message, the possibility of adopting the new religion was at least open for discussion as Dudley recorded the following day:

> A meeting was held today of several of the elders (there being no chiefs in this group of islands), to decide whether they should give up the "*ogeara*" and with it their whole system, and join the new religion. But after long talking they could not decide. They cling much too strongly to their old religion to give it up without a struggle. They seemed to fear that if they did what we wished, their gods, or some men who had power would send boils and all sorts of diseases upon them.[112]

Although the Mota people seemed indifferent to the missionaries' message, they nevertheless treated them kindly and did not cause them any harm. Toward the end of their stay, Dudley was surprised to discover one possible motivation for such good behavior. He wrote in his diary, September 30th, 1860, "The people have got an idea into their heads that if they do not behave while we are here, a man-of-war will come and blow up their island, but who led them to fear this I do not know."[113]

The following year the missionaries were met with even greater friendliness and positive response, with boys volunteering from many villages to go to the Central School in New Zealand. In 1862 the winter school was described as "the most hopeful of all."[114] By this date, the internal endemic hostility between the nine different districts of the island had considerably subsided, enabling Patteson to write that "Now men may walk where they please in Mota, and unless there be some special quarrel between two or more villages, scarcely a bow or club are seen."[115]

Indigenous Innovative Response and the Formation of a Christian Village on Mota.

For the next several years Mota continued to be kindly disposed to the missionaries and sent an increasing number of scholars to New Zealand; however, there was very little evidence of any movement toward Christianity among the islanders. Finally, George Sarawia, who had been one of the most promising scholars from the beginning, approached Patteson with the idea of establishing a model Christian village on Mota. Patteson was elated with the idea and so purchased ten acres of land between two villages, paying off with "trade goods" the sixteen different owners who laid claim to the land and fruit trees.[116]

In 1869 George Sarawia, who had been ordained deacon the previous year, established his Christian settlement with two other couples, and called it Kohimarama, after the school in New Zealand. According to the official Mission report for 1867, the purpose of establishing a separate village on Mota was "so that, as George Sarawia said, we may be able to support one another, and carry on our Christian mode of life without interruption and distraction."[117] Here twenty young men lived at the station and nearly forty came to school daily. It appeared that Selwyn's scheme was beginning to pay dividends, and it was believed that the Banks' Islands would become to the Melanesian Mission what Samoa and Rarotonga had been to the London Missionary Society—a center from which indigenous missionaries had gone to other parts of the Pacific.[118]

The Dynamics of Religious Change and an Indigenous People Movement on Mota.

In 1870 Patteson wrote to Selwyn who had become the Bishop of Lichfield, and informed him that, "Codrington says the time is come, in his opinion, for some steps to be taken to further the movement in Mota. Grown-up people much changed, improved, some almost to be regarded as catechumens."[119] The following year Patteson spent seven weeks at Mota, and shortly after arriving, he wrote on June 9th:

> There is more indication than I ever saw here before of a "movement," a distinct advance, toward Christianity. The distinction between passively listening to our teaching, and accepting it as God's Word and acting upon it, seems to be clearly felt.[120]

During this seven-week visit Patteson baptized a total of 289 persons on Mota, including 231 children, 41 adults, the majority being men, and 17 of the scholars studying with the Mota deacon George Sarawia at his school.[121] Many of the adult baptisms were triggered by the children's baptisms, as Patteson explains in a July 31st letter to his sisters: "They think and speak much of the fact that so many of their children have been baptized, they wish to belong to the same set."[122]

This was the year for which the Mission had been waiting — a vindication for their unique method of evangelization, and a counter-argument against those who had argued that such a plan was "visionary and impracticable."[123] Patteson wrote on August 20th, 1871, one month before he was to be killed at Nukapu:

> I never had such an experience before. It is something quite new to me. Classes regularly morning and evening, and all day parties

> coming to talk and ask questions, some bring a wife or child, some a brother, some a friend. We were 150 sleeping on the Mission premises, houses being put up all around by people coming from a distance.[124]

The mode of conversion was in line with Anglican High Church principles and traditions, being more of a cognitive than an emotional experience for the converts. Patteson continues his letter of August 20th:

> There is little excitement, no impulsive vehement outpouring of feeling. People come and say, "I do see the evil of the old life; I do believe in what you teach us. I feel in my heart new desires, new wishes, new hopes. The old life has become hateful to me; the new life is full of joy. But it is so *mawa* (weighty), I am afraid. What if after making these promises I go back?"

Such a "rational," cognitive approach to Christianity by the islanders pleased Patteson very much, for it was in keeping with his theology and missiological principles. He was elated and overwhelmed with the Mission's apparent success on Mota.

One month later, on the small island of Nukapu in the Reef Islands, Patteson was killed, supposedly in retaliation for atrocities committed by a European vessel recruiting labor for work on plantations in Fiji.[125] The news of his death was a terrible shock to the new converts at Mota. Some felt that with the death of Patteson, the Mission was finished, and the new teaching recently embraced would come to naught. The Mota deacon assured his congregation that since this was God's work and not man's, that everything would continue on, granted, without the supportive Bishop's presence.[126] Indeed, the report for the following year shows that fifty-three more were baptized on Mota. The island continued to be a model to which the Mission could point as justification for its methods:

> It will be seen from this brief sketch of the condition of the Banks' Islands, that the gospel has not only held its ground, but that it has considerably advanced; and by the agency of native teachers.[127]

The euphoria of 1871-1872 collapsed in 1873. In January a hurricane destroyed villages and gardens, and this was followed by heavy rains for an extended period, and by epidemics of dysentery and influenza. Two hundred people died, including at least seventy who had been recently baptized. The Mission Report for 1873 candidly admits, "There had been no progress such as last year, on the contrary there had been considerable falling off everywhere in attendance of school and prayers."[128] Given the depressing conditions in the island, the state of things, while disappointing, was not surprising to the missionaries who noted:

> It would have been no wonder if there had been some dejection among those who had received the Gospel . . . It was natural also

> that something of opposition should be roused by feeling that the new teaching was followed so quickly by a great mortality. It cannot be said, however, that there was any abandonment of his belief on that account by any baptised person; indeed it was very remarkable that baptism was sought by very many who were in danger of death.[129]

In the same year, 1873, George Sarawia was advanced from deacon to priest, principally because of the movement toward Christianity among the Mota islanders. Sarawia died in 1901 after a lifetime of faithful association with the Melanesian Mission. However, due to illness from crippling rheumatism most of his life, he was seldom able to attend to more than his one school called Kohimarama on the island of Mota. Although the missionaries perceived him as lacking energy and great intelligence, they nevertheless appreciated him as a steadfast and faithful example to his people.[130]

The movement toward Christianity on Mota peaked in 1871-1872, and after the disasters of 1873, it never again became the model that the Mission had hoped it would be. The 1874 Mission Report noted, "There is a want of zeal and energy and the evangelization of the whole island languishes."[131] Commodore J. G. Goodenough, on visiting Mota in 1875, did not find an exemplary Christian community in the middle of Melanesia, but rather a dilapidated station in which the islanders were "pleasing-looking people, but very dirty compared with those of Samoa or Fiji even."[132] Hilliard (1978: 61) in his assessment poignantly notes, "Patteson's ideal Christian village had been a theological construction, and when put to the test, the romanticism of the original concept was easily exposed."

Nevertheless, despite the islanders' lack of enthusiasm for the new teaching, and the continual disappointment of the Mission in the "leading Christian island," converts on Mota were slowly, but steadily, added to the church. In 1881, one half of the population of 900 (reduced from 1,430 in 1860) were reported to be baptized on Mota, while 1,000 Christians were reported for the whole of the Banks' Islands, whose population was 5,000. Only one of the nine districts on Mota was reported to still be "dominated by paganism." There were, however, only nineteen to twenty communicants on Mota, demonstrating that while comparatively large numbers were baptized, the Mission reserved this very high level of church membership for a select few.[133]

While missionaries expressed concern over the way many Christians tenaciously held to belief in witchcraft and other traditional customs, it appears from the reports that their greatest interest was in establishing a regular and orderly system in the schools, and in inducing the islanders to build a "proper chapel" after the original building was destroyed by the hurricane of 1882.[134] By 1885, the advent of a new way of life to accompany the cognitive assent given to Christianity was still very unsatisfactory to the missionary in charge of the Banks' Islands. Palmer wrote from an ethnocentric perspective:

> There are places in the district one would wish to see more alive than they are, and there is a great want all through the whole group of general improvement in their ways of life, etc., in what is generally meant by civilization. Their moral life has been vastly improved, but their social habits and ways of living are much what they used to be. How all this is to be altered and improved is the problem.[135]

Despite the lethargic state of Mota after the initial enthusiasm for Christianity had worn off, there were nevertheless some bright spots for the Mission. One of these was the "missionary spirit" of the Mota Church, exemplified by the willingness of individuals to serve as teachers in other islands. Consequently, the spread of Christianity through the Banks' Islands was initially accomplished primarily through Mota teachers, and then later through teachers from the island of Motalava. In 1879, there were eighteen from Mota serving on other Banks' Islands as teachers. For most of this period Norfolk Island was dominated by scholars from the Banks' Islands, most of whom were from Mota. Thus for example, in 1873 there were 184 Melanesians at Norfolk Island with 99 of these from the Banks', including 38 from Mota. In the same year there were 65 scholars from the Solomon Islands. However, eleven years later in 1884, the Solomon Islanders outnumbered the Banks' Islanders at Norfolk Island, 73 to 60.[136]

The *Suqe*: An Encounter between Anglican Christianity and an Indigenous Institution.

In concluding this section on Mota and the Banks' Islands, it is important to discuss the role of the *Suqe* graded society in the conversion of the islanders, and the missionaries' attitude toward it which changed over time.

The *Suqe* (graded society) and *Tamate* (secret society) were clearly the dominant social institutions of Banks' Islands society — the center of ritual and economic life, and the mechanism whereby leadership in the community was established.[137] Patteson had not opposed these indigenous institutions in principle although some of the practices connected with them were distasteful to him. Believing that converts would of their own accord put away practices inconsistent with Anglican Christianity, he chose not to interfere.

The primary objection voiced by teachers and missionaries alike, was the long period of isolation from the community (50-100 days) demanded by initiation from one grade to another, and this necessarily kept people from attending school and prayers on a regular basis.[138]

The Mission interfered initially only by attempting to limit the period of seclusion of initiates to three or even ten days, but this was unsuccessful. The official missionary position held that these institutions were undesirable, in so much as they interfered with the order and regularity of daily Christian activities, i.e., attendance at morning and evening prayers and school. There was no objection to the *Suqe* on moral grounds, and there was no belief among the missionaries that membership in these societies presented any religious competition with Christianity. For example, Codrington writing in 1881, noted:

> In times not very distant the mysterious character of the *Tamate* was still maintained; the women and children believed that real ghosts were present. All supernatural character has probably now disappeared at Mota, and the societies are maintained for the pleasure of the thing, from old associations, and the convenience of a club at the *Salagoro*. It is not only in the Banks' Islands that a secret and a costume have their attractions.[139]

Through John Palmer's long association with the Banks' Islands, it was the apathy shown in church matters, contrasted with the enthusiasm shown for the *Suqe*, that influenced him to eventually oppose it.[140] It was not until H. V. Adams was stationed in the Banks' permanently at the turn of the century that the pervasiveness of the *Suqe* and *Tamate* became clear, and its strong religious character revealed, for the principal ceremonies had always been conducted while the district missionary was away at Norfolk Island, and tabus associated with it were lifted during visits of the *Southern Cross*.[141] Adams learned that the great influence of George Sarawia, on Mota, and indeed throughout the Banks' Islands, was not due to his office as a Christian priest, so much as his high rank in the *Suqe*.[142] It is interesting to note that when the mission attitude began to turn against the *Suqe*, indigenous clergy and teachers condemned it as stongly as some of the missionaries did, but for very different reasons. The main objection raised by the island clergy was that it prevented people from going to morning and evening prayers. The time-consuming preparation for the *Suqe* ceremonies, the seclusion required of candidates, and the general enthusiasm shown by villagers for *Suqe* activities, which was in sharp contrast to the sober church services and discipline of daily school, all presented a competitive challenge to the local clergy. To the missionaries, however, this was of secondary importance, for it was because of its implicit connection to pagan religious beliefs that the greatest objection to it was raised.[143] Toward the end of his life, Robert Pantutun, a Banks' Islands deacon, admitted that the greatest cause of the falling away from Christianity on Mota had been the *Suqe*, because:

> In order to gain rank in it money was needed, and to get it sacrifices were offered as in old days. Rain, wind, sunshine, health, and sickness were all bought from those who had power over these things. He said that he had spoken in every *gamal* . . . and *salagoro* . . . repeatedly and with tears, against this practise of heathenism, but his voice had fallen on deaf ears.[144]

Discussion of the *Suqe* became a hotly debated issue among members of the Melanesian Mission. It was a complex problem the missionaries had to face. In reviewing the evidence for and against the *Suqe*, Durrad concluded:

> It . . . inevitably draws people back into heathenish ways of thinking. Many, perhaps most, think in heathen ways to a very large extent always, but the power of heathen ideas gains the ascendancy when the *Suqe* is strong. I believe this is owing to the belief that to be rich and prosperous you must have *mana*. To get rich is the inevitable trend of men's minds, so that the getting of *mana* is the dominant ambition. Now the *mana* is not that associated with God. It is the *mana* of the *vuis*, the spirits their fathers worshipped. So we find that *Suqe* will inevitably lead back to the recrudescence and the strengthening of all heathen ideas (1920: 18-19).

Fox (1958: 132) reached a similar conclusion in that "where the *Suqe* was strong there the Church was weak."[145]

In summarizing this section, we can see that it was in the Banks' Islands that Christianity was initially embraced in a people movement early in the 1870's, but the depth of religious conviction may not have been great, for such dominant indigenous institutions as the graded and secret societies were still an important foci of social life at the turn of the century. The outward signs of a "new way of life" were the establishment of village churches and schools, the wearing of clothes among converts, and a general cessation of fighting and endemic overt hostility.[146] There were clearly some significant socio-cultural changes as a result of islanders' adopting Christianity, but the missionaries felt that many islanders frequently fell short of the ideal in internalizing their adopted faith.

It is difficult to pinpoint with precision why the Melanesian Mission was successful in advocating change on Mota, while elsewhere, there seemed to be greater resistance in accepting its message. There are a number of factors, however, that may bear on this question of why the Mission was more successful on Mota than elsewere in the initial stage of culture contact in Melanesia.

First, the islanders' initial contact with Europeans was with Anglican missionaries. There were no other competing models to influence the islanders, and so in introducing a new belief system, the missionaries were also the only source of Western material products. This would have tended to intensify rather than diffuse the interaction between islanders and missionaries.

Secondly, in the early stage of contact, the missionaries had a closer relationship with the Banks' Islanders than with other Melanesians. The "winter school" was held on Mota several times, and the language of Mota soon became the *lingua franca* of the Mission. Also, the Mission's first experimental "Christian village" was established by George Sarawia on

Mota. In other words, the Mission's presence on Mota seems to have been greater here than elsewhere, where contact tended to be more sporadic.

Thirdly, and closely associated with the second factor, is the notion that missionaries tended to stay for longer periods of time on Mota. Patteson appears to have been an attractive personality and he spent more time on Mota than on the other islands. The sustained first-hand contact between missionary advocates living with the people seems to be a factor worthy of consideration in attempting to account for the Mission's success here.

A fourth possible factor is the fact that George Sarawia, the Mission's primary indigenous agent in the Banks' Islands, was established high up in the hierarchical graded society. As a Big Man in other domains of village life, he undoubtedly would have had considerable moral and political influence, and his advocacy for adopting Christianity would have been taken more seriously than if he had been only marginal to the community.

These four factors are suggested as working hypotheses for further research. In anthropological analysis, it is frequently easier to account for resistance to change than to explain the acceptance of change; however, I believe that the structural principles underlying these four factors are a useful starting point for further investigation.

As the initial enthusiasm for Christianity was waning in the Banks' Islands, a movement to embrace the new teaching advocated by the Melanesian Mission was underway in the Solomon Islands.

An Indigenous Response to Christianity on Nggela in the Solomon Islands

Attention is now turned to the Solomon Islands and the Nggela Group, or Florida as the Spanish named it, a small, densely populated group of islands midway between Malaita and Guadalcanal (see map, p. 138). During the last quarter of the nineteenth century, while the Melanesian Mission was having very little success elsewhere in the Solomon Islands, Nggela and Santa Isabel were exceptions to the rule, for here a significant movement toward Christianity occurred.[147] But let us first review some of the history of missionary contact here.

Early Stages of Missionary Contact on Nggela.

The first Nggela scholar was taken to Kohimarama in New Zealand in 1862. The Mission's hopes for him as a future evangelist to his own people were not realized, for ten years later, he was the leader in the party that attacked the *Lavinia* in 1872, massacring seven of those on board and plundering its cargo of trade goods.[148]

In 1868 a young Irish priest, Charles H. Brooke, began staying on Nggela under the protective custody of Takua, the renowned Big Man of Boli

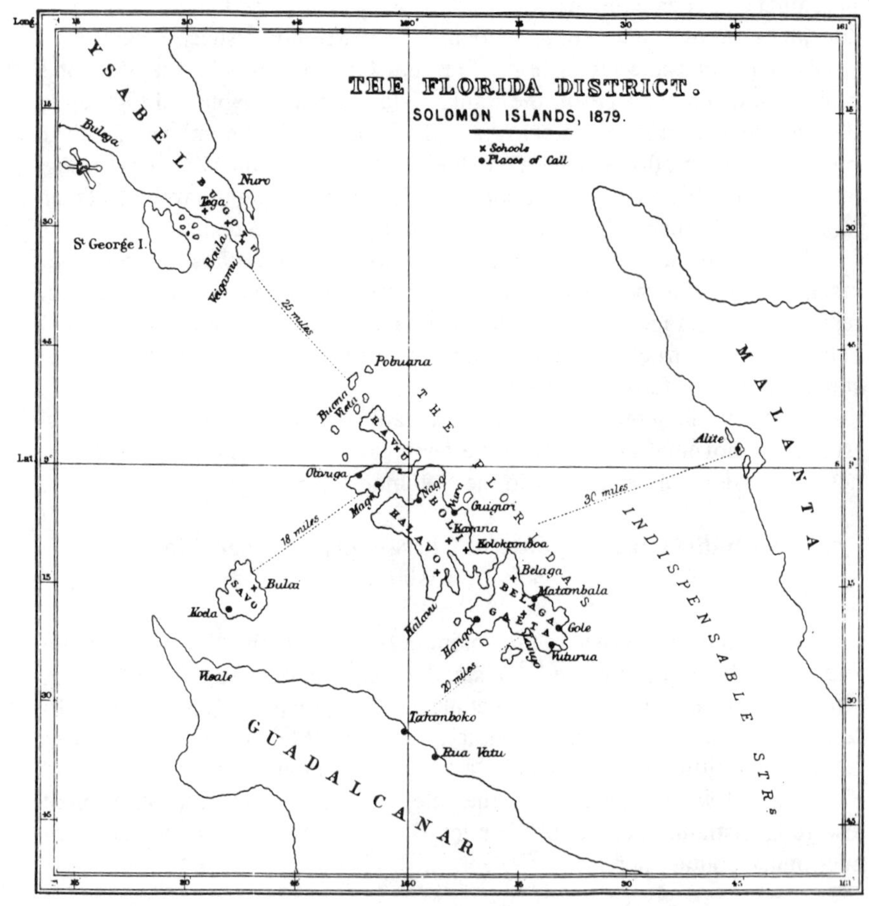

Mission Work on Nggela, Solomon Islands, 1879.

district, and one of the most powerful influences in the entire group. Brooke paid yearly visits of ten to twelve weeks over the next six years, and appears to have struck an alliance with Takua, and to have established friendly relations among the people; however, his influence was limited primarily to the Boli district. He was successful in recruiting young men for training in Norfolk Island, as evidenced by twenty-nine scholars out of a total of fifty-eight from the Solomons that were resident there in 1873 and 1874. Takua took advantage of his patronage of the European missionary, taxing anyone who entered the missionary's house and collecting trade goods from young men as they returned from Norfolk Island, and taxing them as they left.[149] While in the island, Brooke held a school for both old and young scholars, but when he returned to Norfolk Island the school collapsed. Brooke spoke the language fluently, translated the Prayer Book, and wrote some Nggela hymns. He endeared himself to many of the people, but there was little overt response to the Christian message he presented. He revelled in his position as a pioneer missionary on a savage island,[150] but he was quickly dismissed in 1874 when it was revealed that he had entered into homosexual relationships with some of his young scholars.[151]

Missionary and Indigenous Advocates: The Role of Alfred Penny and Charles Sapibuana on Nggela.

In 1875 Alfred Penny followed Charles Brooke in overseeing the mission work on Nggela, and during his ten years saw the transformation of the indigenous society.[152] Fox (1958: 180) described him as "a big bearded man with fine presence who took a deep interest in the customs of the people and in his time the four Gospels and Acts were translated into the Gela language which Penny spoke fluently."

The prime-mover in Nggela, however, was not so much the missionary Penny, as it was the Melanesian Charles Sapibuana, a native of the Gaeta district. He was first encountered by the Mission in 1866 when he went with Patteson to New Zealand. After eleven years of training, he returned to his island in 1877 and began the establishment of a permanent school. The following year he baptized his brother and sister-in-law, and their two children, and a small nucleus of Christians was established at the village of Langgo in the Gaeta district. Penny recalled, in 1885, Sapibuana's immediate influence upon returning from his Norfolk Island training:

> He was soon at work, and at once his power began to be felt, for from the first he set himself against what was wrong with quiet and unflinching determination. Of course he met with bitter and most dangerous opposition, but he passed unhurt through all, though the threats of vengence and the plans to kill him and destroy his property, might well have daunted a less determined man.[153]

In the following year, 1878, Sapibuana's defiance of traditional customs resulted in a power encounter[154] between Christianity and traditional beliefs, and a movement which caught Penny by surprise was underway. Penny recorded that:

> Groups of men and women, after catechumen classes were over in the evening, would come to ask questions about things they had just heard: one group after another, till late at night and for very weariness we could see no more. These people, by refusing to observe all kinds of heathen practices, braved their chief's displeasure, a source of real peril when dealing with men able to take life, and indifferent to its value. They let go their old superstition and faced danger in the strength of the new religion; refusing to attend sacrifices, treading on forbidden ground where sickness once was found through fear, and doing things which once brought death (1887: 184-185).

A Catalytic Event and Subsequent People Movement Toward Christianity on Nggela.

In October 1880, an incident occurred that profoundly influenced the course of events in the following years. Kalekona, the principal Big Man of the Gaeta district where Sapibuana lived, had demanded a human head to restore him to his accustomed position of power and authority. An opportunity came when a surveying party from HMS *Sandfly* landed on a small uninhabited islet, three miles off the coast of Gaeta. Led by Kalekona's son, Vuria, a party of five Nggela men attacked the sailors, killing three immediately and later the head of the party, Lt. Bower, after discovering him hiding in a banyan tree. Such an unprovoked killing brought strong reactions of outrage in England, and so the HMS *Emerald* was sent to Nggela to bring its full force to bear on the islanders with a punitive expedition throughout the Gaeta district, destroying and burning houses, canoes, and coconut trees. All but the village of Langgo, distinguished with its school-house bell, and a white cross marking a grave, were reduced to ashes.[155]

Although the punitive expedition brought massive destruction to the area, it nevertheless failed in capturing and punishing the five offenders, and so HMS *Cormorant* was sent, in May 1881, to investigate and capture the men directly responsible. Bishop John Selwyn (son of the founder George A. Selwyn) played the role of a mediator, convincing Kalekona to give up the guilty men, including his son, in order to avoid the British's inflicting further punishment on the whole district. Three of the five men were delivered, tried, and executed; a fourth escaped, and Kalekona's son, Vuria, was allowed to go free.

The impressive force of the man-of-war was never forgotten, and the power of Europeans to mete out "justice" left a lasting impression. The indigenous society was morally and socially severely disrupted by this event, setting the scene for changes to soon follow when large numbers would forsake their old social and religious system and adopt the one advocated by the all-powerful men from England.[156]

In contrast to progress in the Gaeta district under Sapibuana's leadership, the Mission was discouraged with the state of things at Boli, where they had had the longest contact with the islanders. Writing in 1879, Penny noted that during his annual stay on the island:

> . . . the school attendance had been very fair and everything was going smoothly. But, in spite of what I have said, Boli is very unsatisfactory. Things go on smoothly there and that is all. I cannot see that there is any stir among the people, or any general seeking after Holy Baptism. The contrast between Boli and Gaeta in this respect is very great.[157]

But there were other contrasts which seemed to underscore the Mission's philosophy of employing well-trained native evangelists to convert their own people. Penny continues in his report:

> At Boli there is the feeling painfully clear on my mind that everything hangs on me which is just what it ought not to be. At Gaeta I am equally clear that my being there makes no difference to the routine of the school — and work goes on whether I am there or not.[158]

By 1882, the Christian village of Langgo had grown to 115, and for his role in the progressing movement toward Christianity in the Gaeta district, Charles Sapibuana was ordained deacon at his village in 1882 — the first Solomon Islander to reach this level in the Mission hierarchy. Although there had been a steady increase in Christian converts since 1879, the real movement which was to spread through the island came in 1883. It began with the Big Man Kalekona of the Gaeta district who had been humiliated by the punitive expedition of the man-of-war for his complicity in the *Sandfly* affair. In his report for 1883, Penny vividly describes the turn of events:

> The collapse at Florida began in this way. Shortly before the *Southern Cross* was due at Gaeta, Kalekona called the principal people together in his following who were not Christians, and proposed to them to make a clean sweep of their Tindalos.[159] To this they agreed, and charms, relics, and things of all kinds that had been venerated for generations, some of which were only known to be in existence by tradition, being in the keeping of a privileged few, were put into a bag which was thrown into the sea. After this, Kalekona and his whole party came to the school and asked to be taught.
>
> The news of what the Gaeta chief had done spread rapidly through the neighbouring islands, and opinions were first freely expressed that the outraged Tindalos would punish their deserters with

> sickness or death, but as no untoward event happened at Gaeta, public opinion then declared that, "the power of the good teaching" as they call Christianity, "was too strong at Gaeta." I remember a chief from another island being weather bound at Gaeta last year and adopting this theory also, to account for the failure of his attempts to produce a calm.[160]

It did not take long, however, for Kalekona to demonstrate that this power was not localized only in his district. He went to a neighboring Big Man to collect an overdue debt, but repayment was refused. The debtor then challenged Kalekona:

> . . . to proceed to the usual extreme measures on the ground that his Tindalos would make him and his whole party ill if they took what was their due by force, or damaged his property which he had taken the precaution of making sacred by a charm. On this the Gaeta party set fire to the Tindalo house, and broke up all the bowls and utensils used in sacrifice that they could find. The chief and his people meanwhile looking on and crying dismally, then having seized two large pigs in payment of the debt, they took their departure, and as Kalekona naively remarked in telling this story to me, "there was not one of us ill afterwards."[161]

Belief in the efficacy of the *Tindalos* was visibly shaken. Therefore, the only known alternative, Christianity, was sought by many to fill the religious vacuum.[162] Penny was concerned, however that a high standard be kept in the midst of large numbers desiring to embrace the new religion. He wrote in 1883:

> In dealing with the numbers now seeking Baptism at Florida, I have exercised much caution, thinking it better to urge delay, where any doubt of fitness existed, than to admit a Catechumen into the Church who did not understand his privileges and responsibilities.[163]

The movement which had begun in Gaeta spread to other districts of Nggela, following established patterns of kinship and social organization. By 1886 the 1,000th baptism was recorded within a ten year period.[164] In the late 1880's the number of baptisms per year decreased while the number of scholars attending the village schools increased. By 1896, the Melanesian Mission claimed 3,500 Christians out of a population of 4,000 islanders on Nggela. Schools were operating in every major district, and peace was established throughout the land, the Mission having to deal with only one murder in the preceding fifteen years.[165] Publicly, the Melanesian Mission pointed with pride to Nggela. "Such is the power of the Gospel in lands which once ran with blood," wrote the newly installed Bishop Cecil Wilson in 1896. He looked to Nggela to "become a fountain of life to the cannibal islands which lie all around it" for surely, Nggela "must become a light in a dark place."[166]

The Problem of Indigenous Leadership on Nggela.

On closer inspection, the bright light of Nggela had a few dim spots. For example, as the traditional religious power of the Big Man was undermined, a crisis of leadership occurred in Nggela society. The vacuum created was eagerly filled by Norfolk Island trained teachers, who, feeling the heady prestige of their now important role, wielded authority with aplomb. Increasingly reports were given to the missionary on his annual visitation of the island of misconduct by the teachers, chief of which was the accusation of sexual offences. Not infrequently teachers overstepped their ecclesiastical domain and became embroiled in the political and social life of the village, dismissing people from school and prayers for minor offences, and then demanding a fine for their readmittance. J. H. Plant, who followed Alfred Penny as district missionary for Nggela, lamented in 1890:

> I sometimes wish Christianity was not quite so popular in Florida. My eyes were opened to some of the feelings entertained with regard to it by some of our heathen neighbours. I had a visit from Tandira, a native of Guadalcanal, whose son is at Norfolk Island. He said, "I want the Gospel very much," adding, "I want to be a chief."[167]

To help meet this crisis of leadership on Nggela, J. H. Plant instituted a "Native Parliament" in 1888, to be attended by all the teachers and traditional Big Men.[168] In the first year they met and passed three laws: two dealing with offences for adultery, and one with the problem of trespassing pigs that destroyed gardens and personal property.[169] However, by 1890, Plant was disappointed, for the *Vaukolou* had become more of an excuse for an island-wide feast, than an occasion for parliamentary debate. He wrote, "I hope our Parliament for the future will be less of a *fete* and more of a conference of teachers and Christian Chiefs."[170]

The "transformation" of Nggela society with the innovation of Christianity had another important social consequence. Bishop Cecil Wilson on his first tour of the islands was shocked by the absence of young men and noted:

> Life in Florida is said to be dull for the young men. True there are gardens to cultivate and fish to catch, but what are these when compared with the wonderful things which are to be seen and done in the white man's country? Such questions are rife everywhere amongst the young men, and when the labour vessels come they readily recruit in them to take a turn in the sugar fields of Queensland and Fiji. A whole first class at a school fails to put in an appearance. The question is asked, "where are they?" and the answer is, "They have gone to Queensland."[171]

In some districts the original enthusiasm for Christianity had worn off, as in Belaga where it was said, "Their first love seems to have waxed cold."[172] Bishop Wilson, reflecting the spirit of the times, suggested a solution for the languid spirit that was settling over the now Christianized island of Nggela.

He suggested that:

> These Christians must not only have given up heathen ways, they must help others to do the same. Moreover, they must learn crafts, carpentering, boat building, etc., which shall raise them in the esteem of the surrounding nations, so that they also may ask to be taught the wonderful doctrine which makes nations great. As soon as possible I shall seek missionary carpenters and other tradesmen of the right sort to come and teach these people some of the arts of civilization.[173]

It is evident that not only had a change come to the indigenous societies who had adopted Christianity, but a very different philosophy of mission was emerging, one which perceived the adoption of Christianity as inevitably leading to the Westernization of Melanesian converts.

Summary of the Period of Missionary Contact, 1850-1900

Church Growth in Melanesia.

The statistics of the Melanesian Mission for 1901 are instructive for understanding the results of the methods employed in attempting to introduce Christianity into Melanesia.[174] There were twenty-five islands in which the Mission had some influence. Of this number, three of the Banks' Islands, and Nggela in the Solomons were said to be "practically all Christian." There were 11,318 baptized Christians, but also under church influence were 420 catechumens preparing for baptism, and 1,199 hearers, who were being introduced to Christianity through formal instruction. Just under one-half (5,642) of the total number of converts came from the Solomon Islands, and of this number, 58½ percent (3,300) came from Nggela, and 20 percent (1,137) from Santa Isabel, where there had been a large-scale movement of people toward Christianity in the closing years of the century.

These statistics demonstrate that the positive response to the Melanesian Mission's advocacy for adopting Christianity was very uneven, and they point to the anthropological importance that the people movements in the Banks', Nggela, and Santa Isabel had for Melanesian church growth. There is a definite pattern here. Where a positive response occurred, it involved a movement of people that followed traditional lines of kinship and other forms of social structure, rather than the conversion of isolated individuals away from the corporate group of which they were members.

The Melanesian Mission's emphasis on training islanders to be evangelists to their own people is seen in the 528 teachers, but there were only ten clergy, all trained at the Central School. The European staff, meanwhile, had been considerably augmented by this time, from the original handful at Norfolk Island, to nineteen clergy and nineteen lay-workers in 1903. There were new faces at Norfolk Island, with all but one having joined the Mission since 1886.

The population of the islands with which the Melanesian Mission had contact was estimated at 150,610 in 1895. The percent of the population who were Christian converts at this time was only six percent.[175] After fifty years of contact, by comparative standards for Oceania, this was a very small response.[176] Had it not been for the movements in Nggela and Santa Isabel, which occurred toward the end of this period, the response would have been even less.

An Analysis of Factors Contributing to the Melanesian Mission's Lack of Substantial Success in this Period.

It is evident that the basic fabric of Melanesian society was still intact. Although significant incursions from other European sources had occurred, there was still a great resistance on the part of the majority of Melanesians to abandon their traditional religious system and way of life, and adopt that advocated by the Melanesian Mission. In anthropological terms we can say there was not a sufficient felt need among Melanesians to motivate them to change their culture by adopting new religious beliefs. There are several important factors that appear to have influenced such a poor return for the time and effort the Melanesian Mission spent. Therefore, in concluding this chapter on the contact period, I will briefly discuss four of these factors, namely (1) the labor trade, (2) the "remote control" method of mission operations, (3) the extractionist method of conversion, and (4) the Mission's lack of expectancy for quick and immediate results.

1. The Labor Trade.

The recruiting of Melanesian laborers to work on plantations in Queensland and Fiji began in the New Hebrides in the early 1860's, and moved northward to the Solomons in 1870. Recruits were to be contracted for a period of 3-5 years, and then returned to their homes. However, in the beginning phases of contact, both in the New Hebrides and the Solomons, there were many illegal aspects of the business. Islanders were frequently unaware that they were committing themselves to a minimum of three years on a plantation, and some of the violence committed against islanders in "recruiting" them led many to call it the "Kidnapping Trade" or "Blackbirding."[177] Although nefarious activities associated with the trade in the initial phases decreased, the recruitment of islanders continued into the present century, ending in Queensland in 1904 and in Fiji in 1911.[178] Some labor was recruited for work in New Caledonia and Samoa, but these fields were of secondary importance. During this period large numbers of Melanesians left their homes to engage in plantation work, but many never returned. Corris (1973: 150) estimates that more than 30,000 Solomon Islanders were recruited between 1870 and 1914. Swan (1958: 69-70) gives a conservative estimate of 25,000 recruited from the New Hebrides and Banks' Islands, and only about half of these returned to their islands.[179] The negative impact of the labor trade on Melanesian society was indeed significant.[180]

The labor trade was a major new element with which the Melanesian Mission had to contend, and it presented one of the greatest threats and sources of competition to their work.[181] As early as 1869, Patteson was voicing his concern for the safety of the Mission's voyages through the islands because of the treachery and violence of some of the labor recruiters.[182] Patteson's views on the labor trade were cogently articulated in a Memorandum to the General Synod of the Anglican Church in New Zealand in 1871. This Memorandum is reproduced in Appendix IV.

Patteson became increasingly disturbed when he learned that some recruiters were telling islanders that the Bishop was ill from having broken his leg getting into his boat, and that he was in Sydney and had asked the recruiters to bring the islanders to him.[183] The Mission's indignation with the unscrupulous aspects of the trade reached its height with the murder of Patteson at Nukapu in 1871. In all probability, Patteson was killed in retaliation for atrocities committed by a recruiter who had recently called at the island.

R. H. Codrington was the most outspoken critic for the Melanesian Mission, and in the Report for 1873, he notes that the labor trade:

> . . . is a most serious obstacle in the way of the evangelization of the natives . . . It is not a question of more or less difficulty in carrying on the Mission; it is a question in some islands already whether the population is to be utterly destroyed instead of being evangelized.[184]

Indeed, this was one of the most frequent complaints made—the depopulation and subsequent demoralization of the islanders, especially in the Banks' Group. Although the labor trade unquestionably contributed to severe problems of depopulation in some islands, the introduction of diseases had an equal, if not greater effect. In addition to the problem of depopulation, another obstacle was frequently those laborers who did return, bringing not only habits acquired from intercourse with vulgar Europeans, but worse, firearms, poison, and venereal disease. In every annual report of the Melanesian Mission from 1871 to 1876, a discussion is given to the labor trade, which was perceived to be "the chief obstacle to the progress of the Mission."[185] Although an entire chapter could be given to this topic of the labor trade, reference to previous studies must suffice at present.[186]

2. The Remote Control Method of Mission Operation.

It is apparent that there were serious defects in the Mission's policy of operating by "remote control" from its headquarters on Norfolk Island. One of these defects is that from the islanders' point of view, the periodic visit of the mission ship became an important cog in the Melanesian exchange economy. The Mission needed yams, coconuts, and pigs to feed its cargo of scholars aboard the *Southern Cross*, and for this an exchange of trade goods was made. In addition, the missionaries could not help but give the impression that they were hiring young men and buying wives for them. From the missionaries' point of view, this was an unfortunate, but necessary, means to an important end — the conversion of Melanesians to Christianity. To the Melanesians, it frequently was an end in itself. For example, the islanders on San Cristobal, who had had considerable intercourse with Europeans, and were amongst the first Solomon Islanders to be reached by the Melanesian Mission, never, as a corporate entity, took seriously the Mission's message, but always eagerly awaited its material goods. Thus R. B. Comins, reporting in 1881, thirty years after the first scholar, Didimang, had gone from San Cristobal to St. John's in Auckland, lamented:

> Things were in a sad state here, Stephen's own daughter Rosa, whom he had left to the Mission to be educated and cared for, and who was many years at Norfolk Island, being trained and taught, had returned to her home and heathen ways . . . The people here seem thoroughly callous and forbidding. I tried to make friends with them . . . but their only wish seemed to be to find out what fish hooks and tobacco I had about me and how I could be induced to part with them.[187]

Another problem associated with the Mission's method of operation was the behavior of the islanders which was frequently different during the months the missionary was in temporary residence with them; the private journals of the missionaries frequently reflect this concern. The first weeks after their return to the island seem always to have been spent in "repairing the damage" that had been done during their absence, and just when they began to see their teachers, schools and congregations on a "sound footing" again, it was time for them to pull out and catch the *Southern Cross* back to Norfolk Island.[188] This lack of continuity in the missionary's physical presence among the islanders necessarily made the mission work very disjointed. With such discontinuity it is not surprising that these agents of change had limited influence.

3. The Extractionist Approach to Conversion.

Related to the problem of a remote control method of operation was the philosophy of the missionaries which led them to believe that the most effective way to convert the whole of Melanesia was by extracting a few select islanders out of their own socio-cultural context, exposing them to Christianity and European culture, and then sending them back to win their fellows. The rationale for such a scheme was that they did not want to convert Melanesians to English culture, but to Christianity. This *modus operandi*, however, seems to have negated in practice what the Mission professed in principle. Over and over again, one reads of scholars "lapsing back into heathenism" once they returned to their own society. Although lamentable to the missionaries, such behavior is hardly surprising to the student of culture. To extract a young person from the security of his/her own cultural context and subject him to an alien way of life in order to teach him a new religion might be effective if that person were to remain within the new cultural context, but to do this with the object in mind of returning him to his own society is to misunderstand the dynamics of culture change in the contact situation. Upon returning home to his indigenous society, the scholar would be immediately confronted with a social complex hostile to Christianity. Here he would be forced either to submit to the collective pressure of his village and resume his former role and position in society, thus abandoning his Christian way of life learned in New Zealand or at Norfolk Island, or he could accept a self-imposed ostracism and actively stand as a Christian, albeit a marginal native, opposed to his own social system. As we have seen, both George Sarawia of Mota, and Charles Sapibuana of Florida, took the latter position, forming their own Christian village separated from others, and standing firmly against what they perceived to be inconsistent with the Christian way of life. From the Mission's perspective, however, these men were, unfortunately, exceptions rather than the norm. It was actually easier for a person after receiving training at the Central School to return as a missionary to a society other than his own in order to actively promote and demonstrate an Anglican Christian life-way. We are not surprised, therefore, to discover that in the first fifty years of the Melanesian Mission, those islanders who were successful as evangelists to their "own people" were primarily those who worked in a Melanesian society other than their own.[189] For the most part, however, the threat to group cohesion implied by the individual nature of conversion was too great an obstacle to overcome and the majority of those extracted from their culture and introduced to Christianity at the Central School did very little by way of converting their kinsmen once they returned home.[190]

4. The Missionary's Lack of Expectancy.

Finally, another important factor that contributed to limited results was the missionaries' own attitude toward conversion. The High Church Anglican theology which permeated the Mission demanded a cognitive conversion with strong emphasis on accumulation of correct knowledge, rather than an emotional experience which was more characteristic of the evangelical missions. Also, in contrast to the evangelical missions, there was a noticeable lack of preaching on the punishment of hell-fire for those islanders who had chosen not to adopt Christianity as their own. Thus to become a Christian in the Anglican scheme, was less of a "crisis experience" and more of an evolutionary process, requiring long periods of preparation of up to 1½ years or more, and involving distinct rites of passage. There were four clearly defined levels in the Christian hierarchy.[191] The first step was to become a "hearer"—one who was interested in learning about Christianity through formal instruction. If one desired to be baptized, then one entered the second stage by becoming a catechumen; further instruction was given while the prospective Christian memorized the Lord's Prayer, Ten Commandments, and various Creeds. The third level was baptism, and once one was baptized and acknowledged by the Church to be a Christian, there was yet another, fourth step — that of confirmation, required before one could become a full member of the Anglican Church, and partake of Holy Communion. Out of the 11,318 baptized Christians recorded in 1901, only 2,070, or 17.3 percent were Communicants, which demonstrates that the Mission reserved this top rung of the spiritual ladder for only a select few. The top professional levels of this hierarchy were first deacons, and then finally priests. The possibility of a Melanesian bishop at this time was never even entertained.

The missionaries were so convinced that their methods were the best ones for the situation that they frequently admitted that although they might be slower initially, they were definitely better in the long run. For a theological justification for the slow and uneven progress, they affirmed that, "God is never in a hurry."[192]

External Critics Assess the Mission's Progress.

Outside observers during this period were not so bound by tradition and were thus more critical of the Mission. For example, H. H. Montgomery, Bishop of Tasmania, toured the work in 1892, between the episcopacies of John Selwyn and Cecil Wilson, and recommended that the time had come for a change of policies.[193]

There were mixed reactions to the work of the Melanesian Mission among secular observers. The surgeon-naturalist, H. B. Guppy, for example, declared:

> The quiet heroism of the members of the Melanesian Mission, under circumstances often the most dispiriting and insecure, it would ill become me to praise. It will be sufficient, however, to remark that it has been the only redeeming feature in the intercourse of the white man with these islanders during the last twenty-five years (1887: 271).[194]

Nevertheless, others were equally harsh in their criticism. C. M. Woodford, another naturalist touring the Solomons in the same period as Guppy, recorded in his diary, "I do not believe there is in the whole group one genuine convert, who if the Mission were to retire for a year would remain faithful to it."[195] Sir John Thurston, the Western Pacific High Commissioner, with the model of successful mission work in Fiji before him, reported on his tour in 1894 of the newly established British Protectorate in the Solomon

Islands, that:

> . . . although some twenty-five years have elapsed since the Mission first established its station in this group, it would be a delicate, as well as a really difficult task, to offer any positive opinions upon the results attained. I found the native mind, everywhere possessed with a strong feeling against the Mission, and in many places the natives, upon my expressing surprise and regret, very frankly gave their reasons . . . I merely observe that judging from appearances the Mission has done very little.[196]

Fifty years of missionary contact had seen two areas in Melanesia respond by innovating and accepting the Anglican Christianity advocated by the Melanesian Mission, while other areas seemed impenetrable.

The Cultural Dynamics of the Contact Period.

This chapter has focused on personalities, institutions, and movements, in the contact period of Melanesian-missionary interaction. There has been necessarily a heavy emphasis on history in this chapter, but the purpose of the historical discussion has been to demonstrate the underlying anthropological principles which are important in understanding the dynamics of culture change. We have seen how the missionary, as an advocate of change, employed various methods to attract Melanesians and persuade them of the advantages of converting to Christianity. However, in this period especially, islanders were not always convinced that the missionary's message was meaningful for them. They saw no need, nor felt any urgency to abandon their own religious system. In those places where islanders did choose to innovate and adopt Christianity, they frequently did it in the context of a group movement.

It is also clear from this discussion of the contact period, that there was frequently a goal discrepancy between islanders and missionaries, in terms of converting to Christianity. The Mission's goal was conversion of Melanesians to a new faith as an **end** in itself; but islanders not infrequently considered "conversion" an appropriate **means** to another end. This is not to imply that sincere and genuine Christian conversions did not occur, for the data demonstrate that they did, but the increase in nominality and a waning of the initial enthusiasm for Christianity that occurred on Mota and Nggela seem to indicate that there may have been motives other than simply religious ones in the initial conversion of many islanders.

This chapter has also demonstrated that the Mission did not function in isolation in the contact period. There were other European agents of change — traders, labor recruiters, and others—each making different demands on the island population, and each introducing elements of culture change into Melanesian communities. Missionaries were often forced to compete with these other European agents in order to win a hearing. Thus, the data demonstrate that this period of culture contact was indeed a very dynamic one, and missionaries as agents of change were but one of many elements in the cultural arena.

Given the antecedent conditions discussed in this chapter, I will now proceed to describe and analyze the changes that occurred in what I have called the "Period of Penetration" (1900-1942), as Melanesians continued to respond as innovators, in one way or another, to the Melanesian Mission's presence.

CHAPTER 3 NOTES

1. The offer was first made to his brother William Selwyn, who declined it, later becoming the Lady Margaret Professor of Divinity at Cambridge, cf. Scholefield (1940: 285).
2. The Letters Patent is an official British Government document, declaring the boundaries of the Church of England in a British colony, and hence, the bishop's legal responsibilities. Prebble (1931: 15-20) argues that there was no "clerical error" in the Letters Patent in demarcating the boundaries of Selwyn's New Zealand diocese, because government documents prior to 1841 had stated that the islands within the boundaries of 47° south latitude and 34° north, were known and designated as the Colony of New Zealand.
3. Quoted in Tucker (1879, I: 85). Cf. letter from Selwyn to Edward Coleridge, October 8, 1851, in G. A. Selwyn, et. al., *Extracts from New Zealand Letters during the Years 1851-1852*. Eton: E. P. Williams (1853), pp. 6-7. For further discussion regarding the controversy of the Letters Patent, cf. Prebble (1931: 15-20) and A. Ross (1964: 13-15).
4. G. A. Selwyn to Edward Coleridge, April 12, 1852, in G. A. Selwyn, et al., *op. cit.* pp. 17-18.
5. Patton (1931: 24).
6. McLintock (1966, III: 220). For brief biographical sketches of Selwyn, cf. Mennell (1892: 407-409), Scholefield (1940: 285-288), and McLintock (1966, III: 220-222). The principal biography of Selwyn is Tucker (1879). Additional biographies are Curteis (1889), and Evans (1964). For a discussion of Selwyn's role in the founding of the Melanesian Mission, cf. Hilliard (1970a). A score of popular books and pamphlets on the life of Bishop Selwyn have emerged, cf. Boreham (n.d.), and Creighton (1923).

7. Scholefield (1940: 285).

8. Fox (1958: 2).

9. For further discussion on St. John's College, cf. Davis (1911), and Evans (1964: 99-119).

10. Fox (1958: 5). James Paddon was a most interesting character in the sandalwood trade. For further discussion regarding him and his activities, cf. Swan (1958: 14-17), and Shineberg (1967: 98-108).

11. For a very contrary picture of Paddon, one that portrays him not as a "tutor" but as an obstructionist to missionary work, see the private journals of John Geddie, housed in the La Trobe Library, Melbourne (Reference, MS 8774). John Geddie was a missionary on Aneiteum in the New Hebrides where the Presbyterian Mission began work in 1848. His journals, covering the period 1848-1857, reflect the antagonism he felt from Paddon who had established the first sandalwood station in the Southwest Pacific on this island in January 1844. He and Geddie were competing for influence among the same group of islanders. See Tippett (1973a: 105-125) for a very illuminating analysis of this triangle of relationships involving the islanders, the trader and the missionary.

12. Melanesian Mission, *Isles of the Pacific: Account of the Melanesian Mission and of the Wreck of the Mission Vessel.* Melbourne: Samuel Mullen (1861), p. 1.

13. Armstrong (1900: 9).

14. Quoted in Armstrong (1900: 8).

15. Church of England in Australia, *Minutes of Proceedings at a Meeting of the Metropolitan and Suffragan Bishops of the Province of Australasia, held at Sydney, from October 1st to November 1st, A.D. 1850.* Sydney (1850). Also in Selwyn Papers, MS 273, Vol. 9. Auckland Institute and Museum Library.

16. Patteson (1862: 14-15).

17. This problem caused the death of two Catholic priests on San Cristobal in 1847 when the Marists unsuccessfully attempted to cross the island by passing through the territory of traditional enemies with the coastal people who had initially befriended them. Consequently, they were never seen alive again, cf. Laracy (1976: 20).

18. Church of England in Australia, *op. cit.*

19. Selwyn Papers, *op. cit.*, Vol. 1: 246.

20. Throughout this study I will use the term "scholar" to refer to those

Melanesians who were brought from the islands for training at the Central School. The age variation of the scholars was from young boys of twelve years to men in their twenties. This usage of the term is consistent with all Melanesian Mission literature.

21. Selwyn Papers, *op. cit.*, Vol. 1: 247.

22. *The Island Mission* (1869), p. 19.

23. Today St. John's College is only a theological seminary for training Anglican and Methodist clerics. The acres of land which Selwyn purchased in the country have now become prime residential property as Auckland has expanded. This land is leased to local residents by the Melanesian Mission Trust Board providing an annual income of nearly one million dollars, which is the primary source of revenue for the Church of Melanesia in Vanuatu and the Solomon Islands today.

24. Selwyn to Rev. Edward Coleridge, December 21, 1849, in *Two Letters from Bishop Selwyn.* Eton: E. P. Williams (1850), p. 14. For additional discussion on the difficulty of establishing a multi-cultural environment at St. John's College, cf. Letter from C. J. Abraham to Edward Coleridge, December 6, 1851, in G. A. Selwyn et al., *op. cit.*

25. Eventually the Mission selected young women to go for training to prepare them to become suitable wives for the men trained by the Mission. However, the women always comprised a small number of the scholars in residence at the Central School.

26. For an excellent description and defense of the method adopted by the Melanesian Mission, cf. Codrington (1863), and Patteson (1864). See also, *The Sydney Morning Herald*, Saturday, April 16, 1864, p. 5, for a reaction to Patteson's address.

27. Armstrong (1900: 14).

28. For a detailed description of the 1851 tour, see "Northern Mission" in the *New Zealand Church Almanac, 1852.*

29. A vivid account of this tour is given by Selwyn in a journal letter written to his two sons, dated 17 October 1857, and signed in a most distinguished way, G. A. New Zealand. Selwyn Papers, *op. cit.*, Vol. 1: 298-391.

30. For a complete listing of the scholars who came from Melanesia to New Zealand from 1849 to 1860, and a list of the islands visited during this period, see *Report of the Melanesian Mission, March 18, 1861*, pp. 11-14. Cf. Hilliard (1978: 17-18).

31. Selwyn to Edward Coleridge, August 21, 1849, in Selwyn *op. cit.* The reference to the "Sydney speculator" is undoubtedly Benjamin Boyd.

For discussion of Boyd, cf. Shineberg (1967: 72-73).

32. G. A. Selwyn to his sons, 17 October 1857, Selwyn Papers, *loc. cit.*

33. Sarawia (1968: 1-3).

34. Dunbabin (1925: 3-4). For a brief discussion of the changing patterns of economic exploitation in the South Pacific, cf. Tippett (1956: 10-15).

35. Quoted in Grattan (1963a: 193).

36. Cf. Belshaw (1954: 16), and Corris (1973: 8).

37. For a short period there was even trade in the preserved smoked Maori heads with their elaborately carved tattoos. These were sought by Europeans as curiosity pieces until the New South Wales government imposed a heavy fine in 1831 on anyone dealing in such questionable trade. This exotic trade, however, continued surreptitiously for some time afterward, cf. Brookes (1941: 33).

38. For a very interesting account of one trader's interaction with the islanders, see Cheyne (1971).

39. Shineberg (1967: 156-157). For a brief historical review of commercial enterprises in the Pacific in general and Melanesia in particular, cf. Dunbabin (1925), Brookes (1941: 10-18, 28-37), Morrell (1960: 25-30), Grattan (1963a: 188-196), Shineberg (1967: 1-15), Maude (1968: 178-232), and Corris (1973: 7-9).

40. Fredrick J. Bradford to the British Consul at Papeete, Tahiti, 7 September 1861. Tahiti British Consulate Papers, In Letters, 1857-1866, Vol. 5, MSS 24, item 8. Mitchell Library, Sydney.

    Maude (1968: 170-177) has compiled an annotated bibliography of twenty-one works written either by or from material obtained from Pacific beachcombers and castaways. One reference in particular, a work by Leonard Shaw in Morrell (1832, Ch. 8), describes the castaway's experience of fifteen weeks on Kilinailau (Massacre) Island in the northern Solomons. See also Marwick (1935) for a description of the experience of John Renton, marooned on north Malaita from 1868 to 1875. Additional discussion on beach communities in the Pacific is found in Ralston (1970). Herman Melville's story, *Typee*, is an interesting illustration of a beachcomber's life.

41. Cf. Cheyne (1971), and Maude (1968: 160-161).

42. Shineberg (1966) discusses in detail the role of the sandalwood trade in introducing objects of Western manufacture and origin into the traditional Melanesian economy, and how this, in turn, forced the traders to meet these newly created desires of the islanders if they

were to be successful in their commercial enterprises. In other words, it was frequently the islanders, not the traders, who called the tune. For accounts of this trade, cf. Im Thurn and Warton (1925). Parsonson (1964) in discussing the role of the missionaries in the socio-cultural change of the Pacific islands, argues that the early explorers, followed by whalers, sandalwooders, and traders, brought greater change to the Pacific than did the missionaries.

43. Tobacco was in Fiji before this period of European contact. However, it was the Europeans who taught the islanders to smoke it, cf. Tippett (1973a: 81-90).

44. G. A. Selwyn to his father, June 17, 1848, Selwyn Papers, *op. cit.*, Vol. 1: 449.

45. Patteson, who succeeded Selwyn as head of the Melanesian Mission, held similar views. For example, in a letter written to his father in 1859, he discusses the influences of "lawless traders" in the Pacific:

> The ships of these men are turned into regular abodes of misery and vice. Each man buys for a musket or some article of less value a woman, wherever he may be, turns her adrift when he is tired of her, and gets another . . . You are aware that I do not speak without a real acquaintance with facts. The lawlessness and brutality of these men is often shocking, and we see with our own eyes the inhabitants of the places where they frequent utterly demoralized by them. Diseases are introduced, and feelings of suspicion and hatred engendered, and then comes some irregular enquiry by a Man-of-War, which is almost sure to do more harm than good. (Patteson to his father, 5 September – 20 December, 1859, on board the *Southern Cross*. qMS Bishop John Coleridge Patteson, 1854-1871. Alexander Turnbull Library, Wellington.)

46. Cf. Hilliard (1978: 17). For a thorough examination of early European contact on San Cristobal in the Solomon Islands, cf. Sayes (1976: 39-96).

47. Cf. Belshaw (1954: 50-52), Tippett (1967: 34-35), and Hilliard (1978: 21-22).

48. *M.M.R.*, 1857-1858, p. 27. For further detail of this event, cf. Yonge (1874, I: 359), and Armstrong (1900: 42-43).

49. However, this does not mean that the missionaries always viewed the islanders as the acme of humanity either. Witness Alfred Penny's entry in his diary on December 20, 1883, evidently after a particularly trying day at Norfolk Island: "The cooks in the kitchen gave me a good deal of trouble with their intense stupidity—for crass stupidity commend me to a Melanesian." (Alfred Penny, Diary, 1876-1886, B807-817, Mitchell Library, Sydney).

50. G. A. Selwyn to his father, 15 September 1849, Selwyn Papers, *op. cit.*, Vol. 1: 225.

51. For example, the Presbyterian missionaries working in the southern New Hebrides described their potential Melanesian converts in terms that were never used by members of the Melanesian Mission. In their annual report for 1875, they noted, "We labour among very, very low and fearfully degraded races." (*Twelfth Annual Report of the New Hebrides Mission Vessel "Dayspring" 1875*, p. 19, quoted in Scarr 1967: 123).

    An even more graphic portrayal of the "natives" is given by the missionary, Mrs. Agnes Watt (1896: 90-91) who, in describing her New Hebridean charges, notes, "Oh if you were just here and saw heathenism, with the wild savage look of the miserable dirty creatures, —in all cases perfectly nude. Yet they are immortal, they have souls to be saved; they are degraded, it is true, but Jesus can save unto the uttermost." (Quoted in Swan 1958: 24.)

52. Cf. Armstrong (1900: 16-18), and Fox (1958: 7-8).

53. Letter from Bishop Tyrrell of Newcastle, September 21, 1851, in "Letters from Bishop Selwyn and Others," TS, p. 831. Canterbury Museum Library, Christchurch, New Zealand.

54. Cf. Fox. (1958: 9).

55. G. A. Selwyn to his sons, 17 October 1857, Selwyn Papers, *loc. cit.*. The concept of aristocracy is a main theme in Goldman's (1970) monumental study of traditional Polynesian society.

56. Cf. Tippett (1973a: 193-202) for a discussion of "Missionary Resources and Island Life Histories." He notes the value of indigenously created documents for anthropological research, and provides a partial list of these documents that would be most useful to the Pacific enthnohistorian.

57. Sarawia (1968: 8).

58. Marau (1894: 23). Marau's other motivation for going was to see the graves of his twin brothers who had died at the Central School on Norfolk Island the previous year.

59. Patteson will be discussed in detail below, pp. 116-120.

60. Lady Martin to the Society for the Propagation of the Gospel, July 6, 1851. "Letters from Bishop Selwyn and Others" *op. cit.*, pp. 813-824.

61. George Sarawia who was considered by Patteson to be one of the most promising of the Melanesian scholars during this initial period, admitted that he did not understand the purpose of the Mission in bringing him to the Central School until his fourth visit (Sarawia 1968:

20-21). Cf. Hilliard (1970b: 184-185).

62. *Melanesian Mission*, n.d., ca. 1858. Pamphlet enclosed in Selwyn, *Two Letters, etc.* 279/S, Mitchell Library, Sydney.

63. It is important to note here that group movements toward Christianity or cargo cults away from it start with innovative individuals, who formulate new social norms which the group adopts. Cf. Tippett (1976: 67-82) and Barnett (1953: 116-117), and my discussion of conversion in group movements below, pp. 358-372.

64. *M.M.R.*, March 18, 1861, p. 8. It is important to note here that the Anglican missionaries were not driven by any strong doctrine of hell-fire and brimstone as punishment for those who did not convert to Christianity.

65. It was Selwyn's desire to visit "every island in the Pacific and . . . every village in New Zealand" (Selwyn to Edward Coleridge, December 21, 1849, in Selwyn, *op. cit.*).

    Writing to Edward Coleridge in 1851, Selwyn defends himself against the charge that he has been neglecting his diocese:

    > You say that questions have been raised about my neglecting my own Diocese. Pray inform all complainants that my Diocese extends from the Auckland Islands to the Carolines; i.e. from 50° **south** latitude, to 34° **north**; upwards of 80 degrees of latitude by 20 of longitude; and that having a Diocese so like a rolling pin, I must needs be a "rolling stone;" though I am well aware that such stones, whether heaved by Sisyphus, or borne by torrents, "gather no moss." (Selwyn to Edward Coleridge, 8 October 1851, in G. A. Selwyn, et al., *op. cit.*, p. 6.)

66. Cf. G. Barnett Smith (1893: 404).

67. Parkenham (1892: 317) has noted that, "The earlier missionaries of this century, with scarcely an exception, had sprung from the lower ranks of society, but the time had come when the noble and the great were to consider themselves honored by following in their steps."

    There are numerous biographies of Patteson, written for different audiences and thus for very different purposes. One of the earliest is by Yonge (1874), a large two-volume work compiled mostly from his letters, and one of the most complete and authoritative sources on Patteson. The most recent biography is by Gutch (1971), a semi-scholarly edition written to commemorate the 100th year anniversary of the death of Patteson. The most scholarly treatment of Patteson is found in Hilliard (1970b), in which he begins his essay by noting that:

    > John Coleridge Patteson is perhaps the most familiar figure in the English missionary episcopate of the nineteenth century. Even

> before his death his fame as a pioneer missionary was ensured; and, since then, his reputation has waxed rather than suffered eclipse. The reasons for this are not far to seek. Thanks to his own writings faithfully preserved by an admirable biographer, we can see him as a living man in some completeness. More than this, his violent death at a relatively early age, by earning him a place in the gallery of Christian martyrs, has ensured the growth of a Patteson legend, sustained by a steady stream of popular hagiography (1970b: 177).

68. Fox (1966: 2). Fox (1958: 16) reports that Codrington claimed that Patteson could speak four languages fluently (Mota, Bugotu, Arosi, and Negone) and get along fairly well in sixteen others. Sir William Martin claimed Patteson spoke at least twenty-three languages, cf. Yonge (1874, II: 586-590). See also Gladstone (1879, II: 235-236).

    Codrington wrote of Patteson:

    > The secret of the freedom and affectionateness of the intercourse of the Melanesians with the Bishop did not lie in any singular attractiveness of his manner only, but in the experience that he sought nothing for himself. A stranger would be struck with his bright smiles and sweet tones as he would address some little stranger who came into his room, but none who knew a little of the languages alone could know with what extraordinary quickness he passed from one language to another. A man of his faculty of expression could not speak like a native; he spoke better than a native. He was jealous of the claim of those languages to be considered true languages. His translations of some of the Psalms into Mota are as lofty in their diction and as harmonious in their rhythm, in my opinion, as any thing almost I have read in any language (quoted in Charles 1969: 286).

    For a Melanesian's reaction to Patteson's linguistic skills, cf. Robert Pantutun's reminiscence of his early encounters with Patteson, in *S.C.L.* Vol. 1 (6): 10-11, 1895.

69. Patteson's personality differed greatly from Selwyn's. Contemporaries of Selwyn frequently commented on what a great general in the army, or admiral in the navy he would have been, but he chose to be a Churchman Militant. In contrast to Selwyn's forceful personality, Patteson was more retiring and low-key in his personal relationships with others. Although Melanesians appear to have been attracted to Selwyn, it was with Patteson that many scholars felt particularly close.

70. Many nineteenth century Anglicans also held this view of Patteson, as witnessed by William Gladstone's (1879, II: 262-263) Victorian portrayal:

> The three highest titles that can be given to a man are those of martyr, hero, saint; and which of the three is there that in substance it would be irrational to attach to the name of John Coleridge Patteson?

71. The work of Samuel Marsden in Australia and New Zealand vividly exemplifies this philosophy of mission: that before you could Christianize pagans, you first had to civilize them. In contrast to Marsden, there were a few men like Henry Williams of the Church Missionary Society in New Zealand who believed the missionary's first objective was to evangelize and let the civilizing process follow in due course. Selwyn himself advocated the close relationship between Christianity and Western civilization as a necessary function of evangelization. As Patteson's missiology matured, he increasingly questioned this implicit assumption, although he never totally rejected it, cf. Tippett (1967: 40-41, 1971: 171-196), and Hilliard (1978: 56-59).
72. Patteson to his uncle, Tuesday in Holy Week, 1866, in Yonge (1874, II: 167). See also Yonge (1874, I: 512, 519; II: 354, 357-361, 372-373).
73. Yonge (1874, II: 151).
74. Cf. E. Miller (1973).
75. Yonge (1874, II: 152). See Kraft's (1979: 147ff) discussion on the importance of a receptor-oriented focus in cross-cultural communication of Christianity.
76. Yonge (1874, II: 169).
77. Patteson to Selwyn, 10 February 1859. Letters to G. A. Selwyn, 1858-1859, St. John's College Library, Auckland. See also *M.M.R.*, 1857-1858, pp. 42-47.
78. Yonge (1872: 5).
79. J. C. Patteson (n.d.), *The Melanesian Mission*, p. 18.
80. Quoted in Gladstone (1879, II: 222).
81. Patteson, *A Letter from the Right Reverend John Coleridge Patteson, D.D. to* *** (11 November 1862). Auckland, n.d., p. 16.
82. In the Maori language kohimarama means "focus of light," cf. Yonge (1874, II: 367).
83. The Pitcairn Islanders did not object to the presence of the mission as much as they resented having the land sold out from under them. They had come to Norfolk Island with the understanding that the island was theirs, and that there would be no other residents. Thus selling

1,000 acres of "their" land to the Melanesian Mission did not meet with overwhelming approval. To the contrary, some of the settlers returned to their original home, cf. Armstrong (1900: 88-89). Patteson was aware of this feeling and upon arriving at Norfolk Island and receiving the governor's offer, he wrote in his diary, June 9, 1866, "The people while pleased that we have come but sorc about the land being sold away from them." (Patteson, Diary, 1866, 1870, microfilm Mfm G14419, National Library of Australia, Canberra). Cf. Belcher (1871: 309-330) for a discussion and correspondence regarding the Pitcairners' attitude toward selling the land. A grant of 99 acres was given to the Melanesian Mission, and the remaining land was sold for £2 per acre.

84. Cf. Patteson's letter to his sisters, October 14, 1867 in Yonge (1874, II: 281).

85. The Arnoldian system stems from Thomas Arnold (1795-1842), headmaster and reformer of Rugby school (1827-1842). In attempting to reform Rugby, by making it a school for Christian gentlemen, he relied more heavily upon the prefect system than any previous headmaster. His methods and philosophy of education were adopted in countless English secondary schools, and the Arnold tradition spread to other schools through Rugby pupils and masters appointed to them.

86. Patteson in writing to a friend in 1862 declared:

> But the most important part of his life (the missionary's) work is done in New Zealand. It is here that the future missionaries must be trained for their sake. It is in the quiet regularity of our College life and not amidst the distractions of an heathen island that we must seek by God's grace to qualify these young men for their future work (Patteson, *A Letter*, etc. *op. cit.*, p. 16).

87. For further description of life at the Central School on Norfolk Island, cf. Cowie (1872), Yonge (1874, II: 418-421), Coote (1883: 12-16), "A Visit to Norfolk Island" in *Mission Field* (1884, 24: 382-385), Penny (1887: 30-34), Waddy (1903), Montgomery (1908: 11-21), Coombe (1909).

88. Marau (1894: 23-24).

89. Yonge (1874, II: 54). Cf. *M.M.R.*, 1857-1858, p. 8.

90. Yonge (1874, II: 54).

91. Cf. Patteson's Diary, 1866: September 9, 19, and 25.

92. Patteson to his sister Frances, 14 October 1867, Patteson Papers, quoted in Hilliard (1978: 36).

93. For further discussion of R. H. Codrington and his work, cf. Ray

(1922: 169-171), *S.C.L.E.*, (October 1922, pp. 114-122), Fox (1958: 219-222), Lane (1975: 95-96).

94. Cf. Patteson's Diary, 1866: January 3.

95. Like many of the traditions in the Melanesian Mission, the use of Mota became so entrenched that few ever questioned its continued use. Ivens (1918: 206) amplifies the problem:

> The use of Mota tended, moreover, to cause a depreciation in the estimate of the value of the other languages of the Mission. Mota was the language, and the enlightenment or the importance of a place was measured at times by the ability or otherwise of its people to speak Mota. The unquestioned usefulness and predominance of Mota tended to put all the other languages into the background and had a prejudicial effect on the study of them.

96. For further discussion regarding the Memorial Chapel at Norfolk Island, cf. *I.V.* (1880, pp. 16-27), Armstrong (1900: 206-207), Montgomery (1908: 12-13), Fox (1958: 219, 1962: 11), Cox and Stacey (1971: 47-49), Hilliard (1978: 73-75, 205-206).

97. Montgomery (1908: 12).

98. Cf. Hilliard (1978: 41-43), and Montgomery (1908: 13).

99. Cowie (1872: 9).

100. Australian Board of Missions (1900), part eight, "The Melanesian Mission."

101. In 1896, 116 shirts and 426 pairs of trousers were made by the island girls "training" at Norfolk Island (*M.M.R.*, 1896, p. 2). For a discussion of "women's work" at Norfolk Island, cf. *S.C.L.*, May 1895, pp. 6-7; June 1895, pp. 5-6; July 1895, pp. 7-8.

102. Norfolk Island and the islanders' villages were two very different cultural worlds. For an excellent discussion and analysis of the rural and urban cultural worlds of Africans which is pertinent to this situation, cf. Gluckman (1965).

103. Cf. Hilliard (1978: 41-43).

104. This is not to imply that these terms are antithetical.

105. Codrington to Fison, April 7, 1887. Tippett Research Collection, File TB3, Folder 32, item (p), St. Mark's Library, Canberra.

106. Dudley (1860), (pages unnumbered).

107. *Ibid.*

108. See discussion of the *Suqe* below, pp. 134-136.

109. Dudley (1860). A report for 1860 notes that at the winter school for

Mota, "The greater number of New Zealand scholars, on their return home, went back to their old heathen customs, and the remainder were compelled by their friends against their wills to join them" (Melanesian Mission, 1861: 6).

110. In the context of which Dudley is writing, I believe he is referring to the *salagoro*, a secret men's house in some secluded place where women and children were not allowed to go, cf. Codrington (1891: 73-83).

111. Dudley (1860).

112. *Ibid.*

113. *Ibid.*

114. Patteson, *A Letter*, etc. *op. cit.*

115. *Ibid.*, p. 13.

116. Cf. Yonge (1874, II: 370-371), and Armstrong (1900: 97-98).

117. *M.M.R.*, 1867, p. 3. It is noteworthy that Sarawia perceived a "Christian mode of life" as something separate from, not intergrated into, his normal activities of island life. Such a perception would tend to lead converts to think in terms of sacred and secular aspects of daily living — an idea alien to Melanesian thought.

118. Yonge (1874, II: 353).

119. *Ibid.*, p. 463.

120. *Ibid.*, p. 519.

121. *Ibid.*, p. 546.

122. *Ibid.*, p. 532.

123. Henry Venn to Admiral Vernon Harcourt, April 2, 1852, Church Missionary Society, Outward Letterbooks, Home G/AC 1/9, Church Missionary Society Archives, London. Quoted in Hilliard (1978: 18).

124. Yonge (1874, II: 546).

125. A great deal of literature exists on the death of Patteson, describing the events of his death, and the impact it had in Great Britain and in the Pacific Colonies. Although his death is an historically important event, its relevance to this study is somewhat less significant. Therefore, I have chosen to cite some extant literature rather than describe this event in detail. Cf. Atkin (1871), Fison (1871), Tucker (1872), Great Britain and Colonial Office (1873: 2-11), Armstrong (1900: 120-125), Drummond (1930), Fox (1958: 24-27), Drysdale (1960), Hilliard (1970b: 198-200; 1978: 66-75), Melanesian Mission Broad

Sheet No. 18, August 1970, Gutch (1971: 203-215), Tippett (1973c).

126. *M.M.R.*, 1872, pp. 7-8.

127. *Ibid.*, p. 10.

128. *M.M.R.*, 1873, pp. 16-17.

129. *Ibid.*, p. 16.

130. For a brief biographical sketch of George Sarawia written in 1873 at the time of his ordination to the priesthood, see Dudley (1873: 15-20). Cf. Awdry (1903: 134-141), and Fox (1958: 133-135).

131. *M.M.R.*, 1874, p. 14.

132. Goodenough (1876: 298).

133. *I.V.*, 1881, p. 37.

134. Cf. *I.V.*, 1883, p. 13; 1885, p. 21. In 1897 the missionaries were speaking "very earnestly to the people upon the absolute necessity of beginning a church worthy of the early associations of their island" (*S.C.L.*, February 1897, Vol. 2 [22]: 47).

135. *I.V.*, 1885, p. 26.

136. *M.M.R.*, 1884, p. 8.

137. Cf. Codrington (1881: 287-288; 1891: 110-115).

138. R. P. Wilson discovered in 1897, much to his amazement, that there was no attempt on behalf of the Mota men to continue their Christian religious practices during their time of seclusion in the men's house. He noted, "It is clear that there are one or two chief causes for the want of vitality in the island . . . I questioned them also on the subject of private prayers, and I found that in the "gamals" they never prayed. No wonder the island is lukewarm. The fact of the people not praying is undoubtedly the reason why there is so much deadness and indifference" (*S.C.L.*, February 1897, Vol. 2 [22]: 59).

139. Codrington (1881: 288). Codrington noted as early as 1873 that the *Tamate* or secret society is "now more of a club than anything else" (*M.M.R.*, 1873, p. 17).

140. Cf. Durrad (1920: 2).

141. Cf. Hilliard (1978: 199-200).

142. Cf. Durrad (1920: 18).

143. *Ibid.*, p. 17.

144. *S.C.L.*, April 1911, p. 150. Quoted in Hilliard (1978: 201).

145. This is an example of religious syncretism, where two seemingly

incompatible religious beliefs coexist in a unified belief system. The problem of syncretism is discussed in detail below, Chapter 7, pp. 415-416.

146. In the earliest period of the Melanesian Mission the wearing of clothes was not considered an essential requirement of being a Christian; however, toward the end of this period, (1850-1900), the wearing of European-style clothing was axiomatic with being a Christian, as evidenced by Bishop Cecil Wilson's observations in the village of Matoa on the island of Ulawa in the Solomons:

> Christianity is certainly in possession in Matoa, but the island generally is only in a transition stage, and walking the street of this village, amongst its clean nicely-clothed people, are naked visitors from other places, some utterly regardless of their nakedness, others ashamed of it, and trying to hide themselves behind trees and in houses when the people come together. If they could be baptised and become Christians at once they would do so, but they dread the interval between renouncing their present gods and being received into the kingdom of the true God. During this time when they are nobodies, their forsaken gods might catch and punish them for their desertion. Hence they remain where they are, and are naked. The first step a man takes toward becoming a Christian is to put on a loin cloth. Then he attends classes for a year or more, after which he is baptised (*S.C.L.*, February 1897, Vol. 2 [22]: 5).

147. The movement on Santa Isabel occurred primarily in the 1890's with the support of Henry Welchman — missionary and doctor who resided on the island from 1890 to 1908. I will discuss this movement in detail in Chapter 6, pp. 358-364 as an historical antecedent to understanding the form and function of Christianity on Santa Isabel today.

148. *M.M.R.*, 1872, p. 11; 1873, p. 21. Cf. Fox (1958: 179-180).

149. Cf. Hilliard (1978: 89).

150. *S.C.L.E.*, January 1924, p. 10.

151. Cf. Hilliard (1978: 90). Brooke later wrote anonymously a novel entitled, *Percy Pomo, The Autobiography of a South Sea Islander* (n.d.), the story of a Nggela boy who is enticed onto a labor vessel and sent to New Caledonia. Codrington called it "the best written description of the life of a Florida youth at that period" Fox (1958: 179).

152. Penny (1887) has vividly described his own experiences and the change that occurred on Nggela in *Ten Years in Melanesia*. Penny's personal diaries for the same period are housed in the Mitchell Library, Sydney. Reference B807-817.

153. *I.V.*, 1885, pp. 52-53.

154. I have borrowed this concept from anthropologist A. R. Tippett, who, in his numerous writings, uses the term to describe the ocular demonstration of power that occurs in the conversion process of many societies when they change from animism to Christianity. Cf. Tippett (1967, 1976). See discussion below, pp. 366-367.

155. Cf. Captain W. H. Maxwell to Commodore J. C. Wilson, January 3, 1881, enclosed in Admirality to Colonial Office, March 31, 1881, Colonial Office 225/8, Public Record Office, London. Cf. Hilliard (1978: 91).

156. For further discussion of the events surrounding the *Sandfly* affair, cf. *I.V.*, 1881, pp. 7-12, 75-76, Penny (1887: 153-171), Armstrong (1900: 210-213), and Hilliard (1978: 90-91).

157. *I.V.*, 1879, pp. 78-79.

158. *Ibid.*

159. The Nggela term *tindalo* means the spirit of a deceased ancestor. Cf. Penny (1887: 55-59, 189-196), and Codrington (1891: 124-127).

160. *I.V.*, 1883, p. 92.

161. *Ibid*, pp. 92-93.

162. This is a good example of how Christianity becomes a functional substitute. The identification of elements of Christianity that correspond to those in the traditional religious system, opens the way for substitution; in this case, the belief that Christianity is more powerful than the *Tindalos*. For further discussion on how conversion, and religious change involves the process of innovation as outlined in Appendix II and discussed briefly in Chapter 1, pp. 5-6; see discussion below, Chapter 6, pp. 368-372.

163. *I.V.*, 1883, p. 93.

164. *M.M.R.*, 1886, p. 9.

165. *S.C.L.*, January 1896, Vol. 1 (9): 1-2; February 1897, Vol. 2 (22): 6.

166. *S.C.L.*, January 1896, Vol. 1 (9): 2.

167. *I.V.*, 1890, p. 54.

168. Notable for his absence was Takua, the Big Man of Boli, who had been the Mission's longest ally, but insurmountable obstacles were raised by the missionary which kept him from becoming a Christian, as Penny explains:

> Takua, who, I think, all my friends know by this time, is as

> friendly as possible, and I really believe is sincerely fond of me. He is a very good heathen and there he stops! He is quite satisfied with his state, and talks to me about people who have committed some crime as being "such heathens," and of others he will say, "We will go and teach them." He wishes to be baptised, but I cannot allow him to keep his wives and be baptised, and to tell him to put four wives away and keep one when he has lived with them for the last 15 or 20 years, and they have all grown old together is equally impossible (*I. V.*, 1879, p. 79).

169. *M.M.R.*, 1888, p. 8. Cf. Awdry (1903: 86-90).

170. *I. V.*, 1890, p. 55.

171. *S.C.L.*, January 1896, Vol. 1 (9): 3.

172. *Ibid.*

173. *Ibid.*, p. 2. This is similar to the proverbial problem of "shipping coal to Newcastle," since the Solomon Islanders were such outstanding craftsmen in the construction of canoes. See discussion above, Chapter 2, pp. 55-56.

174. See Appendix III for statistics of the Melanesian Mission for 1901.

175. Montgomery (1896: Appendix I).

176. Cf. Gunson (1978, esp. pp. 217-236) for the most definitive study of Protestant missions in the South Pacific, and of the people movements toward Christianity. See also Tippett (1971). The contrast in the conversion rate between Polynesia and Melanesia is indeed very striking.

177. Cf. G. Palmer (1871), Inglis (1872), A. Markham (1873), Moresby (1876: 84), Alexander (1895: 37), Rannie (1912: 18-19), Paton (1913), Dunbabin (1935: 168, 189, 212, 258-259, 289), Drost (1938: 135), Tippett (1956: 90-94), Morrell (1960: 171-180), Docker (1970), Corris (1973: 25-29). For a contemporary review of the legislation passed in an attempt to control the labor trade, cf. "Pacific Islanders Protection Bill, 1875," and the "Kidnapping Act, 1872." One of the most influential critics against the labor trade was the Fijian missionary-anthropologist Lorimer Fison, whose series of nine long articles entitled, "The South Seas Labour Traffic" was published in the *Daily Telegraph*, from December 21, 1872, to March 15, 1873. For a discussion of these articles and their impact in molding public opinion in Australia, see Tippett (1956: 101-109).

178. With the cession of Fiji in 1874, there was still labor, but it was indentured labor. Much of the indentured labor came from India with the first shipment arriving in 1874. In 1881-1882 there were 114,748

Fijians to 588 Indian laborers. By 1916 the ratio was 87,096 Fijians to 40,286 Indians, and today, the Indian population is just over 51 percent, cf. Tippett (1956: 137).

179. For a discussion of the effect of the labor trade on the depopulation of Melanesia, cf. Alexander (1895: 50-51), Frater (1947), Tippett (1956: 123-126).

180. This would be a rich topic of ethnohistorical research. The labor trade was certainly an agent of culture change in this period, and thus a study of its influence on the cultural dynamics of a changing Melanesian society would yield fruitful results. Most of the studies to date have been compiled by historians rather than by anthropologists, and these tend to focus less on cultural dynamics and more on historical "facts." An example of the kind of study I am suggesting is Linker (1959) who focuses on the relationship between the labor trade and Melanesian acculturation.

181. On the presumed threat of the labor trade to Christianity, cf. Macdonald (1878), and Steel (1880). A more critical summary, written from a less impassioned distance of over twenty years, is found in Ivens (1918: 217-232).

182. Patteson to Lady Stephen, June 19, 1869. Stephen Family Papers, MSS/777/11, Mitchell Library, Sydney.

183. There were many accounts and variations of this missionary drama, cf. Yonge (1874, II: 368, 380), and Tippett (1956: 128-129).

184. *M.M.R.*, 1873, pp. 23-24.

185. *Ibid.*, p. 23.

186. Major studies of the labor trade include Molesworth (1917), Drost (1938), Tippett (1956), McIntosh (1961), Parnaby (1964), Scarr (1970), and Corris (1973). For contemporary accounts, see Romilly (1887), Wawn (1893), Rannie (1912), Cromar (1935), and Giles (1968).

187. *I.V.*, 1881, p. 23.

188. Penny was privately noting in his diary (August 19, 1877) that it would be good if he could spend an entire year on Nggela:

> I or someone must do this and the sooner the better. I firmly believe that great things might be done here if we did not go away just as the inert mass of indifference and deadness began to move. God give me grace and bodily strength to carry out this idea (Penny, Diary, *op. cit.*).

He never did, nor did any missionary spend an entire year in the islands until the very end of the nineteenth century.

189. The following indigenous missionaries are a few examples of those who left their own islands to work and live as missionaries in another society, during this first period of Mission contact: Mano Wadrokal from Mare in the Loyalty Islands worked on Savo, Santa Isabel, Reef Islands and Santa Cruz. Thomas Ulagu from Mota worked on Raga (Pentecost) in the New Hebrides. Joe Gilvelte from Motlav in the Banks' worked on San Cristobal. Ellison Tegortok also from Motlav went to Tikopia, and another Motlav man, Barnabas Serbas, went to North Malaita as a missionary. Robert Pantutun of Mota went to Santa Maria, Maewo and the Torres Islands, and Edward Wogale of Vanua Lava in the Banks' Islands was a missionary for a short time on Nggela, working with Charles Sapibuana, and then later, he went to the Torres Islands. Clement Marau of Merlava in the Banks' was a long-time missionary on Ulawa in the Solomon Islands.

Three interesting exceptions to this pattern were Henry Tagalad who was instrumental in evangelizing his own island of Motlav; George Sarawia, although born at Vanua Lava considered himself a Mota man, who was the first Melanesian priest ordained in the Mission; and Charles Sapibuana, who played a leading role in the conversion process on Nggela. In each of these three places there were significant movements of people toward Christianity in this initial period of Mission contact.

190. Cf. Tippett (1967: 39-40), and Hilliard (1978: 19-20).

191. *I.V.*, 1890, p. 62.

192. Quoted in Hilliard (1978: 114). For an example of this lack of urgency on the part of the Anglican missionaries, see Charles Bice, in *Gospel Missionary*, n.s., 1877, p. 155.

193. Montgomery (1908: 259-262).

194. Guppy (1887: 271).

195. Woodford, Diary, September 25, 1886. Woodford Papers, bundle 30, 1/4. Australian National University, Department of Pacific and Southeast Asian History. Quoted in Hilliard (1978: 113).

196. Sir John Thurston to Lord Ripon, December 22, 1894. Colonial Office 225/45, Public Record Office, London. Quoted in Hilliard (1978: 114).

In contrast to Thurston's negative criticism are the glowing statements made by men of the Royal Navy, and published by the Melanesian Mission in a pamphlet entitled, *The Melanesian Mission: Some Testimony to the Efficacy of its Work in Humanizing, Civilizing and Christianizing the Natives of the Islands of the S. W. Pacific Ocean*, (n.d., ca. 1899).

Excerpts from this pamphlet will not only demonstrate the view that some Europeans had of the Melanesian Mission, but the view that the Melanesian Mission wished to promote of itself.

Rear Admiral Clayton — Commander of HMS *Diamond* on the Australian Station 1885-1887:

> In the Solomon Islands, wherever the influence of the Mission was felt, the change in the character of wild, treacherous islanders was very striking. Progress could be noted; each year they were becoming quieter and more peaceable among themselves and looking to the Missionaries to settle their quarrels. I saw many of the native teachers at times when the white Missionaries had left for the season, and found almost all setting a good example to their fellow-countrymen and acting up to the teaching they had received (p. 9).

Captain H. R. Adams, R.N., HMS *Plyades* — on the Australian Station 1895-1896. In speaking of the Solomon Island pagans, Adams says they believe in Tindalos or "evil spirits" and are frightened to go out in the dark:

> They never venture out without spears or bows and arrows, and they always look carefully round the corners for possible enemies. In the Christian places this is quite different, the natives have quite discarded the use of arms, and indeed, curios of that description cannot be obtained there. The Christian natives appreciate this peaceful state, and call Christianity "The Religion of Peace." . . . The contrast between the Christian villages and those of the heathen is very striking, and could not fail to convince the greatest sceptic as to the successful work of the Mission as civiliser (p. 14).

The Missionary: **REALLY MY FRIENDS, THE LADIES CAN'T LAND UNLESS YOU PUT ON SOME CLOTHES.**

The Clothes.

Fig. 4. "The Gospel of Good News or the Gospel of Good Clothes?"
Ca. 19th Century Cartoon (Source Unknown)

Chapter 4

Melanesian Movements Toward Christianity

In this era of missionary penetration (1900-1942) we encounter a very different arena of culture contact from that of the previous period. The cultural wall isolating Melanesian society from European contact began crumbling in the last half of the nineteenth century. The intensity and frequency of this contact continued to increase at such a rapid rate, that by the end of this period, the wall of isolation had completely collapsed, and there were very few, if any, societies in Island Melanesia living a completely "traditional" way of life.[1] In the previous period (1850-1900), Melanesian culture change had been sporadic and uneven in most societies. For example, many of the "bush" communities in the mountainous interior of the larger islands had undergone very little, if any, acculturation as a result of European presence in Melanesia. Certainly they had been impervious to missionary influence. However, as this chapter will demonstrate, this was no longer the case by the end of this period of penetration.

In this chapter discussion will first be given to the changing cultural context in which the Melanesian Mission functioned, and the adjustments it made under these altered conditions. Next, the spread of Christianity and the patterns of conversion will be described and special attention will be given to the development of an indigenous evangelistic order within the Melanesian Mission. The nature of missionary-islander relationships during this period will be analyzed, and the chapter will conclude with a discussion of the culture change which occurred during this period and the missionaries' role in that change process.

Changes in the Contact Community

As noted above in Chapter 1 (pp. 16–17), in the discussion of the analytical framework for this study, the nature of the "contact community" is an important factor in influencing the kind of cultural change that transpires in any given period of culture contact.[2] The contact communities in this period were in many respects different from those which had preceded them in the nineteenth century, and it is on these newly emerging groups that I now focus my discussion. I will consider the nature of (1) the Colonial Government communities, (2) the Competitive Mission communities, and (3) the European Commercial communities.

Colonialism and Acculturation.

The cause of Empire came to Melanesia with the establishment of a British Protectorate in the Solomon Islands in 1893, and the creation of a Condominium Government in the New Hebrides, following the Anglo-French Convention of 1906.[3] In 1899 the Shortland Islands, Santa Isabel, Choiseul and Ontong Java were added to the British Solomon Islands Protectorate under the Samoan Tripartite Convention which left Buka and Bougainville as part of Germany's New Guinea possession.[4]

The first Resident Commissioner appointed to head the Protectorate government was the naturalist Charles M. Woodford, who began his administration with a small imperial grant-in-aid of a bare £600.[5] Woodford established the headquarters for the infant government on the islet of Tulagi in the Nggela Group, which in addition to being centrally located, was also considerably pacified in contrast to other islands, primarily as a result of the movement toward Christianity which had occurred there beginning in 1883.[6] Ostensibly the Protectorate was established to maintain law and order, a stance it held until the early 1920's. In this regard its major objective was to annihilate headhunting primarily in the New Georgia Group, and to control inter-group hostilities, especially on Malaita. Among other concerns for the Protectorate were the control of labor recruitment, the suppression of the arms traffic, and "the education of the natives."[7] Since the British Government required Protectorates to be self-supporting, Woodford was obliged to devote considerable time to developing and supervising trade in the Solomons. By 1907-1908, revenue from import duties (especially tobacco which was used as the principal currency in European trade with islanders) amounted to £7,430 — a significant increase from the 1904-1905 figure of £1,994.[8]

The Melanesian Mission welcomed the establishment of the Protectorate in the Solomons, not only because the majority of its missionaries were proud Englishmen, but because they believed the presence of a Colonial Government would aid them in their efforts to evangelize Melanesia. Significantly the missionary R. B. Comins accompanied HMS *Curacoa* in 1893 on its cruise through the Solomons, hoisting the Union Jack and explaining to islanders the meaning of the establishment of the Protectorate.[9]

The presence of colonial power in the New Hebrides was a far more complicated issue, which was not resolved satisfactorily until 1980 when the independent nation of Vanuatu came into being. In 1907 the French outnumbered the British, or more precisely, the Australians, in terms of residents in the islands (401 to 228), in claims to land, and development of plantations.[10] It was primarily over problems developing from claims to land by European entrepreneurs that the French and British struck an *Entente Cordiale* in declaring joint control and influence over the group. Most unfortunate were the native New Hebrideans, who were manipulated like pawns on an international chess board of Pacific diplomacy by French and Anglo players, each concerned with his own interests, and each trying to checkmate the other. This cumbersome dual system of colonial rule established its headquarters at Vila on the island of Efate. The British High Commissioner, Sir Everard Im Thurn greeted the new government by declaring in 1907:

> . . . for the first time in history the natives of these islands will be brought under civilized rule . . . it should be clearly realized that this rule over the natives will be as much to their own interests as in the interests of the white men who have settled among them.[11]

Unfortunately for the New Hebrideans, these words were meaningless, for the interests of the indigenes were of secondary importance to the self-serving concerns of the European residents. The Melanesian Mission never did enthusiastically support the Condominium Government, and through time came to view it as a cumbersome, irritating nuisance.[12]

The sustained presence of a Colonial government in Melanesia was quite different from the previous periodic visits of HMS men-of-war cruising through the islands. It brought a new complexity to the inter-cultural arena of European-Melanesian interaction. Grattan, in reference to colonialism in the islands of the Southwest Pacific, notes that:

> Their history from about 1900 to the outbreak of World War II, in terms of Western impact on them, consists in largest measure of an effort by the responsible political authorities to strike a defensible balance between promoting the exploitation of the land resources by white entrepreneurs and safeguarding the native interests (1963b: 337).

There were, of course, differing opinions as to what constituted a proper balance. It is clearly documented, however, that the Melanesian Mission was an advocate of islanders' interests *vis a vis* those of foreign entrepreneurs.

In the 1920's a head tax was imposed on the Solomon Islanders, giving greater support to indigenous belief that the government of the Protectorate was in the islands not to protect indigenes' interests so much as it was there to meddle in native affairs. The Colonial government imposed many new laws at variance with Melanesian culture, altering forever the traditional legal system.[13]

Competitive Missions.

The presence of Colonial governments was only one of several changes in this period, for the era of the Melanesian Mission's proselytizing monopoly was quickly swept away at the turn of the century by other missions entering the field. Its principle of comity, by which it had honored "spheres of influence," was disavowed by most of the newcomers. After having been the sole agent of missionization for fifty years, being forced to compete with other Christians for Melanesian converts dealt a humiliating blow to the self-image of the Melanesian Mission. For the islanders, however, having more than one brand of Christianity from which to choose, enabled them to use their association with different missions as a new form of political alliance. Denominationalism became a functional substitute to support traditional cleavages in Melanesian society.[14] Thus for example, in the Western Solomons it was/is not uncommon for one faction in a village to give allegiance to the Methodist mission while the other supported the Seventh Day Adventists. From a theological perspective, the Melanesian Mission bemoaned the presence of these "impure strains" of Christianity being introduced into Melanesia, but it had failed to occupy the field in the first fifty years, and thus competition was to be expected, even though it was unwelcomed.

After fifty years of absence the French Catholic Society of Mary (Marists) returned to the Solomon Islands in 1898, and established a headquarters off the northeast coast of Guadalcanal on the small islet of Rua-Sura.[15] The Marists quickly expanded their work by establishing mission stations at other settlements along the coast of Guadalcanal. Mission stations were later established at Wanoni Bay in San Cristobal (1909), on Savo (1909), and at Rohinari (1912) and Buma (1913) on the southwest coast of Malaita.

The Anglicans were forced to compete not only with Catholics, but with other Protestant missions as well. Returned Solomon Island laborers who had become Christians in Queensland under the influence of the Queensland Kanaka Mission, requested that missionaries come and establish a branch of the mission in the Solomon Islands, which they did finally in 1902. The mission was renamed the South Sea Evangelical Mission (S.S.E.M.) in 1904; a station was established at Malu'u on the north coast of Malaita in 1905 and in the same year, the mission's headquarters were put down at One Pusu on the southwest coast of Malaita. The mission's work was expanded to Talise on the southwest coast of Guadalcanal and to Wanoni Bay on San Cristobal in 1912.[16]

The fundamentalist theology and a more enthusiastic and extemporaneous worship pattern was a significant alternative to the sober and ritualistic High Church Anglicans. Moreover, the S.S.E.M. did not deprecate the emerging *lingua franca* of Solomon Islands Pidgin as a language, but instead used it as their primary medium of communication to the large audience of returned laborers who had learned it on the plantations of Queensland and Fiji. The Melanesian Mission, in contrast, viewed Pidgin as nothing short of bastardized English — a "language" quite unfit for reverent liturgical worship.[17]

In the Western Solomons, the Melanesian Mission had made only a few contacts and no work had been established. When the Methodist Mission began work there in 1902, followed by the Seventh Day Adventists in 1914, it effectively closed the door to any advancement beyond Santa Isabel for the Anglicans.[18]

The Catholics (Marists) and Evangelicals (S.S.E.M.) were the most significant competitors with the Anglicans for Solomon Island converts, and both the Marists on Guadalcanal and the S.S.E.M. on Malaita gained more adherents than did the Melanesian Mission in the early decades of the century. Bishop Wilson wrote privately to his wife while on tour of Guadalcanal in 1909:

> This coast is dotted with little Roman Catholic Schools. Wherever we have one they try to put two on each side of it. They attract our boys away by offering them education in iron buildings, and our men, by telling them to keep their ghost worship and do very much as they like. It is such an easy religion that the people are greatly attracted.[19]

In their work in the New Hebrides, the Anglicans met with competition from other missions as well. The Roman Catholics (Marists) began work on Pentecost and Omba in 1898, and by 1903 the Australian Church of Christ missionaries were present on Pentecost, Omba and Maewo, attracted to the "fields white unto harvest" from the large contingency of returning Queensland and Fiji laborers, who were more receptive to innovation.

Contrary to the Melanesian Mission's mode of operation, none of these newly established missions itinerated from a headquarters outside of Melanesia. Each one came, intending to stay, and built permanent mission stations and lived in the islands year around.[20]

Although an understanding was reached with the Methodists, and to a lesser extent with the S.S.E.M. regarding "spheres of influence" in the Solomon Islands, the Marists would have nothing to do with such an arrangement, viewing all Protestant missions as heretical.[21] However, by 1924, the long-standing principle of comity which the Melanesian Mission had held from the beginning began to crumble, and Anglican missionaries decided that they were morally obliged to establish a school or church in any village where they were invited, regardless of on whose "territory" they might be "trespassing."[22]

European Economic Contact and Change.

The third significant change occurring in Melanesia at the turn of the century was the increase in commercial activities. Sporadic contact had been maintained with Europeans in commercial ventures since the whaling days began in the early 1800's, but now small-time traders were resident in the islands and increasing in number annually. With the establishment of the Protectorate in the Solomon Islands, trade was actively promoted. Perhaps individual traders felt more secure with the presence of a Colonial government, for there was an increase in resident traders, from a dozen in 1893 to about fifty by 1896. Their activities were centered mainly on the northeast coast of Guadalcanal, New Georgia, and the Shortland Islands.[23] After 1900, however, there was a significant shift away from the small traders to the big company enterprises, as evidenced by the entry of Lever Pacific Plantations,

Ltd. and Burns, Philp & Company, Ltd. into the Solomons in 1904 and 1908 respectively. The establishment of large plantations within Melanesia assured the continuation of wage labor for the islanders since they were recruited as laborers to work the plantations. Grattan (1963b: 338) has cogently noted that European entrepreneurs "were in the islands for what they could make out of them and the natives were regarded as labor supply."[24]

A similar, if not more intense, pattern emerged in the New Hebrides with an increase of resident traders and planters. Burns, Philp & Company became the largest single British landowner or claimant; however, the biggest company, controlling almost three-quarters of all land claimed by Europeans, was the French La Societe Francaise des Nouvelles-Hebrides.[25]

Island Melanesia was no longer cut off from the rest of the commercial world, for steamers plied regularly between the islands and Sydney. Island products, especially copra, were extracted from Melanesia, and Western goods poured in to meet an ever-increasing demand. By 1938, F. Keesing (1941: 311) reported that in the Solomon Islands, 74 ships carrying 64,746 tons of cargo were registered at Tulagi, the administrative headquarters. In the same year, 57 ships carrying 163,163 tons of cargo were registered at Vila in the New Hebrides. Gone forever were the days of the lone mission vessel *Southern Cross* carrying missionaries who enticed islanders away to school with a few fish hooks.[26] A new age was dawning for Melanesia. The Melanesian Mission recognized these changes that were rapidly coming to one of the world's last frontiers of European settlement and commercial development. The official report for 1909 cried out, "The civilised world has broken in upon us."[27]

The cultural context of missionary-islander interaction underwent a significant change during this period. A Colonial government had been established that would suppress headhunting and warfare, replacing these with a new and alien system of law. Commercial activities increased, bringing within the orbit of all islanders the opportunity to engage in wage labor and to buy Western goods. Competitive missions had arrived eager to gather in the harvest of Christian converts which appeared to be burgeoning on the horizon. Traditional Melanesia existed only in the minds of the elders, preserved in anthropological reports of the time. In response to this rapid influx of change from outside their culture, Melanesians were compelled to adapt as best they could to the new conditions.[28] It was not only the islanders, however, who had to adapt in order to function in the new age; the Melanesian Mission had to do so as well.

Mission Reorganization and Adaptation of Institutions

With a rapidly changing Melanesian cultural context during this period, the Melanesian Mission found it necessary to make some changes in its traditional mode of operation. In this section I will discuss four institutional adjustments that were made during this period of penetration: (1) the relocation of the mission headquarters and the establishment of missionaries as permanent island residents, (2) the introduction of women's work in the islands, (3) the organization of the Mission's educational system in the islands, and (4) the development of a medical mission outreach.

Mission Relocation and Missionaries as Permanent Island Residents.

One may wish to inquire as to how the Melanesian Mission responded in the face of these changing conditions which rapidly altered the socio-cultural milieu of Melanesia. The answer is, "slowly!"

The focal point of Melanesian Mission activities in the islands had gradually moved northward, away from the Banks' Islands and the New Hebrides to the Central Solomon Islands.[29] Norfolk Island, as an administrative center for the Mission, had become an anachronism. In the heated debates over mission reorganization, its "hallowed traditions" were a more persuasive argument than the necessity to respond to new conditions. Although discussion on transferring the mission headquarters to the Solomon Islands had begun prior to 1910, the headquarters was not removed from Norfolk Island until the end of 1919, when it was established at Siota on Nggela.[30]

Although in the 1890's some missionaries had begun "experimenting" with the idea of residing in the islands year around, the significance of moving the mission headquarters into the islands meant that the Anglican missionaries, like their contemporary competitors, had come to stay.[31]

As missionaries moved into the islands permanently, their role necessarily changed away from the itinerant school teacher concerned with the training of "his boys" at Norfolk Island, and with their repatriation back into their own society as teachers to their own people. The missionary, now more than ever, was an important model of behavior for the islanders to emulate. In many instances the missionaries wielded far more power during this period than at any other time in the Mission's history. As their role became increasingly one of pastoring Melanesian Christians, instead of converting Melanesian pagans, they were frequently drawn into arenas wider than their ecclesiastical concerns, adjudicating disputes between factions and hostile parties, and becoming more involved in the political-jural domains of Melanesian society as "advisors" to the islanders.[32]

Women's Missionary Work in a Melanesian Context.

Another adjustment to changing times was the beginning of women's missionary work in the islands. The Melanesian Mission had always been a man's mission — preferably staffed with "men of the right stamp," university graduates and English gentlemen. Missionary wives and other women had always been actively involved in the training of the small number of

Melanesian girls at the Central School; but in a typically Victorian stance, the Mission believed that pioneering missionary work in Melanesia was the preserve of men alone. The first woman in the Mission to even briefly visit the islands was Bishop John Selwyn's second wife, Annie, who accompanied him on his episcopal tour in 1886.[33]

The first attempt of a woman to live in the islands was in 1896 when Dr. Henry Welchman brought his young bride, Helen Rossiter, to Nggela, but she died within a few months, underscoring the popular opinion that the islands were no place for women to reside.

Under the episcopacy of Cecil Wilson (1894-1911) women missionaries (two or three together as a group) were introduced into Melanesia and established in districts that had been pacified, if not Christianized, by this time. Thus women's stations were founded on Nggela in 1905, Lamalanga on Pentecost in 1906, Mota in 1909, and at Maravovo on Guadalcanal in 1913. The women carried over into the island stations the same pattern of "women's work" that had been established at the Central School on Norfolk Island. Their efforts were extended to ameliorate what was then held to be the popular missionary view regarding Melanesian women. The essence of that view is captured by Bishop Wilson when he observed that:

> Everybody knows that a woman's lot in a savage country is not a happy one, and the condition of women in the Melanesian Islands is no exception to the general rule. The islander in his savage condition has usually one wife, who is his drudge . . . The women are, in fact, little better than the pigs, and must be treated accordingly.[34]

However, given this appalling condition, there was still hope for Melanesian women, as Wilson concluded:

> Those who have the teaching of the Melanesian Islanders at Norfolk Island say that intellectually the girl is quite equal to the boy, and there is no reason whatever why the island women, however much downtrodden hitherto, should not become the loving helpmates of their husbands instead of their drudges.[35]

If this was perceived to be the problem, then its solution was to take "training" and "teaching" to the women in the islands, since there were limits on the number of young girls who could be extracted from their society and taken to Norfolk Island. It is not surprising then to discover that the "teaching" focused on good Victorian values of cleanliness, obedience, and good manners, with emphasis on reading and writing and understanding Christianity through Bible stories. The "training" was primarily in teaching sewing so that Melanesian women could make their own European-style clothing. Such "training" seems ill-sorted for women in Melanesia, and it is doubtful whether it enhanced their role in village life.[36]

Women's missionary work of this nature was clearly generated from a

European worldview, for the "problem" and hence the "solution" to the problem, were both defined in terms of Western standards for women's roles rather than Melanesians' needs. It is not surprising to discover that few, if any, of these early women missionaries ever closely identified with their Melanesian counterparts. Instead, their attitude was frequently one of revulsion as evidenced by the following ethnocentric report:

> Oh how these women yell and scream after a relation or friend has died! You have no idea how awful it is. I have spoken very much about it, and they were really quieter, though I expect they saw us coming . . . Of course, it is trying, as they do press so close, and, oh, the dirt! to say nothing of skin diseases.[37]

Later in this period the role of the female missionary was primarily that of nurse and teacher in the established medical centers and girls' schools. Speaking of the nurses who worked during this period, Fox (1958: 254) dramatically notes that, "Nothing has been finer in the last 50 years of the Mission than the work of this brave company of women."[38]

Missionaries and Islanders' Education.

Finally, in discussing the Mission's adjustment to changing circumstances, it should be noted that there was an increasing emphasis on "secular" domains of work, by greater involvement in education and medicine. As the initial stage of converting Melanesians from their primal religion to Christianity was accomplished, the Melanesian Mission turned its efforts toward developing "higher" (i.e., more Westernized) educational standards and training, and beginning formal medical work as part of the Christian ministry to Melanesians.

The Mission's system of education was a pyramidal structure with five levels as represented in the diagram below.

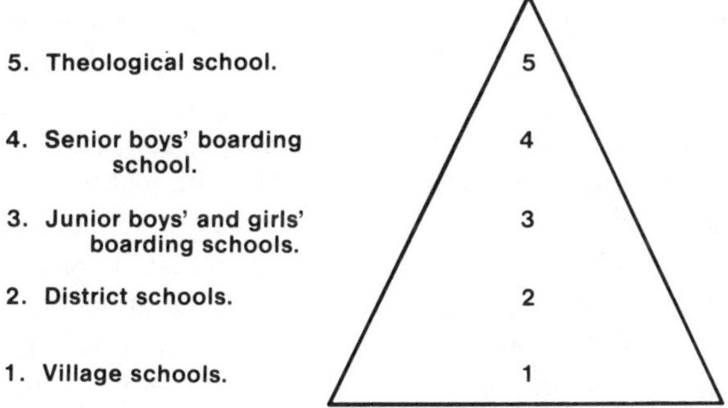

Fig 5. The Hierarchical Structure of Mission Education.

The village school had always been the "bread and butter" of the Mission's educational program, but during this period, missionary emphasis and personnel were occupied with the upper levels (especially levels 3 and 4); the lower levels, manned completely by Melanesians, became of secondary importance. However, this is typical of the period, for missionary work became more institutionalized and less responsive to Melanesian needs at the village level. It was their senior boys' school at Pawa, and their hospital at Fauabu that were used in propaganda literature to portray a positive image of the Melanesian Mission. The understanding and application of Christianity by Melanesians at the village level was eclipsed by the Mission's concern for its institutionalized programs. Fox reflects this trend in the Mission when he concludes that:

> At the end of the first 100 years the Mission boarding schools had multiplied exceedingly. There were still village schools but they were not as good as formerly, in a good many villages there were no schools, and the people were growing up without religious teaching and illiterate . . . The weakness was a lack of trained teachers so that secular training was not of a high standard though character training was excellent. The real weakness was in the village schools. Education at the top was good, but it rested finally on the village schools which were poor (1958: 246).

In contrast to Fox's belief that schools "at the top (were) good," in the Solomon Islands, the Colonial government's view in the 1930's was that there was "very little education of any kind in the Protectorate," since all education was conducted by the missions.[39]

Advancement through the educational ranks depended not only on missionaries' assessments of a Melanesian's intellectual ability, but perhaps more importantly, also evaluation of his moral character and potential for leadership. Those judged to be worthy in this capacity were encouraged to attend the theological college after completing their training at the senior boys' school. In addition, the theological college was the center where refresher courses were given to teachers in the village schools and for the Melanesian clergy.

When the mission headquarters were transferred to the Solomons in late 1919, it spelled the end of St. Barnabas College with its fifty-year history of Norfolk Island traditions. However, the senior boys' school established at Pawa on the island of Ugi in 1922, was meant to take its place.[40] The best scholars from the central primary schools were permitted to advance to Pawa where many of the Norfolk Island traditions were continued, including the establishment of a school farm and the use of Mota, a Banks' Island language, as the primary medium of instruction.

The vexing "language question" arose as early as 1911, in a debate over English vs. Mota for use in the training schools. Mission policy and episcopal edict vacillated on the issue, first deciding in 1916 that English be adopted, then reversing the decision two years later. The question was left unresolved until 1931 when English was chosen as the language of instruction in the schools.[41]

Although Melanesian society was viewed as a "man's world," and the thrust of the Mission had always been toward training Melanesian men, the Mission did establish boarding schools for girls during this period, beginning work on Nggela in 1917, and on Vanua Lava in the Banks' Islands in 1920. As in the boys' schools, the main emphasis was upon "building character" and religious instruction, along with teaching skills in the "domestic arts" such as sewing, needlework and handicrafts.

The thrust of the Mission's education was avowedly religious instruction; however, toward the end of this period, more technical training was introduced. A Mission propaganda piece in 1949 declared that:

> Beginning with Selwyn, through the Norfolk Island days, and ever since, education in the Mission has aimed at the enrichment and enlightenment of the native way of life and never at the substitution of an alien culture.[42]

Despite these claims, the trend during this period was away from the development of religious instruction at the village level and toward institutionalized education for a select few in which an increasing amount of Westernized instruction and training was added to the curriculum. The intrinsic qualities of Melanesian culture were valued less, as missionaries increasingly adopted an evolutionary view of their work, perceiving their task as one of pushing the Melanesian along the road of "progress." Thus the Mission was proud of the fact that some observers had called their senior boys' school at Pawa, "The Eton of the Pacific."[43] By the end of this period there were numerous village schools, twenty or more district schools, four central junior schools, one senior boys' school and one theological college for the training of ordinands.[44]

Missionaries and Medical Work in Melanesia.

In the earlier days of the Mission each missionary, in addition to his many other roles, functioned as an "amateur doctor." For example, in 1886 Bishop John Selwyn administered a judicious remedy of quinine and brandy to the ailing Santa Isabel Big Man, Soga, who quickly made a speedy recovery. Later the incident was cited as one of the important catalysts that led to Soga's conversion.[45] The only exception to the amateur doctor status was Henry Welchman, M.R.C.S., who had trained in England as a general practitioner before joining the Mission in 1888. The first Melanesian Mission hospital in the islands was in memory of Dr. Welchman, built partially from money raised by European traders in the Solomons, and opened in 1912 at

Hautabu, adjacent to Maravovo on Guadalcanal. A coconut plantation was built to finance the hospital, but in 1916 the doctor married the matron and returned to England to serve in World War I, and the hospital closed permanently.

Another hospital was not opened until 1929, when one was established on the southwest coast of Malaita at a place called Fauabu in Coleridge Bay. A leper colony was then built nearby. Under the episcopal leadership of Bishop Baddeley (1932-1947), medical work was emphasized more than previously to coincide with his belief that Christianity was concerned as much with the here and now as it was with the future of men's souls in eternity. He commented, "How are we to preach the love of God to folk whose bodies are covered with yaws or have limbs partly eaten away with horrible sores?"[46]

In step with other missionary organizations of the period, medical missionary work was justified as an effective avenue for evangelization, but under Baddeley, the definition of evangelism was expanded beyond personal salvation. Toward the end of this period the training of islanders at Fauabu hospital began and mother-craft (infant care) work started, although with the numerous Melanesian tabus surrounding women and childbirth, missionaries found this area to be an "uphill battle."

Although the use of Western-style medicine undoubtedly ameliorated some Melanesian diseases and illnesses, it is questionable whether it substantially altered any indigenous beliefs about the causes of human illness. Moreover, to the dismay of the missionaries, their efforts were not always appreciated by the islanders, as evidenced by a Malaita Christian's response to a missionary's plea that he help his own people, because the Mission had helped him. He replied:

> We did not ask you to come. You came because you wanted to, and not because we wanted you to come. As for you, you come here to give us medicine. You get paid for doing it. It is just your job.[47]

During this period the Melanesian Mission responded to the changing context in which they functioned by innovating and adopting some institutional and structural changes in their method of operation. In summary, the most significant of these changes as outlined above were:

1. The transfer of the Mission headquarters from Norfolk Island to the Solomons,
2. The permanent residence of missionaries in the islands,
3. The development of women's missionary work, primarily in nursing and teaching,

4. The shift in educational emphasis, from village instruction to a more "advanced" education and training for a select few,
5. The adoption of English as the language of instruction in the training schools, and
6. The development of formal medical work by establishing hospitals and clinics.

The significance of these changes meant that the Melanesian Mission became a more forceful agent of culture change than in the previous period. Because the Mission became highly institutionalized during this period, and less concerned with developments at the village level, it necessarily became more Western and less Melanesian in its goals and objectives. Structurally the Mission had significantly changed since the days of Selwyn and Patteson.

As an agent of culture change the Melanesian Mission during this period of penetration tended to stimulate overt Melanesian culture change more in the direction of becoming acculturated to Western values and artifacts, than in developing an indigenous Melanesian Christianity suited to meet Melanesian needs and designed to help islanders adapt and live in a changing Melanesian world. The Mission's operations during this period reflect a shift in emphasis from the days of Bishop Patteson when he declared that his goal was to convert Melanesians to Christianity without forcing upon them all the trappings of Western culture. The ethos of the Melanesian Mission during this period increasingly became one of viewing Melanesians as if they were on different rungs of an evolutionary ladder which would progressively lead them from Melanesian lifeways to European mores, and eventually to civilization itself. The cultural sensitivity and appreciation for an indigenous Christianity which had been an important element in the Melanesian Mission ethos at the beginning, now began to disappear during this period. No longer did one hear missionaries talking about a Melanesian Christianity created by Melanesians from a Melanesian worldview. No longer did the Melanesian Mission encourage Melanesian converts to worship God in a Melanesian way, applying Christianity to meet Melanesian needs as the Melanesians themselves felt them.

Phenomenology of Religious Change

In the previous period missionaries attempted to win converts to Christianity by employing a distinctly apologetic strategy. Missionaries perceived their role as one of cognitively convincing Melanesians that Christianity was superior to their own indigenous animistic beliefs, and therefore should be adopted. In this apologetic role, the missionary attempted by various means to convince Melanesians of the many advantages Christianity held for them over their primal religious system. As noted in the previous chapter, however, this apologetic strategy was not highly successful except in a few islands. It failed because the majority of pragmatic Melanesians remained unconvinced that it was to their advantage to abandon their own beliefs and adopt Christianity. Although European culture contact had increased through the nineteenth century, the fabric of Melanesian society and culture had remained, for the most part, intact and Melanesians' belief in the validity of their own way of life was largely unshaken.

The seeds of change, however, were sown toward the end of the nineteenth century, and as noted above, the many external changes brought to Melanesia by increased European contact in this period created a climate for internal change in Melanesian society and culture. To paraphrase Kroeber, the time was ripe for change.[48]

Although the missionary did not abandon his apologetic role altogether, there was a decided shift in emphasis, and in increasing numbers Melanesians were beginning to accept the "package deal" offered by the Mission. In 1903 Bishop Wilson wrote, "Our artillery of persuasion has been peace, reading and writing, callings of the steamer, and knowledge of the Good Spirit."[49] The missionary in this period now became more of a "shepherd" to his flock which continued to increase in size through time. This was indeed the era of European influence penetrating Melanesian society and culture.

Numerical Growth in Christian Converts.

In 1894, at the beginning of Cecil Wilson's episcopacy, the Melanesian Mission registered 8,929 baptized Christians and 122 village schools scattered throughout the islands. Sixteen years later, toward the end of Bishop Wilson's time, these figures had escalated to 14,125 baptized Christians and 352 schools; an increase of 189 percent in the number of schools and 58 percent in overall converts. The Mission remained on a plateau during the period of Cecil Wood's episcopacy (1912-1918). By 1918, there was a drop in the number of village schools to 318, and the number of converts was registered at only 14,194 — an increase of 69 over the 1910 figure. There are no statistics until 1934, six years after what Fox (1958: 73) called the "golden age for the Church in Melanesia" (1919-1928), during the episcopal reign of John Steward. These figures show an overall increase in the number of Melanesian converts (29,081) and in the number of Christian villages associated with the Mission (413). By the end of this period in 1942, there were an estimated 35,000 Christians claimed by the Melanesian Mission. The following table illustrates the growth pattern for this period of Melanesian Mission activity.

Year	Number of Baptized Christians	Number of Village Schools
1894	8,929	122
1910	14,125	352
1918	14,194	318
1934	29,081	413
1942	35,000 est.	no returns

Table 4.1 Numerical Growth in Anglican Congregations.

These are the statistics for this period. I will now discuss their significance in terms of the culture change occurring at this time.

The Relationship Between Education and Christianity.

By this period (1900-1942) the association between "schools" and Christianity was clearly established in the minds of Melanesians. The first step in becoming a convert was therefore to associate with a mission school established in a village. If a pagan village collectively decided that it wanted to become Christian, a deputation would be sent to the district missionary requesting that a school be established in their own village. On Guadalcanal and San Cristobal, which had been especially impervious to missionaries' advocacy for adopting Christianity, there were now many requests for schools. For example, writing to his wife from Guadalcanal in 1909, Wilson noted:

> It is marvelous to see how Christianity is spreading here. Bollen has carried it 80 miles down the coast . . . and bush teachers have just told me that every village in the bush wants a school now.[50]

From Makira Bay, San Cristobal, Bishop Wilson wrote in 1903:

> Yesterday, we came on to a place called Marau. As usual, we quietly discussed the school idea. When they heard it made peace, they said that it would be good. It is queer that all these places would like to begin schooling now. At Makira the chief told us plainly that we might start school as soon as we liked. I don't know how Wilson (the resident missionary on San Cristobal) will find teachers for all these places, but there are openings everywhere.[51]

Missionaries and their schools were a commodity now in demand by Melanesians, for as W. A. Uthwatt noted:

> . . . now the natives themselves are pleading that we may send them men. Where there are heathen, the man in charge of the district frequently receives deputations asking for teachers. They

> will build a school and a house for the teacher, will provide him with food, will come regularly to the daily services, and will send their children to school, if only we will give them a man. They want to be Christian. We cannot meet this demand . . . Never in the history of the Mission has the desire been so urgent or so general (1910-1911: 239).[52]

Indigenous Patterns of Conversion.

This increased interest in Christianity was manifest in different patterns. One of the most dramatic was found on the larger islands where there was a distinction between coastal and bush people.[53] On these islands, Christianity increasingly became a way of life on the coast, for it was here that the various missions established their centers, and it was the beach that symbolically represented the place where Melanesian-European culture contact was most intense. For many Melanesians in the interior of the larger islands, the choice to convert to Christianity and attend the mission school meant migrating from the bush to the coast. Bishop Wilson observed this phenomenon on Guadalcanal, and in writing to his wife in 1903 noted:

> I had a talk with a friendly chief from the next village. He says some friends of his far away in the bush are coming down this year to the Coast to come to school or get one of their own.[54]

With the cessation of warfare and headhunting during this period, life along the coast was far less precarious, and this undoubtedly contributed to the migration of islanders from the bush to the coast.

Another pattern of conversion was the movement of Melanesians from dispersed hamlets to nucleated villages. Thus a general residential pattern emerged during this period, in which pagans in the bush continued to live in dispersed hamlets, whereas Christians tended to live more in villages formed along the coast. Thus for many Melanesians, the choice to innovate and adopt Christinaity carried with it a shift in residential patterns involving migration from hamlets to villages and from the bush to the coast.[55]

Many of the newly created Christian villages formed during the first two decades of this century were the result of returning laborers, principally from Queensland but also from Fiji. This phenomenon was especially marked on the island of Malaita which had contributed such a large percent of the island labor force.

As a result of the "White Australia" policy, legislation was passed in 1901, prohibiting Melanesians from entering Queensland after March 31, 1904, and setting in motion the deportation of islanders back to their "homes."[56] Many Melanesians had undergone significant acculturation in Queensland and had no desire to return to the traditional way of life they had left in the islands. For others, the return to their own villages meant certain death, for they had initially escaped punishment by enlisting on a labor vessel, or had been accused of sorcery during their absence. Another deterrent was that people who had accumulated material goods while working on plantations did not want to return to their villages and be forced to give away everything they had brought with them from Queensland. Having to distribute their cargo was a frequent occurrence, following the indigenous pattern for the redistribution of personal wealth.[57]

Thus many Melanesians, who either returned of their own free will, or were forced home, desired to continue their acculturated life style as best they could in the islands. This led to the establishment of many Christian villages in the islands which cut across traditional lines of political and social structure.[58] As Hopkins observed of the Anglican settlements on Malaita:

> At Gnore Fou and in all our schools there was a mixture of coast men from the islets (artificial islands) with a certain number of bush men. Their common profession as seekers after Christianity united them, but sometimes it was a strain.[59]

The large Christian village of Fiu (pop. 300) on the southwest coast of Malaita was a conglomerate of five different communities in groups of huts. Hopkins noted that it was very difficult for these villagers to eliminate their traditional differences and hostilities, and merge into a common life. "Persecution from without was a great help towards fusing them into one body."[60]

Thus these villages were formed by islanders of diverse ethnic backgrounds who held in common the desire to perpetuate the Christian way of life they had learned in the Colonies, or to seek refuge from their own villages. Guadalcanal and Malaita, from where most of the Solomon Islands recruits had come, were the most affected by the returned laborers. It was here that the establishment of Christian villages by repatriated laborers was most dramatic. For example, by 1908 on Malaita, there were seventy Christian settlements around the coast, twenty-six of which were claimed by the Melanesian Mission.[61] In fact, it was in response to an appeal by returned laborers to the Resident Commissioner Charles Woodford, that Bishop Cecil Wilson appointed Arthur Hopkins to oversee the district work on North Malaita in 1902.[62] After several decades had passed, Hopkins observed that:

> The returned Kanaka[63] excitements were dying down; Missions were making headway; plantation work on neighbouring islands were (sic) an outlet for the most restless. The island was being opened up and the people no longer shut up in their little tribal districts were not necessarily enemies whenever out of them; widened bush paths helped and the many things once *tapu* could now be done harmlessly as experience proved. The thick atmosphere of mutual distrust began to lift and Christian ways were found not to bring disaster either on themselves or others, but rather peace and friendship. Then again the ferment caused by the

> mass return of Kanakas began to abate. They were being absorbed in their village, or in the schools, or on local plantations. Even to primitive intelligence the Christian village with all its imperfections, was a far better place than his own so small and fearful; to those who had gained by civilization it was the obvious place of refuge and hope.[64]

Although less dramatic and intense, there were parallels to the Malaita situation on other islands where Melanesians returned from the labor fields of Queensland and Fiji.

The choice to innovate and adopt Christianity as advocated by the missionaries was of course made by individuals, but the response was frequently a multi-individual response, in contrast to a mass movement.[65] That is, individuals established the new norm for the group which then led to whole groups choosing to become Christian. This frequently meant the establishing of a new Christian village where individuals could practice their understanding of Christian living as a corporate entity. Thus pagan and Christian villages were dispersed throughout a given district, and in some cases, a single village would be divided between Christian and pagan factions.[66]

Melanesian Motivations for Conversion.

The spread of Christianity during this period of penetration (1900-1942), portrays a significant contrast to the previous period of Melanesian-European culture contact. It now remains to try to understand some of the motivating forces behind this movement toward Christianity.[67]

I now move into an area of ethnopsychology which is always a difficult field of inquiry and explanation. It is important, however, to note that what motivates one islander to adopt Christianity may be quite different from that which motivates another. In addition, the level of understanding as to what was being adopted, and what the potential benefits and responsibilities of the new religion entailed, varied considerably from one convert to another. Notwithstanding these qualifying remarks, there emerges in the data a cluster of motivating factors that played an important role during this period. Briefly summarized, these were:

1. The explicit linkage between Christianity and schools, which meant education, and education was the passport for entry into the white man's world.
2. The desire for material objects of European origin, especially tobacco and cloth.
3. The desire for peace.
4. A connection to the outside world.
5. The adoption of Christianity because it was the religion of the

European, and thus it was perceived to be a religion of greater practical validity in the changing contact situation.[68]

6. The adoption of Christianity because of the influence and force of individual missionary personalities that attracted islanders and motivated them to become Christian.

This is not an exhaustive list but it includes the primary motivating influences with the exception of one very important factor. This is the positive emotional experience that some converts had in embracing Christianity. This was communicated to fellow Melanesians and increased the response. It is important to note that not all motivation can be observed or inferred, and undoubtedly there were some who became Christians for the religious experience itself, and not as a presumed guaranteed means to a measurable, materialistic end. Each of the factors enumerated above will now be briefly discussed.[69]

1. Christianity and Schools. Anglican Christianity was presented as a religion of the book — not only was the Bible important, but the Prayer Book was a companion aid to worship of equal, if not greater, stature.[70] Thus literacy was part and parcel of the conversion process. To many Melanesians, it was the European's ability to read and write that seemed to be the key that unlocked the secret to his vast stores of material well-being. Hogbin, through the words of a pagan Solomon Islander, provides us with an emic or insider's view of the value of learning to read and write:

> "You white men are like us," he said to me. "You have only two eyes, two hands, two feet. How are you different? Because you can read books. That is why you can buy axes, knives, clothing, ships and motor-cars. You buy a passage in a steamer and visit places of which we have only heard, where people live in stone houses one on top of the other. You do not have to work hard; you pay us a little money and we work for you, carrying heavy boxes on our backs. All this we know comes from books. If we understood books we could do this. If we could read your books we would have money and possessions" (1939: 180-181).

The Melanesian Mission emphasized the use of the vernacular or of Mota, the mission *lingua franca*, rather than English.[71] Nevertheless, the desire to learn to read and write was a strong motivating factor for many islanders seeking to have a school established in their midst. The importance of learning to read and write is underscored by the Malaita District Officer, reporting in 1932; referring to the Bali sub-district of Malaita, he notes:

> Missionary societies have made certain progress, notably the South Sea Evangelical Mission, and, in the island districts, the Melanesian Mission (Church of England), but the greater majority of the people still carry on the old-time "akalo" worship and have slight use for Christianity except as a means of obtaining "white man's education."[72]

The invitation to the mission to start a school was the symbolic signal that the group was now ready to entertain the possibility of becoming Christian. Elders today still talk about their conversion to Christianity in terms of "going to school," or of pagan days as "before the school came."[73]

2. Material Advantages. The acquisition of Western material goods as a motivation for adopting Christianity and associating with the Melanesian Mission was not new to this period of mission contact. This was a contributing factor behind the acceptance of Christianity in the earlier period of Melanesian-missionary interaction as well. There were now, of course, more sources from which material goods could be obtained, but this desire for imported goods continued to function as a motivating factor for conversion in this period. Hilliard (1978: 166) notes that as late as 1925, the islanders of Santa Catalina, just south of San Cristobal, informed the Mission that they were prepared to have a school as long as gifts of tobacco and calico were forthcoming. Hopkins met with a similar response in the Tai Lagoon of Malaita where he observed that:

> In the early days progress was slow and the welcome warmed by visions of white man's things and gifts. From each islet canoes would shoot out to gather around the boat, and the islets themselves were fringed with brown, chiefly feminine folk. From their united voices arose a shrill cry of "Si firi, si firi," i.e., a bit of tobacco. The male counter-bass from the canoes around would be "tabac, tabac." There were so many islets that it took them quite a while to learn that my boat was not a free automatic tobacco discharging machine. When they discovered that finally, visits would be quicker and the welcome less effusive but more real.[74]

The traditional religion of Melanesians was a pragmatic one, and so concern with social and economic well-being was of paramount importance in religious belief and ritual. It is therefore not unreasonable to assume that their interpretation of Christianity would be similar. That is, the obvious wealth and power of the European was related to his practice of Christianity. Thus by adopting the white man's religion, the Melanesian attempted to insure his own social and material well-being. Because of the nature of this phenomenon, it is difficult to document precise cases of individuals who adopted Christianity for this reason alone. Nevertheless, the increased rise of cargo cult movements in Melanesia after European contact confirms that this was indeed a factor involved in the initial conversion process of some Melanesians.[75]

Related to the linkage between the adoption of Christianity and economic well-being, was the desire by many Melanesians to have a European missionary in their midst. His presence conferred status on the Big Man and his followers who claimed to be his patron. Hopkins recounts the enthusiastic reception he received in 1902 when he was first put down at his station on North Malaita where the residents of the Christian village:

> . . . were there to eagerly welcome us. And their Fera-si-boa (a pagan artificial islet) and other friends were clamorous in their reception and vociferous in their assurances, and in high excitement at the prospect of a white man come to live among them. The white man meant to some, great vague hopes of money, trade, of Government support, of prestige that would make their foes look small.[76]

3. Desire for Peace. The traditional checks and balances of Melanesian warfare were upset in the nineteenth century with the introduction of Western firearms and poisons.[77] As a result, the increase in aggressive behavior expressed in internal feuding and external raiding created institutions that were highly anxiety-ridden. The costs to the islanders began to far outweigh the benefits. Missionaries capitalized on this by stressing the relationship between Christianity and peace. They contrasted the pagan religion which was inextricably bound up with violence, warfare, and in some places, headhunting and cannibalism, with Christianity as a "Way of Peace" where aggressive and violent behavior was inappropriate to the new social norms. G. White (1979) and Jackson (1972, 1975) have documented how Christianity as a way of peace was a persuasive alternative to the anxiety-ridden life of raiding and defense from raiding, in the conversion of so many islanders on Santa Isabel. The dynamics of conversion and the motivation for peaceful living which White describes for Santa Isabel, had similarities elsewhere in Melanesia. He notes:

> Pressure from raiding headhunters engendered the desire for peace on Santa Isabel and missionaries supplied the cultural innovations necessary to institutionalize it. Raiding was eagerly abandoned by Isabel people because it had become a distinct burden during the later half of the nineteenth century when raids by marauding headhunters from the Western Solomons drastically disrupted social life on the island. At the same time, the (Anglican) Melanesian Mission supplied an ideology of peace linked with a ritual-religious framework which could be assimilated to indigenous concepts of mana and the supernatural . . . The suppression of raiding was accomplished more easily through holistic change—supplanting one set of beliefs and practices by another—than it could have been through piecemeal change which eliminated raiding but left the religious and moral system intact (1979: 110).[78]

Peace was desired, and in very pragmatic, Melanesian terms, a Santa Isabel bushman inquired of Bishop Wilson, "What will it cost us to buy this new teaching which gives peace, for we are tired of fighting."[79] On a visit to Choiseul in 1900, Wilson encountered a Big Man who wanted the peace offered by the Mission. He narrates the episode:

> The chief enquired if the ship were a man-of-war, and when we said it was not, but a school ship, he asked, "What is a school?"

> We said, "It teaches, and we have a teaching which gives peace." It took a long time for Bosi to understand; then he said, "Why did you not come before? Two months ago the men of Bilhua over there (New Georgia) came, and they killed thirty of my people and my three sons, and they took my wife and children, and further up the coast they killed thirty more. Why did you not come before with this teaching of peace?" (1932: 239-240).

Whatever the costs entailed, many Melanesians chose to endorse Christianity with the anticipation that a more peaceful and stable way of life would be forthcoming. Clearly, the "Gospel of Peace" as the missionaries described their message, met the felt needs of many Melanesians who wanted to escape from the more anxiety-ridden institutions of their culture. Christianity provided a *modus operandi* with a new behavioral code and a supporting ideology to provide sufficient justification for change.[80]

4. Connection to the Outside World. As noted above, during this period the complete isolation of Melanesian communities from European contact gave way to greater interaction with the white man and exposure to his material goods. Many Melanesians perceived that Christianity in general and the missionary in particular gave them greater access and linkage to the world beyond Melanesia. Access to knowledge of the European's world was sought after, and any action which increased the possibility of gaining more European goods was followed avidly. This factor was more significant in the early part of this period, for experience soon taught them that Christianity and the presence of a missionary did not automatically increase intercourse with the outside world to the degree many Melanesians desired to achieve.

5. Christianity as the White Man's Religion. Another inducement to conversion which was also more significant in the earlier part of the period than in the later, was the fact that Christianity was the religion of the European. Linton (1940) draws our attention to the fact that frequently in programs of directed change the introduced idea is associated with the advocate and so is adopted for that reason. He states:

> If (a novelty) originates outside the group, its association will derive not only from the innovators but also from the donor society. In other words, the attitudes of the receiving group toward the donor group will attach themselves, at least initially, to the elements of culture which contact between the two groups makes available for borrowing. (1940: 484)

The changing cultural context of the period gave Christianity a new prestige it had lacked in the previous period. Since European material objects were esteemed, it was not irrational for the Melanesian to assume that European religion must be superior as well. In addressing this phenomenon, Guiart has suggested that:

> Melanesians and Polynesians discovered functionalism and structuralism for themselves through being confronted with the white

> man's culture and society. Among other fine points, they grasped that religion had a definite function inside our world. They realized that if they were ever to come to our level they would have to accept our religion. At first they ascribed to white men a kind of god-like status; but this view passed. The native people were soon trying to think out how they might become the equals of these pale-skinned, rich, powerful, at times naive or ruthless mortals. The simplest way appeared to be adoption of their religion (1970: 123).

Concomitantly, the validity of the traditional religion was increasingly called into question in the face of changing conditions which significantly altered the traditional Melanesian way of life. Increasingly, depopulation and European contact and control left many Melanesian communities demoralized.[81]

For many Melanesians, the adoption of Christianity served indeed as the "New Way" to respond meaningfully to the new conditions of the twentieth century, which had altered traditional Melanesian society and culture. Their new faith helped to serve as an adaptive mechanism for their continued survival. Belshaw (1954:70) notes that, "Christianity was everywhere regarded as a new form of ritual devised to placate or encourage superior spirits."[82]

As extended contact with the European community soon taught the Melanesians, not all white men subscribed to Christian beliefs and practices. Thus the earlier connection between Europeans and Christianity tended to erode, and by the end of the period it may not have been such an important factor in motivating islanders to adopt Christianity.

6. Influence of Individual Missionaries in Attracting Some Converts to Christianity. In the initial phases of missionary-islander contact, the models of Christianity were those given by the missionaries. Missionaries were also frequently the champions of islanders' rights *vis a vis* government and commercial interests, and this would have undoubtedly influenced Melanesians in their decision to convert.[83] As the number of Melanesian converts increased, however, and there were more indigenous clergy, there were also more models of Christian belief and behavior. Thus during this era the force of the missionary's personality in influencing islanders to convert may have been a more important factor at the beginning of the period than it was at the end. This is not to say his power and influence decreased. To the contrary, it **increased** during this period, but as a magnetic force attracting Melanesians to Christianity, it probably began to wane.[84]

In concluding this section on Melanesian motivations for conversion to Christianity it is important to reiterate that islanders chose to innovate and adopt Christianity from a complex of multiple motivations, both latent and manifest. The six primary motivating factors discussed above functioned together as a whole, and not in isolation from each other. For the most part,

Christianity as advocated by Anglican missionaries was perceived by Melanesians as part and parcel of a total package of European influences. Power over sickness with medicine, the novelty of "schools," the wealth and prestige afforded those who associated with the European missionary and mission, were all important elements in the configuration of Melanesians' response in choosing to innovate and adopt Christianity as their own.

The Melanesian Brotherhood: An Example of Indigenous Organization and Initiative

I now move to a discussion of what one anthropologist called, "One of the most outstanding indigenous movements in the Christian Church throughout the Pacific."[85] This is the creation of the Melanesian Brotherhood by a Solomon Islander in 1925.

During this period of penetration there was an increasing paternalistic trend in the Melanesian Mission, but there was also a corresponding increase in Melanesians' desire for indigenously created and operated institutions within the church.[86] By 1925 Melanesian life in the villages had become dull. Gone were the anxiety-ridden, but exciting, days of endemic raiding, headhunting and cannibalism. The days when a young man could anticipate the adventure of going off to Fiji or Queensland for new experiences were also gone. There were few opportunities outside village life except working on European-run plantations within the islands, or filling a few openings in government service as clerks or policemen. It is against this background of awakened aspirations but limited opportunities that the Melanesian Brotherhood arose. It was an indigenously inspired and organized effort which met a felt need in Melanesian society at that time.

The principal actor in this drama was a young man from Guadalcanal, Ini Kopuria, who had been an outstanding student and leader at the Norfolk Island school.[87] However, he disappointed the missionaries by not returning to the somewhat dull life of a village teacher as they had anticipated he would do. Instead he joined the Native Armed Constabulary in the Solomon Islands, where, given his abilities and leadership, he soon rose to the rank of sergeant. In 1924 he was in an accident which hospitalized him. During his convalescence he underwent an intense religious experience and had a vision, the outcome of which germinated the idea of forming a Brotherhood of Melanesians to take the message of Christianity to the extant pagan villages, first on Guadalcanal, and then throughout Melanesia. He reasoned, "I have visited all the villages as a police sergeant and they all know me; why not go to them now as a missionary?"[88]

Fortunately for Ini, he met with two sympathetic supporters in Arthur Hopkins and Bishop John Steward, who channeled his desire for missionary service into the notion of a monastic brotherhood of Melanesians, whose primary purpose was "to proclaim the teaching of Jesus Christ among the heathen, not to work among Christians."[89]

To implement a strategy for achieving this goal, Ini first cleared his own land which he had given as a headquarters for the Brotherhood, and built a house there for the future brothers who would join him. He then toured with the *Southern Cross* on its first voyage of 1926 through the islands, sharing his dreams with other young men, and appealing for them to join him. He also published his ideas in the Mota language paper, *O Sala Ususur*, which circulated throughout the Mission's area. His appeal netted him six volunteers: three from Santa Isabel, two from the Russell Islands, and one from Guadalcanal.[90]

The Brotherhood was organized into households of not more than twelve brothers each, with an elder brother over each household. This assured the small corporate nature of the working unit. One brother was elected annually to be the head of the Brotherhood, and all were under the authority of the bishop who was designated as the Father of the Brotherhood. This organizational structure provided for a chain of command, but also preserved the spirit of egalitarianism which was so important to the Melanesians. Each brother vowed not to marry, not to take any pay, and to obey those in authority. These vows of celibacy, poverty and obedience were renewed annually on October 28th, St. Simon's and St. Jude's Day, as the brothers gathered together at their headquarters at Tabalia on Guadalcanal. Many stayed in the Melanesian Brotherhood for 4 or 5 years, and a few for life.

The brothers perceived their mission as an evangelistic enterprise in "opening up"[91] pagan villages for teachers and priests to follow in consolidating their efforts by bringing the group from an initial encounter with Christianity to incorporation within the larger context of the whole Church. Thus, one of their early rules was that they would not stay in a village for more than three months. After that, it was the responsibility of others to come in and continue with the village while they pressed on to "open up" new pagan areas. The brothers always went about in pairs, never alone, dressed in a simple black loin cloth and a white sash.[92]

Through the years the brothers gained a considerable reputation among the Melanesians for their *mana*, as several miraculous incidents were associated with their work. For example, one of the often repeated stories involved two of the first volunteers, Dudley Bale and Moffat Ohigita, both from Santa Isabel, who went to a pagan village nearly 8,000 feet up into the mountains of Guadalcanal. After climbing a steep cliff, dragging themselves up by creepers, they entered a village and were kindly received by the local Big Man. By the next morning, however, things had changed, for the village pagan priest had come to the Big Man in the night telling him to "Drive them out. I have seen a third brother (Jesus) with them whose face shines and terrifies me. Let us have nothing to do with them."[93]

The first year of the Brotherhood's operations were unsuccessful, for they were rejected in one village after another. But an unsuccessful beginning was no deterrent, for in 1927 a household was opened on Santa Cruz, and later work began on Malaita and the Polynesian outliers of Sikaiana in 1929, and Ontong Java in 1933. By 1935 the small band of seven brothers had increased to 128, far surpassing the maximum of twenty that Bishop Steward had envisioned it might obtain. An analysis of the list of brothers shows that the greatest number of volunteers had come from those islands which had most recently begun to innovate in accepting Christianity. In a report of the Brothers' Conference of 1935 it was stated that:

> The number of Brothers from different islands is not without interest as a test of their missionary keenness. Mala (Malaita), providing forty-five Brothers, is far ahead of the others, and then come Raga (Pentecost) with twenty-two, while Gela, with its church population of over 4,000, is by far the lowest, as there are only four Brothers from there. The other figures are: — Bugotu (Santa Isabel) 13, Guadalcanar (Guadalcanal) 11, New Britain 9, San Cristoval and Reef Island 8 each, Ulawa 5, Savo 2, and Sikaiana 1. There are none from the Banks' Islands, Tikopia, Santa Cruz, or Laube (Russell Islands).[94]

The Brotherhood spread beyond Island Melanesia to Fiji, New Britain and New Guinea, and today has expanded its missionary outreach to Carpenteria where they are successfully working with the Australian Aborigines. As the New Guinea Highlands were opened up, the Melanesian Brotherhood pursued its evangelistic efforts there. Between 1955 and 1957 the brothers were responsibile for the conversion of forty-five villages involving 9,500 people in New Britain and New Guinea.[95]

As an indigenous organization it succeeded because it met the felt needs of many islanders in a way that was thoroughly Melanesian, outside the European dominated structure of the Melanesian Mission. It provided not only adventure in an otherwise dull environment, but an outlet for religious zeal and presented a challenge for many which led to a greater internalization of their religious experience. It is not surprising then, that many former brothers later became priests and village catechists.

The original plan of the Brotherhood had to be altered through time, for they "opened up" pagan villages faster than they could be supplied with trained teachers to follow up and establish schools. As a result, when the brothers left after three months, the villagers either returned to their traditional religion, or as happened more often, they accepted a teacher from another mission. Fox (1962: 75) reports that this happened in at least thirty places of which he was aware. Today the original rule of working only among pagans has been altered, so that not only do brothers stay longer in pagan villages, but they also go to areas that have been Christian for many years but have lapsed into nominal faith. This "revival" aspect of their work has become increasingly important in later years. It is interesting to note that one of the areas they returned to in this capacity in the early 1960's, was to Mota — the first Melanesian Island to respond to the advocacy of the Melanesian Mission and adopt Christianity back in the 1870's.

One would expect that for a Mission that advocated overtly the goal of an indigenous church, the innovation of an indigenous religious order like the Melanesian Brotherhood would have been welcomed and enthusiastically supported. However, the opposite occurred, and the European missionaries were "critical of the Brothers — unjustly so, so the Melanesians thought."[96] Instead of encouraging them in their evangelistic role, missionaries used the brothers as a cheap labor force for doing all sorts of odd jobs, from rebuilding a church, or helping to move a school, to acting as caretakers of a mission station.[97] Fox notes that:

> They were not regarded as members of a Religious Order — except by the Melanesians, who have always held the Brothers in the highest honour and treated them almost with reverence; but then they know how hard a Brother's life really is, what real sacrifices he makes, and what a deep and true motive for becoming a Brother many of them have (1962: 76).

Not only were the missionaries lethargic in their support for the Brotherhood, but the brothers were frequently viewed askance by the native clergy. In a real sense, the brothers were seen as spiritual competitors for the power and authority of the clergy, who tended to view themselves as the spiritual elites within the emerging Melanesian Christian society and the established Anglican Church, and so they resented any competition. It is not difficult to understand why some clergy felt threatened, for they were the professional, well-trained and established leaders. In contrast, the brothers were mere amateurs. In Melanesia, however, it is one's *mana*, not one's credentials, that is important. Thus while the indigenous Anglican priests may be feared and respected, the brothers are loved and admired by village Christians.

To insure a wide base of support independent of the Mission hierarchy and organization, Ini Kopuria established a village level counterpart to the work of the brothers — a Christian order whereby villagers, through prayers and alms, would support the work of the Brotherhood. This was the Order of Companions of the Brothers, whose efforts were to support their own Melanesian missionaries. Today in many Anglican villages, prayers are said daily or weekly for the work of the Brotherhood, and Companions are required to do something practical in their own villages, such as cleaning the church, keeping the chapel grounds in good order, serving at the Eucharist, collecting firewood for the sick and elderly, etc.[98]

Thus the Melanesian Brotherhood and its village counterpart, the Companions, represent a truly indigenous response to the culture-contact situation. The brothers were no longer simply the missionized; they became the missionaries to their own people, and evangelized in their own Melanesian way. The Melanesian Brotherhood represents the desire for Melanesian initiative and organization in an environment that was increasingly dominated by paternalistic Europeans. Although the circumstances that led up to the formation of the Brotherhood have changed since the 1920's, the Melanesian Brotherhood is still functioning strongly today, adapting to changing circumstances, but continuing to play an important role in the life of the Melanesian church, and helping to meet the needs of many islanders.

During the time of my fieldwork (1977-1978) there were seventy-eight members of the Brotherhood, in addition to many novices undergoing two years of training in preparation for becoming a brother. I had the opportunity to interview many brothers and asked them about their experiences within the Brotherhood and about their motivation for joining the group. I was impressed with the deep level of commitment many had to their Christian faith and the work of the Church. Many told me that it was only in the company of the Brotherhood that they had come to really understand the meaning of Christianity, even though they had been born and raised in nominally Christian villages. As the number of pagan villages has decreased, more of the brothers are voicing concern for their own villages where they see an incomprehensible Christianity practiced in apathy and ignorance.

The Melanesian Brotherhood represents a struggle for indigeneity. It is an attempt by Melanesians to take an introduced religion of foreign origin, and make it their own, adapting it to the island context. It represents the tension between "grass-roots" Christianity at the village level, and institutionalized Christianity as portrayed by the established Melanesian Mission. It has been successful as a Melanesian innovation because its training program has been directed to the local situation and at the level of its participants. It has functioned with clearly defined goals, i.e., evangelism, and has engendered a tremendous spirit of dedication among its participants. It has been an organization whose function has been independent of the professional clergy, providing an opportunity of service for Melanesians whose educational background has not included formal theological training. And finally, it has a strong emphasis on community life which identifies readily with the corporate existence of most Melanesians living in rural villages.[99]

Missionary-Melanesian Interpersonal Relations

In this section discussion will be given to the nature of the missionary-islander relationships as they evolved during this period from the turn of the century to the outbreak of World War II. There are two themes that permeated the dynamic arena of Missionary-Melanesian relationships: (1)

an increase in mission paternalism, and (2) the belief among Europeans that the Melanesians were a dying race. Each of these will be discussed in this section. I will then discuss three different missionaries as paradigm models of behavior found within the Melanesian Mission during this period.

Paternalism in Intercultural Relationships.

Bishop G.A. Selwyn, the founder of the Melanesian Mission, was fond of using the analogy of a "black net floated by white corks" to describe the principle of developing an indigenous network of lay teachers and clergy, guided by the supervision of European missionaries. From our present-day perspective such an analogy is blatantly paternalistic in nature, but its intent in the 1840's was not meant to be so. Selwyn saw the "white corks" as necessary in the beginning, but only as a temporary measure until Melanesians filled that role. Nevertheless, the seeds of paternalism were sown early in the Melanesian Mission, for by 1876, after a brief visit to Mota in the Banks' Islands, missionary John Still wrote:

> They sadly want someone to stir up their dormant energies. The school house begins to look very shabby, and the church wants repairing or rebuilding . . . It shows how difficult it is for these natives to sustain any effort towards advancement when left to depend on themselves. They must have someone to lean upon, **at least for the present** (my emphasis)."[100]

"At least for the present" was frequently the argument given for continued domination by European missionaries which fostered a state of dependency in the Melanesian converts. However, by the time of Bishop Wilson's episcopacy (1894-1911), this incipient paternalism had become very explicit. Speaking of the indigenous village teachers, Wilson wrote in 1902:

> They do better work when their white "father" is nearer at hand than when he is absent, but even in his absence their work will not cease, nor the Church fall to pieces.

Nevertheless, he concludes, "They will never attain to that complete independence for which Bishop Selwyn, our founder used to hope."[101] That is, the white corks would **always** be necessary to support the black net. Acting on this belief, Wilson pursued a vigorous campaign for recruiting more European missionaries. When he was consecrated bishop in 1894 he had a European staff of nine, but by 1902 that had increased more than three-fold to twenty-eight, while there were only ten indigenous clergy and most of these were old men.[102] It is significant that in his seventeen years as head of the Melanesian Mission, Bishop Wilson ordained only three Melanesian priests. The belief in the inherent capacity for Melanesians to become priests and spiritual leaders to their own people, which Selwyn and Patteson had held so strongly, had increasingly eroded away, to be replaced by paternalism.

G. A. Selwyn and especially Patteson, had held strongly to the belief in the inherent capacity for Melanesians to evangelize their own people and raise up a solid indigenous clergy to lead the Melanesian Church. During this period of penetration, however, that belief was replaced by the notion that few were worthy and all would have to be superintended by a European missionary. Speaking of Nggela, W. A. Uthwatt, Archdeacon of the Solomons, wrote in 1910:

> Most of the natives are of the third generation of Christians. Their zeal and enthusiasm are reported to have died away and the villages need constant supervision and encouragement in order that the earnestness of their religion may be maintained.[103]

Such a comment leads one to question the depths to which Christianity had penetrated those Melanesian societies which were ostensibly Christian. It is a telling statement on the degree to which the adopted religion had become integrated into Melanesian society and culture.[104] It is interesting to note that the superficiality of Christianity became a ready rationale for the missionaries to become even more paternalistic. Since the adopted religion had not penetrated the depths of Melanesian experience, islanders lapsed into a state of lethargic indifference, leading missionaries to conclude that the Melanesian converts had to be heavily "supervised" if Christianity was to prevail.

W. J. Durrad was one of those many new recruits who came out to Melanesia under Bishop Wilson. His fresh perspective led him to conclude that for many Melanesians, Christianity was a superficial experience. Writing in 1908 he noted:

> Perhaps it seems presumptuous and absurd to dogmatize, from an acquaintance with only one very small district such as the Torres, on the grasp which the native has of Christianity. But the conviction becomes clearer that Christianity is still largely an exotic in Melanesia. It has not yet laid hold of the spirit and genius of the race. Evidence that this is so is furnished by noticing how readily and spontaneously natives will slip back in any crisis into the old forms which enshrine their faith and the faith of their fathers, the charms, the incantations, and the magic.[105]

The mission adopted the notion that the solution to the superficiality of second and third generation Christians must lie in increasing European supervision over their island children, rather than encouraging indigenous adaptations of Christianity that would clothe it with Melanesian meaning and functional significance. Durrad wrote pessimistically that, "Without adequate supervision it is entirely hopeless to expect the Church in the Banks' Islands to be a living one; certainly it will never be a growing one."[106]

In 1925 it was noted that, "Twenty native Priests are at work. They need white supervision and do not yet fill the place of the white men, but under their guidance do in their own way invaluable work."[107]

Ten years later, the Melanesian Mission had twenty-four European clergy, fourteen laymen, and twenty-six women at work in the Mission, while there were forty-nine Melanesian clergy and more than 700 village catechists. The conclusion drawn by Hopkins was that:

> With the scanty supply of European clergy available for district work it is obvious that the control of the islands and villages, from a religious point of view, is necessarily in the hands of the Melanesian clergy (1936: 35).[108]

Note what had happened during 85 years of missionary activity! The earlier goal of raising up a "native clergy" now seems to have been neatly reversed. Melanesian clergy were given "control of the islands and villages," **not** because this was still a Mission objective, but because there were not enough white missionaries to go around.

The perceived inferior status of Melanesian clergy *vis a vis* European staff, was demonstrated in several concrete ways. For example, wages for indigenous priests and teachers had been a generous £25 and £10 per year respectively in the 1870's, but reduced to £15 and £3 during the first decade of this century.[109] Similarly, Melanesian clergy were increasingly excluded from policy making activities. For example, as one of his last acts before resigning, Bishop Wilson called a conference in 1911 of all the European missionaries to discuss major policy issues, but the Melanesian clergy were excluded. One of the decisions made at this conference was that in the future a conference of Melanesian clergy and head teachers should be held every three years, but this was never to be.[110]

Under the leadership of Bishop Baddeley (1932-1947) the racial distinction between European missionaries and Melanesian clergy was even more exacerbated. Thus for example, when the new *Southern Cross VII* arrived in 1933, the age-old mission tradition of European and Melanesian clergy taking meals together on the ship was discontinued, the excuse being that it was too expensive to maintain such a custom with the growing number of Melanesian clergy. As Hilliard (1978: 272) notes, "To dine with the bishop on board was a special privilege, no longer taken for granted." Despite the efforts of the Mission to hide behind the transparent shield of financial exigency, it is clearly evident that the missionaries' relationships with Melanesians were far more racist and paternalistic than they had been in the earliest period of the Mission.

This theme of paternalism we have been tracing through this period, however, was not a phenomenon unique to the Melanesian Mission. To the contrary, in contrast with other missionary organizations in this same area and time period, the Melanesian Mission was surprisingly egalitarian in its relationship with the islanders. Paternalism in the Melanesian Mission was simply a reflection of an underlying structural principle — the imposition of colonialism on indigenous societies. This principle of structural inequalities was a child of Colonial rule, and the missionary who did not fall victim to such an insidious ideology was a rare individual.[111]

Roland Allen, an Anglican missionary who worked in China at the turn of the century, captures the essence of this missionary paternalism that became so manifest in the first several decades of this century on nearly every mission field:

> We have desired to help them. We have been anxious to do something for them. And we have done much. We have done everything for them. We have taught them, baptised them, shepherded them. We have managed their funds, ordered their services, built their churches, provided their teachers. We have nursed them, fed them, doctored them. We have done everything for them except acknowledge any equality. We have done everything for them, but very little with them. We have done everything for them, except give place to them. We have treated them as "dear children," but not as "brethren" (1962: 143).

The Melanesians as a Dying Race.

A corollary to missionary paternalism was the widespread belief, among economists and other European scholars, that the Melanesians were a dying race whose future, like the Tasmanians, was inevitable extinction. This view was expressed by the Melanesian Mission, as for example in Bishop Wilson's comments written in 1904:

> Ten years ago we had 8,929 baptized people, and now we have not quite 13,000, and yet there have never been less than 1,000 persons baptized in each of these years, and in 1900 the number baptized was 1,800. There have probably been at least 13,000 people baptized in the last 10 years, which would give us, if none had died at all, 22,000 Christians now.[112]

With a loss of 41 percent of baptized Christians in ten years, Wilson concluded:

> Our people are one of those sick children in God's great family . . . They have but a short time to live, and all that can be done is done for them, that their short lives might be brightened. A dying race should not promote contempt, but sympathy, and with sympathy, help. We are placed then by God in His infirmary, to work amongst a dying race; but a race which will certainly die a Christian death.[113]

This belief that Melanesians were doomed to extinction was not peculiar only to the majority of Anglican missionaries, but also reflected a popular notion held by the Colonial government. Charles Woodford, Resident Commissioner of the Solomon Islands, wrote to the High Commissioner, Sir Everad Im Thurn in 1909, that:

> . . . nothing in the way of the most paternal legislation or fostering care, carried out at any expense whatever, can prevent the eventual extinction of the Melanesian race in the Pacific. This I look upon as a fundamental fact and as certain as the rising and setting of the sun.[114]

It is interesting to note that the government responded to the "inevitable extinction of the Melanesians" by turning its concern to ways in which their land could "be shaped to the best advantage of the British Empire."[115] A proposal was submitted to the Colonial Office to import labor from India, as had been done in Fiji, to work the European plantations in the Solomon Islands, thus solving two problems at once for the British Empire — overpopulation in India and depopulation and subsequent underdevelopment of land in Melanesia. To the regret of the High Commissioner and the Lever Pacific Plantations Ltd., the India Office rejected the scheme in December 1911, and the Solomon Islands was saved from what would have been a tragic mistake.[116]

The problem of depopulation was worst in the northern New Hebrides and Banks' Islands, followed by Santa Cruz and then the Solomons. But the pattern in the Solomons was uneven, for Malaita seemed to suffer the least, while San Cristobal experienced severe depopulation. The principal causes of depopulation from 1870 to 1910 had been recruiting for the labor trade, internal fighting with European weapons, and infanticide, but after this period, the introduction of European diseases seems to have been the main killer.

Diseases were transported by ships, and the Melanesian Mission's *Southern Cross* was not immune, frequently leaving a trail of death as it plied through the islands.[117] One of the most serious episodes occurred in 1931 when influenza brought by the *Southern Cross* to Malaita killed 1,100 islanders.[118] The introduced diseases causing the most death were pulmonary illnesses (influenza, tuberculosis, bronchitis, and pneumonia). In addition, other illnesses, when introduced into a population without any immunity, could have a devastating effect. Fox comments on the severity of this problem in San Cristobal:

> Every year an epidemic of dysentery went through the islands. In 1910 there were, near Pamua 5 small bush villages, about 200 people; when the epidemic of that year was over no one was left alive in those villages (1967: 45).

Other introduced diseases such as whooping cough, polio, measles and yaws, as well as leprosy and venereal disease, had a debilitating effect on the population and contributed to depopulation.

Mission villages were not exempt from the wrath of disease, and the Christian God was not perceived as a protector of Melanesians against this scourge. In fact, to the contrary, many villages were loath to accept a school for fear that it would bring disease and death in its train. For example, on San Cristobal, "The Lord of Peace" was preached to a gathering of men by the missionaries, and:

> After two short addresses the natives were consulted among themselves and on the whole they were inclined to have a school. They fully agreed that the Christian religion, which preached peace, was better than their own way of life, but they hesitated because they thought that the white men's religion would mean the introduction of white men's sickness, such as measles and influenza.[119]

Interestingly, it was also the belief of the Resident Commissioner of the Solomons, Charles Woodford, that the population density of the Solomons was "in inverse ratio to the degree of civilisation exhibited."[120]

Introduced diseases certainly were a cause of depopulation. A popular notion in the first few decades of this century, however, held that Melanesians were dying from *tedium vitae*, a loss of interest in life and desire to live. The most articulate exposition of this view was by the anthropologist W. H. R. Rivers (1922) who wrote of the "Psychological Factor" in the decline of Melanesian populations. Rivers was sympathetic to the work of the Melanesian Mission and advocated a vigorous Christianity as a functional substitute that would restore to Melanesians the zest for life they had once had in their traditional society. His views were echoed by members of the Melanesian Mission. For example, Hopkins observed that:

> The islands are now being rapidly brought under the control of alien influences—those of the missionary, the trader and the government official. The efforts made by the natives to adjust themselves to these influences are emotional and exhausting. The reaction tends to lead to ennui and death, unless a real Christian faith vitalizes both the white and the brown. This means mutual service, not one-sided exploitation (1928b: 543).

Similarly, the positive influence of Christianity on Melanesia was articulated by Ivens (1918: 189) who believed that, "Christianity comes to them as a means of insuring both individual and social vigor and only in so far as they become Christian will they be saved from extinction." In an article entitled, "Christian Influences on a Dying Race," missionary Robert Freeth argued in a similar vein, stating that:

> Surely it cannot be mere coincidence that the three most Christian districts in Melanesia are at the same time the only three places which show a marked increase in population. Moreover, it is not unreasonable to judge the general virility of the race by the birth rate (1916: 393).

Freeth (1916: 389), responding to the rhetorical question, what is our duty toward "a race suffering from physical, social, moral and spiritual degeneration?" answered, "As Christians we must be filled with pity towards these childish creatures eking out their existence in ignorance and heathen darkness."

Writing in 1922, Durrad emphatically stated that:

> The great need is for Government action, drastic, decisive and immediate. Nothing short of this will avail to save the Melanesians from extinction. Missionaries can do little or nothing to prevent it because they have no power to make or enforce laws dealing with purely secular matters (1922: 21).

There is little doubt that the perception of Melanesians as a dying race influenced missionary policy at least indirectly, if not directly. If the Mission was called to minister at the deathbed of a dying people, then there would have been less urgency in raising up a native clergy to lead an indigenous Church in Melanesia; by all indications, that Church was doomed to extinction.[121]

Missionary Models: A Study in Contrasts.

Missionization as an external force in culture change is not a monolithic influence, but is a structural configuration composed of mission policies, institutions, and the personalities of individual missionaries interacting with indigenes. It is important, therefore, in understanding the role of the missionary in culture change, that we look carefully at different models of missionary-indigene interaction. In this sense the Melanesian Mission presents an excellent case study, for a gamut of missionary types existed on the mission staff. Three of these missionaries will now be examined as paradigm models of interpersonal relations in the cross-cultural context of Melanesia.

1. Richard P. Fallowes—Agitator and Reformer.

Richard P. Fallowes represents a missionary model of ambivalence and paradox, for while overtly paternalistic, thoroughly enjoying his role as a "White Chief" among "his" islanders,[122] he also "won the confidence and affection of all the people because he was their champion and defender."[123] A graduate of Cambridge and ordained Anglican priest, he arrived in the Solomons in 1929 as "a young inexperienced upstart from (the) UK,"[124] filled with visions of nurturing a Christian Melanesian society, free from impurity, and worshipping God in the best of the ritualistic Anglo-Catholic tradition.[125] He was soon appointed to Santa Isabel as the European district priest where it took only a short time for him to discover that beneath the placid surface of this all-Anglican island, which had become the showpiece of the Melanesian Mission, there was considerable discrepancy between the

Christian ideal, and the actual Melanesian behavior. "Nothing but sickness, sin and sorrow have been my lot," he wrote despondantly to his sister after a tour of his district:

> I wonder if you can realize the sorrow that falls heavily on the heart of a priest as he listens to the confessions of grievous sins of those he had come to love and hope so much of. And here on Bugotu (Santa Isabel) the devil is very active and sometimes I seem all alone in combatting the evil that is around me. . . . The forces of evil are so many and so strong and when those forces destroy the good one has laboured to achieve it brings one very nearly to the breaking point.[126]

And what was this evil force against which the young missionary felt so compelled to do battle? "Adultery is one if not the prevailing sin of the native,"[127] he wrote; it is "the great sin of Bugotu."[128]

Although the Protectorate Government in the Solomon Islands had made adultery a criminal offence with a criminal punishment of fines and jail sentences attached to it, Fallowes maintained "that adultery is a sin against the Law of God and not against the state and therefore should be punishable by the Church alone."[129] The Government District Officer for Isabel was inclined to agree and left the punishment for such misconduct in the hands of the Church. The standard penance for adultery was excommunication from the Church for six months, which was no mean punishment. Being "put out of the Church" meant that the offender was denied attendance at daily prayers in the village chapel, and more importantly, access to receiving Holy Communion. This was a severe social and religious sanction, for as G. White (1978: 225) has correctly noted, "The offender was socially ostracized and placed outside the protective power of the Christian God, open to supernatural attack — if not from God, then from malevolent spirits."

Years later, Fallowes recalled:

> When I arrived I spent a good deal of time depriving the offenders of the Sacraments. That seemed altogether unsatisfactory, so I substituted an alternative punishment — a thrashing voluntarily accepted in every case.[130]

Whether or not this form of punishment was a deterrent to adultery is questionable, but given the choice between being put out of the Church for six months or enduring six hard thrashings from Fallowes' cane, most offenders chose beating over excommunication, because in the words of one islander, "I like to attend Divine service."[131] A thrashing from Fallowes could be severe, as he relates in a letter to his sister:

> Usually the penalty is to be excommunicated from prayers and Mass for six months, but now to the young men I offer an alternative—a thrashing. Since my return two have chosen a thrashing and one to be put out of the church. They know a

> thrashing is good for them. There is never any bitterness afterward. The last boy howled out with pain and my thrashings are no light matter. I broke my stick on the last, the one Mrs. Conolly gave me in Sydney. When it was all over he said in his native tongue, "Very good. It hurt very much. My sin was very bad."[132]

Fallowes recalled forty-five years later:

> I remember the day when two men arrived in a canoe all the way from Kia to Mara-na-tabu (a distance of 110 miles). I greeted them warmly and was taken aback when they said, "we have come to be beaten. Our Chief will not allow us to attend prayers until you have punished us."[133]

Nevertheless, in 1933 the Protectorate Government prosecuted Fallows on thirteen counts of common assault, but he was acquitted on all but three of the charges for which he was fined ten shillings each.[134] Fallowes was more annoyed than threatened by the Government's action, for as he confidently wrote to his sister:

> I have the support of the natives and whites on Bugotu and none more so than those I have beaten. There is not a single complaint from them and it is that which puzzles and annoys the Government officials so. The Head of the Police did his utmost to get these boys to bring a complaint against me, but failed. They remained perfectly loyal.[135]

On the three counts for which he was convicted, Fallowes wrote, "All the witnesses admitted that they had assented to be beaten, but in three cases, the magistrate maintained that it was assent, not consent."[136] The Legal Advisor reported of the proceedings that:

> It was clear that the natives stood in considerable awe of Mr. Fallowes. One witness said, "Priest he strong too much," meaning not that this particular priest was physically strong, but that a priest as such has great prestige.[137]

Fallowes had built his island-wide base of support from activities ranging considerably beyond that of punishing offenders for moral misconduct. On his first tour of Santa Isabel in November 1929, in anticipation of being appointed to the island, he was met with the expectations the islanders had for his role as a European priest among them:

> Up and down Bugotu the news is fast spreading that after a lapse of five years a white priest is at last coming to them. They are saying, "He will help us now. He will teach us how to pray. He will bring us the Bread of Life. He will heal our sores. He will protect us against the government. He will make us happy." But who is sufficient for all these things?[138]

The foundation for Fallowes' multifunctional role was laid in the fact that the whole island was Anglican, and as he wrote in 1930, "The power of the

Church is considerable in Bugotu."[139] As the European "head" of that Church, Fallowes often felt his awesome responsibility:

> No incumbent in England has to deal with the problems I shall be dealing with, or has anything like the same power over his people. What incumbent could inflict such a penance as I have described, or if he did, who would submit to it?[140]

In 1931 Fallowes instituted the office of "Church Chief" — an elected office in every village, which soon became the counterpart, if not the rival, to the Government's appointed village headman, although in at least thirteen villages, both positions were held by the same man.[141] The primary responsibility of the Church Chief was to function as a church warden in maintaining the village chapel, but also to report cases of adultery and fornication. But as the following list of duties illustrates, the village Church Chiefs soon inserted themselves into practically the whole of village life. Their duties are as follows:

1. To help the teachers and fix up any business reported to them by the teachers.
2. To see that the Church, School, and Missionary's house are kept clean.
3. To see that all children go to school and go to Church.
4. To tell all the people that they must work all Saturday cleaning around the Church.
5. To report any adultery or other business to Rado [a self-declared "district" Church Chief] who will in turn report to Fallowes.
6. If they find a man who is not "strong along mission" to report him.
7. To fix up anything which is no good along mission and to work hard in this respect.
8. To fix up all the sins named in the Bible.[142]

Such an all-encompassing list of duties demonstrates the growing power of the Church Chiefs, and with Fallowes as the head of the mission organization on the island, his power likewise grew from purely ecclesiastical matters to involvement in the everyday affairs of island life. Fallowes' archrival was Walter Notere, the Government Headman for the whole of Santa Isabel. It is easy to understand his frustration with the increasing power and authority of Fallowes and his Church Chiefs. In a testimony given to the Government in March 1933, he reported:

> It is now the general practice for the mission headmen to deal with cases of adultery. The result of this is that the mission has grown in power and the government has accordingly lost grip. The mission headmen are now fixing up practically the whole of the ordinary business and the only thing dealt with by the Government are matters which are really serious. There is very little serious crime

> amongst my people and so the missions are practically running everything.[143]

Fallowes suffered a mental breakdown in 1935 and was compelled to leave his engaging work on Santa Isabel. He had increasingly been at loggerheads with Bishop Baddeley[144] so when he returned to the Solomons in October 1938, he came against the efforts of the bishop to block his entering the Solomons, and independently of the Mission, for he no longer had a license to function as an Anglican priest under the auspices of the Melanesian Mission. "So while my religious work was considerably curtailed, my political activities were considerably enhanced," Fallowes later recalled.[145] During the next nine months Fallowes devoted himself to furthering the cause of Solomon Islanders which irritated Bishop Baddeley and embarrassed the Protectorate Government. Although many Europeans perceived Fallowes as a rabble-rouser, manipulating islanders into agitation against colonial authority, this he clearly was not. Instead, Fallowes proved to be a timely channel through which many islanders manifested their considerable latent discontent with the Colonial Order. He provided for them a hope for a better future. By the 1930's, as Laracy (1976: 88) poignantly notes, "Solomon Island converts wanted more than a creed." They wanted better returns from the Government tax and the Mission collections, returns that would promote their own socio-economic welfare. Second and third generation Christians had become disillusioned and disappointed, for the "New Way" of Christianity seemed only to point to the paternalistic Colonial Order and a life of rigid inequality between Melanesians and Europeans.

Returning to Santa Isabel, Fallowes travelled widely throughout the island, discussing topics of great interest to the islanders: the lack of rural dispensaries for better medical care and educational facilities where English and technical training would be taught, the inequality of wages and prices for island products, and the need for Solomon Islanders to have a greater voice in their own political destiny. These were all issues dear to the hearts of many islanders.

Fallowes' village discussions fell on fertile soil, and a desire was quickly kindled for a forum in which islanders could discuss their needs and interests and present their requests to the Government as a united front. The first island-wide assembly of village headmen, Church Chiefs, catechists and priests, was held in the Bugotu district of Santa Isabel in early 1939. This meeting was followed by another one on Savo in April, and the third and last one, on Nggela in June 1939. At each assembly the attendance increased as enthusiasm for what was being called "The Fallowes Movement" spread to the Russell Islands, Guadalcanal, Malaita, and San Cristobal. Not since the late nineteenth century and the days of the Mission instituted *Vaukolo* or "Native Parliament" on Nggela, had there been such an island-wide forum for discussion of issues important to the islanders. Fallowes had struck at the heart of a deeply felt need among Solomon Islanders, and now they were responding.

At the meetings a parliamentary procedure suggested by Fallowes was adopted to facilitate discussion, and a "speaker" was elected to "chair" the meeting. Available for the speaker was an ornately carved chair made by a Santa Isabel craftsman, which soon became imbued with a supernatural power all its own—giving rise to the term "Chair and Rule Movement."[146]

The discussions at these meetings included topics of concern to the islanders relative to their socio-economic well-being, and their desire for greater political autonomy; topics which ostensibly were of equal concern to the Protectorate Government and the Melanesian Mission—better schools and health clinics, higher wages for plantation work,[147] the fluctuating and low price of copra paid to the island producers, and similar concerns—were the topics of discussion. By the end of the third meeting a list of requests had been drawn up to present to the High Commissioner, Sir Harry Luke, who was due to arrive in the Solomons for his first tour in June 1939. Included in the list were requests for medical dispensaries, a technical training school in which English would be taught, a native hostel at the Administrative center at Tulagi, a regulation requiring married men working on plantations to return to their families after two years of service, and a request that the buying price of copra and shell on the Sydney market be publicly posted for the islanders to see. These and a few other grievances with the Protectorate Government were translated by Fallowes and presented to the Government.[148] It is hard from our present-day perspective to perceive these requests as a list of radical demands, but as Hilliard (1974: 113) notes, "Fallowes' political ideas were simple and in themselves unrevolutionary, but in the paternalistic and stagnant atmosphere of the pre-war Solomons they could be explosive."

The overwhelming response of the Solomon Islanders to the Fallowes Movement, and the increasing popularity of this renegade European priest, proved very threatening to the Government and embarrassing to the Melanesian Mission. Thus when the High Commissioner arrived, he summoned Fallowes and lectured him on the proper sphere of activity for a man of the cloth, which did not include political concerns. With Baddeley's encouragement, the High Commissioner summarily deported Fallowes, forcing him to leave on the next steamer out of the Solomons. Fallowes had articulated for the Solomon Islanders their discontent with the Colonial Order and the consequent political and economic inequality they suffered under a paternalistic Protectorate Government and Anglican bishop. The movement caught the imagination of the Melanesians, and although it was suppressed by the Government, it did not die. Politically, Solomon Islanders had "come of age," but they were perceived by most Europeans as still children, dependent on their White Father. Consequently, for Melanesians, a Christianity that did not lead to equality became increasingly suspect by second and third generation Christians. This frustration was expressed by a Big Man on Nggela, who noted:

> We have only been taught the Gospel, but nothing yet about trade and commerce. We have been Christianized for 78 years now. The Church people are anxious for collections, and the (Government) for taxes, but where is the money? Here in the Islands wages and prices are very small, not enough for taxes and church collections.[149]

Fallowes symbolized for many islanders not only their opposition to the Government for failing to promote their economic development and socio-political advancement, but also their reaction to the increasing mission paternalism of this period. The same Nggela Big Man declared:

> Clergy and teachers, chiefs and people belonging to the Solomon Islands have said together, "We follow Fallowes. Whoever is foolish shall follow the Bishop and Hipkin (a missionary) who desire to blind our eyes and shut our ears and want us different from the people of England."[150]

The only support Fallowes received from his former missionary colleagues came from Charles Fox.[151] Bishop Baddeley and others failed to comprehend the significance of a peaceful effort to articulate deeply-felt Melanesian aspirations. This is all the more ironic when we realize that only months before Baddeley urged the deportation of Fallowes, he had stated in a radio broadcast in Sydney that he was "looking forward to the day when Melanesians will be able to take their part in the government of the Islands."[152] That day was dawning, but an embarrassed and threatened bishop was incapable of understanding and appreciating the significance of the movement. The Fallowes Movement, as Hilliard cogently notes, highlighted the discrepancy between what the Melanesian Mission **said** its goals were, and what it actually practiced. He states:

> By exposing a division between the white staff of the Melanesian Mission who supported the government in uncomprehending opposition, and its native teachers and clergy who played a leading part in voicing the aspirations and discontents of the people of the central Solomons, the Fallowes movement showed that the mission's quasi-establishment position was essentially a personal association between European missionaries and European heads of the government, born of a common background and community of mind, and did not embrace the indigenous church which the missionaries had come to the Solomons to build (1974: 116).[153]

2. Bishop Walter H. Baddeley — Paternalist.

Walter Hubert Baddeley (1894-1960) was Bishop of Melanesia from 1932 to 1947. Hilliard (1978: 260) in summarizing his personality noted that, "Baddeley shared many traits with George Augustus Selwyn. He was autocratic, brisk, self-assured, 'the very picture of health,' with an unsentimental, hearty manner, which impressed men of affairs." He was a man among men with his fellow Colonial comrades in government and business. He once wrote:

> No one imagines that the Solomon Island traders and planters came into the islands originally for philanthropic reasons. They came to make their livings. But they have made—and this cannot be denied — a very big contribution to the building up of the native society as we have it today, and to the establishment of British prestige among our Solomon Island people.[154]

Building up the prestige of the British seems to have been more important to Baddeley than empathetic understanding of Melanesian society and culture. He embodied the Colonial ethos of paternalism which was characteristic throughout the Colonial world during this period. Fox writes of Baddeley:

> He had not the deep understanding of Melanesians possessed by Patteson and Steward, nor did he speak their languages, nor had he lived as a district priest among them, as both those two great bishops did (1958: 91).

Baddeley was an efficient administrator with a military style, leading one missionary nurse to recall that he had commanded the missionaries as if they were his troops. "The only discipline he understood was military discipline," commented another missionary who served under him in the 1940's.[155]

Although not mentioning Baddeley by name, Fox, speaking in the context of the post-war reaction to Colonialism, notes:

> The chief drawback to British rule is the colour feeling of the British race. It is clean contrary to the teaching of the Christian faith but it is found in Christian missionaries as well as in Government officials. Some time ago there was a bishop, not of the present time, who would have said he had no colour feeling, but a very good and very loyal native priest who was talking to me one day said, "When an English priest goes to see the Bishop he finds him perhaps standing at the top of the steps of his verandah, and as soon as the Bishop sees him he says, 'Come in, old chap, and have a cup of tea.' But if I, or another Melanesian priest, goes to see him he stands at the top of the steps and says, 'Well, what have you come here for?' It hurts" (1962: 134).

The emphasis of Baddeley's episcopal reign was upon this-world-humanitarian endeavors rather than supernatural other-worldliness. He wrote:

> For my part I don't think the Christian Gospel is primarily concerned with life hereafter. I think the Christian Gospel is profoundly concerned with men's lives here and now. It is concerned with the whole man, his body and his mind as well as the spiritual part of him.[156]

Institutionalized medical work increased in the Mission under Baddeley, and many district schools or boys' boarding schools were established with a higher standard of education.[157] During Baddeley's episcopacy, the number of ordained Melanesian clergy rose from twenty-eight in 1932 to eighty-one in 1947, but the paradox of his leadership is that they had far less power and voice in the running of their own church than the previous indigenous clergy had had. For example, there were no synods or conferences called during his time, as there had been under Bishop John Steward. Melanesia became Baddeley's domain of rule and under him many mission links with the past were relinquished. As one missionary has recalled, "He resented all of us who had been in the Mission before him and got rid of us one by one," replacing them with his own "yes men."[158]

The irony of Baddeley's leadership is that in his efforts to run a tight ship and help the Melanesians, he in fact undermined the very idea of a "Native Church" of which he so often spoke publicly. His concept of redeeming the "whole man" included health and education, but not political and economic independence for the Melanesian Christians. He operated from a dependency theory which corresponded to other parts of the world where the Black man became the White man's burden.

Village Christianity under Baddeley was eclipsed in favor of institutionalized Christianity, established in Mission-sponsored programs of medical and educational work. The village schools failed to fulfill their function of teaching the basic tenets of Christian faith to the children of the second and third generation Christians. Missionaries became increasingly institutional caretakers, stationed at educational, medical, and administrative centers, while the development of a basic understanding of Christianity at the village level was relegated to a place of secondary importance. It is not surprising to discover that nominal adherence to Christianity by Melanesians became increasingly manifest under Baddeley's leadership. This nominalism produced a generation of "Christians" who were abandoned in a theological wilderness, having left their traditional religion far behind, but finding in Christianity a faith that did not answer their needs. Increasingly Christianity became less understood. It became more of a set of formal worship patterns, and less integrated and related to the everyday affairs of village living.

As a missionary model, Baddeley represents the image of Colonial paternalism. In his efforts to "serve Melanesia" he controlled his own empire with tight organization. While espousing the age-old goal of a "Native

Melanesian Church" Baddeley's policies and actions demonstrated little belief in the capacity of Melanesians to develop their own indigenous church, and he made few efforts to encourge them in that direction.

"Baddeley was a disaster for Melanesia," reminisced one former missionary. I believe Baddeley was a failure for Melanesia because he seemed more preoccupied with promoting the image of the Melanesian Mission, than with encouraging the development of a Melanesian Church and an indigenous Melanesian Christianity.

Being a military man at heart,[159] Baddeley's finest hour came in 1942 when the Japanese invaded the Solomon Islands. Baddeley refused to flee, choosing instead to seek refuge in the mountainous bush villages of Malaita. His courageous act is frequently cited as being responsible for the Resident Commissioner, W. S. Marchant's decision to stay in the Solomons as well.[160] Baddeley was a popular figure among the Allied troops in the Solomon Islands[161] and for his efforts during the war and his relationship with the American troops, he was awarded an Honorary Doctorate of Sacred Theology (S.T.D.) by Columbia University in November 1944, and the U. S. Medal of Freedom in May 1948.[162]

3. Charles E. Fox — Empathizer.

C. E. Fox (1878-1977) was first drawn to Melanesia when Bishop Cecil Wilson, himself a great cricketer and member of the 1884 Kent XI (the only county to beat Australia that year) brought a team from Norfolk Island to play schools in New Zealand in 1895. Fox played against them in Napier. They won, but it was his encounter with them there that so fascinated him with Melanesians. Seven years later he joined the Melanesian Mission at Norfolk Island. Later he wrote:

> So it was that vocation came from a natural fascination for queer languages and a love for cricket, and when I saw the Melanesians it was a case of love at first sight and ever after.

He then continues philosophically:

> It does not seem to me much use if a man goes to people he does not like, for if he does not like them he will never understand them. There have been some in Melanesia and it is better for them to go back.[163]

Fox set out on what was to be a long missionary career, intent on understanding Melanesians. Eight years after joining the Melanesian Mission he produced his first scholarly work, *An Introduction to the Study of Oceanic Languages* (1910). Charles Fox, the anthropologist, was greatly influenced by his association with W. H. R. Rivers, which began in 1908 while Rivers was touring Melanesia.[164] Fox recalls that first meeting while on board the *Southern Cross* enroute from Norfolk Island to the Solomons:

> I had looked on ethnology as a vague, picturesque, and highly imaginative subject, and not at all as an exact or scientific study. I now became deeply interested in it and of course more and more drawn to the man himself. He recommended books to me, and by the time we reached San Cristoval, I was committed to ethnological work.[165]

Anthropology did not create in Fox an interest in understanding Melanesians, for this was deeply rooted in his being before he ever met Rivers. However, it did give him critical tools with which to pursue his interests and inquiries.[166]

In 1920 he took a further step toward understanding Melanesians. He wrote to W. J. Durrad of the experience:

> Well last January, I made up my mind to try life as a Melanesian and I took the plunge. I performed *haimarahuda* with Martin Taki; that is to say we exchanged possessions. I went into his house and he into mine, and except for a few private mementos of friends I kept nothing, e.g. got an old razor for my Gillette (still have), lost my pipes, hat, shoes, clothes, European food, cooking utensils, tobacco, gum, money (including that in the bank, £40) etc. On the other hand I gained the aforesaid razor, sufficient clothes, 2/6, a clay pipe, a yam garden, various coconut trees and property in land. We also exchanged names.

During this time Fox lived as a Melanesian and spent one month working on a plantation so he could understand what young Melanesian men experienced there. He wrote to Durrad:

> I have never in all my life been so happy as I often have been in these months. I have been treated by Melanesians as a Melanesian and learnt many things. But sometimes I have been very hungry, and sometimes I have had ulcers and been ill without medicine or bandages.[167]

Shifting roles opened up to Fox a whole new world of interpersonal relationships with Melanesians. He continued in his letter to Durrad:

> You have no idea how great a difference it made. I got to know the women for the first time, to find out how they chaff the men continually. I was treated entirely differently, with less respect but with infinitely greater friendliness.[168]

The European community's response to Fox's experience was mixed. Some were very angry and full of contempt. An S.S.E.M. missionary wrote him a "scathing letter full of (biblical) texts," while a Marist father wrote him "a loving letter." Bishop Steward "was full of sympathy" and supported Fox in his unique experience.

In 1932 Fox was asked to become the seventh bishop of Melanesia, but unfortunately for the future course of the Melanesian Mission, he declined to accept the nomination, and Walter Baddeley was chosen in his place. In the same year, Fox took another step to further identify with the islanders. Instead of accepting the nomination for bishop, he joined the Melanesian Brotherhood. Here he served for eleven years under the authority of several Head Brothers, one of whom had once been one of his students at Pawa. Baddeley brought an end to Fox's time in the Brotherhood, by requiring him to withdraw in 1943. Fox found real identification with the Melanesians during this time, and later wrote:

> My own years in the Brotherhood were some of my happiest years in Melanesia. It is impossible to convey in words the friendliness, and the fun among the Brothers; or the goodwill and comradeship towards them of all Melanesians (1962: 79).

In an interview with a newspaper reporter in 1977, Fox fished from his collar a medallion of the Melanesian Brotherhood, and said, "The Queen gave me the C.B.E. (1974), but I value this more."[169]

Fox, more than any other missionary, went beyond mere lip-service in articulating the possibility and need for a Melanesian Christianity. He was a missionary in the best tradition of Bishop Patteson, but he went further than Patteson because of his anthropological perspective and critical skills. He regretted much of the culture change that had come to Melanesia, unnecessarily, he felt, because of the impact of the missionary. In an age of colonialism and paternalism, Fox was an empathetic observer and participant in Melanesian culture and society.

When I interviewed him in New Zealand in February 1977, at the age of 98, the one theme he impressed on me, time and again, was, "I am a Melanesian." He was so insistent on referring to himself as a Melanesian, that I followed this up during my fieldwork in the Solomon Islands. Without question, *Doktor Fockis*, as he is affectionately called in Pidgin, was held in high esteem by all those with whom I talked, and in many ways, he had become a culture-hero in twentieth century Melanesian folklore. But in response to my question, "Was Dr. Fox really a Melanesian?" the answer was "No." However, this was quickly followed by the comment, "But he came closer than any other European missionary we have known to truly understanding us and being one of us."[170]

Fox's diaries over a seventeen-year period (1942-1959) are full of incidents of Melanesians coming to him, seeking his help and advice. An entry for September 13, 1950 is typical: "Asked to bless houses, native medicine and water to pour on a grave to keep the ghost quiet." Two weeks later on September 27th, he recorded: "Called at 2 a.m. to a woman dying in childbirth. After some prayers she was delivered safely of her baby and both doing well."[171]

Fox finally left the Solomons in 1973, but in his retirement in New Zealand, he carried on a heavy correspondence with many Melanesians. He was a missionary and agent of change who was highly approachable and islanders were not afraid to discuss beliefs and practices with him that were at variance with Mission doctrine and teaching. But more importantly, Fox was a man of *mana*, and it is this quality that drew Melanesians to him. Without doubt, Fox became as much of a Melanesian as a European could become.

He once wrote about the difficult hill one must climb if one wants to live meaningfully as a missionary in Melanesia. There are difficulties with a new language, isolation and loneliness, climate, etc. that one must overcome:

> More than half who come do not get over it; to those who cross it the reward is rich. The malaria gets less, the language becomes like your own, you have plenty of Melanesian friends, you never want again to be anywhere else . . . Of course you must have a sense of humor.[172]

Analysis of Missionary Models.

The three missionaries discussed above — Fallowes, Baddeley, and Fox — can be analyzed as behavioral models in a larger interpretive framework than simply their interaction with Melanesians.[173] As leadership models they are characteristic of "ideal types" found in any social system.

Drawing on the seminal ideas of Talcott Parsons, I will delineate leadership in a social system in terms of the following dimensions: (1) Instrumental-Expressive, (2) Formal-Informal, and (3) Authoritarian-Laissez-faire. These dimensions depicted on an axis in a social system are diagrammed as follows:

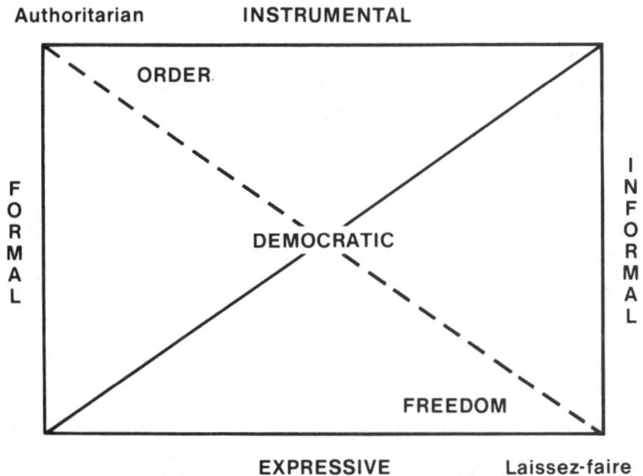

Fig. 6. Dimensions of Leadership in a Social System.

As can be seen by this diagram, formal, authoritarian, and instrumental qualities of leadership tend to cluster, emphasizing **maintaining order** in the social system. In contrast, informal, laissez-faire, and expressive leadership qualities tend to cluster and emphasis is upon **allowing freedom** in the social system. The median point in this diagram is termed democratic. It is here that a balanced equilibrium is maintained between the tensions toward freedom or order found in the social system.

Data on the three missionary models discussed above seem to fit quite well into this schema of leadership dimensions in a social system. The authoritarian – democratic – laissez-faire axis is a useful heuristic device for plotting the three missionary models discussed above. This can be diagrammed as follows:

Authoritarian	Democratic	Laissez-faire
X	X	X
Baddeley	Fallowes	Fox

Fig. 7. Missionary Models and Leadership Dimensions.

Baddeley was a missionary who emphasized formal and instrumental qualities combined with an authoritarian personality to maintain **order** in the colonial structure of European dominance. He appears to have never questioned the structural inequalities between Europeans and Melanesians in the colonial era, and he saw his role as one of carrying out "missionary work" **within** that context rather than in opposition to it. He therefore perceived Fallowes as a threat to the Mission and Government, a threat to the paternalistic status quo of the Colonial Order. It is not surprising to discover that he never got on well with Charles Fox, who, as a missionary model, was the antithesis of Baddeley.

In contrast to Bishop Baddeley, Charles Fox combined informal, expressive and laissez-faire attributes in his relationships with Melanesians. He was more concerned with assuring Melanesians' cultural integrity and personal freedom than in preserving the Colonial Order. For this reason, he was frequently severely criticized by his missionary colleagues, but his approach of philosophical laissez-faire behavior in his interpersonal relationships with

Melanesians endeared him to the islanders. Fox was more concerned with reaching across cultural boundaries and establishing meaningful relationships with the islanders than he was in preserving the status quo of the colonial era which guaranteed the missionary a privileged position but fostered inequality between Europeans and Melanesians.

As a missionary model, Richard P. Fallowes falls in between Baddeley and Fox at the democratic position on the authoritarian—laissez-faire axis. While frequently paternalistic in his behavior with Solomon Islanders, he nevertheless championed their right to have a voice in governing their own political and socio-economic affairs. As a model of missionary behavior, Fallowes approximates the center of tension between freedom and order, formal and informal, instrumental and expressive dimensions of leadership in a social system.

As this brief analysis of three missionary types in the Melanesian Mission demonstrates, missionaries, as agents of change, do not fit neatly into any stereotypic modes. It is true that there are frequently structural similarities in missionary-convert interaction in most culture contact situations; but, given these underlying similarities, there is a divergence of missionary personalities which influences the nature of the cross-cultural interaction. This factor must always be taken into consideration when discussing the role of missionaries as agents of culture change.

Today the popular notion of a missionary is frequently based on some misconceived nineteenth century caricature of a Victorian Englishman going out to "civilize the natives" and destroying their culture in the process. Such a caricature represented by Abner Hale in James Michener's (1959) *Hawaii* is a misleading generalization. As the above brief analysis has demonstrated for the Melanesian Mission, there were very different missionaries even within the same mission of the same period of mission history. Any study, other than a very superficial one, will quickly reveal that missionaries have never conveniently fit into a stereotypic model. Different mission organizations at different periods of mission history will have very different missionary types within their ranks. We grossly oversimplify a complex situation when we assume a uniformity of missionary types across all denominations and through every period of history.

Melanesian Responses to Missionary Advocacy of Change

In concluding this chapter, it is important to focus briefly on elements of Melanesian society and culture that underwent change during this period of penetration. The missionaries who advocated certain indigenous changes in conjunction with Christian conversion, did so in a dynamic arena in which other European forces impinged on Melanesian society as well. The missionary did not advocate change in isolation, but in the context of other European agents of change. The colonial governments in Melanesia imposed new and alien laws, and then exacted taxes from the islanders to help pay for their enforcement. European planters introduced wage labor into what was previously a subsistence economy, and traders supplied the Western goods readily purchased with the income derived from the islanders' work. The net effect was to reduce the craftsmanship of many traditional utilitarian objects which were now easily purchased. Melanesians were thus brought insidiously to greater dependence on European goods in place of their own traditionally manufactured and produced items. As the desire for European foods and utensils increased, Melanesians became more reliant on a cash economy for their purchase. Tinned meat, biscuits and tobacco were no longer luxuries — they had become necessities.[174]

Although it is difficult to analytically separate changes that occurred as a result of missionary influence from those which occurred from government and commercial penetration, it is nevertheless important to consider several areas of Melanesian society and culture that were influenced by missionary contact during this period of penetration. The following topics will be briefly discussed: (1) changes in Melanesian religion and worldview, (2) changes in Melanesian social organization, and (3) the conflict between Melanesian behavior and Western Christian ethics.

Changes in Melanesian Religion and Worldview.

By the end of this period there were approximately 35,000 baptized Christians on the books of the Melanesian Mission. Given that by the end of the first fifty years of the Mission's activities there were only 12,000 Christians, and that many Christians were victims of the tremendous depopulation during the first three decades of this period, the approximate total of 35,000 represents a substantial increase in the number of converts for this second period of Mission activity. In this study of culture change, however, I am interested in more than just the statistical data of mission membership; of greater importance is understanding the dynamics of conversion and the meaning Melanesians imputed to their adopted religion.

During this period there are numerous references in the Mission literature to the fact that although there were increasing numbers of Christian converts, there was also a corresponding decrease in the level of understanding and practice of Christianity by those converts. Although the adoption of Christianity was widespread across linguistic and ethnic boundaries, the emerging Melanesian Christianity appeared to many missionaries to be only a superficial expression. I cited earlier in this chapter Durrad's belief that, "Christianity is still largely an exotic in Melanesia. It has not yet laid hold of the spirit and genius of the race."[175] Writing about Motalava, reputed to be the best of the Banks' Islands, Durrad continued in a similar vein:

> There is all through manifest a total lack of real interest or understanding of what is our aim and hope to establish. Christianity

> seems foreign still. It is in many native eyes a white man's "custom" that has been laid upon them. They do not disbelieve it, but their faith does not issue in energetic action.

And speaking of Mota, which had been the first of the Melanesian islands to respond to the Mission's message, he added, "The island is largely heathen still at heart."[176]

The often cited analogy of the white corks and black net was questioned during this period, but it was **not** the continuation of the white corks, as an objective analyst might expect, but the ability of the black net to fulfill its responsibility that was questioned. Thus Ivens concluded that:

> . . . it cannot be questioned that up to the present time the native Christians, teachers and people alike, fall short in the performance of their part in the casting of the Gospel net. The truth of the matter would seem to be that the native church has not yet risen to a sense of its duty in the work of evangelization; Christianity has seemed to the converts to be more a thing brought from outside and to be accepted along with the rest of the white man's things than a matter vitally concerning themselves and depending on their cooperation (1918: 192).

On Santa Isabel, in the village of Sepi, which was at one time the heart of the Christian movement on that island, Richard Fallowes recorded in his diary in 1932:

> . . . not a very satisfactory visit. Little Church enthusiasm and scarcely any schooling going on. The candidates for confirmation I found to be in a tragic state of ignorance. Willie the teacher means well, but he gets little support.[177]

It appears that a serious goal discrepancy occurred between what missionaries advocated, and how Melanesians interpreted the message and responded to it.[178] I have argued elsewhere (Whiteman 1974) that in missionary proselytizing the message of Christianity proceeds through two distinct and different cultural filters in the process of communication. The first filter is the missionary's own interpretation of the biblical paradigm and church tradition which influence his decision in what he chooses to communicate as "essential Christianity." The second filter is that of the Melanesian innovator, whose cultural precepts influence his perception of the message. Thus in the process of communicating across cultural and linguistic boundaries there are many alterations, additions and subtractions that are made to the message of Christianity. Is it little wonder then, that missionaries of the Melanesian Mission were discouraged with the Melanesian response to their advocacy for change?

The goal for missionary advocates was a Christian society in a Melanesian context, where commitment to Christian principles would be the primary motivating factor in converts' choices of belief and action. The goal for many

Melanesians was successful adaptation to a changing environment. As noted above (Chapter 2, pp. 64-67) the essence of traditional Melanesian religion was to ensure control of the Melanesian universe. As this universe underwent change through increasing depopulation and European interference and domination in the affairs of village life, the old order of beliefs and ritual seemed less reliable in meeting the new demands of the changing situation. Thus for many, "conversion" to Christianity was an appropriate response to a changing world. As the Colonial Order became established in Melanesia, Christianity was perceived by many to have an important function in that new order, and thus by its adoption, it was hoped that Melanesians' welfare would be assured. Thus for many islanders, the adoption of Christianity was seen as an adaptive mechanism for survival in the new Colonial Order. It was, therefore, a pragmatic choice, concerned more with materialistic and social well-being than with the validity of metaphysical absolutes.

In this period, while missionaries bemoaned the superficiality of conversion and lack of understanding and knowledge of basic Christian doctrine, they seem to have contributed to it instead of taking measures to alleviate the problem. For example, the Melanesian Mission's impressive record of translations of Bible portions and other aids to worship and religious instruction declined both in quality and quantity during this period. Whereas in the previous period converts had undergone very careful and thorough instruction before being admitted to the Church, during this period this practice declined as well. Today islanders still talk about the rapid-fire method of confirmation practiced by Bishop Baddeley on his hurried island tours, instead of his taking time for a careful examination of potential Church members. The underlying assumption was that children of second and third generation Christians had received the requisite knowledge from their parents. However, during this period there was greater emphasis on Mission institutions, to the neglect of village instruction and training. Village-related Christianity was eclipsed in favor of Mission institutions where training of a select few was encouraged and emphasized.

Thus in many ways, Christianity was poorly understood and practiced by Melanesian converts; although missionaries bemoaned this state of affairs, they inadvertently contributed to it. The traditional religion had been altered somewhat by the incorporation of new Christian beliefs, but conversion for many did not imply the annihilation of all traditional beliefs. For many the Christian God was more powerful than ancestral spirits, but belief in the latter continued. The worldview of many Melanesians was altered to include an increasing number of "secular" explanations of cause and effect in human affairs, but most clung tenaciously to belief in the efficacy of magic, especially during times of crisis.

Changes in Melanesian Social Organization.

There were several areas of Melanesian social organization that changed during this period; a brief discussion will be given to three of them: (1) changes in village patterns, (2) changes in leadership, and (3) changes in marriage.

1. Village Patterns.

Writing in 1918, W. G. Ivens observed that:

> The comparative scantiness of the population is the real difficulty in the evangelization of Melanesia. There must be an assembling of the scattered units of population in the islands, and since one of the first results of the propagation of Christianity in Melanesia is the gathering together of the people in a community where hitherto they have been living as scattered units all over the face of the land, it seems obvious that the initiative in the program of work will be with the missions (1918: 191).

Not only was the adoption of Christianity signaled by a move from scattered hamlets to nucleated villages in many areas of Melanesia,[179] but in the larger islands such as Malaita and Guadalcanal, it was associated with significant population shifts from the interior to the coast. Since the centers of traditional Melanesian religion were located in ancestral shrines and sacred groves, a move to the coast was often symbolic of a convert's rejection of pagan loyalties and allegiance to new ones.

Coastal villages sprang up as island gateways to the Western world — the European's material goods, medicine and religion were all more readily accessible on the coast than in the interior. Coastal villages also reflected the coming of peace and an end to internecine hostility. For example, in the last half of the nineteenth century, when Santa Isabel was under increasing threat of attack from headhunters in the Western Solomons, they built large tree houses in which to retreat, and constructed fortified villages perched atop a ridge, which supposedly gave them greater protection from the enemy. With the coming of peace, these elaborate precautions were abandoned and village structures were altered to reflect these social changes.

Christianity expanded the Melanesian's definition of "who is my brother" and thus members of an adjacent village or ethnic and linguistic group were no longer automatic enemies. In this sense, Christianity gave to Melanesians an ideological basis for expanding their social relations, and village structures in this period reflect this change.[180]

2. Leadership.

In Melanesia, as noted above (Chapter 2, pp. 58-60), leadership was based on achieved status in an egalitarian society. Rather than chiefs with inherited authority as in Polynesia, the Melanesian model of leadership, with some exceptions, is best personified in the concept of a Big Man — one who rises to a position of influence through his own achievements. The epistemological base for a Melanesian Big Man was religious knowledge. His authority was supported by the traditional ideology which held that in order to become a Big Man, one must acquire *mana* or supernatural power. A man with *mana* manifested his power as a successful warrior, an entrepreneur, and/or "priest." Validation of his authority occurred in successful raids and through large feasts where ostentatious displays of his wealth were redistributed among his followers.

The effect of Christianity on Melanesian leadership patterns introduced changes in two dimensions. First, by converting to a new ideology, the traditional "religious" base of a Big Man's leadership was undermined, for he had relied on power from the ghosts and spirits of deceased ancestors. Allegiance to the Christian God meant that theoretically Melanesians were equalized in their access to supernatural resources. *Mana* was now available to everyone from the God of the Universe, rather than issuing only from certain ancestral spirits in one's lineage. This ideological shift from particularism to universalism undercut a Big Man's corner on the supernatural market. In addition, the ideology of Christianity valued peaceful and submissive behavior in contrast to the traditional ideology which gave value to aggression as expressed in the Melanesian warrior. Big Men were aggressive manipulators of the social environment who gained power and influence through a conscious effort of promoting their own enterprise. In contrast, Christianity called all converts to become servants, and warned that those who promoted themselves first would end up last.

Secondly, concomitant with the introduced religion were new roles of leadership which provided a functional substitute for traditional leadership roles. These roles advocated by the Melanesian Mission were those of village teachers or catechists, deacons and priests. As pacification ended internecine warfare, Mission institutions took on a more prominent and comprehensive role in Melanesian society. The catechists, deacons and priests became increasingly important and powerful in the new Christian village, for they fulfilled a dual function of cultural brokers between Melanesians and Europeans, and as dispensers of supernatural power, for they were perceived by villagers to have greater access to the new source of *mana* than did the laity. Thus as the traditional leadership roles, based on aggression and supported by *mana* derived from ancestral spirits, became obsolete and began to wane, the new roles of mission elites waxed, supported by a new ideology and alternative source of power.[181]

3. Marriage.

A third area where the impact of Christianity brought culture change in Melanesian social organization is that of Melanesian marriage.[182] One of the most significant changes was the Mission prohibition on polygyny that accompanied conversion to Christianity. A man's wife performed an important economic function, and thus traditional Big Men were dependent on multiple wives to provide a sufficient economic base for their entrepreneurial activities. A man could not give a large feast if he lacked the sufficient economic base in foodstuffs, and pigs, and thus with only one wife, his access to potential resources was limited. Multiple wives represented a Big Man's prestige and wealth, for indeed, in many ways their economic function was the source of his wealth.

The Melanesian Mission also advocated limits on bride price, which during this period began escalating on some islands. On Santa Isabel, bride price was eliminated altogether. The lowering of bride price was designed to decrease competitive behavior in the new emerging Christian society, but it was a bone of contention for many Melanesian women who perceived it as an attempt by the Mission to devalue their worth.

The structure of male-female relations was also altered as a consequence of conversion. Whereas the lowering of bride price may have been perceived by some women as lowering their net value, the ideology of Christianity placed a higher value on women in a society dominated by men. Also, Christianity gave women equal access to *mana*, where in the traditional order "religious knowledge" had been, for the most part, restricted primarily to men. Missionaries were frequently appalled by the mere drudges they perceived Melanesian women to be. One is led to believe, however, that this assessment came more from evaluating women in terms of European models of behavior, than from any in-depth understanding of the function of women in Melanesian society.[183]

The diaries of missionaries are replete with entries in which they have been called upon to settle marriage disputes. Much of Henry Welchman's time on Santa Isabel was spent in attempts to reconcile unhappy marriages between islanders. Although it would have been promoted as an ideal, it is difficult to assess the degree to which the adoption of Christianity made for "happier marriages" among Melanesian converts.[184]

The Conflict of Melanesian Behavior with Western Christian Ethics.

Contrary to the opinions of some European observers that pagan Melanesians had no system of morality, the traditional order did have a comprehensive moral code that guided the behavior of individuals in their relationships with each other and in their articulation with the group.[185] The definitions of moral behavior varied at points with Western ethics, but it is erroneous to conclude that Melanesians functioned independently of any ethical parameters. The traditional moral system was held intact by Big Men and the power of *tabu*.

With the introduction of Christianity the basis of morality shifted. What

Dutton describes for Nggela, is true of a generalized process that occurred in other parts of Melanesia as a result of missionary contact:

> What happened in Gela as a result of the Christian Impact was that by and large the old authority was replaced by a new one. The old morality based on the village structure, maintained by custom, enforced by tabu, and the very real authority of the elders, gave way to a new authority taught by the Church, enforced by Canons of Discipline, and the very real power of excommunication used by the clergy to discipline the erring. The force of excommunication lay partly in a fear of God's avenging power, a real sense of having transgressed God's law and not kept the faith, and a shame at being excluded from the new community which gave the Melanesians a real sense of belonging (1969: 85).

In some spheres of activity the ethical system of the Mission was less demanding than the traditional one.[186] For example, the punishment for adultery prior to missionary contact had been death for the offenders in many Melanesian societies. However, the "New Morality" issued in less drastic sanctions against offenders, for excommunication was substituted for the death penalty. It is difficult to evaluate and document whether or not there was an increase in the incidents of adultery and fornication as the power of the old sanctions decreased and was replaced by mission-directed sanctions. However, mission documents, both public and private, attest to a large number of converts who "fell into sin" — the popular euphemism for adultery and fornication. It was a problem that plagued the laity, but was not isolated there, for there are several celebrated cases of tried and trusted Melanesian priests of long standing who were found guilty of "falling into sin" with their parishioners. This led to a crisis of confidence in the Melanesian clergy, and undoubtedly was a contributing rationale for increased paternalism and domination by the European missionaries during this period. Adultery and fornication were seen by most Europeans as the sin of the islanders — a sin of epidemic proportions, and as one Solomon Island bishop informed me, this is still the case today.[187]

A strong case can be made to suggest that for many Melanesian converts, Christianity was perceived as an alternative form of *tabu*. An important theme in Christianity is the notion of the Love of God for Mankind, and Christ as a reconciler, which the missionaries emphasized in contrasting their religion with the fearfulness and dread of the pagan religion. Nevertheless, many Melanesians followed the moral code out of fear. The Christian God was often perceived in the Old Testament sense, as one who would mete out severe punishment for sin. Thus sickness, "natural" disasters and misfortune, were frequently interpreted as punishment from God for the sin of an individual.[188] In many areas the sanctions of sorcery were more powerful in enforcing moral behavior than was the Western ethical system.

Consequently, when sorcery was forbidden, along with killing and hostile aggression, it lifted a very powerful traditional sanction from such things as petty thievery, etc.[189]

Thus the Melanesian response to missionary advocacy of change resulted in the decline of some powerful sanctions and the substitution of new rules of behavior appropriate to the New Order. However, to conclude that this represents a shift from **immoral** pagan Melanesians, to **moral** Christians, is to misunderstand the ethical system enforced before the advent of missionary contact.

Summary

I have called this era of Melanesian culture change the period of penetration — the penetration of European acculturative influences that transformed Melanesian society and culture within a span of less than fifty years. Although this study focuses on the Melanesian Mission as an agent of change, I have stressed that missionaries functioned in a context of other impinging influences. Colonial governments brought new laws, commercial enterprises introduced a cash economy, and other mission organizations arrived to compete with the Anglicans by introducing variants of the new religion.

Not only were Melanesians required to adapt to a rapidly changing socio-economic and political environment, but the Melanesian Mission was also forced to respond by reorganizing and adapting its own institutional framework to the exigencies of the new context. In doing so, missionaries became permanent residents in the islands, replacing the old itinerant pattern of the previous period. In the process, some missionaries gained positions of dominance and authority in their host societies, as their role expanded beyond that of ecclesiastical concerns. Mission priorities shifted to educational and medical institutions and increasingly missionary personnel became occupied with administrative positions as institutional caretakers, thus losing touch with Melanesians at the village level.

A paternalistic ethos invaded the Mission, giving it a different stamp under Bishop Baddeley than that it had had under Bishop Patteson's leadership. But this was more than simply a reflection of the different bishops' personalities — it reflected and represented a structural change that was a product of the Colonial Order. Nevertheless, there were individual missionaries such as Charles Fox who defied this paternalism, choosing instead to empathetically identify with the very Melanesians to whom he introduced Christiantiy as an alternative belief system and standard of behavior.

Melanesians responded in this period by choosing to innovate in adopting many of the artifacts, much of the behavior, and some of the beliefs advocated by the European agents of change. Most welcomed were the Western material goods introduced by the traders, and least welcomed was the intrusion of colonial administrators into the affairs of village life, instituting an alien legal system and then taxing Melanesians to help finance its enforcement.

The introduction of Christianity brought greater changes than either government or commercial influences. And throughout this period, Melanesians increasingly chose to adopt the new religion as their own. They did so for a multitude of reasons. The "New Way" promised peace, which was very welcomed by the end of the nineteenth century. There were also many points of identification between Melanesians' traditional religious beliefs and Christianity, and the ritualistic form introduced by the Melanesian Mission was especially attractive, for Melanesians had always used ritual as a means of gaining *mana*. Thus, for many Melanesians, conversion to Christianity meant substituting a new ideology and ritual for obtaining the traditional ends of social and material well-being. The adoption of Christianity became a rational response to a rapidly changing world, increasingly dominated by Europeans. The traditional ideology and ritual were appropriate to the traditional order, but much of that order disintegrated during this period, and thus Christianity functioned as an adaptive mechanism in aiding the transition of Melanesians from the old order to the new.

Owing to the superficial nature of many Melanesians' conversion to Christianity, the initial enthusiasm of first generation Christians began to wane with subsequent descendants of the converts, so that by the end of this period much of village Christianity had become apathetic and routine-bound. The founding of the Melanesian Brotherhood in this period represents a Melanesian attempt to develop an indigenous organization free from the domination of European missionaries and Melanesian clergy. It demonstrates that although Christianity had become a listless and meaningless routine for many island converts, there were still young volunteers for whom the initial dynamism of conversion had not waned.

Increasingly Christians became discontent with their socio-political status, for although the "New Way" had brought some welcomed changes, it also seemed increasingly bound to the colonial system of structured inequalities between Europeans and Melanesians.

If we can anticipate the next chapter, it is against this background that activities in the next period following World War II must be understood. Melanesians had become increasingly acculturated, but also increasingly dominated by the paternalistic Colonial Order. Reaction against this order occurred in the Marching Rule Movement, but continued until the Melanesian Anglicans had their own autonomous Church of Melanesia in 1975, and the Solomon Islanders had their own independent nation in 1978. For Melanesians in the New Hebrides, independence came in July, 1980, with the founding of the new Pacific Island Nation of Vanuatu.

CHAPTER 4 NOTES

1. Perhaps the only place in Melanesia where traditional culture was unaltered would have been in some parts of the New Guinea Highlands.
2. See discussion above, Chapter 1, pp. 16-17.
3. A thorough historical treatise regarding the British Solomon Islands Protectorate (B.S.I.P.) is found in Scarr (1967: 252-256, 258-270). See also Morrell (1960: 331-349). For a brief summary of the establishment of the B.S.I.P. cf. Grattan (1963b: 393-394). For a discussion of the establishment of the Anglo-French Condominium in the New Hebrides, cf. Jacomb (n.d.), Latham (1927), Mander (1954: 467-476, 489-491), Morrell (1960: 349-360), and Scarr (1967: 218-251). Cf. Cooper (1979: 25-41).

   Colonialism in the Southwest Pacific had been clearly established by this time, for Britain had annexed Fiji in 1874. France had annexed New Caledonia and the Loyalty Islands as early as 1853, and the New Guinea region had been carved up between the Dutch in 1828, and Britain and Germany in 1884.
4. Cf. Moses (1969).
5. Scarr (1967: 262).
6. For discussion of this movement see above, Chapter 3, pp. 137-144.
7. Scarr (1967: 262). It is interesting to note that the B.S.I.P. never took an active part in education until the 1970's, but left this sphere of acculturation to the Christian missions, cf. B.S.I.P. *White Paper* No. 3. For discussion on education in the Solomon Islands, cf. B. Palmer (1977), and Boutilier (1978).
8. Scarr (1967: 266).
9. Cf. *Mission Field* (1893), 38: 447-452, "Hoisting the Flag in the Solomon Islands." For a discussion of the Melanesian Mission's relations with Woodford and the B.S.I.P. Government, see Hilliard (1978: 132-136). For a wider treatment of the Melanesian Mission's relationship to British Colonialism in the Solomon Islands, cf. Hilliard (1974).
10. Grattan (1963b: 404).
11. Quoted in Grattan, *Ibid.*
12. For a brief synopsis of Anglican missionaries' attitudes to the Condominium Government, cf. Hilliard (1978: 239-242). Fox (1958: 43, 122, 142-143, 145) has been one of the most outspoken critics of the

Condominium Government. For a more general discussion of Protestant missionary attitudes, cf. Forman (1972).

13. For an example of this problem in the Solomon Islands, cf. Hogbin (1935).

14. Cf. Beckett (1971), and H. Ross (1978).

15. Laracy (1976: 39).

16. Young (n.d. [1925]: 256).

17. Cf. *S.C.L.E.*, January 1943, pp. 7-8, September 1954, p. 230. For a less severe criticism of Pidgin, cf. Fox writing in *The Melanesian Messenger*, Christmas 1966, pp. 2-4. Although Fox lived for seventy years in the Solomon Islands and spoke several languages fluently, he never spoke Pidgin. Islanders frequently told me of missionaries who had served many years in the Islands but who refused to speak Pidgin. Students in the Mission's schools were also forbidden to speak it.

    George Warren who served in the Mission's schools for twenty-five years, captures the attitude most of the Anglican missionaries had toward Pidgin. He is discussing an American doctor going to Melanesia:

    > . . . to prove that pidgin is a real language. I don't know whether you know pidgin, but it makes you shudder. It is one of those things we have fought against always, for it is a barrier to knowledge of every sort. For a sane white man to talk about it as a language is ludicrous (*S.C.L.E.*, September 1954, p. 230).

18. There was an attempt in the mid-1920's to begin work on New Britain but it failed and the Mission withdrew, content with Santa Isabel as its northern boundary. Cf. Fox (1958: 210-214), and Hilliard (1978: 243-246, 277-279). Cf. *S.C.L.E.*, July 1949.

    The histories of these various missions in the Solomon Islands, written by the missionaries themselves, and thus uncritical in the main, are Young (n.d.) for the South Sea Evangelical Mission, Luxton (1955) for the Methodist Mission, and Raucaz (1925, 1928) for the Catholic Marists. Critical studies of the non-Anglican Protestant missions are found in Hilliard (1966: Chs. 6-8) and for the S.S.E.M. (1969). A critical study of the Catholic mission in the Solomons is found in Laracy (1969, 1976). For a comparative study of the Methodists and Anglicans, cf. Tippett (1967), and for a more recent history of the Methodist Mission, cf. R. Williams (1972).

19. Wilson to his wife, September 5, 1909. Extracts from letters to his wife 1900, 1903, 1904, 1909. TS in possession of the Reverend Canon John C. J. Wilson, Otane, New Zealand.

20. The Marist missionaries were especially long-term residents. Vacations for missionaries were not introduced until 1925, and then only

six months leave was allowed after fifteen years of service (Laracy 1976: 71).

21. This policy of comity was reinforced, if not enforced, by the first Resident Commissioner, C. M. Woodford, who pursued a policy of keeping the missions from competing with each other, by disallowing land purchases by a mission if he believed it would be competing with another mission already established in the area. Cf. Hilliard (1966: 121-128; 1978: 134-135), and Laracy (1976: 43).

22. Laracy (1976: 43), Hilliard (1978: 142). For a discussion of Melanesian Mission relations with other missions, cf. Hilliard (1978: 136-144).

23. Laracy (1976: 35). For an interesting account of the Solomon Islanders from the perspective of a European entrepreneur during these years just prior to 1900, cf. Nerdrum (1902).

24. Cf. Grattan (1963b: 395-396). Judy Bennett of the Research School of Pacific Studies, Australian National University, has recently completed a doctoral thesis on the history of the commercial enterprises of traders and planters in the Solomon Islands up to World War II. The problems of land tenure resulting from the proliferation of plantations in the Solomon Islands has been the recent (1980) doctoral study of Ian Heath at La Trobe University, Melbourne.

25. Grattan (1963b: 404). Cf. Thompson (1971).

26. Hilliard (1978: 167) reports that:

    > By 1912, the white population of the protectorate exceeded five hundred and there were fifty planters on the coastal plains of northern Guadalcanal. More than 4500 Solomon Islanders were employed as labourers on local plantations. In a single week of 1911, eight steamers — two warships, five trading vessels and a mission-ship—anchored at Tulagi and Gavutu.

27. *M.M.R.*, 1909, p. 14. Quoted in Hilliard (1978: 166).

28. For a general discussion of changes brought to Melanesia as a result of European contact during this period, cf. Hogbin (1958: 163-206), and for the Solomon Islands exclusively, cf. Hogbin (1934).

29. In a, "Memorandum on the Future of the Melanesian Mission" written for private circulation in 1919, it was noted with despair that despite the changing conditions, the Melanesian Mission had been slow to respond to the new opportunities for evangelism:

    > The small number of white workers placed in the Solomon Islands is utterly inadequate to the great task before them. The population of the Solomons (including Bougainville) is estimated at

210,000. We have only eight white Priests working there. The population of the southern groups (Banks', Torres and New Hebrides) is small compared with the Solomons; but we have five white Priests here and four at Norfolk Island. Thus the less important islands receive, in proportion, much more attention than the important ones" (*Memorandum* . . . , p. 5).

30. Cf. Hilliard (1978: 205-206). An interesting document, written by T. C. Cullwick (ca. 1910), gives financial, practical and spiritual justification for retaining Norfolk Island as the Melanesian Mission headquarters. It is a good example of the kind of arguments that were waged against moving from that center of hallowed mission traditions. It is titled, "In the Matter of the Proposal to Move the Headquarters of the Melanesian Mission from Norfolk Island to the Solomon Islands and also to give up Norfolk Island as a Training College and the *Southern Cross* as a Missionary Vessel." St. John's College Library, Auckland.

31. A significant exception to the pattern of itineration, where a missionary moved back and forth between his island district and Norfolk Island, was that of Dr. Henry Welchman who was instrumental in the large group movement of conversion to Christianity on Santa Isabel. Welchman was one of the first missionaries to not return in the "summer" months to Norfolk Island, and from 1903 until his death in 1908, he stayed in the islands devoting himself to the work on Santa Isabel (Fox 1958: 197; E. Wilson 1935: 53). Prior to Welchman the renegade missionary A. C. Forrest had resided continuously throughout the year at Santa Cruz (Ivens 1918: 204). For a brief discussion of the "infamous" Forrest, cf. Hilliard (1978: 185-186).

32. The private diaries of the missionaries demonstrate this more than any other documentary source. For example, Henry Welchman's diaries are replete with entries about his activities in trying to solve domestic disputes and marriage problems.

33. *M.M.R.*, 1886, p. 17.

34. Cecil Wilson, *Women of Melanesia* (Sydney, n.d. [1904] pages unnumbered). For a contrasting islander's view of women on Santa Isabel, cf. Bogesi (1948: 215-216).

35. Cecil Wilson, *loc. cit.*

36. Even a Norfolk Island-trained girl was not always appreciated or welcomed, for her kinsmen complained that her training ruined her for garden work, her most important occupation, and made her a recalcitrant wife so that she would not listen to her husband (Hilliard 1978: 150).

37. *S.C.L.E.*, April 1907, p. 47. Quoted in Hilliard (1978: 151). Cf. Melanesian Mission, *About Melanesia No. 6*: "Lady Missionaries and One of the Empire's Best," being an Extract from "A Trader in the Savage Solomons" (n.p., n.d.), *About Melanesia No. 7*: Native Women of the Solomons, "Mother's Union Work" (Sydney, n.d.).

38. On the early work of women missionaries at Norfolk Island, cf. *S.C.L.*, May 1895, pp. 6-7; June 1895, pp. 5-6; July 1895, pp. 7-8. For a discussion of women's missionary work in the islands, cf. E. Wilson (1915: 121-128), Hopkins (1927: 63-73), Fox (1958: 45), Hilliard (1978: 149-153).

39. W.P.H.C., 3561/1930, F. Ashley to M. Fletcher, October 29, 1930. For a review of the various missions' educational programs and the government's attitude toward them in the Solomon Islands, cf. Boutilier (1978: 139-161). See also B. Palmer (1977).

40. For a vivid description of life at Pawa, cf. Fox (1962: 38-46). Fox was headmaster of All Hallows' Senior Boys' School, Pawa, on the island of Ugi, from 1924 to 1932. Cf. *S.C.L.E.*, July 1949, pp. 135-138.

41. Mota continued to be used as the language of instruction at the theological college until the mid 1950's. For further discussion on the "language question" and subsequent debate within the Melanesian Mission, cf. Hilliard (1978: 203-205).

    T. C. Cullwick (n.d.) was a strong adherent of keeping Mota as the mission *lingua franca*, and wrote:

    > If the knowledge of Mota goes the power of personal influence (which counts for so much in a work like this) of the Bishop and of those who take his place, will, to a great extent, be lost as he cannot possibly gain such a knowledge of the various languages as will enable him to place himself in such a close personal relationship which the thorough knowledge of a language common to himself and his teachers gives him: English for many years to come cannot possibly take its place.

42. Melanesian Mission, *Pacific Progress 1849-1949. Being the Illustrated Centenary Book of the Diocese of Melanesia.* London: The Melanesian Mission (pages unnumbered).

43. Cf. *The Melanesian Messenger* (Easter 1967), p. 15.

44. For a history of the Mission's educational work, from one of its own members, during this period, cf. Fox (1958: 225-247), cf. Hopkins (1927: 48-62, 86-95; 1936). An example of mission propaganda to promote the understanding of the Melanesian Mission's work in education is found in, *About Melanesia No. 8*: Training Young

Melanesians. This pamphlet gives an insider's view of the mission's educational methods. A critical study of all mission-school education in the Solomon Islands during this period is found in Grover (1940), cf. B. Palmer (1977), Boutilier (1978: 139-161).

45. Cf. Fox (1958: 34-35).

46. Quoted in Fox (1958: 253). For further reference to Baddeley's philosophy of mission and his emphasis on medical work, cf. *S.C.L.E.*, April-July 1944, pp. 13-19; April-July 1945, pp. 25-28.

47. *The Reaper* (September 1938), 16(8): 4. Wellington, New Zealand. Quoted in Hilliard (1978: 270). For a brief historical review of the Melanesian Mission's medical work, cf. Fox (1958: 248-254), and Hilliard (1978: 267-270). See also, *About Melanesia No. 4*: Medical Work in Melanesia, Hopkins (1927: 74-85), and E. Wilson (1936).

48. Kroeber (1948: 364).

49. C. Wilson, Extracts from letters . . . , *op. cit.*, September 12, 1903.

50. *Ibid.*, August 25, 1909.

51. *Ibid.*, September 15, 1903.

52. Quoted in Hilliard (1978: 163).

53. For discussion on the distinction between bush and salt-water people, see above, Ch. 2, pp. 60-61.

54. C. Wilson, Extracts from letters . . . , *op. cit.*, September 27, 1903.

55. For a discussion of the distinction between pagan settlements in the bush and Christian villages on the coast in northern Malaita, cf. Hogbin (1939: 212), and H. Ross (1973: 99-104; 1978: 180-182).

56. For a discussion of the repatriation of Solomon Islanders from the plantations of Queensland and Fiji, cf. Ivens (1918: 230-232), Hopkins (*Autobiography*, pp. 90-96), and Corris (1973: 126-148).

This original legislation called for the deportation of islanders who had lived for many years in Queensland, and would have deported all but 691 islanders. However, considerable pressure was mounted against the Queensland government to expand the exemption clauses. A. I. Hopkins went to Australia to represent the Melanesian Mission in alerting the government to some of the defects in the original proposal (*Autobiography*, pp. 155-157). Exemptions were finally made for anyone who had resided in Queensland for at least five years prior to September 1, 1884, for those who had been in Australia before September 1, 1879, or who had resided in Australia for twenty years prior to December 31, 1906. Others exempted from deportation were islanders who were registered owners of freehold land in Queensland, male islanders married to non-Pacific women, and islanders suffering from illness or those of extreme old age. In 1906 there were 6,389 Melanesians in Queensland scheduled to be deported. Approximately 4,800 of these were Solomon Islanders, and 2,500 of these were from Malaita. (Queensland Legislative Assembly, *Votes and Proceedings 1906*, Vol. 2: 103.) Cited in Corris (1973: 129-130).

57. Cf. Hopkins, *Autobiography*, p. 92. Ivens (1918: 232).

58. Hopkins (*Autobiography*, p. 159) notes that Christian villages were established by beginning "schools" which "were open to those afraid to land at their village or those who came back Christians."

59. Hopkins, *Autobiography*, p. 46.

60. *Ibid.*, pp. 46-47.

61. Hilliard (1969: 47-49), Corris (1973: 136).

62. Hopkins, *Autobiography*, pp.25-26.

63. Kanaka is an Hawaiian word meaning man. However it has been used to describe Melanesian laborers in Queensland and as a gloss for natives in Papua New Guinea. For further discussion, cf. Ivens (1918: 218).

64. Hopkins, *Autobiography*, p. 192.

65. The term "mass movement" carries a negative connotation and implies people acting in a fearful, hysterical manner as an irrational mass; there is nothing irrational about multi-individual group movements. The importance of individual decision making is often lost when the term mass movement is used. In contrast, the term multi-individual movement, first articulated by H. G. Barnett, more accurately portrays the character of the communal group. In communal societies people frequently make decisions after considerable discussion, and act on them in group patterns. The solidarity of the group is maintained this way, for the decision to innovate and change is not made unless the group is unanimous. Thus in multi-individual people movements, individuals are not submerged in a blind mass, or subjected to the "tyranny of the group." Their individual personalities are maintained, and by deliberate individual choice, people act as a group. This is quite different from action implied by the notion of a mass movement. Tippett (1971: 198-220) discusses the concept of multi-individual people movements as it relates to group movements in conversion to Christianity. He demonstrates that the concept of mass movement is very inaccurate to describe the cultural dynamics of multi-individual people movements and notes:

> Church growth studies demonstrate that responses to the gospel have been more effective where missionary advocates have directed their appeals to autonomous decision-making groups, who have power to act, rather than to individuals who have to rebel against the group to act alone . . . The bulk of the church in the Pacific has been won by people movements; that is, not isolated individuals, but by individuals acting within their own social patterns and by means of their own decision-making mechanisms. (1971: 200-201).

For an interesting study of the whole village approach to evangelism employed by the Lutherans in New Guinea, see Keysser (1980). See also Tippett (n.d., b: 24-29), Barnett (1953: 15).

66. Cf. Tippett (1967: 319-329).

67. Speaking of Pacific Islanders in general, Hogbin (1958: 71) asks:

> Why did the natives without any objective proof believe the missionaries? And why did they abandon so much of what had hitherto served to orient their lives? Their pagan religion had guaranteed a measure of security, but they dismissed these beliefs as superstitions, ceased attending the ceremonies, treated their priests with disrespect, burned the images or sold them to museum collectors, and allowed the temples to fall in ruins . . . Our problem in this instance is thus to account not for an unexpected rejection of an innovation but for a surprising acceptance.

68. Belshaw (1954: 70) notes that, "Christiantiy was everywhere regarded as a new form of ritual devised to placate or encourage superior spirits."

69. Discussion of Pacific Islanders' motivations for converting to Christianity is found in Hogbin (1939: 179-184) for Malaita, Firth (1970: 320-326) for Tikopia, Guiart (1970) for Melanesia in general and the New Hebrides in particular, and Hogbin (1958: 70-75) for a general discussion.

70. For further discussion on the Prayer Book, see below Ch. 6, p.335.

71. It is not surprising to discover that in the 1930's among Nggela and Santa Isabel converts, who were now second and third generation Christians, there arose some discontent with the Melanesian Mission for not teaching them English in the schools. They realized that their own language, or the Mission *lingua franca*, Mota, would not give them access to the wider European world as the English language would do (W.P.H.C., 2594/1931, J. Barley to M. Fletcher, December 9, 1931).

72. *B.S.I.P., Annual Report 1932*, Office of District Officer, Auki, January 25, 1933, p. 4. W.P.A., BSIP 27/VI/1 Malaita District Annual Report 1930-1936.

73. For a broader discussion on the relationship of literacy to conversion in Oceania, Cf. Parsonson (1967). See also Belshaw (1954: 73), and for Nigeria, cf. Peel (1968b: 139-140).

74. Hopkins, *Autobiography*, pp. 52-53.

75. Cf. Guiart (1970). Belshaw (1954: 71) states that, "The early adherence to Christianity . . . must be explained in terms of social and material advantage."

76. Hopkins. *Autobiography*, pp. 28-29. Cf. Corris (1970: 263). Laracy (1976: 71-72) notes that to induce conversion the Catholic Marists employed a strategy of "paternal indulgence of their parishoner's material desires." He quotes a missionary writing in 1902 who noted:

    > 'To win a little tobacco . . . (The Solomon Islander) will promise whatever you wish. In his honeyed language he will regale your ears with the names "friend" . . . "brother" . . . "chief" . . .' Filling the pipes of thirty-five bushmen, he reflected, 'it is by these gifts that the missionary wins the affection of the natives.'

77. Cf. McKinnon (1972: Ch. V; 1975).

78. For more on the relationship between the headhunting crisis and conversion on Santa Isabel, see discussion below, Ch. 6, pp. 359-364.

79. C. Wilson (1932: 235).

80. For an excellent discussion of the role of the Methodist Mission as a peace-maker on Choiseul, cf. Tippett (1967: 190-200). It is important to realize that the notion of peace had many indigenous patterns, and thus the concept introduced by the Mission was not novel. See, for example, Brown (1910: 255-260), Fox (1924: 311-313), Ivens (1927: 161, 304), C. Wilson (1932: 36, 40), Scheffler (1964, 1965: 222-223, 237-239). Christianity simply provided an alternative mode for implementing peace; a mode complete with religious beliefs and ritual symbols for islanders to adopt in the new social order of peaceful coexistence. On the pacification of Melanesia, see the symposium edited by Rodman and Cooper (1979).

81. See discussion below on depopulation and demoralization of Melanesian societies in this period, pp. 202-205.

82. For a discussion of the updating of religious ritual to serve traditional Melanesian ends, see above, Ch. 2, p. 66.

83. Speaking about the influence of missionaries in the Pacific, Hogbin (1958: 72) notes:

    > Like the other white men, they also appeared to be rich, owned so many possessions, and obviously knew so much. In addition, they were in a position to win more personal respect and even love. They alone of the permanent foreign residents in the colony

followed a calling that compelled them to live side by side with the native community and learn the vernacular tongues. They visited the afflicted, tended the sick, and were interested in the humblest villager and prepared to work for his well-being.

84. Three different models of missionary-islander interaction during this period are discussed below, pp. 205-219. It will become clear in that discussion that many missionaries had gained considerable power in the Christian Melanesian communities.

85. Interview with Dr. Gerald A. Arbuckle, Taradale, New Zealand, February 7, 1977.

86. This paternalistic trend is discussed later in this chapter. See discussion below, pp. 199-202.

87. Fox (1962: 70) who served longer than any other member of the Melanesian Mission stated that Ini Kopuria was "one of the two ablest Melanesians I have known." In writing Ini's obituary, Fox stated:

> He was not popular with the white staff who thought him conceited . . . He thought it all wrong that every Melanesian because of his colour, should be inferior to every white man because of his colour, yet he felt there was this feeling even within the mission (*S.C.L.E.*, January 1946, p. 7).

88. *S.C.L.*, June 1946, pp. 22-23. Quoted in Hilliard (1978: 227).

89. This is the first rule of the Brotherhood. For a partial list of the Rules of the Melanesian Brotherhood, see Appendix V.

90. One of the Isabel volunteers was Dudley Bale who later became a priest. Although retired, he was still alive and active during the period of my fieldwork (1977-1978) and gave me several interesting interviews.

91. To "open up" a pagan village is the islanders' own term for their evangelistic activity.

92. The uniform of the Brothers has symbolic meaning as well. The black loincloth "means the heathen who are still in darkness. The white sash is the light of Christ, shining in the midst of the heathen" (*The Melanesian Messenger*, December 1962, p. 17).

93. Quoted in Fox (1962: 72). For other miracle stories of the Melanesian Brotherhood, cf. *The Melanesian Messenger*, April 1, 1962, pp. 11-12.

94. *S.C.L.*, January 1936, p. 15.

95. Melanesian Mission, *Proceedings of the Diocesan Synod 1962*, p. 69. Cited in Tippett (1967: 51).

96. Fox (1962: 76).

97. *Ibid.*
98. *Ibid.*, p. 77.
99. I am indebted to Dr. Gerald Arbuckle for many of these insights as to the Melanesian character of the Melanesian Brotherhood. For additional discussion on the Melanesian Brotherhood, cf. Steward (1928, 1936), Lycett (1935), Hopkins (*Autobiography*, pp. 206-207), Newbolt (1939: 111-122), Fox (1958: 193-195; 1962: 67-79; n.d.b., ca. 1972), Tippett (1967: 50-53), Naban (1976: 87-93), Hilliard (1978: 227-232), Macdonald-Milne (n.d., ca. 1981). See also *S.C.L.E.*, January 1946, pp. 5-7; May 1955, pp. 53-54; June 1962, pp. 44-48; September 1963, pp. 90-94, 97; *The Melanesian Messenger*, May 1960, p. 6; April 1962, pp. 11-12; December 1962, pp. 16-20; December 1964, p. 12. For a discussion of the role of the Brotherhood in converting Tikopia to Christianity, cf. Firth (1970: 341-342).
100. John Still, "Letter from a Wolverhampton missionary in New Zealand," June 29, 1876. Newspaper clipping, A.J.C.P. M804, microfilm, N.L.A.
101. *M.M.R.*, 1902, p. 12.
102. *Ibid.*, p. 8.
103. *M.M.R.*, 1910, p. 56.
104. See discussion below on the integration of Christianity into contemporary Melanesian life, Chapter 6, pp. 372-392.
105. *M.M.R.*, 1908, p. 44.
106. *S.C.L.E.*, July 1912, p. 117.
107. Melanesian Mission (1926), *Melanesia*, p. 25. In 1926 there were 27 Melanesian clergy including deacons and priests, 20 European clergy, 8 laymen, and 17 women workers.
108. Hopkins (1936) discusses in detail the composition of the Melanesian Mission in terms of the White corks and the Black net. Although the metaphor originated with Bishop George Selwyn, its meaning appears to have undergone considerable change, to the point where it was believed the black net could never function without the support of the white corks.
109. Hilliard (1978: 155).
110. Fox (1958: 47-48), Hilliard (1978: 202-203).
111. For a discussion of missionary paternalism and its relationship to Marching Rule, a post World War II nativistic movement in the Solomon Islands, cf. Whiteman (1975: 361-366), and Ch. 5, pp. 266-272, in this study. As I have suggested, the impact of these structural inequalities imposed on societies under the domination of

foreign rule, was a phenomenon throughout the colonial world. An example of this is found in a lucid discussion of the structure and function of early expatriate communities in northern Nigeria (Salamone 1978).

Early in this period Ivens wrote a pamphlet entitled, *Hints to Missionaries to Melanesia*. In chapter five, entitled "Management of Natives," he warned the new missionaries:

> A native quite understands the white man's stooping to conquer, but he has a very keen sense of what their teaching ought to be, and he expects them to show him an example of dignity. To follow Christ and to "empty" oneself is very different from being familiar (1907: 24).

112. *M.M.R.*, 1904, pp. 14-15.

113. *Ibid.*, p. 16. Writing privately to his wife while on an episcopal tour of the islands in 1904, Wilson lamented, "About 10,000 Christians must have died in the 10 years I have been here. I hope some of them are thankful for the work we do for them" (Extracts from letters . . . , *op. cit.*, July 10, 1904).

114. C. M. Woodford to Sir Everad Im Thurn, December 26, 1909, enclosure in Thurn to C.O., January 24, 1910. C.O. 225/90. Public Record Office. Quoted in Scarr (1967: 293).

115. Sir Francis May to C.O., December 8, 1911. C.O. 225/98. Public Record Office. Quoted in Scarr (1967: 294).

116. Scarr (1967: 293).

117. Durrad (1922: 5-6), E. Wilson (1936: 71).

118. W.P.H.C. 1214/1932, Malaita District Report 1931. Cf. Hilliard (1978: 156).

119. *S.C.L.E.*, July 1912, p. 110.

120. W.P.H.C. 82/1898 (i), Woodford to Im Thurn, February 21, 1908. Quoted in Scarr (1967: 292).

121. F. Keesing (1941: 54) based on data collected in the late 1930's, reported that although there were areas in Island Melanesia where population decline was reversed, the overall trend appeared to be somewhat downward, whereas in New Guinea, the population was reported to be increasing. For further discussion of depopulation in Melanesia, and the Pacific in general, cf. Rivers (1922), Buxton (1925-26), Pitt-Rivers (1927), Roberts (1927), Hamlin (1932), Lambert (1934), Bernatzik (1935: 70-71), Mander (1954: 321, 479-480).

122. Fallowes, Letters to his sister, 1929-1934, N.L.A., February 17, 1930.

123. Fox (1958: 20).

124. Personal communication from R. P. Fallowes, February 20, 1978.

125. For discussion of the Anglo-Catholic tradition in the Melanesian Mission, see below, Ch. 6, pp. 333-334.

126. Fallowes, *op. cit.*, September 7, 1929.

127. *Ibid.*, August 29, 1929.

128. *Ibid.*, February 17, 1930.

129. *Ibid.*

130. Personal communication from R. P. Fallowes, February 20, 1978.

131. BSIP 1/III MP 479/33, item 1, W.P.A. Report from D. O. Ysabel to Resident Commissioner, March 8, 1933.

132. Fallowes, *op. cit.*, May 15, 1931.

133. Personal communication from R. P. Fallowes, February 20, 1978.

134. BSIP 1/III MP 380/33, enclosure 10 A, W.P.A. P. C. Hubbard, Legal Advisor to Resident Commissioner, Tulagi, June 26, 1933.

135. Fallowes, *op. cit.*, April 19, 1933.

136. *Ibid.*, June 24, 1933.

137. BSIP 1/III MP 380/33, enclosure 10 A.

138. Fallowes, *op. cit.*, November 8, 1929.

139. *Ibid.*, February 17, 1930.

140. *Ibid.*

141. BSIP 1/III MP 479/33. Report submitted by the Acting Commandant Armed Constabulary, 5 March 1933, to the Acting Resident Commissioner.

142. BSIP 1/III MP 479/33, p. 16. List of orders given by Fallowes to the Mission Headmen, supplied by Walter Notere.

143. *Ibid.*, p. 14. For an excellent discussion of the tensions between Church and State on Santa Isabel during this period, cf. Hilliard (1974: 112-116), and G. White (1978: 210-230). Wilfred Fowler, a District Officer on Santa Isabel during Fallowes' time, has written a book about his experiences. He devotes an unflattering chapter to "The Missionary" —Fallowes, disguised as "Woodley" (1959: 23-55).

144. Fallowes' diary (1931-1934, N.L.A.) has several entries about his personal tangles with Bishop Baddeley, who, on one occasion (March 18, 1934), lost his temper with Fallowes, saying that he was "able to

defy the Government, but shall not defy him."

145. Personal communication from R. P. Fallowes, March 13, 1979.

146. Cf. Belshaw (1958: 488-489).

147. BSIP 27/VI/1, Malaita District Annual Report 1930-1936. January 14, 1936, The Office of the District Officer, Malaita, Annual Report 1935, p. 14. W.P.A. By an ordinance of the King in 1935, the minimum wage in the Solomon Islands was reduced by one-half, from £1 per month to 10 shillings.

148. BSIP F43/14. Fallowes to High Commissioner, June 12, 1939.

149. *Ibid.* Statement of John Palmer Pidoke, "Chief of Gela," June 1939, enclosure in R. P. Fallowes to High Commissioner, 15 June 1939. Quoted in Hilliard (1978: 284).

150. *Ibid.*

151. Personal communication from R. P. Fallowes, February 20, 1978; March 13, 1979.

152. *S.C.L.*, October 1938, p. 11. Quoted in Hilliard (1978: 284).

153. For further discussion of the Fallowes Movement, also known as the Chair and Rule Movement, cf. Worsley (1957: 171-172), Belshaw (1958: 488-489), Hilliard (1974: 113-116; 1978: 282-285), and G. White (1978: 230-240). See also the following W.P.A. file numbers: WPHC 3307/1938, Sir Harry Luke to C.O., November 27, 1939; WPHC 2195/1940, Ysabel, Guadalcanal and Eastern Solomons District Reports 1939; BSIP F43/14/1.

154. Quoted in Fox (1958: 96).

155. Interview with Sr. Helen Barrett, Fauabu, Malaita, March 1978. Personal communication from R. P. Fallowes, February 20, 1978.

156. Quoted in Fox (1958: 95). Cf. *S.C.L.E.*, April-July 1944, p. 19.

157. Fox (1958: 87).

158. Personal communication from R. P. Fallowes, February 20, 1978.

159. In World War I, Baddeley commanded an infantry battalion of the East Surreys in France, and was decorated D.S.O. and M.C. with bar, for his valiant military efforts.

160. Colonial Office (1946), *Among Those Present*, pp. 7-11.

161. Cf. Van Dusen (1945: 58-61).

162. *S.C.L.E.*, January-April 1945, p. 15; July 1948, p. 39; October 1948, p. 58. For the President's Citation of Baddeley for his efforts in World War II, cf. *S.C.L.E.*, October 1948, p. 58. For further

discussion on Baddeley, cf. Fox (1958: 83-96), and Hilliard (1978: 259ff).

163. Fox (n.d.c. [1956]) *Melanesian Memories*, Ch. 2, p. 2.

164. When I interviewed Fox in February 1977, he stated that he regretted being influenced so much by Rivers and the "English School of Diffusionism" when he wrote his classic ethnography, *The Threshold of the Pacific* (1924).

165. Fox (1924: vii).

166. Fox's most significant anthropological contribution was *The Threshold of the Pacific* (1924). G. Elliot Smith in the preface to Fox's book, notes (1924: vi):

> Just before his death, Dr. Rivers received the manuscript from which the present book has been prepared. It is difficult to convey an adequate idea of the profound impression the study of Fox's manuscript made on him. Rivers regarded it—and with ample justification—as one of the most important, if not the most important, piece of field-work that has ever been done in social anthropology.

In addition to his major 1924 work, Fox published at least nine articles and notes in *The Journal of the Polynesian Society*, and numerous enthnographic descriptions of Melanesian society and culture in the Mission's official publication, the *Southern Cross Log*.

167. Fox to Durrad, July 8, 1920. Durrad Papers, MS Papers 171, Alexander Turnbull Library, Wellington, New Zealand.

168. *Ibid.*

169. Hugh Young, "The Living Legend," *The Solomons News Drum*, July 1, 1977, p. 3.

170. Interview with Bishop Dudley Tuti, February 1978.

171. Fox's diaries are housed in the Church of Melanesia Archives, Honiara, Solomon Islands.

172. Fox (n.d.c. [1956]), *loc. cit.* At the age of 99, Charles Elliot Fox died in New Zealand on October 28, 1977, corresponding with the festival of St. Simon and St. Jude, the day on which the founding of the Melanesian Brotherhood is annually commemorated. The rumor in the Solomons and published in the local newspapers was that Fox had wanted to die on that date. His body was brought back to the Solomons, and he was buried in his Brother's uniform at Tabalia, the headquarters of the Melanesian Brotherhood. Following the burial, an enormous Melanesian feast was given in his honor. One Melanesian after another stood and gave an extemporaneous tribute about their friend, *Dr.*

Fockis. It was a moving experience for me, and his words spoken to me six months previously had a ring of truth: "I am a Melanesian."

173. I am indebted to stimulating discussions with Professor Richard M. Thomas for the following analysis of missionary types in a larger interpretive framework of leadership in a social system.

174. For a contemporary study of Solomon Islanders who have successfully combined participation in the cash economy with subsistence activities leading to development without destruction, see Whiteman (1982).

175. *M.M.R.*, 1908, p. 44.

176. *S.C.L.E.*, July 1912, pp. 115-116.

177. Fallowes, Diary, *op. cit.*, April 12, 1932.

178. Cf. Bates (1971) for a contemporary discussion of goal discrepancy as it relates to tensions between missionary organizations and native churches in Africa.

179. As late as 1936, the Malaita District Annual Report 1936, notes that the people of Malaita do not live in villages: "Two or three houses in a small clearing, containing a family is all that one finds, and in a day's walk, one sees remarkably little of the inhabitants. The only villages in the true sense are certain Mission settlements around the foreshores of the Island" (BSIP 27/VI/1, Malaita District Annual Report 1930-1936, p. 15).

180. Cf. Hilliard (1966: 546), and M. Wilson (1971: 105).

181. For an excellent discussion of changing leadership roles on Santa Isabel resulting from islanders' adoption of Christianity, cf. G. White (1978, esp. pp. 131-197). See also, Hogbin (1939: 223-226) for North Malaita, Scheffler (1964b, 1965: 28) for Choiseul, and Tippett (1967: 139-146) for the Western Solomons in general.

182. Cf. Hilliard (1966: 503-509).

183. There were of course exceptions in missionary perceptions of Melanesian women. One of these was Charles Brooke, in charge of the Mission's work on Nggela (1867-1874). Hilliard (1978: 150) notes that:

> Brooke was one of the few missionaries to perceive that Nggela women, for example, occupied an influential social role in village affairs, as messengers, mediators between enemies, and negotiators of loans.

Hilliard goes on to note that:

> Nevertheless, the customary exclusion of women from certain religious and social activities, and the fact that all the teachers of

Christianity were male, effectively ensured that women inhabitants of school villages were as a rule much less affected than men by the new teaching.

184. One of the problems created by church rulings instead of customary laws regulating marriage, is that the Anglican Church did not recognize the importance of clan boundaries in demarcating the limits of marriageable partners. This has created a serious problem at times when members of the same clan intermarry—breaking their traditional laws but not violating church rules.

185. For a contemporary study of a pagan ethical system in the Solomon Islands, cf. Cooper (1970).

186. A number of informants on Malaita said that they had become Christian because of the high cost of maintaining traditional shrines. They claimed that it took so much time and energy to attend these in order to appease the ancestral spirits, that Christianity appeared to be a far less taxing belief system, and so for this reason, they were primarily attracted to it.

187. For a discussion of chastity on Malaita, cf. Hogbin (1939: 209-211).

188. *Ibid.*, pp. 195-197.

189. Cf. Hogbin (1935).

Chapter 5

Toward Independence and Indigenization

The previous period (1900-1942) of Melanesian culture contact introduced penetrating socio-cultural changes in island life: Colonial government had established *Pax Britannica*, Christian missions had introduced various models of Christian belief and behavior, and increasingly islanders had chosen to convert to the new faith. European planters had alienated large tracts of land in establishing plantations, and used islanders as their labor supply.

In the 1930's the world-wide economic depression was felt in Melanesia. The bottom fell out of copra prices, the main island export, and wages paid to Melanesian laborers were reduced from £1 per month to 10 shillings.[1] However, islanders felt more than simply the effects of economic depression. Socio-political depression was even more deeply felt under the heavy-handed domination of paternalistic European government officials, missionaries and planters. Discontent with this Colonial Order was expressed throughout this period but it became increasingly manifest in the late 1930's. The catalyst which triggered general restlessness and impatience with the socio-political status quo was the impact of World War II which introduced a flood of new things and new ideas.[2]

In this chapter discussion will center on the evolution of socio-political institutions as Melanesians attempted to adjust to European paternalism. Hence the chapter title, "Toward Independence and Indigenization." Brief discussion will first be given to the impact of World War II on the islands, followed by a study of a Melanesian socio-political movement known as "Marching Rule." This important movement occurred in the Solomon Islands and symbolized the islanders' attempts to resolve the contradictions between their indigenous values and introduced Western institutions. The final sections of this chapter will focus on Melanesians' attempts to gain greater control of the Anglican Church which was firmly established but still dominated by European missionaries.

World War II and Its Impact on Melanesian Acculturation

The Solomon Islands, as an isolated backwater of the Pacific, was suddenly brought to the world's attention in 1942. After bombing and subsequently occupying the strategic port of Rabaul on New Britain in

January 1942, the Japanese pushed on toward the Solomon Islands. They began dropping bombs weekly on the small capital of the Protectorate at Tulagi in February, and by May had launched a full-scale invasion. In July they set about building an airfield on the coastal plains of Guadalcanal in anticipation of a further thrust south and east.[3] The American counter-offensive, beginning in August, aimed at first capturing the airfield and then pushing the Japanese back toward New Guinea and eventually to their own country. Guadalcanal became the scene of some of the most bitter fighting in the Pacific theatre.[4] Thousands of Allied troops (Americans, Fijians, and New Zealanders) poured into the Solomon Islands and eventually drove the Japanese out. In addition to Guadalcanal, parts of the Western Solomons were also the scenes of Japanese and American combat. However, the greatest impact of the war on the islands was not so much the Japanese invasion as it was the American liberation.[5]

In response to the Japanese invasion most of the Europeans in the Solomons fled, but a few remained behind, including the Resident Commissioner W. S. Marchant.[6] But in effect, the Protectorate Administration had collapsed in the face of the Japanese invasion, a fact which did not go unnoticed among the islanders.[7] It was the American troops, not the British, who came to the aid of the islanders in routing the Japanese from the islands. By March 1943, the battle for the central Solomons had been won and the combat zone moved northwestward. However, the Americans did not leave the Solomons, for Guadalcanal and Nggela became staging bases for operations in the northwest, and Solomon Islanders, primarily from Malaita,[8] were employed by the Americans in the volunteer Labor Corps.[9] Between 1943 and 1945 hundreds of thousands of American troops passed through the Solomons, bringing with them an ensemble of material wealth never before realized nor scarcely imagined by the islanders — huge quantities of food, mechanical equipment, large supplies of tents, stretchers, mosquito netting, electric lights, jeeps, trucks, etc. Much of this material was treated casually as if there was "plenty more where that came from," and it was liberally doled out to islanders working in the Labor Corps. Belshaw comments on this sudden influx of material goods:

> I estimated that every one of the 6,000 people of Gela in the Solomons acquired a stretcher bed and mosquito net in this period. In the Russell Islands in the Solomons, so I am told, villagers acquired and owned telephones, and electric lighting systems, and rebuilt their houses entirely of timber. The equipment was still working satisfactorily in 1947, one year after the Americans had left.[10]

But the Americans introduced more than just tons of material goods; they introduced anti-colonial ideas and a spirit of egalitarianism between Europeans and islanders. Despite the fact that American Blacks functioned in segregated units and were assigned to supply duties rather than combat, islanders perceived them to be in a far more egalitarian relationship with the White troops than they themselves were with European planters, government officials and missionaries.[11] Roger Keesing cogently notes the challenges this new situation presented to the British colonialists:

> The ex-colonial officers who commanded the Labour Corps faced difficulties in trying to maintain status and prestige on behalf of a British establishment that had crumbled in the face of Japanese invasion and been humbled by massive American power and successful liberation. They did their best to preserve a heavy-handed control in the racist pre-war colonial style and to prevent the "natives" from getting "uppity" in the face of American largesse and egalitarianism. Their confiscation of goods the Labour Corps men had accumulated[12] and attempts to preserve pre-war style segregation and subordination[13] only heightened resentment among the Malaitans and anticolonialist sentiment among American military personnel (1978b: 48).

An Anglican missionary who stayed in the Solomons through the war years, observed in 1945:

> Labour is difficult—the natives have been badly spoilt through the generosity of our Allies, who have showered them with dollars and clothing, which we never allow them to have as it weakens their chest . . . Also the most stupid thing is to give them boots, poor children, (that is what they are in many ways) —they come in with horrible sores on their feet from boots which do not fit, socks filthy and feet poisoned. It also makes them think we are mean — but they see through it and just laugh and say: "Americans are another kind" comparing them to Chinese or other nationalities.[14]

In the New Hebrides the impact of the war was far less than in the Solomon Islands. Three American bases were established there, but none in the area of the Melanesian Mission work. The greatest impact of the war was to increase the cash economy through wage labor,[15] but for the most part, island life continued uninterrupted. Plantations thrived during this time as there was a good market for copra since those in the Solomons were put out of operation. The inept Condominium Government continued to function as usual.

World War II is a distinct watershed in Melanesian culture-contact history for it opened the way to an ideological revolution which profoundly changed the attitudes and perspectives of both islanders and Europeans toward policies and programs to be pursued in the post-war years.[16] Although reaction to the Colonial Order had antecedents prior to the war, the post-war developments and concerns for independence and indigeneity became more manifest, more vocal and more determined. In the following section I will focus on one of the most significant of these protest movements.

Marching Rule

Following close on the heels of the war was another eruption in the Solomon Islands. Only this time it came from within. It was the popular movement known as "Marching Rule"[17] which captured the allegiance of thousands of islanders, marshalling native enthusiasm and baffling colonial administrators. The Solomons had never before witnessed such a show of indigenous unity, nor had the Administration ever been so impotent in dealing with "Native Affairs."

A brief review of the colonial context is necessary in order to understand the cultural milieu in which the movement emerged. As noted above (pp. 172-173) colonialism appeared in the Solomons toward the end of the nineteenth century with the British establishing a Protectorate over the islands in 1893. During the first twenty-five years of British Administrative presence very little legislation was enacted that affected the islanders directly. In 1920, however, tax regulations were put into effect, calling for an annual tax to be paid by Solomon Islanders.[18] This was followed by labor regulations in 1921 and native administration regulations in 1922 when an attempt was made by the Colonial Office to initiate indirect rule after the model they had followed in East Africa.

The nature of the administrative judicial structure gave almost complete powers to the District Officer. In the absence of any memorandum clearly stating objectives and methods for effecting indirect rule, the quality of administrative justice was highly dependent on the personal attributes of the District Officer.[19] District Officers before the second World War tended to be men with either a military or plantation background. Cadets with pre-service training, as established by the Colonial Service in the mid-1920's did not reach the Solomons until the outbreak of World War II.[20]

Lacking a thorough understanding of indigenous leadership patterns, the Administration often appointed "chiefs" who in fact had no parallel authority among their own people. This undermining of traditional leadership and imposition of an artificial structure on the indigenous cultural pattern led to pre-war resistance by many Solomon Islanders particularly in the central and eastern districts.[21]

Thus on the eve of the 1942 Japanese invasion there was considerable discontent and frustration among Solomon Islanders with the British Administration. As Belshaw (1947: 190) notes, "It is not difficult to account for the glee with which law books were burnt and houses looted after the evacuation of European inhabitants of the region in 1942." The time was ripe for Marching Rule!

It is believed that the movement originated in the Solomon Island Labour Corps (S.I.L.C.) on Guadalcanal in 1943 and subsequently spread to the mountain villages in the Kwaio and 'Are' are districts of Malaita via repatriated members of the S.I.L.C. By 1945 the movement had spread to North Malaita and then on to Ulawa, San Cristobal and Guadalcanal. By 1947 the movement reached its peak, spreading to Santa Isabel, Nggela, and some of the outlying Polynesian islands in the Solomons.[22] It was estimated that at its zenith, 95 percent of the Malaita population supported Marching Rule.[23] We will now turn our attention briefly to summarizing (1) the doctrine and beliefs of the movement, and (2) the organization of its members.

Doctrine and Beliefs of Marching Rule.

The doctrine and beliefs of the Marching Rule movement had both positive and negative elements from the perspective of the European community and the British Administration. As Allan notes, writing in the Colonial journal, *Corona*:

> This movement which has combined admirable and progressive objects with preposterous and mystical promises and terrorist tactics, has developed a studied system of civil disobedience which unfortunately compares more favourably with similar campaigns in far less primitive countries (1951: 93).

A dominating tenet of Marching Rule doctrine, articulated in numerous ways, was an expression of anti-European sentiment. Allan (1950: 26) notes that, "Marching Rule has become an intangible symbol, adherence to which involves blind refusal to comply with Government orders and complete disassociation from the whiteman and his works." One of the most important manifestations of anti-European sentiment was the refusal of islanders to work on European-run plantations. Malaita was the center of Marching Rule activities, and also the primary source of island labor for working the plantations scattered throughout the Solomons. Thus the islanders' boycott of European plantations had disastrous consequences for the economy of the Solomon Islands struggling to regain financial solvency after the war. The small plantations in particular were devastated as a consequence of the boycott. Cochrane (1970: 91) notes that, "By the early 1950's only those planters who had shown that they were prepared to treat Solomon Islanders in a humane and fair way managed to obtain workers."

In addition to the labor strike, anti-European sentiment was expressed by a boycott against missionaries; however, it was selective, with some missionaries being forced to leave altogether, while others were able to continue their work without a great deal of interruption. An analysis of this differential treatment will proceed below (pp. 266-272).

Most scholars have tended to emphasize the importance of a variant of the classic Melanesian cargo cult myth in the Marching Rule doctrine. Allan (1950: 54-55) claims that the success of the movement derived from the successful propagation of a myth prophesying that on a given day, to be revealed by the leaders, the Americans would return in their Liberty ships to Malaita and there on the beaches disgorge tons of cargo: cigarettes (preferably "Luckies"), twist tobacco, candy, tinned food, knives, fish hooks and lines, calico, and the 101 items found in the Army PX or local trade store.[24]

Solomon Islanders clearly distinguished between the British and the Americans, claiming that the British refused to disgorge their cargo, while it was the Americans who would be the saviors of the Solomon Islands.[25] Such a contrast between Americans and British was consistent with their experience with the two different nationalities. It was the Americans who had been so liberal in doling out money and goods as evidenced by the estimated quarter of a million dollars left behind in the Solomons. Those islanders employed by the British in the National Defense League and the Labour Corps earned only £1 a month, whereas one who was employed by the Americans or worked as a free laborer could take advantage of the "fringe benefits" and easily make £12-14 a month. The contrast between British and Americans was significant and came to play an important role in the development of the supporting myth of Marching Rule.

In the course of my fieldwork I interviewed informants who had participated in Marching Rule in Malaita, and I came to the conclusion that although variants of a "cargo" ideology were present, it was far less significant as a formative element than most scholars have realized.[26] If scholars with preconceived notions are looking for "cargo" in Marching Rule to fit a convenient typology to "explain" the movement, then they will have little difficulty in documenting stories of "cargo." However, I am convinced that the cargo ideology was **not** a central doctrine of the early leaders, but occurred when all else had failed, in the later stages of the movement, and then on the periphery of it.[27]

The dominant theme in Marching Rule was the desire for Solomon Islanders to preserve their indigenous identity. Informants claim that Marching Rule was first and foremost a "custom movement," not an anti-British movement or cargo cult. Indeed, as the movement transpired and gained momentum, anti-European sentiment did increase, and cargo myths were propagated, but these were not the goals of the original leaders. One informant on Malaita claimed that when Marching Rule took this unfortunate turn, it in fact spoiled the original goals of the movement. Laracy (1971: 103) is therefore correct in asserting that, "Marching Rule was a socially and culturally reintegrative movement — not just an acquisitive and anti-British one."[28] Roger Keesing has also recognized the role of custom, by noting that one of the key elements in the doctrine of the movement was:

> . . . to codify "Custom," particularly related to ancestors, taboos, lands and the sex code; and while conceding that criminal offences of homicide, assault, and theft be dealt with under Protectorate law, to demand jurisdiction over customary matters (1978b: 50).

Let it not be implied that Marching Rule was a contra-acculturative movement. It was not. Islanders did not want to return completely to pre-contact days. Their primary goal was to preserve the integrity of Melanesian values while selectively choosing elements of the introduced European culture and contextualizing them for their own use.[29] Thus, from the viewpoint of the Protectorate government, among the "positive" elements of Marching Rule were:

1. The desire for better schools,
2. A policy of agricultural improvement and innovation,
3. A policy of urging Marching Rule members to use the medical services of the missions (however, they refused to pay for such services),
4. A plan of concentrating into villages,[30]
5. The conviction and policy of encouraging better housing throughout the island,
6. The belief that the elderly must be cared for as they had been traditionally,[31]
7. The sense of unity.[32]

The Government vacillated in their response to the movement. Initially they ignored it, then they encouraged it, but finally, when it was too late, they attempted to suppress it.[33]

Organization of Marching Rule.

The one feature that caught the Administration and European community by complete surprise was the organizational finesse shown by Marching Rule leaders and adherents. With the exception of that of New Caledonia and Fiji, the political prowess of Melanesians was viewed as one of the most primitive (in a pejorative and descriptive sense) in the whole of Oceania. Many Europeans assumed that Melanesians were simply incapable of any united effort approaching that of a nationalistic movement.[34] Yet, without doubt, the single, most significant element in Marching Rule was its organization, uniting heretofore disparate entities and amalgamating cultural and religious differences. Leadership for the movement was not provided by a single, visionary prophet and his close-knit band of disciples, characteristic of many Melanesian cargo cults. To the contrary, leadership for the movement came from several highly competent individuals emerging in different localities.[35]

Malaita was divided into nine districts corresponding roughly to the administrative districts on that island.[36] Each district was instructed to choose a "Head Chief." These men convened together occasionally to discuss broad policy, but for the most part, they ran the movement in their own districts according to their own ideas. The organizational structure was very hierarchical; beneath the "Head Chiefs" were sub-districts with "full chiefs," villages and towns with their own "leader chiefs" and even individual clans represented by a "line chief."

Codification of Marching Rule law, comprising a mixture of traditional norms and contemporary aspirations, was an important activity. To insure compliance with the law, Marching Rule courts were established in 1947, complete with jurisdiction including punishment and incarceration for infraction. It was understood that the more serious offences such as murder would have to be tried in Administration courts and were thus under the jurisdiction of the District Officer. As can be seen, there was clearly a role for the European to play in the Marching Rule regime, but it was determined by Marching Rule members, not by Europeans.

This organizational framework was highly efficient in initiating and executing communal projects. It was couched in military idiom, and as Cochrane (1970: 90) has noted, "The whole military organization was more impressive than that of the British. The ceremony was more elaborate, the drilling more rigorous, and the discipline more harsh." It was clearly the organization of Marching Rule that threatened the Protectorate government. Light fun and jest could be made of primitive natives believing in a cargo myth, but when these same "relics of the stone-age" suddenly began organizing in a unified and sophisticated manner, this was quite another matter with which to deal. It clearly caught the Europeans off guard.

Administration Response to Marching Rule.[37]

Marching Rule initially started as a secret movement. Elaborate steps were taken to insure that the Government not discover its existence. However, as the movement gained strength and organization, instructions were sent down from the leaders to begin operating in the open. The Government's initial response was to sublimate the enthusiasm for better schools, agricultural innovation, etc. into Government sponsored or approved programs. The official statement about the movement in the 1948 *Annual Report* was as follows:

> Between the years 1945 and 1947 administrative officers treated the movement with respect and attempted to turn its undoubted vigour into more productive channels; more especially urging that the energy put into the Marching Rule would be better employed in the properly constituted Local Native Authorities which Government was doing its best to assist and establish. These local authorities, as constituted, had ample power and opportunity to give plenty of scope to the aspirations of Marching Rule leaders had they wished to cooperate.[38]

By July 1947, when an estimated 95 percent of the population of Malaita had joined Marching Rule, and it had spread to other islands, the Administration claimed to have received complaints from islanders against false imprisonment in Marching Rule jails, high-handed action by leaders, and "terrorist tactics" against the minority of islanders who refused to join Marching Rule.[39]

The Government was thus "forced" to step in. From its point of view, the initial positive thrust had now deteriorated into an emphasis on hero-leader worship, cargo cult ideology, and general terrorist behavior.[40] Mass meetings, and what was interpreted as mass hysteria, increased as well as open threats, by some, against British lives.[41] With the advent of the indigenous Marching Rule courts, the Administration became alarmed at such "insurrection" and took immediate steps to quash the movement by arresting the nine "Head Chiefs" on Malaita in August 1947.[42]

The November 1947 issue of *Pacific Islands Monthly* reported:

> In a leaflet printed in Honiara, and widely distributed, the Administration made a direct appeal to the native people, in very simple English, and explained why Marching Rule had been arrested and why Marching Rule was "not good." The leaflet gave a list of eight offences committed by the Marching Rule leaders, including obstruction of the work of Government; retention of money collected without explanation; fining and imprisonment of the people; forcing people to work in Marching Rule gardens; establishment of "scouts" over the people to make them afraid; preventing the people from making copra themselves or working for planters; lying to the people and the Government. "These things are not good," said the leaflet. "The Marching Rule must finish now . . . There is only one good law to make the people happy. This law is Government Rule" (*P.I.M.*, Vol. 18 [4]: 9).

The arrests were coincidentally timed with the arrival of British war ships passing through the Solomons, returning to Hong Kong from Australia.[43] Such a display of power did much to affirm the authority of the Administration and at least from their point of view, the ships' arrival was quite timely.

Vouza, the Marching Rule leader on Guadalcanal, was sent along with a few others to Fiji where he was given a course in local government. The Administration hoped that in seeing the Fijian model of government, he would be convinced of the "errors of his way" and return to the Solomon Islands and persuade others that Marching Rule was wrong and futile.

The arrest of so many leaders broke the back of the movement on Guadalcanal and Santa Isabel. However, on Malaita, and to a lesser extent on San Cristobal, the movement simply regrouped, organized with new leaders, and went underground, shifting the center of activity and resistance from South Malaita to the north of the island where an S.S.E.M. elder and teacher by the name of Irofalu became the dominant personality. The movement now took the form of passive resistance. Fox describes some of the tactics that were used:

> The people took to passive resistance, refused to pay taxes, refused to obey all orders of the Government and went quietly to gaol [jail], about two thousand of them; in some villages only the women remained. The Government hoped that the women, left to do all the heavy work the men usually did, would persuade their men-folk to give in; it was not realised that the women were in the movement as strongly as the men (1962: 131).

Rumors began circulating that war between Britain and the United States was imminent. The initial doctrines of Marching Rule now became garbled and the original goals of the movement were no longer sharply defined. During this phase, the cargo myth became more pronounced, as many looked forward to the day when free goods would be dumped on the shores of Malaita.

By 1950 leaders of Marching Rule signaled the Administration that they were ready to negotiate a truce. In September of that year they presented the High Commissioner with their demands when he visited Auki. They requested that they have a council for the whole island of Malaita and a flag,[44] the freedom to put their own leaders on the Council and to be able to pay them tribute.[45] The Administration felt that their wishes were already being honored by the existence of the 1947 Regulation that had established local government on a sub-district basis on Malaita. Marching Rule leaders, however, insisted that there be a council on an island-wide basis. The Administration released the original nine "Head Chiefs" of the Marching Rule movement after they had been imprisoned for nearly three years. The Resident Commissioner was satisfied that the power of these men could be turned to the advantage of good government, law and order, and so released them on the King's birthday, June 8th, 1950. Allan says that:

> These men, considerably chastened after two years' imprisonment, agreed to the conditions of the licence, returned to the sub-districts and are now endeavouring to persuade the remainder of the recalcitrants to obey the law. In this, the majority of the released men are succeeding (1951: 97).

Cochrane provides us with the final sequence of events leading up to the end of Marching Rule:

> In January 1953 the High Commissioner for the Western Pacific attended the first meeting of the council at which the "big men" were installed. "Marching Rule" was then finished on Malaita. The Malaita men made their peace separately with the Government. They made no demands on behalf of other Melanesians. And on the other islands "Marching Rule" died as councils were established and the Melanesians were allowed to elect their own "big men" to serve on them (1970: 93).

Analysis of Marching Rule.

Now that we have briefly reviewed the Marching Rule movement and its subsequent decline, we will now turn our attention toward understanding why the movement developed, what causal factors were responsible, and why certain behavior on the part of the Administration led to its overt demise. Another question to consider is what, if anything, did the Solomon Islanders gain through Marching Rule?

A number of anthropological scholars have investigated Marching Rule, emphasizing different elements in explaining its origin and development.[46] A synthesis and evaluation of some of these studies will now proceed below. We will review the research of (1) Belshaw, (2) Allan, (3) Worsley, (4) C. E. Fox, and (5) Cochrane.

1. Belshaw's Analysis.

One of the earliest scholars to analyze Marching Rule was C. S. Belshaw (1947, 1948, 1950a, 1950b, 1954). The central theme of Belshaw's analysis is economic, as represented by one of his earlier statements, that:

> Basically the movement was economic; the natives had become accustomed to a high monetary income received from the large-scale sale of curios and fruit, and had been taught by the Americans that their demand for high wages was legitimate (1947: 191).[47]

Belshaw disposes of two popular explanations for Marching Rule. The first is that of the coercive and dictatorial powers of a single leader's being responsible for the movement. As the data demonstrate, there were unquestionably outstanding leaders in the movement, e.g., Nori, Timothy George, Vouza, Brown Zalamana, et al., but the movement was not crystalized around any one of them. Belshaw (1950b) notes that in the absence of mechanical instruments or a police state, no leader can force his people to follow him. In fact, quite to the contrary, traditionally if Melanesians did not want their "leader" they simply packed up an entire village and moved — leaving the local "Big Man" without much of a following.

Secondly, Belshaw rejects the notion that Marching Rule was a reaction against a particular organization or event. He cites the rather rigid and narrow biblical interpretations of Presbyterian proselytizing as not sufficient to explain the rise of the John Frum movement in the New Hebrides,[48] any more that the war was a sufficient cause to account for the genesis of Marching Rule in the Solomons.

Belshaw prefers to focus on the position of the Melanesian community *vis a vis* the modern world. He notes that none of the Melanesian communities involved in cult activities has remained isolated from European influence. They have all been sufficiently exposed to European material goods and lifestyles to gain a selective appreciation for them; yet none of them has been able to take full advantage of living under these conditions and having equal access with Europeans to similar resources.[49] Belshaw observes that:

> These people, then, have all been in contact with thriving European communities, but none of them have been able to participate in vigorous activity leading to a higher standard of life. I think it is most significant that the two extremes of Melanesian life do not appear so far to have succumbed to these cults, though they have problems of their own. On the one hand, we have the thriving native settlements in or near such towns as Port Moresby, Rabaul, Vila, and in New Caledonia, and areas of intensive missionary industrial work. Here the people are in the grip of modern life — and have little time or inclination to organize into cults. On the other hand, we have areas such as the interior of New Guinea and Malekula, where cults continue in their native form, unmodified by European intrusion (1972: 526-27).

Thus, according to Belshaw, those who are most susceptible to movements such as Marching Rule, are those who are in a "half-way" position, between total isolation from Europeans on the one hand, and freedom to actively participate, as equals, in the European economy and way of life, on the other. If we agree with this explanation, then the islanders of Malaita, the stronghold of Marching Rule, represent a classic example of the "half-way" Melanesian.[50]

In support of his economic explanation, Belshaw gives us a good "emic" view of Marching Rule which also shows the considerable envy and hatred of the white man felt by many of the islanders:

> We don't want the white man around here any more, but we'd like to do things the way he does — for instance, run our schools and maybe live the way he does. No, we don't know who will teach us after the white man has gone, but we don't worry; our leader will find a way, and we'll have our own missionaries and teachers. Anyway, the white man will help us. We'll get good pay for our labour and have plenty of money. Our leader will pay £12 a month out of his own pocket to everybody that works for him. He has three haversacks full of dollars and is a rich man. We want to be like white men, but we won't observe government laws because our leader hasn't told us we should. We know the talk that the Native Councils were set up so we could administer our own laws, but we'd rather have our own leader tell us what to do. We'd cut off our hands if he told us to (1947: 192).

Belshaw must be credited with a positive analysis, for although he acknowledges that the movement appeared to be highly emotional, "It rests on a foundation of sound reasoning and most welcome ambitions for a higher economic and political status" (1947: 192).

2. Allan's Analysis.

We now turn our attention to C. H. Allan's analysis of Marching Rule (1950, 1951, 1960).[51] Allan was a District Officer in the Solomon Islands during the manifest period of Marching Rule, working on Santa Isabel and later on Malaita.[52]

Allan uses Ralph Linton's (1943) "Nativistic Movements" framework to categorize and account for the Marching Rule phenomenon. He summarizes the movement as comprising the following aspects:

> (1) the belief in the arrival of "cargo" and the return of the Americans, (2) the cult of the hero-leader and the recognition of a hierarchical organisation, (3) the desire for social welfare and development, (4) the imitation of the white man and particularly the Americans, (5) the urge to spread the movement and proselytise others, (6) the idealisation of the past, and (7) the establishment of the movement initially as a secret society (1951: 99).

He concludes by noting that:

> Though many of these characteristics are incompatible with one another, they must be seen as the manifestations of a people beset by disillusion of the past and fear of the future. They are the result of the fusion of new religion and practices with age-old social institutions and beliefs. They provide refuge and consolation as an unpractical solution to ever-increasing difficulties (1951: 99).

Allan believes that a dominant theme throughout Marching Rule was an envy of the white man, and concludes that the acceptance of Christianity has been for the Solomon Islanders a means to an end — the end being the possession of "cargo."

Allan should be given credit for emphasizing the pre-war historical factors that had led to tremendous discontent which culminated just as World War II erupted in the Pacific. He cites the following as the most significant antecedent conditions responsible for the growth of stress and strain contributing to Marching Rule:

1. A long period of labor traffic, with Malaita being the most affected of the Solomon Islands, resulting in the emergence of ugly relationships between the people, their leaders, and the Europeans.
2. This period being followed by indentured labor on the European-controlled plantations in the islands.
3. The Government policy of letting education reside solely with the missions, the Administration's significant disregard for indigenous customs, and the very little financial expenditure going toward social and welfare development programs for the Solomon Islanders.
4. The system of taxation being introduced and interlocked with indentured labor. That is, one could not pay the Government tax unless one

worked for a European who would then pay in the currency required for paying the tax.

5. The growing domination of Government headmen by S.S.E.M. teachers who gained enormous spheres of control, especially in northern Malaita.
6. Signs of growing cultural fatigue in the 'Are'are district of Malaita, as well as,
7. An influenza epidemic that broke out in the same area just prior to the Japanese invasion, killing hundreds of people.
8. Excitement over the self-government movement on Santa Isabel and Nggela encouraged by R. P. Fallowes of the Melanesian Mission.
9. The growing popularity throughout the island of the fundamentalist doctrine preached by the S.S.E.M.

Allan (1950: 92) cites the above factors as antecedent conditions that created a climate for Marching Rule, but it was the war, acting as a catalyst, that triggered the psychological conflict and cultural fatigue that had been building up over a long period of time. Allan concludes his analysis by drawing on the work of Philleo Nash (1937) and postulating the following analytical definition of Marching Rule:

> Marching Rule is a nativistic movement which has arisen in a community deprived of many of its traditional institutions and values by culture contact, European and otherwise, in the plural and singular, and has been crystalized by cataclysmic events. It seeks the reestablishment and propagation of original value patterns by the creation of a myth or fantasy basically related to these value patterns. The myth or fantasy symbolizes both acceptance and rejection of extraneous cultures and represents the psychological conflict of the old and new values. The manifestations of the new urges, attitudes, and ideas representing both old and new values, exist side by side within the cult in a state of apparent contradiction (1950: 93-94).[53]

Allan's analysis is essentially negative. It reflects the Protectorate Administration's concerns in emphasizing cargo cult ideology, terrorist tactics and resistance to Government authority and views Marching Rule as "an unpractical solution to ever increasing difficulties." Marching Rule, for Allan, represents a contra-acculturative movement. He fails to see the Colonial Order as problematic for Melanesians, and appears to lack a deep understanding of indigenous values. It is unlikely in his role as a District Officer that he was in a position or frame of mind to undertake an empathetic ethnographic study of the people subject to his authority. Allan has confused the desire for indigenization with contra-acculturative actions. Marching Rule was not contra-acculturative. It was a **selective-acculturation** movement, as well as a repudiation of the structural inequalities in the Colonial Order. Solomon Islanders were not against change—but they wanted change on a selective basis, and they wanted to make those choices on the basis of Melanesian, not European, values and culture.

3. Worsley's Analysis.

Let us now examine the work of Peter Worsley (1957) who has given us a well documented account of Marching Rule within a Marxist framework as part of his evolutionary scheme. He attempts to demonstrate the development of millenarian movements as they change from religious emphasis and expressions toward political concerns. In Worsley's scheme, Marching Rule is an example of a movement placed on the religious-political continuum near the political end of the axis. He states, regarding the movement:

> We have here, in fact, a modern nationalist body with overwhelming popular support; we leave the realm of the Coming of the Cargo and we enter the world of nationalistic politics. Marching Rule, then, was not a cult, but a political party. We see the final consummation of this transition to completely orthodox politics in another important post-war movement, which shows an even clearer abandonment of the millenarian dream — the Paliau movement (1957: 182-183).

Worsley de-emphasizes the role of the cargo cult myth in Marching Rule, pointing instead to economic and political factors as considerably more important in understanding the movement. He notes:

> The demands for minimum wages, for improved education and social services, for independence and self-rule, for national self-expression, etc. are the important features of Marching Rule, not the lingering myths of Cargo (1957: 182).[54]

Worsley also points to pre-war antecedents of the movement, particularly the increasing economic and political agitation of the 1920's and 1930's, as exemplified by the murder of District Officer W. R. Bell and company in 1927,[55] and the depression of the 1930's which hit the copra market particularly hard.[56] Worsley also gives considerable weight in his analysis to the effect of the war on the Solomons, especially the presence of Black American troops, who seemingly were on a par with the Whites.[57]

In support of his political and economic thesis he points to the Western Solomons which suffered considerably more from the war than did the central and eastern districts, yet Marching Rule never gained a footing in the area. He attributes this to the fact that Native Councils had been effectively established and that copra production had revived after the war.

Worsley's emphasis on economic and political oppression as a major causal factor in Marching Rule and similar movements, can be seen in his concluding chapter where he states that:

> Millenarian beliefs have recurred again and again throughout

> history despite failures, disappointments, and repression, precisely because they make such a strong appeal to the oppressed, the disinherited and the wretched (1957: 255).

Worsley gives us a positive analysis by emphasizing the political aspirations of Solomon Islanders and the reaction of islanders against oppression. The weakness of his argument, however, lies in his failure to understand the importance of the indigenous context in which Marching Rule was manifest. Solomon Islanders wanted cultural integrity and personal dignity. Marching Rule was an expression of this desire, for domineering Europeans had failed, by and large, to honor this essence of Melanesian experience.

4. Fox's Analysis.

C. E. Fox's work is that of a missionary-anthropologist who gives us a slightly different emphasis from that of the preceding analysts. Fox (1967: 65-66) counts the following among the factors responsible for the rise and development of Marching Rule:

1. The great shock of World War II on the Solomons.
2. The resentment of expatriated laborers from Queensland.
3. The desire to follow native customs, as both Church and State had been trying for two generations to make Melanesians as British as possible.
4. The desire for local expression in government using indigenous procedures to arrive at consensus on decisions.
5. The contrast of the affluent and generous Americans with the British, it being reported that the Americans left at least $250,000 in cash in the Solomons.
6. The influence of American talk about the evils of colonialism, naively assuming (says Fox) that if the Solomon Islanders were given immediate independence they would be a good and democratic people living in peace and happiness like Americans.

Fox gives considerable weight to the causal effect of American troops' anticolonial rhetoric, and their generosity and friendliness with Solomon Islanders which introduced a new model of European-Melanesian relationships in the racist and paternalistic Colonial Order.[58]

Fox's most significant contribution, as one who lived in the Solomon Islands for half a century, is his understanding of the underlying problem in the islands, of which Marching Rule was merely symptomatic. As important as the American influence may have been in triggering the movement, Fox (1962: 130) says that it was much more deeply rooted than simply a desire for American goods. He cogently notes elsewhere that:

> "Marching Rule" has been called by Europeans a Cargo Cult, a desire for European goods. It was partly that, but only partly; it

> was a desire to return to the old way of life and the old customs, and to reject the British way of life and customs — to be Melanesians not British (1967: 66).

Marching Rule was a reaction to the strain of Melanesian-European relations in general. He claims the chief problem in British Rule in the Solomons lay in the insidious racism manifest in both Christian missionaries and government officials — a sense of superiority over the Melanesians whom they had come to "serve." Fox notes that outright despising of Melanesians was common, or worse, condescending and treating them as a "child race." Such an attitude is, of course, a worn-out dogma from the Victorian era, but it is clear that it was very much alive and manifest in many members of the European community in the Solomons. Fox contrasts such an attitude with that of friendship, and ends by noting that:

> Your friend may differ from you, in ability, in knowledge, in character, but there is equality in friendship nevertheless, and this is what we ought to give other races. It is not easy because the Melanesian's background is so different from ours. But it can be done, and the more easily if you know his language and his way of life; and it is the only thing he cares about. All Melanesians say the British have given them justice. I never heard any say we have given them friendship (1962: 134).[59]

5. Cochrane's Analysis.

The final scholar whose analysis I wish to review is Glynn Cochrane (1970).[60] He draws on the work of the scholars examined previously, but he comes to a somewhat different conclusion regarding an explanation and understanding of Marching Rule and similar movements.

In an extremely cogent critique of theories previously put forth to explain "cargo cults" Cochrane (1970: 145-158) rejects the following explanatory hypotheses, claiming that they are inadequate for a complete understanding, giving only partial explanations at best:

1. **Psychological "Explanations."** These do not give us a deeper level of understanding since they tend to categorize rather than really explain the phenomena.[61]
2. **"Prophet" Theories.** These theories tend to emphasize personal attributes of the individual rather than focusing on the nature of the "prophet's" relationship with his followers. In other words, such an explanation ignores the all-important structural relationship that exists within the society of which the "prophet" and "followers" are members. In the case of Marching Rule, the pattern of leadership was very similar to that of the traditional Big Men.
3. **Political Theories.** Cochrane (1970: 150) says that, "Such theories imply that the cults have given rise to a completely new form of

political organization. They also imply that the natives have nationalistic aspirations in the European sense of the term." Marching Rule was political in that it was responsible for maintaining social order. It did not create, however, a new political unit. On the contrary, it was simply a process of intensification within the traditional organizational structure. That is, the process of maintaining social order remained the same.

Cochrane (1970: 152) also disputes the claim that Marching Rule was essentially anti-European. He argues that too much emphasis has been given to this theme, and that what hostility did exist, was not an expression of ethnic intolerance, for Europeans were assigned roles in the new regime, e.g., handling the more severe crimes in court, operating the communal farms, paying rent and leasing native-owned land, etc. Moreover, anti-European expression was highly selective. Non-cooperation was directed toward the British, but not toward the Americans who were expected to bring the cargo and overthrow the Protectorate government. Many Roman Catholic and Anglican missionaries were neither boycotted nor experienced hostility, whereas European planters and S.S.E.M. missionaries were rejected. What then is the explanation? Cochrane (1970: 152) contends that, "Hostility was related to the amount of force thought necessary to compel a group, or class, or individual to recognize indigenous sets of status." We will return to this notion below (pp. 272-273).

4. **Theories about Cargo and Economic Deprivation.** As noted above, the notion of economic deprivation played a significant role in the analyses of Belshaw and Worsley. The underlying assumption in such an explanation is that World War II triggered Marching Rule because the contact with American troops increased the sense of economic deprivation felt among the Melanesians *vis a vis* their position with Europeans.

An explanation in terms of economic deprivation suffers from the same weakness as the political hypothesis advanced above in that it assumes that Melanesians have the same aspirations as Europeans, i.e. that the pattern of wants for the Melanesian is equivalent to that of Europeans. Cochrane argues that these theorists have misinterpreted what cargo really is to the Melanesian; it is **not** simply an accumulation of more material goods, or a preference for European foods and clothing per se. Rather, "cargo" contained items that were bound up with indigenous notions of status. The all-important difference between a "Big Man" and a "rubbish man" is expressed in terms of material wealth. Thus to the Melanesians, the European wealth was simply an expression of their status as "Big Men." The "cargo" served as a marker of status, not as an end in itself. Cochrane (1970: 155) argues that, "Cargo was not only access to goods, but access to goods with a particular moral relationship."

Europeans have too often focused on cargo as nothing more than "material goodies," and this has frequently led them to misinterpret the true meaning of cargo. They have too often missed its symbolic importance and yet, it is by looking at cargo as symbol (Schwarz 1980) that we can begin to understand the deeper underlying meanings and the human yearnings that give rise to these "cargo" movements.

As an alternative explanation to the theories critiqued above, Cochrane's seminal contribution is in alerting our focus away from the overt and manifest expressions of Marching Rule toward the covert and latent factors responsible for its development.[62] He advances the notion (1970: 163) alluded to above, that Marching Rule and similar movements emerged because they were "spontaneous reactions against status deprivation. They were attempts to force Europeans to recognize indigenous concepts of status." A continuous theme throughout Cochrane's analysis is that the objective of Marching Rule was not to force Europeans to abdicate, but to cooperate. Indigenes were not asking to be left in isolation, to return to pre-contact days; they were asking that they be respected as human beings and dealt with accordingly, not simply treated as "natives" by the Europeans. Cochrane argues convincingly that Marching Rule ended on Malaita not because the Administration finally wore the movement down by arresting thousands of adherents, but because in 1953 indigenous concepts of status were finally recognized by the Government.

Benefits Derived from Marching Rule.

In the minds of many Solomon Islanders today, Marching Rule was successful. Developments in the following years, giving islanders a greater voice and role in their own political destiny, seemed to vindicate their initial aspirations.[63]

Tippett (1967) has made a significant contribution to the Marching Rule literature by providing an indigene's assessment of the movement over a decade after it had elapsed. In an interview with a Malaita man, the informant declared that, "Marching Rule was one of the best things that had happened in Malaita and that most of the things they had fought for they had won" (1967: 206-207).[64] Tippett (1967: 207) asked him to specify what they had gained as a result of Marching Rule, and without hesitation, he ticked off five points on his fingers:

1. We wanted the unity of all Malaita with a president or a paramount chief. We now have that.
2. We wanted a council under that president, where affairs of concern to all Malaita could be discussed. Now we have it.

> 3. We wanted representatives from all the different areas of Malaita, so discussions could be effective. Now we have this.
> 4. We wanted Solomon Island magistrates to try local cases, and not Europeans who knew nothing of customary law. We now have them.
> 5. If Malaita was to be taxed at all, we wanted that revenue expended on the development of Malaita. This is now being done.

Tippett goes on to note that:

> My informant was convinced that without Marching Rule none of these things would have been achieved. He put his finger on three important problems — the unity of Malaita, the unfamiliarity of white officials with customary law and attitudes, and the distribution of revenue derived from taxation. These have been points of distrust with Administration policy over the years: administration from outside, judgments from outside, and expenditure of local revenue outside. They represent three passionate cries — the cry for entity, the cry for justice, and the cry for development (1967: 207).

I see Tippett's "three passionate cries" as expressions of indigenous desire for recognition of their status as men, an important factor discussed in the work of Fox and Cochrane.

Marching Rule and the Missions.

It was noted above that non-cooperation with Europeans was selective. Marching Rule members distinguished between Americans and British, viewing the former as liberators, and the latter as oppressors.[65] But they also responded differently to the various missionary organizations and their representatives. I want to explore further the nature of this differential response, for in many ways, Marching Rule was an indigenous response, not only to Colonial rule, but also to generations of islander-missionary interpersonal relationships. Why were some missionaries free to go about doing their work while others were severely hampered and even ostracized?

The four missionary organizations working in the central and eastern Solomons at the time of Marching Rule were:

1. Melanesian Mission,
2. Roman Catholic (Marist),
3. South Sea Evangelical Mission, and
4. Seventh Day Adventists.[66]

The following table gives the number of missionaries and number of adherents for each of these four missions in 1949 (after Shevill 1949: 142).

		Missionaries		
Mission	Adherents	male	wives	female
M.M.	32,605	9	2	13
R.C.	8,776	37	0	25
S.S.E.M.	14,000	11	10	10
S.D.A.	4,128	12	–	3

Table 5.1. Missionaries and Adherents, Solomon Islands – 1949.

Allan (1950: 53) states that during the war the South Sea Evangelical Mission and the Seventh Day Adventists evacuated their missionaries from the islands, while the Anglicans and Catholics stayed behind.[67] He goes on to note that:

> While their Catholic and Melanesian Mission adherent members of the marching rule boycotted them for a time, their relations have never been broken off completely. In the case of the other two Missions [S.S.E.M. and S.D.A.] apart from a few extreme followers, the European missionaries upon their return found themselves completely ignored by their former flock. The S.D.A. was a relatively weak organization, and many of the natives merely transferred their allegiance to one of the other Missions. The S.S.E.M. is still flourishing. The people attend the churches frequently, the services are conducted by native teachers most of whom are marching rule leaders. If European teachers arrive to take a service, their presence is politely ignored and the church becomes empty. It is therefore not too much to say that the S.S.E.M. is today a native church with close affiliation to marching rule (1950: 53-54).

Many S.S.E.M. teachers became leaders in Marching Rule, especially as the locus of leadership shifted to North Malaita in the later phases of the movement. In contrast, there were few Marching Rule leaders among the Anglicans, and Fox (1962: 131) states that none of the Melanesian Mission indigenous clergy joined the movement.[68] This is not to imply, however, that Anglicans did not join, for they did. Marching Rule attracted all denominations and united Christians and pagans alike. Nevertheless, the fact that very few of the Melanesian Mission indigenous clergy joined, in contrast to the S.S.E.M. teachers who endorsed and led the movement, is, I believe, a significant statement reflecting the nature of the relationships between indigenes and their respective missionaries.[69]

I will now examine more closely the policies and personnel of the Melanesian Mission *vis a vis* those of the South Sea Evangelical Mission, for if we are to adequately account for the different ways in which these two missions "survived" Marching Rule, we must first study those factors that bear on missionary-indigene interaction leading up to the period of this post-war movement.

As the previous two chapters have demonstrated, the Melanesian Mission had a long history of cross-cultural sensitivity in their approach to winning Melanesian converts.[70] They had pursued a liberal policy of respecting indigenous customs, and had consciously worked toward establishing a Melanesian Christianity, led by an increasing number of ordained indigenous clergy. Highly qualified and trained personnel of the calibre of Patteson, Codrington, Ivens, Hopkins and Fox, to name a few, had stamped the Melanesian Mission with an ethos of anthropological awareness and cultural empathy, rarely equaled among missionaries in the South Pacific. Shevill, commenting on this orientation of the mission, states that:

> Although it has been argued with some degree of truth that the Melanesian Mission did not help sufficiently in preparing the people for industrialization, no mission in the Pacific has approached the work of evangelisation in a more scientific and scholarly fashion. Its agents have never attempted to impose white civilisation upon a native people. They have aimed at, and succeeded in producing a generation of native Christians with a native culture, but with a Christian faith (1949: 104-105).

In contrast to the Melanesian Mission, the S.S.E.M. has been far less tolerant of indigenous customs and has shown little appreciation for Melanesian culture.[71] According to Dr. Northcote Deck, head of the S.S.E.M., older Melanesian pagans, "besotted with sin and demon worship," were "almost animals in mind and thought habits." Although young pagans were, "more outwardly attractive," they nevertheless, were "only splendid animals . . . devoid of most of the finer feelings of life."[72] Missionaries saw little in the traditional Melanesian culture worth preserving as islanders converted to their brand of Christianity.[73] The majority spoke only Solomon Islands Pidgin and evidenced little interest in learning a local language, relying instead on interpreters for communication with the islanders. This effectively prevented them from establishing close interpersonal relationships with the islanders. But then there was little desire to do so. Missionaries lived apart from Melanesians, culturally and spatially, in grand missionary compounds, alienated from their island converts. It is also noteworthy that the majority of S.S.E.M. missionaries were women, in striking contrast to the Melanesian Mission's male-dominated staff.[74]

Although I have noted a distinct paternalistic trend in the history of the Melanesian Mission,[75] S.S.E.M. missionaries, in contrast, were far more paternalistic and reluctant to pursue a policy of indigeneity in their work. Cochrane, drawing on interviews with Solomon Islanders, notes that:

> Mission teaching and the mission way of life emphasized that

> there was a difference between natives and Europeans. The mission continued to encourage its members to work on plantations, and Solomon Islanders were taught to know their place. Native officials in the mission were discriminated against; they had to speak respectfully to Europeans, they were not invited to eat or stay at the houses of their European superiors, and they were taught that service of any kind to Europeans was the highest form of native attainment (1970: 80).

The pattern of interpersonal relationships between the two missions and their respective congregations was very different; however, there were more theological similarities than differences between the two groups. But the differences that did exist may have an important bearing on the problem under discussion.

Ecclesiastically there is far more structure in the Anglican congregations. Village catechists are under the authority of district priests, who are in turn, subject to the authority of the bishop. Theologically, the Bible is an important source of knowledge and a guide to Christian belief and behavior, but its interpretation is guarded in Church Canons and tradition. In addition, Anglican Christians rely on the Prayer Book with its creeds and catechism as theological contextual guides to biblical interpretation. Worship is formal and liturgical.

In contrast, the S.S.E.M. fundamentalist theology emphasizes biblical authority as the only guide for faith and action, and there is far greater freedom for individual interpretation. Worship and prayer are extemporaneous, unguided by a formal liturgy and Prayer Book. Church organization follows the congregational pattern with the local pastor-teacher responsible only to the elders in each village. Lacking a hierarchical structure and with greater local autonomy, S.S.E.M. churches are far freer to do as they please.

Finally, another important difference between the Melanesian Mission and the S.S.E.M. was in their proselytizing objectives. S.S.E.M. missionaries were concerned primarily with soul-winning and with renewing lethargic Christians through revival services. Thus their mission was narrowly defined in terms of "spiritual" goals, and as Hilliard (1966: 400) has observed, "Native education, economic development and health were regarded as incidental to the paramount spiritual ideal and therefore of little importance."

In contrast, the objectives of the Melanesian Mission were increasingly modeled after the notion of the "Redemption of the Whole Man" —his spiritual, physical and mental needs were to be met if the Good News of the Gospel was to have any meaning for Melanesians.

The pattern that emerges from the data shows that the Melanesian Mission and S.S.E.M. had distinctly different approaches to mission, different philosophies regarding the Indigenous Church, and different attitudes toward, and relationships with, the islanders.

Although Marching Rule was anti-British and promulgated traditional values, it was not anti-Christian. In fact, the amazing aspect of Marching Rule, from the Europeans' perspective, was its ability to amalgamate Christians and pagans, and bring together adherents of different missions who had heretofore been at odds with one another. A spirit of brotherhood and unity prevailed among Marching Rule members. Christianity played an important role in the movement, and many of its goals and objectives were expressed within a framework of Christian ideology and articulated through Christian idiom and symbols.[76]

Marching Rule's endorsement of Christianity, however, did not lead to its members' embracing all the European missionaries. S.S.E.M. missionaries suddenly found themselves completely alienated by their island converts who would have nothing to do with them. The ground work had been laid over two generations by paternalistic missionaries who refused to acknowledge any value in indigenous Melanesian culture. Thus when the breach came between Mission and Church, it was severe, and the S.S.E.M. never completely recovered.[77] An illustration from O'Reilly (1948) underscores the severity of the breach between islanders and S.S.E.M. missionaries:

> In North Malaita, the people expelled their missionary in 1947 saying, "You have taught us all that was in the Bible. You have taught us to read. Now let us manage our religion ourselves." Again, people now demanded payment for small services which they had always performed free for missionaries in the past. On being accused of ingratitude by a missionary who had spent his whole life educating them and curing the sick, natives replied: "But it's your work, isn't it?"[78]

And I might add, this is precisely the point! Melanesians did not perceive "mission work" as an indigenous enterprise, but as something foreign, imposed from the outside. It is clear from this illustration that a missionary's personal motivation and commitment to the work is of little consequence if his relationship with the islanders is paternalistic and he refuses to allow them to take over key leadership positions and develop their own culturally meaningful modes of expression.

Marching Rule proved to be a difficult time for the Melanesian Mission, but none of its missionaires were ostracized. In an address to English supporters of the Mission in Britain, Bishop Caulton discussed some of the difficulties the Mission had experienced with Marching Rule, but then noted:

> Some of the missionaries [S.S.E.M.] have suffered very badly and are taking it hard, and I feel that it is largely due to the way Bishop Baddeley remained there during the war that we have not suffered. They cannot bring anything up against us and so they have remained loyal . . . The reception I got was more friendly than had been given to our own men six months previously. Some of the

> non-Anglican missionaries had been badly received. We have not been treated like that and I was warmly welcomed everywhere.[79]

Charles Fox lived on Malaita (1949-1952) during Marching Rule and was unhampered in his movements about the island. An inspection of his personal diaries during this period reveals that his advice and counsel were actively sought by islanders. Touring Melanesian Mission villages that had gone Marching Rule, he recorded in his diary, "Went to Ubuna and talked of Marching Rule. Here and everywhere I got a tumultuous welcome" (November 11, 1948).[80]

In some districts Marching Rule adherents boycotted Melanesian Mission schools and in one case a school was closed for lack of attendance.[81] Bishop Caulton in his report for 1949, noted that:

> The most harm [from Marching Rule] has been done in our District Schools where in some of the more ardent Marching Rule areas there is a reluctance to send children to school. The idea being that education is intended to produce workers for, or imitations of, the white man.[82]

Marching Rule adherents also boycotted government and mission clinics for a time, and on one occasion the Melanesian Mission hospital at Fauabu on Malaita was nearly closed down.[83]

Although individual missionaries were treated well by Marching Rule members, the Mission nevertheless lost some converts to the Roman Catholic Mission.[84] The Melanesian Mission as the Church of England in the Solomon Islands had always been seen as the unofficial religious voice of the Protectorate government, and in the early days of contact, the Melanesian Mission bishop and the Resident Commissioner were seen by many islanders as two sides of the same Colonial coin. Since Marching Rule was clearly anti-government, the decision to join became problematic for many Melanesian Anglicans. The Melanesian Mission preached against the movement, in contrast to the Marist Mission which approved of it. The years of Marching Rule for the Marists were good ones indeed, for as the Marist missionary, Bernard van de Walle wrote in 1947:

> The Marching Rule has done only good for the advancement of our religion. The lagoon is ripe, there are fine villages [formed under Marching Rule] of sixty to eighty people where formerly there were only one or two families.[85]

Marching Rule produced a windfall of Marist converts for the Catholic Mission. As Laracy has noted:

> The baptism rate doubled in San Cristobal and trebled on Malaita, where Catholic numbers increased 42% rising from 5,410 to 7,694 between 1946 and 1950. Not only did the movement from heathenism accelerate but many Anglicans shifted their allegiance (1971: 108).[86]

The Melanesian Mission, like the Protectorate government, misunderstood Marching Rule.[87] One unsympathetic missionary defined it as:

> . . . a very ill-advised movement with much that is bewildering and hard to believe in, but probably in some ways a movement showing the growing pains of a comparatively primitive people trying, so to speak, to find their feet.[88]

In 1948 Charles Fox in his understanding and empathetic way, attempted to channel the enthusiasm for Marching Rule into an organization called *Patana* (Partner) — a partnership between Melanesians and Europeans rather than hostile confrontations, "which thousands of them really wanted," Fox (1962: 132) recalled. He continues:

> A large number urged me to set Patana going and promised to join. But the Resident Commissioner, who at that time was out to kill Marching Rule by putting, if need be, the whole population in gaol [jail], asked me to give up Patana. So I did. Partnership is however the only real solution (1962: 133).[89]

The Melanesian Mission laid most of the blame for Marching Rule at the door of World War II in general, and the American troops in particular.[90] It was almost with a sigh of relief that the Mission reported:

> It is felt that the departure of the last contingent of American troops at the end of 1949 may have dashed the remaining hopes of the members of the movement that the U.S.A. would take over the administration of the Islands from the British.[91]

The Melanesian Mission failed to understand that Marching Rule was far more than simply a reaction to the war and influence of American troops. It was a response to the effects of European culture contact over a period of many decades. In conclusion, in terms of the missions, the anti-European sentiment of Marching Rule and expression of hostility toward and/or boycotting of missionaries were functions of the relationship that had been established and developed over many years between missionaries and indigenes.[92] Where Melanesians were treated as equals by the Mission, Marching Rule had an insignificant effect. Where Melanesians had been treated as inferior and subordinate to the European missionary, Marching Rule brought a devastating blow to that relationship.

Marching Rule and the Theory of Relative Deprivation.

I now want to bring together several disparate lines of inquiry pursued in this study of Marching Rule in an attempt to provide a more inclusive theoretical framework in which to understand the movement.

The unifying theme running through the different analyses of Marching Rule, and underlying the differential response to the S.S.E.M. and Melanesian Mission, is the notion of relative deprivation.

David Aberle (1970: 209-214) has made a significant contribution in applying this concept to the broader context in which movements like Marching Rule develop. Relative deprivation is defined as "a negative discrepancy between legitimate expectations and actuality."[93] Four types of deprivation are then delineated: (1) possessions, (2) status, (3) behavior, and (4) worth.

We can see all four types expressed in the Marching Rule movement. Belshaw emphasized the important role the material wealth of the war had in increasing the sense of economic deprivation, corresponding to Aberle's first type. Cochrane waged a convincing argument for the importance of status deprivation as a causal factor in Marching Rule. In Aberle's third type, deprivation in the area of behavior, the codification of indigenous customs and the development of Marching Rule law provide ample evidence that this was an important area of deprivation experienced by many Solomon Islanders.

Deprivation in terms of worth, Aberle (1970: 211) says, refers to a person's experience of others' estimation of him. This is essentially a phenomenological category in which factors such as the integration of world-view, self concept, and interpretation of experience play a significant role. It is here that indigenes felt the difference between the two missions discussed above. I would argue that the relative deprivation of worth was higher (particularly among the leaders) for those Solomon Islanders associated with the S.S.E.M., and thus the expression of hostility toward its missionaries was greater. It is important to recognize that Marching Rule was not a rejection of Christianity, but it expressed a repudiation of its European representatives — namely, the paternalistic missionary along with all others who were not prepared to recognize the inherent worth of the islanders and establish a relationship of moral equivalence with them.

While I acknowledge the importance of the first three types of deprivation, I would contend that the concept of deprivation of worth gives us a more complete understanding of the driving force underlying the Marching Rule movement.

Melanesian Acculturation and Revitalization

The preceding analysis of Marching Rule demonstrates that the movement was a Melanesian attempt at what Wallace (1956) calls revitalization. It was a "deliberate, conscious, organized" effort by Solomon Islanders "to create a more satisfying culture" (1956: 279). In Melanesia there was a florescence of revitalization movements following World War II. Most of these sprang from a foundation of pre-war experience and conditions, and were thus a Melanesian reaction to acculturation under colonial regimes. As an example of a revitalization movement, Marching Rule was not a phenomenon unique to the Solomon Islands as will be shown, but it was part of a pattern of responses to acculturation which occurred after the war, from the New Hebrides to New Guinea.

Wallace (1956) postulates five stages of a revitalization movement: (1) initial steady state, (2) period of individual stress, (3) period of cultural distortion, (4) revitalization, and finally (5) a new steady state. Drawing on Wallace, Nida (1960: 145) diagrams the five stages of a revitalization movement in terms of the society's energy expenditure in responding to acculturation. He does this in the following manner:

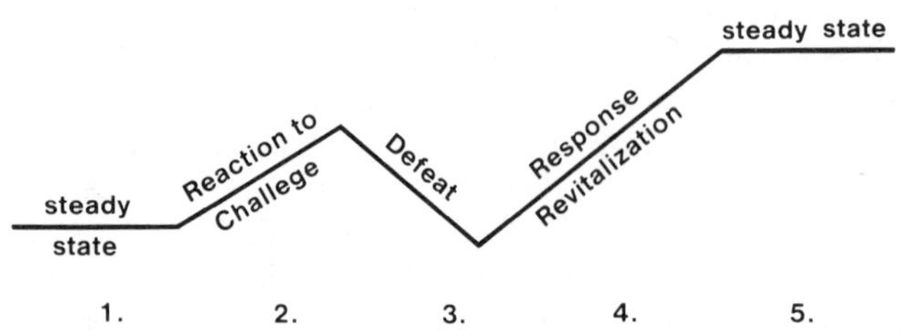

Fig. 8. Stages of Revitalization in Terms of Energy Expenditure.

This response pattern to acculturation, Nida (1960: 145) says, can be accomplished in one generation, but it frequently takes three generations. This pattern stands out clearly when applied to the present ethnohistorical study in Melanesia. The following table lists the five periods of this study with the corresponding five stages in a revitalization movement as diagrammed above.

Stages of Revitalization	Mission Contact History
1. Initial Steady State	1. Pre-contact (before 1850)
2. Reaction to Challenge	2. Contact (1850-1900)
3. Defeat	3. Penetration (1900-1942)
4. Revitalization	4. Absorption (1942-1975)
5. New Steady State	5. Autonomy (after 1975)

Table 5.2 Stages of a Revitalization Movement and Melanesian Mission Contact History.

According to Nida, if this response pattern takes three generations to run its course, then the first generation after contact ends with frustration. The second generation experiences a time of disillusionment, and the third generation makes a new adjustment through revitalization. This pattern appears to fit the data of the Melanesian Mission history amazingly well.

Witness the words of a third generation Christian Big Man from Nggela who participated in the Fallowes movement in the late 1930's:

> In the year 1820 (sic) Bishop Selwyn commenced the commandments of Jesus and the law Queen Anne had laid down in England and taught and instructed the heathen of New Zealand called Maoris. After 50 years they were allowed equality with white men in regards to wages and prices . . .
>
> In the year 1801 (sic) Bishop Selwyn and Bishop Patteson promised to minister like that among the heathen of Melanesia following the words of Jesus; and the law of Queen Anne which she laid down to the people of England, to teach them the Way of Jesus, and to instruct them about work and wages, and after 50 years to give them equality with whites in the matter of wages and prices . . .
>
> We have only been taught the Gospel, but nothing yet about trade and commerce. We have been Christianized for 78 years now.[94]

Throughout Melanesia the colonial pre-war period had been one of cultural defeat for the islanders. World War II had been such a cataclysmic event that it was easy for colonial administrators and missionaries to seek explanation for these revitalization movements in terms of indigenous reactions to the effects of the war. Seldom did they look beyond the threshold of the war in searching for antecedent conditions, perhaps because it was the pre-war period that was a product of their own misguided policies and activities. In the diagram and Table 5.2 above, it is obvious that the timing of World War II was significant as a catalyst in "triggering" post-war movements, but it is also clear beyond question that the foundation from which they sprang was laid in the pre-war era. The revitalization movements may have been hastened in coming by the impact of the war, but they were not caused by it.

It is not the intention of this study to discuss the theoretical significance of Melanesian revitalization movements, or to outline in detail the development of these post-war activities, for this has been done elsewhere.[95] It is important, however, to appreciate the plethora of these movements in setting the background against which independence activities in the Melanesian Mission occurred.

The following revitalization movements which were functioning just prior to and/or began after World War II will be briefly reviewed. Spatially distributed from the New Hebrides to New Guinea, they include: (1) the John Frum movement, (2) Naked Cult, (3) Moro Movement, (4) Doliasi Custom Movement, (5) Silas Eto's Christian Fellowship Church, (6) Hahalis Welfare Society, (7) Paliau Movement, and (8) Tommy Kabu Movement.

1. John Frum Movement.[96] The John Frum movement which began in 1941 on the island of Tanna, increased in activity in the post-war years. It was a repudiation of Christianity in general and the Presbyterian Mission in particular. It was extremely hostile to Europeans, and called for a return to the traditional customs of polygyny, dancing, kava drinking, etc. Christian villages established by the Presbyterian Mission ceased to exist overnight, as islanders returned to the bush and beyond the influence of the missionaries. Cargo cult ideology became important and model "airfields" were constructed in anticipation of the day when the Americans would return and land with the cargo.

2. Naked Cult.[97] Further to the north on the island of Espiritu Santo in the New Hebrides, a movement known as the "naked cult" became manifest from 1944 to 1948. Unlike Marching Rule, the Naked Cult was a rejection of traditional morals, rules of exogamy and marriage payments, as well as a rejection of European material goods. Paradoxically, however, a strong cargo cult ideology was emphasized and islanders who viewed the Americans as their saviors from oppression, anxiously awaited their return, believing they would then usher in a golden era of immortality. The term "naked" was applied to the cult as members of the movement were encouraged to go naked and to have sexual intercourse in public.

3. Moro Movement.[98] In the central Solomons the Moro Movement began on the weathercoast of Guadalcanal in the late 1950's, and is still active today. It is a "social movement that seeks to reduce discrepancies perceived and conflicts generated by culture contact."[99] The Moro Movement is an extension of Marching Rule, with emphasis on a return to traditional customs. However, on the peripheries of the movement a cargo cult ideology developed with Americans, especially "Black Americans" playing an important role. In some villages the date of August 8th, 1958, was prophesied as the day the Americans would return, and pick up the faithful followers of the movement and transport them to the United States. Nevertheless:

> . . . the avowed purpose of the movement was to improve living conditions . . . through independent self-help. No assistance from the Government was sought.[100]

4. Doliasi "Custom" Movement.[101] In the mountainous interior of North Malaita a short-lived phenomenon known as the Doliasi "Custom" Movement occurred from 1963 to 1966, climaxing in 1965. According to Cochrane:

> The movement combined admirable and progressive objects with a studied system of non-cooperation and a deep-rooted belief in the efficacy of the traditional way of life (1970: 106).

It had many parallels to Marching Rule, including the desire to codify customary law, and the abandonment of Malaitans of their scattered hamlets in the bush and coalescing on the coast to build "custom headquarters." But unlike the former Marching Rule adherents, they did not remain long, returning to their hamlets after several weeks. Another departure from

Marching Rule is that there were no Christians in the Doliasi Movement.[102]

5. Silas Eto and the Christian Fellowship Church.[103] In New Georgia, Western Solomons, another type of revitalization movement was underway in the 1950's. Led by a charismatic prophet, Silas Eto, it culminated in a breakaway movement from the established Methodist Mission in 1961. Its adherents subsequently founded the Christian Fellowship Church, with Silas Eto at its head as the self-proclaimed "Holy Mama"[104] and fourth member of the Divine "Trinity." This syncretistic movement with a strong economic organization was a reaction to fifty years of missionary paternalism, where the acquisition of "Christian knowledge" did not lead to egalitarianism with the missionaries who advocated the adoption of this "New Way of Life." Today the movement has reached a new steady state, and the Christian Fellowship Church with Silas Eto at its head is an important and stable social entity in the Western Solomons.

6. Hahalis Welfare Society.[105] Further to the northwest, on the island of Buka, there has been a continuity of revitalization movements at least as far back as 1913 with the emergence of the Lontis Cult which began under German administration.[106] The latest manifest expression of revitalization activities appeared in 1957 and became known as the Hahalis Welfare Society. Ten years later, Tippett (1967: 211) reported, "The movement is still strong and appears to have settled at a strength of about 6,000 persons."

The Hahalis Welfare Society has emphasized economic development in conjunction with a strong anti-government stance. In addition, it has developed a syncretistic ideology with a sharp break from the Christian (and for that matter, traditional) sexual code. One of its unique features was the establishment of a "Baby Garden"—an institutionalized prostitution where young girls, on the consent of their parents, were made available to satisfy the sexual desires of the male members of the Welfare Society. The Catholic Mission was especially affected, for when the Baby Garden was denounced by the the Marist missionaries, Society members simply left the Mission and formed their own *sori lotu* — an independent church, claiming, "We (will) pray to God in our own way so that he may be sorry for us."[107]

Moving now to Papua New Guinea, two post-war revitalization efforts that were contemporary movements with Marching Rule in the Solomons will briefly be reviewed.

7. Paliau Movement.[108] The Paliau Movement (1946-1954) was an acculturation effort among Admiralty Islanders who had been influenced by the enormous influx of American troops to a base established on Manus during World War II. It was a movement of popular discontent with Australia's governing of the area. It advocated a breaking with the past by abandoning bride price and polygyny, mortuary feasts and the use of traditional dog's teeth as currency for exchange. It also emphasized socio-economic development, peaceful coexistence and political unity among a formerly disparate people. Communal activities were advocated to replace individual enterprises in an effort to promote the advancement of island life. Paliau's program was often cloaked in Christian idiom, but its goals were avowedly secular. Although large numbers of Catholics defected from the mission, the movement never became anti-Christian. Schwarts provides a salient summary of Paliau's goals for his revitalization movement:

> He offered a program of planned cultural change that would give its followers a new way of life immediately, a new coherent ordering of native society that would serve as a vehicle for continued change in the direction of the ultimate goal—culture modeled after European society (1962: 266).

The Australian Administration initially misunderstood and opposed the movement, imprisoning Paliau for six months in 1950. The original goals were also complicated and deflected by a cargo cult ideology called the *Noise* that sprang up briefly as a parallel movement. Nevertheless, by 1953 a United Nations Mission reported that in the area under the influence of the Paliau movement it had encountered "one of the most orderly, progressive and prosperous communities . . . anywhere in the Territory."[109] The Paliau movement had reached a new steady state, and:

> . . . its adherents were the people who pressed for the establishment of a Council which now, composed of these as well as many people not associated with the movement, has shown excellent results.[110]

8. Tommy Kabu Movement.[111] Perhaps the most secularized post-war revitalization movement was that of Tommy Kabu in the Purari Delta of Papua. The primary objective was economic development, and so the Purari economy was reorganized on a communal and cooperative basis. Many traditional elements of Papuan culture were rejected and Christianity was endorsed as the official religion of the movement. In addition, women were elevated to equal status and participation with the men in the movement's activities. There was no anti-European sentiment and cargo cult ideology played an insignificant role.

The dominant leader of the movement was Tommy Kabu, the only Papuan to serve with the Royal Australian Navy and one who had been in Australia for training. He continually stressed his close association with Europeans to validate his leadership. Efforts were made to unite six similar ethnic-linguistic groups in the area by encouraging everyone to speak Police Motu, the *lingua franca* of Papua. Emphasis was on cooperation across traditional linguistic and cultural boundaries, and the traditional basis of status was rejected in favor of one founded on European norms and material values. The archetype of the "New Men" became the business man, who represented the road to equality with Europeans. As in other movements discussed above, villages were relocated and construction of houses was improved over the traditional model.

The response of the Australian administration was ambivalent, mistrusting the movement to a degree and refusing to support its economic enterprises. Eventually the business projects began to collapse, primarily from lack of indigenous experience with the European dominated economic world. As business waned so did indigenous enthusiasm for the movement, and as the "practical" side of the movement became increasingly impractical, the genesis of cargo cult ideology began to appear. Maher notes that:

> Although they did not dominate the scene, some people were openly cynical of the projects of the business men, and more than a few people were beginning to talk in terms of the general idea of Cargo Cult (1958: 90).

In summary, all these movements, briefly outlined above, were Melanesian attempts at revitalization. They were organized efforts to create a more satisfying culture in the post-war period. Guiart (1951) has called them the "Forerunners of Melanesian Nationalism."[112] Whether the movements were short lived or continued on to a new steady state, the goals and aspirations became part and parcel of the post-war era. Writing nearly fifteen years after Marching Rule formally ended, Davenport and Coker observed that:

> The sentiment of Marching Rule as a high point of unity, of purpose, of co-operative achievement, and enhanced self-importance proudly lingers on even today, not only on Malaita but throughout those parts of the British Solomons that had been caught up in it (1967: 128-129).

Whether these revitalization movements emphasized "cargo cult" ideology or "practical cooperation," it appears to me that the one theme common throughout is the desire of indigenes for racial equality with their Colonial masters. Wallace (1956: 276) notes that in areas such as Melanesia, where indigenes were subjected to direct coercion by a foreign police power, the response has not been so much one of "revival," as in the case of North American Indians, but an "importation" of the Europeans' culture, as Melanesians attempted to identify with their oppressors. He states:

> An important variable in choice of indentification is the degree of domination exerted by a foreign society, and . . . import-oriented revitalization movements will not develop until an extremely high degree of domination is reached (1956: 276).

The data from Melanesia support Wallace's hypothesis in a convincing manner.

In this chapter I have thus far given considerable attention to the Marching Rule movement and briefly reviewed other revitalization movements in an attempt to set the scene against which activities in the Melanesian Mission can be meaningfully understood in this post-war era. Melanesians began calling for a New Order, one that would contrast with the racist and paternalistic Colonial Order. How did they articulate and achieve their aspirations for indigeneity and independence, and how did the missionaries respond to their legitimate desires? These are the primary questions that will be addressed in the following discussion as we examine the Solomon Islanders' attempt to form their own independent Church Association.

The Church Association: A Case Study[113]

By 1949 Marching Rule on Malaita had entered the phase where cargo cult ideology and the prophesy of Americans' returning gained ascendancy. Rumors were fueled by the actual return of a contingent of 1,000 American troops to carry out a survey of the Solomon Islands. During this phase, the Anglican Church was most affected, for nearly all of the catechists were jailed for the sake of Marching Rule, and there was no one left to carry on the daily church services of morning and evening prayers. Moreover, many villagers lost interest in attending daily prayers:

> Our clergy were exceedingly sorry about this, because of the teachers' negligences, for the Church seemed to be alienated and neglected; because of their perplexities and anxieties, there were not many people who could afford to go to church for daily services, while some other people were on the lookout for the arrival of the Americans.[114]

In this difficult and perplexing situation a South Malaita priest, Fr. Willie Masuraa, concerned with the apostasy of his people, had a profound vision in which the idea of the Church Association was revealed to him. The next morning he began to write down some of the rules in Mota, and then called two others to help him: a layman, Timothy Faifu, and another priest, Fr. Willie Au. The three met in secret, discussing the idea, and developing the rules over a six-month period. The rules were worked out with biblical references justifying each section. They were then translated into English by Timothy Faifu and given to Bishop Caulton for his approval. The District Commissioner of Malaita, suspecting that this might be another form of Marching Rule, asked to examine the note book, and after studying it, gave his approval.

With the consent of the Bishop and the District Commissioner of Malaita, meetings were held to explain the purpose of the Church Council, as it was initially called. There was criticism from some, but there was enough support from others to make a beginning. On June 11, 1953, a third meeting was held at Ngorefou, Malaita — Hopkins' old station at the north end of the island. The Melanesian Mission availed the *Southern Cross* to collect people from around the island and special effort was made to ensure that nearly all the ex-

Pawa boys were present. The meeting lasted three days, ending with the Malaitans adopting the plan of the Church Association and electing Fr. Leonard Alufurai as its first president.

In late July, 1953, thirty-nine Melanesian clergy and nine Europeans convened the first General Synod to be called since 1928.[115] The main purpose was to nominate a successor to Bishop Caulton, who was resigning, but on the third day, the Synod discussed the Church Association. After modifying the rules and rewriting the text, it gave its approval and urged that other islands would follow Malaita's lead in adopting it. The "Rules of the Church Association" as adopted by the Melanesian Mission Synod are found in Appendix VI.

Willie Masuraa — Founder of the Church Association.

Before discussing the rules and significance of this movement, a brief biographical sketch of the founder, Fr. Willie Masuraa, will be helpful. His father, Rev. Luke Masuraa, Fox says, was:

> . . . an heroic figure on South Mala 50 years ago. Luke had many escapes, was wounded and often under fire from the Mala heathen of those days. Brave, fiery, and energetic he served the Church well, but he was not in favour with some of the European staff, who called him rough and rude, for if he saw what he thought was slackness in anyone, Melanesian or European, he said so very plainly, and forcibly (1964: 20-21).

This portrayal of Willie's father is appropriate, for Fox called Willie Masuraa a "true son of his father . . . even smaller than his father, but with his father's strength of character and more than his father's ability."[116]

Born around the turn of the century, Masuraa was educated at Pawa, and then later joined the Melanesian Brotherhood. Following this experience, he became captain of the *Mavis*, one of the Mission's small vessels, and later he chose to enter the priesthood. He was ordained in 1942. By 1957 Bishop Hill had made him a Canon of the Honiara Cathedral, and in 1964 he was appointed Rural Dean of South Malaita. Fox (1964: 21) claims that Willie Masuraa had more influence than any other priest on Malaita, speaking three of the Malaita languages (Lau, 'Are'are, and Saa), and knowing his people through and through.[117]

The Socio-cultural Context of the Church Association.

The development of the Church Association on Malaita must be understood in the context of Marching Rule which had influenced the island so greatly. Thus, the primary argument in promoting the Church Association by Masuraa and his cohorts, was that Malaitans could get the things they wanted by supporting the Church Association, and according to Timothy Faifu, they were explicit about taking over the running of the Church from the Europeans as soon as possible; and this could be done only if they became self-supporting.[118]

The Church Association was portrayed as a viable alternative to Marching Rule, creating an avenue whereby Mclancsians could begin to have control over their own affairs. This was explicitly stated, "The Mission and the Government will teach and guide and show us everything for Church Schools and work and ways how to find money and how we are to stand by ourselves."[119] The official Mission version declared:

> This Association has been formed after much prayer, and we believe it comes from the guiding of the Holy Spirit. It has only one aim — to help and strengthen the Church in Melanesia by getting the people to love and support the Church more than they have done before.[120]

Fox noted that the movement of the Church Association, coming from the Melanesians themselves was:

> . . . of greater importance than any since Ini Kopuria began the Native Brotherhood. It is a movement of self-support, but it is far more than that; for they propose to build their own boarding schools and hospitals and to pay for them, besides entirely supporting their own priests and teachers, and to send out missionaries not only to the remaining heathen parts of Mala [Malaita], but beyond Melanesia, and to support them themselves.[121]

The Rules of the Church Association.[122]

The rules as originally developed by Willie Masuraa and translated by Timothy Faifu are written below without alteration. They should be compared with the version adopted by the 1953 Melanesian Mission Synod, in Appendix VI.

Church Council of South Malaita

(1) God's Law

1. Chapters, Mt. 22: 35-40; Mk. 12: 28-34; Lk. 10: 25-28.
2. We have two important things to do: (1) To Love God. (2) To love our Neighbour.

We cannot love God truly if we are thinking of ourselves.

The Church Council

All the Truth of the Church

The Church Council of S. Malaita will stand upon all these chapters. Mt. 22: 35-40; Mt. 16: 18-19; Jn. 21: 15-19.

The Collection

The Collection stands upon all these chapters. Acts 4: 36-37; Acts 2: 42-47; Acts 5: 1-4; Rom. 13: 6-8.

Two Shillings

Two Shillings stands upon all these chapters. Mt. 17: 24-27; Lk. 21: 1-4.

The Bag of Money

The bag of money stands upon all these chapters. Jn. 12: 4-6; Jn. 13: 29-30.

The Laws of the Church Council

To the Church of S. Malaita let us try and follow all the laws and Rules of the Church Council and what is written in this book, which says, Let us try to follow or copy the FAITH of our Lord Jesus Christ.

Before the Meeting, read these chapters. Mt. 22: 35-40; Mt. 16: 18-19; Jn. 21: 15-19.

The Work of Jesus

1. When Jesus began his work on the earth he chose 12 men to help him in his work. And with them they got a bag of money, and that money was used for their food. Jn. 13: 29-30.
2. The Faithful men went about preaching the Resurrection of our Lord, and those who believed, sold all their possessions of lands or houses, and brought the money and laid it at the Apostles' feet. Acts 4: 26-37; Acts 2: 42-47; Acts 5: 1-4; Rom. 13: 6-8.
3. The bag of money helped them to buy their food and to help the poor. Jn. 12: 4-6; Jn. 13: 29-30.

The Church

1. The Life of the Church=Jesus Christ. Jn. 14: 5-7.
2. The Life of all the schools, and all the works of it= The Money. 1 Cor. 16: 1-2.
3. The Life of money=The Bag of money. Acts 4: 32-35.

4. The Life of the Bag of money=The collection. Acts 10: 1-2.
5. All this collected money which offered to God by Christian men, the Church used it for the goodness of the Church in all the world. Acts 11: 29-30.

What Shall the Church Do?

1. The Life of the Church=Collection. Acts 4: 32-35.
2. The Church must give their collection each year. Lk. 19: 8.
3. The collection will be 2/-. Lk. 21: 1-4.
4. Each baptised member. Acts 2: 41-45.
5. Copra can be used as your collection. Lev. 2: 1-2.
6. Any village has a plantation of coconuts belonging to the Mission—They can make copra, when selling it, and they get the money, part of that money must be given to the Church according to the Law. The remainder will be kept by their chief.
7. Other villages have no plantation belonging to the Mission, they will give 2/-, or anything which can be sold for money. 2 Cor. 9: 7-9.
8. A village has not a plantation of coconuts belonging to the Mission but have their own plantation they can use it for copra for their Collection, which is 2/-.
9. A porpoise teeth will do for a collection.
10. Shells can be given for a collection. Acts 4: 36-37.

Going to the Plantation

1. Anyone belonging to the Melanesian Mission of S. Malaita go out for work on the plantation such as trading companies, LPPL, Honiara or anywhere, must give 5/- and 3/- for thanksgiving offering to God.
2. Anyone who goes out for work on plantation but already given his collection, 3/- more will be for thanksgiving offering towards God.
3. Anyone goes out for 1 year labouring but his money was already given, (5/-) but work again for another year, on his arrival he must give 5/- for that year. Rom. 15: 26.
4. Any man who goes out and work for six month, but already given his collection (5/-) for that year, he will give 1/6 for thanksgiving offering.

5. Any man work for six month, but does not give his collection, he will give 2/- for collection, 1/6 for thanksgiving offering.
6. Any male or female working on a plantation for all their lives, or living in some other villages but belonging to the S. Mala Church Council, must give or send his collection each year in accordance with the Law of the Church Council for all his life. 2 Cor. 9: 5; 2 Cor. 8: 7.
7. To all the crews on the ship, the members of the S. Mala Church, Will you listen and hear all the Laws of the Church Council of S. Mala wants you to follow and to keep all the Laws, and the Rules of the Church Council orders you to give your collection each year.
8. Those who say that they have no money or refuse to follow the Rules of the Church Council, or not even try to believe all the Laws; or despise to hear and listen, or to keep it, or not to follow; and don't want to give collection, the Church Keeper will get some money out from their own bag of money from the Church and will be given to the Church Council. Afterwards, they will try hard to find some money and pay back what they owed to their Church or Chapel.

(2) The Church Council

All the Lives of the Church

1. All members of the Church must give their collection in accordance with the Law of the Church Council.
2. Each baptised member of the Church on S. Mala to give 2/- each year.
3. The priests of S. Mala to give £2 each year.
4. Any other S. Mala priests working on another island to give £2 a year.
5. The deacons of S. Malaita to give £1 each year.
6. S. Malaita deacons working on another island, also to give £1.
7. Any white resident priest on S. Mala to give £2 each year.
8. Any white resident deacons on S. Mala to give £1 each year.
9. Any white resident woman missionary to give £1 each year.

10. The Archdeacon to give £2.10.
11. The Bishop to give £3 a year.
12. Any member of the Government belonging to the Church to help with this collection for the Church and for schools for the children. Acts 10: 1-2.
13. Dressers belonging to the Church on S. Mala to give £1 each year.
14. Headmen belonging to the Church on S. Mala to give £1.
15. Teachers in Junior Schools £1.
16. Teachers in District Schools 15/-.
17. District Preachers on S. Mala to give 5/- each year.
18. Village chiefs 3/-.
19. Village teachers 3/-.
20. Storekeepers on S. Mala £1.
21. Those holding special positions in Government or Trading Companies or with the Mission £2 a year.
22. Hope that the Government and the Mission will be able to give contributions each year to the S. Mala Church Council. Lk. 11: 9-13.
23. This collection for the Church Council must not interfere or take place of ordinary Church collection or with Government tax.

It is right to see the Bishop, the Archdeacon, the R.C., and the District Commissioner first. If an agreement is made between you and me, I will ask the Archdeacon to help me put the money in the Bank at Honiara.

(3) All the Members of the Church on S. Mala.

Several Rules of it for Money

1. Those who cured from sickness to give 1/- thanksgiving offering, and pray to God. Mt. 8: 2-4.
2. To give a tenth of the food from the garden each day: the food is kept for sale, if not able to be sold, it will be given to the sick, poor or visitors. The Leader of that village will take care of the food, and to see that the food is properly used. Mt. 23: 23.

3. Each village to plant a coconut plantation for the Church, as some villages are already done. Ex. 13: 1.
4. To plant food and tobacco, and to make things such as bowls for the Church.
5. Villages to have pigs, fowls, ducks for sale for the Church.
6. The Church Council to choose a team of men to go to work with the Government, Traders or Mission.
7. If they earn £2 a month, one pound for Church Council and one pound for themselves. Ex. 13: 1-2; Mt. 23: 10-12.
8. The name given to this group of men will be, "Team of Consolation." Acts 4: 32-37.
9. This team to make their promises to the Bishop or Priests at the Altar. They promise to do what is told by the Church Council, and would be honestly so what is good to God and men.
10. It is good for young men who went to Pawa, Alangaula, or District Schools would be able to join this team of S. Mala. Acts 6: 3-6.
11. The Council to find a man who will offer his land for Farming (like S. Barnabas who offered his land for the Apostle's sake) and this Team could work on that land, planting different kinds of food. When their work increases, some of the fruit can be used for food, most of the fruit for sale for the sake of the Church Council. Acts 4: 36 to end.
12. It is not necessary that this land should be owned by the church.
13. This team can use some of the produce, if they see that their work is increasing. 1 Cor. 9: 8-11.
14. The Church Council hopes the Mission and the Government will help them to get a market for their produce. 1 Cor. 4: 9-13.

Their Special Jobs

1. The Church Council to find a man who is suppose to be the Head for this work.
2. There will be an Officer some where for the work.
3. There will be Leaders in each village to look after everything.
4. There will be a Clerk for the work.

(4) The Church Council

The Laws of the Church on S. Malaita

The Laws of the Church shall be discussed. If the District Council has been hold up on this island of S. Mala, and also the Custom.

(5) The Church Council

The Laws of the Church on S. Malaita

The Laws and the ways how to make prayers, and how to teach the people, shall be made up later.

(6) The Church Council

The Rules and Helping of the Church on S. Malaita

1. It is right for the Mission and the Government to help and support the Natives.
2. The Mission and the Govt. will point out for Natives the, TRUTH OF THE CHURCH, and also for the BODY.
3. Both the Mission and the Government could send to us different kinds of seeds and fruits, that when planting them, we will have more money when we sell them.
4. You will help us more than before, and send to us more materials we needed for our work.
5. Also the Mission and the Government will look after all our Schools.
6. Try and show us all good examples for both South and N. Malaita as we know that both islands are still very strong with their work till today.
7. You will help us in our work with money, and to hold up TRUTH in the eyes of the people.

(7) The Church Council

The Rules of "Rest in mind" of the Church on S. Mala

The rules for "Rest in mind" will be discussed later, till the Church Council has been already stand on this island.

My Promises

1. The Church on S. Mala will try their best to add more money into their Bag of money each year, till the Bishop will see that the money is ready for work, before I could try to use according to its work.
2. The collection on Christmas, Easter, and in Holy Communion, the Church on S. Mala has no right to touch them, unless the Bishop allows it.
3. When using the money, the Church has to help some other islands that are not able to help themselves, and also for all the schools in Melanesia.
4. The Church Council is ready to help some other islands who asks for help.
5. The Mission and the Government will Lead, Guide and show us every thing for Church Schools and work and ways how to find money, and how are we to stand by ourselves.

— By Rev. William Atkin Masuraa

The Native Melanesian Society

In the year when the "Native Melanesian Society" begin to use the money, or when they start to work with the money, that is in the bank, before they have to choose out four Communities.

1. No. 1 Community, for farming and Carpenter. These men will show and teach the people how to work or growing things or feed things such as pigs, fowls, anything that is necessary for sale for money for the use of the Native Melanesian Society.
2. No. 2 Community, for Church and District Schools and all the works of the Church.
3. No. 3 Community, for hospital and all its work.
4. No. 4 Community, to deal with money and banking, and how to find out money that comes in and goes out for the use of the "Native Melanesian Society."

Important—Money is the **Root** for this work which we like mostly. I think No. 1 Community will start to work first. No. 2, 3, 4 will be started later, if the money is already kept in the bank.

Organizational Structure of the Church Association.

As is apparent from a cursory review of the rules, the primary activity of the Church Association was to collect money from its members. An Association leader was chosen for each village, and an island-wide president of the Association elected to oversee its activities. Four separatc committees were planned—a committee for (1) farms, (2) church and schools, (3) medical work, and (4) accounting. The head of each of these committees met with the president of the Association in forming the Central Committee which made decisions on allocating money for different projects, and keeping the bishop informed of the Association's activities. It is interesting to note that the original rules went into great detail regarding the collection of money while the committee structure played a rather minor role. In the version endorsed by the 1953 Synod, however, the description of the committees' work was greatly expanded and more power given to the bishop as proclaimed by the statement that, "A report shall be sent to the Bishop each year of what the Committee wants to do, and nothing shall be done and no money spent unless the Bishop agrees."[123]

Ideological Frame of Reference.

One would expect a voluntary association related to the Church to have some religious justification, but one of the amazing features of Willie Masuraa's Church Council rules was the degree to which the rules were explicitly tied to biblical injunctions. He wanted strong inducements to encourage people to give money, and therefore alluded to many traditional Melanesian values as expressed in the biblical narrative. A theological analysis of these biblical injunctions reveals that Masuraa was attempting to set up a Melanesian society on the model of the early Christian Church, which has many parallels with traditional Melanesian culture. For example, Acts 4: 32-37 is cited seven times. This is an important reference, for it describes the unity of believers and the communal spirit of the early Church, where everyone shared what they had for the benefit of the corporate group. This passage describes people selling their possessions and contributing the money to a general fund and then redistributing the income among the believers according to their needs.

There are fifteen different references from the Gospels, some cited more than once. Most of these deal with paying the temple tax, or making a thanksgiving offering to God. The justification for demanding members to pay at least two shillings comes from Luke 21: 1-4, the story of the poor widow who dropped two little copper coins into the temple treasury. There are fifty-one biblical references in the text of the rules, but some of these are repeated several times. Seventeen of these deal explicitly with money or giving and sharing. In essence the biblical references give religious sanctions for building a "new" economic order among Melanesians. I say "new" because this call to a more communal way of life is consistent with traditional patterns, but is now given a new religious frame of reference.

One of the most interesting biblical references cited in the rules is I Corinthians 4: 9-13, used to support the following statement:[124] "The Church Council hopes the Mission and the Government will help to get a market for their produce." The reference from the Good News Bible reads:

> For it seems to be that God has given the very last place to us apostles, like men condemned to die in public as a spectacle for the whole world of angels and of mankind. For Christ's sake we are fools; but you are wise in union with Christ! We are weak, but you are strong! We are despised, but you are honoured! To this very moment we go hungry and thirsty; we are clothed in rags; we are beaten; we wander from place to place; we wear ourselves out with hard work. When we are persecuted, we endure; when we are insulted, we answer with kind words. We are no more than this world's refuse; we are the scum of the earth to this very moment.

There are perhaps several possible interpretations here, but I see the passage as a revealing statement of the Melanesians' perceptions of themselves *vis a vis* the dominant European missionaries and Government officials. As I suggested in the discussion of Marching Rule, deprivation of personal worth was the primary causal factor that led to the revitalization activities in the post-war Solomon Islands. In the passage quoted above, if the Melanesians are identifying themselves with the Apostles as the "scum of the earth," and I believe this is an accurate interpretation, then this is good evidence to support the hypothesis that the pre-war colonial period had left Melanesians in a state of significant deprivation of their personal worth. It is out of this context that the Church Association arose, and to its cultural significance, we will now turn for discussion.

The Significance of the Church Association.

The most significant aspect of this movement is that it was an entirely Melanesian enterprise, born of desires for economic, political and religious revitalization. There are several features of this movement that should be highlighted.

One of these is the Band of Consolation which was to be made up of men who left their village and island to work for Government, for the Mission or on plantations. They would vow to give £1 per month back to the Association. The absence of young men from the village had become an increasing problem because those who gained a good education in the Mission schools were equipped to work in European enterprises where they could make a good salary. Although mission educational standards improved during this period, this education also militated against graduates returning to a meaningful village life and making a contribution there. In other words, mission education tended to alienate people from a meaningful life in the village. Thus the Church Association rules attempted to recoup the loss of these people from village life by requiring them to reinvest some of their income back into their home communities. If by their absence they were prevented from making a physical contribution, they could at least make a financial one.

Another important feature was the establishment of Church Association farms. This was designed to be a communal activity, much like the Marching Rule farms, which were modeled after the huge American truck farms established on the Guadalcanal plains during the war. Profits from the farms were to be given to the Church Association and agricultural advice given to people everywhere to improve the quality of their gardens.

Writing in 1954, Charles Fox underscores the significance the movement had for the islanders:

> It is a strong new Melanesian movement which seems likely to spread through all the Islands. The days the Synod spent in considering, revising and adopting the rules were days of special importance, because of the quiet, steady enthusiasm of the Melanesian priests for something that was all their own and would put fresh and vigorous life into their Church.[125]

Melanesian Reception and Mission Perception of the Church Association Movement.

The Church Association was started on Malaita and Nggela in June 1953, and in each case, a church Big Man was elected president of the Association. Guadalcanal began the Church Association in September 1957. Farms were started on Malaita and Nggela and within a few years there was sufficient money in the bank to enable Malaita to buy a rice huller and Nggela to purchase a rotary hoe. The start was slow, and all the original objectives were not met initially, but the Church Association belonged to the islanders — it was their own creation. Now when they gave, they were not contributing to a Mission collection that swallowed up the money into some amorphous fund. They now gave to advance their own island. Fox wrote in 1964:

> This idea of Canon Willie has had a deep effect on the Melanesian Church. As it spread from island to island its form has altered a little, but the idea has always been kept. Sacrificial giving in Melanesian ways was the idea and that has been held firm. Before it took root on Gela the annual giving amounted to about £30, now to nearly £600. The whole idea of the Church Association and the manner of giving was thoroughly Melanesian.[126]

By the 1960's the Church Association had been established in one form or another in nearly all the Anglican areas. But its reception was uneven. For example, on Santa Isabel it was enthusiastically supported, but on Malaita the initial enthusiasm began to wane.

In addition, a parallel indigenous organization, the Village Union, was developed to organize communal labor for the benefit of the church. This is how it functioned. A voluntary labor force would clear land, prepare new gardens and work on plantations. One pound per day would then be paid by the beneficiary of the group for its labor, regardless of the number of workers. This money, in turn, would then be given to the Church Association. Such a scheme enabled individuals to have the benefit of a corporate labor force, and also contributed money to the islanders' church at the same time. It was a Melanesian origination which involved islanders in the life of their church on a cooperative labor basis rather than on a cash giving basis, and as such, it followed indigenous lines of communal activity.[127]

The Melanesian Mission's reaction to the Church Association is interesting. Bishop Caulton hailed it as "a momentous thing that marks a step forward in the development of the Church in Melanesia."[128] Nevertheless, the Mission soon came to see it as a convenient source of additional income, and praised it publicly more than it encouraged it privately. An example of this is provided from Fox's personal diary, written early in 1959:

> It was arranged for *Baddeley* to take Philip and me to Hakama [The Nggela Church Association farm] to make a start (at last after 5 months) with the hoe, but the Archdeacon stopped this and said *Baddeley* must go to Honiara. Another setback for the Church Association. It has to struggle against the complete apathy for its welfare at the [hands of the] Mission authorities.

As the Church Association developed in the islands, it became polarized with the Mission. The Church Association represented Melanesian activities and interests; the Melanesian Mission, those of European missionaries. Islanders saw the Church Association as belonging to themselves, whereas the Melanesian Mission was perceived to be the concern of European missionaries. Such a polarization was unfortunate, but given the socio-political context, it seems to have been inevitable. The Church Association fulfilled many of the same functions for Melanesian Anglicans that Marching Rule had tried to fill. Because the Church Association was less radical and threatening, from the Government's and Mission's perspectives, it was viewed as a legitimate avenue through which Melanesians could aim at actualizing their aspirations.

Missionary Responses to Melanesian Aspirations for Indigenization and Independence

On May 30th, 1954, Alfred Thomas Hill, the former headmaster of All Hallowes School, Pawa (1938-1953), was the first Bishop of Melanesia to be consecrated in the islands. This event had important symbolic significance for the islanders as it represented the first time Melanesians were able to witness the impressive and solemn ceremony.[129]

Hill's episcopacy (1954-1967) is interesting, for although he was a strong, ethnocentric and paternalistic leader, he nevertheless advanced a number of concerns in an effort to increase the indigeneity of the Anglican Church in Melanesia. Before coming to Melanesia in 1936, among other things, Hill had been captain of a 20,000 ton ocean liner. He was a perfectionist, and ran the Mission like a tight ship. A man with a quick temper and headstrong drive, he is nevertheless remembered by Melanesians, above everything else, as a "pastoral bishop." Speaking to a gathering of supporters of the Melanesian Mission in England in 1955, Hill remarked:

> Our Melanesian children are growing up. Melanesia today is very different from the Melanesia of pre-war days; these children of ours are awakening from their long, long sleep. They are becoming aware of their responsibilities, and are increasingly anxious to become more self-supporting. The movement known as "Marching Rule" was an expression of this awakening, though a warped one. Questions are being asked, "What of the future — are we to be given opportunities which will enable us to take a more active part in our own affairs?" Such questions reveal a healthy desire to "grow up" and to accept additional responsibility, a desire that should be encouraged. Our Melanesian clergy have the task of leading their people along the Christian road to attain the ultimate goal. It is my wish that they should be given increased responsibility, and I propose to select four of my outstanding priests to accept the position of Rural Deans within the very near future. Of course, these men lack the culture and background of their European colleagues, but many of them are men of much wisdom and ability. This move will be an act of faith, and later the time will come to make an even greater act of faith — the appointment of a Melanesian as an Assistant Bishop.[130]

By 1956 Dudley Tuti of Santa Isabel and Leonard Alufurai of Malaita were appointed rural deans of their respective islands, with district priests under their charge. However, handing over the leadership of the Church to the Melanesians was more apparent than real, for as Charles Fox wrote in his diary on March 8th, 1956:

> Bishop having announced he was giving the Melanesian clergy more power has ingeniously made all the white clergy deans or archdeacons so that the gap is greater than before. It ensures the domination of the Melanesian Church by Europeans.

By 1961 there were Melanesian rural deans for Santa Isabel, Nggela and Savo, Guadalcanal, San Cristobal, Malaita, Santa Cruz, Reefs and Taumako — a total of seven. There was no Melanesian rural dean appointed to the New Hebrides by this date. A European archdeacon was appointed over the Melanesian rural deans in the Solomon Islands, and a European archdeacon was assigned to oversee all the Melanesian clergy in the New Hebrides.[131] This hierarchical mission structure can be diagrammed as follows:

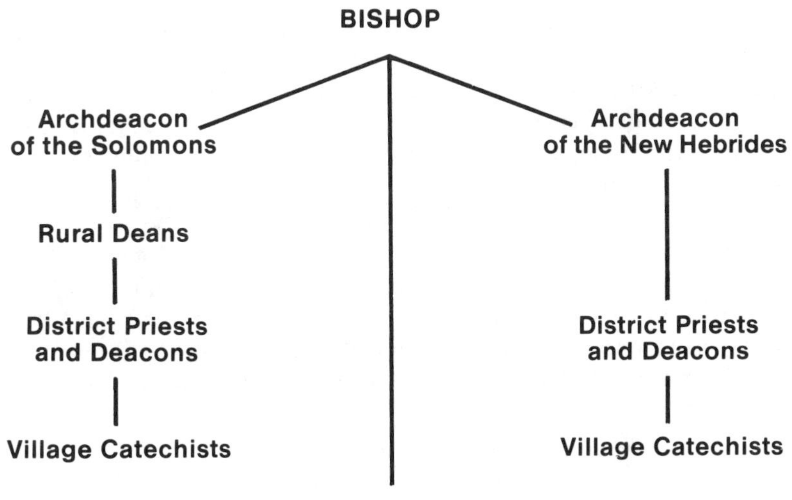

Fig. 9. Organizational Structure of the Melanesian Mission.

In 1963 the staff composition of the Melanesian Mission included a European bishop and 13 clergy (70% from England), 21 teachers (71% from New Zealand), 10 medical personnel (60% from New Zealand), and 12 Europeans in auxiliary activities such as transportation, building, maintenance, printing, etc. This comprised a total European staff of 57.

The number of Melanesians working in the Church included 101 clergy, 820 catechists, 80 members of the Melanesian Brotherhood, 292 teachers, 81 medical personnel, 69 working on the Mission's ships, and 101 in auxiliary capacities. The total number of European missionaries to Melanesian workers was 57 to 1,546, a ratio of 1 to 29.

Europeans were no longer active at the village level, but executed administrative and institutional roles — all positions of power.[132] However, in contrast to the organization of the Anglican Church in Papua New Guinea and Polynesia, Melanesia appeared very indigenous indeed, for as Coaldrake observed:

> Whatever the cause there is a wider and deeper spread of the Church in the Island community. It is not just that one finds whole regions completely and exclusively Anglican for that can also be found in Papua. In Melanesia in such areas the community as a whole has a life which is the life of the Church in a Melanesian pattern. The clergy are Melanesian entirely from the Rural Deans outward (1963: 1).

Coaldrake's observations are those of a European mission executive, comparing one area of the Pacific with other regions, but they do not articulate the Melanesians' desire for greater authority and autonomy in their own affairs. Melanesians had come a long way since the pre-war days, but for many, progress toward equality with whites was still painfully slow. The church had seemingly become more indigenous, but a subtle distinction between European privileges and Melanesian responsibilities still existed.

Melanesians in the 1960's were not calling for a boycott of all European missionaries. Islanders were not asking for a moratorium on missions. The observations of the General Secretary of the New Zealand Anglican Board of Missions is most revealing at this point. Being present at a discussion in which the question "What kind of Missionaries do we want and need?" was raised, he notes:

> I found the discussion and conclusions reached about this perhaps the most stimulating part of the meeting. The Indigenous members had trenchant and sometimes startling things to say and the summary of conclusions will be an essential reference for sometime ahead. To give one example: under the heading "We do however wish to exclude" there is the following list:
>
> 1. Those with an urge but no qualifications.
> 2. Those seeking a satisfaction they are not able to find at home.
> 3. Those who know it all before they come.
> 4. Those who assume that that which is different is "lower."
> 5. Those who have a need to be paternal or maternal.[133]

Melanesians were prepared to have missionaries but they did not want inequality with them.

An illustration which focuses sharply on Melanesian perceptions of inequality in the Melanesian Mission is a tragedy that occurred in 1955. A young missionary recruit from England in a moment of fury killed a young North Malaita boy at Maravovo school. He was brought to trial, charged with the murder and given a death sentence, which was never carried out, as he was removed from the Solomons and sent back to England. The Melanesian Mission underwent the expenses of bringing a defense lawyer and psychiatrist to the Solomons on behalf of the young missionary.[134] Seven years later, three Melanesians wrote a letter to the editor of *The Melanesian Messenger*, in which they expressed their dissatisfaction with the way the Melanesian Mission had provided for the defense of the young missionary. They cried:

> For the Mission to do it was wrong. It was wrong because the Mission knew that *X* was committing the murder of the boy, yet the Mission paid the defense Lawyer. Is a European's life worth more than a Blackman's life in the Presence of God? If so who creates a Blackman? For the Mission to pay for a defense Lawyer, it looks as if *X's* life is worth more than the boy's.[135]

The three Melanesian authors then proceeded to cite a list of tragedies that had occurred to the Mission and the Government after the trial of the missionary:

> 1. In 1957 Rev. D. Hoey and Mr. C. Ross drowned. [Both were members of the Melanesian Mission.]
> 2. In 1958 MV *Melanesian* with about 60 souls lost and the MV *Betua* wrecked.
> 3. In 1959 MV *Margery* sank.
> 4. In 1960 *Southern Cross 8* went aground at the Maravovo beach.
> 5. In 1962 the well Beloved *Southern Cross 9* who has not yet done enough Service for God's Church in Melanesia was wrecked.[136]
>
> These are the greatest losses in the Mission and the Government . . . This may sound very, very silly to you but we believe this is the cause of these losses.[137]

This illustration points vividly to the Melanesians' worldview and perceptions of the inequality between islanders and Europeans. By 1962 voices were raised asking for greater equality and more leadership for Melanesians in the Church. Bishop Hill, shortly after he became the head of the Melanesian Mission talked about the possibility of a future Melanesian assistant bishop, but as one islander declared:

> We still do not know when we shall have Melanesian Bishops. But we all know we must have Bishops from among ourselves to be our Leaders in the Church of Melanesia, men who understand us and our ways, which white men can never do. So let us all pray that this day may come soon, when our Leaders in the Church here are men from our own people.[138]

Their prayers were soon to be answered, for in August 1963, Bishop Hill wrote to his Melanesian Congregation:

> We are now about to have Bishops, priests and deacons as well as brothers and lay workers who are Melanesians. It has become a

> Melanesian Church . . . and I would now say that in the future we call ourselves the "Church of Melanesia." The words "Melanesian Mission" will still be used in connection with our offices but not for the other functions of our work. This will necessitate the need for all Melanesians to realise more than they have in the past their duty to give for the support of their own Church. We are long past the infant stage, we are now like the young men earning their own living.[139]

On November 30th, 1963, two Solomon Islanders, Dudley Tuti of Santa Isabel, and Leonard Alufurai of Malaita, were consecrated assistant bishops. Both men were outstanding leaders among their own people, and were the first two Melanesians to be appointed rural deans in 1956. Both were fairly acculturated, being products of the Mission's educational system. Each of them had studied in New Zealand, including time at St. John's Theological College in Auckland, the school founded by Bishop George Selwyn as his original training center for Melanesians.[140]

This was a significant step for Melanesians, symbolizing the day when they would become a completely autonomous church with their own indigenous leaders at the top of the hierarchical organization. In actuality, however, the assistant bishops became "errand boys" for an aging and failing European bishop. They were at Bishop Hill's beck and call and were used in the strenuous work of pastoral visiting, hopping from one island to another as the bishop directed. They were kept ignorant of the financial operations of the church, and in effect had very little power.

The real power lay with the European archdeacons, and of course the final authority in all decisions was Bishop Hill. The church looked more Melanesian, but it was still very much a European mission organization, with power residing in the hands of the missionaries. Thus the appointment of Melanesian assistant bishops was a tremendously important symbol of an emerging indigenous church, but it was more cosmetic than real; the actual transfer of power and authority to the Melanesians themselves had not yet occurred.

Worn out and tired and failing in health, Bishop Hill retired in 1967 after thirteen years as bishop and thirty-one in the Melanesian Mission. His episcopacy had been a very difficult one, but under his leadership many innovations occurred within the Mission, among which, I would count the following to be the most important:

1. He called three Synods in 1957, 1962, and 1965 and at the 1957 Synod involved Melanesian laymen for the first time.
2. He appointed Melanesians as rural deans beginning in 1956.
3. Two Melanesians were consecrated assistant bishops in 1963.
4. He instituted regular retreats and conferences on an island-wide basis for Melanesian clergy and laymen.

5. Melanesian clergy pay was raised in 1958 from £11 to £25 for deacons, and from £18-21 per year to £35 for priests.
6. A catechist training college was instituted.
7. In the theological college the medium of instruction was changed from Mota to English.
8. As a former headmaster of Pawa school, Hill made education the priority of his episcopacy, and thus the standard of education was raised considerably.

The paradox of Bishop Hill's episcopacy is that he assumed that in order for the church to become autonomous and indigenous, it would have to first raise its Melanesian leaders to European standards. In his mind, when Melanesians approximated European standards, they would then be ready to run their own church. It is apparent that he did not understand the true nature of indigeneity, for one does not promote an indigenous church by encouraging the indigenes to become more Westernized.

Upon Bishop Hill's announced resignation, a Sacred Synod was called to nominate his successor. There were no Melanesians put forth as possible candidates to succeed him. After three ballots one of the European staff was leading, but there was no clear majority. The final decision was therefore made by the New Zealand Bench of Bishops who elected John Wallace Chisholm, who was then an assistant bishop in New Guinea.

He was enthroned as the 10th Bishop of Melanesia on September 24th, 1967. It did not take long for the new bishop to realize all was not well with the Anglican Church in Melanesia. Addressing the Diocesan Standing Committee, six months after his consecration, he declared:

> When a Bishop is called to a Missionary Diocese such as this — he comes to make the work live and grow —he is called to stir the waters —he is expected to give a lead, not for his own glorification or honour, but for the good of the whole Church committed to his care. And this is what I see my vocation in Melanesia and the reason why God called me in the way He did. It is to make the Church live and grow. But is our church alive and is it growing? On paper it all reads so well — we can point to our schools, Colleges, Hospitals, workshops and ships and be thrilled by them all — but deep down is this the whole truth? As I go about the Diocese I see quite another picture — I see a Church which is tired and sick, making little or no impact on our people, either in rural or urban areas. I see a band of clergy — certainly large in number — but many of them ill equipped to do the work expected of them. I see a splendid structure of rural deans, archdeacons, and so on, expected to lead in their areas and yet at a loss to know how to give that lead; I find Brothers and Catechists not really understanding what their true work is.[141]

Chisholm was also concerned that the Melanesian assistant bishops be more than showpieces and that they take over positions of greater responsibility and authority. A month after his consecration, he declared:

> The Concelebration at the Enthronement was no empty symbol, but to us all a most meaningful act of togetherness and I am seeking ways and means by which this may be even more powerfully spelt out than at present. I intend that Bishop Leonard and Bishop Dudley will ordain men of their own areas of jurisdiction and be responsible for them. I wish to investigate how they may exercise greater responsibility in the future — and my mind on this matter, is that they should take over more and more of the responsibilities of the Archdeacons of the Central Solomons and Malaita.[142]

The tone of Chisholm's episcopacy was set early. He was intent on leading the Melanesian Mission from a Diocesan status to that of an independent and autonomous province. Bishop Dudley Tuti called him the "Master Builder" for he "changed our Diocese into a Province."[143] At Diocesan conferences in January and November 1973, discussion was given to "the proper and orderly way" in which the Diocese of Melanesia associated with the Anglican Province of New Zealand could become a separate and autonomous Province of Melanesia. There were very complicated legal and ecclesiastical issues to be resolved, and in this work, Bishop Chisholm was truly a "Master Builder."

By 1975 the stage was set, and Sunday the 26th of January, the Church of Melanesia was inaugurated — no longer the Melanesian Mission, no longer a missionary diocese in the Province of New Zealand, but now an independent and autonomous Province of Melanesia, a member of the worldwide Anglican Communion.[144] Legally and ecclesiastically the Church of Melanesia was now autonomous. Nevertheless, a more important cultural question, to be discussed fully in the following chapter, is whether or not this autonomous church was truly an indigenous one. Had the long awaited goal of Selwyn and Patteson finally been realized?

Within four months of the inauguration of the Province of Melanesia, its first archbishop was dead. John Chisholm had died suddenly of cancer at the age of 52. His death was a great shock to the new province, and many islanders wondered, "What will we do now?" In his eight-year reign, he had given the Melanesian assistant bishops more responsibility and authority. The thrust of his whole episcopacy had been to lead the church to independence, while at the same time, increasing its indigeneity.[145]

The Council of Bishops met shortly after Chisholm's death and elected a Melanesian priest, Norman Kitchener Palmer, as the new archbishop. On November 1st, 1975, more than 5,000 people attended his consecration as the first Melanesian archbishop. Eight days later, the new archbishop, in turn, consecrated a Tikopian, Caspar Uka, as an assistant bishop.[146] The islanders after 125 years of missionary contact had their own Church of Melanesia.

Summary

This period of absorption (1942-1975) is characterized by changes significantly different from the previous two periods of missionary contact and cultural change. The dawn of this period witnessed Melanesian Anglicans agitating for their rightful place in the island world—a place free from paternalism and domination by a foreign power. In the twilight of the period, the Melanesian Mission relinquished its power, took a polite bow and left the center stage.

This chapter has focused on a period of Melanesian acculturation in which revitalization movements played a very important role, as islanders attempted to create a more satisfying culture—a blending of cultures, based on traditional Melanesian values, but allowing for selective innovation of changes advocated by European agents of change.

Marching Rule and the innovation of the Church Association were both important landmarks in the islanders' pilgrimage to independence — an independence that led first to the birth of a Melanesian Anglican Church in 1975, and then to the birth of the Solomon Islands Nation in 1978, and the island nation of Vanuatu in 1980.

In this chapter I have also focused on the missionaries' responses to these movements. Marching Rule was misinterpreted as a Melanesian mystical mirage, reinforcing the missionaries' preconceived ideas that the islanders were far from capable of handling their own affairs, and reinforcing their belief that a paternalistic missionary policy was in the best interest of everyone. The Church Association received a more favorable reception, for it appeared far more "rational," more "practical," and thus more legitimate. But Mission endorsement fell short of enthusiastic support, for if the Church Association had been too successful, there would have been no further need of European missionaries. Or would there have been?

Bishop Hill responded by apparently relegating greater responsibility to islanders, but in actuality, the locus of power remained firmly in the hands of the European missionaries. The church looked more Melanesian than it had at any previous period in the history of the Melanesian Mission, but then looks can be deceptive. And thus, although Bishop Hill recommended that the term "Melanesian Mission" be replaced by the term, "Church of Melanesia," the Mission was still dominant. Nevertheless, in the evolutionary change from a Mission to a Church, the organic possibility of an indigenous church was beginning to be realized and to take shape.

It was the fortunate combination of a courageous and foresighted Bishop John Chisholm, and the outstanding Melanesian leadership of Bishops Dudley and Leonard that ushered in the culmination of that evolutionary process in the form of the Church of Melanesia. And it was an accident of history that dismissed the last European leader in that process, but the time was ripe for his shoes to be filled by a Melanesian.

This chapter has dealt primarily with institutional changes in leadership and has demonstrated the evolution from predominantly European to increasingly Melanesian roles in that process of change. The cultural content and existential meaning of these changes, however, has not been analyzed here. It awaits us in the next chapter when I examine contemporary Anglican Christianity in the islands, and ask whether the Church of Melanesia is only an autonomous Anglican Province, or whether it is also an indigenous Melanesian Church.

CHAPTER 5 NOTES

1. By an Ordinance from the King in 1935 the minimum wage was reduced to half. BSIP 27/VI/I, Malaita District Annual Report 1935., W.P.A.
2. A great deal of the literature cites the impact of World War II as triggering many Melanesian cargo cults, but it is important to note that in almost every case, pre-war antecedents are responsible for creating the conditions in which a "cargo cult" movement became an appropriate post-war response.
3. For a discussion of the Japanese strategy for conquering the Pacific, cf. D. Oliver (1961: 373-374), Grattan (1963b: 519-523).
4. Today the city of Honiara, capital of the Solomon Islands, is located on the very battleground of some of the heaviest fighting on Guadalcanal. As one walks down Mendana Avenue, historical markers give a blow-by-blow description of the battle that ensued there. The airstrip built during the war (Henderson Field) is now a commercial airport, connecting Honiara with other islands in the Solomons and with Fiji, Naura, Australia and Papua New Guinea.

   Official sources describing the American involvement in the Solomons are Morrison (1949) and Craven and Cate (1950). The Battle for Guadalcanal is found in Craven and Cate (1950: 26-91) and Morrison (1949 Vol. V). See also, "The Battle for Guadalcanal" in *Among Those Present* (Colonial Office, 1946: 23-41).

5. The Japanese impact became more of a negative influence as they began to lose the war. In terms of their relationship with the Solomon Islanders, Mander states that:

   > The Japanese apparently did not attempt to establish friendly relations with the natives; not only did they press the headmen to reveal the whereabouts of the British troops but took food much needed by the natives, molested their women, and after the fortunes of war turned against them, they raided native gardens, killed pigs, and so menaced the food supplies that many of the Solomon Islanders suffered extreme hunger (1954: 329).

   The Western Solomons suffered the most under the Japanese, for here entire villages were annihilated.

6. See discussion of Baddeley and Marchant above (Chapter 4, p. 214). Bishop Baddeley reported that remaining with the Resident Commissioner were five other officers. The Roman Catholic missionaries remained, "Mr. Deck and 5 of his men of S.S.E.M.; some of the Methodist staff up West; and our 16 selves. There were a few planters and others who chose to remain. In all we were about 100" (*S.C.L.E.*, July 1943, p. 24).

7. Charles Fox recorded in his diary for January 27, 1942:

   > Government moved to Auki. People starting to scatter about—no guides for the future—people pretty calm but rather afraid.

   By February 20th he recorded:

   > Unless the Government does something to show that they still function there will be trouble all along the coast. The people think there is now no Government.

8. This was consistent with the pattern of wage labor in which the Malaitans had engaged as far back as the 1870's when the labor trade began.

9. The islanders were under the command of British officers, many of whom were locally commissioned ex-planters, but they worked closely with the American troops in road-building and runway repair, unloading cargo and working on the large 1,600 acre truck farms on the Guadalcanal plains to provide fresh vegetables for the military troops in Melanesia (R. Keesing 1978b: 48).

10. Quoted in Mander (1954: 330).

11. Cf. Laracy (1971: 98) and Roger Keesing (1978b: 48-49).

12. Keesing's footnote: "Keesing and Fifi'i, n.d., give detailed eyewitness accounts of the confiscation and public burning of goods earned and accumulated by Labour Corps volunteers. These incidents became

focal points of resentment."

13. Keesing's footnote: "In the pre-war Solomons, when addressed by Europeans, Melanesians were forced to stand at attention, pipes taken from mouths, and to address the Europeans as 'Master.' In Tulagi, Melanesians were required to dismount from their bicycles and stand while Europeans passed" (J. Fifi'i, personal communication).

14. Estelle Field to Miss Rice, 28 October 1945. Letter Book of typed copies to Miss Rice, Oxford. A.J.C.P. M804.

15. Bishop Caulton observed that, "The natives are making a great deal of money at present. This is encouraging them to adopt an artificial way of living, and they are patronizing bakeries instead of working in their gardens as they used to do" (*S.C.L.E.*, July 1948, p. 44). Cf. D. Oliver (1961: 377-378).

16. For additional discussion of the impact of the war in this area, cf. Colonial Office, *Among Those Present: The Official Story of the Pacific Islands at War.* See also, Van Dusen (1945: 27-62), Mander (1954: 329-331), D. Oliver (1961: 376-378), Fox (1962: 119-126, 1967: 56-61), Laracy (1976: 110-117).

17. "Marching Rule" says Allan (1950: 27) is an anglicized version of Masinga Rule, which in the 'Are'are language on South Malaita means "brotherhood." Other terms compiled by Worsley (1957: 173) include Masinga Lo, Maasina Rule, Martin Lo, Masinga Law, Mercy Rule, Masian Rule, etc. Cochrane (1970: 95) claims, "The name 'Marching Rule' came from the opening phrase of the old S.S.E.M. hymn which was sung on the way to work in the mission gardens: 'we're marching along together . . .' "

    D. G. Kennedy (1967) argues that the original Pidgin term, of which "Marching Rule" is an English corruption, was *Masini Rulu*, which properly translated is "Marchant's system-of-government." Kennedy, a District Officer on Nggela, attempted in 1940-1941, to implement an experimental form of local government modeled after East African indirect rule, and suggested by Resident Commissioner Marchant, who had recently transferred to the Solomon Islands from East Africa.

    Allan (1950: 27) notes that on Malaita the movement has sometimes been referred to as "work b'long Nori"—Nori being the leader of the movement, and on Guadalcanal, the term "movm'nt b'long Sgt. Vouza"—Vouza being the leader on Guadalcanal.

    The term "Marxian Rule" or "Marx's Rule" as reported in the *Pacific Islands Monthly* and overseas newspapers, was not uncommonly used in reference to the movement, the implication being of course, that it was communist inspired. In refutation of such a claim, Allan (1950: 27) says, "No evidence has been discovered of any relationship between marching rule and communism. The idea of 'Marxian Rule' is the creation of a Russo-phobic journalist without foundation."

18. Fox (n.d.a: 58) once wrote regarding the Solomon Islanders and taxation:

> The Melanesians used to ask Government officials why they were taxed. I remember a District Officer being asked that, and his answer was, "It is for your protection. If we were not here, the Germans or Japanese would come in and take your islands and treat you very badly." Afterwards the boy who asked the question, said to me with irony, "Now I understand, it is like a big boy sitting on a little boy and beating him, and the little boy says, 'Why are you beating me?' and the big boy says, 'Why, if I were not beating you, a bigger boy than I would be doing it much worse. Where is your gratitude to me?' " They feel very much treated as inferiors.

19. Cochrane (1970: 74-78) develops this theme a bit more. He notes:

> While on patrol the D.O. was accompanied by an armed detachment of Native Constabulary. "Government" for the Melanesian was a single D.O. in the same way that in traditional times it had been a "big man." The Melanesian's only contact with Government was when the D.O. made his rounds: "The difficulty is that such visits must nearly always be disciplinary; the District Officer does not have time to give complimentary and friendly visits" (quoting Hopkins 1928: 236). The D.O. was a harsh disciplinarian. He gave executive orders like a traditional "big man," and he sent the Melanesians out to work as if they were his dependants (1970: 76-77).

20. Cochrane (1970: 76). There was quite a difference between pre-war and post-war Colonial Service Officers. Post-war officers were introduced to the principles of social anthropology during their training. From a short clipping in the *P.I.M.*, September 1947, p. 69, under the heading, "Leftist Officials and BSI Agitators" the following is quoted:

> "Much of the labour trouble in the British Solomons," said an old resident of the Protectorate, "is due to the attitude adopted by the numerous young officials now arriving from the Old Country, and who for the most part have been inoculated with the Socialist virus. There are now over 150 officials in the group, where in pre-war days there were only about 50. The correct post-war policy," he continued, "should have been one embracing strong disciplinary measures among the natives."

21. The resistance was greatest in Malaita and Guadalcanal. The episode

surrounding the murder of District Officer W. R. Bell in October 1927, is symptomatic of the discontent felt by the Solomon Islanders. H. C. Moorhouse, appointed to inquire into the circumstances of the murder, concluded his report and recommendations by noting:

> I am afraid that at the present moment the majority of natives look on the district officer merely as a tax gatherer or one who metes out punishment, and the first task should be to dispel that idea (1929: 13).

I would suggest further that an objective evaluation of the D.O.'s role would come fairly close to that perceived by the Solomon Islanders. It was Administration policy to let social services such as medicine and education reside with the missions. Cf. Mander (1954: 318-327).

22. Allan (1950: 30) says that it never caught on in the outlying Polynesian islands, although it was well known and talked about. On Nggela, the administrative and commercial center of the Solomons, the Marching Rule movement was short lived. Fox's account is most interesting:

> Soon after I moved to Gela, Marching Rule reached that island. The leaders burned with zeal to spread it, they were fanatics who could not be reasoned with. One of them came to Gela and went from village to village. He gathered the people into the churches, preaching fervently, mentioning that the British were referred to in the Bible as wolves clothed in sheep's clothing. He went thus through some twenty villages, and all the people in every village but one (Belaga) joined the movement. But Marching Rule was really impossible for Christians because it preached hate for all who did not belong to it. A week later I followed this fanatic through the same villages, taking two Gela friends with me, and all the people who had joined left it again, though they did not get back their dollars. That was the end of Marching Rule on Gela; it never got a footing again, and the refusal of Gela to join it had a good deal of influence (1962: 132).

When I interviewed Fox in February 1977, he spoke about what a marvelous movement Marching Rule had been, and called the Government "silly asses" for repressing it. I then asked him why he had spoken out against it on Nggela, and he replied, "To avert civil war on the island, since Little Gela had supported it, while Big Gela had not joined in, and there was bitter strife between the two factions."

For a discussion of the brief period of Marching Rule activity on Santa Isabel, cf. White (1978: 246-255).

23. Malaita District Annual Report, 1947. W.P.A.

24. The Melanesian Mission reported in 1949 that: "Marching Rule still goes strong in places. There was a fantastic story going round that the

Americans had dug a tunnel from America which came up in the bush in Ulawa, and that the bush was full of troops" (*S.C.L.E.*, July 1949, p. 110).

25. Americans have played a significant role in many post-war Melanesian cargo cults, e.g., John Frum in the New Hebrides (Guiart 1952), Johnson Cult on New Hanover (Billings 1969). For a similar reaction to Australians *vis a vis* the British in New Guinea during the war, cf. Read (1947).

    The notion that the Americans will help the Solomon Islanders was still alive during the period of my fieldwork (1977-1978). Many suggested to me that after the Solomon Islands gained their independence in 1978, perhaps the Americans would return and help the islanders.

26. Roger Keesing (1978b) is the most recent scholar to turn his attention to Marching Rule. He argues that the emphasis on cargo is an artifact of the European investigators of Marching Rule and not of central importance to the goals and aspirations of the movement's members.

27. For a discussion of the "cargo" emphasis in the later phases of the movement on Santa Isabel, cf. G. White (1978: 250-251).

28. In my earlier study of Marching Rule (Whiteman 1975) I overemphasized the importance of cargo and underestimated the important role that the desire for preserving Melanesian culture played, particularly in the formative stages of the movement. This is a good lesson in the epistemology of anthropological investigation, (cf. Salamone 1979), for my initial research relied on government reports or studies compiled by former District Officers (Allan 1950, 1951; Belshaw 1947, 1948, 1950a, 1950b, 1954; Cochrane 1970) and did not benefit from field work and interviews with former participants in the movement.

29. For a similar response among the Seneca see the study of Handsome Lake by Wallace (1969).

30. For years the Government and missions had urged the people to abandon their scattered villages and hamlets in the bush and relocate on the coast in nucleated villages. Except for the string of "mission villages" along the coast, most Malaitans (of which half were estimated to be pagans in 1942) still lived in the interior. Nevertheless, in 1946 new "towns" were built on Malaita, situated on the coast, composed of people who heretofore had lived in scattered hamlets in the mountainous interior. A Marching Rule "town" was a model combined of features advocated by the missions and Government, and those of the American army camps which had been seen during the war years on

Nggela and Guadalcanal. Allan (1950: 46) notes that a tremendous amount of work went into the erection of these "towns" and he suggests several reasons for the considerable industry which Malaitans exhibited:

(1) The conviction and policy of Marching Rule to encourage better housing throughout the island;
(2) The belief that the British would come and take the island away from the people, so some form of defense was needed;
(3) The desire to emulate the Americans and their army camps in hopes that some day they would return to rule Malaita;
(4) The belief that at some unspecified date in the future some ghost-like American vessels of war would arrive off their coast to distribute freely tremendous quantities of material goods possessed heretofore by the Europeans, but for which the Malaitans had had to pay hard earned shillings. So they wanted as many people as possible ready to receive the goods when the greatest *ngwane-inotos* (Big Men) of all time arrived on the coast.

Cf. Worsley's (1957: 252) discussion of the Marching Rule "towns" *vis a vis* the separatist activity of many cargo cult movements, corresponding to Van Gennep's "rites of separation." Cf. Laracy (1971: 103) on the establishment of Marching Rule "towns."

31. As a result of young men going off to work on the plantations, the traditional way of providing for the aged had fallen into disregard. Marching Rule expressly forbade anyone going off to a plantation to work and thus leaving their elderly kin to fend for themselves. To insure this, it was required that anyone accepting plantation work must be paid £12 a month; a substantial increase from the standard 10-20 shillings per month.

32. This sense of unity may have evolved as a result of the organization of Marching Rule rather than by any deliberate ideological tenets designed to bring the people together. Nevertheless, it was very real, a strong and dominant belief among the members. Fox gives us his assessment of the unity he observed in the islands:

> Deep differences in language, in custom, in government divided the people of the different islands. The inhabitants of one island were foreigners to those of another, and used to be killed at sight. There were no common leaders. Yet here in Marching Rule was something uniting them all. Those who joined said: "Now we are all one." It seemed incredible. It astonished those of us who knew them best. I talked to a native of North Mala and asked him why he had joined and why he liked Marching Rule. He said, "Because it has made us Melanesians all one. We are all brothers now. Before it began if I had tried to walk to South Mala through the

> central districts of Koio and Areare I should have been killed long before I got to South Mala. But now the Koio and Areare people say to us, 'Come through when you wish, we are all one.' " And the same thing was said to me on San Cristoval, many of whose people are hereditary enemies of Mala men. "But now," they said to me, "we are all one with the Mala people." And so it was too in the other islands. British rule had not united them, Christianity had not united them, and here they were suddenly swept into a unity never dreamed of before by this new movement for independence and self government. It amazed us all (1962: 128-129).

33. Cf. *Annual Report of the British Solomon Islands Protectorate 1948* (1949: 26-29); *Annual Report . . . 1949 and 1950* (1951: 37-42).

34. Cf. Worsley (1957: 174-175), and Fox (1967: 66).

35. The two initial leaders on Malaita were Nori, a young pagan 'Are'are man who converted to the Marist mission in 1947, and who had had considerable contact with Americans during the war, and Timothy George of Sa'a who was highly acculturated to European ways, having been born in Queensland and having lived there for some time. As the movement progressed on Malaita the leadership shifted from the southern part of the island to the northern half, where S.S.E.M. "teachers" became the powerful leaders. Vouza was the leader of the movement on Guadalcanal; for his intriguing story see MacQuarrie (1948). Brown Zalamana carried the message of Marching Rule from Guadalcanal to Santa Isabel where he became the dominant, although short-term leader. Brown was a member of the Isabel Council during my fieldwork, but lost his bid for re-election in July 1977. I had an excellent interview with him in January 1978 concerning his activities during Marching Rule and his ideas for indigenous development today.

    One of the important elements that most of the leaders seem to have had in common was their considerable experience with Europeans, either during the war, or in the pre-war Civil Service, or through working for European entrepreneurs or missionaries. In discussing the leadership of Marching Rule *vis a vis* the leadership of the Government councils which failed in the central and eastern Solomon Islands, Allan (1950: 40) noted, "The Government council was something which was initiated by Europeans and was imposed from without Malaita while the marching rule arose from and belonged to the people."

36. Roger Keesing (1978b: 251-252) notes that the political structure of Marching Rule was along the lines created by District Officer W. R. Bell (1915-1927) who in 1922 organized an administrative structure

with a Head Chief for each sub-district of Malaita, a Full Chief for each passage, and a communal meeting village for each "line." Cf. R. Keesing (1968).

37. The Archives of the Western Pacific High Commission have a "closed period" of thirty years which means that most of the Government documents related to Marching Rule were not available for my inspection. By 1983 the documents covering the entire period of Marching Rule activities will be available and should throw additional light on the Administration's attitude and response to Marching Rule. I have been limited to using only published records, combined with eyewitness accounts, and supplemented, if not corrected, by statements of informants who participated in the movement.

38. *Annual Report of the British Solomon Islands Protectorate 1948* (1949: 26-27). If Marching Rule adherents really believed that they had "ample power and opportunity to give plenty of scope to their aspirations," then why did Marching Rule ever develop, and appear in a **parallel** political structure in **opposition** to the Government?—a question the Administration apparently failed to comprehend.

39. Fox (1962: 131) reports that in the Melanesian Mission, "None of the Melanesian priests of the Mission joined it, and so they were persecuted, ostracised, sent to Coventry, and had their goods stolen with impunity. They had a very hard time."

40. *Annual Report of the British Solomon Islands Protectorate 1949 and 1950* (1951: 37-39).

41. Cochrane (1970: 90) says that the object of Marching Rule was to force the British to cooperate, not to kill them. From an interview with Vouza, Cochrane claims that during the six years of full-scale Marching Rule activity, only one Government supporter was killed.

42. *P.I.M.*, (March 1948, p. 29) reported that at the trial of twenty-nine Marching Rule leaders, which concluded on February 14, 1948 after twenty-five days of deliberation, "Six of the accused were found not guilty; nine were sentenced to six years' imprisonment with hard labour; the remaining received sentences ranging from five years to one year." The article fails to note that the nine Marching Rule leaders of Malaita, sentenced to six years of hard labor, were convicted for violation of the Unlawful Societies Act of 1799, and the Seditious Meetings Act of 1817 (R. Keesing 1978b: 52).

43. *P.I.M.*, October 1947, p. 17.

44. This is a significant point. For years the Administration had tried to give the Protectorate a sense of unity. For one thing, it would be easier

to control. However, since there had been no indigenous pattern of unity the Administration's efforts to amalgamate the cultural hodgepodge of the Solomons had been to no avail. Now, suddenly here was Malaita, undoubtedly the most heterogeneous of all the islands, calling for recognition as an entity. Marching Rule came to the fore when the Malaitans were ready to be seen as an entity. And what better way to symbolize that unified entity than through their own flag?

P.I.M., (November 1947, p. 9) carried a photograph of the flag and made the following comment: " 'The design was very neat and effective,' said Major Robinson, 'and it was no native job — undoubtedly the flag had been designed for them by some European. But no one has been able to discover the origin of the flag.'

"The size of the flag was approximately 48 inches by 30 inches. It was a blue flag with 10 horizontal stripes in yellow. The central design — apparently a bow and arrow — was in white as also were the letters NUC, which stand for Native Union Council."

45. This is an enactment of the traditional "Big Man" role and function. Cf. Cochrane (1970: 93) for further discussion.

46. The subject of Marching Rule deserves a dissertation-length ethnohistorical study, which to date has not been done. Three of the scholars evaluated below (Belshaw, Allan, and Cochrane) all served time in the Solomon Islands as District Officers. The most recent studies of Marching Rule are Laracy (1971) who pays particular attention to the Marist missionaries' relationship to the movement, Whiteman (1975) who discusses Marching Rule in terms of its significance for applied anthropology, and R. Keesing (1978b) who cogently argues that Marching Rule is one of several politico-religious movements in a history of Malaita anti-colonial sentiment, and attempts to resolve the contradictions between exogenous European influence and endogenous values and traditional Melanesian culture.

47. This is not all the Americans taught the islanders. The full impact of the G.I.'s on the Solomon Islanders is yet to be thoroughly analyzed, but there is little doubt that there was something of the "Spirit of 1776" in the G.I.'s encouragement given to the islanders to "throw off the yoke of the oppressor." After all, it was the English from whom the Americans had demanded independence, and in this sense, the Americans and the Solomon Islanders had something in common.

48. For a recent "emic" view of John Frum, cf. Rice (1974).

49. This corresponds to Merton's (1957) notion that the goals and aspirations are clearly present in the individual's mind and value system, but he lacks the institutionalized means of achieving them,

thus frustrating the individual and leading to a state of anomie; cf. Durkheim (1951).

50. The notion of a half-way Melanesian is a good example of a marginal person as developed in the theory of marginality. For further discussion on marginality theory, cf. Park (1928), Stonequist (1937), Hughes (1949), Kerchoff and McCormick (1955), and Dunning (1959).

51. Allan (1974) has also provided some interesting oral history accounts of antecedent activities that bear on an indigenous understanding of Marching Rule.

52. Allan later became Sir Colin Allan and returned to the Solomon Islands as Her Majesty's Governor to see the islands through the final stages leading to independence in July 1978.

53. Allan's quote is a perfect description of the "marginal man," cf. Stonequist (1937).

54. For a similar interpretation of Melanesian "Cargo Cults" and the status of Marching Rule within this schema, cf. Guiart (1951).

55. For a detailed ethnohistorical account of the Bell murder at the hands of the Kwaio on Malaita, cf. R. Keesing and Corris (1980). See also Moorhouse (1929) and "A Short statement on the matters leading up to the murder of Messrs. Bell and Lillies and 13 native officials at Kwai'ambe, Sinerango, Malaita on the 4th of October 1927" (BSIP 27/I/14, W.P.A.). On the pacification of Malaita, cf. Boutilier (1979).

56. The copra market remained depressed until after the war when in 1948 prices began to rise.

57. From the islanders' perspective, black and white G.I.'s appeared equal, but in fact, there was considerable racism and discrimination. Cf. Laracy (1971: 98) and R. Keesing (1978b: 48-49) for further discussion of the influence of black soldiers in the Solomon Islands.

58. One effect of the American presence in the Solomons was manifest in the entrance fee required to join Marching Rule on Malaita; one American dollar for adults, and five cents for a baby — you could not join with the equivalent sum in British shillings or native money (Fox 1962: 127).

59. A very similar theme is expressed in Burridge's account of Tangu (New Guinea) and European interaction:

> When Tangu encounter Europeans, or get into trouble with administrative officers, they would want, instinctively, to be able to "quarrel it through." But this they cannot do. Instead, they are punished, warned or forgiven — each a unilateral act which

> erases all meaning from equivalence. Nor can the situation be explained away simply in terms of different cultural conventions. The fact is that when Tangu face a European, eye to blazing eye, within arm's length, the sap runs dry. Tangu submit. And they know that they do so. But they would like it to be otherwise. "Are we dogs?" they cry in impassioned fury. — "Are we not men as they are?" (1960: 215).

60. Cochrane's study has been severely criticized, and his book does have several errors of fact. R. Keesing (1978b: 55) is the most critical and notes that, "Cochrane in discussing Doliasi's movement, neglects to mention that as Acting D.O., North Malaita, he was actively engaged in trying to subvert and discredit the movement." I am aware of the shortcomings of Cochrane's work, but I nevertheless believe he has given us a useful analytical framework for a partial explanation and interpretation of Marching Rule.

61. Cochrane (1970: 145) says, "There can be no advance in knowledge about these movements when they are termed: 'escapist' (Linton), 'projection into phantasy world' (Berndt), 'phantasy substitute for political action' (Mair), 'irrationality' (Firth), and 'automania' (Williams)."

62. R. Keesing (1978b) has made a significant contribution in a similar fashion by noting that Marching Rule and other movements preceding and following it on Malaita have been simply manifestations of underlying themes running through the history of "cult" activities on this island. According to Keesing (1978b: 70) these focal themes are, "The resolution of contradictions between Fundamentalist Christianity and ancestral culture, anticolonial hostility, the valuation and codification of custom as a symbol of past strength and integrity, and the internal transformation of communities."

63. This notion was emphasized by Brown Zalamana when I interviewed him in 1978. Cf. G. White (1978: 250).

64. For a discussion of what the Solomon Islanders did **not** gain through Marching Rule, cf. Cochrane (1970: 93-95).

65. Islanders continue today to distinguish between different European nationalities — Americans, Australians, New Zealanders and Englishmen. The task of establishing rapport with islanders in the field was greatly facilitated by the fact that my wife and I were Americans. Many were eager to share their wartime experiences with us and recount their fond memories of American troops.

66. Dovey (1950: 37-38) probably drawing on Shevill (1949: 142) cites the following post-war statistics of mission membership in the Solomons:

(1) Melanesian Mission—32,605 adherents in 339 villages; (2) Roman Catholics—8,776; (3) Seventh Day Adventists—4,128 adherents centered around 86 native stations mostly in the Western Solomons; (4) South Sea Evangelical Mission—14,000 members in 350 churches. Laracy (1971: 104) claims that, "In 1942 nearly half of Malaita with a total population possibly underestimated at 40,000, was Christian—9,000 S.S.E.M., 5,000 Anglican and about 4,000 Catholic."

67. This is not altogether correct. Deck (1945: 15) says that five men stayed during the War, "to seek to care for their converts, the bulk of whom lived on Malaita." Cf. "The Bishop's Report 1942" *S.C.L.E.*, July 1943, p. 24.

68. Bishop Caulton in his "Report for 1949" spoke of Marching Rule and stated that, "This movement still persists, but it is a great tribute to the loyalty of our clergy that not one of the Melanesian priests or deacons has joined it, though it means that they suffer a certain amount of estrangement from their people" (*S.C.L.E.*, April 1950, p. 196).

Bishop Caulton's pronouncement is not altogether true. It may be true that no clergy on Malaita joined the movement, but there were at least two priests on Santa Isabel who did, including Ben Hageria, who had been active in the Fallowes Movement, and was a priest of long-standing with the Melanesian Mission. The leader of Marching Rule on Santa Isabel was Brown Zalamana, a catechist who had spent eight years in the Melanesian Brotherhood, and then had briefly studied for the priesthood until interrupted by the war. For further discussion of Zalamana cf. G. White (1978: 252-255).

69. Melanesian Mission indigenous clergy may have had much more to lose and little to gain by joining Marching Rule compared to the S.S.E.M. teachers, for their salaries were paid by the Mission. In contrast, all the S.S.E.M. teachers received no pay from their mission, but were supported solely by the generosity of their local congregations. Cf. Hilliard (1966: 396).

70. I have also been free to point out policies and personnel who were not as cross-culturally sensitive as they might have been. But in the main, members of the Melanesian Mission were far less ethnocentric than their fellow European counterparts in government, business and other missions.

71. In discussing the differences between the various missionary organizations in Island Melanesia Belshaw notes:

> There are of course many differences, from the administrative point of view, between these various bodies. In their attitude to native life, all were at first intolerant and sometimes brutal in the

> deliberate shock they administered to native custom. After this initial phase which was due largely to ignorance, various degrees of tolerance have been adopted. Generally speaking, the small Protestant groups are still uncompromising on such matters as the consumption of pork (the primary source of meat), singing and dancing, smoking and dress. The Catholics and Melanesian Mission, and in recent years the Presbyterians, have been much more sympathetic, and have been content to make slow progress in a spirit of compromise (1950b: 46).

For further discussion on the differences between the Melanesian Mission and S.S.E.M., cf. Hogbin (1939: 173-219), and Tippett (1967).

72. *Dr. Deck's Letter*, October 1922, pp. 3-4. Quoted in Hilliard (1966: 399).

73. Conversion to Christianity in the S.S.E.M. meant not only a shift in religious allegiance, but implied turning one's back on one's own Melanesian culture and embracing the ways of the white man. Missionaries took a stand against such Melanesian behavior as dancing, feasting, smoking, chewing betel and other behavior patterns offensive to a more conservative and puritanical philosophy. As Cochrane (1970: 79) has observed, "Mission teaching was 'light' on theology and 'heavy' on Christian ethics."

74. Hilliard (1966: 397) notes that about one-third of the S.S.E.M. missionaries resided at their headquarters located at One Pusu on Malaita, and that, "In 1923 there were eight women missionaries and one man resident at One Pusu; in 1939 seven women and two men."

75. See discussion of paternalism above, Chapter 4, pp. 198-202.

76. Cf. Laracy (1971: 105-107) and G. White (1978: 254). The number of Christian converts on Malaita increased during Marching Rule. In 1942 less than half (18,000) of the Malaitans were Christian, but by 1950 it was estimated that one-fourth of the island still remained pagan. This represents an increase of approximately 15,000 Christian converts. Cf. *S.C.L.E.*, February 1952, p. 366; Laracy (1971: 104).

77. Today the South Sea Evangelical Church is an autonomous and independent Melanesian church. But interestingly, there is still a South Sea Evangelical Mission with a small band of missionaries operating independently of and sometimes in contention with the local church.

78. Quoted in Worsley (1957: 175).

79. *S.C.L.E.*, July 1948, pp. 43-44.

80. For further reference to Fox's freedom of movement during Marching Rule cf. Fox to Durrad, August 17, 1947. Durrad Papers (MS Papers 1171, p. 30), Alexander Turnbull Library, Wellington, New Zealand.

81. *S.C.L.E.*, January 1950, p. 179; April 1950, p. 196; July 1950, p. 221; November 1951, p. 349.

82. *Ibid.*, April 1950, p. 196.

83. *Ibid.*, October 1948, p. 63; January 1950, p. 176.

84. Laracy (1971) gives us a well-documented study of the Marist Mission during Marching Rule.

85. Quoted in Laracy (1971: 108).

86. Fox recorded in his diary (April 30, 1948) while touring Malaita:

> The people want to go to Rome because of Reynolds' [Archdeacon of the the Solomons] Pastoral [Letter], "To all the Faithful of the Church of Melanesia I command you all to leave Marching Rule at once," with orders to have it read in all the Churches which Wa did, but did not excommunicate all his people as ordered. None left Marching Rule and Rome was ready to have them.

87. Bishop Caulton, writing in 1949 declared:

> The most disturbing event of recent years has of course been the war. The suspension of the normal order of things and contact with all the tremendous organisation of modern warfare has produced a sense of unsettlement among some sections of the native community which is quite a new feature of life in the islands. It has shown itself in the movement known as "Marching Rule," which has persisted since the war. Although it differs in some respects in different localities its chief attitude is one of passive opposition to the present Government. Its adherents are possessed by a strange and crude fanaticism which is very difficult to dispel, and it is by no means easy to convince them that they have not reasoned out their position far enough. Those of them who are agitating for independence do not realise that they are a long way from being capable of exercising such authority and that their welfare is best served by being subject to an external authority which is ready to give them such control of their own affairs as they are capable of using rightly. Until they come to realise this, their present discontent needs to be handled with wise understanding.
>
> We can best assist the people in this time of unrest by teaching them the Christian duty of subjection to lawful authority, which in this case is protective and in no way repressive; and by helping them to see that their development will be best assured by remaining under tutelage rather than by premature independence,

> especially as their idea of independence is that isolation which they enjoyed in the past and which can never return ("Message from the Bishop," *100 Years Christian Progress in the Pacific 1849-1949*. Melanesian Mission, n.d., pages unnumbered).

See also, S. G. Caulton, "The Marching Rule Delusion," *P.I.M.*, August 1950, pp. 77-79.

88. H. V. C. Reynolds, *S.C.L.E.*, February 1952, p. 366.

89. Cf. "Partners," *The Melanesian Messenger*, 8 October 1958, pp. 2-3. A similar idea was developed by the Marist Fr. Bernard van de Walle who founded the Catholic Welfare Society in March 1950. It was immediately and enthusiastically accepted by the islanders, but also proved too threatening to the Government who did not want to be upstaged by the missions, and thus ordered it to be dissolved in September 1950, cf. Laracy (1971: 111-112).

90. Cf. *S.C.L.E.*, July 1948, p. 43; July 1949, p. 122, 138; July 1950, p. 221; October 1950, p. 242.

91. *Ibid.*, January 1951, p. 269. In Fox's correspondence with Durrad during this period, he writes frequently about the influence of the Americans on the Solomon Islanders, cf. Durrad Papers, *op. cit.*

92. Tippett (n.d.b) discusses this differential response to missions in terms of the types of movements that emerge. He identifies three forms of religious innovation in Melanesia: (1) the nativistic movement or "cargo cult," (2) the Indigenous Church, and (3) the Independent Church. He argues that the different non-traditional forms of religiosity expressed in Melanesia were reactions primarily to the "manifest operations of white traders, settlers, and especially public servants, administrators and missionaries [which] influenced the precise form of the Melanesian reaction" (n.d.b: 18).

    The nativistic cult and independent church are reactionary responses to a mission organization that has been paternalistic and remained in authority over "its people." The indigenous church is the culmination of an evolutionary process rather than a revolution, and represents the efforts of missionaries and indigenes alike in developing a structure appropriate to the given cultural context.

93. Aberle (1970: 209).

94. Statement of John Palmer Pidoke, "Chief of Gela," June 1939, enclosure in R. P. Fallowes to High Commissioner, 15 June 1939. BSIP F43/14/1. Quoted in Hilliard (1978: 283-284).

95. For a general discussion of these movements, cf. Hogbin (1958: 207-233). A good review of cargo cults, including a "Missionary Response"

to them is found in Strelan (1977). See also Steinbauer (1974, 1979). Two excellent studies of cargo movements in Irian Jaya are Kamma (1972) and Godschalk (1977). The most significant theoretical discussions encompassing a phenomenon wider than just Melanesian cargo cults are found in: Barber (1941), Linton (1943), Wallis (1943), Wallace (1956), Lanternari (1963), Clemhout (1964), Aberle (1970), and LaBarre (1971). Bibliographies of Melanesian cargo cults are found in Leeson (1952), Worsley (1968: 289-293), and New Guinea Research Unit (1972). Some of the most important theoretical studies of post-war Melanesian revitalization movements include the following: Belshaw (1950a, 1951), Bodrogi (1951), Guiart (1951, 1970), Firth (1955), Inglis (1957), Stanner (1958), Worsley (1957, 1968), Watters (1960), Newman (1961), Jarvie (1963, 1964: 55-128, 1966, 1972), Oosterwal (1967, 1973), Burridge (1969), Christiansen (1969), Cochrane (1970), Eliade (1970), and Mair (1971).

The Melanesian Institute of Goroka, Papua New Guinea, has recently (1980, 1982) held two conferences on Religious Movements in Melanesia. The scope of the Religious Movements project is wider than traditional cargo cults, and includes revival movements and pentecostal movements within the churches as well as the emergence of independent churches. The papers from these conferences will be forthcoming, published by The Melanesian Institute.

96. Cf. Belshaw (1950a), Guiart (1952, 1956), Worsley (1968: 152-160), Rice (1974). See also, *P.I.M.*, January 1950, pp. 67-70, February 1950, pp. 59-65.

97. Cf. J. Miller (1948), Belshaw (1950a), and Worsley (1968: 148-152).

98. Cf. Davenport and Coker (1967), and O'Connor (1973).

99. Davenport and Coker (1967: 172-173).

100. *Ibid.*, p. 134.

101. Cf. Cochrane (1970: 97-118); *The Melanesian Messenger*, August 1966, p. 8.

102. For a discussion of general Neo-Marching Rule activities in North Malaita during this period, cf. H. Ross (1973).

103. Cf. Tippett (1967: 212-266), Tuza (1970), Harwood (1971, 1978), and *P.I.M.*, July 1978, pp. 18-20.

104. In Solomon Islands Pidgin, "Mama" is the word for father.

105. Cf. Tippett (1967: 209-212), Rimoldi (1971), and Laracy (1976: 135-140).

106. Cf. Worsley (1968: 114-122).

107. Laracy (1976: 136-137).

108. Cf. M. Mead (1956), Schwartz (1962), and Worsley (1968: 183-193). For Paliau's own life story, cf. Maloat (1970).

109. *Report of the U.N. Visiting Mission to Trust Territories in the Pacific, Reports on New Guinea*, 12th Session, New York, 1953, p. 10. Quoted in Worsley (1968: 192).

110. *Ibid.*

111. Cf. Maher (1958, 1961), and Worsley (1968: 193).

112. Cf. Cranswick (1952). In the discussion of these revitalization movements above, I have drawn on diverse theoretical orientations. For example, political interpretations as in Guiart and Worsley are quite distinct from psychocultural interpretations as in Wallace and Schwartz.

113. The following discussion of the Church Association has been reconstructed from *S.C.L.E.*, February 1954, pp. 145-146, 153-156; February 1955, pp. 16-18; May 1955, pp. 45-48. *O Sala Ususur*, Easter 1954, pp. 28-30; All Saints' Tide 1954, pp. 36-38; Easter 1955, pp. 10-12; St. Andrew's Tide 1955, pp. 2-5. *The Melanesian Messenger*, October 1958, pp. 16, 18; All Saints' Tide 1959, pp. 2, 15, 17-18; May 1960, pp. 7, 12; August 1963, pp. 26-30; Easter 1964, pp. 20-22; August 1964, p. 4; December 1965, pp. 18-25. Coaldrake (1963), Peterson (1966), and Tippett (1967: 183-184).

114. Timothy Faifu, *The Melanesian Messenger*, December 1965, p. 19.

115. *S.C.L.E.*, February 1954, p. 150.

116. Fox (1958: 170, 1964: 21).

117. For additional biographical sketches of Willie Masuraa cf. *S.C.L.E.*, June-September 1957, pp. 77-78; *The Melanesian Messenger*, Easter 1964, pp. 20-22; Peterson (1966: 219-220). For a brief sketch of Willie Au who worked with Willie Masuraa in formulating the rules of the Church Council, cf. *S.C.L.E.*, June-September 1957, pp. 78-79.

118. Peterson (1966: 219).

119. See Rule No. 5 under section entitled, "My Promises" on page 289 below.

120. *Rules of the Church Association*, Rule No. 2. See Appendix VI.

121. *S.C.L.E.*, February 1954, p. 155.

122. The copy from which these rules have been taken is in the possession

of Rev. Stephen Brooker, General Secretary of the New Zealand Anglican Board of Missions, Wellington.

123. *Rules of the Church Association*, Section 9, "The Central Committee," Rule No. 2. See Appendix VI.

124. Rule No. 14 under section entitled, "All Members of the Church on S. Mala." See p. 287 above.

125. *S.C.L.E.*, February 1954, p. 156.

126. *The Melanesian Messenger*, Easter 1964, p. 22.

127. Coaldrake (1963: 5-6), Tippett (1967: 183).

128. *S.C.L.E.*, February 1954, p. 146.

129. Cf. *ibid.*, November 1954, pp. 252-255; May 1955, pp. 39-40.

130. *The Reaper*, February 1956, p. 6 (New Zealand Anglican Board of Missions, Wellington). See also, *S.C.L.E.*, August 1955, pp. 84-85.

131. *The Melanesian Messenger*, Easter 1961, pp. 10-18; December 1961, p. 10.

132. Coaldrake (1963: 2).

133. *Report of the General Secretary on a Visit to the South Pacific, 9 May — 12 July, 1966*, p. 2. Church of Melanesia Archives, Honiara.

134. For further discussion on this tragedy, cf. *S.C.L.E.*, June 1956, pp. 33-34.

135. *The Melanesian Messenger*, December 1962, p. 27.

136. The authors are in error here. The *Southern Cross IX* did run aground on a reef and it took over two weeks to get it off, but the vessel experienced only minor damage. Cf. *S.C.L.E.*, March 1963, pp. 4-5.

137. *The Melanesian Messenger*, December 1962, p. 28.

138. *Ibid.*

139. *Ibid.*, August 1963, pp. 2-3.

140. For further biographical sketches of these two men, cf. *The Melanesian Messenger*, August 1963, pp. 11-12; *S.C.L.E.*, September 1963, pp. 80-81; 1966, p. 33; Naban (1976: 94-95). For details regarding the consecration of the assistant bishops, cf. *The Melanesian Messenger*, January 1964, pp. 5-8, 10-22; *S.C.L.E.*, March 1964, pp. 10-19.

141. "Address to the Standing Committee, March 29, 1968." Church of Melanesia Archives, Honiara.

142. "Address to the Standing Committee, October 21, 1967." Church of Melanesia Archives, Honiara.

143. *Wantok*, Vol. 1 (1): 3 (n.d. [1976]), Wellington. See also, "Minutes of the Provincial Council Commencing on 15th July, 1975 In the Council Chamber, Church House, Honiara," Senior Bishop's Address, pp. 1-3. Church of Melanesia Archives, Honiara.

144. Surprisingly the "Melanesian Mission" is still alive and well today. Operating out of headquarters in London, it has continued the English Committee, employs a priest as secretary, and has the annual meeting on St. Barnabas Day at the same Mary Summer House. The "Melanesian Mission" publishes a newsletter, *Melanesian News*, and an *Annual Report*. In 1976 its income was £40,977 and expenditures £27,399, including a grant of £11,000 to the Province of Melanesia (*Melanesian Mission, Annual Report 1977-1978*, p. 24).

The continued existence of the "Melanesian Mission" as a separate entity from the Province of Melanesia is most amazing. Its primary function must be to serve European interests in the history of the Mission, for the Church of Melanesia has little need for such an organization. Traditions die hard!

145. For Chisholm's obituary, cf. *P.I.M.*, July 1975, p. 72.

146. For brief biographical sketches of Palmer and Uka, cf. Naban (1976: 99-101).

Chapter 6

The Problem of Indigenous Christianity

In this study I have followed historically the process of culture change in Melanesia *vis a vis* the history of the Melanesian Mission. Beginning with a pre-contact model of Melanesian society and culture, I have documented the initial period of missionary contact and followed the Melanesian Mission's strategy for converting islanders from animism to Christianity. The success and failure of this strategy has been analyzed. It has been noted that when missionaries initially contacted Melanesians they had to "earn a hearing," for they were clearly guests in their hosts' society. It is interesting to note, however, that as islanders through time began to adopt Christianity, they also, concomitantly, became increasingly dominated by the missionaries — the greater the penetration of Christianity into Melanesian society, the greater the paternalistic domination of converts by those agents of change who had advocated adoption of the new religion. The previous chapter discussed the Melanesians' reaction to this paternalistic domination as islanders began clamoring for greater independence and responsibility in their own affairs. In their cries for independence they were successful, as both mission and Government relented, ushering in a new era of autonomy into Melanesian culture history.

Throughout this study there has been evidence of what F. E. Williams (1935) called, "The Blending of Cultures."[1] The interaction of Melanesians with European agents of change has produced a blending of cultures in a new form that is neither wholly Melanesian nor wholly European, but a blending of elements from each. Williams (1935: 7) identifies three stages or tasks in the process of culture change leading to a new blending of cultures: (1) maintenance, (2) expurgation, and (3) expansion. The Melanesian Mission overtly encouraged Melanesians to **maintain** a great deal of their traditional culture—dancing, singing, arts and crafts, language, social organization, etc.[2] Nevertheless, the ideology of Christianity was incompatible with some elements of traditional Melanesian culture, and thus conversion implied the **expurgation** of activities such as headhunting, cannibalism, warfare, infanticide, widow strangling, sorcery, and other cultural values that idealized violence and aggression. Moreover, the Melanesian Mission advocated not only functional substitutes to fill the void left by the abandonment of these and other cultural elements, but it **expanded** the islanders' society through education, medicine, and an ideology that advocated peace and unity among believers, inculcating a sense of community that extended far beyond the traditional bounds of kinship. New sets of social status and roles were introduced for islanders to occupy as well. Thus the Melanesian Mission advocated the maintenance, expurgation and expansion of cultural elements. The result of this advocation by the Mission and adoption by Melanesians is diagrammed below:[3]

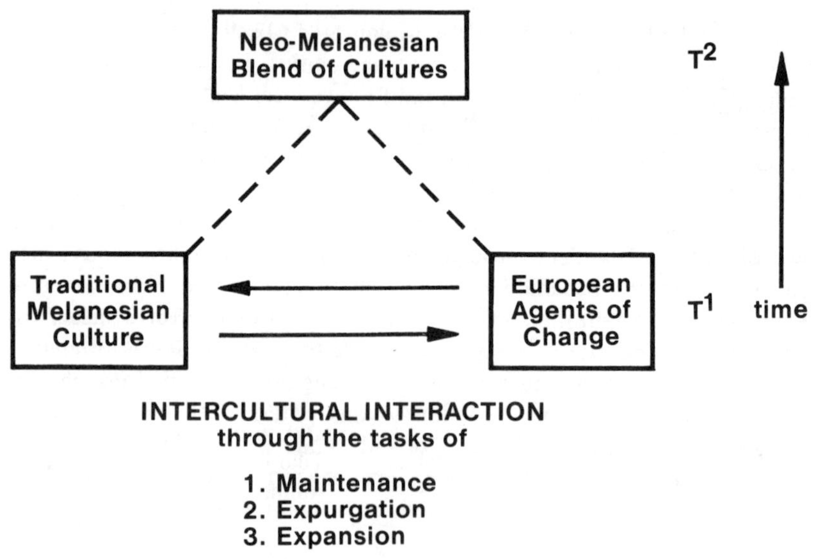

Fig. 10. The Blending of Melanesian and European Cultures.

Today, contemporary Anglican Christianity in Melanesia is a product of both change and continuity; it is the net result of 125 years of culture change in which Melanesian-European interaction has produced a blending of cultures. It is this cultural blend that was the focus of my fieldwork in the Solomon Islands from April 1977 to April 1978 and for several months in 1981. My primary objective was to discover the form and function of Christianity in the islands — to investigate the outcome of the Melanesian Mission's evolution into the Church of Melanesia.

This chapter analyzes Anglican Christianity in the islands today, and pursues the question of whether or not the **autonomous** Church of Melanesia is an **indigenous** Melanesian church. The chapter will deal first with the organizational structure of the Church of Melanesia (COM), and a discussion of Christianity at the village level will then follow. Particular attention will be paid to the tension which exists between these two levels, and the efforts being made by church leaders to reduce that tension. As background to understanding Christianity in the village today, I will then discuss conversion as an innovative process in which people change religious allegiance and orientation from animism to Christianity. The focus of this discussion will be on the people of Santa Isabel. The chapter will conclude with an analysis of the degree to which the COM and Christianity in general has become integrated into contemporary Melanesian society.

Organizational Structure of the Church of Melanesia

Geographically the Province of Melanesia is divided into five dioceses: (1) Ysabel, (2) Malaita, (3) Central Melanesia, (4) Temotu, and (5) Vanuatu (New Hebrides). The following table and map (see pp. 326-327) give the distribution of islands within each diocese.

DIOCESES

Ysabel	Malaita	Central Melanesia	Temotu	Vanuatu
Santa Isabel	N. Malaita	Guadalcanal	Santa Cruz	Torres Islands
Russells	S. Malaita	Nggela	Reef Islands	Banks' Islands
Gizo Town	Ontong Java	Savo	Vanikolo	Maewo
	Sikaiana	San Cristobal	Utupua	Aoba
		Santa Ana	Duff Islands	Raga
		Santa Catalina	Tikopia	Espiritu Santo
		Ulawa	Anuda	Vila Town
		Ugi		Noumea Towa

Table 6.1. Islands and Dioceses in the Church of Melanesia.

The ecclesiastical head of each diocese is a bishop. The first two Melanesian assistant bishops, Dudley Tuti and Leonard Alufurai, became Bishop of Ysabel and Bishop of Malaita respectively. Both men retired in 1981 and were replaced by young Melanesian clergymen with parish experience and theological training in New Zealand — Ellison Pogolamana of Santa Isabel and Willie Pwaisiho of Malaita. The Diocese of Temotu was created in 1980, with Amos Waiaru serving as its first bishop. Harry Tevi of Raga, was consecrated Assistant Bishop of the New Hebrides in February 1979, and now serves as the Bishop of the Diocese of Vanuatu.[4]

Archbishop Norman Palmer is also Bishop of the Diocese of Central Melanesia. As Archbishop of the Province of Melanesia, Norman Palmer represents the Church of Melanesia to the worldwide Anglican Communion, but he has no jurisdiction in the other dioceses of the province.[5] In this sense diocesan bishops are independent of the archbishop, but of course all must

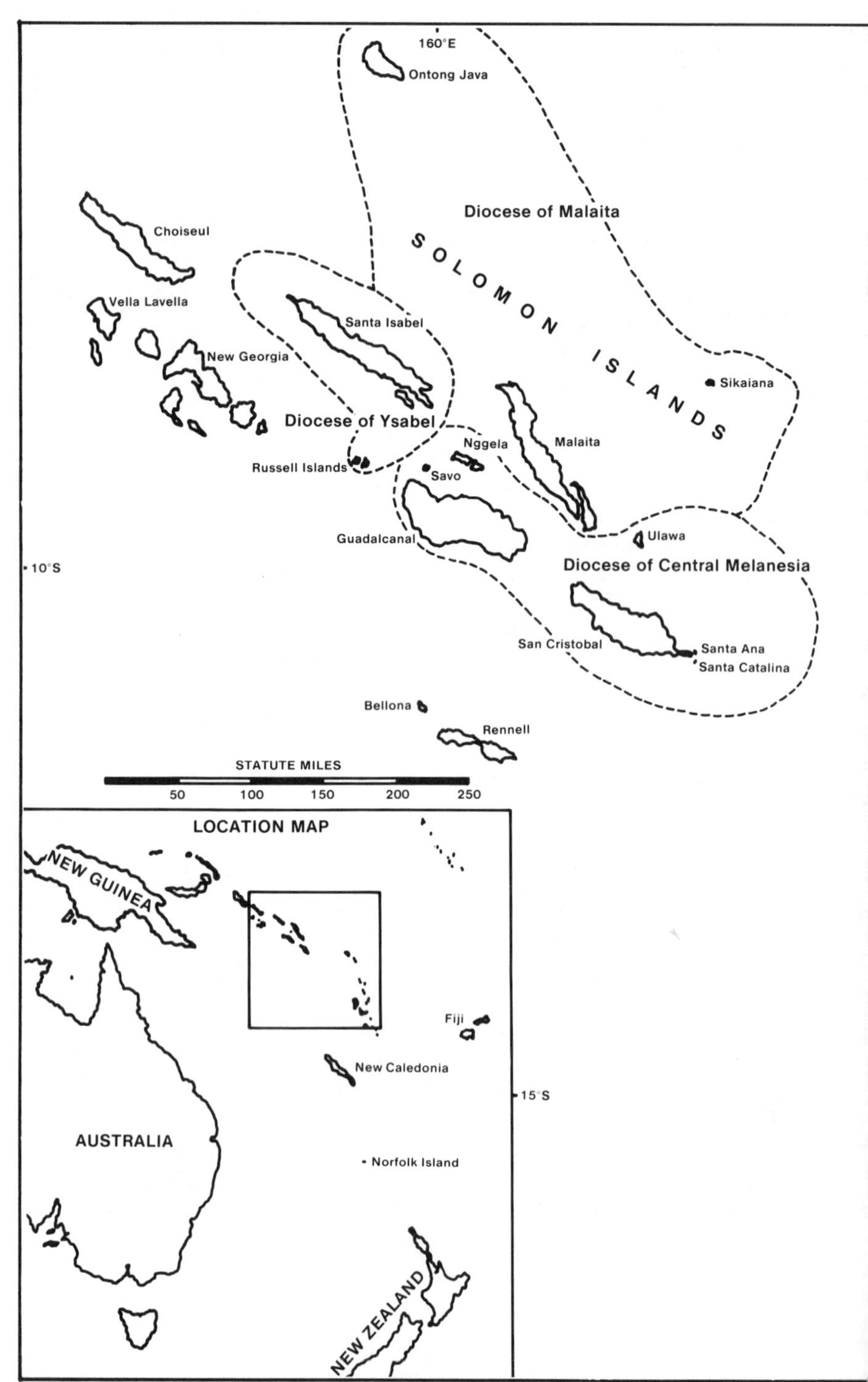
160°E
Ontong Java
Diocese of Malaita
SOLOMON ISLANDS
Choiseul
Vella Lavella
Santa Isabel
New Georgia
Sikaiana
Diocese of Ysabel
Nggela
Malaita
Russell Islands
Savo
Guadalcanal
Ulawa
10°S
Diocese of Central Melanesia
San Cristobal
Santa Ana
Santa Catalina
Bellona
Rennell
STATUTE MILES
50
100
150
200
250
LOCATION MAP
NEW GUINEA
Fiji
New Caledonia
15°S
AUSTRALIA
Norfolk Island
NEW ZEALAND

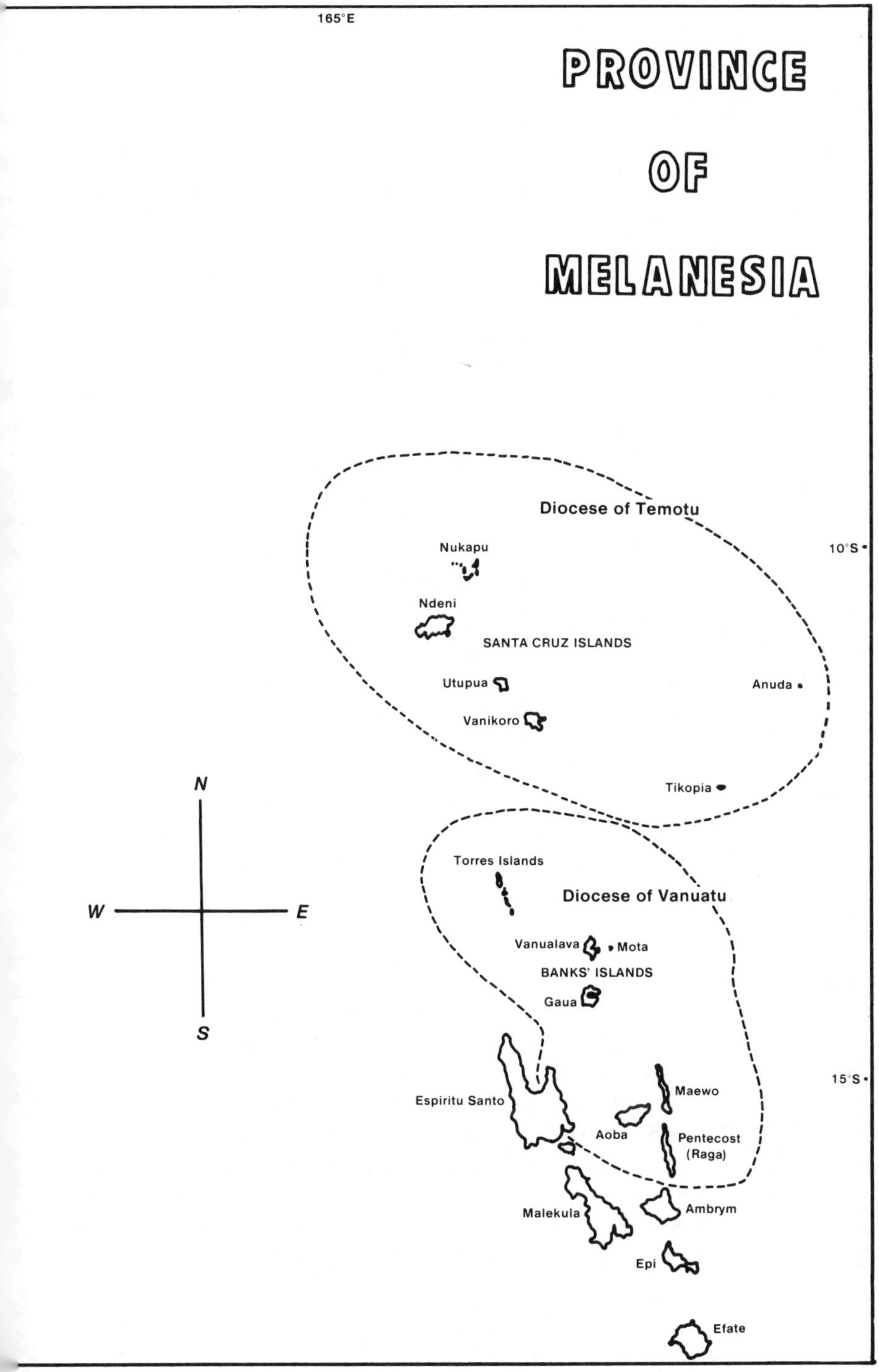

165°E

PROVINCE OF MELANESIA

Diocese of Temotu

Nukapu

Ndeni

SANTA CRUZ ISLANDS

Utupua

Vanikoro

Anuda

Tikopia

10°S

Torres Islands

Diocese of Vanuatu

Vanualava

Mota

BANKS' ISLANDS

Gaua

15°S

Espiritu Santo

Maewo

Aoba

Pentecost (Raga)

Malekula

Ambrym

Epi

Efate

N

W

E

S

abide by the *Canons of the Province of Melanesia* — the offical charter for this socio-religious organization.

Provincial Structure.

Articulation of the individual dioceses occurs at the provincial level in the form of the Provincial Council, the Council of Bishops and the Provincial Synod, with the archbishop functioning as chairman of all three bodies. The Provincial Synod is the legal and ecclesiastical body for making church laws for the province, and it has final authority in matters of spiritual discipline.[6] The Provincial Synod is called by the archbishop at his discretion, but seldom more than every three to four years.[7] The Provincial Council which meets annually, acts as a standing committee of the Provincial Synod, serving from the close of one synod to the opening of the next.[8] In this way the independent island dioceses come together as a Melanesian entity, and islanders see their church as something larger than the village chapel or even islandwide diocese. It is through the Provincial Synod and Council that the COM functions as an ecclesiastical entity. But there is also an administrative arm of the church, known collectively as the provincial headquarters. Overseeing the administration of all the COM's activities is a provincial secretary, appointed by the archbishop.[9] During the time of our fieldwork the provincial secretary was an Englishman whose wide experience as a corporation executive and amateur yachtsman made him ideally suited for his unique work. Although he ran the administration of the church in a very efficient and cost-conscious manner, befitting English standards, he was nevertheless sensitive to the problems of indigenization in the church, and was training a Santa Isabel man who gradually took over the full responsibilities of the provincial secretary in 1982.

The provincial headquarters resembles a business corporation with several departments and organizations under its large umbrella-like structure. The financial operation of the provincial headquarters will be discussed below.

Diocesan Structure.

In comparison to the provincial structure, individual dioceses are relatively small organizations. The bishop as the head convenes the Diocesan Synod which meets every three years. The Diocesan Council acts as a standing committee serving from the close of a session of the Diocesan Synod to the opening of the next. Santa Isabel, which is similar to other dioceses, is divided into various districts, with a District Committee organized to ensure that decisions approved by the Diocesan Synod or Council are put into action and carried out at the district level. The District Committee also functions to aid the villages in the general development and activity of the church in that district.[10] The members of this committee consist of the district priest, a catechist and two laymen chosen from each Village Committee. The Committee meets at least every six months.[11]

Beneath the District Committee, in the hierarchical organizational structure of the diocese, is a Village Committee, whose members consist of the village headman and a village catechist, and not more than ten others elected by the village. If there is a member of the local government council residing in the village, he is invited to be a member of the Village Committee, which is supposed to meet at least monthly, called by the elected chairman.[12] Thus the structure of the Diocese of Ysabel allows for representation and participation of islanders from the village level upward in the affairs of their own church. The diocesan structure is diagrammed as follows:

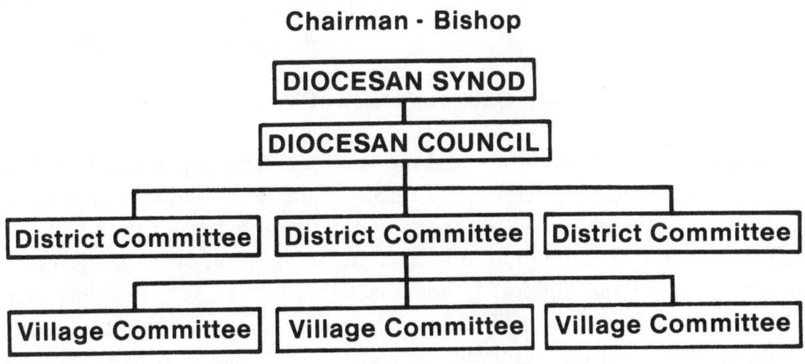

Fig. 11. Diocesan Structure in the Church of Melanesia.

If one were to draw an organizational chart of the Church of Melanesia today (see Fig. 12, p. 331), on paper the distance between the village churches and the provincial headquarters would be very short. In reality, they are worlds apart. The COM organization to most villagers is vague and confusing, bearing little concrete relation to their village life and personal concerns. In this way, the COM provincial headquarters is perceived by most islanders in the same way as the former Melanesian Mission headquarters was. That is, it is an entity "out there" that functions in mysterious European ways. Likewise, those who live in Honiara and work in the provincial headquarters can easily lose touch with the realities of village life. This tension between village church and provincial headquarters is more than a contrast between rural and urban ways — it is a contrast between Melanesian and European worldviews.

To keep this large provincial organization financially afloat, a large amount of income is required. Most of this is generated by the COM Trust

Board.[13] The following table is based on estimates of income for 1977-1978, in Australian dollars.[14]

DONORS	INCOME	PERCENT
Melanesian Trust Board, New Zealand	A$410,000	70.0%
New Zealand Anglican Board of Missions	68,800	11.7
Leper Trust Board	37,500	6.3
Anglican Board of Missions - Australia	34,000	5.8
Miscellaneous	19,000	3.2
Melanesian Trust Board, London	17,000	2.0
Associates of Melanesia	1,000	0.1
TOTAL:	$587,300	100%

Table 6.2. Estimated Income, Church of Melanesia – 1977-1978.

A very small percent of the total income required to operate the province is generated from within Melanesia through islanders' own contributions to the church. This problem will be discussed in detail below when the question of Christian stewardship and the indigenous integration of the church at the financial level of self support is addressed. Suffice to say, that one of the most important factors contributing to the islanders' perception that today's provincial headquarters resembles yesterday's Melanesian Mission is the large intake of overseas capital to sponsor activities within the province. As in the days of the European missionaries before, money continues to flow into Melanesia from across the sea.

Christianity in the Village: Belief and Practice

This study has documented that in the 125 years of Melanesian Mission contact in the islands, the Mission's policies and personnel regarding the evangelization of Melanesia moved further and further away from the village context toward an institutional setting — hospitals, schools, technical training centers, and so on. More often than not, when islanders left these mission institutions and returned to village life, they left behind many of the practices they had been taught there. Many islanders reasoned that perhaps these things taught by the Europeans, such as new farming techniques, or "better" methods of pig raising, or domestic hygiene, etc. were appropriate for Europeans, and indeed, were rational choices to follow in the European-dominated institutions, but they were not Melanesian ways; they were not

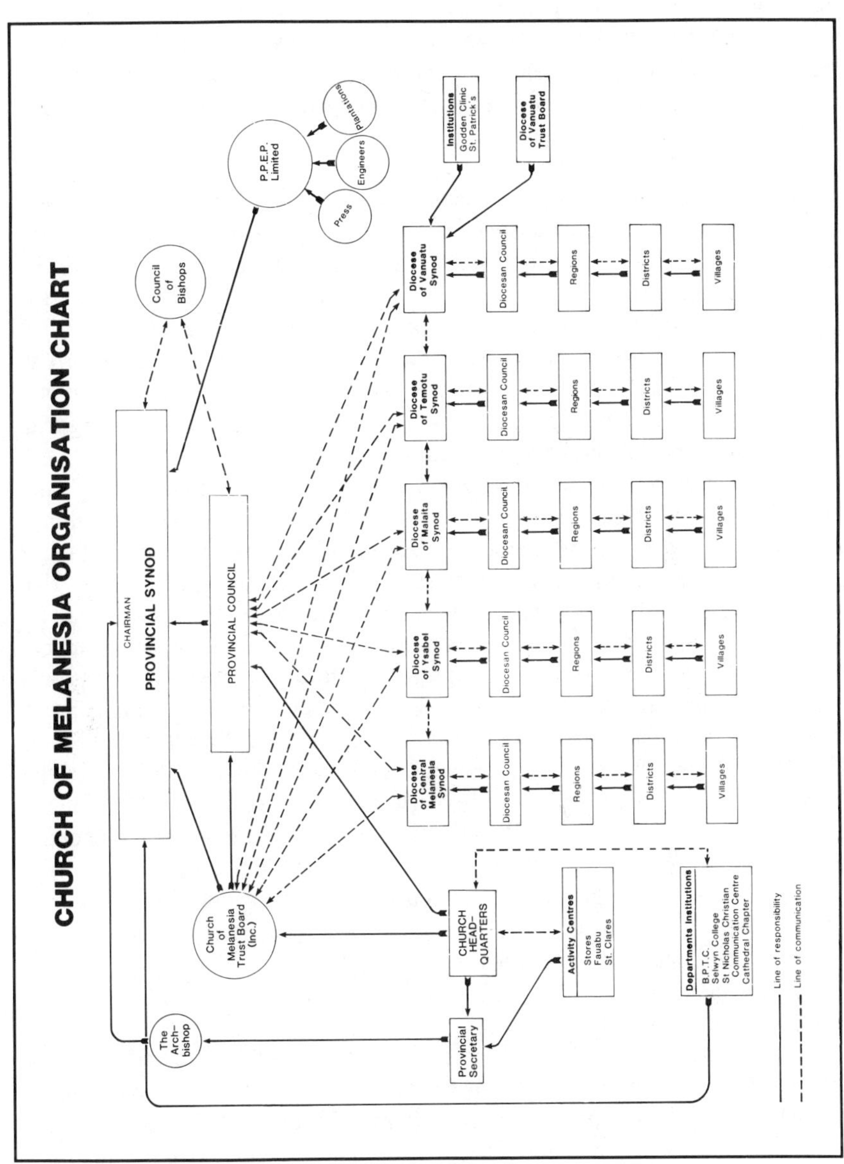

Fig. 12. Church of Melanesia Organization Chart.

the ways taught to the islanders by their fathers. And so, just as easily as young island boys had shed their clothing when they returned to their village from "school" in New Zealand over one hundred years earlier, so did islanders in this generation leave behind much that was taught to them when they returned to their village life.[15]

Of course all was not lost, forgotten or left behind at the mission stations. New ideas and innovations did trickle into village life and initiate changes, but, by and large, the changes were far less than what the missionaries had hoped for. In approaching the question of Christian belief and practice it should not be surprising to discover a similar pattern. Often what the missionaries taught in the mission institutions failed to be effectively transmitted to the village level; this is exactly what one finds with regard to Christian belief and practice.[16] What was understood by villagers was not identical with what was taught to Melanesians training for the Anglican priesthood at the Mission's theological college.

The primary reason for the failure of complete transmission of beliefs and practices was because the missionary was often unfamiliar with the village context in which those ideas and behavior patterns were received. In fact, it is quite possible, if not probable, that a missionary could spend twenty-five years in Melanesia[17] and never really know Melanesians. What do I mean by this? I mean that it was possible for a missionary to never know the islanders in their village context, because he interacted with them only in the Mission's institutional setting. And of course, the Melanesians would frequently feel like strangers in these Mission institutionalized settings. This is why Charles Fox[18] and a few others were so unusual; they realized the artificiality of the Mission's institutional setting, and so attempted to live closer to the village context. It is only in the context of routine living in the village that one could come to know, understand and appreciate the islanders' worldview.[19]

This leads us to the following section, for it was only by living in a Melanesian village myself, that I came to understand something of the islanders' perception and practice of Christianity.

Fieldwork on Santa Isabel.

During the course of our fieldwork, my wife and I were resident in a village of 150 people in the Maringe district of Santa Isabel. I had selected this island chiefly because the mission literature had pointed to Santa Isabel with pride. Here conversion to Christianity had occurred rapidly and extensively, and Santa Isabel was called a "Missionary Island" sending forth evangelists to other parts of Melanesia.[20] Except for a few Seventh Day Adventist villages with a total population of approximately 100, the entire island and population of over 10,000[21] claims allegiance to the Church of Melanesia.

"The entire island is Christian," we were told, and if we wanted to encounter any heathen (their term) we would have to go to Malaita or possibly the mountains of Guadalcanal, but we wouldn't find any heathen on Santa Isabel. Villagers were highly offended, indignant and yet amused one day when two Jehovah's Witnesses missionaries from Malaita visited our village in an attempt to convert Isabel Christians. "Why don't they go back to their own island of Malaita where there are some heathen, instead of wasting their time here?" a villager strongly protested.

It was because Santa Isabel was ostensibly an all-Anglican island that I chose to live there during my fieldwork. Nevertheless, I made numerous trips to other areas of the Solomons, traveling southeast as far as Tikopia for comparative purposes. I reasoned that if Santa Isabel was the "best" of the Melansian Mission's products, it would yield a standard for comparison with other areas which were acknowledged as "weaker."

I will now turn to a discussion of Christian beliefs and practices as inferred and observed in Anglican villages in the Solomon Islands. I will begin by first giving a sketch of Anglican theology, then a discussion on the function of village priests and catechists, and conclude by developing a model of contemporary belief and practice as found in the village today.

Anglican Theology.[22]

The Melanesian Mission was always in the "High Church" tradition of the Church of England.[23] Whenever a new bishop was appointed, among the usual preferred qualifications were that he be a young, single man with the right churchmanship. Right churchmanship meant at least a moderate High Churchman, not an Evangelical, and increasingly it came to mean one who was in the Anglo-Catholic tradition.[24] Under Bishop Cecil Wilson (1894-1911) many missionary recruits within this theological tradition entered the Melanesian mission field. The first bishop to be identified as an Anglo-Catholic however, was Bishop Cecil Wood (1912-1918) who was also the first to wear a cope and mitre.[25]

By the mid 1920's the Anglo-Catholic tradition had become established in the Mission, influencing the form of worship in the decades ahead. The cultural significance of an Anglo-Catholic tradition within the Melanesian Mission meant that there was far more emphasis on elaborate and colorful ritual. The rite of Holy Communion became increasingly emphasized as the single, most important act of worship for the Christian.[26] Colored vestments worn by the priest during Holy Communion, the use of incense in the service, and the terms "Mass" and "Eucharist" were introduced, replacing the Mota word *ganarongo* (holy feast), initiated by Patteson. In addition, a sung Eucharist was introduced, priests were called "Father" and the authority of the bishop, the "Father in God," was validated by reference to biblical and church tradition:

> The Bishops take the place of the Apostles. They have the powers Jesus gave to the Apostles. They are the Rulers of the Catholic Church. Father Bishop is the Ruler of the Church of Melanesia.[27]

As ritual became more important, and the liturgy of the Prayer Book was emphasized, scripture and sermons became less important. Priests in training were taught how to conduct a worship service **properly**. Homiletics and pastoral counseling were not emphasized, and Melanesian priests soon became what one contemporary has called "Mass machines" — dispensers of holy food in the celebration of the Eucharist.[28]

There is little doubt that the elaborate ritual of an Anglican worship service was attractive to many Melanesians for their traditional religion had been highly ritualistic. But Anglican ritual is not sufficient in itself to account for Melanesians' adopting Christianity, as evidenced by islanders' converting to Christianity within the South Sea Evangelical Mission. Many Solomon Islanders were attracted to this brand of Christianity with its loose congregational structure and with emphasis on the Bible and extemporaneous prayer, rather than on the Prayer Book and a formal liturgy. Nevertheless, the Anglican formal worship pattern and hierarchical ecclesiastical structure has given tremendous stability to the church in an area where religious schisms are not uncommon. There have been at least two such schisms in the history of the Melanesian Mission, but they were both small movements and neither one made a significant impact on the church.[29]

In contrast, members of the South Sea Evangelical Church (SSEC) are prime candidates for splintering from their church and forming either new sects or joining other sects and denominations. An interesting example of this phenomenon is the Remnant Church on North Malaita, formed about 1962 by a man called Kweiga. He was a former Marching Rule leader, and former SSEM and SDA member before breaking away to form his own church, which is a syncretistic movement combining SSEM and SDA teaching with traditional beliefs and practices.[30] Likewise, proselytizers of the Jehovah's Witnesses and Bahai faiths find most of their converts among members of the SSEC and SDA rather than the Church of Melanesia.

There are several factors responsible for the more solid COM organization *vis a vis* the more loosely structured SSEC. Discussion of these differences will also throw light on the structure of the Church of Melanesia today.[31] I will discuss briefly the role of the (1) clergy, (2) Prayer Book, and (3) corporate emphasis, as they relate to the stability of the Church of Melanesia in comparison with the South Sea Evangelical Church.

1. **Clergy.** The Church of Melanesia has a professional clergy and an organization in which everyone knows where they fit in the hierarchical structure: village catechists are responsible to district priests who in turn are responsible to the bishop of the diocese. The South Sea Evangelical Church

has essentially no professional clergy, for very few people have been ordained. Generally only middle-aged men who have lived a life of distinguished service have been ordained. With their congregational form of church government, the appointment of village pastors is informal and in no way binding as is the ordination of Anglican deacons and priests. Moreover, the COM Constitution and Canons give clearly defined guidelines for orthodox Anglican beliefs and practice, and thus lend stability to the church as an organization with a clearly defined charter.

2. Book of Common Prayer. In the COM worship centers around the Prayer Book. This *Book of Common Prayer* works as a unifying factor, for as the central item in worship, it prescribes a **common** service for all members of the church. In contrast, the focal point of an SSEC service is the sermon preached by the local pastor, and thus the congregation, as an entity, is more dependent on the quality of the preaching. Moreover, the unity of the group tends to focus around the personality of the pastor and so with frequent changes of pastoral assignments, the local congregations can become unstable in their practices and beliefs. Thus, the Anglican Prayer Book as central to the worship service is more stabilizing than the SSEC service which depends on the preaching and personality of a local pastor.

3. Corporate vs. Individual Emphasis. The religious emphasis in the COM has been on corporate groups such as the family and village community. For example, when an infant is baptized it is the decision of the child's family, and becomes a community-wide affair. Frequently, as in the case of Santa Isabel to be discussd below, islanders converted to Christianity in corporate groups, following traditional lines of kinship or other frameworks of social structure. In the COM, as in traditional Melanesian society, religion is a community activity and not just an individual experience.[32]

In contrast, the emphasis in the SSEC is on individual conversion, with converts making a cognitive decision, choosing Christ as their "personal savior." Individual Christians are encouraged to "work out their own salvation" through Bible reading and personal prayer. One can see that this emphasis on the individual's relationship could lead to atomization of the church with people desiring to go their own individual ways. The structure and ideology of the SSEC would tend to encourage this, while that of the COM would discourage it.

This contrast was vividly brought to light on Santa Isabel during our fieldwork. An Ellis Islander, trained through Campus Crusade for Christ in the Philippines, was introducing techniques of personal evangelism to a group of Anglicans taking a three-month course at the Diocesan Training Center. As part of the course, he was teaching the students how to give a personal testimony comprised of three parts: (1) my life before I was "saved" (i.e. before I became a Christian), (2) how I was saved, and (3) my new life afterward. These concepts were incomprehensible to the Anglican students, for they had always been "saved," since they were baptized as infants and became full members of the Church when they were confirmed as adolescents. Students were confused and perplexed, for the Campus Crusade type of testimony had little bearing on their religious experience within the Anglican Church of Melanesia. This approach, however, would have been immediately understood by members of the SSEC.

In summary, it is clear that the structure and ideology of these two churches tend to lead to stability among Anglican congregations, but to splintering among SSEC members. Since there are more ecclesiastical and theological options available to the Evangelicals, when a new doctrinal alternative is advocated by some prophet or proselytizer, there is already a predisposition to embrace the new idea or practice in order to "try it out." In contrast, COM members would tolerate little alteration in the staid liturgical format. For example, under Bishop John Chisholm (1967-1975) liturgical "reforms" were introduced to simplify the worship service, reducing the ritualistic content. I interviewed numerous informants who claimed that the weakness of the church today was due to the changes introduced in the liturgy during Bishop John's tenure.

To summarize this section, and without going into greater detail at this point, I would suggest that the following are the key points of Anglican theology in the COM that have particular cultural significance for this study:

1. The primacy of Holy Communion as a religious rite for Christians, but available only to those who are confirmed members of the church. Today most people are confirmed in early adolescence.
2. Baptism as the second most important sacrament, and means of formal induction into the Christian faith. Today this occurs in infancy when the parents and godparents of the child present him/her to the priest, naming the child as they do so.
3. The central role of the Prayer Book, providing creeds, prayers and scripture for the believer to follow and use in worship.
4. The importance of daily liturgical prayers and elaborate and colorful ritual in the rite of Holy Communion.

The Function of Anglican Priests in Contemporary Melanesian Society.

In the Church of Melanesia, as of January 1978, there were 225 clergy, including active and retired, deacons and priests. As the following table illustrates, most of these men have been ordained since 1970.[33]

Year of Ordination	Number	Percent
1929	1	0.4
1930's	14	6.2
1940's	23	10.2
1950's	26	11.6
1960's	43	19.1
1970-1977	118	52.5
TOTAL	225	100%

Table 6.3. Church of Melanesia Clergy – 1977.

Today deacons are ordained shortly after they have completed a four-year course of theological education at the Bishop Patteson Theological Centre, Kohimarama on the island of Guadalcanal. Their ordination to the priesthood normally follows within a year or two. This is a striking difference from the pattern of ordination in the nineteenth and early twentieth century when deacons were seldom advanced to the priesthood until they had stood the test of long years of faithful service to the Melanesian Mission. Some were deacons for as long as twenty years before being ordained priests. Another significant difference between the priests of today and those of yesterday is their ages at ordination. Most men today are in their mid to late twenties at the time of ordination, whereas before, a man was often in his thirties or forties when he was ordained. This difference in age is related to the whole question of vocation.

In the days of the Melanesian Mission, a man was generally "called" to train for the priesthood by a missionary priest or bishop. Those who had demonstrated outstanding character and talents in teaching, as members of the Melanesian Brotherhood, as bosuns of one of the Mission's vessels, or in some other capacity of work were approached by the Mission authorities and urged, or sometimes told, to enter training for the priesthood. The strength of that system was that those who were finally ordained were frequently mature men with wide experience. The weakness of the present system is that young men are now advanced to positions of authority and responsibility but lack the experience and maturity of men who are ordained at a later age. Traditionally in Melanesia, young men seldom became Big Men. This was a position of honor which was achieved through years of successful activity by mature men who had proven themselves to the group. Obviously a young graduate from today's theological college is in no similar position, and yet he is given authority as if he were.

Today those who want to enter the priesthood normally initiate the process themselves and frequently they do so shortly after they have gone as far as they can in the regular educational system. The present-day educational system in the Solomon Islands is geared toward producing a select few who will go overseas for a university degree. Consequently, many of those who apply to enter theological training are those who have not been successful in getting an opportunity to pursue a university education.

There is no shortage of applicants for theological training today. In 1976, one hundred and twenty applied to study at Kohimarama, but only sixteen were allowed to enter.[34] It will perhaps be useful to briefly discuss why young Anglican Melanesians are motivated to enter the priesthood today. In numerous interviews with deacons, priests, and theological students, I inquired as to why they had chosen this profession. Invariably the reply was, "I want to serve my people."[35] This may in fact be a contributing factor, and it is certainly a commendable one, but I suspect in most cases that it was neither the only motivation nor the dominant one in desiring to become a priest in the Church of Melanesia.

The traditional avenues of Big Men leadership have been changed radically through the influence of Christianity and pacification.[36] Today a very important avenue through which one can rise as a Melanesian Big Man is that of the priesthood in the Church of Melanesia. Being an Anglican priest is not a guarantee of becoming a Big Man, but it certainly gives one an edge over one's secular competitors. There are several reasons for this. A priest is believed to have greater access to *mana* than does the layman, he has greater knowledge of the wider world through his Europeanized educational training, and he is far wealthier than the majority of his parishioners whom he "serves." In essence, an Anglican priest can acquire all the attributes of a traditional Big Man — *mana*, and hence prestige, knowledge, and wealth. The qualities are the same and provide continuity with the past, but the institutionalized means of achieving them have been changed through the influence of Christianity and pacification. I will now turn to a brief discussion of these three avenues through which a Melanesian Anglican priest can become a Big Man today.

1. The Priest as Man of *Mana*.

The priest, as the specialist in religious knowledge, is the archetype of the man of *mana* in contemporary Anglican villages. He is the one qualified to give Holy Communion — the most important ritual act for acquiring *mana*. For example, Hagesi notes that:

> People go to Church only to ask for what they want or need, but when they don't feel confident to do it themselves, they ask the priests and teachers to do it for them. Thus priests and teachers

> are treated like magic practitioners and sorcerers in former days. It is clear that the beliefs and attitudes of the people towards prayer and worship are a mixture of pre-Christian and Christian beliefs (1972:63-64).

Traditionally men of *mana* were highly respected but also feared, and today this has not changed, although the source of *mana* has changed. A vivid example of this occurred shortly after we arrived in the Solomon Islands in April 1977. An earthquake, measuring 7.4 on the Richter scale, caused severe damage to the weathercoast of Guadalcanal, as landslides destroyed gardens and villages, burying people alive. Three days before the earthquake struck, Archbishop Norman Palmer visited a village in this area where the people wanted to build a big, new, permanent-style (i.e., out of Western materials) church building. However, the same village had failed to contribute its yearly assessment to the general fund to aid in the running of the church. The archbishop became very cross with the people for refusing to pay their general assessment while accumulating money to build their new village chapel, and so he refused to grant them permission to construct the church. Three days later the earthquake destroyed the village, burying five villagers alive. After this tragedy villagers firmly believed that the earthquake had been sent by the archbishop because he had gotten cross with them during his visit. The archbishop, perceived as a man with superior *mana*, would be capable, in the minds of these villagers, of causing such great destruction.[37]

All priests are perceived to have more *mana* than the average layman. Nevertheless, villagers do not view all priests as men of equal *mana*. There is a definite ranking order of those who have more than others, and it is not surprising to discover villagers discussing the powerful priests in the past, *vis a vis* the recent graduates from the theological training center. Thus, for example, on Santa Isabel islanders still talk about the strong leaders and men of *mana* that the first two priests, Hugo Hebala and Ben Hageria, were perceived to be. Indeed, Hugo Hebala, ordained in 1920 as the first Santa Isabel priest, was the acknowledged leader of all the Melanesian clergy in the Mission during the 1920's and up until his death from cancer in 1931. He was believed to be a man with great *mana*, and today numerous legends are told of minor miracles he performed. Villagers confess there are no priests today who have the *mana* of Fr. Ben Hageria, and especially Fr. Hugo Hebala.[38]

A more recent example of a powerful priest renowned for his *mana* is Eric Gnhokro, a Santa Isabel man who died in January 1975. He was a man of extraordinary powers, but one who always attributed the power behind his unusual feats to the faith of those who believed that God could produce miracles, rather than to any inherent magical power of his own. Described as a very humble man, who carried a traditional walking stick with inlaid carving, Gnhokro is credited with the following miracles:

1. Gardens on the small island of Tasia in the Maringe Lagoon were being destroyed by swamp hens until he came over with his stick and commanded them to leave, which they did, permanently.
2. Frequently while traveling on ships in unusually rough seas, he would hold out his stick and command the sea to be calm, and it was.
3. He would drive rats from villages simply on command.
4. A killer shark was menacing people in the Maringe Lagoon until Gnhokro announced one day at Evensong that the next day the shark would be found dead on the beach. It was.
5. In a dry place where pigs would normally have liked to wallow in the mud, Gnhokro went and blessed the ground, and shortly afterward, water came bubbling up.
6. Gnhokro is credited with "moving a mountain" at Kia, on the northwestern end of Santa Isabel. I was told that there had been a large hill between the village and a river which required negotiating every time. Today one can see the place that is now flat where there was once a hill, until Eric Gnhokro commanded it to move.

There are other miraculous feats attributed to this priest, such as turning water into gasoline, redirecting the paths of rivers, healing, etc.[39] Perhaps Eric Gnhokro is an unusual and outstanding example, but the point is made that priests are perceived as men of *mana*, while acknowledging that some priests are perceived to have much more *mana* than others.[40]

2. The Priest as a Man of Knowledge.

As I discussed in Chapter 2 (pp. 64–67) what is analytically defined as "religious" knowledge was traditionally the most important to Melanesians. Nevertheless, there has been an inevitable secularization of Melanesian culture resulting from contact with Western missionaries and other agents of change. Thus today, broader and more Westernized knowledge is increasingly valued. A good education (i.e. formal, Western) is increasingly recognized as a legitimate way to "get ahead," providing an avenue for socio-political "advancement" as Melanesian society becomes increasingly acculturated to Western standards and values.

There has always been an emphasis on "upgrading" the standards in training men for the priesthood in the Melanesina Mission. This is reflected in the training of priests today. Graduates of Bishop Patteson Theological Centre at Kohimarama have courses in human behavior, social structure, social change, administration and accounting, ethics, homiletics, Greek, Hebrew, church history, pastoral counseling, theology of development, theology of science, and numerous courses in biblical theology.[41] Such an education tends to expand a priest's worldview and perspective, and increasingly, young graduates are being sent overseas for additional training beyond their four-year theological course at Kohimarama.

Some priests have used their educational knowledge and experience as a springboard for participation in national politics. Thus, for example, two Malaita priests, Leslie Fugui and John Gerea have served as elected members of the Solomon Islands Legislative Assembly. In Vanuatu, Walter Lini, a COM priest who studied at St. John's College in Auckland, entered the political arena and became president of the Vanuaku Party which boycotted the general elections in November 1977, and established an independent "Peoples Provisional Government." Although this provisional government disbanded in April 1978, Walter Lini, as Deputy Chief Minister in the New Hebrides, played an important role in leading his country toward independence in 1980.[42] Today he is Prime Minister of the young nation of Vanuatu.

Thus, for some students who fail to achieve the highest standards in the government's educational system, the alternative is theological education in the COM. As Melanesians become more acculturated, advanced education is becoming highly valued. Thus a priest, as a man of *mana*, is respected and feared for his power, but he is also admired and envied for his educational experience.

3. The Priest as a Man of Wealth.

At the time of our initial fieldwork (1977-1978), all COM clergy received their salary from provincial headquarters in Honiara. They did not rely on funds generated from village contributions for their welfare, and so they were financially removed from and independent of the parishioners for whom they were ecclesiastically responsible. The provincial headquarters of the COM, aware of the inherent weaknesses of such a salary system, has attempted today to put more responsibility on each diocese for the priests' salaries. Now, instead of a priest's paycheck coming directly from the COM headquarters in Honaira as it did in 1978, today a block grant is given to each diocese based on its Anglican population. From this money the diocese pays its priests and runs its programs and activities. The priests are still not directly reliant on the villages they serve for their financial support, but by shifting the responsibility from the provincial headquarters to the diocese, an effort is being made to have the priests rely more on the people they serve for their financial support.[43] Today COM clergy are wealthy by village standards.[44] The following table gives the salary schedule for COM clergy:[45]

CATEGORY	SALARY PER YEAR
Married priest	$660
Single priest	$440
Married deacon	$616
Single deacon	$396
Senior priest	$935
Urban supplement: e.g., Honiara	$250
Semi-urban supplement: e.g., Kira Kira, Graciosa Bay, Lolowai	$125
Retired clergy pension	$ 78

Table 6.4. Salary Schedule for COM Clergy Per Year – 1977.

There are no available statistics on the average income per household in the village. Most islanders are tied predominantly to a subsistence rather than a cash economy, and generally have only sufficient funds to purchase necessities such as tobacco, clothes, kerosene and occasionally packaged foods in the local trade stores. Earning the annual Isabel Council tax of $11 represents an economic hardship for many.

In the village where we resided on Santa Isabel, many villagers worked at a nearby plantation owned jointly by five villages (see Whiteman 1982). They worked on alternate months for a salary of $11 per month, or $66 per year. There are opportunities open to most villagers to turn island produce such as copra (dried coconuts) into cash income. But, even given this opportunity, most villagers would still make far less than the COM priests. Moreover, in addition to their generous salaries, many priests receive income from economic projects such as plantations, cattle raising, ownership in trade stores, etc.

Church of Melanesia priests, as men of *mana*, knowledge and wealth, are indeed Big Men today. Nowhere is this more evident than on the island of Santa Isabel. When a priest enters a village, people run to beat the slit gong and bang on empty gas cylinders to announce his arrival. This ritual occurs again when he departs from the village. At local feasts and patronal festivals (to be discussed below) priests are always given positions of honor and are served an abundance of the best food. Not infrequently they are given small gifts and they usually make speeches to the large gathering of people at the festivals — all appropriate behavior for a Melanesian Big Man.[46]

Each district priest normally has charge of eight to ten villages. His main duties include baptizing, marrying, and burying, and most importantly, administering Holy Communion at least once a month to each village in his charge. This is the ideal, but in actual practice, his touring schedule may take him to a village far less often. The priests are essentially their own men, planning their itineration through their districts according to their own whims and desires. Although many villagers fear the power of the priests, there are, nevertheless, those who are critical of their behavior and were free to voice their criticism to me. Many priests were accused of abusing their power, and of being lazy in not visiting the village more frequently. The strongest criticism was raised against those priests who came to the village only to give Mass and did little or no teaching or pastoral counseling.[47]

The nature of the structural relationship that priests have with villagers creates a situation readily open to abuse by all but the most scrupulous and conscientious of the clergy. There is, of course, a wide variety of performance in priestly activities and villagers are quick to point out "good" priests from "bad" ones.

Syncretistic Beliefs and Practice in Contemporary Melanesian Society. The words of a Melanesian Anglican theology student serve as an appropriate introduction to this section:

> For us in the Solomons the Bible is literally a story about God and how he has made a group of islands and people to live in the group. These people disobeyed their God and he became angry, and so the people killed the magic man Jesus to appease their angry God. That is the whole story.[48]

What are the contemporary Melanesian perceptions of Anglican Christian beliefs introduced by the Melanesian Mission? How do Melanesians interpret and understand the Bible and the Prayer Book? What are their attitudes toward the ritualistic Anglo-Catholic tradition of worship that has been introduced into the islands? These and similar questions will be addressed in this section as I probe into the meaning Melanesians ascribe to their understanding and practice of Anglican Christianity.

But first a word of caution. I have emphasized throughout this study the inherent danger in making broad generalizations regarding Melanesian society and culture. This must be emphasized again in regard to the following discussion on religious beliefs and practice. Today there is tremendous variability from island to island in the the way Melanesians have come to understand Anglican Christianity. Local church leaders underline this point when they speak of the Church of Melanesia as being "weak" in this region, or "stronger" on that island. And there is, of course, variability in individual interpretation and understanding. On the higher abstract level, however, the model of Melanesians' beliefs and practices is most valid. As one moves closer to empirical reality at the idiosyncratic level, there will be exceptions to this general model as I will outline below. To construct this model we will need several components. I will first discuss Melanesian interpretations of traditional Christian concepts, followed by a discussion of Christopagan or syncretistic ideas and then conclude this section by focusing on contemporary Melanesian magic in village life and beliefs regarding the supernatural.

1. Melanesian Reinterpretation of Christian Concepts.

Although the Melanesian Mission, early in its history, adopted the language of Mota from the Banks' Islands as its *lingua franca*, it never used an indigenous word for the Christian concept of God.[49] Indigenous terms were used for other concepts, such as *ganarongo* (holy feast) to describe Holy Communion.[50] Today many Melanesians perceive God in terms of the Old Testament model of a Jealous God, a God of Vengeance and Anger, a God to be feared, one who will punish for breaking tabus.[51] Disasters such as earthquakes and cyclones are interpreted as acts of God in punishment for Melanesians' disobedience, and illness is often attributed to the wrath of God for one's sin and disobedience. Hilliard is correct in noting that:

> It is this image of God as an external lawgiver and judge . . . and of religion as primarily a matter of obedience to concrete injunctions, which lies at the heart of Solomon Islands Christianity (1966: 522).

Against this background it is not surprising to discover that the Christian doctrine of a God of Love does not carry the same valence of meaning as does the concept of a God of Anger. The God of Love is poorly understood and not well integrated into Melanesian Anglican theology.

Similarly, the doctrine of the Trinity and Resurrection, while given formal assent as important elements of Christian theology, are nevertheless concepts that villagers find hard to comprehend and appreciate. There were certainly no equivalent concepts within traditional Melanesian religion.[52]

Under the influence of the Anglo-Catholic tradition in the Melanesian Mission, greater emphasis was given to the role of saints and their function in intercessory prayer. Many Melanesians perceive the prominent saints as "ghosts" whom they call upon for help. In a similar pattern of interpretation, angels are called "spirits."[53]

The doctrines of Atonement and Incarnation are not equally understood or appreciated. Although atonement is not stressed in Anglo-Catholic theology, nevertheless, islanders in the Church of Melanesia have given this doctrine special emphasis and importance in their corpus of theological beliefs. Hymns with this theme are frequently selected over others for use in worship. It is not surprising that Melanesians should readily identify with the doctrine of Atonement, for sacrifice played a prominent role in traditional religion.[54] On the other hand, many islanders have a difficult time understanding the Incarnation—God becoming man. One bishop informed me that, "Our people clearly understand the concept of God in the Old Testament as it is very Melanesian, but the Christ of the New Testament is a figure that very few at the village level understand. Christ is understood as a man, but not as a God." Villagers can easily perceive God as a spirit, but the notion of a spirit becoming a human being, as in the doctrine of the Incarnation, is quite incomprehensible to most villagers.

When it comes to the Bible, there is not an equal understanding of and/or appreciation for Old and New Testament material. The Old Testament stories appear much closer to Melanesian life-ways and are better understood, for they emphasize ritual and ceremony. I found that Pauline theology in the New Testament was especially alien to many islanders' way of thinking. This accords with Kraft's observations that:

> It is predictable for cultural reasons . . . that Euro-Americans would be more attracted to the Pauline epistles. Africans and many others, however, with cultures more similar to Hebrew culture than ours is, are more attracted to the Gospels and Old Testament. For their preference, unlike Luther's, is for narrative presentation of events rather than for philosophical analysis of their significance (1979: 234).[55]

There are many Christian concepts and religious practices that Melanesians understand and experience through an essentially animistic worldview.[56] I will now briefly discuss how this animistic framework influences contemporary Melanesian attitudes toward Holy Communion and prayer.

Holy Communion.

I was not long into the course of my fieldwork before I came to see the Anglican Melanesians' worldview as full of animistic beliefs. I had not expected to find it, as all my preliminary research, limited primarily to histories of the Mission by either protagonists or missionaries themselves, had led me to believe that the traditional animistic worldview had been eradicated with conversion to Christianity. But this is not the case, for animistic beliefs are at the core of the worldview of many Anglican islanders today. A form of "split-level Christianity" has emerged, with an overlay of overt Christian practices on top of a foundation of covert animistic beliefs. Nowhere is this more apparent than in Melanesians' attitudes toward and perceptions of Holy Communion.[57]

As mentioned above, the sacraments of Holy Communion and Baptism are the only two "which all must receive to have everlasting life."[58] The *Melanesian Prayer Book* defines a sacrament as "something we can see which is a sign of what God does for our spirits, which we cannot see."[59] In the sacrament of Holy Communion, the "something we can see" is bread and wine.[60] Melanesians perceive the act of communion as the most effective ritualistic means for acquiring *mana*. As Hagesi (1972: 66) has noted, "The consecrated bread and wine are not mere symbols but they are literally the real Body and Blood of Christ because they have the *mana* of Christ."

Mana can be dangerous, for like magic, it can rebound and cause harm. Thus Holy Communion is an "awe-ful" act, demanding fasting and a careful preparation beforehand. If any tabus have been broken, e.g., stealing, adultery, swearing, etc., then reconciliation must be made before one participates in this rite.[61] Normally a priest comes to a village the night before Holy Communion is to be given. Following Evening Prayer, a service of preparation for Holy Communion begins. On numerous occasions I have observed villagers who were not attending the daily service of Evensong, make a rush for the village chapel when the service of preparation for Holy Communion began. The results of tabulations kept while we lived at Gnulahage, Santa Isabel, will enable one to better understand the villagers' preference for attending the rite of Holy Communion over the daily services of Morning and Evening Prayer. It is first necessary to have an understanding of the composition of the population in this village. This is provided in the following table.

	Adults (age 15+)	Children	
Male	41	29	
Female	45	35	
Total	86	64	Total village population = 150

Table 6.5. Population of Gnulahage, Santa Isabel – 1977.

The following figures are based on the average (Monday—Saturday) attendance of villagers at Morning and Evening Prayer on a daily basis. The average attendance at Morning Prayers on Sundays when a priest was not present to give Holy Communion is also given in the table below, and should be compared with the average attendance at services when a priest was present and Holy Communion was administered.

	Adult Males	Adult Females	TOTAL	Percent of Village Adult Population
Daily Morning Prayer	13.1	19.9	33	38%
Daily Evening Prayer	9.4	17.1	26.5	31%
Sunday with No Holy Communion	32.9	44	76.9	89%
Service of Holy Communion	41	45	86	100%

Table 6.6. Mean Attendance at Anglican Worship Services Gnulahage, Santa Isabel – 1977-1978.

As this table illustrates, there is tremendous variance between attendance at daily morning and evening prayers, and attendance at services of Holy Communion.

Villagers call the bread and wine of Holy Communion "holy food" and believe it makes them strong — strong physically and spiritually. An interesting index of a person's prognosis for recovery from illness is whether or not he shows improvement after taking Holy Communion. I met this on Malaita where a priest gave Holy Communion to a man who was dying in a hospital in the mid-afternoon. In the evening the priest returned to the hospital to see if the man had shown any improvement. He had not, and he died the next day. In conversation with the priest, I learned that when the man had not shown any signs of improvement after taking Holy Communion, the priest predicted he would in fact die the next day.

Prayer.

One meets a similar pattern in the Melanesians' attitude toward prayer. Traditionally prayer played an important role in Melanesian religion; individuals offered prayers to their ancestral spirits to receive assistance for daily activities such as hunting, fishing, raiding and fighting, etc. For especially important communal interests involving the whole village, formal prayers were said by the village priest. Much of the magical power believed to be in the prayers was conveyed through the words themselves. That is, *mana* was received by uttering the words, in a formal and ritualistically prescribed manner. In this sense, the Anglican Prayer Book serves as a functional substitute; it is a book of formal prayers, for all occasions, and many villagers believe that they receive *mana* simply by uttering the words of the Prayer Book.[62] An Anglican priest, converted from his pagan religion on Malaita, informed me that he was attracted to the Melanesian Mission rather than the S.S.E.M. because of the Prayer Book; the extemporaneous prayer of the Evangelicals appeared to him to be sacrilegious in contrast.

This traditional attitude toward prayer, for the most part, has been conveyed to Christian prayers in the COM. A village catechist conducts the service in a formal manner, reading prescribed collects (prayers) for the day in addition to any others he chooses to include. There is congregational participation in some of the service, but it is the catechist who is perceived as the religious specialist, for he knows the correct techniques for conducting the service and reading the prayers. Prayers are seldom said outside the chapel, and very few villagers pray privately. Praying in the COM is a corporate and formal act, not an individual and spontaneous one. The emphasis is on correct ritual procedure, not on comprehension or meaning derived from the prayers. There are two lines of evidence that support this conclusion.

The first is in regard to the villagers' attitudes toward attending prayers. As the above table demonstrates, the mean average attendance at daily morning and evening prayers attracts only about one-third of the adult population. On several occasions the dismal turnout of only a handful of villagers at Evening Prayer incurred the ire of the catechist, who then reprimanded those present for the poor attendance. Such episodes were viewed by the rest of the community as highly ironic. The catechist went out of his way to assure me that it was his responsibility to make certain that people attended prayers and that he was only doing his job. On inquiring why people did not attend in greater numbers, I was told that villagers were too busy with the gardens and other work, but that it really was not necessary to be physically present as long as one was mentally present, for the prayers said at church were for all people in the village regardless of whether they were present or not. That is, *mana* would be restored vicariously to those who were not present through the prayers said by those who were.

A second line of evidence, supporting the notion that there is power in simply saying the words of the prayer and believing that God will hear them and act accordingly, is the fact that many of the prayers are incomprehensible to those attending the service. There are two reasons for this.

(1) The catechist frequently reads the collects in an inaudible and hurried, mumbled manner, so that those present can neither hear nor understand what is being said. On discussing this with villagers, they frequently confessed that they could not understand the prayers being read, but then added that understanding was not particularly important. There were, of course, exceptions to this norm, and a few did complain because they did not know what was going on as they followed along parrot-fashion.

(2) The second reason is the language of the Prayer Book itself. Today many of the prayer books printed in vernacular languages are artifacts of a Melanesian Mission era several generations past, and thus the language used is archaic, much like the King James version of the Bible is for English speakers today. Moreover, many of the vernacular prayer books are full of errors and some are poor translations. However, there are still many villagers who worship in a language other than their own, and thus prayers are said with little if any comprehension of their meaning. This problem was woefully apparent to Bishop John Chisholm shortly after he became bishop in 1967. Addressing the Standing Committee of the diocese, six months after his consecration he stated:

> Another factor which has contributed to the general malaise of the Church is that we expect our people to worship in a foreign language. In some islands I have visited it would seem that the people do not understand a single word of what is being said—and often being said badly—and there are large numbers of people who have never heard the Gospel in their own tongue, and have never received the Sacraments in their own languages. Is it not a lot to expect of these people that they will live a virile church life when they do not understand what it is all about? Is this the truth that will make them free—when that truth is hidden from them by a strange language?[63]

The church on Santa Isabel serves as an example of this pattern of people worshipping in a language other than their own. Melanesian Mission inroads on the island were first made in the Bugotu district at the southeast end of the island. Large numbers of islanders had migrated to this area to seek refuge from headhunters attacking from the northwest end of the island and from New Georgia. Therefore, when the people-movement toward Christianity occurred around the turn of the century, the Bugotu district and hence the Bugotu language had a dominant role in the newly Christianized Santa Isabel society.[64] The New Testament, selected Old Testament books, and the Prayer Book were translated and used throughout the island for worship, despite the fact that the Bugotu language was only one of several spoken on the island.[65]

It was not until 1973 that an abbreviated Prayer Book was written in the language of the Maringe district. It included a liturgy of Morning and Evening Prayer, Holy Communion, and Infant Baptism.[66] During the course of my fieldwork this translation was used in Gnulahage where my wife and I lived; however, at least once a week the Bugotu Prayer Book was used for the entire service. Moreover, villagers in the Hograno district who speak the Maringe language, did not use this translation at all, but relied instead on the Bugotu Prayer Book and Hymnal.

During the course of my fieldwork I conducted a socio-linguistic survey of Santa Isabel, discovering seven viable language groups on the island.[67] Testing for intelligibility between languages, it was determined that three languages (Bugotu, Maringe and Zabana) would have to be used in a vernacular literature program in order to reach everyone on the island through a language they could understand. What was most revealing was that the Bugotu language was understood by only one other speech community (Gao). Thus the total number of islanders who could understand the Bugotu language was only about one-fourth of the island's population.[68]

One may question why, then, the majority of Santa Isabel islanders continue to use a language they do not understand in their Christian worship. Even more perplexing is why Maringe speakers continue to use the Bugotu Prayer Book. The response I received to this latter question was that villagers like to use the Bugotu Prayer Book because they got tired of the routine with Maringe, or that Bugotu was easier to read than Maringe. Nevertheless, I believe the underlying reason is that, "It doesn't really matter." That is, it makes no difference whether one understands the language or not, for the function of prayer is not to convey meaning to the worshipper, so much as it is to provide *mana* through its ritualistic use, and this does not require an understanding of the words used in the prayers.

We have now seen how two acts of religious ritual, Holy Communion and prayer, introduced as Christian forms into Melanesia by Anglican missionaries, have been reinterpreted by indigenous Christians. Their perception and understanding have been vastly different from that of the missionaries who introduced these ritualistic forms, and thus, the meaning islanders have derived from these rites has also been different. It is clear then, that Holy Communion and liturgical prayer as cultural forms introduced by the Melanesian Mission do not have the same meaning for the islanders who adopted them as they did for the missionaires who introduced them. This problem of transferring meaning associated with a cultural form across cultural boundaries is, however, one that agents of change frequently encounter. In discussing this problem, Linton cogently notes that:

> . . . most culture elements are transferred in terms of objective form stripped of the meaning which is an integral part of them in their original context. At most they may carry over vague associations of sacredness or importance derived from the observed behavior and attitudes of the donor group in connection with them (1940: 486).

Linton's notion of a loss of meaning with the transference of cultural forms corresponds with Kraft's idea that there is a:

> . . . direct relationship between the foreignness of imposed cultural forms and the tendency of many to regard the forms as **sacred in themselves** and to miss the intended meanings (1977: 193).

I now want to proceed to a discussion of Melanesian beliefs and practices that are not reinterpretations of religious ritual introduced by European missionaries, but rather are beliefs and practices that have been a part of Melanesian life-ways reaching far back into the pre-contact period; this is the notion of islanders' contemporary belief in and practice of Melanesian magic.

2. Magic: Its Form and Function.

Shortly after I arrived in the Solomon Islands I was attending a village feast honoring its patron saint, and there I met a young Melanesian deacon who was about to be ordained to the priesthood. In our discussion together he confided, "There are many problems in the Church on Isabel." As I was still very much of a newcomer to the island, I was eager to learn his perspective on the church and so I asked him to give me some examples of what he perceived as "problems" in the church. He was at first hesitant to enumerate many, but said, "We call ourselves Christians but we serve two masters." He then proceeded to elaborate on how much people relied on magic, especially during times of crisis to meet their needs for emotional and physical security. He said he believed that even today, the majority of people on Santa Isabel attributed the cause of death to magic. It did not take me many months in the field before his insights were confirmed by my own observations and inquiries. I found most Solomon Islanders were quite free to discuss the topic of magic with me. It was also interesting to learn that most people believe magic is used even more on other islands, than on their own. Thus, for example, Santa Isabel islanders claim that magic is far more prevalent in the Western Solomons than on their own island. Likewise, Malaitans claim that magic is practiced far more on Santa Isabel than on Malaita. Many informants indicated that in Honiara, the main urban center, magic is used a great deal because islanders are outside the safety and protection of their own village.[69]

Following Sir James G. Frazer's (1890) codification of sympathetic magic, both homeopathic (imitative) and contagious magic are found on Santa Isabel today. Moreover, there are two kinds of magic — (1) magic done with hostile intentions to harm another person (sorcery or "black" magic) and, (2) well-intentioned magic performed for a variety of helpful purposes ("white" magic).[70] A brief discussion of these two types of magical beliefs and practices in contemporary Solomon Islands society (focusing especially on Santa Isabel) will be helpful in demonstrating the pervasiveness of magico-religious thinking among Melanesian Anglican Christians in village life today.

(1) Sorcery.

Comparatively speaking, the conversion of islanders to Christianity has reduced considerably the fear of sorcery from what it was in pre-Christian days. Compared to former times, islanders today feel free to walk about and are no longer paranoid about leaving bits of food, betel husks, tobacco or clothing about for fear that someone might work evil magic over them. But I say "comparatively," for there is still fear among some, and general caution among most islanders, over becoming victims of sorcery.[71] If fear from sorcery has declined, the belief in the **power** of sorcery nevertheless remains unshaken, and accusations are sporadically made against likely candidates suspected of using this magic to bring harm, sickness and even death to others. An informant told me one day that, "People don't need guns and spears to kill because they have magic."

Rooting out sorcery from the society has been a periodic activity of priests and others ever since the majority of the population converted to Christianity around the turn of the century. The famous Santa Isabel priest, Hugo Hebala, frequently turned his attention to this problem; writing in 1925 he noted:

> This last year I determined hotly within myself to make a thorough search amongst all the people for every old heathen thing that still remained hidden in their hearts, to get rid of them entirely. And one man was appointed, Walter Gagai by name, to go through all the villages, seeking out every person, and questioning them. And he succeeded completely. He sought for and found some things belonging to old times that they were still keeping hidden. And they all made full confession of everything, great or small, not one thing of any kind could they keep hidden in their breasts; and all of them in every village promised earnestly to renounce entirely those bad things of olden days, and to cleave with all their might

> to the teaching of Jesus Christ as the only Savior. Thus has the Church of Bugotu been cleansed anew, in order to establish the law of God Almighty, Creator of all things; and the hearts of the people have been emptied of the old heathen things.[72]

Hugo Hebala was optimistic, for in the following fifty years sorcery might have been diminished, but it was not eradicated. Eric Gnhokro, a priest from a later period, known for his extraordinary powers campaigned actively against sorcery. Informants claim that his method was highly successful in reducing sorcery. He demanded that after people attested that they did not use sorcery, that they then kiss the Bible. It was claimed that if someone lied and then kissed the Bible they would die within six months time. I asked my informant if anyone had ever died as a result of this ordeal, and I was told that some did, including a family of two brothers and a sister, all renowned for their practice of sorcery. They died within three months of kissing the Bible after proclaiming that they had not been sorcerers.[73]

During the period of our fieldwork a Fataleka man from Malaita was going from village to village on Santa Isabel in an attempt to discover those who were still practicing sorcery. Known for his divining skills, he was "uncovering" many villagers, including several in the village in which we lived, who were practicing sorcery.

The most common type of sorcery practiced on Santa Isabel is a form of contagious magic known locally as *khorapa'u.* A piece of human bone, preferably that of some well-known and powerful deceased Big Man, is normally used in this magical rite. The sorcerer takes a piece of leftover food or tobacco or feces (which is claimed to be the most potent and deadly material available) of the intended victim, inserting it into the human bone he/she is using. It is claimed that as soon as the sorcerer does this, the intended victim begins to feel sick. The sorcerer can program the speed of his/her victim's demise. The victim will begin to improve if the sorcerer takes the food or feces out of the bone and puts it in the sun, but if the sorcerer puts the material and bone into a fire, the power of the magic increases rapidly and the victim soon dies.

Another form of sorcery, employing the technique of homeopathic (imitative) magic, is called *churumala.* In this magical rite a person desiring to harm another finds that person's footprint and stabs it with a stick or some similar object, much in the same manner that vodun (voodoo) dolls are stuck with pins. It is claimed that the victim will soon begin to feel pain in the foot which gradually moves up the leg and eventually to the head at which time the victim dies.

In all acts of sorcery the intent is hostile and antisocial. The main motivation for performing sorcery is said to be jealousy and envy of another person's wealth or prestige. The act, combining ritual paraphernalia and certain words which are uttered, is always done in private.[74]

(2) Magic with Helpful Intentions.

Although sorcery (black magic) is still practiced today, it is a pale second to the practice of magic done with positive or helpful intentions in mind (white magic). The belief in the efficacy of magic provides the primary matrix of the islander's worldview, and Santa Isabel villagers practice it for all kinds of occasions. Magic ritual is used to insure successful hunting and fishing, and to a lesser extent, success in gardening. "Love magic" is used, as well as numerous magical techniques frequently combined with herbal remedies for treatment of illness and injury. "Custom medicine" is preferred over "Western medicine" and is normally consulted first before going to a clinic or hospital. Not infrequently, the two approaches to healing are used in tandem. For example, one day a village friend came to our house to ask for some aspirin as his eighteen-month-old daughter had a fever. He mentioned that his brother's wife's mother was visiting the village and that she was especially skilled in magical techniques for relieving this kind of illness. He said she had worked over his daughter, holding the child's back, uttering magical words and blowing on her skin. I then asked him why he wanted to use aspirin. "I want both kinds of medicine—custom and white man's," he said, "they can both work together." He left our house, confident that his daughter would soon be feeling better.

The entire corpus of magical techniques used for positive rather than negative purposes are subsumed under an indigenous term — *fa blahi* (to make holy). It is interesting to note that this same term, *fa blahi*, is used in the Maringe Prayer Book in the blessing and the conclusion of Holy Communion.[75]

A syncretism of traditional and Christian beliefs is seen clearly in the practice of magic on Santa Isabel today. The phrase, "In the name of the Father, Son and Holy Spirit," is frequently attached to the "custom words" of the traditional formulae while the practitioner makes the sign of the cross which is believed to give greater potency to the magic and insure success. The number "three" has also taken on special significance, the use of which can be observed in village life. For example, for many illnesses a potion made from tree bark (*popoji*) is given to the ailing person who always sips three clam-shells full of the liquid.[76]

Although there are numerous kinds of magical formulae and each is used for a specific purpose, the average villager may know personally only two or three of them. Individuals are renowned for their use of magic for specific cases. That is, people are specialists, not general practitioners in the art of magic. For example, an elderly man in our village is known for his magic to prevent centipede bites from becoming excruciatingly painful, and many villagers attest to the efficacy of his treatment. Another person in the village is a specialist in performing magic on dogs in preparation for hunting wild pigs in the bush. A brief list will illustrate the numerous uses to which white magic is put today:

1. **"Custom Medicine"** — cures for headache, sore throat and minor mouth irritation, coughing, fever and chills from malaria, diarrhea, constipation, bites from centipedes, boils, filariasis, tuberculosis, pain in different parts of the body, to stop bleeding from a cut, to heal broken bones, and to make infertile women bear children.
2. **Miscellaneous Magic** — cutting a cat's whiskers to make it friendly, giving a certain plant to a woman to eat before she becomes pregnant to assure that she'll have a boy, chewing ginger (a root believed to have strong magical powers) when someone is angry with you to reduce their anger, chewing ginger when you go to a trade store to purchase something so that the money you give in payment for the item will return to your hand, tying a string around one's leg for protection while playing soccer. In addition, magic is used in hunting, fishing, paddling a canoe, to seduce a lover, etc.

To conclude this section on magic done with good intentions and for helpful purposes, I will briefly discuss the use of love magic (*fa tani*) on Santa Isabel, which is used by both married men and women having trouble with their marriage, and by unmarried men and women desiring to marry a particular person. All magical formulae are inherited and/or sold for a consideration, and such is the case with love magic. I knew of at least two men in different villages near where we lived who had this special technique (magical words) which they sold to those interested. The prices for their magical formulae were competitive—one charged $8.00 and the other $10.00. Once the words were purchased they were uttered over a leaf, a piece of tobacco, clothing, etc. Then this object was put under the sleeping mat of the person the purchaser desired to seduce and marry. The same effect is caused by uttering the words over food which is then given to the person to eat.

Another form of *fa tani* is to take a certain wild flower in the bush, say the magical formula over it, and then wear it in the hair. When the one you want looks at you, he/she will have a spell cast that will drive him/her to desire to be your lover. "Does *fa tani* really work?" I often inquired. "Oh yes! Everytime," was invariably the reply. There were several in the village in which we lived who claimed to have been "victims" of *fa tani*, and at least one person had used it to patch up a marital dispute after his wife had "thrown him out of the house." The power of love magic was never doubted, but many were critical of its use because they claimed that many unhappy marriages were contracted under the spell of *fa tani*. It was believed that the power of the magic would eventually wear off and then living together could quickly become more of a trial than a joy.

I have gone into some detail in this section to demonstrate how magic is used and its pervasive role in the everyday life of Santa Isabel islanders. Although some of the COM clergy claim that compared to the previous two generations, the use of magic is on the wane, it is nevertheless prevalent today. When people become ill they normally rely on "custom medicine" and then go to the clinic for "white man's medicine," and as a last resort, turn to the church and seek the prayers of a priest. Although death is still blamed on sorcery, and accusations of sorcery are made sporadically, there is nevertheless an increasing belief in what Westerners regard as "natural" causes of death.

It is noteworthy that although all missionaries preached against sorcery, and most dismissed "white magic" as "ignorant superstition" that would be eradicated through education, they nevertheless contributed to and reinforced a "magical" worldview (as opposed to a "scientific" one). This was done through the use of functional substitutes. For example, priests would bless canoes, canoe houses, fishing nets, gardens, houses, or "whatever was the custom of the people in their heathen state."[77]

On Santa Isabel many islanders traditionally wore charms made from ginger root as a protective device from malevolent supernatural elements. Taking note of this, the missionary R. P. Fallowes wrote to his sister in England, requesting that among other things, she send out small inexpensive crosses to wear around the neck, for as he observed, "Charms were very much in demand in the days gone by and the people feel happier wearing the Sacred Symbol around their necks."[78]

In 1902, missionary Walter Ivens introduced Christian substitutes for the traditional rituals used in porpoise hunting on Small Malaita. As Hilliard notes:

> On this occasion Ivens dedicated six canoes and a new canoe house, composed special prayers for starting, finding and driving the "game," while the fishermen prepared themselves by seclusion, fasting and prayers (1966: 518).[79]

Today priests continue to function in blessing many different things that are important in the life of the villagers; e.g., canoes, houses, gardens, etc. In late April or early May each year, the Church of Melanesia has Rogation Celebrations — a time of asking God for His blessing on different things. Throughout the Rogation Week, the priest goes to the river, gardens, plantation, cemetery, houses, clinics, schools, the beach, etc., praying for God's blessing on the various areas of importance to islanders in their daily life.[80]

It is clearly evident that an essentially animistic framework for interpreting events in the world still functions in the minds of many contemporary Melanesians. Consequently, magical techniques for controlling one's world abound, even though there is little, if any, religious allegiance or worship given to ancestral spirits. Thus, as G. White (1978: 181) has so cogently stated, "Mission procedures have supplied a supplement rather than a substitute for traditional techniques." This corresponds to Schapera's study of the Kxatla in Africa, in which he notes:

> The greatest failure of the Church, and of Western civilization generally has been in regard to magic and sorcery . . . it is difficult to account for the persistence of these beliefs and practices in contrast with the almost complete disappearance of ancestor worship (1936: 239-240).

3. Contemporary Melanesian Beliefs Regarding Supernatural Beings.

To conclude this section on village-level Christianity I will briefly discuss contemporary Melanesian attitudes toward supernatural beings. Although the traditional Melanesian pantheon of spirits has been supplemented by a corpus of Christian spirits (God, Jesus Christ, Holy Spirit, saints, martyrs, Satan, angels) it has not been replaced. For many, conversion to Christianity has meant a shift in allegiance to new spirits, spirits that are perhaps more powerful, but it has not denied the existence of the old ones.

Thus, today villagers frequently discuss the activity of spirits and/or their encounters with them. In the course of my fieldwork I met this on numerous occasions. For example, one evening one of our friends returning from a short trip to another village, went and visited briefly with his sister in the house adjacent to ours, and then came to see us. We conversed for some time, and then as he prepared to leave, he said it was now safe to go to his own home. I, of course, wanted to know the meaning behind such a statement and so I asked him. I discovered that his wife's sister, who had recently had a baby, was temporarily living with them. He said that after walking about in the bush, as he had done, it would have been too dangerous to have gone directly to his own house where the baby was, for when a person comes in from the bush, he brings a spirit with him. The object of going to other houses first is to confuse the spirit, if not to neutralize the potential harm the spirit could cause, especially to a newborn baby.

Villagers believe that evil spirits exist and they were free to describe them to me. For example, one in particular which lived in the bush was described as having long black hair and being wild and dangerous. On the other hand, some ancestral spirits are perceived as benevolent and helpful to their living descendants. For example, there are people who are specialists in calling ancestral spirits in order that one may communicate with them. I was given a vivid description of this activity called *na'itu naghe*, by a man who had consulted a woman medium on several occasions. He informed me that he had paid her five shillings on his very first visit, but had paid nothing after that. This is the episode as he related it to me:

The woman summoned the spirits by calling out their names and then taking a leaf of a special plant that grew alongside her house,[81] and breaking it as she called out the names of the ancestral spirits. After the spirits were called the client sat down in the woman's house and waited. He stressed that it was important that one's lamp be kept low, for a bright light would keep the spirits from coming. When the spirits arrived, he could hear them, for they made a whistling sound similar to that of wind blowing through the cracks in a wall. After they arrived, the medium introduced the spirits to her client and then she retired for the night, leaving him to converse with them at will. "The spirits talked Maringe language," my informant declared, "and they always spoke in a very clear, distinct manner, very different from that of a human being."

My informant claims to have had conversations with these spirits on several occasions. There was no doubt in his mind that this was a conscious experience, not a dream or trance, and that the spirits were real entities, despite the fact they could not be seen. As empirical proof for their existence he informed me that on one of his encounters he was smoking a European cigarette while talking with the spirits. He said they commented on how they liked the smell and so he offered the cigarette to them. He claims that a spirit came and took the cigarette from between his fingers and that he could feel a cold "hand" on his when it was taken away. The spirit then crossed the room and "smoked it very nicely." As the spirit "inhaled," the cigarette glowed in the dark.

There are many other kinds of encounters that individuals experience that confirm their belief in the existence of spirits. For example, although a traditional shrine (*phadagi*) is no longer used today for worship, it is nevertheless a sacred place, and one must be careful to avoid disturbing it. On visiting several phadagi(s), I was always cautioned not to ask too many questions or talk too loud while at the shrine. On one occasion, I trekked up to the top of a steep hill to visit the grave of Figrima, a famous nineteenth century Big Man who converted to Christianity late in his life. As we reached the top of the hill and stood around the grave, large black clouds rolled in and we were soon drenched with rain. There was no doubt in anyone's mind (except mine) that our visit to the grave site had caused the rain. As we left the village that morning it was a bright sunny day, but I learned later that the villagers had predicted that it would rain because we were going to visit the grave of such an important Big Man.[82]

These are only two of many examples I could use to illustrate the principle that belief in traditional spirits is an integral part of the corpus of beliefs for contemporary Anglicans in Melanesia. Most Santa Isabel islanders believe that the spirits of departed ancestors reside on the nearly uninhabited adjacent island of San Jorge. A great deal of "empirical" evidence is cited to support this notion, such as islanders hearing congregational singing on the island when someone has died, pathways that are always swept clean on the island despite the fact that islanders seldom visit the area, and other examples to demonstrate that "someone" lives there.[83]

In this section on Christianity at the village level I have attempted to demonstrate that Christian beliefs and practices introduced by the Melanesian Mission were interpreted by islanders within a Melanesian animistic framework. In addressing this question on the relationship between the traditional animism and introduced Christianity, Hilliard cogently notes:

> In practice . . . accommodation between the two was superficial. Christianity was modified by its new environment and appears to have made only slight impact upon indigenous religious concepts. Individual Christian doctrines, whenever possible, were assimilated by the islanders into their traditional belief system and interpreted in a sense often very different from that intended by their European teachers (1966: 521-522).

Today the missionaries are gone, and the old Melanesian Mission has evolved into the autonomous Church of Melanesia (COM). The Christianity brought by the missionaries over one hundred years ago has made its impact on Melanesian society and culture, but as Hagesi (1972: 48) observes of his own society, "Many people still practice magic and still talk of spirits and ghosts as something more helpful and relevant in their life."

This dual system of animistic and Christian beliefs needs to be explored in terms of the conversion process, for we are interested in discovering the cognitive reorientation that occurs when a group of people like the Santa Isabel islanders choose to innovate and adopt Christianity. In the following section I will therefore discuss the dynamics of conversion to Christianity on Santa Isabel. I believe that an ethnohistorical evaluation of that process will help to explain the type of Christianity practiced on that island today.

Christian Conversion as Innovation: Santa Isabel, a Case Study

Although the general pattern of conversion from animism to Christianity in Oceania has been one of multi-individual group movements,[84] the acceptance of Christianity by an island population the size of Santa Isabel, within a single mission, is indeed a remarkable phenomenon of culture change in Melanesia, and worthy of anthropological investigation and analysis. Justifiably the Melanesian Mission pointed with pride to this island as an example of effective missionary work in which the traditional society and culture were dramatically changed with the acceptance of Christianity.[85]

In this section discussion will focus on the process whereby islanders abandoned their old ways to embrace the "New Way" of Christianity advocated by the Melanesian Mission. I will first describe the nineteenth century cultural context out of which the islanders emerged when they chose to innovate and adopt Christianity. This will be followed by a brief review of the missionaries' role as agents of change, and conclude with a theoretical discussion on the process of conversion.

Headhunting and Raiding in Nineteenth Century Santa Isabel.

By 1880 the traditional society of Santa Isabel had been thrown into disequilibrium and demoralization, primarily because of the intensification of headhunting and internecine warfare and raiding. It is primarily this state of affairs that set the stage for conversion to Christianity on Santa Isabel.[86]

The origins of headhunting in the Solomon Islands are unknown. The earliest historical records of the Spanish (16th century) and the French (18th century) do not reveal the practice of headhunting as it was developed in the last half of the nineteenth century.[87] The first recorded observations of the practice were made by the trader Andrew Cheyne when he visited the island of Simbo (Eddystone) in the Western Solomons in February 1844.[88]

Ethnohistorical evidence indicates that the New Georgia Group was probably the center of the headhunting complex, spreading outward to other islands. The practice appears to have reached the Bugotu district at the southeast end of Santa Isabel by the 1850's.[89] Bishop Patteson visited Santa Isabel in 1861 aboard HMS *Cordelia* at a time when headhunting and internecine raiding were intensifying.[90] Returning the following year in the *Southern Cross*, Patteson anchored off the coast of Sepi. The Big Man Bera who held sway over the entire Bugotu district came on board and presented Patteson with a white cockatoo as a token of goodwill.[91] In 1863 Patteson obtained four boys from Santa Isabel for schooling in New Zealand, one of whom died in a typhoid fever epidemic at Norfolk Island in 1868.[92] When Patteson visited Santa Isabel in 1866 he observed elaborate precautions that had been taken to guard against raiding and headhunting. In addition to fortified villages atop hills and ridges, islanders had built places of refuge in the tops of high trees in which they slept at night.[93]

From the 1860's to the mid 1880's there was increasing external pressure from the raids of headhunters from Kia (northwest end of Santa Isabel) and New Georgia, as well as internal pressure of raiding, which drove the remaining population of the island to the southwestern Bugotu district where they sought alliance with and protection under Bera, the most powerful Big Man in the area.[94]

During this period of social upheaval the Melanesian Mission made little progress. A colony of Santa Isabel refugees was established on the island of Savo, and here the Mission placed Mano Wadrokal, a Loyalty Islander. In 1874 the refugees moved back to Santa Isabel, relocating at Nuro, where the small colony of Christians lived in constant dread of headhunters. In 1876 they moved again, back to their former place at Mahaga where they came under the protection of Bera. But Mano Wadrokal, an arrogant teacher with a fiery temperament came into conflict with Bera in 1878, resulting in Bera's tabuing anyone from attending school, and two of Wadrokal's friends fatally shooting two of Bera's men. Needless to say, it was a setback for the Mission, and Wadrokal was removed from Santa Isabel.[95]

The only bright spot on Santa Isabel for the Melanesian Mission during this period was the mountainous village of Tega, formed as a refuge against headhunting and raiding under the Big Man Samson Ingo.[96] This situation at Tega, where a Christian Big Man offered refuge in a protective settlement, was a microcosm of things to come on Santa Isabel.

Although Bera was friendly to the Mission, he never endorsed Christianity. In fact he was viewed as a real obstructionist to the work of the Melanesian Mission.[97] While offering protection to some against the headhunting raids from New Georgia and northwestern Santa Isabel, he also led devastating headhunting expeditions himself, annihilating the population of the Maringe Lagoon, and inhabitants of Vati Lau Island in Nggela. His raiding extended as far as Estrella Bay on the northeast coast, to half-way up the southwest coast of the island.[98] On Friday, May 16, 1884, Alfred Penny, the missionary overseeing the work on Nggela and Santa Isabel, recorded in his diary, "The news of Bera's death has come from Ysabel, it seems too good to be true."[99] Although Bera never accepted Christianity, at the time of his death he called some of the people around him, telling them to:

> Let no one be killed for me. Do no damage to the food or to people's property when I am dead; there has been enough of this. I did it when I succeeded to the power I am now dying from; I have done so often. Soga and Vou must succeed me and share my power. I charge them to see these commands are carried out.[100]

Bera's death was a turning point in the history of Santa Isabel—a landmark signifying the end of an old era and the beginning of a new one.

Penny recorded on May 22, 1884, that "Soga and Vou came to see me. They are very amenable and want to have a teacher. We have arranged for Devi to go there and begin school."[101] A school, however, would not be allowed in Soga's village for several more years.

Of the two appointed to succeed to Bera's hegemony, Soga quickly came to the fore in establishing his Big Man leadership, partially through raiding and headhunting activities.[102] Contrary to some scholars (Fox 1958: 34, 198; Jackson 1975: 71; Hilliard 1978: 88) Soga was not the son of Bera, but according to my informants, Bera was the brother of Soga's mother — a fact not surprising in a matrilineal society.

In June 1886, a severe influenza epidemic swept through the island, and Soga became seriously ill. Bishop John Selwyn visited him in his illness, and mixed up a concoction of quinine and brandy, which he and the others present tasted before administering it to Soga. The Big Man recovered in a week, sending a large present to Selwyn, and requesting that a school begin in his village, and finally allowing some boys to go to Norfolk Island for training.[103] Two weeks later, a party of headhunters from New Georgia arrived seeking to buy heads for 7s 6d apiece. Soga sent for Selwyn to support him in refusing "to turn over to them, in cold blood, some wretched slave or shrieking woman, whose head might be borne back to their own country."[104]

In the Mission literature, Selwyn's successful doctoring of Soga is frequently cited as the turning point for the Melanesian Mission on Santa Isabel. Soga was at first hesitant to have a school established in his own village, fearing that he would offend the spirits of his ancestors (*tidatho*) and that if he allowed it, he would die like other Big Men who had given permission for schools to be established.[105] But by 1888, Soga made a decision to admit a teacher into his own village and supported him fully. The Mission report for that year noted that Soga:

> . . . who in days gone by was a renowned warrior and dealer in heads, now comes to school most regularly. He has put away all his wives save one, and the other day, when some of his old friends from a neighbouring island visited him in order to buy heads he would have nothing to do with them.[106]

The following year Soga applied for Christian baptism, and was given the name Monilaws, after Robert Monilaws Turnbull, missionary in Bugotu at the time of his baptism.[107] The Melanesian Mission saw this event as an important catalyst that hopefully would trigger a people movement toward Christianity on Santa Isabel. The official report for 1889 noted that:

> The death some years ago of the great and very powerful chief Bera, raised to prominence a man of much shrewdness and intelligence, who for some time past has followed his old spirits, and his head-hunting proclivities. This man's name was Soga. For many months past he has been favourable to Christian teaching, and on the appointment of Hugo Gorovaka as teacher at his village, he allowed his wives and children, and his people generally, to attend school and church freely: and this year, by God's grace, has seen him abandon his old habits and evil ways, and, professing himself an humble follower of the Lord Jesus, apply for Christian baptism. At Mr. Turnbull's wish Mr. Bice baptized him along with the one wife he had chosen, and about seventy of his people. A more important and encouraging event has perhaps never occurred in Melanesia, and it is hoped, and much to be prayed for, that by God's grace and continued blessing Monilaws Soga may hereafter become a second Ethelbert to his people at Ysabel.[108]

The Mission was not to be dissappointed in its prestigious new convert, for in retrospect, the above report was prophetic. Hundreds of islanders followed the lead of Soga and accepted Christianity immediately. The cultural context in which Soga's conversion took place had "preadapted" Santa Isabel for rapid change and revitalization. This preadaptation was primarily the result of headhunting in at least three important ways:

1. It had shifted the population of Santa Isabel to the Bugotu district,

islanders migrating to the region to be under the protection of Bera, and later Soga.

2. It was through headhunting and providing protection from headhunters that traditional leaders such as Bera and Soga had expanded their influence over such a large population.
3. Finally, headhunting had so disrupted social life and demoralized the people that they were anxious for a solution to the problem—one that would hopefully restore a balanced equilibrium to their society.[109]

Headhunting and raiding had escalated to such an extent that they were out of control, and the traditional checks and balances to contain such activity were no longer operative.

Into this arena were added three important ingredients that helped to revitalize Santa Isabel society:

1. The ideology of Anglican Christianity, as advocated by the Melanesian Mission, provided a new value orientation and cultural framework for revitalization.
2. By endorsing Christianity, Soga, the supreme Big Man of Santa Isabel, provided the authority and leadership pattern through which the introduced change was legitimized. Thus when Soga became a Christian, he established a new group norm. That is, because he was a person of central importance, and not just marginal to the society, his behavior set a new norm for the rest of the group to model.
3. Dr. Henry Welchman, who was the first European missionary to reside permanently on Santa Isabel, did much to sensitively guide the revitalization of Santa Isabel society under the aegis of a Christian ideology and cultural code. Welchman's association with Santa Isabel began in May 1890, and over the next 18 years until his death in 1908, he was an important participant-observer in the transformation of life on Santa Isabel.

Jackson, in speaking of Welchman, notes that:

> His attitude to the islanders and their way of life was in the best tradition of George Selwyn and Patteson: he considered that Christianity did not necessarily entail an alteration in the Melanesians' "native civilisation," with its "fixed and well-known laws, of relationship, land, morals."[110] Welchman illustrated his word by living as much as possible in the manner of the islanders, and establishing a close durable relationship with the people (1972: 62).[111]

Soga and Welchman worked closely together to establish a new order on the island. Soga had built his reputation as a paramount Big Man through the activities of headhunting and raiding, but he now converted his traditional Melanesian form of power — a combination of *mana*, wealth, prestige and fear — into a European form of civil, judicial, and administrative control over the islanders.[112] Welchman worked through this indigenous structure, advising and supporting Soga in his activities, advancing the cause of evangelization on the island. One gets an insight into Welchman's theory and method of missionary work through his personal diary. For example, at a gathering of Big Men (Welchman's term) assembled at the village of Sepi, where he and Soga resided, Welchman wrote on Friday, July 29, 1892:

> The Christians came to church and I preached to them from Revelations 11:15. Pointing out to them their duty in ruling their people in the fear of God. After a short interval we assembled in Soga's men's house and there had a long talk. I began by pointing out the change that had taken place in Bugotu in the past . . . years, and how it was due to nothing but Christianity. When I spoke of the old impossibility of such a meeting as that in the old times and of the meeting of a few being accompanied by the exhibition of weapons there were emphatic expressions of assent. Then I pointed out that neither I nor the teachers wanted to take power out of their hands, but rather to guide them how to use their authority justly.[113]

Always conscious of the necessity of working through the prevailing social structure, if meaningful and lasting change was to be implemented, Welchman relied heavily on his alliance with Soga in guiding young converts and shaping the new order. Another entry in his diary (August 23, 1892) demonstrates this principle in action:

> Sent for Soga and talked with him about affairs of state. Told him it would never do for the people to think that now he was a Christian and would not murder them that they could behave as they liked toward him with impunity—that I believed he was trying to rule justly and therefore they ought to listen the more to him and when he summoned them to trial he was to accept no excuse and punish them severely if they did not appear. That Christianity did not take away his power but rather established it in righteousness. That his part was to sift patiently every case, to seek and decide justly and then to punish the right person and not to take vengeance on the innocent.[114]

In the years that followed, increasing numbers of Santa Isabel islanders adopted Christianity, supplanting a life of violence and disruption with one of peace and prosperity. Soga's death in 1898 created a significant vacuum of leadership that was never quite filled, but the movement toward Christianity was sufficiently established by that time to enable it to continue beyond his death.

By 1901 the Melanesian Mission recorded 41 teachers at work in 15 village schools, with 447 confirmed members of the church, including 145 confirmed that year. There were 1,137 baptized Christians including 186 adults and 21 children baptized that year. There were 185 catechumens preparing for baptism and 290 hearers who were interested in learning more about Christianity—a total of 2,100 under the direct influence of the Mission.[115] This steady growth continued, and by 1903 the Melanesian Mission claimed that nearly all of the people of Santa Isabel had adopted Christianity.[116]

Theoretical Significance of Conversion.

The above brief description of the cultural context in which conversion to Christianity on Santa Isabel took place will now serve as a backdrop for a more theoretical discussion of conversion as a process of culture change.

How does one define Christian conversion? I find the definition provided by missionary-anthropologist Louis Luzbetak gives one a solid basis for discussion:

> "Conversion" means a "turning" away from the old ways toward new ways, a basic reorientation in premises and goals, a wholehearted acceptance of a new set of values affecting the "convert" as well as his social group, day in and day out, twenty-four hours of the day and in practically every sphere of activity—economic, social and religious. The changes effected must become living parts of the cultural organism (1963: 6).

Although the subject of religious conversion has seldom attracted anthropological inquiry,[117] most of the studies that have been done tend to ignore the active role which the individual performs in his move from one religious self-definition to another, and tend to treat the individual as an object of a conversion experience, as someone who is converted, rather than looking at the individual as the subject of that experience, as someone who converts. Anthropological analysis of conversion should be concerned more with explaining it, rather than simply attempting to "explain it away," by recourse to predisposing socio-cultural factors, background circumstances or situational contingencies. Such analyses tend to rule out empirical considerations of the active role of the subject himself.[118] The socio-cultural and historical setting are very important in understanding religious conversion, and for this reason, I have briefly outlined above the socio-cultural context in which conversion on Santa Isabel took place. But conversion cannot be explained solely in terms of this setting. Writing from a sociological point of view, B. Taylor notes that:

> . . . the crucial task for a sociology of conversion is not to impose determinism upon the actions of individuals but to consider the actual determinisms as they appear to the convert, and to assess his self-determination; its concerns are not with "predispositions" or with "preordination," but with the ways in which the converting individual disposes himself and experiences a process of self-ordination to the adoption of a converted identity (1974: 18-19).

In what follows, I will present a processual model for dealing with religious conversion, and then demonstrate how Barnett's model of innovation, discussed in Chapter 1 (pp. 5–6 and Appendix II), can be used in accounting for individual converts' active role in the conversion process.[119]

Although the Mission literature tends to emphasize conversion as an event, symbolized in baptism, it is nevertheless a process. In fact, this is implied in the Mission's own categories of islanders as diagrammed below:

heathen → **hearers** → **catechumens** → **baptised** → **confirmed**

Fig. 13. Processual Model of Anglican Conversion.

Becoming a Christian in any cultural context is a process, but different stages tend to be symbolized in events, or rites of passage. Conversion is essentially a process of **separation** from an old context, followed by **incorporation** into a new one, and with this, comes a substantial change of identity.[120]

The pattern of conversion throughout most of Oceania has involved group movements.[121] As discussed in Chapter 3 (pp. 128-144), this was the pattern on Mota and Nggela, and it certainly was the case for Santa Isabel. Tippett defines **group** conversion as:

> The process of multi-individual experience and action of a group, through its competent authority, whereby a group changes from one conceptual and behavioral context to another, within the operations of its own structure and decision-making mechanisms regardless of whether or not the external environment changes (1976: 4).

This process can be diagrammed in terms of units of time as three distinct periods: (1) the Period of Awareness, (2) the Period of Decision, and (3) the Period of Incorporation. The movement from one period to another passes through a specific point — the Point of Realization, and the Point of Encounter, indicated as R and E in the following diagram:

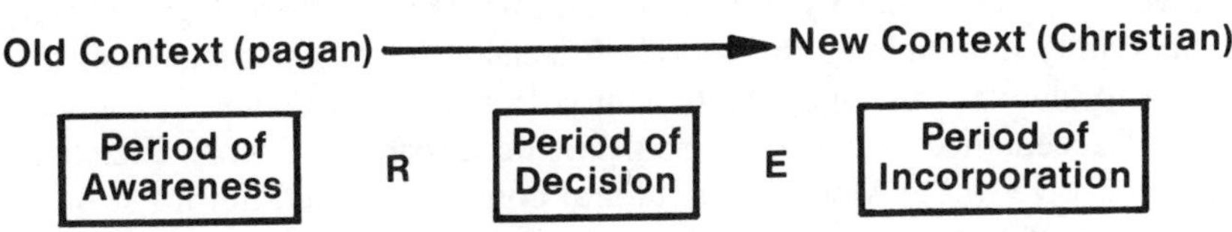

Fig. 14. Schema of the Conversion Process.

Let us now examine the Santa Isabel data in light of this processual model.

Period of Awareness.

Awareness may be accidentally or intentionally stimulated, clearly or vaguely felt, of short or long duration, but it is a necessary beginning point for any innovation. On Santa Isabel, this period of awareness began under the internal pressures from the headhunting crisis that so disrupted social life. As the internal situation increasingly disintegrated, direct advocacy of an alternative way of life was promulgated by the Melanesian Mission. As the headhunting and raiding crisis increased so did greater exposure to Christianity. Although the period 1870-1886 was seemingly unfruitful in terms of the number of converts, it was nevertheless during this era that the foundation for a period of awareness was being laid.

Point of Realization.

The point of realization is a conscious experience that terminates the period of awareness and commences the period of decision. Individuals and groups come to a point where they realize that the passage from the old context into the new is more than an idea; it is a meaningful possibility. It is at the point of realization that the advocate for change plays such a decisive role. Potential converts can remain in a state of awareness for years (as did the Big Man Bera of Santa Isabel) without ever being brought to the point of realization that real change is a possibility for them. The greater the advocate's understanding of the socio-cultural context, the better he can focus his advocacy for change in meaningful terms that help stimulate the point of realization for indigenes. Without a sense of the context in which he advocates the change his message may "fall on deaf ears," or "scratch people where they do not itch," and thus be perceived as irrelevant and meaningless.

Period of Decision.

The period of decision for a communal group may last a long time while village or family discussion continues. It is in this way that a multi-individual decision is made. Individual members of the group, through thoughtful discussion, come to agreement, reach a consensus, and choose to make a decision as a group. Once a group reaches the period of decision, there are three possible outcomes: (1) Rejection, (2) Modification, or (3) Acceptance (See Chapter 1, pp. 7-8).

On Santa Isabel the period of decision for many islanders which led to conversion, began shortly after Bera died in 1884. When Soga endorsed Christianity it stimulated the period of decision for many islanders as they chose to innovate and adopt Christianity. In many ways, their decision was one of acceptance and modification, for the missionary Henry Welchman was sensitive to the Melanesian cultural context, and did not insist on the total acceptance of Anglican Christianity with all its English forms. Welchman advocated change through the indigenous social structure, leaving intact the decision-making units of the society.

Point of Encounter.

The point of encounter is a dramatic experience for both individuals and groups, and climaxes the period of decision. Through discussion the group has ironed out individual differences and is now ready to act in union. As Tippett notes of the encounter process:

> The act itself must be an occular demonstration with a manifest meaning to Christian and pagan alike. It must leave no room for doubt that the old context may still have some of their allegiance, or still hold some power over them . . . **There is clearly a relationship between the manifest form of encounter and the subsequent stability of the new religion,** or to state the principle the other way—**avoid the encounter and increase the reversions** (1976: 14-15).

This point of encounter was met in the discussion of the Nggela Big Man, Kalekona, and his destruction of his *tindalos* in the people movement toward Christianity on that island in the 1880's (Chapter 3, pp. 140-142).[122] Similarly in Welchman's diaries there are numerous references to ancestral shrines (*phadagi*) being destroyed, **not** by the missionary, for he is not the competent authority, but by the converts who had reached a point of encounter in the conversion process.[123]

Period of Incorporation.

The period of incorporation usually begins with an act of incorporation, an event, in which the converts who have chosen to separate themselves from the old pagan context are now incorporated into a new Christian one. In the Melanesian Mission this was the rite of baptism, and in the case of Santa Isabel during Henry Welchman's time, this was not a meaningless symbol, for he demanded a high standard of faith, knowledge and practice in those converts whom he baptized.[124]

It is in the period of incorporation that converts take on a new identity, and in the case of Melanesia, the group now functioned as a meaningful entity that spread beyond the traditional boundaries of geography, kinship and alliance. Converts were incorporated into a group of Christians which was formally identified as a church. It is in this period of incorporation that converts come to either feel that the adopted religion is their own, an important indigenous element of their society, or they tend to perceive it as foreign and alien to their way of life.

The data from Melanesia demonstrate that after some converts have been incorporated into the church, they may in the second, third or even fourth generation after initial conversion, leave the church as they attempt to fulfill deeply felt aspirations through religious movements such as cargo cults. The John Frum split from the Presbyterian Mission, the Silas Eto breakaway from the Methodists in forming the Christian Fellowship Church, and the erosion of Catholics into the Hahalis Welfare Society are examples of these phenomena which were briefly discussed in Chapter 5 (pp. 275-277).

Although the above three periods (Awareness, Decision, Incorporation) seem to account for conversion itself, a fourth period is needed to account for the post-conversion era, after which a church tends to become either indigenous and integrated into the society and culture of the converts, or people leave the church in a neo-pagan revitalization movement. After further research, Tippett (1976: 60-66) concluded that the data demanded an extension of his original model to include a period of maturity, introduced by a point of consummation or confirmation. Thus the original model is expanded to include this period, and is diagrammed as follows:

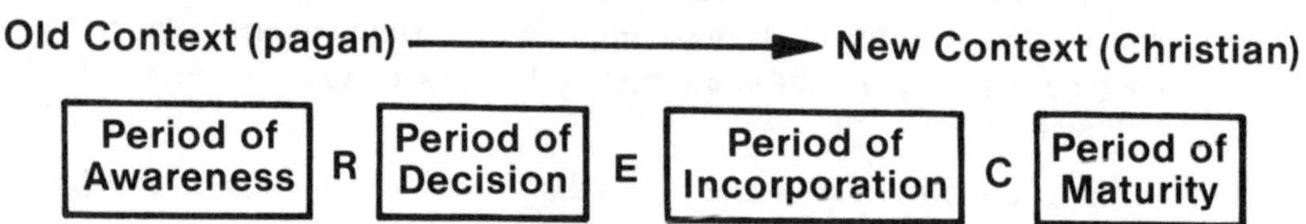

Fig. 15. Processual Model of Conversion and Post-Conversion Activity.

The additions to this model now call for discussion.

Point of Confirmation.

In the Anglican Mission there was an event in which a baptized Christian who had been incorporated into a Christian fellowship group was now advanced further to full membership in the Anglican Church. This act was symbolized by the rite of confirmation which then made the convert eligible to partake of Holy Communion. This was the ultimate religious rite for Christians in the Melanesian Mission. Often baptized converts were postponed for many years before becoming confirmed members of the Church, until they had demonstrated by faith and action that they were truly deserving and committed. Today, in contrast, the adolescent children of Christian parents are confirmed as a matter of course. There is no longer a lengthy period of waiting before this sacred status is bestowed on one.

Period of Maturity.

When it comes to analyzing the period of maturity we find ourselves in the area of what Bidney (1953: 163ff) calls metaanthropology,[125] for we are dealing with a deepening experience of religious belief, and this is a very difficult area to empirically assess, yet it is an integral part of the scientific data. It is during this period of maturity that Melanesian Christians develop their subjective feelings that are the basis for their manifest behavior. This behavior, in turn, can be formally observed in an indigenous island church, or its counterpart—a breakaway neo-pagan revitalization movement.[126]

Conversion and Innovation.

As the processual model developed above attempts to demonstrate, Christian conversion is a movement from one faith to another. It is not a movement from no faith to faith, as many missionaries have erroneously assumed; it is not a new experience in the sense that one's belief emerges from nothing. Conversion is a cultural change, and cultural change implies antecendent conditions. In the case of Melanesians, conversion involved an attitudinal and cognitive change from belief in, and allegiance to, ancestral spirits and numerous other spirit beings believed to control the cosmos. At the base of traditional Melanesian religion was the belief in the power of *mana*. Converts brought to the interaction setting with the missionary an entire corpus of animistic beliefs; they did not come with a religious *tabula rasa*. Thus conversion from animism to Christianity occurred through a recombination of elements and relationships. In other words, it was a Melanesian innovation.

In Arnold van Gennep's (1960) terminology, conversion involves a rite of **separation** from an old pagan and animistic context, and a rite of **incorporation** into a new context of Christian beliefs and practices. Conversion is culture change, change from one context to another, and as such, it is fundamentally a process of innovation. Perhaps by employing Barnett's model of innovation, discussed briefly in Chapter 1 (pp. 5-6) and outlined in more detail in Appendix II, the relationship between conversion will become explicitly clear.

The potential convert comes to the contact situation with an established configuration of religious ideas, and he interprets the missionary's message in terms of his pre-existing configuration, and **not** in terms of the advocate's mental sets.[127] If conversion (an innovation) is to occur, the indigene must discover an element in the missionary's message that is in common with an element in his own religious system. In the case of Melanesians, there were numerous points of contact and identification between their indigenous belief system and the system of Anglican Christianity introduced by missionaries: items such as prayer, ritual, sacrifice, sin and reconciliation, etc.[128] For the purpose of illustration, let us take the concept of power as a point in common between the indigenous religious configuration and Anglican Christianity advocated by the missionary. This can be diagrammed as follows:

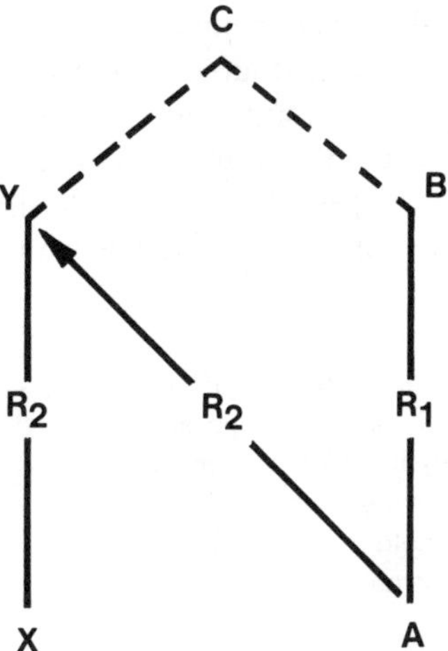

Fig. 16. Conversion in the Context of Innovation.

A Melanesian (A), performs magico-religious rituals (R_1) in order to propitiate ancestral spirits (B). The Christian missionary (X), worships (R_2) the spirit of Jesus Christ (Y). A Melanesian with his indigenous configuration of AR_1B, which we call the prototype, encounters the missionary advocate's stimulus configuration XR_2Y. Now, for an innovation (conversion) to occur, the following two steps are necessary: first, identification, followed by substitution.

Identification. The Melanesian (A) believes that by propitiating (R_1) his ancestral spirits (B), he will obtain *mana* (C), or power. Likewise, the missionary (X) believes that by worshipping (R_2) Jesus Christ (Y), he is promised authority (*exousia* — ἐξουσία) over all other powers (*dunamis* — δύναμις).[129] The point of common identification between the missionary and the Melanesian is **power** (C). That is, for the Melanesian, *mana* (CB) is equivalent to the missionary's *exousia* (CY). The potential convert identifies CY in the missionary's configuration with CB in his own. Thus, the first step in innovation (conversion) has been completed, and now the way is open for the second stage, substitution.

Substitution. The relationship of ancestral spirits (B) to the acquisition of *mana* (C) is **not** an isolated configuration, but it is a sub-whole of a larger, more inclusive configuration, namely AR_1BC. With the expanded cognitive formation of ABC, substitution is now possible because in the process of identification, BC was perceived as equivalent to YC; thus YC substitutes for BC in the indigenous configuration ABC, and a **new** configuration AR_2YC is formed as indicated by the arrow in the diagram. An innovation has occurred. In this case, it is conversion, and the Melanesian (A), now worships (R_2) Jesus Christ (Y) and obtains power (C).

It is unlikely that a Melanesian would substitute allegiance to Christ for allegiance to ancestral spirits solely on the basis of the missionary's theological argument. As discussed in Chapter 2 (pp. 66-67), traditional Melanesian religion was pragmatic, and thus any potential convert would have to be convinced that the power that comes from being a Christian is greater than the power that he receives from propitiating his ancestral spirits. This is precisely why a power encounter was so important in the conversion process — stimulating potential converts to move from the period of decision to the period of incorporation. Tippett underscores the importance of this when he notes:

> In dealing with the psychological processes of conversion in cross-cultural situations, as for example in a missionary program in a communally-structured animist society, it is of basic importance for the evangelist (missionary or national) to recognize that the convert (individual or group) is not just moving from non-faith to faith. He has first to cut himself off from an old, pre-Christian, but nevertheless positive faith; and to demonstrate this in an ocular

> manner in forms socially meaningful to his fellow-countrymen. This may be by burning his fetishes, burying his mana-charged bones or skulls, throwing his sacred paraphernalia into the sea or river, eating his taboo totemic food, destroying the ancestral grove, or some such visible demonstration. Without this, his fellow-countrymen regard the conversion as insincere and likely to be impermanent (1973b: 101).

Tippett goes on to note the importance the concept of conversion-as-innovation has for the potential indigeneity of the adopted religion:

> Where the Christian advocate (missionary or national evangelist) assumes that the process of conversion is merely a passage from a state of nonfaith to faith, he tends to bring about a foreign or westernized conditioning to the resultant congregation, and this can be quite disruptive socially. On the other hand, if he recognizes that something very positive is being surrendered and allows the converts (who are the real innovators) to express themselves through a meaningful act of separation, he tends to retain much more indigeneity in his new congregation (1973b: 101).

What then is the significance of this discussion on conversion for shedding light on the contemporary religious beliefs of Solomon Islanders? I think there are at least two points where this discussion can help our understanding of contemporary beliefs.

(1) If conversion is innovation, as I have argued, then it follows that some elements of the traditional religious configuration in the minds of Melanesians would continue to persist. If conversion was from nonfaith to faith, then one might expect the convert to have identical faith, in form and function, with that of the person who introduced it. But conversion is **not** a change from nonfaith to faith; instead, it is a shift from one faith to another, from allegiance to ancestral spirits to allegiance to Jesus Christ. Therefore, some elements in the traditional configuration will persist, even though the basic orientation and allegiance of the person has changed.[130] The Melanesians' faith will be different from the missionaries' because their pre-Christian configuration is different. And this is what I mean when I speak of an indigenous Melanesian Christianity — a Christian belief system that has some elements of Melanesian thought in it, one that is meaningful to Melanesians in terms of their cognitive configurations, and one that meets the needs of individuals and groups immersed in a Melanesian environment.

Thus today, one finds many traditional elements in the Solomon Islanders' belief system, and where Christianity is perceived to be foreign, it is because islanders have not been encouraged to indigenize it, but instead, have been persuaded that the missionary's model is the only legitimate model of Christian belief and practice.

(2) Another point that bears on the contemporary situation is that third and fourth generation Christians are **not** experiencing what I have described here — conversion as innovation from animism to Christianity in the context of a society in disequilibrium from the effects of headhunting and warfare. In Anglican villages today, islanders do not think in terms of conversion from animism to Christianity. They perceive infant baptism as the crucial religious rite that makes one a Christian, and later, the rite of confirmation which incorporates an adolescent into the church as a communicant. It is a predictable, cultural evolutionary process, without the points of encounter experienced by the first generation Christians. I think this may help to explain the general lack of enthusiasm for Christianity that third and fourth generation Anglican converts have. There is no significant contrast now between the old (pagan) and the new (Christian) context, because islanders are born into the new context, and thus the dynamism of religious experience that many first generation Christians have, tends to be lacking in most third and fourth generation Anglican Christians in the Solomon Islands today.

Summary of Conversion as Innovation.

In summary we can see how important it is to understand the socio-cultural context of headhunting and warfare on Santa Isabel as a precursor to the revitalization of the society in the form of a people movement toward Christianity. The religion introduced by missionaries was a viable solution out of a cultural trap that had been precipitated by the escalation of headhunting and internecine warfare. Although the socio-cultural context in which conversion occurred is an important element in any explanatory hypothesis, it is nevertheless inadequate by itself. For this reason, I have attempted to show how conversion is an innovative response made by individuals, albeit in the context of the larger group. As an innovation, conversion to Christianity involves a recombination of cultural elements and relationships, and thus there is frequently continuity of some cultural elements from the pre-conversion to the post-conversion era. I have also attempted to demonstrate in this section that conversion is a cultural process, not simply a crisis experience — a process involving distinct evolutionary periods and eventful points in the movement from a pagan to a Christian identity.

The Integration of Christianity in Melanesian Society and Culture

When the Melanesian Mission introduced Anglican Christianity into Melanesian society, it introduced far more than simply an alternative belief system. Although missionaries advocating conversion to Christianity were **primarily** concerned with islanders' changing their beliefs and giving allegiance to Christian doctrines, the concomitant changes that occurred with conversion exceeded changes in islanders' ideology. New elements of material culture, new behavioral patterns, new ritual, new social roles, etc. were part and parcel of the "New Way of Life" advocated by Anglican missionaries and adopted by Melanesians.

As I have discussed previously in this chapter, and indeed, implied throughout this study, socio-cultural change in Melanesia was the result of missionaries' **advocation** and the islanders' **innovation**. The changes advocated by missionaries were frequently reinterpreted by Melanesians, and so the "change" was often far less, or very different from the missionaries' preconceived notions of what an ideal Christian Melanesian society should be.[131] Credit must be given, however, to the Melanesian Mission for at least conceiving of the possibility of a Christian society that was also Melanesian. Most of the other missionary organizations in this area tended to view "Christian" and "Melanesian" as antithetical categories. To these types of missionaries the concept of a Christian Melanesian society was a contradiction of terms for they saw little redeeming value in the traditional Melanesian culture.

In this section I will address the problem of socio-cultural integration in terms of the degree to which Christianity has become integrated into Melanesian society and culture. But preliminary to this discussion, it will be helpful to first focus on the concept of socio-cultural integration.

This concept has played an important role in studies of culture change. Pre-World War II cultural theorists tended to see healthy functioning cultural systems as highly integrated in a state of equilibrium and stability. Conversely, any social change, especially rapid change, was perceived as likely to lead to disequilibrium, maladjustment and dysfunction of the cultural system. It is noteworthy that in the post-war era there has been a shift from static to dynamic thinking, and so the concept of integration is presently perceived as a quality of culture that is never perfect, never completely coherent and harmonious. But neither is integration ever absent. There is always some integration of cultural elements despite contradictions, tensions and inconsistencies between the parts of the whole. If there was a complete absense of integration between cultural elements a society could no longer exist.

Although the concept of socio-cultural integration has been frequently used by anthropologists in studies of culture change, it nevertheless remains a somewhat vague and illusive concept.[132] In my mind, integration is essentially a structural property in which the elements of culture, in the form of ideas, behavior patterns, and material products, are integrally related to each other, forming a relatively coherent cultural system. The degree of integration for any cultural element is related to its articulation and compatibility with other cultural and sociological variables within the social system.

Thus if a particular cultural element is said to be highly integrated into a socio-cultural system, this means it is compatible with, and has structural linkages to, many other elements within that socio-cultural system. For example, the automobile is highly integrated into American society. Its obvious purpose is transportation, but it has become such an integral part of what we call the "American Way of Life" that it performs many more functions than simply transporting people from one place to another. For example, we use the automobile as a status marker for prestige in our highly materialistic society. It functions as a symbol of rugged individualism and the spirit of freedom which we prize so much. Teenage couples use an automobile as a haven of privacy, but cease to use it for this function once they are married. The automobile has profoundly affected our work habits, our family relationships, the organization of our voluntary associations such as churches, our buying patterns, and so on. In fact, the automobile has become so integrated into so many aspects of our culture that it may very well prove to be the largest obstacle in preventing Americans from responding appropriately to the present-day energy crisis.

In this study I am concerned with trying to understand how well the various cultural elements associated with Christianity, as advocated by the Melanesian Mission, have become integrated into contemporary Melanesian village life among members of the Church of Melanesia. I have found Spicer's (1961) discussion of culture change in American Indian societies to be a helpful approach in sharpening the focus of this concept of socio-cultural integration as it relates to culture change. He notes:

> What has been most interesting about contact situations has been the wide variety in the results of contact. Every contact involves some degree of social and cultural integration, but there is a wide range in what become more or less stabilized situations with varying degrees of integration (1961:519).

Spicer suggests four types of socio-cultural integration which I have found to be analytically most helpful in analyzing the degree to which change advocated by the Melanesian Mission has become integrated into contemporary Anglican villages in the Solomon Islands. These four types are defined as follows.

1. Incorporative Integration. The model of incorporative integration refers to:

> . . . the transfer of elements from one cultural system and their integration into another system in such a way that they conform to the meaningful and functional relations within the latter . . . Incorporative integration is a type of tradition combination which results in totally new forms being accepted into a culture in such a way that they enhance the existing organization of that culture (1961:530).

Incorporative integration is not disruptive to the society. Although new forms are adopted they are used to express traditional meanings and fulfill traditional functions.

2. Assimilative Integration. This form of integration is the very opposite of incorporative integration, for here the emphasis is upon "the acceptance and replacement of cultural behaviors in terms of the dominant society's cultural system" (1961:531). In this model of integration there is no attempt to harmonize the introduced cultural elements with the indigenous cultural system.

3. Fusional Integration. This model of integration is similar to F. E. Williams' notion of the blending of cultures discussed in this study (Chapter 1, pp. 10-12; Chapter 6, pp. 323-324). A common example of fusional integration is where cultural forms introduced by the dominant society become fused with meanings from the subordinate society and a syncretism results. Spicer notes that:

> The essentials of fusion are that elements of two or more distinct cultural traditions be involved, that they are combined into a single system, and that the principles in terms of which they combine not be the same as those governing the cultural systems from which they come (1961:532).

4. Isolative Integration. In this model of integration, cultural elements introduced into a society are adopted, but they remain isolated from other aspects of the society and become compartmentalized. Spicer notes that:

> . . . in isolative integration the accepted elements lack linkage with other complexes, despite serving very similar or identical functions. The lack of linkage leads to their being isolated with the culture in a distinct subsystem of meanings (1961:533-534).

These four models of integration will serve as focal points in the following analysis. I will argue that an important index of indigeneity is the degree to which introduced change has become integrated into a society by those members who have adopted the new idea, institution, artifact, etc. as their own.

When I use the term "indigenous" I am referring to the way in which indigenes perceive and identify particular cultural elements introduced into their society. If they perceive them as their own, and identify them as "our custom" then these elements have become internalized into the culture. That is, they have become indigenous despite their origin.[133] I believe that introduced cultural elements that are well integrated into the receptor's society, are also more likely to become indigenized. And conversely, the more indigenized an element becomes, the more likely it will become a well integrated cultural element within that society.

In this section I am specifically concerned with evaluating the degree to which the Church of Melanesia, as an autonomous Anglican Church, is in fact an indigenous church. To rephrase the problem, one can ask, "Is the Church of Melanesia only an autonomous Anglican Province, or is it also an indigenous Melanesian church?"

I had been in the Solomon Islands less than a week when I was told by non-Anglican informants that of all the missions in the Solomons, the Melanesian Mission had been the most influential and successful, for they had set as their goal the establishment of a Melanesian church. They had of course fallen short of the mark at times, as this study has documented, but it had nevertheless been the conscious aim of the Mission, and thus today, the Church of Melanesia is more of an Island church (as opposed to a European one) than any of the other denominations in the Solomons. These and similar remarks seemed to reinforce what the Mission literature had indicated. That is, Anglican missionaries had not come to Melanesia with the intention of converting islanders into **English** Christians, but had come believing that Christianity could transform, without destroying, Melanesian culture. That is, the essential integrity of Melanesian society remained, allowing it to function in equilibrium, even though particular cultural elements in that society were changed.

Today the Church of Melanesia appears to be very much of an island enterprise. Although the provincial headquarters resembles a European business corporation, the clergy in the Church are all Melanesians,[133] and indeed, at every turn, islanders are functioning in responsible roles throughout the province. There are no longer any European missionaries dominating the scene. Just because all the missionaries have gone home, does this imply that the Church is automatically indigenous? Certainly not, and yet this notion was at the basis of many peoples' thinking in the not so distant era of "missionary go home" and the "moratorium on missionaries." It is still an unquestioned assumption among some churches today. If one is to evaluate the degree to which the church is indigenous one must look beyond the professional clergy to different levels of socio-cultural integration in the context of Melanesian village life. The degree to which Anglican Christianity has become integrated into contemporary Melanesian society can be analyzed in terms of many different cultural dimensions. I have chosen to briefly discuss indigenous integration in six of these dimensions: (1) material culture, (2) worship patterns, (3) behavior, (4) socio-ceremonial life, (5) financial self-support, and (6) beliefs.

1. Material Culture.

As I discussed earlier, Christianity was introduced into Melanesia as a "package deal." Included with the new ideology were also elements of material culture. This association of material culture with Christianity is seen, for example, in the construction of village chapels. Here is a place where men and women perform religious ritual **together**, which is indeed an innovation. Traditionally, the mixing of men and women in religious activities would seldom, if ever, have happened.

When it comes to the dimension of material culture, one is struck by the high degree of indigenous forms used in the church. Most village chapels are built in an indigenous style of architecture using local materials of sago palm leaf, timber and bamboo for construction. In recent years, however, on some islands, there has been a growing trend toward villages competing with each other in building large chapels, using cement, sawn lumber and corrugated iron roofing. Although still incorporating indigenous architecture, these "permanent style" chapels have become prestige symbols. Nowhere is this more evident than on the island of Santa Isabel, where villages of only 150 people will raise up to $5,000 to build a chapel capable of seating 600 people. The cost of the building is also a status symbol, and news of the expenditure travels quickly from one village to another. In one village I was surprised to discover the total cost of the church prominently displayed above the church door for all to see, admire and envy:

St. Mark's Chapel
Kolotubi
$4,330.12

One bishop in the province has become so alarmed at this new trend that he has forbidden the construction of village chapels out of anything but local materials.

The Melanesian Mission encouraged islanders to maintain and further expand their indigenous arts and crafts. Thus they have produced richly ornamented altars, crosses, lecterns, baptismal fonts, candlesticks, etc., frequently using the medium of inlaid of mother-of-pearl from the Nautilus shell.[134] The interior of many village chapels is striking, especially on Santa Isabel, where indigenous art forms have been employed to create a distinctly Melanesian atmosphere.

In many ways, village chapels serve as functional substitutes for traditional shrines and club houses, the main difference being that **both** men and women participate in activities associated with this structure. The chapel is nearly always the dominant architectural feature — the largest structure located in the center of the village. Following the Anglican tradition, most village chapels are laid out east to west, regardless of whether or not this is in line with the village pattern.

Villagers perceive chapels in much the same way they traditionally perceived shrines and club houses. That is, they are believed to have *mana* and are therefore *tabu*.[135] The only activities that take place inside are daily formal worship services, and occasionally choir practice in the evenings. Announcements important to villagers are made outside the chapel after everyone has filed out. Village-wide meetings are held in the open or around a Big Man's house, never in the chapel. Smoking twist tobacco and chewing betel nut are part and parcel of every village gathering, but people never do this in church. Pipes are generally left outside. The village chapel is a sacred place, the center of religious activities. This discussion of the village chapel leads us logically into the next dimension of culture — the pattern of worship that takes place within the chapel.

2. Patterns of Anglican Worship in the Village.

Christianity for many Melanesians has become what Hagesi (1972:97) calls "church-centered." For example, the word "Jesus" or the names of the disciples and apostles have for many years been *tabu*. The only place appropriate or safe to mention them was in the village chapel, the holy place. This belief is slowly disappearing with the introduction of "sunday school" songs for children, which are sung around the village and contain these sacred names. For many, Christianity is an exercise of religious ritual that takes place in the chapel, divorced from daily activities such as gardening, fishing and hunting. This church-centered worship pattern was observed by Tippett more than a decade ago in an Anglican village on North Malaita. He notes:

> My impression was that religion was associated with the church building, which was always there for anyone to use and was regarded as sacred. Pipes, knives and other secular things were never taken inside and put in the pocket or under the seat. They were left outside. One by one they would take a last draw from the pipe, then set it in the fork of a tree or a cleft in a rock, and go on into church (1967: 318).

If the church architecture and furnishings tend to be highly indigenous, the worship pattern inside the building is considerably less so. Daily morning and evening prayers follow closely the Church of England *Book of Common Prayer* (1662) in a liturgical style of formal prayers, creeds and scriptural anthems. The *Kalendar and Lectionary* for the COM provides the structure for daily scripture reading, weekly topics and concerns for prayer, and the daily color of the altar cloth to be used. It also lends uniformity of worship throughout all the Anglican churches. Hymn selection is varied but shows a strong soteriological emphasis. This formal service of standing, sitting, kneeling, reciting and singing lasts fifteen to twenty minutes. At the close of Morning Prayer most women remain in the chapel for a few minutes to recite a prayer for the Mothers' Union,[136] and in the evening, village members of the Companions remain to recite a formal prayer for the Melanesian Brotherhood. There are, of course, many villages in which membership in these two voluntary associations is weak, but on Santa Isabel, both have strong membership with considerable village participation.

I have discussed previously the problem of worshipping in a language that villagers do not understand or with a translation of the Prayer Book that is so archaic it has lost much of its original meaning, assuming the correct meaning was assigned in the initial translation (Chapter 6, pp. 348-349). This tends to underscore the foreignness of worship and may be a contributing factor in villagers' imputing an aura of magic to the incomprehensible prayers and readings, believing it is not necessary to understand what is being said, since one receives *mana* simply through their recitation.[137] Although villagers may not understand the content of the Prayer Book, Bible and Hymn Book, they nevertheless consider them to have *mana* and to be *tabu*. In many villages these are used only in the chapel and left there with the other "holy paraphernalia" when people leave the chapel and return to their houses.

The music in the church is primarily Victorian English hymns and Gregorian and Merbecke's plain-song. On Santa Isabel, a woman is assigned the task of starting the hymn — a role she plays with pride, and one of which she can become very possessive. Although there is a rich Melanesian tradition of poetry and music in many societies, there has been little effort in the past to incorporate this into the Anglican worship service. There is, however, a growing awareness today among some islanders for the need to incorporate indigenous tunes into the worship pattern. Some innovations have occurred in the music of worship in Lau (North Malaita) and Arosi (San Cristobal) and are being developed elsewhere in the province.[138] A Solomon Islander's perception of Anglican worship underscores the non-Melanesian character of the service. He says:

> When Christianity came, Christian music was understood as calm and dignified. Music is therefore restricted. There is no freedom of expression, shaking of the body and dancing etc.
>
> One of the reasons that the Church is often dull is that we have been taught to hide our emotions. We are suppose to sit in church and be pious, with a long face and not move. On Sundays when the service is too long with a boring sermon, people go to sleep. But if there is one place where we should have joy it is in the Church.
>
> Church Music that is dull has no joy. Over the years we have been taught to distrust anything that is of the body. If the body responds in Church it is regarded as sinful. How then do we explain David dancing in front of the altar before the Lord (II Samuel 6: 14)?[139]

I have discussed above the importance of Holy Communion and the magical framework in which it is interpreted. Although there are many traditional parallels to this rite, the way in which it is performed is alien and non-Melanesian. Hagesi claims that:

> Holy Communion is something from outside the Solomons. It does not have the Melanesian pattern of fellowship and bread and

> wine are something known to be uncommon for the people. It is not the fruit of their labour that is being offered. The people go for Holy Communion because they have to, but really it is something alien and mysterious. They do not understand what it means and a mixture of Christian and pre-Christian beliefs are bound up with it (1972:90-91).

Despite the splendid Melanesian tradition of ritual, poetry and music, it has not been integrated nor incorporated into the life of the Anglican Church in the islands. There have been a few experimental services in which islanders have attempted to express their worship through traditional symbols and activities. Islanders were quick to point out that when Holy Communion was performed in this manner the meaning it conveyed to them was far greater than the standard COM service. These have been occasional experimental services and to date have not entered the life of the village congregations. The bishops of the COM have tended to be quite conservative when it comes to "tampering" with the formal worship service. They have been hesitant to do anything other than perpetuate the pattern taught to them by the European missionaries.

The pattern of Anglican worship in Melanesia is today more reminiscent of the Church of England in England than of Melanesian modes of worship. This alien pattern of worship has undoubtedly contributed to many islanders' perception that:

> Christianity is still regarded as a foreign religion, something which is imposed on the people from outside; whereas it should now be founded on the life of the Solomon Islands society and express itself in the patterns and thought-forms of the people.[140]

In summary, it is evident that although there is a great resource of traditional Melanesian culture from which the Church of Melanesia could draw to indigenize and better integrate the worship pattern, it has not done so heretofore. It is still relying primarily on the pattern of worship introduced by European missionaries. Nevertheless, there is a minority of priests and others who are charting new avenues and exercising creative thinking about ways in which Anglican worship can become Christian worship in a Melanesian way.

3. The Integration of Christian Modes of Behavior.

Christianity has been influential in changing behavior in Melanesia. But one should be cautious and not assume that all behavioral changes are the result of conversion to Christianity. It is difficult, if not unproductive, to attempt to analytically separate all motivational forces that impinge on contemporary Melanesian behavioral patterns. Nevertheless, Christianity has provided a convenient rationale as an ideological base for behavioral changes.[141] In discussing the relationship between behavioral changes and an introduced set of values, Barnett notes that:

> Profound social and economic changes have followed upon the indoctrination of one ethnic group with the values of another. The acceptance of an idea entails the acceptance of some correlate which supports or complements it (1953: 93).

Thus the adoption of Christianity, which values peace and solidarity, meant adopting extra-religious ideas and behavior as well.

The most significant of these changes has been the reduction of overt violence, and indeed, the complete eradication of violence-laden customary practices such as headhunting, raiding, widow strangling, human sacrifice and cannibalism. Christianity was identified initially as the "Way of Peace" and thus its adoption provided an ideological rationale for a shift from violent to peaceful behavior as part and parcel of conversion to Christianity.[142] In discussing the contrast of life today with life before Christianity came, the predominant theme in conversations with islanders is the contrast of peaceful ways now with violent ways before. A retrospective evaluation of pagan days may tend to exaggerate the violent aspects of pre-Christian life, but given this possible tendency among some informants, there is still, nevertheless, an abundance of ethnohistorical evidence to support the claim that the pre-Christian life in Melanesia was violence-laden.

It must not be assumed however, that aggressive behavior was a cultural ideal for all aspects of pre-Christian Melanesian society. In fact, it was proscribed within the limited boundary of one's own kin group which was the moral basis of society. The primary impact of Christianity on Melanesian society was the expansion of the definition of "Who is my brother?" beyond the narrow confines of kinsmen to include all human beings — even, or especially, one's traditional enemies. G. White cogently articulates this process of change in the moral order when he notes that:

> The behavioral ideals expressed in Mission morality emphasize the virtues of cooperation, obedience and the denial of hostility or aggression in all contexts. It is not so much the content of these ideas as the shift from a particularistic to a universalistic morality which is innovative (1978: 395).

It is this shift from the particular to the universal that expanded the boundaries of the moral community which then provided avenues for expansion in other areas. Thus, for example, the migration of people from scattered bush hamlets to the larger aggregates of coastal villages was facilitated by conversion to Christianity and the adoption of a broader base of morality beyond the confines of kinship.[143]

There is, of course, some discrepancy between this Christian ideal and actual behavior, but the important fact remains, that the adoption of Christianity has influenced a Melanesian shift in cultural focus, away from violent and aggressive behavior toward peaceful relations beyond the boundary of the kin group. In this behavioral sense, Christianity is well integrated into contemporary Melanesian society. The prescribed model of behavior is one that emphasizes the solidarity of the community. Thus, attributes of kindness, humility, peacefulness, obedience, etc., all of which contribute to group cohesiveness, are those which are highly valued today.[144]

Another important behavioral arena which demonstrates the integration of Christianity into Melanesian society is that of male-female relationships. Traditionally there was a sharp demarcation between male and female spheres of activity. If men represented the sacred domain, then women represented the profane. It was men who were the dominant socio-political leaders, and men who were the specialists in religious ritual. Melanesia is still very much of a "man's world" today, but the social gap between men and women has narrowed considerably under the influence of Christianity. The ideological position of Christianity *vis a vis* men and women, at least in theory, makes no distinction between male and female — salvation is for all.

Through the organization of the Anglican Mothers' Union, introduced into Melanesia by missionaries in the 1930's, women in the village have an important framework for socio-religious activities. The efforts of the Mothers' Union are designed to stimulate an applied Christianity in the homes of its members. Although the Mother's Union is not uniformly strong throughout the COM, it is well organized on Santa Isabel, with the Maringe district having the most active participation of village women. Women travel to other villages of distances up to ten miles or more to participate in the monthly meetings, and local village bazaars are held occasionally to raise money for specific projects. This freedom of women to "walkabout" is hailed by many of the islanders today as one of the most significant behavioral changes made possible by the adoption of Christianity.

In the same way that islanders today seem to exaggerate the violent nature of pre-Christian Melanesia, so too they tend to downgrade the role that women traditionally had in comparison to their freedom of movement and equality of status today. Allowing for such retrospective inflationary evaluations, it is nevertheless clear that the behavior of women is substantially different today from what it was in the pre-Christian period, and this is primarily due to the influence of an ideology that tends to promote equality of the sexes.

There has also been another change, but not one advocated by the missionaries. This has been the increase in adultery with the coming of the church. Although Christian ideology strongly forbids adultery, the punishment prescribed is less severe than what traditional Melanesian morality usually demanded — the killing of both guilty partners. With the institutions of confession to a priest, and absolution in Holy Communion, forgiveness is easily obtained.[145]

I have highlighted only two areas of Melanesian behavior, the reduction of overt violence and a change in male-female relationships, that have been influenced by the islanders' adoption of Christianity. There is, of course, a continuous strain between the old and the new, the ideal and the actual, but a new social identity and behavioral expectations have indeed penetrated Melanesian society.

4. Anglican Christianity and Melanesian Socio-Ceremonial Life.

For many Anglican communities in Melanesia the church is the focus of village social life. This is perhaps most evident on the island of Santa Isabel where the church takes precedent over the government as the dominant institution around which social activities are organized.[146] In many ways, the ceremonial and social calendar is set by the church, with the Anglican "Christian Year" of important "Red Letter Days" providing the pattern and rhythm of socio-religious occasions. Baptism and confirmation are important *rites de passage* in the life of an Anglican, and are thus occasions for celebrating and feasting. The most important day however, in terms of a village's socio-religious identity is the annual "Church Day," commemorating the patron saint of the village. Each village chapel is named for a saint, martyr, or even a Mission personality such as Bishop Patteson or Charles Fox, or a famous indigenous priest such as Hugo Hebala.[147]

On this day Holy Communion is celebrated, usually with more than one priest in attendance, and a large feast is provided by the host village for all the guests who have come from other villages. Preparation for the day's important activities begins weeks and months in advance. Occasionally special gardens of taro and/or sweet potato are grown, men organize parties for hunting wild pig, and others go fishing or in search of mud clams. Tinned meat, bread, rice and tea are usually served to honored guests, i.e., priests, village catechists, and other visiting dignitaries, and this entails an outlay of cash. Thus the village usually organizes to make several bags of copra, which when sold at 8¢ per pound can provide ready income for such occasions. These feast days can become lavish occasions, and villages tend to compete with each other for the most food prepared, the most priests in attendance, the most people, the best dancing, the biggest bazaar, etc. In one extreme case, a village on Nggela a few years ago spent $5,000 on a feast day, although that same village had not made its annual assessment (church tax) to the general operating fund of the church.[148] Competitive feasting between rival Big Men is a traditional Melanesian pattern. Although the occasion has changed, and the new pattern is a church celebration of a village's patron saint, these feasts, in many ways, represent new means by which old cultural values are realized.

In addition to the annual celebration of a village's patron saint, Christmas and Easter are also occasions that stimulate social activities. For example, on Santa Isabel an entire village will visit another village to serenade them with Christmas carols. The host village then provides a feast for their guests, who may spend several days in the village. Occasionally a village will travel a considerable distance over rough terrain or charter a ship. It is, of course, expected that the host village will reciprocate the following year or two later. If a village should be so fortunate as to have one of its young men ordained to the priesthood, then this becomes another great occasion for feasting and celebrating. This is always a great day in the life of a village, as is the dedication of a new village chapel.

The church also provides occasions that stimulate additional socio-economic activities. For example, in addition to the Mother's Union bazaars noted above, a village will use similar occasions to raise money for a new "permanent" style church, or some other type of community-wide project. The village participates together in first providing and then buying from each other island produce such as coconuts, sugar cane, betel nut, fish, wild pig, crabs, etc. Traditional puddings are made and sold along with bread and tea. It is a great festive occasion and by village standards, also economically remunerative, for it is not uncommon for a village to be able to raise $50 or more in one day.

Thus the monotonous routine of daily village life is broken by socio-religious celebrations provided by the church. On Santa Isabel, even "secular" occasions such as the opening of a trade store or building a house, are made "sacred" by calling on the priest for his prayers and blessing. This is, of course, followed by a feast for all in attendance.

To a European observer, accustomed to greater separation between institutionalized religion and daily secular activities, the closeness of the relationship between the church and daily life is most striking. In fact, I have come to the conclusion that the primary function of the COM in Anglican villages in Melanesia is more social than religious, if we can draw an analytical distinction between the two. By this I mean that people look to the church more to organize their social occasions than to meet their spiritual needs. It is the church that sets a daily pattern of morning and evening prayer, and it is the church that provides the primary *rites de passage*, and the opportunities for celebrations and festivals. As a social framework regulating village life, it is indeed well integrated into contemporary Melanesian society. The rhythms of socio-ceremonial life pulsate with church-related activities, on a daily basis, and a yearly cycle.

5. The Church of Melanesia and the Problem of Self-Support.

When it comes to the cultural dimension of self-support, one discovers that the Church of Melanesia is far from indigenous, for it depends on overseas aid and income generated from the COM Trust Board to cover nearly one hundred percent of its operating costs.

A theme one hears continually from the bishops and the provincial headquarters is the need for "Christian Stewardship," i.e., for villagers to contribute a greater share of the operating cost of "their" church. Nevertheless, these cries for greater giving appear to fall on deaf ears. To illustrate the severity of this problem I have constructed the following table (Table 6.7, p. 386) of local giving for the year 1977. Each diocese promised to raise twenty percent of their own operating costs, but as can be seen, this was not met.[149]

As can be seen by Table 6.7, only the Diocese of Ysabel came close to meeting its promised assessment, which would have been only twelve percent of its own operating cost, and this does not include the salaries paid to its clergy.

Table 6.8 (p. 386) gives the amount of income that is provided for each diocese from the provincial headquarters which draws from outside funds (cf. Table 6.2., p. 330).

As can be seen by these tables, the local village contribution toward meeting the church expenditure ranges from a high of nine percent in the Diocese of Ysabel to only one percent in the Diocese of New Hebrides (Vanuatu). The evidence is clear; this is not a self-supporting church. It is reliant almost completely on funds from outside Melanesia.

This lack of self-support is a perplexing problem to church leaders and they are stymied in creating ways to stimulate "Christian Stewardship." Although most of the COM rhetoric is aimed at convincing people that it is their Christian duty, or that giving to the church is an index of their love for God, it has heretofore produced limited results. In many ways this lack of giving at the village level is a legacy from the Melanesian Mission. "They never taught us anything about stewardship," the archbishop informed me, "They just gave us what we asked for."[150]

This lack of giving by Melanesians is an interesting anthropological problem, for it is more than a statement of a people's economic resources. It is a statement about what they perceive to be culturally significant and important. Thus, for example, contributing to the general operating fund of the COM is not as important for most villagers as is building their own chapel, or hosting an elaborate feast on their festival day.

For most islanders, the Church of Melanesia is simply an extension of the former Melanesian Mission. Melanesians did not perceive the Mission as their own, nor do they perceive the COM as their **own** church, for they are continually asking what the COM will do for them, rather than what they can do for the church.[151] In contrast, the village chapel, or a feast prepared on a "Church Day" **does** belong to the villagers; it is an emblem of their social identity. For something that is perceived as their own, there is plenty of incentive to raise money through cooperative communal activities. Money and resources are available to do what the village perceives as culturally important. Thus far, the operating cost of the COM has not fallen into the same cognitive category as building a local chapel or holding a large feast. Until it does, the COM will continue to be perceived by most villagers as a

Diocese	Number of Anglicans	Promised Giving	Actual Giving	Percent of Promised	Amount per Anglican Promised	Amount per Anglican Actual
Central Melanesia	37,157	$15,672	$8,529	54.4%	$0.42	$0.23
Ysabel	12,710	8,819	8,684	98.4%	0.69	0.68
Malaita	16,501	9,941	3,302	33.2%	0.60	0.20
New Hebrides	15,000 (est.)	9,163	1,587	17.3%	0.61	0.10
TOTAL	81,638	$46,455	$22,102			

Table 6.7. Analysis of Local Giving in the Church of Melanesia, 1977.

Diocese	Clergy Pay	Capital Grant	Diocesan Grant	Provincial Expense	Institutions' Expense	Total Provincial Contribution	Ratio of Local Giving to Provincial Expenditure
Central Melanesia	$ 53,138	$ 3,500	$18,779	$ 75,710	$101,088	$252,215	$1 : $29.57
Ysabel	21,114	3,500	7,553	25,897	34,579	92,643	1 : 10.67
Malaita	25,943	13,500	12,035	33,622	44,892	129,992	1 : 39.37
New Hebrides	23,265	7,000	36,350	30,563	55,200	152,378	1 : 96.02
TOTAL	$123,460	$27,500	$74,717	$165,792	$235,759	$627,228	$1 : $28.38

Table 6.8. Analysis of Provincial Grants made to the Church of Melanesia Dioceses, 1977-1978.

Tables 6.6 and 6.7: COM Statistics.

Missionary Institution — not an Indigenous Church, and local giving to support it will continue to remain sparse.

6. The Integration of Christian Beliefs.

In 1977 the archbishop called for a year of "Spiritual Renewal" in the Church of Melanesia. Church leaders believed that Anglican Christianity in Melanesia was in a lethargic state and in need of revitalization and renewal. In numerous discussions I held with church leaders, it was invariably declared that the church was weak, that Christianity at the village level was poorly understood, imperfectly practiced and relegated to a position of irrelevance by many. It is true that for many present-day second, third and fourth generation Christians, Christianity as a religion lacks much of the initial dynamism it had in the past. Many of today's Christians have had no experience of "metanoia," i.e., they have been born into the faith, not converted to it. The dynamics of conversion in the first generation of Christians are often lacking in the second and third generations. This is primarily because the cultural context, out of which the first generation was converted, has changed dramatically for the subsequent generations of Christians.

Although traditionally Melanesians may have analytically separated the sacred from the profane, they did not do so psychologically, for life was seen whole, with the "spirit" world and the "natural" world inextricably intertwined in the everyday affairs of living. Today "work" and "worship" are seen as separate entities, and worship is increasingly an activity carried on within the confines of the village chapel. This divorce of Christianiy from everyday life is indeed the antithesis of traditional Melanesian religion where one was continually in touch with the spirits, enlisting their help in every activity.

There is also a sense among many villagers today that Christianity does not have the power their old religion had. As one informant noted, "In the heathen religion when we prayed we got results — when we prayed for rain, it rained. But today there is no power in our religion. What is wrong?" As noted in Chapter 2 (pp. 72-75), power is/was the essence of Melanesian religion, and so Christian priests like Hugo Hebala and Eric Gnhokro were seen as manifestations of the vitality and validity of Christianity because through it, they demonstrated miraculous feats of power.[152] Today this is believed to be lacking among laymen and clergy alike, although there are always individual exceptions.

Undoubtedly, one of the contributing factors to the general feeling among many islanders that there is no power in their faith is that many continue to perceive Christianity as the religion of the European missionary, for as Hagesi (1972:86) notes, "Christianity is still regarded as a foreign religion, something which is imposed on the people from outside."

For many Melanesians the practice of Christianity is motivated out of fear as much, if not more than, out of love and understanding. They attend the formal worship service out of a sense of obligation and fear of the consequences for not attending. This, of course, is not the model of Christianity the Anglican missionaries intended to introduce, but it appears to be the model that many islanders have adopted, for it is a highly salient one for many in the village today.

There is an increasing drift among Melanesian Anglicans, away from the "true Christian" toward the "nominal Christian." Tippett (1967: 308-318) interprets this process in terms of stages in drift from "nuclear" to "marginal" to "nominal" Christians. Islanders today recognize these different categories of Christians, and speak of them in terms of "Committed Christians" and "Christians-in-name-only." In recognition of the growing number of nominal Christians in the COM, church leaders have developed what they call "Team Ministries" that travel to the villages to teach, encourage and revitalize the people. The Melanesian Brotherhood has been increasingly used to revitalize nominal Christian communities, a significant shift from its original objective to work only among pagans. It is interesting to note that with this end in mind, the Brothers were sent to Mota in the early 1960's — Mota, the first island to convert to Christianity in the Melanesian Mission, was in need of revitalization.

This pattern of nominalism throughout the Church of Melanesia is one that has leaders duly concerned; thus, the call for a year of "Spiritual Renewal" in 1977, the creation of Team Ministries in the dioceses, and the reorientation of the Melanesian Brotherhood. In 1979-80 a "Commitment Programme" was inaugurated. Its aims are to foster Christian growth and deepen the understanding and commitment of Anglican Christians, promote stewardship and develop a more effective program of pastoral care.

This growing nominalism and apparent lack of integration of Christian beliefs with everyday life is undoubtedly the product of a long period of Melanesian Mission activity. I believe the primary reason for this present state is the Mission's lack of teaching at the village level. Of course this was not always the case, for as I have documented in this study, missionaries were greatly concerned with the quality of basic Christian teaching for the first generation of converts. But with subsequent generations of Christians, the Mission shifted its emphasis away from village-level teaching to institutionalized settings, leaving in abeyance the basic Christian knowledge and understanding of villagers. In light of the ethnohistorical documentation of changes in Mission policies and attitudes, the contemporary lack of integration of Christian faith with Melanesian experience, is not surprising. In fact, it is quite understandable. Nevertheless, for today's leaders in the Church of Melanesia, struggling with a newly created autonomous church, the inheritance of this legacy from the Melanesian Mission presents a most lamentable and perplexing problem.

Summary and Theoretical Significance.

There is a pattern that emerges in the six cultural dimensions of integration discussed above. The data demonstrate that the degree of indigenous integration is very uneven, varying differently with the cultural dimensions considered in our analysis. If this is diagrammed schematically, with the different cultural dimensions on the horizontal axis, and the vertical axis signifying high and low integration, it can be seen that as one moves along the horizontal axis from beliefs to material culture, the degree of indigenous integration (indigeneity) increases. The set of Christian beliefs introduced appear to be the least integrated, while the ceremonial festivals and material artifacts associated with the church appear to be more highly integrated.

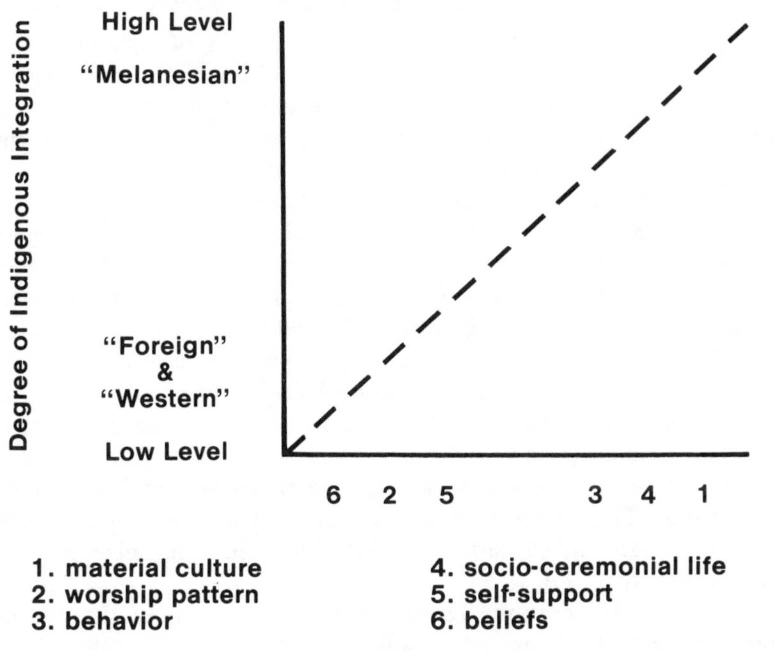

Fig. 17. Indigenous Integration and Cultural Dimensions of Contemporary Melanesian Anglicans.

An example of this relationship between integration and the different cultural dimensions is the village chapel which may employ indigenous architecture and artifacts, but the worship service taking place inside that structure is far less indigenous. Moreover, when villagers leave the chapel they leave behind any notions of an applied Christianity, choosing instead to rely more on traditional magic to meet their daily needs, especially during times of crisis.

This compartmentalization of Christianity seems to indicate that it is not highly integrated into the islanders' Melanesian worldview, but rather it is perceived as a ritual activity that occurs inside the chapel, and is unrelated to concerns of village living outside the church. It has become a "split-level Christianity," with Christian rituals on the surface and traditional beliefs below. Thus at the belief (6) end of the horizontal axis (see Figure 17), Christianity is not very indigenous, but still quite foreign and Western to many Melanesians.[153]

Let us now return to Spicer's four categories of integration discussed above (pp. 372-373), to see if his heuristic device can be helpful here in understanding the unevenness of integration in the total cultural package introduced by Christian missionaries. Let us review these categories in terms of the six cultural dimensions discussed above and portrayed in Figure 17.

1. **Incorporative Integration.** Many of the items of material culture associated with the introduction of Christianity fall into this category. For example, the chapel building is for many a functional substitute for the traditional sacred men's house, and many of the artifacts within the building, although manifestations of introduced forms like the cross, have nevertheless employed traditional motifs and artistic skills in their manufacture. The socio-ceremonial functions of the church festivals also fall into this category, for in many ways, they are new forms used to express traditional meanings, and in this sense are quite indigenous. That is, they are very Melanesian.

2. **Assimilative or Replacive Integration.** Of the six cultural dimensions analyzed above, the one that most clearly fits into this category is that of behavior. Inter-cultural violence in the form of headhunting, raiding, cannibalism, and other forms of violence such as widow-strangling, human sacrifice, and infanticide are no longer upheld as appropriate models of behavior. In this sense, there is a significant difference between the pre-Christian and Christian eras. The former cultural ideals have been replaced with greater emphasis on peace and solidarity as islanders attempt to actualize their new Christian identity.

3. **Fusional Integration.** There are certain elements of the worship pattern such as Holy Communion, baptism and liturgical prayer that appear to be representative of this type of integration. Although they are new forms introduced into Melanesia by Anglican missionaries, they have been reinterpreted in such a way that the meaning the missionary advocates attached to them is not the same as the meaning Melanesians have ascribed to these religious rituals. There has been a fusion of cultural elements between Western forms and Melanesian meanings, resulting in a syncretistic product.

4. **Isolative Integration.** In essence this type of integration is at the opposite end of the continuum from incorporative integration. For, although elements advocated by an outside agent of change are adopted, they become compartmentalized and unrelated to other aspects of the culture. Much of the

worship pattern, many of the beliefs, and certainly the attitude toward the church's self-support appear to be good examples of isolative integration. They are elements that exist in the Melanesians' socio-cultural system, but they tend to be compartmentalized from their everyday activities, for they appear to remain foreign and Western rather than perceived as indigenous and Melanesian.

It is unlikely that this is what the missionaries intended to communicate to potential converts, but it is evident that this is the way their message has been interpreted. Many aspects of "being a Christian" were associated with "being a European." As long as missionaries communicated that a Christian Melanesian church should resemble a European Christian church in both form and function, then, even though the church is superficially adopted, it is not perceived by Melanesians as belonging to themselves. The model of Christianity emerging from this kind of Westernized institution tends to become compartmentalized in the minds of indigenous Christians, and not deeply integrated into the society of those who adopt it.

Throughout this study I have drawn on the seminal work of Homer Barnett in distinguishing between Melanesians as innovators and missionaries as advocates in the culture change situation. As this study has documented, Anglican missionaries for over 125 years have advocated the adoption of Christianity, and Melanesians through time, have responded by innovating and accepting the proposed change. Nevertheless, the Melanesians' interpretation and practice of Christianity have been conditioned by their cognitive maps and cultural models, which of course are different from those of the European missionaries who advocated adopting the new religion.

Unless the missionary, as an advocate, can learn what these cognitive maps and cultural models are—that is, unless he comes to understand the Melanesian's worldview—his approach as an advocate to the islanders will be from his own worldview, and thus the Melanesians' response to his message will be uneven. In some cultural domains the change advocated by the missionary may very well meet the felt needs of a Melanesian and thus integration will occur in his own life and culture. In other domains, the change advocated by the missionary will be reinterpreted by the indigene according to pre-existing mental maps and cultural models, or it may be ignored altogether as irrelevant and meaningless. Therefore, as an agent of change, the importance of the missionary's understanding the worldview of the receptor, cannot be overemphasized. I would hypothesize that the degree to which proposed change becomes indigenously integrated into the receptor's culture, is proportional to the degree to which the change advocated by the missionary is commensurate with the worldview of the innovator.

The history of the Melanesian Mission shows this pattern. In some areas proposed change was accepted and integrated into the lives and culture of the Melanesian innovators. In other areas it was not, and today, this unevenness of indigenous integration is very evident at the village level. For example, the church building may be very Melanesian looking, but the worship service inside is not. Also, the Christian ideas proclaimed in the worship service do not become a vital part of an applied Christianity in everyday activities. This compartmentalization of Christianity seems to indicate that it is not highly integrated into the Melanesian worldview, but is rather an activity focused on the bishop or priest that occurs inside the chapel and is unrelated to concerns of village living outside the church building. And as we have observed in this study, this is the antithesis of the way religion functioned in traditional Melanesian society.

This is, of course, the pastoral challenge of not only the Anglicans in the Solomon Islands and Vanuatu, but of many churches throughout Melanesia. How can the Christian church become something more than just a new form of social organization? How can it become a Melanesian church and how can the Christian gospel come to be a viable living force integrated with the whole of life in Melanesian communities? These are some of the important missiological questions being raised today in this post-colonial era of church and mission.

At the beginning of this section I posed the question of whether or not the autonomous Church of Melanesia was indeed an indigenous church.[154] The data demonstrate that in 125 years the Melanesian Mission did, in fact, produce an independent and autonomous "Church of Melanesia," but today, that church is struggling to become truly indigenous and Melanesian. How could a church become independent and not be indigenous? Legally and ecclesiastically the Church of Melanesia is an independently operated Melanesian institution, but phenomenologically and culturally, it still remains primarily a Europeanized institution located in Melanesia. An institution such as a church does not automatically become indigenous simply because Melanesians have replaced Europeans in positions of leadership. This is a necessary, but not a sufficient condition for indigenization. In the following chapter I will discuss in detail some important anthropological principles that bear on the problem of indigenizing Christianity in Melanesia, or for that matter, indigenizing any institution that is introduced from outside.

Chapter Summary

This chapter has focused primarily on the findings of my fieldwork in the Solomon Islands. I have attempted to analyze the form and function of Anglican Christianity in the Solomon Islands at two different levels — (1) the institutionalized Church of Melanesia, and (2) the understanding and practice of Christianity at the village level.

The organizational structure of the COM has been seen as a predominantly Westernized institution that tends to be divorced culturally from the realities of village-level Christian beliefs and practices. I have suggested that at the village level the understanding and practice of Christianity is a mixture of traditional Melanesian meanings with introduced Westernized forms.

In the ethnohistorical discussion of Christian conversion as an example of innovation, I have attempted to provide an historical and theoretical perspective for understanding contemporary islanders' attitudes toward and beliefs about Christianity. This discussion was followed by an analysis of the degree to which various aspects of the cultural package associated with the introduction of Christiantity by Anglican missionaries have become more or less integrated into the contemporary Melanesian socio-cultural system. The data demonstrate that the acceptance, understanding and practice of Christianity is today very uneven. Some aspects of the new religion advocated by Anglican missionaries have indeed become indigenized and well integrated into Melanesian society, but other aspects have remained isolated, obtrusive and foreign to the Melansian way of life.

In the final chapter of this study I will attempt to analyze why the missionaries' cross-cultural communication was only partially successful, and I will suggest some models of cross-cultural communication that I believe are relevant for any agent of culture change.

CHAPTER 6 NOTES

1. Cf. Chapter 1, pp. 10-12, for a dicussion of Williams' model of culture change.
2. Cf. Hilliard (1966, Ch. 9) for a comparison of the Melanesian Mission with other Protestant missions in the Solomons regarding missionaries' attitudes toward traditional Melanesian society and culture. See especially pp. 495-497, 516-518.
3. Linton's (1940:469) definition of culture change corresponds with this diagram, for he notes that, "Culture change normally involves not only addition of a new element or elements to the culture but also the elimination of certain previously existing elements and the modification and reorganization of others."

   See also Malinowski's (1945) concept of a "third culture" which has certain similarities to Williams' model.
4. The appointment of an assistant bishop for the New Hebrides was announced in the *Church of Melanesia Newsletter*, October 1978 (No. 26), p. 6. At that time the Bishop of the New Hebrides was a

European. He was later succeeded by Harry Tevi, who was elected the bishop of that diocese on February 1st, 1980 and installed the next day.

5. See Article 9 of the Church of Melanesia *Constitution* for the archbishop's duties.

6. See Article 7 and 17 of the COM *Constitution*, and Title D, Canon 1 and 2, *Canons of the Province of Melanesia* (1975), pp. 40-43.

7. The archbishop called the Third Provincial Synod to begin September 24, 1979 (COM *Newsletter*, April 1979, No. 29, p. 4.).

8. See Title D, Canon 3, *Canons of the Province of Melanesia* (1975), pp. 44-45.

9. See Article 12, COM *Constitution*, and Title C, Canon 5, *Canons of the Province of Melanesia* (1975), pp. 38-39.

10. For a list of duties of the District Committee, see Canon 13, Diocese of Ysabel, *Proceedings of the Second Diocesan Synod* (1976), p. 49.

11. Cf. *Ibid*, pp. 48-49.

12. On the Village Committee and its duties, see Canon 13, Diocese of Ysabel, *Proceedings of the Second Diocesan Synod* (1976), pp. 46-47.

13. The Church of Melanesia Trust Board, Inc. formerly the Melanesian Mission Trust (Board) was established in New Zealand in 1862, comprised of farm land at Kohimarama, investments in English securities, and private donations. It grew primarily out of land investments made by Selwyn when he purchased farm land outside Auckland. As the city expanded so did the value of the land, and today the COM Trust Board has assets of over A$1,000,000. Cf. Appendix 14 to Provincial Council Agenda 1977, COM Archives, Honiara.

14. COM Budget Summary 1977-1978 for the Province, Schedule 1, COM Archives, Honiara.

15. Cf. Tippett (1967: 119-135) for an illuminating and cogent discussion of the problems of mission institutions and education.

16. This phenomenon is a function of what Bates (1971) has called goal discrepancy between Mission and Church. Kraft (1979: 147-166) approaches this problem in terms of models of communication. See also Herskovits (1967: 182-194) on cultural focus and reinterpretation, as well as his more general discussion of the process of culture change (1945).

17. Most of the missionaries in the Melanesian Mission had a tenure of less than five years.

18. For discussion of Fox see Chapter 4, pp. 214-217.

19. This has some important cultural and theoretical implications especially as it relates to transactional analysis theory in the social sciences, and especially the work of Goffman, Barth and others. It is a case of where the institutional setting shapes the nature of the interaction. Islanders presented their "front stage" identity when interacting with missionaries on mission stations, but their "back stage" identity never became known to the missionary, because this was acted out in the islanders' own arena of village life.

20. Fox (1958: 197) says that through the work of missionary-doctor Henry Welchman (1890-1908), "The Santa Isabel Church became the strongest in Melanesia as well as the most generous and most missionary." On Welchman's role in the conversion of Santa Isabel, see my disscussion below, pp. 362-363.

21. In 1976 the population of Santa Isabel was 10,420, including 10,365 Melanesians, 30 Polynesians, 1 Micronesian, 6 Europeans, 1 Chinese and 17 Others. Appendix I, Solomon Islands, *Annual Report* 1976, p. 147.

22. The topic of Anglican Theology is a subject that deserves far more extensive coverage than allowed in this study. One of the best treatments is Neill (1958) which also includes an extensive bibliography. See also Wand (1948, 1961) and Higgins (1958). For an interesting comparison of Anglican Provinces around the world, including Melanesia, cf. Johnson (1963).

23. The original (1689) distinction between "high" and "low" churchmen marked a political distinction rather than a religious one. By the early nineteenth century there were at least three spectrums within the Anglican Church: High Church, Low Church, and Evangelical. After 1860 Low Church and Evangelical perspectives tended to merge. The basic distinction between High Church and Low Church Anglicans is their attitude toward ritual and dogma. High Church Anglicans have emphasized far more ritual in worship and have been more catholic than evangelical in doctrine. Cf. Neill (1958: 178-181, 232, 398-399), and Wand (1961: 96-100, 104-118).

24. In the spectrum of Anglican Theology, Anglo-Catholic and Evangelical thought would occupy two polar positions. The Anglo-Catholic revival in the first three decades of this century had roots in the Oxford Movement of the mid-nineteenth century, cf. Olland (1963). It was a move to instill greater catholic doctrine and practices into the Church of England, and resulted in greater frequency of communion, more colorful ritual, a change in liturgical character, replacing Matins with

the Sung Eucharist, an increase in hymn singing which was an inheritance from the evangelicals, and a revival of monastic communities. For further discussion, cf. Knox (1923), Olland (1925), Lacey (1927), Stewart (1929), Wand (1961: 100-103, 134-148), Lloyd (1966) O. Chadwick (1966-1970, Pt. 2: 308-325, 347-358), and Simcox (1968: 178-184).

25. For further discussion of Bishop Wood, cf. Fox (1958: 55-63) and Hilliard (1978: 208-210).

26. For a comparison of other Protestant missions' attitudes toward Holy Communion in the Solomon Islands, cf. Hilliard (1966).

27. Melanesian Mission, *The Faith of the Church*, p. 17. Quoted in Hilliard (1978: 234).

28. For further discussion on the history of the Anglo-Catholic tradition in the Melanesian Mission, cf. Hagesi (1972: 56-61), and Hilliard (1978: 232-236).

29. The two movements were (1) The Danielites on North Pentecost (Raga), and (2) The Charles Kuper Movement. The Danielites which flourished in the 1930's and early 1940's centered around a single prophet figure, cf. *The Melanesian Messenger*, August 1965, pp. 23-26, and Hilliard (1978: 285-287).

"The True Church of Kuper" was a movement begun by Charles Kuper of Santa Ana in 1959, after his application to attend the Melanesian Mission's theological college had been denied on racial grounds. His father was a European planter, his mother a Solomon Islander. The movement was short-lived and attracted primarily relatives of Kuper. When he was unable to save his own son through prayer, the validity of his leadership was severely questioned and his following quickly dwindled away. Kuper himself returned to the Anglican Church in 1971 after a serious illness which he interpreted as a punishment from God for his renegade activities. Cf. Davenport (1970), and Hagesi (1972: 69-70).

30. Cf. "The Remnant Church," *The Melanesian Messenger*, Easter 1966, p. 9.

31. I am indebted to Gary and Linda Simons for parts of the following discussion. The Simons, conducting linguistic research, had experience in SSEC villages. While I was in the Solomon Islands, I discussed and corresponded with them regarding the similarities and differences in the COM and SSEC.

32. Cf. "What Role for Religion in Melanesia Today?", *P.I.M.*, March 1979, p. 45.

33. This information has been compiled from COM, *Plan of Daily Prayer for Church Workers and For Departed Servants of the Church 1978*. Honiara: Provincial Press. Of this total number of priests, there have been forty-seven (20.9%) ordained as deacons or priests since the inauguration of the Province of Melanesia in January 1975.

34. Interview with Archbishop Norman Palmer, July 1977.

35. Similar evidence was found in a study completed in 1971 among students for the Catholic priesthood and religious life in Papua New Guinea. A great majority gave as their main motive for entering this vocation, the desire to help their people. Cf. Knoebel (n.d.) and Langenkamp and Knoebel (1971).

36. Cf. G. White (1979).

37. One informant explained that priests are like a sign—pointing the proper way to live, and so if islanders disobey the priests, they are afraid they will be punished. My informant stated that because of this fear, many are motivated to live according to the laws of the church.

38. Writing to his sister on April 2, 1930, R. P. Fallowes noted:

> My Bush Priest is here, Ben Hageria, once a headhunter in the old days, and of course a heathen then. He is known as "Ben the Fearless" and will jump into water and kill a crocodile and dive under a shark and slit it open with his knife. . . He is a chief in his own right. He is thought much of here . . . and has great "mana" among the people (Fallowes, Letters to his sister, 1929-1934, N.L.A.).

Ben Hageria died in January 1961, having gone blind several years before, but never losing command of his following in the Hograno District. In January 1978 I walked across the island of Santa Isabel to attend a feast-day in the village of Kolomola for the annual commemoration of the death of this famous priest. It was a large celebration of several hundred people from numerous villages in the Hograno district. Many speeches were made recalling the memory of this important ancestor. I met his wife Carolyn who was in her nineties at that time, but has since died.

For additional information on Hugo Hebala, cf. Fox (1958: 201), Hilliard (1978: 218-220), and G. White (1978: 174-175, 185-189). Today his death is commemorated every April 21st in Buala, and a church at Horara in the Bugotu district is named after him. White (1978: 194) notes that deceased priests on Santa Isabel, especially of the stature of Hebala and Hageria, are now treated in much the same way as renowned ancestors were traditionally treated, and have become symbols of a social identity for their descendants.

39. Cf. G. White (1978: 190).

40. It is interesting to note that Eric Gnhokro was resented and opposed by many of his colleagues in the priesthood, in much the same manner as priests were unsupportive of the work of the Melanesian Brotherhood. They held tenaciously to their monopoly on *mana* and evidently were threatened by such acts of supernatural power as many of the Brothers and Eric Gnhokro displayed.

41. Course list—1978. Bishop Patteson Theological Centre, mimeo.

I recall once while traveling on a ship with a third-year theological student entering into a delightful and yet surprising (to me) discussion with him on the theology of Rudolf Bultmann. I was interested in his perception of German theologians and how he felt their perspective would relate to his future work as a priest. He said that although he enjoyed reading and thinking about this kind of theology, he really could not see how to relate it to people back home in his village. In fact, the general criticism of his theological education was that although it had been very interesting, it was too Westernized and he was confused about how to apply what he had learned to the context of Melanesians in the village.

42. Cf. *P.I.M.*, April 1979, p. 27.

43. For further discussion on this change in the mode of paying priests' salaries, see COM *Newsletter*, April 1979, No. 29, p. 4.

44. They are also paid far more than other clergy in other churches in the Solomon Islands. Although there are no official figures on mean income for village wage-earners, Herlihy (1977: 21) in her research gives as the mean *per caput* (per head) income of a sample on Santa Isabel at $20.37, and on San Cristobal at $16.85.

45. These figures are based on a salary schedule for 1976 (Minutes of the Provincial Council Meetings Held in the Council Chamber, Church House, Honiara, Commencing on Wednesday July 21st, p. 14., COM Archives), and a recommendation that the 1977-1978 budget include a ten percent raise in all clergy pay (Appendix 3 to "Provincial Council Agenda 1977," p. 2., COM Archives).

46. Although priests stand out in terms of their social position in the community today, most are not as prominent as the priests of former years. For example, it was not unusual for Hugo Hebala or Ben Hageria to have an entourage of twenty to thirty "carriers" to accompany them on tours through their districts.

47. My observations of many of the priests on Santa Isabel accorded with villagers' evaluation of them. Without wanting to push the analogy too far, in the course of my fieldwork, I slowly came to perceive the priests

as having many similarities with the priests of the Medieval Church. They were/are powerful men in the society, and in order to preserve their dominant position, they did/do little to encourage acquistion of knowledge and understanding among the laity.

48. Hagesi (1972: 88-89). For an SSEM Malaita man's story of Christianity, cf. Hogbin (1939: 185-187).

49. Cf. Codrington (1891: 121-122n). In other areas of Melanesia, indigenous terms have been used for God. Thus, for example, the Neuendettelsau Lutheran Mission in Papua New Guinea adopted the indigenous term *Anut* (Bel language), or *Anutu* (Yabem language) to represent the concept of the Christian God, cf. Frerichs (1969: 86-87), Ahrens (1974: 26).

50. Ivens (1927: 16) wrote, "In rendering the word Spirit — i.e., Holy Spirit — the Melanesian Mission has used a set of words which denote either ghosts of a higher order like Figona of San Cristobal and Florida, more or less uncreated, or else beings who are not thought of at all as having once been human."

    In Arosi the word *fagarafe* was used for prayer, which Fox (1924: 100) says, "Means, then a request to a spirit or ghost for help and is in no sense a charm." Fox (1924: 99) also notes that the first word in the Arosi language used for prayer was *rihungai*, but it was later discovered that this was a very poor choice of words to use in translating the concept of prayer. In the Bugotu language of Santa Isabel, the term *kilo au* was used to refer to the Church, and means to call out away from; thus, those who became Christians and joined the Church, were those who were called out of darkness, out of heathen ways. See also Hogbin (1939: 188) for indigenous To'ambaita terms applied to Christian concepts on Malaita.

51. Hogbin (1939: 189) states that Malaitans' perception of God is that of "an unlovely tyrant who has the power to keep men good but instead allows them to be tempted and then punished." For additional discussion on Melanesians' concept of God, cf. *S.C.L.*, December 1912, pp. 114-116, Hogbin (1939: 191), and Hilliard (1966: 522).

52. Cf. Hilliard (1966: 521), Ivens in *S.C.L.*, September 1901, pp. 105-108; *M.M.R.*, 1920, pp. 19-20.

53. Hagesi (1972: 54) also notes that the beautiful and ornate Bishop Patteson Memorial Chapel at Norfolk Island was more than a beautiful building invoking the sacred memory of a martyr. To the Melanesians who worshipped there, "It meant much more . . . simply because it was closely associated with Patteson and therefore, the Melanesians at this stage worshipped the ghost of Patteson in this chapel."

54. Cf. Hogbin (1939: 190).

55. Cf. Kraft (1979: 227-235) for an expanded discussion of this phenomenon. It is interesting to note that the theological students I interviewed and priests who had studied at St. John's College in Auckland, all voiced a preference for studying Hebrew over Greek. They noted that Hebrew was relatively easy for them, but Greek was very difficult. Grammatically Melanesian languages resemble Hebrew, an observation Bishop Patteson made on many occasions in his correspondence with Sir William Martin and Professor Max Muller. Also phenomenologically, Hebrew would be closer to a Melanesian worldview than Greek would be. Cf. Appendix I "Letter from Bishop Patteson to Professor Max Muller" in Yonge (1874, II: 581-585).

56. Cf. Belshaw (1954: 69-75).

57. Cf. Hogbin (1939: 190) and Hagesi (1972: 64-65).

58. *Melanesian Prayer Book*, Catechism (1973), p. 254. COM.

59. *Ibid.*

60. Communion wafers are made locally using a flat iron, similar to a waffle iron, held over an open fire. The wine, on the other hand, is all imported from Australia. There is a great resistance among church leaders to substitute local products such as taro or sweet potato and coconut juice for the bread and wine. The SSEC on the other hand has contextualized Holy Communion somewhat by using local products. Cf. Hagesi (1972: 90-91).

61. Cf. Hagesi (1972: 66). Hilliard (1966: 523) notes how an epidemic on Nggela in 1902 which killed a large number of elderly people who had recently been confirmed, caused a near panic when it was rumored that the epidemic was "a judgement on those persons for venturing to approach such a holy ordinance" (*Island Voyage and Report 1902*, p. 33).

62. Cf. Hogbin (1939: 202-203).

63. Bishop John Chisholm's address to Standing Committee, March 25, 1968. COM Archives.

    Bishop Chisholm's concern for the use of vernacular languages in village worship was a significant contrast to Bishop Hill's policy of encouraging villagers to adopt English. However, there are still many places today in the Solomon Islands where Anglican worship is conducted in a language other than the people's own. Many of today's leaders of the COM are concerned with this problem and greater emphasis is being given to training islanders to do translation work. Summer Institute of Linguistics (SIL) personnel have now entered the

Solomons and are conducting translation workshops on different islands. Also a SIL team has recently been assigned to Santa Isabel where they are presently learning the Maringe language and will be involved in translation consultation with the Santa Isabel islanders.

64. The dynamics of this conversion process on Santa Isabel will be discussed below, pp. 358-372.

65. Although the Old Testament was translated by George Bogesi in the 1950's (*The Melanesian Messenger*, All Saints' Tide 1959, p. 5) to my knowledge it has never been published. The Book of Genesis was published in 1973. The Book of Common Prayer was first published in the Bugotu language in 1882, with subsequent editions printed in 1902, 1918, 1927, 1954 and 1975. The Bugotu Hymn Book was first published in 1905, with the last edition in 1961. For a complete list of Bugotu publications, cf. Linda Simons (1977: 13).

66. Collects and Psalms or other orders of service have not yet been translated and published in the Maringe language. However, a Maringe hymn book was published in 1975.

Ethnologically the Maringe language is more correctly termed A'ara. The word "Maringe" comes from a prominent rock near the village of Nareabu in the Maringe Lagoon. Since most islanders do not refer to their language as A'ara, and publications in the vernacular refer to this language as Maringe, I have chosen to continue with the popular usage of the term, by referring to this language as Maringe rather than A'ara. G. White (1978) prefers the term "A'ara" with sound ethnological justification for doing so. The Summer Institute of Linguistics (SIL) team on Santa Isabel are now calling this language "Holo" which means "bush"—*cheke holo* is the language of the bush. Along with "Maringe" and "A'ara" this is also an appropriate term for this language. Since the SIL team is beginning to produce stories and Bible portions in the Holo language, this term may soon replace "Maringe" as the most widely used term for this language.

67. Cf. Whiteman and Simons (1978).

68. Writing in 1954, George Bogesi, a Santa Isabel man, noted that:

> It is well known that Ysabel has many dialects. Bugotu language was used as an "Official" language for Church purposes. The real Bugotu people cannot speak either Gao, Mereinge, Koakota, Kia, Zazao, or Hograno languages and vice versa. The Bugotu language has been in use from the [18]80's until the present day, but believe it or not, only about 5 to 10 per cent of the people mentioned can speak it, even brokenly. It has been in use for over 70 years, yet the majority of the people, other than the real Bugotu people, do not understand it (*O Sala Ususur*, Easter 1954, No. 86: 43-44).

69. Hogbin (1958: 242) citing Redfield in his Yucatan research, notes that fear of black magic is stronger in the capital city than in the village.
70. For a discussion of magic and sorcery in the Solomon Islands, cf. Tippett (1967: 10-16).
71. Cf. Black (1963: 177).
72. *S.C.L.E.*, August 1925, p. 123.
73. G. White (1978: 189) notes that Hugo Hebala employed the same method used by Eric Gnhokro and obtained similar results.
74. For further discussion on the various types of sorcery on Santa Isabel, cf. G. White (1978: 113-116).
75. COM, *Buka Tharai Ka Cheke Maringe* (1973), p. 17.
76. An interesting point worthy of further investigation is the role the numeral three may have played in the pre-contact period in various Melanesian societies.
77. Melanesian Mission, *The Constitutions, Canons and Regulations of the Missionary Diocese of Melanesia* ... (1924), p. 14. Cited in Hilliard (1966: 518).
78. R. P. Fallowes, letter to his sister, November 17, 1932. Cited in G. White (1978: 184).
79. Cf. *S.C.L.*, January 1902, p. 165; July 1902, pp. 21-22; January 1903, p. 90, Ivens (1930: 170).
80. Cf. "Rogation Procession" in the *Melanesian Prayer Book* (1973), pp. 297-302. See also Hopkins, *Autobiography*, pp. 205-206; Hagesi (1972: 101-102). For further discussion on various aspects of "Christian magic" in Melanesia, cf. Hogbin (1939: 202-203), Belshaw (1954: 74-75), Hilliard (1966: 518-525), and G. White (1978: 182-188).
81. This plant is called in Maringe, *nahogle*, and is imbued with mystical powers. It is always found planted in cemeteries and often around a traditional shrine (*phadagi*). The plant has either red, purple or green leaves, "just like the Church's colors," my informant exclaimed, "except there is no white leaf." In the Anglican ritual of worship, these four colors — red, purple, green and white — are used as symbols throughout the Christian Year, each one used during a certain period, or for a specific occasion.
82. For further discussion on the corpus of indigenous spirits in Santa Isabel, cf. G. White (1978: 111-113).
83. For a European's encounter with the "Ghosts of San Jorge," cf. Grover (1973). See also G. White (1978: 188-189).

84. Tippett (1976) has put together five of his "Research in Progress Pamphlets" under the title, *The Phenomenology of Cross-Cultural Conversion in Oceania.* Pamplet No. 11 (1976: 1-51) written originally in 1967, focuses on Religious Group Conversion in Non-Western Society, drawing material from Polynesia and Melanesia to demonstrate the nature of multi-individual group movements. See also Tippett (1971).

85. Cf. Armstrong (1900: 272-274, 359-360), Awdry (1903: 62-71), Montgomery (1908: 240-255), E. Wilson (1915: 99-120), Fox (1958: 195-200).

86. For further discussion on headhunting in the Solomon Islands see above, Chapter 2, pp. 62-63. Cf. Guppy (1887: 13-40), Woodford (1888, 1890a: 140-159), Codrington (1891: 297, 345)), Somerville (1897), Goldie (1908), Hocart (1922, 1931), Tippett (1967: 147-159), Jackson (1972, 1975), G. White (1979), Zelenietz (1979).

87. Headhunting as practiced in the Solomon Islands in the nineteenth century must be distinguished from the Melanesian custom of removing the heads of the dead of those killed in warfare. Headhunting involved raiding expeditions for the sole purpose of obtaining human heads, cf. Romilly (1887: 74).

88. Cheyne recorded on February 3rd, 1844:

> Visited the Head chief's village this afternoon on the low island & on landing the first thing that met my view, was the wall plates of a large canoe house strung with human heads, of both sexes, and apparently of all ages. Many of them appear to have been recently killed, and the marks of the tomahawk were seen in all. I was horrified at the sight and felt quite sick until I got away again. Dornin informed me that they had a few days previous to our arrival returned from a war expedition in which they had come off conquerors and had brought home with them — including men, women and children — no less than ninety-three human heads — and that it was a universal custom throughout New Georgia to exhibit them as trophies in their canoe houses (1971: 303-304).

89. Cf. Codrington (1891: 135-136, 345), Ivens (1930: 185-187, 1936: 26), Bogesi (1948: 210).

90. Armstrong (1900: 73).

91. Montgomery (1908: 244).

92. Armstrong (1900: 73).

93. See Patteson's description of these tree houses above, Chapter 2, pp. 89-90, footnote No. 81. See also Patteson, n.d.c. "Ysabel Island" (A Story for Children), enclosed in a letter from J.C. Patteson to Lady Stephen, October 31, 1866. Stephen Family Papers, MSS 777/11,

Mitchell Library, Sydney. For additional discussion of the Santa Isabel tree houses, cf. Foljambe (1868: 215-216), Anonymous *The Island Mission* (1869: 263-266), Yonge (1874, II: 196-198), *The Island Voyage 1879*, pp. 56-57, Armstrong (1900: 86-87), and C. Wilson (1932: 233).

94. For further discussion on Bera, cf. Penny (1887: 64-68), Wawn (1893: 219, 223, 225), Awdry (1903: 57-61), Jackson (1972: 42-43, 46-51). Nearly the entire population of the central portion of Santa Isabel was driven out under threat of attack by headhunters, or killed outright. Touring this area in the 1880's Woodford (1890a: 154) noted of the northern coast of the island, "I found village after village along the coast deserted, the former inhabitants having been killed by head-hunting canoes from this part of the group," i.e., the Western Solomons.

95. *The Island Voyage 1878*, pp. 14-15.

96. Cf. *The Island Voyage 1879*, pp. 94-95. In 1886 Samson Ingo died and his village ceased to be as important to the Melanesian Mission advance on Santa Isabel (*The Island Voyage 1886*, p. 5).

97. Penny (1887: 65) said that Bera "was the worst obstructionist I had to encounter." Bishop John Selwyn's opinion of Bera was also unfavorable; he noted that, "At the old station in Mahaga lives a chief named Bera, who, as far as I could gather, was at the bottom of the murders that were committed in the district" (*The Island Voyage 1875*, p. 37).

98. Woodford (1890a: 183-186), Wawn (1893: 219, 225), Bogesi (1948: 210).

99. Alfred Penny, Diaries 1876-1886, B 807-817, Mitchell Library, Sydney.

100. Awdry (1903: 61).

101. Alfred Penny, Diaries.

102. Cf. *The Island Voyage 1886*, p. 9.

103. *Ibid.*, pp. 11-12.

104. *Ibid.*, p. 14.

105. *The Island Voyage 1887*, p. 63.

106. *M.M.R.*, 1888, p. 6.

107. E. Wilson (1915: 103).

108. *M.M.R.*, 1889, p. 5.

109. Cf. Jackson (1972: 52; 1975: 69), and G. White (1979: 123-124).

110. Jackson is citing C. E. Fox (n.d.) *History of the Melanesian Mission*, typescript, Auckland, p. 47. Fox cites one of Welchman's reports, but no date is given.

111. Welchman's biography is written by E. Wilson (1935) and is based primarily on his personal diaries. This source provides a wealth of information, enabling the ethnohistorian to document the changes that occurred in this traditional Melanesian society and culture following the introduction and subsequent adoption of Christianity. Welchman's diaries and correspondence are housed with the Melanesian Mission, London. They are also available on microfilm: "Missionary Life in the Melanesian Islands," Diaries, 12 vols. 1889-1908, and correspondence. A.J.C.P. M728, M805-806.

For additional discussion on Henry Welchman, cf. Fox (1958: 197-198), and Hilliard (1978: 173-176).

112. Jackson (1972: 62).

113. Henry Welchman, Diaries.

114. *Ibid.*

115. Statistics of the Melanesian Mission for 1901. See Appendix III.

116. *Melanesian Mission Report Issued by the English Committee 1903*, London (1904), pp. 40-42.

117. There nevertheless have been some significant anthropological studies of religious conversion, including Rapoport (1954), Skinner (1958), Messenger (1960), Peel (1968a), Parrat (1969), Horton (1971), Fisher (1973), Salamone (1972, 1975, 1976), and Pauw (1975).

118. Cf. B. Taylor (1974).

119. Studying religious conversion as a cultural process in which the active role of the convert is emphasized has been the focus of research by Herskovits (1943), Aquina (1967), Sahay (1968), Guiart (1970) and Salamone (1975, 1976). One of the most cogent and significant theoretical discussions of conversion is Hiebert's (1978a) article on "Conversion, Culture and Cognitive Categories." His insights have profound implications for cross-cultural evangelism.

120. Alan Tippett's (1976) writing on cross-cultural conversion in Oceania I have found to be very seminal and stimulating. Much of what follows owes a debt to his theoretical inspiration.

121. Cf. Tippett (1971) for a study of people movements toward Christianity in Polynesia. Cf. Tippett (1967: 42-43).

122. See discussion above, Chapter 3, pp. 139-142. For an interesting discussion of power encounter among the Western Dani, in which

sacred objects were destroyed by an indigenously inspired movement, cf. O'Brien and Ploeg (1964). Cf. Tippett (1967: 100-118).

123. Cf. E. Wilson (1935: 86-87, 99-101), Tippett (1967: 109), and G. White (1978: 167-168).

124. Cf. Tippett (1967: 44), and Hilliard (1978: 174-176).

125. For a similar discussion dealing with the metahistorical problems in history, cf. Gottschalk (1969: 245-255).

126. Cf. Tippett (1967: 60-66).

127. Barnett warns that:

> . . . only confusion and artificiality can result from a structuring of acceptance issues in terms of the thought processes of an observer or a novelty introducer rather than in terms of the mental prototypes and identifications of the actual acceptors and rejectors. The observer's fallacy, or the error of rationalism, is one against which all of us must be on guard. It is easy to succumb to it unawares (1953: 339).

128. Cf. Richardson (1974) for an interesting account of the way in which Christianity was introduced into a Melanesian culture in terms of the indigenes' cultural categories. Richardson appears to be a culturally sensitive and anthropologically informed missionary who lived among the Sawi of Irian Jaya. He presented the message of Christianity in terms of an indigenous concept of a "peace child" which was a traditional mechanism for ending internecine hostility. Further research has led Richardson to speak in terms of "redemptive analogies" in the missionary-indigene contact situation. He argues that in every culture there are indigenous models (redemptive analogies) that a missionary can use in communicating cross-culturally the message of Christianity (Richardson 1981). Such a missionary strategy would be in line with Barnett's model of culture change.

129. In the Good News Bible, Luke 10: 19 states: "Listen: I have given you authority (*exousia* — ἐξουσία), so that you can walk on snakes and scorpions and overcome all the power (*dunamis* — δύναμις) of the Enemy, and nothing will hurt you."

130. For an excellent study of the persistence of values despite conversion among the Igbo, cf. Salamone (1975).

131. Elsewhere (Whiteman 1974) I have discussed this problem of cross-cultural communication in terms of the biblical message being interpreted through two distinct and different cultural filters in the process of communication — the cultural filter of the missionary who selects what he believes is important to communicate, and the cultural filter of

the indigene who interprets the missionary's message in terms of his pre-existing, traditional non-Christian worldview.

132. Levine (1968) has a cogent discussion on the history and use of this concept in anthropology. See also, Gillin (1948: 498-531), Landecker (1951), Parsons and Shils (1954: 202-204), Hogbin (1958: 46-54), Herskovits (1967: 109-127), Tippett (1967: 83). Sapir (1924) gives us a unique approach to the problem of socio-cultural integration in terms of culture as either genuine or spurious.

133. Europeans are used primarily in education. Both at Selwyn College, the COM secondary school, and at the Bishop Patteson Theological Centre, there are European instructors, but they form a small minority of the teaching and administrative staff. As of 1981 a small staff of three European nurses ran the medical program at Fauabu hospital on Malaita.

134. Anglican priests and bishops wear a cross around their neck as a symbol of their ecclesiastical role. In the Solomon Islands these are generally carved from turtle shell and inlaid with mother-of-pearl — a distinctive Solomon Islands medium innovatively employed in a new form.

Waite (1969) has written an excellent study of traditional Solomon Islands sculpture. Unfortunately she seems to have assumed that when missions came traditional art ceased to be produced. She could have explored for instance, the many ways in which traditional Solomon Islands sculpture has been incorporated into the Melanesian Anglican church.

135. Cf. Hagesi (1972: 62-63).

136. The Mothers' Union is a world-wide Anglican society introduced into Melanesia first by Mrs. Gwendoline Mason on Malaita in 1931 (*S.C.L.E.*, May 1931, pp. 70-71) and shortly afterward on Santa Isabel by Mrs. Emily Sprott (*The Melanesian Messenger*, All Saints' Tide 1958, p. 23). According to the *Mothers' Card*, the aim of the Mothers' Union is "to put forth the teaching of Christ in marriage and family life." Its objectives are:

(1) To understand and follow Christ's teaching about marriage and help others to do the same.
(2) To help mothers and fathers to bring up their children in the Faith and Life of the Church.
(3) To help Christians everywhere in the world to join together in prayer, worship and work for others.
(4) To make known to all peoples good ways to keep family life strong and protect children.

(5) To help those people who have family troubles.

The Mothers' Union prayer, said at the conclusion of Morning Prayer, is:

> Almighty God our Heavenly Father, you gave marriage to be a way to bless men and women. We thank you for the happiness of family life. Pour out on us your Holy Spirit that we may truly love and serve you. Bless those who are married and all parents and children. May we know your Presence and peace in our homes. Fill our homes with your love and use them for your glory. Bless the members of the Mothers' Union all over the world. Unite us in prayer and Worship, in love and Service. Make us strong by your will, through Jesus Christ Our Lord. Amen (COM, The Mothers' Union Members' Card).

137. This is reminiscent of many American Roman Catholics who have preferred the use of Latin in the Mass to that of English which was widely introduced with many other reforms following Vatican II.

138. In a good study of traditional Lau music and poetry on Malaita, Ellison Suri (1976) suggests ways in which this rich heritage could be incorporated into Anglican worship in the Solomon Islands.

139. Suri (1976: 48-49).

140. Hagesi (1972: 86). Both Hagesi (1972) and Suri (1976) have been critical of Westernized Christianity as a model of worship for Solomon Islanders, and thus have made some interesting suggestions for indigenizing Christian worship, contextualizing it for Melanesians.

141. Cf. Hogbin (1958: 70-75), Burridge (1978: 12-18).

142. Cf. G. White (1979).

143. Cf. Hogbin (1958: 182), M. Wilson (1971: 90-99), and Pauw (1975).

144. For an excellent discussion of the "Christian Person" as a model and symbol of social identity on Santa Isabel, cf. G. White (1978: 392-416).

145. For a similar pattern of behavior among the Anang of Nigeria, cf. Messenger (1959, 1960).

146. Cf. G. White (1978), especially p. 388.

147. On Santa Isabel there is a church named after each of these personalities: Horara—Hugo Hebala, Tasia—Bishop Patteson, and Kolosori—Charles Fox.

148. Interview with Archbishop Norman Palmer, July 1977.

149. Tables 6.7 and 6.8 are adapted from, "1976/7 Local Giving and Provincial Grants for 1977/8," COM Archives.

150. Krass (1974: 141-147) contrasts two missionary approaches used in northern Ghana. In one approach the missionary provided all the materials for building a new church; in the other, the missionary gave a little aid, but encouraged the people of the village to raise their own resources for the church. The first approach led villagers to perceive the church as the **missionary's** church; after all **he** built it. The second approach led villagers to see the church as **their own**.

151. For example, the Government Council on Santa Isabel returns twenty-five percent of the head tax back to the village to be spent by the village on whatever it chooses. In village after village I encountered people asking the bishop why the diocese did not follow the same plan and give back to the village twenty-five percent of the church collection. Villagers perceive that their annual assessment ($84 for villages in the Maringe district) is nothing other than a church tax.

152. Tippett (1967: 5-6, 100-111; 1973d: 88-91) discusses this problem in terms of a "power encounter" of Christianity with traditional religion. The concept of a power encounter is most appropriate to Melanesia where indigenes measure the validity of religion on the basis of its power, not on the plausibility of an intellectual argument or logical proof. The classic Western "proofs" for the existence of God would not hold the interest of traditional Melanesians. They would be more concerned with whether or not this God had any power, and on that basis, he would be proved or disproved.

153. M. Kraft (1978) utilizing an ethnoscience methodology has produced an excellent study of the relationship between Christian conversion and alteration in worldview, among the Kamwe of northeastern Nigeria.

154. This question was the focus of an earlier article (Whiteman 1981a) in which I traced the evolution of the Anglican Church in the Solomon Islands, from a foreign mission to an independent church. A similar theme for the South Pacific has been pursued by Latukefu (1974).

Chapter 7

Missionaries as Agents of Cultural Change

The emphasis of this concluding chapter is primarily theoretical rather than historical or ethnographic. An attempt will be made to draw together several theoretical themes that have permeated this study. This will be done by first discussing the concept of indigenization as it applies not only to the arena of missionary activities, but also to programs of directed culture change in general. Next, attention will focus on religious change in terms of the process of indigenization. A distinction between syncretism and indigenous Christiantiy will be made. This analytical distinction will be illustrated by a brief review of indigenous Christianity in Africa. Finally, in this first section, I will discuss the difference between Christianity as a belief system and Christendom as a Western cultural tradition, and argue that the missionaries' confusion of these two entities has retarded the development of indigenous Christianity which most missions espouse as their primary objective.

Missionaries and cultural change will be the focus of the next section. A processual model of change is proposed and applied to the case study of the Melanesian Mission. An evaluation of the Melanesian Mission's activities that either encouraged or thwarted indigenization of Christianity will then follow. This section will conclude by suggesting criteria whereby we can evaluate missionaries as either the destroyers of traditional cultures, or in a more positive function, as cultural brokers in the arena of rapid socio-cultural change.

Some general principles of cross-cultural communication as they relate to missionary activities and agents of change in general are discussed in the next section. The emphasis will be on receptor-oriented communication where the worldview of the indigenous recipients is taken seriously by the outside advocates of change.

A summary of the entire study will conclude this chapter. Some methodological and substantive conclusions from the study will be drawn and suggestions for further research made.

Indigenization

The concept of indigenization has been used throughout this study. It is important now to focus more sharply on the term and to understand its meaning in a context wider than that of missionary activity.

Indigenization is a cultural process in which indigenes attempt to take something borrowed from outside their culture and make it their own. The word *indigene*, from the French, literally means "inborn." Thus something that is indigenous to a society is something that originates there, is created in that culture and is thus native to it. Indigenization therefore is a process in which **indigenes** (not foreigners) attempt consciously or unconsciously to take something borrowed from another culture and to alter it in such a way that it becomes adapted to their culture and truly their own. For example, a borrowed cultural element may perform a certain function in the adopters' society that is quite different from its function in the originators' society. By altering the function of the cultural element to fit the new cultural context, indigenes have in fact indigenized the borrowed element. They now identify it as their own, fulfilling a meaningful function in their society.

Another form of indigenization takes place when a borrowed cultural element performs a traditional function in the receptors' culture, similar to the function it performs in the originators' culture. In this sense, the borrowed cultural element becomes a functional substitute; the form may be Western, but it performs an indigenous function. Thus, indigenization is simply another form of culture change — taking elements external to the culture, and altering and adapting them in such a way that they become internalized within the borrowers' culture, taking on an indigenous form, function, use or meaning.[1]

This concept of indigenization has important practical implications for an agent of change, whether one is concerned with rural economic development, political change or religious conversion. If the change one advocates can easily become indigenized, then it is more likely to be adopted and internalized and thus integrated as a permanent part of the society—lasting long after the agent of change is removed from the scene. There are numerous examples of Peace Corps projects or United States AID programs that have failed, primarily because the change advocated by Americans did not become indigenized by the recipient society.[2] Instead, it remained alien and foreign to the culture.

Therefore, if change agents are to be successful they must advocate change in such a way that members of the recipient society can readily indigenize it, making it their own. This will necessarily involve reinterpretation so that the introduced idea, behavior, or material artifact can take on an indigenous form, function, use or meaning. Unless this does happen, "acceptance" will only be superficial, and neither long-lasting nor integrated into the society.

The theoretical implications of indigenization are equally intriguing, for essentially, indigenization is a process of innovation, and corresponds to Barnett's model of culture change as discussed in Chapter 1 (pp. 5-6) and Appendix II. The external change advocated is combined in an internal recombination of cultural elements so that the resulting configuration is qualitatively new. Thus indigenization as a cultural process is a manifestation of Barnett's six processes of recombination, discussed in Appendix II. It is a "creation only in the sense that it is a new combination, never in the sense that it is something emerging from nothing" (Barnett 1953: 181).

The implications this carries for the agent of change is that indigenization must be done by the recipients, the innovators, the indigenes. That is, it cannot be done by the external advocate or agent of change. Therefore, as members of the receiving society perceive points of identification between their own cultural configuration and the item (idea, behavior, artifact) being introduced, they will more readily accept it and proceed to indigenize it. The task, therefore, of the agent of change, is to advocate the adoption and acceptance of an idea, behavior or artifact, in such a way that it facilitates identification and indigenization rather than obscures it.

Indigenization and Christianity.

With the above discussion giving us a brief introduction to the practical and theoretical significance of indigenization, we now want to consider the relationship between Christianity and indigenization. The question that looms large in this discussion is whether or not Christianity can ever become indigenized when it is introduced into a culture by an outsider. Perhaps the words of F. B. Welbourn will provide the best introduction to the problem under discussion. He notes:

> The Christian faith has its origin in (whatever else he was) a Palestinian Jew of the first century, found its first literary expression primarily in the common Greek of the day, its first intellectual framework in Greek philosophy and its first hierarchical model in the political organization of the Roman Empire.
>
> . . . At every point it has both helped to mould, and itself been moulded by, the total society in which it has lived and preached. There seems to be an inalienable core, which enables one Christian to recognize another across very considerable differences of cultural expression; but what that core is no one group of Christians has ever been able to define to the complete satisfaction of any other; and the particular culture through which the core is expressed has been knit from many factors which have no necessary relationship to the original Christianity (1961: 169-170).

This study has focused on socio-religious change advocated by Anglican missionaries in Island Melanesia. Bishop Patteson, early in the history of the Melanesian Mission advocated an indigenous Melanesian Christianity, rather than assuming that conversion to Christianity implied an automatic conversion to Victorian English values and culture. This study has documented the success and failure of the Melanesian Mission in introducing Christianity in a way that facilitated its indigenization to Melanesian life-ways.

The question before us, of both theoretical and practical interest, is whether or not Christianity introduced by Western missionaries can ever become indigenized into the cultures of those who adopt it. We are now into the area of what Bidney (1953: 163ff) calls metaanthropology, and at the interface of theology and anthropology. This is an area of research that has received inadequate attention, primarily because most theologians lack training in anthropology, and do not adequately understand the concept of culture,[3] and because most anthropologists have little interest in theological concerns.[4] Nevertheless, it is an area ripe for research and pregnant with theoretical issues of importance to contemporary anthropology and missiology.

The process of indigenizing Christianity is similar to that of indigenizing other cultural elements introduced into a culture. The critical tension, however, is between maintaining an essential core of values and beliefs that are clearly identified as Christian (by both advocate and innovator) and expressing this faith in forms that are indigenously meaningful. In other words, there appears to be a fine line between syncretism on the one hand, and indigenous Christianity on the other.[5] And of course, this is the problem encountered by any culturally sensitive missionary, intent on introducing Christianity in such a way that points of identification are easily made by the receptors. There is always the risk of syncretism. But the alternative is also problematic, for if the missionary is culturally insensitive and makes no attempt to communicate Christianity in such a way that it can be easily indigenized, converts, in their striving after meaning, may very well distort the message and develop a syncretistic system of beliefs, in reaction to an incomprehensible and culturally irrelevant gospel.

Perhaps some definitions are in order at this point. I would define religious syncretism as a fusion (blending) of culturally disparate beliefs and practices, so that the resultant form is a new configuration, distinct from both original systems of belief and practice.[6] Religious syncretism is essentially a response to the problem of meaning. In the interaction between Christianity and animism, if the newly introduced Christian forms are given pagan meaning, then syncretism results — the new belief system is neither Christianity nor is it traditional primal religion; it is a mixing of both, and thus the product is qualitatively new.

Herskovits' research in West Africa, the Carribean and Brazil provides vivid illustrations of religious syncretism where Roman Catholic saints in the New World are identified with counterparts in Africa.[7] Thus Catholic worshippers participating in Catholic ritual, led by Catholic priests, were nevertheless syncretistic in their beliefs, for the deities they invoked and their ideology and ceremonialism were Dahomean and Yoruba. The religious meaning derived from the worship was mainly African and animistic. In religious syncretism the striving after meaning causes Christianity to be fused with traditional animistic beliefs in such a way that the essential qualities of Christianity are lost, for the meaning derived is primarily animistic, and the ritual performed is primarily magical.

In contrast to a syncretistic Christianity is indigenous Christianity. Granted, there is a fine line of analytical distinction between the two, and anthropologists have seldom made the careful distinction, but an increasing amount of data demands that we do so in our analysis of religious change.[8] I define indigenous Christianity as the expression of Christian beliefs and meanings in forms that are culturally appropriate for the adherents of that faith. Here the emphasis is upon the retention of Christian meaning, but the expression of that meaning in diverse cultural forms that are meaningful to indigenous converts. Instead of a syncretistic **fusion** of traditional and Christian beliefs and practices, indigenous Christianity leads to a **replacement** of traditional cultural elements by **functionally similar** Christian elements, fulfilling indigenous needs.

Tippett's (1975a: 28) insights into the problem of indigenous Christianity seem especially appropriate at this point. He notes:

> The universal human problems — finding one's way in the darkness, comforting the bereaved, encouraging the discouraged, preserving the family, solving the personal disagreements—will all have their peculiar formations in any culture different from our own. No religion can be indigenous unless it comes to grips with these universal problems in their culture-bound forms. When the laughing and crying, the feasting and mourning, the instructing and singing are truly culturally patterned, then we are looking at indigenous Christianity — here the gospel is at work in an experience of incarnation. And this is a far cry from syncretism (1975a: 28).

The development of an indigenous Christianity is a cultural process whereby an initially foreign message is accepted, taking on a form that is more compatible with the cultural context of the receptors. And as Taber (1978: 54) notes, good indigenization makes the Christian message intelligible in terms of receptor categories of thought and imagery and also relevant to the existential concerns of the receptors. Indigenous Christiantiy thus sharpens the focus of the gospel, whereas syncretism diffuses and confuses the gospel.

Now that the terms of definition have been carefully spelled out, and an analytical distinction drawn between syncretictic Christianity and indigenous Christianity, the next question to pursue is whether or not indigenous Christianity exists anywhere outside the Western world, or if it is only a theoretical fabrication. Let us briefly turn our attention to Africa.

The profound traditional African religiosity seems to have pre-adapted Africans for developing their own indigenous Christianity once they have been given the opportunity. Today, Christianity is undergoing unprecedented growth[9] and an indigenous Christianity is clearly visible on the African continent.

One of the most interesting examples of an African attempt to indigenize Christianity is the emergence of a plethora of Independent Churches. Although the number of African Independent Churches has increased dramatically in the post-colonial era, the phenomenon itself has a history of at least one hundred years. Most of the African Independent Churches have their historical roots in Protestant missions and are reactions against paternalistic and Westernized missionary organizations. They are not reactions against Christianity but against the formal expression of that faith as taught by well-intentioned, but anthropologically uninformed missionaries. Since the appearance of Bengt Sundkler's (1948) classic study, *Bantu Prophets in South Africa*, academic scholarship has turned its attention to this intriguing phenomena with an increasing number of publications.[10]

The majority of African Christians, however, have stayed within the traditions of the missionary-founded churches, but this does not mean they are complacently modeling their missionary antecedents. Indeed, the post-colonial era in Africa has witnessed an astounding increase of interest in generating models of African Christian theology. As the shackles of colonialism have been thrown off, Africans are attempting to rediscover their cultural heritage which for three generations or more was denegrated by most Europeans.[11] This has led to new attempts to clothe Christianity with African garments — using African forms of expression so often discouraged by missionaries in the past. An interesting dialogue is occurring on the continent as Africans attempt to affirm their Christian faith in ways that are their own, developing through a dynamic process, not syncretistic cults, but African forms of indigenous Christiantiy.[12]

Africa has been highlighted in this discussion of indigenous Christianity because of the many different cultural and theological expressions that appear on that continent, and also because of the vast amount of material available to any student of this phenomenon. Nevertheless, indigenous theologies are being developed in other areas of the Third World which are distinct from what is being developed in Africa, but the common goal, an attempt to make Christianity more meaningful in their own cultural context, is the same. For example, Kosuke Koyama (1974) writes of *Waterbuffalo Theology* in Asia, and Jung Young Lee (1979) talks of the *The Theology of Change* from an Oriental perspective. Other significant work on indigenous Christianity in Asia is that of Holth (1968), Beeby (1973), Widjaja (1973), Peter Lee (1974), Gerald Anderson (1976), and Song (1977, 1979, 1982) to name a few. In Latin America the emphasis on liberation theology is another form of indigenizing Christianity.[13] In more general terms, the seminal writing of Visser't Hooft (1967), Von Allmen (1975), and Taber (1978) have made significant theoretical contributions to the problem of indigenous Christianity. The best articles on this topic have been brought together in one volume, edited by Kraft and Wisley (1979).

It is evident that the development of indigenous Christianity in the post-colonial era is more than a passing fad. It is a movement gaining momentum, whose sociological and historical ramifications may prove to be even more significant than the Protestant Reformation. Indeed, Walbert Buhlmann (1978) is suggesting that the church in the Third World is not only ceasing to be under the domination of the West, but that the center of gravity for the Christian Church is shifting rapidly toward this Third Church in the Third World. It is hoped that in the near future anthropologists will respond to this growing phenomenon, for it presents a promising area of study in a dynamic arena of culture change, pregnant with research possibilities.

This discussion of indigenous Christianity in other parts of the world has been a brief divergence to document this interesting phenomenon. But what about Melanesia? Are Melanesians beginning to seek after an alternative form to Western Christianity introduced into the islands by the historical missions? The answer is a resounding "yes," although it does not compare to the phenomenon in Africa. For example, the plethora of cargo cults is in many ways, anthropologically speaking, a Melanesian equivalent to the Independent Churches and syncretistic movements in Africa. That is, it is an expression of a striving after meaning, for unless the introduced forms of Christianity meet the needs of converts, they will make adjustments either in the direction of indigenizing Christianity, or in the direction of syncretism and cargo cults.[14]

There is a growing concern among converts for developing an indigenous Christianity in a Melanesian context, employing traditional forms to express the new meaning found in Christianity. Although the literature is meager compared to that of Africa, it is nevertheless growing in quantity and quality. For example, the theses of Tuza (1970), Hagesi (1972), Suri (1976) and Tavoa (1977) are creative attempts by Melanesian students to develop a Melanesian indigenous Christianity. The recent workshop in the Solomon Islands on "Melanesian Culture and Christian Faith" and in Vanuatu on "New Hebridean Culture and Christian Faith: Two Heads and Two Hearts" are other examples of growing interest being shown by islanders in the problem of developing an indigenous Christianity for Melanesia.[15] Another indication of this growing interest has been the establishment in 1968 of The Melanesian Institute for Pastoral and Socio-economic Service, an ecumenical research organization investigating the relationship of Christianity to Melanesian society and culture.[16]

As the evolution from Mission to Church continues throughout Melanesia, and islanders continue taking over responsibilities from missionaries, there will be an increasing move toward indigenizing the faith as well as the structures of that Melanesian church.[17] As this study has shown, the Melanesian Mission has evolved into an independent and autonomous island church, but it is not yet completely an indigenous church. This will undoubtedly come in time as Melanesian Christians, in their striving after meaning, develop their own Melanesian theology and worship in a manner more appropriate to Melanesia, and not simply a copy of Canterbury.

Christianity and Christendom

One of the primary obstacles on the road to indigenization has been the identification of Christianity with Christendom. These two entities have often been unwittingly merged into one in the minds of many missionaries as they have advocated the acceptance of Christianity by their host society. Despite the popular notion to the contrary, as illustrated in the cartoon in Chapter 3 (p. 170), the two concepts are not synonymous, for Christianity is a belief system rooted in the historical person of Jesus of Nazareth, and Christendom is a Western cultural tradition, influenced pervasively by the Christian religion, but not identical nor synonymous with it.

Viewing Christianity and Christendom as inseparable leads to cultural imperialism on the part of the missionary. A more biblical perspective sees Christianity and culture in a creative, continuous tension. If there is no tension, Christianity can become swallowed up by culture and lose its prophetic impact on society. If the tension is too great and too negative then Christianity cannot effectively relate to people embedded in their own culture. A way out of this dilemma, shunning both extremes, is to adopt a positive but critical attitude toward culture. Bleeker captures this perspective when he notes:

> The moment Christianity allies itself too closely to worldly norms, it loses its purity and grandeur. If, on the other hand, it keeps aloof from the culture around it, it will fail to be effective . . . Christianity does not retire from the world as a matter of principle, it is not hostile to culture but critical of it. The Christian attitude to the world is positive rather than negative (1965: 37-39).[18]

The European Christian missionary is a product of Western cultural traditions and denominational distinctives, but his self-proclaimed task is to disseminate a message of Good News which claims to be universal and not culture-bound. Many missionaries in the past, and not too few in the present, lacking anthropological insight and an understanding of the concept of culture, have confused Christianity with Christendom, and the gospel of Christ with Western cultural traditions and denominational distinctives. This, of course, has often resulted in gross misunderstanding and frustrating endeavors. Nida brings this problem clearly into focus when he notes that:

> Bathing frequently, brushing one's teeth, abstaining from beer, tobacco and betel nut, and refusing to eat clams or oysters have all been preached by various missionaries as symbols of the "new life in Christ Jesus" (1954: 255).

One of the results of this confusion between Christianity and Christendom in the minds of missionaries has been that they have often advocated that indigenous cultural elements be displaced or altered, not because they violated Christian principles of belief or practice, but because they offended the missionaries' sense of propriety, derived from their Western norms and values. The words of the nineteenth century missionary statesman, Rufus Anderson (1875: 61) poignantly illustrate this confusion, for in articulating the goal of the work of the American Board among American Indians, he stated that the objective was "to make them English in language, civilized in habits, and Christian in their religion." Hopefully these words represent a bygone era, but they illustrate a missionary approach that is the antithesis of encouraging converts to develop their own indigenous Christianity. This missionary strategy is the advocation of Christendom, not simply the proclamation of Christianity, and as such, is the epitome of cultural imperialism.

Theoretically it is important to make this distinction between Christianity as a belief system, and Christendom as a Western cultural tradition, because too often anthropological analysis of religious change has ignored this distinction, and instead, has lumped the influence of Christianity and the influence of Western cultural tradition into one monolithic enterprise called missionization. Unfortunately this tends to obscure fine details that are important in the study of culture change, for indigenous innovators do not simply respond passively to Christianity as a unilateral force, but are highly discriminating and selective in their choices for change. Therefore, any analysis of Christian missions and their effect on culture change needs to be done from two different perspectives — the Christian or religious, and the Western or cultural influence.

This distinction also has important practical implications for missionaries as agents of change. In this era of post-colonial missions the model of cultural imperalism as part and parcel of evangelism is an anachronism that should be housed with the archives of the colonial period. But if missionaries are going to avoid the pitfalls of cultural imperalism, they will have to advocate the adoption of Christianity as a religion, and not Christendom as a cultural tradition.[19] Only by internalizing this philosophical distinction can they develop a methodology of partnership with their host society and aid in the development of, and clearing the way for, a truly indigenous Christianity to emerge.[20]

Missionaries and Culture Change

In this section an attempt will be made to deal comprehensively with changes advocated by the Melanesian Mission during the five periods delineated in this study and listed below:

Period V	Autonomy	1975-present
Period IV	Absorption	1942-1975
Period III	Penetration	1900-1942
Period II	Contact	1850-1900
Period I	Pre-contact	prior to 1850

The following processual model of change, based on acculturation theory, is useful as a heuristic device to demonstrate the nature of culture change resulting from European and Melanesian interaction through time.[21] I postulate four conceptual stages in this dynamic process, illustrated in the following figure.

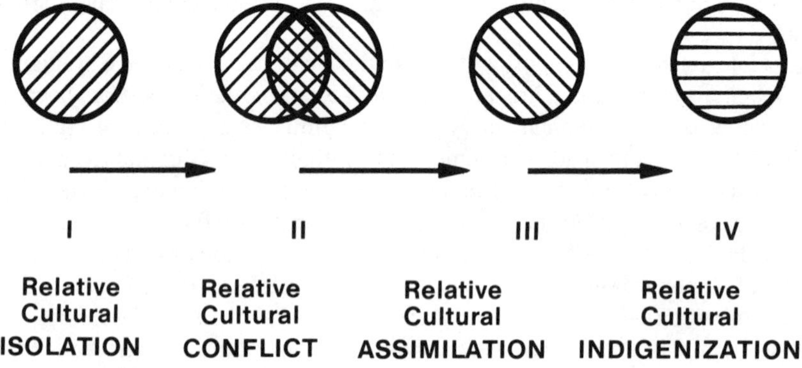

Fig. 18. Processual Model of Culture Change.

The five periods of this study correspond to this processual model in the following way:

PERIOD		STAGE
I. Pre-Contact	pre-1850	I. Isolation
II. Contact	1850-1900	
III. Penetration	1900-1942	II. Conflict
IV. Absorption	1942-1975	III. Assimilation
V. Autonomy	1975-	IV. Indigenization

Discussion.

Stage I. Relative Cultural Isolation.

In this stage the indigenous society and culture remains relatively isolated from external European influences. Although a few items of material culture may be introduced through intermittent contact with Europeans, the structure of the relationship is such that any culture change occurring is non-directed.

Period I and II of this study correspond to the stage of Relative Cultural Isolation. In the pre-contact period Melanesians had infrequent contact with Europeans—explorers, whalers, sandalwooders, and traders. There were, however, no sustained European communities in the islands whose purpose it was to directly advocate change in the indigenous communities. Sundry material artifacts entered the island communities in exchange for island products, but the nature of the indigenous society and culture remained relatively unaltered. Nevertheless, as I have stressed above in this study, this period of relative isolation from European contact does not imply a static Melanesian cultural arena, for it was very dynamic with continuous change occurring, but change occurring in a system isolated from European influence and control.

Period II of this study has been called the period of contact. This was the era of the Melanesian Mission's initial thrust into the island world. For most of the islanders, their contact with the Mission introduced them to their first exposure to Christianity. But Melanesians were being exposed to other things in addition to a new religion during this period. Although contact with whalers decreased after the 1860's, that with traders increased, such that by the end of this period (1900) there were traders living permanently in the islands. During this period the labor trade made its demands on Melanesian society, bringing considerable injustice in its train, and for islanders, wider exposure to the European world outside Melanesia. Thus, although the Melanesian Mission was the only missionary organization present, it nevertheless was competing with other influences.[22]

To gain the goodwill of potential converts the Mission was forced to operate in a method similar to that of other Europeans, namely by trading items of Western manufacture, not only for exchange of goods and services, but also for potential converts. Although the success of the Mission in proselytizing was limited during this period, there were nevertheless areas such as Mota, Nggela and Santa Isabel that underwent significant socio-cultural change toward the end of this period of contact. The reduction of internecine warfare and the stabilizing of society were perhaps the most significant social changes. The acquistion of new values and behavioral codes commensurate with the new religion clearly brought about significant socio-cultural changes in those communities where Christianity was adopted.

Stage II. Relative Cultural Conflict.

The third period of this study, a period of missionary penetration into Melanesia (1900-1942), corresponds roughly to the stage of relative cultural conflict. This is represented in Fig. 18 by two circles overlapping, where a conflict of values and life-ways is generated between those of traditional Melanesia and those of the colonial power. Marching Rule, although discussed in the next period, belongs to this stage of relative cultural conflict. Marching

Rule and the Fallowes movement are symptomatic of the kinds of latent cultural conflict that seemed to permeate Melanesia during this period of the colonial era. European colonialism made increasing demands on the Melanesians—demands on their land, demands on their labor and demands on their culture. The structural relationship between Europeans and Melanesians was one of dominance and submisssion, with racism and paternalism permeating European attitudes. Cultural conflict was also manifest in the disease, death, depopulation and demoralization that characterized many Melanesian communities during this period.

The Melanesian Mission was no longer the sole agent of Christian proselytizing. Its monopoly on the field gave way to competition with other missions for converts. And converts there were—village after village formally accepted Christianity, and the migration from scattered hamlets in the mountains to nucleated villages on the coast was one of the most graphic expressions of the conversion process during this period of penetration. Among second and third generation converts, toward the end of this period, Christianity frequently became routinized and dull, as the initial enthusiasm characteristic of many first generation Christians began to wane.

Because of increasing European dominance and penetration into more areas of Melanesian life, it is often difficult to analytically separate mission influence from that of government and commerce. The most significant changes brought about by the Mission during this period were undoubtedly those introduced through its hospitals and especially its schools. Education became the primary vehicle to greater social mobility and participation in the wider society in a world dominated by colonial interests. Mission schools became the primary agent of enculturation to European values and lifestyles, which included at least nominal adherence to Christian beliefs and practices. In the case of the New Hebrides and the Solomon Islands, the government was all too willing to allow the missions this responsibility, channeling its meager funds instead into administrative and police activities.

Stage III. Relative Cultural Assimilation.

The fourth period, one of absorption (1942-1975) in this study, can be seen as a stage of relative cultural assimilation. Cultural assimilation is a process whereby the members of the subordinate society begin to incorporate values and roles of the dominant society into their culture. Thus for example, a Melanesian Big Man no longer gains his renown from being a warrior as he may have done in the stage of cultural isolation. Instead, he becomes a Big Man through successful participation in Europeanized political, economic or ecclesiastical institutions and structures.

This period of absorption begins with World War II and its cultural impact on Melanesia, and ends with the independence of the Church of Melanesia. This period corresponds fairly well to the stage of relative cultural assimilation. Changes introduced in this period came from the multiplex functions and activities of the dominant European-controlled institutions. Thus, for example, this period led to greater involvement of islanders in the political destiny of their own country, culminating in Independence for the Solomon Islands in July 1978, and Independence for the New Hebrides in July 1980. During this period the ecclesiastical structures of the Melanesian Mission gave way to greater and more meaningful participation by islanders in the life of their church. Also the influence of a cash economy increased significantly during this period, making inroads into what was traditionally a subsistence economy where people lived primarily from the produce of the land and sea with few imports from outside.

The primary change for this period, which can be associated with the Melanesian Mission, continued to be introduced through the schools, enculturating islanders in how to function successfully in a Melanesian world dominated by European interests. Nevertheless, the Melanesian Mission was the first to take the lead in promoting independence and voicing confidence in the capacity of Melanesian leadership to function in the Europeanized institutions of the church. Later (1978 and 1980) the British and French colonial powers followed suit by granting independence to Melanesians in the political field. Thus the changes introduced in previous periods by the Melanesian Mission continued to be important in this period, but the significant difference was the evolution of a foreign mission society into a localized Melanesian church—a vivid illustration of cultural assimilation.

Stage IV. Relative Cultural Indigenization.

The essential features of this stage of cultural change are a return to traditional elements and values that were subjugated under the domination of European influence. This stage does not imply a nativistic retreat and regression back to the pre-contact world, but it does mean a valuing of things that are a part of the indigenous cultural heritage. The process of Africanization in the post-colonial era is but one of several outstanding examples of this process. In Melanesia, this process of relative cultural indigenization is only beginning. For example, one of the bishops of the Church of Melanesia told me that when he was a young student in the mission schools he came to believe that his own culture was woefully inferior to that of the Europeans, and that the only way for him to "get ahead in the world" would be to model European behavior, not emulate Melanesian life-ways. Being a gifted and charismatic leader, he rose through the ranks of the mission hierarchy, espousing European values and encouraging his own people to modernize through education and economic development. He saw no future for Melanesian culture, and so he measured success in accordance with the degree of assimilation to European values and life-ways. The more Europeanized Melanesians became, the more successful they would become. Today his tune has changed, and he regrets his former philosophy and practice. He has done an about-face in his attitude toward Melanesian culture and today is a leading spokesman for the preservation of things Melanesian, and for indigenization of the church and government. He no longer has an inferiority complex *vis a vis* his own Melanesian cultural heritage. He has not become anti-European, he is simply pro-Melanesian.

The process of relative cultural indigenization is not an easy one, for the relics of colonialism permeate much of the society. It is easy for post-colonial leaders to mimic the ways of their colonial masters before them, and, in a new kind of exploitation, usher in an era of neo-colonial totalitarianism. It is interesting to note that in Melanesia, there has been a basic continuity of traditional values through time.[23] This constitutes a valuable resource on which islanders can draw as they produce a new cultural creation and prepare for the future, not by retreating from the present and returning to the past, but by reshaping imported institutional structures in light of Melanesian designs for living.

The period of autonomy in this study ushers in the stage of relative cultural indigenization. The era of the Melanesian Mission has come to an end, but the era of the Church of Melanesia is just beginning. Mission impact and influence will undoubtedly continue to be felt for years, but the Church of Melanesia is now a Christian fellowship group of Melanesian believers. It is the islanders themselves who will be the architects for designing how that church will function in their own society. As the process of indigenization begins, some of the functions and forms of the church introduced by the missionaries will undoubtedly undergo change, but there is little evidence that the church will disappear and be seen only as a religious relic of the colonial past. This new era presents numerous opportunities for anthropological investigation. The cultural process of moving from assimilation to indigenization should be at least as interesting as is the process of change from cultural isolation to assimilation, which heretofore has been the primary focus of anthropological studies of culture change. The classic methodology of a study and subsequent restudy will be a very useful tool for measuring culture change in the process of indigenization.

Summary of Cultural Changes in This Study

In summarizing the cultural change documented in this study it will perhaps be useful now to return to the analytical framework discussed in Chapter 1, pp. 16-17. This framework, adapted after Spicer (1961), has guided my thinking and organized my research throughout this study. It has proved to be a useful methodological tool in investigation and will now be used as a heuristic device to distinguish the different periods of this study in terms of the predominant contact communities in each period and the general type of change that has resulted from Melanesian contact with these communities. The following framework expressed in very general terms, but tied to historical events, enables one to see the change resulting from 125 years of culture contact in Melanesia (Table 7.1, p. 426). It combines the five periods of this study with the four stages of culture change outlined above.

The Melanesian Mission and Indigenization: An Evaluation

Although this study has focused on culture change in general, the particular emphasis has been on the Melanesian Mission as an agent of change. The question that needs to be considered in this concluding chapter is what actions on the part of missionaries led to the indigenization of Christianity in Melanesia, and what actions inhibited it. I consider indigenization to be a positive goal in any program of directed change. Therefore, inasmuch as missionaries promoted indigenization, I would evaluate them positively, and where they obstructed and inhibited it, I would evaluate them negatively. There are several positive factors that can be enumerated that promoted indigenization of Christianity in Melanesia:

1. Intercultural Understanding. The general positive and empathetic attitude demonstrated toward Melanesians, especially by early missionaries, is a significant factor. They treated the islanders as human beings with dignity, not as ignorant savages to be abused; they declared without qualification a confidence in the islanders' capacity to understand and internalize Christian beliefs and practices. Moreover, the founders of the Melanesian Mission stated as their objective the growth of a Melanesian Church, led by Melanesian clergy, worshipping in a Melanesian way. This "Melanesian ethos" in the Mission's early period was eloquently articulated by Bishop Patteson on numerous occasions. The subsequent history of the Melanesian Mission steered a course contrary to this stated goal, but this does not detract from the initial objective of establishing an independent Melanesian church. It is unfortunate that this culturally sensitive ethos which was characteristic of the Melanesian Mission during its early years of operation, did not continue throughout the Mission's history.

2. Translations. A second factor is the strong emphasis on vernacular translations of the Bible and Prayer Book. Granted, what was selected as important for translation was done from a European viewpoint, but the emphasis upon getting material into the language of converts was a positive step toward indigenization. This emphasis was also more characterisic of the earlier rather than later phase of the Mission's activities.

3. Leadership. Thirdly, the Mission advanced Melanesians into leadership positions in the Church through their system of catechist-teachers, and the ordination of deacons and priests. For example, if one compares the record of the Marist Mission in the Solomons with that of the Melanesian Mission,

PERIOD	HISTORICAL EVENTS		CONTACT COMMUNITIES	STAGE	TYPE OF CHANGE
V. 1975- present	1980 1978 1975	Vanuatu Independ. Solomon Islands Independence COM Independ.	Multinational corporations	Indigenization	Impact of urbanization and modernization.
IV. 1942-1975	1946- 1953	Marching Rule	American and Japanese military, Missions, Plantations, Government officials.	Assimilation	Acculturation to European lifeways and values.
III. 1900-1942	1942 1927 1922 1906- 1914 1906	World War II Murder of Bell on Malaita Head tax imposed Laborers return to Melanesia Anglo-French Condominium—N.H.	Competitive Missions, Plantations, Government officials, and Traders.	Culture Conflict	Migration from scattered hamlets to coastal villages. Acceptance of European material goods and religion.
II. 1850-1900	1893 1871 1860- 1870	Protectorate in Solomon Islands Patteson killed Labor Trade commences	Labor recruiters, Resident traders, Anglican missionaries.	Isolation	Acceptance of European material goods and selective acceptance of Christianity.
I. before 1850	1820- 1860 1767- 1840 1568	Whalers & Traders French & English Explorers Mendana discovers Solomon Islands	Traders: beche de mer, turtle shell, sandalwood, etc. Whalers, Explorers.	Isolation	No substantial change in Melanesian way of life. Introduction of selected artifacts.

Table 7.1. Culture Change in Island Melanesia: An Overview.

the difference in this regard is readily apparent. The Marists insisted on celibacy as a prerequisite for ordination to the priesthood, the Anglicans did not. The first Melanesian ordained priest in the Anglican Mission was George Sarawia in 1873. In contrast, the first Solomon Islander to reach this status among the Catholic Marists was Michael Aike of Malaita, ordained in 1966. In 1972 the Marists had only thirteen indigenous priests in the Solomon Islands, including seven in the diocese of Bougainville.[24] Moreover, the Melanesian Mission symbolically displayed even greater confidence in the Melanesians' capacity for leadership within the church by elevating two Solomon Islanders to the level of assistant bishop in 1963.

4. Cultural Tolerance. Fourthly, the Melanesian Mission adopted a stance of relative tolerance toward indigenous customs. Instead of lumping them all together and branding them as heathen or demonic, many missionaries were careful not to deliberately destroy that which they evaluated as morally neutral *vis a vis* Christianity. With this attitude of tolerance, it is not surprising that the Mission attracted men who combined cross-cultural empathy with scholarship and keen observation, producing some excellent ethographies. The greatest of this group was probably R. H. Codrington, but C. E. Fox made some very significant anthropological contributions as well. Others included Penny, Ivens, Hopkins, and Durrad. Encouraged by relatively empathetic understanding and scholarly insight from missionaries like these, the indigenous adaptation of Christianity to a Melanesian context was enhanced rather than thwarted by the Mission.

5. Independence. Fifthly, and perhaps the most important landmark on the road to indigeneity, was the granting of independence to the Church of Melanesia in 1975. The Church of Melanesia is no longer the "mission field" of the Melanesian Mission, but an independent and autonomous province within the world-wide Anglican Communion. Nevertheless, a self-governing church is not synonymous with an indigenous church. Self-governance is a necessary but not a sufficient condition for an indigenous church. With Melanesians now in control of their own church the progress toward indigeneity may continue, but there is no guarantee that this will be so.

On the negative side of evaluation there are also several factors that inhibited or obstructed indigeneity. Many of these are the reverse side of what I have already enumerated as positive factors. They include the following:

1. Method of proselytizing. The approach of extracting people from their cultural context and teaching them about Christianity in a Europeanized environment, may have appeared to the founders to be the only viable option open to them. Nevertheless, it led to meager results in the first fifty years and tended to lead islanders to associate Christianity with Europeans, rather than perceive it as a vital force within their own Melanesian society. Those areas where there were significant people movements toward Christianity in the first fifty years, namely Mota, Nggela and Santa Isabel, are also the areas where there was a more sustained missionary presence living with and among the islanders.

2. Paternalism. This doctrine of cultural superiority became manifest in the Melanesian Mission from the turn of the century onward. It was an attitude toward indigenous life that pervaded the colonial world, and so it is not surprising that many missionaries of this period should also reflect the times in their relationships with islanders. Paternalism was displayed in numerous ways. For example, the concept of Christian stewardship was never taught in a convincing manner since the missionaries saw themselves in a benevolent role of helping the islanders, rather than emphasizing that Melanesians should learn to help themselves. Paternalism was the manifestation of a lack of confidence in the capacity of Melanesians to sustain the Christian religion as their own, integrated meaningfully into their society and culture.

Although I am suggesting that paternalism in the Melanesian Mission was a problem that thwarted indigenization, the Anglican missionaries must be evaluated in the broader context in which they functioned. Compared with other missions of the same time period and geographical area, the Anglicans appeared far less paternalistic. For example, the Presbyterian Mission in the New Hebrides and the Methodist Mission in the Western Solomons were both very paternalistic, and in time, each reaped the rewards; each area was the scene of a significant nativistic movement away from the church — the John Frum Movement in the New Hebrides, and the Silas Eto Christian Fellowship Church in the Western Solomons.[25]

3. Hierarchical control. One of the outworkings of paternalism was that the missionaries maintained tight control of the hierarchical structure of the Mission. Although the Mission must be commended for its relatively good record in ordaining indigenous clergy, it nevertheless maintained control at the top through European missionaries. The Mission tended to revolve around the person of the bishop, and not all bishops had the cross-cultural sensitivity that Patteson and Steward displayed. If the Melanesian clergy had been given positions of authority, especially over their European counterparts, it would have given the islanders a greater sense that the church was really theirs. Instead, the church was frequently identified with the Mission. It was an institution to employ European priests or to entertain missionary circles back in England with dramatic tales of the natives. Even with the appointment of two Solomon Island assistant bishops, the Melanesian leadership and authority in the church was more apparent than real. The power resided with the European missionaries who controlled the Mission ecclesiastically, financially and legally.

4. Foreign worship and church structure. Another way in which the Melanesian Mission inhibited indigenization was through its imposition of a foreign worship pattern and ecclesiastical structure. Instead of encouraging Melanesians to use their rich cultural heritage of drama, dance and song in worship, as the Methodists did in Fiji, the Anglicans tended to be rigid and uncreative. New hymns using indigenous tunes were not introduced and created by Melanesians to reflect their encounter with Christianity. Instead, they were translated and sung to the same tunes as hymns in England. Drama was not used to express Christian meanings. Instead, Melanesian clergy were instructed in homiletics as if they were European seminarians and taught to preach and to perform the religious ceremonies accurately according to formulae established by Canterbury. Melanesian forms and structures were ignored as unsuitable for Christian worship. This, of course, led to the feeling among many converts that Christianity was a foreign religion — the antithesis of indigenization.

5. Translations. I have cited the Melanesian Mission's admirable record of translation work in the first fifty years as a positive contribution to indigenization. The reverse side of this good record is that in the last seventy-five years missionaries increasingly took translation work less seriously. If the proclamation of a missionary's message is intended to be "Good News," it can hardly be perceived this way if it is interpreted as unintelligible news. And yet, for many Melanesian congregations, this was the situation since they did not have the Prayer Book or Bible in their own language. The Mission tended to rely too heavily on Mota as the language of worship throughout Melanesia. This was fine for Banks' Islanders who understood it, or for the young Norfolk Island scholars who learned it, but it was inadequate for everyone else. On islands such as Santa Isabel where several languages were spoken, the Mission seemed content to use only the first language translated (such as Bugotu) for the other speech communities on the island. Granted, the legion of languages in Melanesia required a herculean task of translation, but without every villager worshipping, reading or hearing in a language he understood, the process of indigenizing Christianity met with a very serious obstacle. It is indeed noteworthy that as the church has become independent and is now striving to become indigenous, the bishops have set translation work as a high priority in their dioceses.

Missionaries as Cultural Destroyers or Cultural Brokers?

In this discussion of missionaries and cultural change, it is important to consider an issue on which a great deal of anthropological and literary ink has been spilt. The issue is whether or not the accusation, made by anthropologists and novelists alike, that missionaries have been in the vanguard of cultural destruction, is indeed a justified claim. This is a very sensitive issue among anthropologists who characterize themselves as the champions of cultural preservation among the thousands of different ethnic and linguistic communities in the world. The missionary is often portrayed as the antithesis of the anthropologist — one whose objective is conversion, not the perservation of cultural differences.[26] Is this caricature of the missionary a fair one, or is the missionary more accurately portrayed as a cultural broker instead of a destroyer of cultural differences?

Any generalizations will be inadequate because of the diversity of missionary types that exist. Also, missionary attitudes toward other cultures have changed through time, and on the whole, have become more anthropologically informed, and thus more tolerant of cultural differences. A general pattern, however, does emerge in terms of missionaries' attitudes toward indigenous cultures. On the whole, Catholic missionaries, especially since Vatican II, have tended to be the most tolerant and understanding, conservative fundamentalist missionaries the least. Many culturally sensitive missionaries have probed the indigenous cultures for points of contact with Christianity, and have viewed their efforts as one of accommodating the gospel they bring to the indigenous cultures that receive it. Many of these missionaries have made superb ethnological contributions in the course of their missionary work.[27] On the other hand, other missionaries have considered indigenous cultures to be a religious *tabula rasa* on which they have come to erect a structure of Christian belief. They have tended to perceive little value in any elements of the indigenous culture, and so have attempted to Westernize as much as Christianize their potential converts. It is these missionaries who are often the target of those persons who value highly indigenous cultural diversity. But it is a gross misjudgment to assume that all missionaries have been of this type.

Missionaries have seldom been an isolated acculturative influence, but have often been part and parcel of Western expansion into the Third World. Sometimes they have preceded commerce and government; more often they have followed. This expansionism of the West has wrought tremendous socio-cultural change wherever it has impinged on indigenous societies. Thus change has been inevitable. To accuse the entire missionary enterprise of being a tool of colonialism is a polemic that will not stand against the documentary evidence to the contrary. Of course, there have been some notorious exceptions such as Shirley Baker of Tonga,[28] but the majority of missionaries have tended to fulfill the role of cultural brokers and have resisted theocratic empire building.[29]

Many missionaries have been cultural brokers in the sense that they have eased the transition for indigenes from isolation to contact with the Western world. Frequently traditional religious systems have been found wanting by indigenes in the face of rapid socio-cultural change due to depopulation, commercial exploitation, and/or political domination. Under these circumstances Christianity has often been adopted as a functional substitute, as a more effective system of beliefs to aid dejected and demoralized indigenes in accounting for and reconciling such rapid changes in their traditional way of life. Missionaries in their role as cultural brokers have often functioned as interpreters of this rapid change coming from Western intrusion into indigenous societies. They have frequently functioned as a buffer zone to ease the culture shock from change that was inevitable. In their role as cultural brokers, missionaries have aided indigenes in the transition from a face-to-face world of particularistic concerns to participation in the wider society where they will come into contact with universalistic concerns as the world becomes a global community. Unfortunately for many ethnic groups cultural isolation is no longer an option today. Therefore, inasmuch as missionaries have helped to articulate villagers with the wider society, they have performed an important role as cultural brokers.[30]

I am not attempting here to give an apologetic defense of, nor justification for, the missionary enterprise. I am only suggesting that any wholesale condemnation of missionaries as cultural destroyers is both superficial and inaccurate. I would suggest the following criteria be applied to any analysis of missionaries as agents of change before they are categorized as either cultural brokers or cultural destroyers:

1. Different mission organizations have vastly different attitudes toward indigenous cultures. While all missionaries are concerned with conversion to Christianity, their methodologies for proselytizing vary considerably from one group to another. Therefore, **each mission must be evaluated on a case by case basis**, and not all lumped together into a single category of missionization. This lumping together obscures the important differences that exist between them.

2. **Missionaries must be evaluated in terms of the historical context in which they functioned.** For example, I believe that paternalism is always a negative attribute and an inappropriate attitude in cross-cultural relationships, but missionary paternalism in the heydey of colonialism must be evaluated differently from paternalism in the post-colonial era of missions. The historical context in which missionaries function today is not the same as it was in the colonial era, and so we cannot fairly evaluate missionaries of the colonial era from today's vantage point and by today's standards and insights.

3. **An evaluation of missionaries must not only consider the historical context, but also the cultural milieu in which they serve.** The modern missionary movement has been part and parcel of Western expansionism both politically and economically. Missionaries must therefore be evaluated in terms of the roles they played *vis a vis* Western intrusion into indigenous societies. Thus it is inaccurate to evaluate them as if they have been the only agents of change, assuming there would have been little or no cultural change

in these indigenous societies if only the missionary had stayed home. Without question, missionaries have been very significant agents of change in the last 150 years, but they have not been change agents in isolation. While they have advocated conversion to Christianity, other representatives from the West have brought political and economic changes. Whereas missionaries have used persuasive influence, colonial governments have had coercive power to enforce change they deemed necessary in indigenous societies.[31]

4. Finally, the fourth criterion applied to an evaluation of the missionary enterprise is grounded in the theoretical framework of this study, namely, missionaries are the advocates of change, indigenes are the innovators. It is misleading to portray missionaries as simply cultural destroyers actively manipulating passive natives. The receptors of the missionary's message and activity have an equally active role in the process of innovation. They are not passive recipients, but active participants, reinterpreting, modifying, accepting and rejecting change advocated by the missionary. Often the message of the missionary has been accepted as a means to an end quite different from what the missionary proposed. **It is in the transactional strategies employed by indigenous innovators that we find the real locus of change—not in what the missionary advocates.** Thus, any framework for evaluating missionary activity must include the innovative strategies employed by indigenes. When the active indigenous response is taken into consideration it often alters one's perception of the missionary's role.

Summary

This study has attempted to employ these four criteria in evaluating the activities of the Melanesian Mission over a 125-year period. If an evaluative axis were constructed with the missionary as a cultural broker at one end, and as a cultural destroyer at the other, I believe the evidence for the Melanesian Mission would establish it nearer to the cultural broker end of the axis as illustrated below:

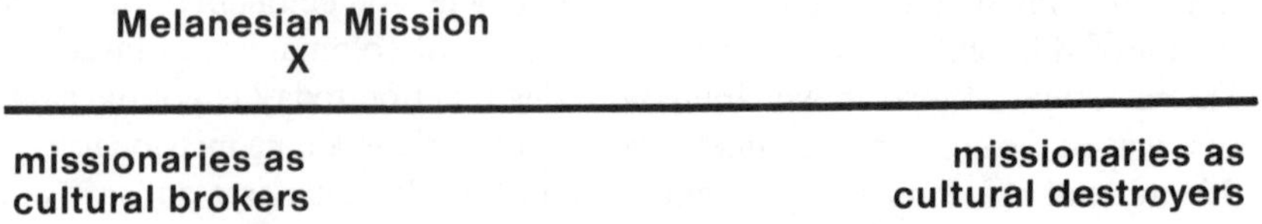

Melanesian Mission
X

---

missionaries as cultural brokers	**missionaries as cultural destroyers**

Fig. 19. An Evaluative Axis for Missionary Activity.

I recognize that the above scale is not based on criteria that have been empirically measured on a scale of 1-10, but the ethnohistorical evidence leaves no doubt that an evaluation of the Melanesian Mission should be placed closer to the cultural broker end of the axis. Within the Melanesian Mission itself, there were missionaries such as Charles Fox who represent the archetype of the cultural broker, while others could more aptly be described as cultural destroyers. Nevertheless, the Mission as a whole, during its 125-year history, tended to attract people who were culturally sensitive and not overly ethnocentric in their relationships with Melanesians.

Principles of Cross-cultural Communication for Agents of Change

This case study of the Melanesian Mission as an advocate of change has some important theoretical and practical implications that reach beyond the confines of the Melanesian cultural arena of missionary-indigene interaction. Therefore, in this section I will discuss some principles of cross-cultural communication that are important to missionaries and other agents of change.

Anthropological science has made us vividly aware of the tremendous diversity of cultures despite the commonality of man. It has also documented the pervasive function that culture has in shaping our values, our behavior, and even our conception of the world. The 5,000 or more languages, in the world[32] are not simply alternative symbolic systems that reflect the same reality; it is believed that they represent different realities altogether. Some languages of course, such as German and English, are symbolic systems representing nearly the same reality, but others such as English and Hopi reflect quite different realities, for they each impose a different order on the world.[33]

Because of linguistic and cultural diversity, communication across linguistic and cultural boundaries is indeed very complex and very difficult, but normally not impossible. To communicate effectively, however, the communicator has to do more than simply learn the language of the receptor. He must also be aware of the receptor's worldview and culture in which he is embedded. As Kraft (1979:147) notes, "The purpose of communication is to bring a receptor to understand a message presented by a communicator in a way that substantially corresponds with the intent of the communicator."

Effective communication is difficult to achieve, for what is **intended** by the communicator and what is **understood** by the receptor, are often not identical, even when communication takes place between members of the same speech community and culture, who hold similar values, similar worldviews and similar norms of behavior. It is, of course, even more difficult to assure that the receptor understands what the communicator intends when none of these are held in common. Owing to these complexities, successful communication must be measured **not** by what is said, but by what the receptor understands. If the receptor understands what the communicator intended, then communication between the two has been successful. Even though the communicator may be articulate and eloquent, employing vivid illustrations to get his message across, he has failed if his listeners do not understand what he has intended to communicate.

When two human beings interact they are communicating to each other in more ways than simply through verbal exchange. There are many messages being sent between the two, many of which lie below the conscious level of both communicator and recipient. Often these paramessages distract from, or confuse, the main verbal message, so that what the communicator says is contradicted or superseded by the paramessages that communicate a different behavior, or attitude, etc. The popular phrase, "One's actions speak louder than one's words," captures this principle of communication.[34]

For example, the Melanesian Mission, in an attempt to earn the goodwill of the islanders upon initial contact, doled out gifts of fish-hooks, steel axes, cloth, and sundry other "trade" items. The missionaries intended that this "paramessage" be used to facilitate the communication of their main message — the Good News of Jesus Christ. But frequently islanders enthusiastically received the paramessage that said, "We want to establish goodwill," but ignored altogether as meaningless or irrelevant the missionaries' main message. Thus in some cases the behavioral paramessage confused or detracted from the missionaries' main verbal message. I believe Nida (1954: 251) has touched a crucial point when he notes that, "It is not primarily the message but the messenger of Christianity that provides the greatest problems for the average non-Christian."

The Problem of Form and Meaning.

One of the most important areas of culture that contributes to the problem of cross-cultural communication is the relationship between cultural forms and the meanings they convey. Cultural forms are the obvious, observable and audible parts of culture such as material artifacts, behavior, ceremonies, words, etc. and they are always culture specific. That is, they do not convey any universal meaning, but are related to a specific meaning which is determined by the cultural context in which they are employed. Thus a form transplanted from one culture to another seldom, if ever, carries the same meaning across cultural boundaries. The people who adopt an introduced form will assign a meaning to it that is different from the meaning assigned to it in the original culture.[35]

For example, missionaries introducing the Bible to Mazatecos Indians in Mexico used an indigenous term for the concept of "God's Word." This society of Indians had a culture that was pervaded by the belief that one could have supernatural experiences by eating hallucinogenic mushrooms. Therefore, the Mazatecos considered the mushroom a means of getting a message from God. Thus the form (word) used by the missionaries to translate "God's Word" meant to the receptors "eating the sacred mushroom."

Since all kinds of ritual precaution and tabus surrounded the use of the mushroom, these people interpreted the term for "God's Word" in the same category of meaning as "eating the sacred mushroom." Consequently they were afraid to read the Bible for fear they would break the same tabus imposed on ritual mushroom eating, and therefore go crazy, or their children would die, or some other calamity would befall them. After more than a year the missionaries finally discovered the way the Mazatecos were interpreting what they had intended to communicate, so they changed the form and used a different set of terms that meant, "This book teaches us about God." The alternative term conveyed a different meaning to the Mazatecos that was now closer to what the missionaries had orignially intended to communicate. Consequently, they were no longer afraid to read the Bible.[36]

There are numerous examples in the literature of indigenes applying a particular meaning to a form used by a missionary that is very different from what the missionary had intended to communicate. The religious rites of water baptism and Holy Communion are two such forms that are particularly susceptible to this problem of reinterpretation.

Cultural forms are important because of the **meaning** they convey, and not because there is any intrinsic value in them. A form in and of itself is useless—only when it imparts meaning to someone does it take on a useful function. We often forget this because in our habitual day-to-day activities we do not pause to analytically separate the meaning from the form. We treat them psychologically as a whole unit. And of course this is precisely where we run into difficulty when we attempt to communicate to someone who does not derive the same meaning from the form we use, whether it be a word, an act or an object. We say something or do something in an attempt to communicate a specific meaning, but the words we use or the behavior we adopt have a very different meaning for the receptor, and thus our communication is ineffective. We frequently insist on using certain cultural forms because they have certain meanings for us, and because of our cultural conditioning, it all seems so natural, so right. Therefore when we see others employing different forms to communicate the same meaning it strikes us as strange, weird or even wrong. And yet, this is the nature of culture in which every human being is embedded.[37] It is clear that effective communication must be receptor-oriented, and as Kraft (1979: 7) notes, the anthropological perspective in cross-cultural communication forces us to take our hearers seriously if we expect them to take us seriously.[38]

This seems to be the heart of the missionary problem, or for that matter, the crucial dimension of any program of directed cultural change. How does one advocate change across cultural boundaries without a loss of meaning? For the missionary the problem is how to communicate the meaning of Christianity in forms that will be meaningful to the receptors in another culture.

Receptor-oriented communication means that the advocate of change must transpose himself into the indigenous frame of reference of the potential innovators. Too often advocates of change have demanded that the receptors get into their Western frame of reference before communication between the two can take place. When this happens, frequently each side of the cultural-linguistic barrier misunderstands the other. For example, if the colonial administration in the Solomon Islands had been capable of understanding the frame of reference of the islanders, they would have seen Marching Rule, not as a negative reactionary movement, but as a dynamic and positive attempt by Melanesians to bring cohesion to their worldview and affirm the integrity of their Melanesian cultural traditions. The "solutions" to Marching Rule were determined from a European perspective and were thus inadequate. An emic (insider's) analysis of "problem areas" is critically important if a meaningful solution is to obtain.

How does this insight into cross-cultural communication relate to missionary advocacy for conversion to Christianity? With this perspective we can see that when missionaries fail to be receptor-oriented in their communication, or refuse to transpose themselves into the frame of reference of their potential converts, they frequently are advocating a cultural conversion to a Western worldview and lifeway, not simply conversion to Christianity within their own indigenous culture. The following model will perhaps be helpful in illustrating this point:

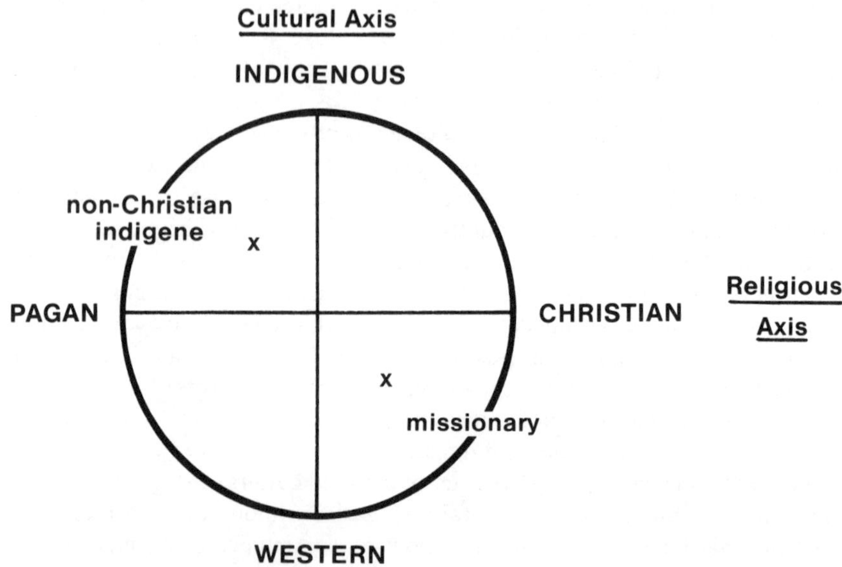

Fig. 20. Religious-Cultural Matrix in Missionary-Indigene Interaction.

This schematic field distinguishes Christianity as a meaningful message on the Religious Axis (Pagan-Christian) from Christendom as a Western cultural tradition on a Cultural Axis (Indigenous-Western).[39] The missionary embedded in the Western-Christian quadrant must overcome the religious and cultural barriers[40] to encounter the non-Christian indigene embedded in the Pagan-Indigenous quadrant. If the goal of the missionary is the planting of an indigenous church (and many say this is their objective), then a missionary who is culturally sensitive and anthropologically informed, should communicate his message of the gospel in such a way that converts move from the Pagan-Indigenous quadrant to the Christian-Indigenous quadrant as diagrammed below:

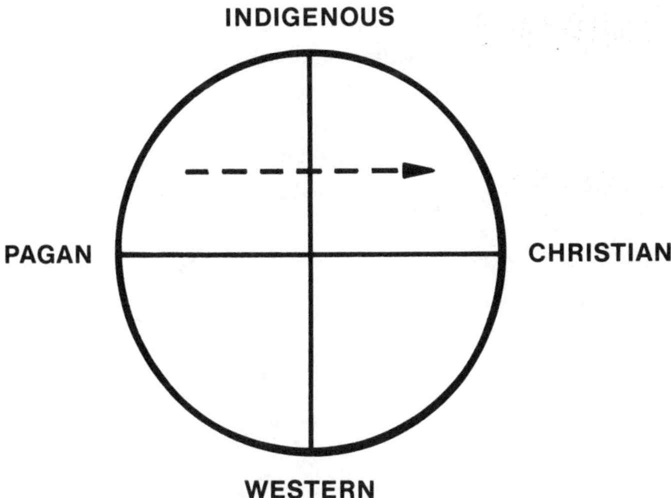

Fig. 21. Cross-cultural Sensitivity in Missionary Advocacy.

Following this approach, the missionary will be receptor-oriented in his communication with potential converts. He will communicate a message that is meaningful to them where they are, embedded in their pagan-indigenous culture. But he will encourage a response to the gospel that is dynamically equivalent to the response the first Christians made nearly two thousand years ago.[41] In this way new converts move from the Pagan to the Christian quadrant on the Religious Axis, but remain within the indigenous sphere on the Cultural Axis. When this occurs, the adopted Christianity is more likely to become functionally integrated into the indigenous society and culture. Its formal expression may be quite different from that of the missionary's expression; these indigenous Christians may act differently than the missionary, they may worship differently, they may structure their churches differently, etc., but they will nevertheless be Christians. They will be practicing a form of indigenous Christianity that is appropriate to their cultural context.

This was the stated objective of Bishop Patteson; his goal was to introduce Christianity in such a way that it would become Melanesianized by island converts. Although this model outlined above is perhaps a hypothetical ideal, it has been actualized in part and to a degree at different periods of the Melanesian Mission's activity in the islands.

In contrast to this model, a great deal of missionary work has been aimed at producing a response of formal correspondence to Western ways. Under this program, evangelizing and civilizing go hand in hand. This approach has been followed by well-intentioned missionaries, who, lacking anthropologically informed insights into cross-cultural communication, simply have not realized that alternative methods were possible. As a result, they have encouraged (insisted?) indigenous converts to move from the Pagan-Indigenous quadrant to the Western-Christian quadrant as diagrammed below:

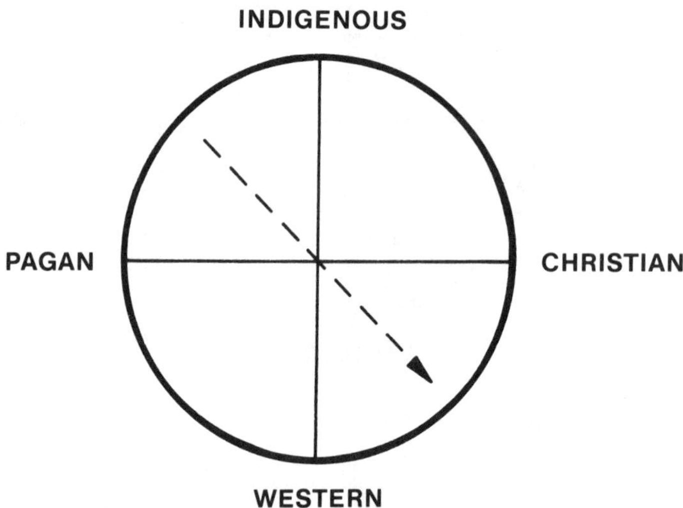

Fig. 22. An Ethnocentric Approach in Missionary Advocacy.

With this ethnocentric approach to culture change missionaries insist that to become a Christian an indigenous convert must also adopt much of the Western cultural package. He must behave like the missionaries, worship as they do, structure his church as they do, etc. When this approach is followed it does not encourage indigenous converts to express Christian meanings in forms appropriate to their culture. Instead, it often leads to indigenous converts, especially in the second and third generation, following one of two paths: (1) they drift back either to the Pagan-Western quadrant, a phenomenon seen in nominal Christianity and among many Third World elites who have been trained in Europe and America, or (2) they drift back to the Pagan-Indigenous quadrant of which many of the Melanesian "cargo cults" are an expression. These phenomena can be diagrammed as follows:

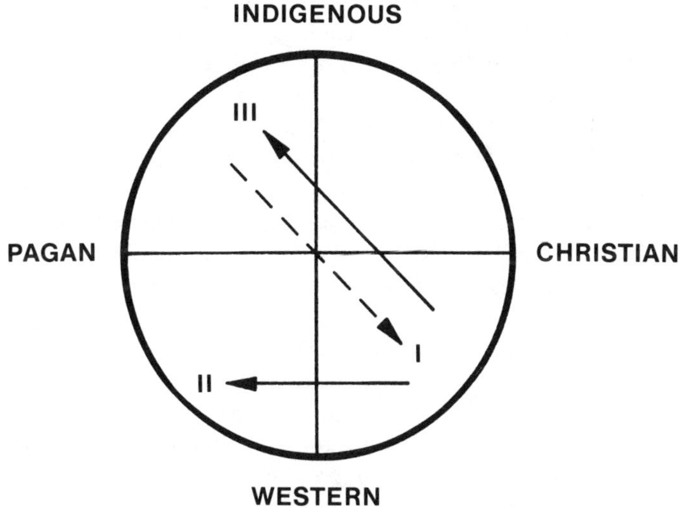

I. Initial conversion to "Western" Christianity
II. Drift toward nominalism after conversion
III. Cargo cult movement after conversion

Fig. 23. Possible Consequences of an Ethnocentric Approach in Missionary Advocacy.

Although this model of communication and advocacy for culture change has been developed on the basis of missionary-indigene interaction, [42] I believe it is applicable to any agent of change whose goal is to introduce a new idea, artifact or behavioral mode. Communication must be so structured that indigenization of the advocated change is maximized.

Equality of Interpersonal Relationships.

Another important principle of cross-cultural communication is that relationships between advocate and innovator be constructed in terms of equivalence, not in terms of dominance and submission. It is important to establish and maintain an equality of status between fellow human beings *qua* human beings (as opposed to missionaries and natives) across cultural and linguistic boundaries. It is of crucial importance that anthropologists or agents of change do not develop an attitude characterized by what Levi-Strauss calls "a state of affairs in which one part of mankind treats the other as object."[43] I am not suggesting a program of annihilating differences in order to establish equality; this would only lead to cultural sterility and uniform monotony. Cultural differences should be encouraged but we should not allow them to become a license for discrimination in which the essential worth of a people is denied. This insight is basic to any program of community development and directed change, and unless it is recognized and implemented, the good intentions and benevolent humanism of any development program will surely fall short.[44]

One of the significant attributes that characterized Charles Fox as a missionary in the Melanesian Mission was his appreciation of cultural differences, and his treatment of islanders as people with dignity and worth, not simply as natives who were objects for conversion by the Mission or exploitation by the government and European entrepreneurs. He was a far more effective advocate of change than those who perceived their missionary role as one of benevolent paternalism.[45]

There are undoubtedly numerous other factors that are important in effective cross-cultural communication.[46] I have not attempted to develop an exhaustive list of principles and factors, but only to highlight and emphasize a few. Essentially the interaction setting of advocate and receptor is one in which individual persons, often representing drastically different cultures, attempt to form an interpersonal relationship. A relationship that engenders mutual trust, understanding and respect will be more effective than one that instills hostility, antipathy and misunderstanding. Any agent of change intent on introducing new ideas, products, techniques, equipment, or ideologies into another culture must be sensitive both inter-personally and inter-culturally. An attempt must be made to understand the worldview of the recipient and communicate in terms that are meaningful to it. Programs of directed cultural change that fail to operate in terms of the receptors' frame of reference will frequently be misunderstood and ineffective. Ethnocentric change agents are those who do not consistently operate in terms of their host society's frame of reference, and the failure in their attempts to introduce change is illustrative of the consequence of such an approach. The model for the successful change agent, articulated by Goodenough (1963), is one in which there is cooperation in change — not forceful, threatening or intimidating change. As I trust this study has amply documented, there is considerable impact from the way a change agent structures the interaction situation. He can engender trust and confidence in understanding, or he can provoke mistrust and hostility. The former leads more readily to the acceptance and indigenization of advocated change, the latter obstructs it.

Summary and Conclusions of this Study

This has been a study in socio-cultural change. The approach has been ethnohistorical, ethnographic and theoretical. The focus of this research has been on analyzing the process of change that has resulted from the interaction of indigenous populations with European missionaries. The cultural arena has been Island Melanesia, where members of the Anglican Melanesian Mission advocated socio-religious change in those island societies with whom they came into direct contact.

The theoretical position adopted in this study has been that innovation is the basis of culture change. The missionary has therefore been analyzed as the **advocate** of change, the recipient Melanesians as the **innovators.** I have argued that the dynamic cultural matrix of missionary as advocate and indigene as innovator is an ideal arena in which to further our understanding of the complex factors involved in the change process. In this connection, Beidelman (1974:242) has noted that, "It is remarkable that despite the profusion of theory and descriptive writings on social change, on the whole missionary activities have remained outside the scrutiny of social scientists." This study of the dynamic interaction between Melanesians and missionaries, each influencing change in the other, has been an attempt toward filling that lacuna in anthropological research.

The study of culture change necessarily involves a diachronic dimension. I have therefore employed an ethnohistorical approach in analyzing a long period of contact and interaction. I have relied heavily on primary sources in the form of records, reports, journals and letters created by the missionaries who lived in the islands and spoke the language of the people with whom they worked. This approach to the data has allowed us to see more clearly how missionary policies and methods changed through time, as well as the differential response of the Melanesians at different periods in the history of their interaction with missionaries.

The ethnohistorical methodology employed in this study would be useful in studying colonial groups such as administrators, traders, planters and other agents of change. Studying these agents in the colonial era from an anthropological perspective would yield a more dynamic and complete socio-historical picture of the recent past. There is an enormous body of documents housed in the archives that can be utilized with less passion and more objectivity now that the colonial era is past. It is interesting to note that many of the post-colonial regimes continue to use similar structures and to have goals similar to those of their colonial predecessors. By consulting the colonial records that have good historical depth one has an excellent opportunity to study the problems of directed socio-cultural change.

In addition to archival research and ethnohistorical analysis, this study has relied on the results of a year of fieldwork in the Solomon Islands where the main goal of my research was to discover the form and function of contemporary Anglican Christianity. The purpose of doing an ethnohistorical study in which archival research and fieldwork were combined was to present a holistic and diachronic view of culture change. By combining two distinct, yet complementary, research strategies, I believe a more comprehensive understanding of the missionary as an agent of change has been obtained. Either method in isolation would not have yielded the holism I have attempted to achieve.

The conclusions drawn from this study are both methodological and substantive, and include the following.

Methodological Conclusions.

(1) A study of culture change must utilize a diachronic approach; the greater the historical depth, the richer and more meaningful the analysis.

(2) A missionary organization as an agent of change is an excellent focus of attention for further study into the complexities of culture change, since missionaries have been one of several influential factors in promoting rapid change in non-Western cultures in the last 175 years. As Beidelman (1974: 236) notes, "The problem of planned social change, of communication and exercise of power between culturally different groups, remains one of the most important and pressing sociological issues." Missionaries have gone everywhere in the world with their gospel, and everywhere they have gone they have been agents of socio-cultural change. I believe this study demonstrates the value of analyzing their activities.

(3) A third methodological conclusion is that the approach I have used in this study, namely combining fieldwork with archival research, is one that could be successfully employed in numerous other types of studies of the process of culture change. I discovered that the archival research gave me a meaningful historical framework in which to understand the experiences of my fieldwork. Likewise, since the fieldwork focused on the end product of 125 years of missionary activity, it gave me a valuable perspective for understanding the historical documents that I otherwise would not have had. Personalities, mission policies and procedures made more sense anthropologically in light of the changes they had influenced. I believe the value of an ethnohistorical approach to an acculturation study has been convincingly demonstrated in the course of this research.

Substantive Conclusions.

(1) Missionaries as agents of change can advocate the acceptance of certain beliefs and practices in their host society, but in the final analysis, it is the indigenes who make the choice to innovate through acceptance, modification or rejection of the missionaries' proposals. This study has demonstrated the active role indigenes play in the process of culture change. As Tiffany (1978:305) notes, "There has been a tendency among anthropologists to view missionization as an exogenous force unilaterally impinging upon passive recipient peoples." This study has demonstrated the superficiality and inaccuracy of such a view. Rather, it is more in line with Guiart's assertion that in Oceania it is more appropriate to:

> . . .think of Christianity as a living factor inside the social structure, as being in many ways an entirely new phenomenon; the reinterpretation of occidental traditional religious ideas and structures by people who have chosen to make use of them as their own (1970: 122).

(2) To label all missionaries as the destroyers of indigenous cultures in the name of Christianity and Western Imperialism is a gross misjudgment of their activities. Missionaries have seldom functioned in isolation from other agents of change. They have frequently been part and parcel of Western expansionism, and in that dynamic arena, they have often functioned as cultural brokers, providing a cultural buffer zone between the indigenous society and the impinging changes brought by colonialism and commercial activities. In terms of the Melanesian Mission, its missionaries tended to function more in the capacity of cultural brokers than of cultural destroyers.

(3) A third substantive conclusion is that this study has shown the complexities of missionary activity *vis a vis* changes in indigenous societies. Not all missionaries, including those serving under the same mission organization, have the same attitude toward the cultural differences of their host society. Some are very ethnocentric, while others are unusually sensitive and empathetic in dealing with cultural differences. The approach of a mission to its task of evangelism is not a constant, but a variable that changes through time. For example, paternalism was more evident in some phases of the Melanesian Mission's history than at other times. Finally, this study has shown how some activities and attitudes on the part of missionaries increased the indigenization of proposed change, while others inhibited and thwarted it.

CHAPTER 7 NOTES

1. The use of these concepts in anthropological analysis is derived from Linton (1936: 402-410). I find them to be particularly useful in analyzing the process of indigenization which can be related with more analytical refinement to each of these four concepts.

2. Numerous examples of failures can be found in the books on social change by Spicer (1952), Paul (1955), Erasmus (1961), Niehoff (1966), Arensberg and Niehoff (1971), and Foster (1973).

3. See, for example, the way the concept of culture is used in the work of Niebuhr (1951) and Tillich (1959).

4. There are some outstanding exceptions to this pattern such as the work of Nida (1954, 1960, 1968), Luzbetak (1963), Tippett (1967, 1973d), Law (1968), Mayers (1974), Loewen (1975), Kraft (1977, 1979), and Barney (1981).

5. This tension is discussed in a symposium entitled *Christopaganism or Indigenous Christianity?* edited by T. Yamamori and C. Taber (1975). Four approaches to the problem are addressed in twelve papers. The most useful articles are those by Tippett who presents an anthropological perspective, and those by Beyerhause writing from a theological point of view.

6. The etymology of the term syncretism can be traced back to its original use as a political term. Plutarch relates that on the island of Crete, rival Greek tribes were usually involved in minor warfare against each other, but when threatened by an external attack on the island, the rival groups united in a military alliance.

   Hendrick Kraemer (1938, 1956, 1960, 1962) more than any other scholar has dealt with the theological problem of syncretism. For an anthropological discussion on syncretism, cf. Barnett (1953: 49), Herskovits (1967: 190-193), and Peel (1968b). An excellent case study is found in Madsen (1957). For a vivid portrayal of syncretism, see Pozas (1962), and Tippett's (1975a: 20-26) analysis of syncretism as portrayed in this monograph.
7. Cf. Herskovits (1937c).
8. Sahay (1968) in his excellent study of the cultural impact of Christianity on indigenous ethnic groups in India, is an example of an anthropologist who does make this distinction. He postulates a processual model of religious change involving the following five processes that roughly correspond to the beginning and later phases of growth in Christianity: (1) Cultural Oscillation, (2) Cultural Scrutinization, (3) Cultural Combination, (4) Cultural Indigenization, (5) Cultural Retroversion. His third process, cultural combination, is essentially syncretism, and is not associated with any particular generation of Christian converts. However, it is important to note that Sahay distinguishes syncretism from indigenization as a separate though similar cultural process.
9. Cf. Buhlmann (1978: 149-154). See also Barrett (1982, esp. pp. 4, 778) for statistics on Christianity in Africa.
10. Sundkler's (1948) study listed 800 independent churches in South Africa alone. A second edition (1961) based on further fieldwork and research, listed 2,200 such churches. One of the most comprehensive surveys is Barrett's (1968), *Schism and Renewal in Africa*, in which he analyzes the phenomenon of independence in 6,000 contemporary religious movements. The literature on modern African religious movements is indeed voluminous, numbering at least 1,500 published materials as of 1966.

    For an outstanding anthropological analysis of an African Independent Church, cf. J.D.Y. Peel's (1968) study of Aladura among the Yoruba. See also Turner (1967, 2 vols) for further discussion on the Aladura Church. Another important movement is Jamaa in Zaire, analyzed by J. Fabian (1971). F.B. Welbourn (1961) gives us an excellent study of some Independent Churches in East Africa, focusing on "The

Missionary Culture and African Response" which is particularly relevant to this study. See also his later study, Welbourn and Ogot (1966).

For a comprehensive listing of material on African Independent Churches, see R. C. Mitchell and H. W. Turner (1966). This bibliography is brought up to date at regular intervals in the *Journal of Religion in Africa*.

11. Perhaps the most comprehensive attempt at Africanization at the national level is found in Zaire. Since 1971 President Mobutu has instituted a program and developed an ideology of **authenticity**, in an attempt to strip the country of any vestiges of colonialism. For a critique of this movement *vis a vis* Christianity in Zaire, cf. Mushete (1978).

12. I do not wish to imply that there are no syncretistic cults in Africa, for this would be misleading. I am here emphasizing the fact that many Africans have rejected syncretism and have chosen instead to develop an African Christian theology. For an excellent discussion of religious movements including African Independent Churches, see H. W. Turner (1981).

The student interested in this phenomenon is confronted by an impressive quantity of published and unpublished materials. One of the leading spokesmen for developing an African theology is John S. Mbiti (cf. 1970, 1971, 1972, 1979). Several recent symposia have been published dealing with African theology and the relationship of Christianity to Africans' society and culture. See for example, Fashole-Luke, et al. (1978), especially the articles by Omoyajowo (pp. 96-110), Opoku (pp. 111-121), Tutu (pp. 365-369), Kibicho (pp. 370-388), Setiloane (pp. 402-412), Peel (pp. 443-454), Shorter (pp. 531-544), and Ndofunsu (pp. 577-596). For an excellent collection of recent essays on African Theology, see also Appiah-Kubi and Torres (1979) *African Theology en Route*. Cf. Baeta (1968) and Dickson and Ellingworth (1971).

Some excellent studies on the relationship of Christianity to different African cultures are Pauw (1960) for the Tswana, Williamson (1965) for the Akan, Murphree (1969) for for the Shona, and Bhebe (1979) for the Ndebele in Western Zimbabwe. More general studies of this nature are found in Westermann (1937) writing in the colonial period, and more recently, Beetham (1967), Oosthuizen (1968), M. Wilson (1971), Nyamiti (1973), and Shorter (1973, 1977). Finally, a recent comprehensive bibliography on *Christianity in Tropical Africa*, prepared by Ofori (1977) lists no less than 2,859 entries, illustrating the vastness of the literature on this topic.

Donovan (1982) has written an intriguing and fascinating book based on his experience of seventeen years of missionary work among the Masai in East Africa. Through his interaction with these Africans and the impact of their worldview on his understanding of mission, he came to "rediscover Christianity." As we from the West turn to those Christians in non-Western cultures, I believe there will be many "rediscoveries" awaiting us.

13. The literature on liberation theology is indeed vast. Some of the most significant writing on this topic is Alves (1969, 1972), Laurentin (1972), Gutierrez (1973) and Segundo (1973-74, 1976). For a critique of these and other Liberation Theologians, cf. Dunn (1980: 179-286). A recent collection of essays on the topic is Gibellini (1979).

14. On the relationship between cargo cults and Christianity, cf. Oosterwal (1967, 1973), Aherns (1974), Steinbauer (1974, 1979), Strelan (1975, 1977a, 1977b) and Forman (1982: 154-163). See also Murphy (1974), *The Church and Adjustment Movements*, for an excellent collection of essays on this topic.

15. Wright (1978, 1979). Two excellent articles concerned with doing theology in the Melanesian context of Papua New Guinea are Ahrens (1978) and Flannery (1978a). In an illuminating discussion, Flannery (1979) illustrates how the depth of Melanesian myths and symbols are an important starting point for the development of an indigenous Melanesian Christian theology. She notes in conclusion, that:

> Because they can reveal so much of what makes up the fabric of people's lives, symbols and myths can be an avenue for locating key themes and forms for genuinely Melanesian Christian worship and theology (1979: 448).

Cf. Flannery (1978b). McGregor (1982) vividly illustrates how in his early missionary work he and his missionary colleagues failed to appreciate and understand the symbolism and mythology caught up in a fish *sing-sing* festival among the Wape people in the Lumi area of Papua New Guinea. He calls for a cultural sensitivity and an acknowledgement that a valid indigenous Christian theology that speaks to the tensions of Melanesian life will not and cannot ignore traditional values, worldview and beliefs.

For the South Pacific in general see discussions of the indigenous view of Christianity in Koskinen (1957) and Forman (1982: 89-101).

16. The Melanesian Institute, located in Goroka, Papua New Guinea, publishes two journals, *Point* (biannually) and *Catalyst* (quarterly). These journals carry numerous articles on topics related to the problem of indigenous Christianity in Melanesia. For example, one of the most significant collections of essays published to date on this topic is

Knight (1977), *Christ in Melanesia: Exploring Theological Issues.* See especially the articles by Aherns (pp. 61-86), Pech (87-121), Fugmann (pp. 122-133), Gaquarae (pp. 146-153), Gibbs (pp. 166-177), Trompf (pp. 208-225), Carley (pp. 226-241), and Burrows (pp. 242-255).

17. There are several studies that deal with this process of foreign missions evolving into independent churches in Melanesia. See for example, Pilhofer (1962), Tippett (1967), R. G. Williams, (1972), Threlfall (1975) and articles by Grossart (pp. 641-653), Hannett (pp. 654-665), R. G. Williams (pp. 666-680), and Murphy (pp. 681-705), on the indigenous church, in *The Politics of Melanesia*, Fourth Waigani Seminar, Marion Ward (ed.), (1970). The movement from Mission to Church in the South Pacific is the topic of Forman's (1982) book and Latukefu's (1974) article. See especially Forman (1982: 164-181).

18. Regarding the distinction between Christianity as a religion and Christendom as a Western cultural tradition, Freeman notes:

> That Christian missionaries have been agents of social change is a matter of record; missionaries have been regarded as civilizers, innovators and disruptors of non-Western societies, and consequently it has been easy to assume that Christianity and Western civilization would be considered as interchangeable when missionaries preached the Gospel to unenlightened heathens (1965: 115).

Freeman goes on to note that the classical debate over whether one had to become civilized or evangelized first:

> . . . has tended to obscure the fact that Christianity has traditionally been critical of this world and has, in its emphasis upon individual salvation, been inclined to deny both the values and practices of Western civilization . . . The literature of the Indian convert cannot be understood as documenting the unity of Christianity and White civilization, for the conversion narrative was for both White and Indian an other-worldly ideal which explicitly rejected white society (1965: 115).

Today more and more missionaries are beginning to question this traditional view of equating Christianity with Western cultural values. This fact has caught the attention of the popular press as evidenced by *Time* magazine's (December 27, 1982 Vol. 120 No. 26, pp. 50-56) cover story on the "The New Missionary." Cf. Stott and Coote (1979) and Winter and Hawthorne (1981: 361-538).

19. For further discussion, cf. Whiteman (1974).

20. For a lucid discussion of indigenization of Christianity *vis a vis* missionary methods in Micronesia, cf. Hezel (1978).

21. I am indebted to Professor Richard M. Thomas of Southern Illinois University for this idea. In his dissertation (1964: 129-132) he discusses three zones of cultural change: (1) relative cultural isolation, (2) relative cultural conflict, and (3) relative cultural assimilation. My addition to his model is postulating a fourth stage (zone) of relative cultural indigenization.

22. I am referring now to the Melanesian Mission's area extending from the northern New Hebrides to the Solomon Islands. The Presbyterians had of course been active in the southern and central New Hebrides since 1848, and the Marists had made an abortive attempt (1845-1847) in the Solomon Islands. Essentially the Melanesian Mission was without competition from other missions during this fifty year period.

23. For an excellent study emphasizing the continuity of values through change, cf. Cronin (1970).

24. Laracy (1976: 159).

25. For discussion of the John Frum movement and the Christian Fellowship Church, see Chapter 5 (pp. 275-276, 277).

26. On the relationship between anthropologists and missionaries, cf. Nida (1966), Salamone (1977), Hiebert (1978b), Hughes (1978), and Stipe (1980).

27. In addition to Codrington, Fox and Ivens of the Melanesian Mission, other outstanding anthropological contributions from Pacific missionaries have been made by Lorimer Fison, George Brown, William Ellis, Thomas Williams, William E. Bromilow, R. K. Rickard, George Vicedom, Gottfried Oosterwal, Louis Luzbetak, and Alan Tippett. Africa has been the scene of numerous anthropologically minded missionaries who have made significant contributions to the science of man. Among these are Dan Crawford, Henri Junod, Edwin W. Smith, Diedrich Westermann, Alexander Heatherwick, Bengt Sundkler, F. B. Welbourn, John V. Taylor, Harold W. Turner, and Aylward Shorter. There are many other missionaries who could be cited, representing different areas of the world and different eras of missionary activity.

    Alan Tippett (1977) has edited an excellent collection of anthropological writing by Protestant missionaries, presenting ninety-three selections from sixty-one different missionaries. Tippett notes in his introduction (1977: xi), "The editorial problem was not in finding material to cover the whole field of anthropology, but in deciding which selections to make out of a multitude of riches."

    The extant anthropological writings by missionaries are indeed numerous, cf. Rosensteil (1959) and the collections of articles edited by Smalley (1967, 1978) which include anthropological articles written mostly by missionaries.

28. Shirley W. Baker was a Methodist missionary in Tonga and chairman of the Tonga district for the Wesleyan Church. In the 1880's he rose to increasing power and influence. Taufaahau, or King George, as he was often called, appointed Baker prime minister of the Kingdom of Tonga. Baker also played an important role in the emergence of the Tonga Free Church which remained Methodist in polity but became independent of the former mission church. It became the state church and held the allegiance of the vast majority of Tongan Christians. In 1890 Baker was forcibly deported from Tonga by British authorities, but the Free Church continued. For further discussion see Rutherford (1971).

29. For further discussion on missionaries and colonialism in the Pacific cf. Martin (1924), Koskinen (1953), Gunson (1965, 1969, 1978: 280-300), Forman (1972) and Hilliard (1974). The general topic from a global perspective is addressed by Neill (1966) and Dunn (1980: 9-50).

30. In his study of religious change among the Bukusu in western Kenya, De Wolf (1977) argues the point I am making here. Rather than a wholesale condemnation of the missionary enterprise, he evaluates missionaries in terms of the colonial context in which they functioned. He concludes his study by noting (1977: 209) that, "The mediating function of the churches in the process of social change consisted of their encouragement of individual social mobility."

31. In a discussion of missionaries and administrators in Africa, De Wolf (1977: 159) notes that:

    > The difference between colonial administrators and missionaries is aptly reflected in the distinction which Peter Nettl (1969: 17-18) has drawn between power and influence. Power may be defined as something which causes the restructuring of actions without altering preferences. One is made to do something irrespective of whether it is one's preferred course of action. Influence is the reverse in that it restructures or alters preferences. Someone is persuaded to do something and does it because he now prefers it to that which he wanted before.

32. The 1978 edition of *Ethnologue*, published by the Summer Institute of Linguistics, lists no less than a total of 5,103 languages spoken in the world today. Barrett (1982: 108) says there are 7,010 distinct living languages in the world today. The total number of languages according to different scholars tends to vary, depending on how one distinguishes between dialects and languages, cf. Voegelin and Voegelin (1977).

33. This perspective, a debated one in anthropology today, is known as the Sapir-Whorf hypothesis, after the seminal linguistic work of Edward Sapir and Benjamin Lee Whorf. In essence, the Sapir-Whorf hypothesis suggests that the structure of the language one habitually uses influences the manner in which one understands his environment and perceives the world. For a collection of Whorf's writings, see *Language, Thought and Reality*: Selected writings of Benjamin Lee Whorf edited and with an introduction by John B. Carroll (1956). A collection of Sapir's work has been edited by David Mandelbaum (1963) and is entitled, *Selected Writings of Edward Sapir in Language, Culture and Personality*.
34. The work of Edward T. Hall (1959, 1966, 1976) in the area of proxemic analysis is especially helpful at this point. The way people communicate with their bodies and with gestures is culturally conditioned, and of course, is different from one culture to another, which complicates the process of communication across cultural boundaries. For a recent popular treatment of this problem, see Hall's article, "Learning the Arabs' Silent Language" in *Psychology Today*, August 1979, pp. 45-54.
35. For an excellent discussion of the relationship between form and meaning in language, cf. Malinowski (1949). He argues that the meaning derived from linguistic terms (forms) is understandable only in terms of the context of the situation in which those words are used. Thus, he argues, any linguistic translation must be accompanied by a cultural translation in order to preserve the meaning in the process of translating across cultural boundaries.
36. Pike and Cowan (1959).
37. For further discussion on the relationship between form and meaning, especially as it relates to missionary cross-cultural communication, cf. Nida (1960: 33-93), Mayers (1974: 193-200), Hesselgrave (1978), and Kraft (1979, especially pp. 64-69).
38. Cf. Kraft (1979: 147ff.).
39. See the discussion relating to this distinction above (pp. 418-419) and also in Whiteman (1974).
40. On cultural, social and psychological barriers to change, cf. Foster (1962: 64-142).
41. On the distinction between dynamic equivalence and formal correspondence models of conversion, see Kraft (1973, 1979: 261ff.).
42. For further discussion related to missionary communication, cf. Whiteman (1979, 1981b).

43. Cf. Carpenter (1974: 192-196).
44. For further discussion of this principle as it relates to agents of change, cf. Whiteman (1976).
45. See Chapter 4, pp. 214-217, for discussion of Charles Fox.
46. See, for example, Kraft (1979: 360-381, especially pp. 366-370) for an excellent discussion of factors influencing the advocacy of change. Although Kraft is writing in the context of missionary communication, his insights are applicable to any program of directed cultural change.

Appendix I

"Memorandum for the Study of Acculturation"

Outline for the Study of Acculturation

I. Definition

"Acculturation comprehends those phenomena which result when groups of individuals having different cultures come into continuous first-hand contact, with subsequent changes in the original cultural patterns of either or both groups." (Note: Under this definition, acculturation is to be distinguished from *culture-change*, of which it is but one aspect, and *assimilation*, which is at times a phase of acculturation. It is also to be differentiated from *diffusion* which, while occurring in all instances of acculturation, is not only a phenomenon which frequently takes place without the occurrence of the type of contact between peoples specified in the definition given above, but also constitutes only one aspect of the process of acculturation.)

II. Approach to the problem

A. Listing of materials available for study

1. Published materials of prehistoric contacts (to indicate how acculturation has characterized human contacts from early times), as well as of contacts between primitive groups, between primitive and literate groups (both mechanized and non-mechanized), and between literate groups of either or both categories.
2. Unpublished materials of studies in acculturation which are completed or in progress.

B. Classification of the above materials

1. Do these studies treat of entire cultures or specific phases of culture?
2. If the studies are restricted ones, what phases of the culture are treated?
3. What are the motivations of the studies (insofar as this affects the type of material treated), e.g., are they scientific, or are they designed to aid in the formulation of administrative, educational, or missionary policy?

C. Techniques employed in the studies analyzed

1. Direct observation of acculturation in process.
2. Recent acculturation studied through interviews with members of acculturated groups.
3. Use of documentary evidence which gives historic testimony concerning early contacts which have resulted in acculturation.
4. Deductions from historical analyses and reconstructions.

III. Analysis of acculturation

(Note: The significance of physical type in determining attitudes operative in acculturation, as well as the importance of the concomitant occurrence of race-mixture or its prohibition, must not be overlooked as a factor which may pervade any situation, process, or result envisaged in this section.)

A. *Types of contacts*

1. Where contacts are between entire groups; or are between an entire population and selected groups from another population, e.g., missionaries, traders, administrators, special craftsmen, pioneers and their families, and immigrant males (all these considered with special reference to the elements of culture likely to be made available by the members of such special groups to the population among whom they live).
2. Where contacts are friendly, or are hostile.
3. Where contacts are between groups of approximately equal size, or between groups of markedly different size.
4. Where contacts are between groups marked by unequal degrees of complexity in material or non-material aspects of culture, or both, or in some phase of either.
5. Where contacts result from the culture-carriers coming into the habitat of the receiving group, or from the receiving group being brought into contact with the new culture in a new region.

B. *Situations* in which acculturation may occur

1. Where elements of culture are forced upon a people, or are received voluntarily by them.
2. Where there is no social or political inequality between groups.
3. Where inequality exists between groups, in which case any of the following may result:
   a. political dominance by one group, without recognition of its social dominance by the subject group;
   b. political and social dominance by one group;
   c. recognition of social superiority of one group by the other without the exercise of political dominance by the former.

C. The *processes* of acculturation

1. *Selection* of traits under acculturation:
   a. the order in which traits are selected (in specific cases);
   b. the possible relationships to be discerned between the selection of traits under the various types of contacts leading to acculturation, and the situations in which acculturation may occur (as set down under III A and B above);

- c. partial presentation of traits under forced acculturation:
  - a’. types of traits permitted and forbidden to receiving group;
  - b’. techniques employed by donor group for imposing traits;
  - c’. types of traits whose acceptance can be forced;
  - d’. limitations of forced acceptance;
- d. resistance of receiving group to traits presented to them:
  - a’. reasons for this resistance;
  - b’. significance of understanding resistance to traits as well as acceptance of them.

2. *Determination* of traits presented and selected in acculturation situations:
   - a. traits presented by the donor group because of
     - a’. practical advantages, such as economic profit or political dominance;
     - b’. desirability of bringing about conformity to values of the donor group, such as humanitarian ideals, modesty, etc.;
     - c’. ethical and religious considerations;
   - b. traits selected by the receiving group because of
     - a’. economic advantages;
     - b’. social advantages (prestige);
     - c’. congruity of existing culture-patterns;
     - d’. immediacy and extensiveness of changes necessitated in certain aspects of the culture by the adoption of functionally related traits;
   - c. traits rejected by receiving group.
3. *Integration* of traits into the patterns of the accepting culture:
   - a. the factor of *time* that has elapsed since the acceptance of a trait.
   - b. the element of *conflict* produced within a culture by the acceptance of new traits at variance with pre-existing ones, and the degree of conflict which ensues;
   - c. the process of *adjustment* in acculturation;
     - a’. modification and reinterpretation of traits taken over;
     - b’. modification of pre-existing patterns resulting from the taking over of new traits;
     - c’. displacement of older traits in a pattern by new ones;
     - d’. “survivals;”
     - e’. transfer of sanctions;
     - f’. shifts in cultural focus caused by acculturation.

IV. *Psychological mechanisms* of selection and integration of traits under acculturation

A. The role of the individual

1. As member of the selecting group; personality of the first individuals to accept foreign traits and their position in society as influencing selection and acceptance of new traits.
2. As member of the donor group; personality of the individuals who are in contact with the receiving group, their attitudes and points of view, and the way in which the group to which they belong is regarded by members of the receiving group, as making for favorable and unfavorable reception of traits.
3. The individual as member of a special group in his society (priestly class, sib, secret society, etc.) and his position in this group, as accelerating or retarding acceptance of new traits.

B. Possible consistencies in personality types of those who accept or reject new traits.

C. Differential selection and acceptance of traits in accordance with sex lines, differing social strata, differing types of belief, and occupation.

D. Initial hostility and subsequent reconcilliation of individuals to the new culture as a factor in integrating new culture-traits, and caused by

1. intensity of contact;
2. duration of contact and resulting habituation to new cultural elements;
3. social, economic or political advantages resultant upon acceptance;

E. Psychic conflict resulting from attempts to reconcile differing traditions of social behavior and different sets of social sanctions.

V. The *results of acculturation*

A. *Acceptance*: where the process of acculturation eventuates in the taking over of the greater portion of another culture and the loss of most of the older cultural heritage; with acquiescence on the part of the members of the accepting group, and, as a result, assimilation by them not only to the behavior patterns but to the inner values of the culture with which they have come into contact.

B. *Adaptation*: where both original and foreign traits are combined so as to produce a smoothly functioning cultural whole which is actually an historic mosaic; with either a reworking of the patterns of the two cultures into a harmonious meaningful whole to the individuals concerned, or the retention of a series of more or less conflicting attitudes and points of view which are reconciled in everyday life as specific occasions arise.

C. *Reaction*: where because of oppression, or because of the unforeseen results of the acceptance of foreign traits, contra-acculturative movements arise; these maintaining their psychological force (a) as compensations for an imposed or assumed inferiority, or (b) through the prestige which a return to older pre-acculturative conditions may bring to those participating in such a movement.

From: R. Redfield et al. (1936), "Memorandum for the Study of Acculturation," *American Anthropologist* 38: 149-152. Reprinted with permission of the Social Science Research Council.

The above Memorandum should be compared with that of Leonard Broom, Bernard Siegel, Evon Z. Vogt and James B. Watson, "Acculturation: An Exploratory Formulation." This document came out of the Social Science Research Council Summer Seminar on Acculturation in 1953, and was published in *American Anthropologist* 56: 973-1000 (1954). It is reprinted in Bohannan and Plog (1967: 255-286).

Appendix II

Barnett's Model of Innovation

The essence of Barnett's theory of culture change is that, "Innovation does not result from the addition or substraction of parts. It takes place only when there is a recombination of them (1953: 9)." The emphasis then in this model is on the recombination of cultural elements. Barnett has developed the following diagram to illustrate his recombination thesis.

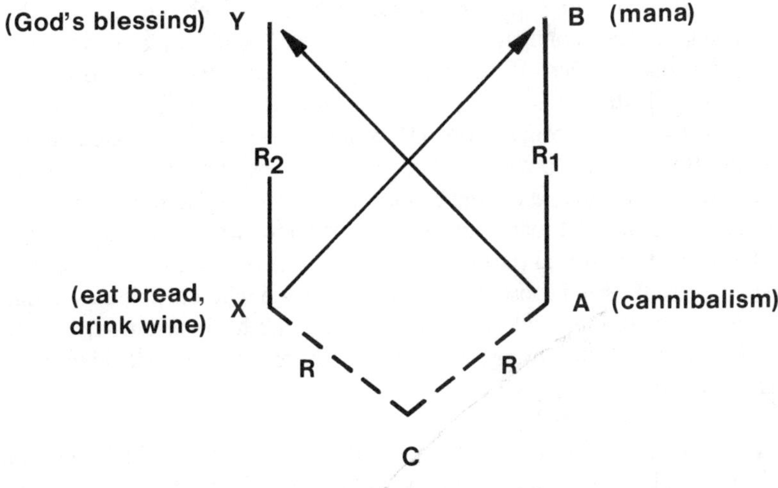

Fig. 24. Innovation as Configurational Recombination.

I will briefly summarize the elements within this diagram, relating them to specific cultural content.

1. AB is a mental configuration—an idea of a family, a bow and arrow complex, a religious ritual, etc.
2. In the configuration AB there is a relationship (R_1) that exists between the parts of that configuration and is represented as AR_1B. Let us say that AR_1B represents an idea of a Melanesian religious ritual, in which A—correct actions, is related (R_1) to B—expected supernatural results, in this case the acquisition of *mana*.
3. XY is also a configuration with the relationship R_2 obtaining between its parts. For purpose of illustration let us say that XR_2Y represents the idea of Holy Communion advocated by Anglican missionaries in contact with Melanesians who practice the religious ritual AR_1B.
4. The relationship R_2 between the parts in the configuration XY may, or may not, be the same as the relationship R_1 between the parts in the configuration AB. Frequently in the innovation process they are different.

We now have an indigenous configuration AR_1B, which Barnett calls the prototype, and an alien configuration XR_2Y (stimulus configuration) advocated by Anglican missionaries. What must happen for an innovation to occur? The following illustration should clarify the process.

In the indigenous configuration AR_1B, let A represent ritualistic cannibalism and B the *mana* (power) which accrues to the one who performs the ritual act. In the introduced configuration XR_2Y of Holy Communion, let X represent the eating of bread and drinking of wine, which are said by the missionary to be the literal partaking of the body and blood of Jesus, and Y represent God's blessing (power) that accrues to one who participates in this ritual. How does the innovative process occur if the Melanesian adopts the religious ritual advocated by the missionary? There are two steps, identification and substitution.

Step 1—Identification. The first step in the process is identification, and this begins by discovering a common point between X and A. There are two forms of identification: (1) convergent analysis, and (2) convergent incorporation.

(1) In convergent analysis X is analyzed and something in it, which is also discovered in A, is represented by C in the diagram (in our example it is eating human flesh and drinking blood). The relationship between C and X is the same (in the mind of the innovator) as that between C and A. Thus CX and CA are taken to be the same. In our example two wholes, X (Holy Communion) and A (ritualistic cannibalism) are broken down (analyzed) to discover a point in common between them.

(2) Identification can also take place through convergent incorporation, where instead of breaking down two wholes, to discover a point in common,

two new wholes are built up (synthesized) to include a common denominator, thus binding together two previously unconnected wholes. This is done by taking two distinct configurations, A and C, and synthesizing them into a unit, with the relationship (R) obtaining between its parts. The net result is the same as that of convergent analysis, for CA and CX become equivalent in the mind of the innovator. Both processes lead to identification which is a prerequisite to substitution, the next stage in the innovative process.

Step 2—Substitution. The fact that the innovator has identified CA with CX is not an innovation, but simply indicates that in some respects, the two are equated and treated alike, and thus given the same meaning or perhaps have the same function. By equating CA with CX, the innovator is drawing on something familiar to him (CA) to account for something that is presented to him (CX). It is important to note that the missionary advocate does not equate cannibalism with communion, but the innovating indigenes do so, and thus frequently derive a magical view of communion. Once this identification is made by the indigenous innovator, between something familiar and something presented to him, there are then several possibilities for substitution.

Assimilation.

One of the most important processes in terms of frequency of occurrence is assimilation. It must be remembered that CA is now perceived as a configuration, a whole, not simply A related to C. CA next becomes incorporated as a subwhole of a larger, more inclusive configuration. It does this by recalling the correlate or associate B, to which it was previously related by the relationship R_1. The expanded configuration or prototype now becomes CAB. With the cognitive formation of CAB, substitution is now possible, for as we recall, CA is peceived as equivalent to CX. Thus CX substitutes for CA in the configuration CAB, and a new configuration CXB, is either deliberately or unwittingly formed. In either case CAB (the indigenous prototype)assimilates CX because CX is synthesized with B in the same way as is CA. Thus the new configuration CXB comes into being and is indicated in the diagram by the arrow drawn from X to B. An innovation has occurred. CX is joined to B in the same relation R_1 as is CA. The configuration CXR_1B is an innovation for it is qualitatively different from either of the two pre-existing configurations CXY or CAB.

Assimilation is a very common process. It occurs, for example, when things are treated as if they were the same even though one knows that a detailed exploration would reveal that they are not. Barnett notes that assimilation is a routine phenomenon as illustrated by the following example.

> If we do not have a hammer available when we need one, we use anything like a hammer that we can find; it may be our first, a stick, a stone, a wrench, or a shoe heel. (1953: 209)

Projection.

A second form of substitution leading to an innovation is projection. Again CA and CX are perceived as equivalent in the mind of the innovator, and this opens the way for substitution of CA for CX. However, Y in the configuration XY is not abandoned or lost, but acts as a second stimulus in conjunction with X. Since CX is present in the context of the second stimulus Y when CA is substituted for CX, CA is now projected onto the stimulus field and a new innovative configuration CAY is formed as indicated by an arrow from A to Y.

Like assimilation, projection is a common process, and occurs for instance, in misreading labels and in many other types of errors where false apprehensions and past memories are projected into the situation.

The distinction between projection and assimilation in culture change has been lucidly demonstrated by Adair and Vogt (1949) in their study of Navaho and Zuni war veterans. They note that Zuni who are predominantly assimilative did not take on American customs and behavior patterns in the context of the U.S. Army. In contrast, the Navaho who are more projective in their identifications, adopted American behavior patterns in the Army and were overtly more acculturated than their Zuni counterparts. In our example, if projection were the process of innovation (CAR_2Y) then the Melanesian would project cannibalism as a ritual onto the introduced stimulus field, in order to obtain God's blessing. In the case of our example however, Melanesians follow the pattern of assimilation, not projection. Assimilation (CXR_1B) occurs when the Melanesian partakes of Holy Communion (X) with the belief (R_1) it will give him *mana* (B).

Of all the possibilities of recombination in the process of innovation, Barnett has reduced them to the following six processes:

1. X is combined with B in the relationship R_1 (XR_1B).
2. X is combined with B in the relationship R_2 (XR_2B).
3. A is combined with Y in the relationship R_1 (AR_1Y).
4. A is combined with Y in the relationship R_2 (AR_2Y).
5. X is combined with Y in the relationship R_1 (XR_1Y).
6. A is combined with B in the relationship R_2 (AR_2B).

The important factor in Barnett's thesis is that innovation is, "a creation only in the sense that it is a new combination, never in the sense that it is something emerging from nothing" (1953: 181).

The processes of innovation discussed above are concerned with how an **individual** creates change in his mind. How does Barnett's model help us deal with cultural change in a society? Individual change is not culture change until it becomes a part of the group norm and is shared by others in the society. As Barnett notes, the anthropologist's "primary concern is with the socialized aspect of ideas instead of with the idiosyncratic. The idea-in-common is the proper area for his exploration, for this is culture." Since ideas are lodged in the minds of individuals, however, and not in some mystical "group mind," he states that:

> Cultural explanations of human behavior can be given, but they always imply or necessitate psychological assumptions. They presuppose certain real explanatory elements in the observed relationship between behavioral patterns (1953: 12).

Barnett's concept of multi-individual ideas is a most useful way of relating individual ideas to group behavior. This socio-psychological view of culture has tremendous analytical utility in dealing with the dynamics of culture change.

Appendix III

Statistics of the Melanesian Mission for 1901

ISLANDS	Native Clergy	Teachers	Schools	New schools during 1901	Total Baptised	Total Communi-cants
New Hebrides Islands:						
Opa —	—	31	26	10	444	8
Raga —	—	77	50	11	1298	30
Maewo —	—	16	8	—	301	47
Total —	—	124	84	21	2043	85
Banks' Islands:						
Merelava —	1	14	5	—	320	115
Merig —	—	3	1	—	36	8
Santa Maria —	—	50	19	2	680	81
Mota —	1	18	7	—	500	168
Motalava —	2	34	10	—	1000	352
Vanua Lava —	—	17	7	—	470	70
Roua —	—	2	1	—	37	5
Ureparapara —	—	3	2	—	103	20
Total —	4	121	52	2	3146	819
Torres Islands:						
Loh		6	2	—	150	69
Toga	1	5	2	1	39	6
Tegua		4	1	—	174	48
Total —	1	15	5	1	303	123
Santa Cruz Islands:						
Santa Cruz —	—	10	2	—	101	21
Reef Islands —	—	8	4	—	23	6
Total —	—	18	6	—	124	27
Solomon Islands:						
San Cristoval	—	24	8	3	155	5
Ugi	—	7	3	1	4	4
Bugotu —	—	41	14	1	1137	447
South East Mala —	1	31	10	—	649	44
North West Mala —	—	2	1	—	30	6
Ulawa —	1	20	6	—	351	40
Florida —	2	105	35	1	°3300	°450
Guadalcanar —	1	16	6	1	10	§16
Savo —	—	4	1	—	†6	4
Total —	5	250	84	7	5642	1016
Grand Total —	10	528	231	31	11318	2070

Baptised during 1901		Confirmed during 1901		Catechumens	Hearers	Remarks
Adults	Children	Males	Females			
126	48	—	—	115	640	English Clergy, 2.
509	131	13	2	158	1698	No statistics for Maewo
26	18	—	—	26	50	received for 1901.
661	197	13	2	299	2388	Those given are from 1899.
20	9	16	23	—	110	English Clergy, 2.
—	1	1	3	—	—	
74	19	16	3	—	500	°Population practically
—	14	47	37	—	°	all Christians.
—	23	53	50	—	°	
5	22	—	—	—	50	
—	1	—	—	—	°	
—	—	—	—	—	—	
99	89	133	116	—	600	
?	?	9	15	—	20	These statistics are
35	?	2	—	—	170	only approximate.
24	?	14	12	—	20	
59	?	25	27	—	210	
5	1	6	4	26	?	English Clergy, 2.
6	1	—	—	10	52	
11	2	6	4	36	52	
—	11	—	—	36	71	English Clergy, 6.
—	—	—	—	7	91	°Approximately correct
186	21	67	78	185	290	§These are clergy and
42	17	11	15	100	50	teachers, and not
—	—	—	—	—	70	Guadalcanar Christians,
10	10	12	10	42	32	and therefore not
236	173	111	138	°40	°400	counted among the
1	—	—	1	10	173	Baptised of Guadal-
—	—	—	—	—	22	canar.
475	232	201	242	420	1199	†These were baptised by Rev. J. Ruddock, and
1305	520	378	391	‡755	4509	had lapsed, but most of them are now attending school again. ‡Also 15 at St. Barnabas

Appendix IV

Bishop Patteson's Memorandum on the Labor Trade—1871

The object of this memorandum is to inform the General Synod of the means frequently adopted in the islands of the S.W. Pacific to produce labourers for the Queensland and Fiji plantations.

I am not now concerned with the treatment of these islanders on the plantations, which I have never visited. My duty is to state that which has occurred in these islands, and to make known the character of the trade which is carried on there.

Assuming that the Government of Queensland and Her Majesty's Consul at Levuka, Fiji Islands, do all that lies in their power to guard this traffic from abuse, and assuming that they succeed in affording some security to the islanders while on the plantations, it is certain that they do not and cannot restrain lawless men from employing unjust means to procure so-called labourers in the islands: they cannot know what is done by the masters and crews of the numerous vessels engaged in the trade; they are absolutely without power to enforce any regulations as to the number of persons kept on board, the amount of food given to them, the treatment of the sick, and the general management of the whole transaction.

Whatever measures may be proposed or adopted to secure humane and just treatment of these islanders while in Queensland and Fiji, there is absolutely no check whatever upon the proceedings of the men engaged in procuring these islanders for the labour markets of Queensland and Fiji. No regulations can prevent men who are bound by no religious or moral restraint from practising deception and violence to entice or convey natives on board their vessels, or from detaining them forcibly when on board.

Much is said about engagements and contracts being made with these islanders. I do not believe that it is possible for any of these traders to make a *bona fide* contract with any natives of the Northern New Hebrides, and Banks, and Solomon Islands. I doubt if any one of these traders can speak half-a-dozen words in any one of the dialects of those islands; and I am sure that the very idea of a contract cannot be made intelligible to a native of those islands without a very full power of communicating readily with him. More than ten natives of Mota Island have been absent now nearly three years. The trader made a contract with them by holding up three fingers. They thought that three suns or three moons were signified. Probably he was very willing that they should think so, but he thought of at least three years.

Something has been said about the benefits to the islanders by bringing them "into contact with civilisation." What kind of civilisation they may see on the plantations I do not know, for I have not visited them; neither can I say that I have seen many natives who have been returned to their homes, from whose conduct I might judge of the effects of their "contact with civilisation." The reason is simple. Out of 400 or 500 Banks Islanders who have been taken away, I have not heard of, much less seen, one-tenth of that number brought back.

But there is no instance that I can remember of any one of these natives exhibiting on his island any proof of his having received any benefit from his "contact with civilisation," much less of his conferring any benefit on his people.

The few that have been brought back to the Banks Islands bear a bad character among their own people.

But I am not now concerned with the treatment of these islanders on the plantation, nor with the effect of their intercourse with white men, or upon themselves or their people.

The African slave trade was put down as a thing evil in itself, a disgrace to humanity, and a practical repudiation of Christianity. People did not stop to inquire further. It was enough that men were stolen away from their homes and taken away by force.

There is no check at present upon the traders engaged in procuring "labourers" for Queensland and Fiji. Many of these men, whether they are technically and legally slavers or not, are acting in the spirit of slavers. Sir William Manning admitted in the Daphne case that "this system of so-called emigration is likely to degenerate, and probably sometimes has degenerated, into a practice approaching a slave trade and perhaps actually amounting to it." It is, indeed, a mockery to speak of it as a system of emigration.

A most impartial and dispassionate writer in *Blackwood's Magazine*, who had spent some time in sailing among these islands, and had twice visited Fiji, speaks of the "nefarious nature of many of the transactions (of the masters of vessels sent to procure labourers for the Queensland and Fiji plantations) which have undoubtedly, in not a few instances, been nothing less than kidnapping." I leave the statements of some of our scholars to speak for themselves. But I know that throughout the Northern New Hebrides and the Banks Islands, deception and violence are frequently practised. I know the lawless character and the lawless conduct of persons now engaged in the trade, whose names I am not at liberty to divulge. One person writes to me mentioning by name four vessels carrying on "rough work" with the New Hebrides natives. "You know," he says, "that these men have no scruples of conscience, and so long as they make money are perfectly dead to any code of laws, human or divine. I tell you of this (he adds) confidentially, as I have only had the information as a friend and inform you for your own protection when amongst the islands."

A captain of a whale ship writes to me: — "The natives of these islands would come off in former years, bringing such articles of trade as their islands afford, for which we paid them hatchets, tobacco, fish-hooks, &c. They trusted us, and we trusted them. At times our decks were crowded. This, when slavery commenced, was all to the slaver's advantage, for the natives were easily enticed below, the hatches put on, and the vessel was off. Now, no native comes on board the whale ship, and we, in our turn, dare not land. Again, we used to carry people from one island to another, when they wished it, and they would give us hogs and other articles. This also has been taken advantage of, and the natives carried into slavery instead of home. Should we be wrecked, our lives must go for those that have been stolen, and the natives will be condemned and called bloodthirsty, &c.; and yet what will the natives have done? Not certainly right, but no more than civilised people have done in many cases. I hear that they use your name to decoy natives from their islands, and I also hear from good authority that they inquire very particularly of the whereabouts of the *Southern Cross*."

We experience, to some extent, the evil effects of this traffic which has been described in this last extract. In many islands where we were already on more intimate terms with the people, we are now obliged to be very cautious. Unless we are so well known as to be thoroughly trusted, we have to begin again, to some extent, the task of disabusing their minds of the natural suspicion and distrust which these "nefarious practices" excite.

As for using our names and inventing any stories about us which may induce natives to go on board their vessels, that is the common trick adopted by some traders. There are some,—I trust very few—men sailing in these vessels who have taken a voyage in the *Southern Cross*, and the fact that they have been on board the mission vessel gives a plausibility to their story. In several of these islands some of our scholars are living; they speak a little English, and communicate more or less readily with any white men. Of course they use their influence to dissuade their people from going in such vessels. They know nothing about the Queensland and Fiji plantations, but they know quite enough of the character of these vessels to warn their people against going in them.

Many natives of Tanna, Vate, and of the Loyalty Islands, are employed by these traders for the boating work. These men are amongst the most reckless and mischievous of the whole number of persons concerned in the trade.

Naisilene, the Christian chief of Mare, has forbidden any native of that island to go on board any one of these vessels. It would be well if white men were to follow his example.

In conclusion, I desire to protest by anticipation against any punishment being inflicted upon natives of these island who may cut off vessels or kill boats' crews, until it is clearly shown that these acts are not done in way of retribution for outrages first committed by white men. Only a few days ago a report reached me that a boat's crew had been killed at Espirito Santo. Nothing is more likely. I expect to hear of such things. It is the white man's fault, and it is unjust to punish the coloured man for doing what, under such circumstances, he may naturally be expected to do. People say and write inconsiderately about the treachery of these islanders. I have experienced no instance of anything of the kind during fourteen years' intercourse with them; and I may fairly claim the right to be believed, when I say that, if the Melanesian native is treated kindly, he will reciprocate such treatment readily. The contact of many of these traders arouses all the worst suspicions and passions of the wild, untaught man. It is difficult to find any answer to the question, Who is the savage, and who is the heathen man?

Imperial legislation is required to put an end to this miserable state of things. Stringent regulations ought to be made, and enforced by heavy penalties, as to the size and fittings of vessels licensed to convey natives to and from the South Sea Islands to Queensland and Fiji. All details should be specified and vigilantly carried out as to the number of natives that may be put on board, their food, clothing, payment, term of labour, reconveyance to their homes.

Two small men-of-war ought to cruise constantly in the islands, and especially in the neighbourhood of Queensland and Fiji, to intercept vessels bringing natives to those parts, and to examine into the observance or non-observance of the regulations.

It is manifestly to the planter's interest to discourage the lawless practices now going on in the islands. If he wishes to have a willing, good-humoured set of men on his plantation, it is evident that they must come to him willingly, and receive from him such treatment that they will work for him cheerfully.

At present many of these islanders are brought to the plantations in an angry, sullen, revengeful state of mind. Who can wonder at it? The planter pays a heavy sum now—amounting, it is said, in some cases, to £10 or £12 per head—for the so-called "passage" given to these "imported labourers." I do not believe that the planters themselves justify or desire the continuance of these proceedings in the islands. It may be that only a few persons would be found willing to come if their free consent was required, and that compulsion is necessary if labourers are to be procured at all. In this case it is not too much to say that free labourers must be sought elsewhere, among the Chinese or other people who are able to protect themselves from injustice.

But my belief is that there will be always some, not many, islanders willing to leave their homes for a time, if once it is thoroughly known by experience that they will be treated kindly and fairly, and brought home at the proper time. Curiosity, excitement, the spirit of adventure, will always induce some men to volunteer for any employment that is not distasteful, with people who treat them honestly and fairly.

There are some two or three vessels honourably distinguished from the rest by fair and generous treatment of the natives. One such vessel was at anchor for some weeks in Vanua Lava harbour. I do not know its name.

Ganevierg (the Leper Island lad) speaks of a whaler, a three-masted vessel, which was visited by some of the people. It came on to blow, and the Leper Islanders were kept on board all night, well fed, and sent ashore with presents the next morning. He could not tell me the name of the vessel, but she was a whaler, and such treatment of natives is customary with such vessels.

I regret that I am unable to attend the General Synod, and that I lose the opportunity of giving further explanations of the real character of this traffic.

(Signed)

J. C. Patteson
Norfolk Island
Missionary Bishop

Norfolk Island
11 January 1871

From: "Memorandum to the General Synod of New Zealand", 11 January 1871, Great Britain, *Parliamentary Papers*, vol. 43, 1872 (C. 496), pp. 107-109.

Appendix V

A Partial List of the Rules of the Melanesian Brotherhood

1. The work of the Brotherhood is to proclaim the teaching of Jesus Christ among the heathen, not to work among Christians.
2. Let each Brother remember the Lord's words, "I am among you as he that serves."
3. The Brothers shall be divided into companies, each called a Household. The Father and Chief Brother shall so divide them as they think fit.
4. A Household shall consist of from four to eight Brothers.
5. The Brothers of each Household shall choose one among them to be Elder Brother, and the Elder Brother shall look after the Brothers of his Household, and they shall obey him, and do whatever he tells them.
6. One Brother shall be chief among all the Brothers, under the Father. The Chief Brother shall look after all the Households, and visit them if he can, so that they may all follow with one mind in the same customs.
7. Each Brother when he joins the Brotherhood, and afterward each year on the day of St. Simon and St. Jude, shall take this vow:

   > In the Name of the Father and the Son and the Holy Ghost. I vow while a member of the Brotherhood, to remain unmarried, to take no pay and not to disobey the Father, or the Elder Brother of my Household. I take this vow before God and this gathering of His people.

8. The Bishop shall be the Father of the Brothers.
9. The Brothers of each Household shall meet together four times every year, October 28th, January 25th, April 25th, July 25th.
10. If any dispute occurs among the Brothers, they shall tell it to the Father, and he shall decide it, and no one shall dispute his decision.
11. The Brothers shall go two by two to the villages where their Elder Brother shall send them, and they shall not remain more than a month in one village.
12. No Brother shall work alone.
14. Each Elder Brother of a Household shall report once a year to the Father the work of his Household.

17. If a Brother is asked by a Priest or one in charge of a district to help him in his work, the rule of the Brotherhood shall not hold, the Brother shall ask permission of the Father, and if this is granted, the Brother can do the work.

24. When they leave a village they shall choose someone to say prayers morning and evening with the people, and if he is able, to teach them a little.

29. These rules can be changed when all the Brothers meet together with the Father, but not by a single Household, nor by all the Brothers alone (without the Father).

35. If any Brother sees something in the conduct or words of another Brother which he thinks is wrong, he shall not talk to anyone about it, nor shall he allow it to rankle in his heart, but he shall speak about it before all the Brothers of his Household when they meet together.

    (There is a special form for this, the Elder Brother of a Household or the Chief Brother when the whole Brotherhood meets once a year, asking each in turn, beginning with the most junior, if he has anything to say about any other Brother. The Brother in question replies, and all discuss it.)

37. Every Brother shall pray daily for the heathen and all the Brothers.

From: C. E. Fox (1958: 268-269), *Lord of the Southern Isles.*

Appendix VI

Rules of the Church Association

1. The name is to be THE CHURCH ASSOCIATION.

2. This Association has been formed after much prayer, and we believe it comes from the guiding of the Holy Spirit. It has only one aim—to help and strengthen the Church in Melanesia by getting the people to love and support the Church more than they have done before. So we begin this Association trusting in the help and guidance of Almighty God.

1. The Foundation.

The Foundation on which the Association is built is the Great Law of GOD—that we love GOD and our neighbour. We are members of one family and we must love and help one another—St. Matthew 22: 35-40.

2. What the Association will do.

The Association will help the people, first by strengthening the life of the Church: then by helping the life of the people by schools, medical work, and by teaching good ways of gardening and farming.

We hope the Association will spread all through the diocese of Melanesia, and it will be the work of those islands where it is strong to help the other islands that are not yet strong.—Romans 15: 1.

3. The Mission and Government to help.

The Mission and Government will help as much as they can to support the Association, especially by providing what is wanted for the farms, schools and hospitals. At first help will be wanted with money, to get the work started.

4. How Christians helped the Church in the early days.

1. Our Lord and His Apostles had a bag of money with which they bought what they needed, and also used it to help the poor.—St. John 12: 6; 13: 29, 30.

2. Then in the early Church everyone wanted to help by giving ALL HE HAD.—Acts 2: 44-47; 4: 34-37.

3. There was a regular collection of money from the Christians.—1 Cor. 16: 1, 2.

4. This money was used to help those who were in need.—Acts 11: 29, 30; 1 Cor. 16: 3.

The Church can do its work well ONLY WHEN EVERYONE HELPS by giving.

THE RULES OF THE CHURCH ASSOCIATION FOLLOW THE WAY OF THE CHURCH IN THE BIBLE.

5. The Collection.

1. It shall be the duty of every baptised person to give 2/- each year to the Church Association.

2. People in special positions will give more, like this:

Bishop—£3
Archdeacon—£2/10/-
Priests, Anyone in Special position in Government or Trade or Mission—£2
Deacons—£1
Lay Workers in Mission, Dressers, Headmen, Storekeepers, Junior School Teachers—£1
District School Teachers— 15/-
District Teachers, Village Chiefs, Village Teachers— 5/-

3. Copra, porpoise teeth, shell, or anything that can be sold for money can be given for the Collection.

4. If a village has a Mission plantation and makes copra from it, half the money must be given to the Association and half to the village Church Fund.

5. Those going away to work will give their 2/- for the Collection, and 3/- for a Thankoffering for each year they are working. If they go for less than a year they will give part of the Thankoffering. If they do not send the money, the keeper of the Church money in their village must pay for them until they return.

6. The Collection must not interfere with the ordinary Church collection at Christmas, Easter and other days; which collections also go to the Church Association.

7. None of these Collections must interfere with the Government tax.

6. Other ways of helping.

1. Those who recover from sickness shall make a thankoffering of 1/-.

2. Money may be raised in the following ways. One tenth of the garden food each day may be kept for sale. If it cannot be sold, the village leader will see that it is used to help the poor and sick, and others in need.

3. Villages may plant coconuts, tobacco and food, for helping the Church; also make mats, bowls, baskets and other things that can be sold.

4. Pigs, fowls, ducks can also be sold to help the Church.

7. A Team of "Consolation" (Acts. 4: 32-37).

1. The Association shall choose a number of men who will help by going away to work with Government, Traders or Mission.

2. These men will give at least £1 per month out of their wages to the Church Association.

3. They shall solemnly make their promise to the Bishop or the Priest at the Altar.

4. Young men who have been to school could help very much in this way.

8. The Officers.

1. There shall be one Head of the Association in each Island where it is set up. He shall be called the President.

2. There shall be a leader of the Association in each village.

9. The Central Committee.

1. The President and the head of each of the five Committees shall be a Central Committee to decide what shall be done and how the money shall be spent.

2. A report shall be sent to the Bishop each year of what the Committee wants to do, and nothing shall be done and no money shall be spent unless the Bishop agrees.

3. The Committee shall set apart a sum of money each year to be given to the Bishop either for the general work of the Church in Melanesia, or for some special work such as a school, or for some island that is in need of help.

10. The Five Committees.

There shall be Five Committees to look after the work of the Association in each island.

1. A Committee for Farms.
2. A Committee for Church and Schools.
3. A Committee for Medical Work.
4. A Committee for Mission.
5. A Committee for Money.

11. The Committee for Farms.

1. It will help the Association if some land is given for farming.—Acts 4: 36, 37.

2. These farms will be worked by teams of young men, and the food that is grown, and the pigs and fowls they have, will be sold.

3. It is hoped that the Mission and Government will help by finding ways of selling the produce.

4. The farm workers will help and teach any villages that want to do good farming on their own land.

12. The Committee for Church and Schools.

1. This Committee will look after schools and see where they should be placed.

2. They will decide what salaries they think are right for the priest, deacons and teachers in schools and villages. They will also pay for such Church and school materials as they can.

3. They will help as much as they can such works as the Colleges and other schools in the Mission.

13. The Committee for Medical Work.

1. This Committee will look for suitable places where a hospital or dispensary can be set up.

2. They will find suitable persons to be dressers and nurses.

3. They will help these hospitals and dispensaries with money from the Association fund.

14. The Committee for Missions.

1. This Committee will remind the Church in Melanesia of our Lord's last command.—St. Matthew 28: 19.

2. It will look for new members for the Brotherhood and give any help the Brothers need.

3. It will plan what help can be given to Missions to the heathen outside Melanesia, and try to get any Missionaries needed for this and to support them as they are able.

4. A Brother should be a member of this Committee if possible.

15. The Committee for the Money.

1. All things about the money shall be done by this Committee.

2. All money given to the Association shall be carefully written down by the clerks who keep the books and be kept in the Bank, except as directed in the next clause.

3. The Association shall keep sufficient cash in hand to meet current expenditure.

4. The books kept by the clerks, and the Bank book, shall be checked every quarter by the Bishop, or by someone appointed by him, to make sure they are correct.

5. All money for paying clergy and teachers shall be paid by the Association to the Bishop, so that the Bishop shall pay the salaries of clergy and teachers.

6. Any money given by the Government shall be received first by the Bishop who will pay it over to the Association.

16. Who shall agree to these Rules.

1. Nothing shall be done that the Bishop does not agree to, and these Rules must be agreed to by the priests of the island where the Association is set up.

2. When there is a Synod, the Rules shall be put before them, and anything that is done must be agreed to by Synod.

3. If it is wanted to change any rule, or to make new rules, this must be done with the agreement of the Bishop, and of the Synod if there is a Synod at that time.

THIS IS IMPORTANT, BECAUSE WE MUST KEEP THE UNITY OF THE CHURCH IN THE DIOCESE OF MELANESIA.

ISSUED BY THE AUTHORITY
OF THE SYNOD OF MELANESIA

Pawa,
July, 1953.

From: Southern Cross Log (English ed.), February 1954, pp. 156-160.

Glossary

acculturation — the process by which culture is transmitted through continuous, direct contact between groups of people with different cultures.

agent of change — a person who attempts to introduce change into a culture, whether it be social, religious or technical change. Frequently, but not always, the agent of change is a member of a culture different from the one into which he wishes to introduce change.

animism — the belief in spirits, including the spirits of dead people (ancestors) as well as spirits that have no human origin.

catechumen — a new convert to Christianity receiving instruction in basic church doctrines before baptism.

communicant — a person who partakes of or receives Holy Communion.

conversion — an experience associated with a definite decisive adoption of religion. In the context of this book, conversion means the adoption of Christianity by individuals or by groups of individuals.

cultural integration — the way in which different elements of a culture relate to one another, forming webs of logic and interconnection between the various parts.

culture history — the historical development of a particular culture based on reconstruction from prehistoric data, archaeological investigation, oral traditions and written records.

diachronic — referring to the historical or developmental approach to the study of culture (*see* synchronic).

emic — the perception of a phenomenon as seen and experienced by an inside participant of a particular group or culture (*see* etic).

ethnocentric, ethnocentrism — the belief that one's group has a way of life, set of values and beliefs, and patterns of adaptation that are superior to all others.

ethnohistory — a research methodology and set of techniques for studying culture through the use of written and oral traditions, and for exploring the regions where history phases into anthropology.

ethnology — the comparative study of culture emphasizing theory more than cultural description.

etic — the perception of a phenomenon by an outside observer of a culture, employing "scientific" and "objective" critera for description (*see* emic).

idiosyncratic level — pertaining to the individual and personal level and expression of a specific culture.

indigenization — the process of taking something from outside the culture, adopting and adapting it in such a way that it naturally belongs to the culture and becomes native to it.

innovation — any thought, behavior, or thing that is new because it is qualitatively different from existing forms.

internalization — the action or process of making something an intrinsic or essential attribute or quality.

internecine — referring to warfare for the sake of destruction and slaughter; murderous.

mana — a non-individualized supernatural force independent of specific supernatural beings.

people movement — the rational, conscious, decision of individuals within a group who choose to convert from an old religion to a new one. The term "people movement" is frequently used in reference to a group of individuals who collectively convert to Christianity. A people movement is distinct from an irrational, unreasoning mass movement.

synchronic — referring to the functional approach to the study of culture, emphasizing a given point in time rather than the historical development of a culture (*see* diachronic).

worldview — the central set of concepts and presuppositions that provide people with their basic assumptions about reality. People in different cultures often have very different worldviews or views of the natural and supernatural world.

Bibliography

Aberle, David

1970 "A Note on Relative Deprivation Theory as Applied to Millenarian and Other Cult Movements." In Sylvia Thrupp (ed.), *Millenial Dreams in Action*, pp. 209-214. New York: Schocken Books.

Adair, John and Evon Vogt

1949 "Navaho and Zuni Veterans: A Study of Contrasting Modes of Culture Change." *American Anthropologist* 51: 547-561.

Ahrens, Theodor

1974 "Christian Syncretism: A Study from the Southern Madang District of Papua New Guinea." *Catalyst* 4 (1): 3-40.

1977 "Concepts of Power in a Melanesian and Biblical Perspective." In Knight (ed.), *Christ in Melanesia: Exploring Theological Issues*, pp. 61-86. Goroka: The Melanesian Institute.

1978 "Local Church and Theology in Melanesia." *Point 2*, pp. 140-158. Goroka: The Melanesian Institute.

Alexander, James M.

1895 *The Islands of the Pacific: From the Old to the New.* New York: American Tract Society.

Allan, Colin H.

1950 The Marching Rule Movement in the British Solomon Islands Protectorate. Dip. Anthropology thesis, Haddon Library, Cambridge.

1951 "Marching Rule: A Nativistic Cult of the British Solomon Islands." *Corona* 3 (3): 93-100.

1957 *Customary Land Tenure in the British Solomon Islands Protectorate.* Honiara: Western Pacific Commission.

1960 "Local Government and Political Consciousness in the British Solomon Islands." *Journal of African Administration* 12: 158-163.

1974 "Some Marching Rule Stories." *The Journal of Pacific History.*

Allen, Jim

1976 "New Light on the Spanish Settlement of the Southeast Solomons: An Archaeological Approach." In Green and Creswell (eds.), *Southeast Solomon Islands Cultural History: A Preliminary Survey*, pp. 19-29. Wellington: The Royal Society of New Zealand, Bulletin No. 11.

Allen, Jim and R. C. Green
1972 "Mendana 1595 and the Fate of the Lost Almiranta: An Archaelogical Investigation." *The Journal of Pacific History* 7: 73-91.

Allen, Roland
1962 *Missionary Methods: St. Paul's or Ours?* American edition. Grand Rapids: Wm. B. Eerdmans.

Alves, Rubem
1969 *A Theology of Human Hope*. Washington: Corpus Books.
1972 *Tomorrow's Child: Imagination, Creativity and Rebirth of Culture*. New York: Harper and Row.

Amherst of Hackney, Lord and Basil Thompson (eds.)
1901 *The Discovery of the Solomon Islands by Alvaro de Mendana in 1568*. 2 vols. London: Hakluyt Society.

Anderson, Gerald H.
1976 *Asian Voices in Christian Theology*. Maryknoll, NY: Orbis Books.

Anderson, Rufus
1875 *Foreign Missions, Their Relations and Claims*. Boston.

Andersson, Efrian
1968 *Churches at the Grass Roots: A Study in Congo-Brazzaville*. London: Lutterworth.

Anonymous
1869 *The Island Mission: Being a History of the Melanesian Mission from Its Commencement.* Reprinted from *Mission Life,* London.

Appiah-Kubi, Kofi and Sergio Torres
1979 *African Theology en Route.* Papers from the Pan-African Conference of Third World Theologians, December 17-23, 1977, Accra, Ghana. Maryknoll, NY: Orbis Books.

Aquina, Sister Mary
1967 "The People of the Spirit: An Independent Church in Rhodesia." *Africa* 37: 203-219.

Arensberg, Conrad M. and Arthur H. Niehoff
1971 *Introducing Social Change: A Manual for Community Development*. 2nd ed. Chicago: Aldine.

Armstrong, E. S.
1900 *The History of the Melanesian Mission*. London: Isbister.

Artless, Stuart (ed.)
1936 *The Church in Melanesia*. London: Melanesian Mission.

Atkin, J.

1871 Unfinished Letter of Rev. J. Atkin, September 21, 1871. Taurarua, New Zealand: Henry Hill, St. Stephens.

Australian Board of Missions

1900 "The Jubilee Festival of the Australian Board of Missions, 1850-1900: The Commemoration in Sydney, Illustrated Handbook and Programme of Services and Meetings, August 19th to August 26th Inclusive." Sydney.

Awdry, Frances

1903 *In the Isles of the Sea: The Story of Fifty Years in Melanesia.* 2nd ed. London: Bemrose and Sons.

Azariah, Vedanayakam Samuel

1954 *Christian Giving.* London: Lutterworth.

Bachofen, J. J.

1861 *Das Mutterrecht.* Basel: Benno Schwabe.

Baeta, C. G. (ed.)

1968 *Christianity in Tropical Africa.* Studies Presented and Discussed at the Seventh International African Seminar, University of Ghana, 1965. London: Oxford University Press.

Barber, Bernard

1941 "Acculturation and Messianic Movements." *American Sociological Review* 6: 663-669.

Barbetti, M. and H. Allen

1972 "Prehistoric Man at Lake Mungo, Australia, by 32,000 B.P." *Nature* 240: 46-48.

Barger, W. K.

1977 "Culture Change and Psychological Adjustment." *American Ethnologist* 4: 471-495.

Barnes, J. A.

1954 *Politics in a Changing Society: A Political History of the Fort Jameson Ngoni.* London: Oxford University Press.

Barney, G. Lynwood

1981 "The Challenge of Anthropology to Current Missiology." *International Bulletin of Missionary Research* 5: 172-177.

Barnett, Homer G.

1940 "Culture Processes." *American Anthropologist* 42: 21-48.

1941 "Personal Conflicts and Cultural Change." *Social Forces* 20: 160-171.

1942a "Cultural Growth by Substitution." *Research Studies of State College of Washington* 10: 26-30.

1942b "Invention and Cultural Change." *American Anthropologist* 44: 14-30.

1953 *Innovation. The Basis of Cultural Change.* New York: McGraw-Hill.

1961 "The Innovative Process." In *Alfred Kroeber. A Memorial.* Kroeber Anthropological Society Papers No. 25. Berkeley: University of California.

1965 "Laws of Socio-Cultural Change." *International Journal of Comparative Sociology* 6: 207-230.

Barrau, J.

1958 *Subsistence Agriculture in Melanesia.* Honolulu: Bernice P. Bishop Museum, Bulletin 219.

Barrett, David B.

1968 *Schism and Renewal in Africa.* Nairobi: Oxford University Press.

1982 *World Christian Encyclopedia: A Comparative Survey of Churches and Religions in the Modern World, A.D. 1900-2000.* New York: Oxford University Press.

Bates, Gerald E.

1971 "Mission/Church Tensions in Africa as a Function of Goal Discrepancy." *Practical Anthropology* 18: 269-278.

Beaglehole, J. C.

1966 *The Exploration of the Pacific.* 3rd ed. London: Adam and Charles Black.

Beckett, Jeremy

1971 "Rivalry, Competition and Conflict among Christian Melanesians." In L. R. Hiatt and C. Jayawardena (eds.) *Anthropology in Oceania.* San Francisco: Chandler.

Beeby, H. D.

1973 "Thoughts on Indigenizing Theology." *South East Asia Journal of Theology.* 14 (2): 34-38.

Beetham, T. A.

1967 *Christianity and the New Africa.* New York: Fredrick A. Praeger.

Beidelman, T. O.

1974 "Social theory and the Study of Christian Missions in Africa." *Africa* 44: 235-249.

1982 *Colonial Evangelism: A Socio-Historical Study of an East African Mission at the Grassroots.* Bloomington: Indiana University Press.

Belcher, Lady

1871 *The Mutineers of the Bounty and Their Descendants in Pitcairn and Norfolk Islands.* New York: Harper and Brothers.

Bellwood, Peter

1975 "The Prehistory of Oceania." *Current Anthropology* 16: 9-17, 24-28.

1979 *Man's Conquest of the Pacific: The Prehistory of Southeast Asia and Oceania.* New York: Oxford University Press.

Belshaw, C. S.

1947 "Native Politics in the Solomon Islands." *Pacific Affairs* 20: 187-193.

1948 "The Postwar Solomons." *Far Eastern Survey* 27 (8): 95-98.

1950a "The Significance of Modern Cults in Melanesian Development." *Australian Outlook* 4 (2): 116-125. Reprinted in Lessa and Vogt (1972: 523-527).

1950b *Island Administration in the South-west Pacific.* London: Royal Institute of International Affairs.

1950c "Changes in Heirloom Jewellery in the Central Solomons." *Oceania* 20: 169-184.

1951 "Cargo Cults." *South Pacific* 5 (8): 167.

1954 *Changing Melanesia: Social Economics of Culture Contact.* Melbourne: Oxford University Press.

1964 *Under the Ivi Tree.* Berkeley: University of California Press.

Berkhofer, Robert F.

1963 "Protestants, Pagans and Sequences among the North American Indians, 1760-1860." *Ethnohistory* 9: 201-232.

1965a "Faith and Factionalism Among the Senecas: Theory and Ethnohistory." *Ethnohistory* 12: 99-112.

1965b *Salvation and the Savage: An Analysis of Protestant Missions and American Indian Response, 1787-1862.* Lexington: University of Kentucky Press.

Bernatzik, Hugo Adolf

1935 *South Seas.* New York: Henry Holt and Company.

Bhebe, Ngwabi

1979 *Christianity and Traditional Religion in Western Zimbabwe, 1859-1923.* London: Longman.

Bidney, David

1953 *Theoretical Anthropology.* New York: Columbia University Press.

Billings, Dorothy K.

1969 "The Johnson Cult of New Hanover." *Oceania* 40: 13-19.

Black, Robert H.

1963 "Christianity as a Cross-cultural Bond in the British Solomon Islands Protectorate as Seen in the Russell Islands." *Oceania* 33: 171-181.

Blackwood, Beatrice

1935 *Both Sides of Buka Passage: An Ethnographic Study of Social, Sexual and Economic Questions in the Northwestern Solomon Islands.* Oxford: Clarendon.

Bleeker, C. J.

1965 *Christ in Modern Athens: The Confrontation of Christianity with Modern Culture and the Non-Christian Religions.* Leiden: E. J. Brill.

Boas, Franz

1903 "The Decorative Art of the North American Indians." Reprinted in *Race, Language and Culture* (1940). New York: Macmillan.

1911 Review of Graebner "Methode Der Ethnologie." Reprinted in *Race, Language and Culture* (1940). New York: Macmillan.

Bodrogi, Tibor

1951 "Colonization and Religious Movements in Melanesia." *Acta Ethnografica Academiae Hungaricae* 2: 259-292.

Bogesi, George

1948 "Santa Isabel, Solomon Islands." *Oceania* 18: 208-232, 327-357.

Bohannan, Paul and Fred Plog (eds.)

1967 *Beyond the Frontier: Social Processes and Cultural Change.* Garden City, NY: The Natural History Press. American Museum Sourcebooks in Anthropology.

Boreham, F. W.

n.d. *George Augustus Selwyn, D. D.: Pioneer Bishop of New Zealand.* London: S. W. Partridge and Company.

Bougainville, Louis de

1772 *A Voyage round the World.* John Forster (trans.). (Reprinted) Amsterdam: N. Israel (1967).

Boutilier, James A.

1978 "Missions, Administration, and Education in the Solomon Islands, 1893-1942." In Boutilier et al. (eds.), *Mission, Church and Sect in Oceania*, pp. 139-161. Ann Arbor: University of Michigan Press.

1979 "Killing the Government: Imperial Policy and the Pacification of Malaita." In M. Rodman and M. Cooper (eds.), pp. 43-87. Ann Arbor: University of Michigan Press.

Boutilier, James A., Daniel T. Hughes, and Sharon W. Tiffany (eds.)

1978 *Mission, Church, and Sect in Oceania.* ASAO Monograph No. 6. Ann Arbor: University of Michigan Press.

Bowler, J. M., A. G. Thorne, and H. A. Polach

1972 "Pleistocene Man in Australia: Age and Significance of the Mungo Skeleton." *Nature* 240: 48-50.

Bradford, Frederick J.

1861 Letter from F. J. Bradford, Acting Mate of the Melbourne Barque *Onyx* to British Consul, Tahiti, 7 September 1861, containing observations on his residence on San Cristobal. Tahiti, British Consulate Papers, Vol. 5: In – letters, 1858-1866, Uncat. MSS, Set 24, Item 8. Mitchell Library, Sydney.

Brenchley, Julius L.

1873 *Jottings During the Cruise of H.M.S. Curacoa among the South Sea Islands in 1865.* London: Longmans, Green and Company.

Brooke, C. H.

n.d. (1881) *Percy Pomo; or the Autobiography of a South Sea Islander.* London: Griffith, Farran, Okeden and Welsh.

Brookes, Jean Ingram

1941 *International Rivalry in the Pacific Islands, 1800-1875.* Berkeley: University of California Press.

Brookfield, H. C. and Doreen Hart

1971 *Melanesia: A Geographical Interpretation of an Island World.* London: Methuen.

Broom, Leonard, et al.

1954 "Acculturation: An Exploratory Formulation." *American Anthropologist* 56: 973-1000.

Brown, George

1910 *Melanesians and Polynesians: Their Life Histories Described and Compared.* London: Macmillan and Co.

Brown, Paula

1978 *Highland Peoples of New Guinea.* Cambridge: Cambridge University Press.

Brunet, Auguste

1908 *Le Regime International des Nouvelles-Hebrides: Le Condomininium Anglo-Franxais.* Paris.

Bühlmann, Walbert

1978 *The Coming of the Third Church.* Maryknoll, NY: Orbis Books.

Bulmer, Susan and Ralph Bulmer

1964 "The Prehistory of the Australian New Guinea Highlands." *American Anthropologist* 66 (4) part 2: 38-76.

Burridge, Kenelm O. L.

1960 *Mambu: A Melanesian Millennium.* London: Methuen.

1969 *New Heaven, New Earth: A Study of Millenarian Activities.* Oxford: Blackwell.

1978 "Missionary Occasions." Introduction to *Mission, Church and Sect in Oceania.* James A. Boutilier, et al. (eds.). Ann Arbor: University of Michigan Press.

Buxton, P. A.

1925-1926 "The Depopulation of the New Hebrides and Other Parts of Melanesia." *Transactions of the Royal Society of Tropical Medicine and Hygiene* 19: 420-454.

Cappell, Arthur

1938 "The Word Mana: A Linguistic Study." *Oceania* 9: 89-96.

1962 "Oceanic Linguistics Today." *Current Anthropology* 3: 371-428.

1969 "Non-Austronesian Languages of the British Solomons." *Pacific Linguistics*, Series A. Occasional Papers No. 21: 1-16.

Carmack, Robert M.

1972 "Ethnohistory: A Review of its Development, Definitions, Methods and Aims." *Annual Review of Anthropology* 1: 227-246.

Carpenter, Edmund

1974 *Oh What a Blow that Phantom Gave Me.* New York: Bantam.

Chadwick, Owen

1966-1970 *The Victorian Church.* In 2 parts. London: Adam and Charles Black.

Charles, Elizabeth

1969 (Orig. 1886) *Three Martyrs of the Nineteenth Century: Studies from the Lives of Livingston, Gordon and Patteson.* New York: Negro Universities Press.

Cheyne, Andrew

1971 *The Trading Voyages of Andrew Cheyne, 1841-1844.* Edited by Dorothy Shineberg. Canberra: Australian National University Press.

Chowning, Ann

1977 *An Introduction to the Peoples and Cultures of Melanesia.* 2nd ed. Menlo Park, CA: Cummings.

Christiansen, Palle

1969 *The Melanesian Cargo Cult: Millenarianism as a Factor in Cultural Change.* Copenhagen: Akademisk Forlag.

Church of England in Australia
1850 "Minutes of Proceedings at a Meeting of the Metropolitan and Suffragan Bishops of the Province of Australasia, held at Sydney, from October 1st to November 1st, A.D. 1850." Sydney.

Church of Melanesia
1973a *Buka Tharai Ka Cheke Maringe.* The Book of Common Prayer, with a Liturgy for Melanesia in the Language of Maringe, Santa Isabel, Solomon Islands. Honiara: Provincial Press.
1973b *Melanesian Prayer Book.* A Book of Common Prayer in Modern English, Translated by C. E. Fox. Honiara: Provincial Press.
1974 *The Constitution of the Church of the Province of Melanesia.* Honiara: Provincial Press.
1975 *Canons of the Province of Melanesia.* Honiara: Provincial Press.
1977 *Plan of Daily Prayer for Church Workers and for Departed Servants of the Church 1978.* Honiara: Provincial Press.
1977-1979 *Church of Melanesia Newsletter.* Honiara: Provincial Press.

Clarke, C. P. S.
1932 *The Oxford Movement and After.* London: A. R. Mowbray and Company.

Clemhout, Simone
1964 "Typology of Nativistic Movements." *Man* 64: 14-15.

Coaldrake, Frank W.
1963 "Chairman's Report, Visit to Melanesia." The Australian Board of Missions 30th April - 2nd May, 1963. Agenda 8c. Mimeo. Stanmore, NSW: Australian Board of Missions Archives.

Cochrane, Glynn
1970 *Big Men and Cargo Cults.* Oxford: Clarendon Press.

Codrington, R. H.
n.d. *Lecture Delivered at Nelson, September 25, 1863.* Torquay.
1881 "Religious Beliefs and Practices in Melanesia." *Journal of the Anthropological Institute* 10: 261-315.
1885 *The Melanesian Languages.* Oxford: Clarendon Press.
1891 *The Melanesians: Studies in Their Anthropology and Folklore.* Oxford: Clarendon Press.

Collins, Lloyd R.
1977 "The Innovation Process in a Modern Industrial Complex." *Human Organization* 36: 282-290.

Colonial Office (Great Britain)

1946 *Among Those Present: The Official Story of the Pacific Islands at War.* London: HMSO.

Compte, Auguste

1830-1842 *The Positive Philosophy of Auguste Compte.* Translated and condensed by H. Martineau. London: Kegan Paul, Trench and Trubner (1893).

Conkling, Robert

1974 "Legitimacy and Coversion in Social Change: The Case of French Missionaries and the Northeastern Algonkian." *Ethnohistory* 21: 1-24.

Conley, William

1976 *The Kalamantan Kenyah: The Study of Tribal Conversion in Terms of Dynamic Themes.* Nutley: Presbyterian and Reform Publishing Company.

Conway, G. R. G.

1946 "Translation of the Report of Dr. Barros to Toledo, Governor of Peru, on His Examination of Members of Mendana's Expedition of 1567 in June 1573." *American Neptune* 6 (April): 139-151.

Cook, S. F.

1976 *The Conflict Between the California Indians and White Civilization by Sherburne F. Cook.* Berkeley: University of California Press. (The six essays reprinted here were written in the 1930's and published as volumes of the Ibero-American series between 1940 and 1943.)

Coombe, Florence

1909 *School-days In Norfolk Island.* London: SPCK.

Cooper, Matthew Owen

1970 Langalanga Ethics (British Solomon Islands). Unpublished Ph.D. dissertation, Yale University.

1979 "On the Beginnings of Colonialism in Melanesia." In M. Rodman and M. Cooper (eds.), *The Pacification of Melanesia,* pp. 25-41. Ann Arbor: University of Michigan Press.

Coote, Walter

1883 *The Western Pacific: Being a Description of the Groups of Islands to the North and East of the Australian Continent.* London.

Cormack, James E.

1944 *Isles of Solomon.* Washington: Review and Herald Publishing Company.

Corris, Peter

1970 "Kwaisulia of Ada Gege: A Strongman in the Solomon Islands." In J. W. Davidson and Deryck Scarr (eds.) *Pacific Island Portraits,* pp. 253-265. Canberra: Australian National University Press.

1972 " 'White Australia' In Action: The Repatriation of Pacific Islanders from Queensland." *Historical Studies* 15 (58): 237-250.

1973 *Passage, Port and Plantation: A History of Solomon Islands Labour Migration 1870-1914.* Melbourne: Melbourne University Press.

Cowie, W. G., Bishop of Auckland

1872 *Notes of a Visit to Norfolk Island, the Headquarters of the Melanesian Mission in November 1872.* Auckland: Wm. Atkin, Church and General Printer.

Cox, Philip and Wesley Stacey

1971 *Building Norfolk Island.* Melbourne: Thomas Nelson.

Cranswick, G. H.

1952 "Cults: Nationalism in the Pacific." Field Survey No. 7. *Australian Board of Missions Review* 40 (7): 101-103.

Craven, Wesley Frank and James Lea Cate (eds.)

1950 *The Pacific: Guadalcanal to Saipan, August 1942 to July 1944, the Army Air Forces in World War II.* Vol. 4. Chicago: University of Chicago Press.

Creighton, Louise

1923 *G. A. Selwyn, D.D.: Bishop of New Zealand and Lichfield.* London: Longmans, Green and Company.

Crocombe, Ron (ed.)

1971 *Land Tenure in the Pacific.* Melbourne: Oxford University Press.

Cromar, John

1935 *Jock of the Islands: Early Days in the South Seas.* London.

Cronin, Constance

1970 *Sting of Change: Sicilians in Sicily and Australia.* Chicago: University of Chicago Press.

Cullwick, T. C.

n.d. (ca. 1910) In the Matter of the Proposal to Move the Headquarters of the Melanesian Mission from Norfolk Island to the Solomon Islands and also to Give Up Norfolk Island as a Training college and the *Southern Cross* as a Missionary Vessel. (Printed document) St. John's College Library, Auckland.

Culwick, A. T.

1935 "Culture Change on the Fringe of Civilisation in Africa." *Africa* 8: 163-170.

Curteis, G. H.

1889 *Bishop Selwyn of New Zealand and Lichfield: A Sketch of His Life and Work.* London: Kegan Paul, Trench and Company.

Dark, Philip J. C.

1957 "Methods of Synthesis in Ethnohistory." *Ethnohistory* 4: 231-278.

Davenport, William H.

1962 "Red Feather Money." *Scientific American* 206 (3): 94-104.

1964 "Notes on Santa Cruz Voyaging." *Journal of the Polynesian Society* 73: 134-142.

1970 "Two Social Movements in the British Solomons that Failed and their Political Consequences." In Marion W. Ward (ed.) Fourth Waigani Seminar, *The Politics of Melanesia*, pp. 162-172. Canberra: Research School of Pacific Studies, Australian National University.

Davenport, William H. and Gulbun Coker

1967 "The Moro Movement of Guadalcanal, British Solomon Islands Protectorate." *Journal of the Polynesian Society* 76: 123-175.

Davidson, James W.

1942 European Penetration of the South Pacific, 1779-1842. Unpublished Ph.D. thesis, Cambridge.

Davis, John King

1911 *History of St. John's College, Tamaki, Auckland, New Zealand.* Auckland: Abel Dykes.

De Wolf, Jan J.

1977 *Differentiation and Integration in Western Kenya: A Study of Religious Innovation and Social Change among the Bukusu.* Paris, The Hague: Mouton.

Deacon, A. B.

1934 *Malekula: A Vanishing People in the New Hebrides.* London.

Deck, Northcote

1945 *South from Guadalcanal: The Romance of Rennell Island.* Toronto: Evangelical Publishers.

Delfendahl, Bernard

1981 "On Anthropologists vs. Missionaries." *Current Anthropology* 22: 89.

Dickson, Kwesi and Paul Ellingworth (eds.)
1971 *Biblical Revelation and African Traditional Beliefs.* Maryknoll, NY: Orbis Books.

Diocese of Ysabel (Church of Melanesia)
1976 *Proceedings of the Second Diocesan Synod, Held at Jejevo 25th August to 29th August, 1976.* Honiara: Provincial Press.

Dissertation Abstracts International
1970 Retrospective Index, Vol. 5 (Social Science). Xerox.

Docker, Edward W.
1970 *The Blackbirders: The Recruiting of South Seas Labour for Queensland, 1863-1907.* Sydney: Angus and Robertson.

Donovan, Vincent J.
1982 *Christianity Rediscovered.* 2nd ed. Maryknoll, NY: Orbis Books.

Dovey, J. Whitsed
1950 *The Gospel in the South Pacific.* London: World Dominion Press.

Drost, E.
1938 *Forced Labor in the South Pacific, 1850-1914.* Iowa City: Iowa State University Press.

Drummond, H. N.
1930 *John Coleridge Patteson. An Account of his Death at Nukapu, and Description of St. Barnabas Chapel, Norfolk Island, Dedicated to his Memory.* Parkstone (Dorset): Ralph and Brown.

Drysdale, M.
1960 Public Reaction in New Zealand to the Death of Bishop Patteson, 1871. Unpublished M.A. thesis, University of Otago, Dunedin.

Dudley, B. T.
1860 *Journal of a Winter Spent on Amota Banks Is. Lat. 13°45′S, Long. 167°40′E.* Auckland: Melanesian Mission Press.
1873 *Who is Sufficient for these Things?* A Sermon Preached in St. Paul's Cathedral Church, Auckland, New Zealand on St. Barnabas' Day, June 11, 1873 on the Occasion of the Ordination of George Sarawia. Auckland: Upton and Company.

Dunbabin, Thomas
1925 "Whalers, Sealers and Buccaneers." *Journal and Proceedings, the Royal Australian Historical Society* 11: 1-32.
1935 *Slavers of the South Seas.* Sydney: Angus and Robertson.

Dunmore, John
1969 *The Fateful Voyage of the St. Jean Baptiste.* Christchurch: Pegasus Press.

Dunn, Edmond J.
1980 *Missionary Theology: Foundations in Development.* Washington: University Press of America.

Dunning, R. W.
1959 "Ethnic Relations and the Marginal Man in Canada." *Human Organization* 18: 117-122.

Durkheim, Emile
1951 *Suicide.* New York: The Free Press.

Durrad Papers
1920-1955 Papers and letters relating to C. E. Fox. (Collection contains an unpublished typescript by Fox entitled "A Missionary in Melanesia" with an introduction and notes by Durrad.) MS Papers 1171, Alexander Turnbull Library, Wellington, New Zealand.

Durrad, Walter John
1920 *The Attitude of the Church to the Suqe.* Melanesian Mission Occasional Papers No. 1. Norfolk Island: Melanesian Mission Press.
1922 "The Depopulation of Melanesia." In W. H. R. Rivers (ed.), *Essays on the Depopulation of Melanesia,* pp. 3-24. Cambridge University Press.

Dutton, Alan G.
1969 Ethics in a Gela Context. Unpublished B.D. thesis, St. John's College, Auckland.

Dyen, Isidore
1965 *A Lexicostatistical Classification of the Austronesian Languages.* Bloomington, IN: International Journal of American Linguistics, Memoir 19.

Edge-Partington, T. W.
1907 "Ingava, Chief of Rubiana, Solomon Islands: Died 1906." *Man* 7: 22-23.

Eliade, Mircea
1970 " 'Cargo-Cults' and Cosmic Regeneration." In Sylvia Thrupp (ed.), *Millennial Dreams in Action,* pp. 139-143. New York: Schocken Books.

Elkin, A. P.
1936 "The Reaction of Primitive Races to the White Man's Culture: A Study in Culture Contact." *The Hibbert Journal* 35: 537-548.

1953 *Social Anthropology in Melanesia: A Review of Research.* London: Oxford University Press.

Erasmus, Charles J.
1961 *Man Takes Control.* New York: Bobbs-Merrill.

Ethnohistory
1961 "Symposium on the Concept of Ethnohistory." Vol. 8: 12-92, 256-280.

Evans, John H.
1964 *Churchman Militant: George Augustus Selwyn, Bishop of New Zealand and Lichfield.* London: George Allen and Unwin.

Evans-Pritchard, E. E.
1962 "Anthropology and History." *Essays in Social Anthropology,* pp. 46-65. London: Farber and Farber.
1964 "Social Anthropology: Past and Present." *Social Anthropology and Other Essays,* pp. 139-154. New York: The Free Press.

Fabian, Johannes
1971 *Jamaa: A Charismatic Movement in Katanga.* Evanston: Northwestern University Press.

Fallers, L. A.
1965 *Bantu Bureaucracy: A Study of Integration and Conflict in the Political Institutions of an East African People.* Cambridge: Heffer.

Fallowes, Richard Prince
1929 Account of Voyage. MS 2478, National Library of Australia.
1929-1934 Letters written by the Rev. Richard Fallowes, Melanesian Mission, to his sister in England, Feb. 17, 1929 - Dec. 27, 1934. (Typescript) MS 2478, National Library of Australia, Canberra.
1931-1934 Diary. MS 2478, National Library of Australia.
1978-1979 Letters to the author (personal correspondence).

Fashole-Luke, Edward, Richard Gray, Adrian Hastings and Goodwin Tasie (eds.)
1978 *Christianity in Independent Africa.* Bloomington: Indiana University Press.

Fenton, William N.
1962 "Ethnohistory and its Problems." *Ethnohistory* 9: 1-23.

Firth, Raymond
1940 "The Analysis of Mana: An Empirical Approach." *Journal of the Polynesian Society.* 49: 483-510.
1955 "The Theory of Cargo Cults." *Man* 55 (142): 130-132.

1959 *Economics of the New Zealand Maori.* 2nd ed. Wellington: R. E. Owen, Government Printer.

1970 *Rank and Religion in Tikopia: A Study in Polynesian Paganism and Conversion to Christianity.* London: George Allen and Unwin.

Fisher, Humphrey J.

1973 "Conversion Reconsidered: Some Historical Aspects of Religious Conversion in Black Africa." *Africa* 43: 27-40.

Fison, Lorimer

1871 "The Murder of Bishop Patteson." *Sydney Morning Herald,* November 18, 1871.

1872-1873 "The South Seas Labour Traffic." *Daily Telegraph.* (Fison wrote this series of articles under the *nom de plume* of Outis.)

1907 *Tales from Old Fiji.* London: Alexander Moring.

Flannery, Wendy

1978a "Theology in Context in Papua New Guinea." *Point* 1, pp. 55-94. Goroka: The Melanesian Institute.

1978b "Melanesian Myth: Medium and Message." *Point* 2, pp. 103-127. Goroka: The Melanesian Institute.

1979 "Symbol and Myth in Melanesian Cultures." *Missiology* 7: 435-449.

Fleurieu, M. L. C.

1791 *Discoveries of the French in 1768 and 1769, to the South-East of New Guinea, etc.* London: John Stockdale.

Foljambe, C. G. S.

1868 *Three Years on the Australia Station.* London.

Forman, Charles W.

1972 "Missionaries and Colonialism: The Case of the New Hebrides in the Twentieth Century." *Journal of Church and State* 14: 75-92.

1982 *The Island Churches of the South Pacific: Emergence in the Twentieth Century.* Maryknoll, NY: Orbis Books.

Fortes, M.

1936 "Culture Contact as a Dynamic Process." *Africa* 9: 24-55.

1938 "Culture Contact as a Dynamic Process." In *Methods of Study of Culture Contact in Africa.* Memorandum 15, International Institute of African Languages and Culture.

Foster, George M.

1962 *Traditional Cultures and the Impact of Technological Change.* New York: Harper and Row.

1973 *Traditional Societies and Technological Change.* 2nd ed. New York: Harper and Row.

Fowler, Wilfred
1959 *This Island's Mine.* London: Constable.

Fox, Charles Elliot
1910 *An Introduction to the Study of Oceanic Languages.* Norfolk Island: Melanesian Mission Press.
1924 *The Threshold of the Pacific: An Account of the Social Organization, Magic and Religion of the People of San Christoval in the Solomon Islands.* London: Kegan Paul, Trench, Trubner and Co.
1958 *Lord of the Southern Isles, Being the Story of the Anglican Mission in Melanesia 1849-1949.* London: A. R. Mowbray and Company.
1962 *Kakamora.* London: Hodder and Stoughton.
1964 "Canon Willie Masuraa." *The Melanesian Messenger,* Easter, pp. 20-22.
1966 "Pidgin." *The Melanesian Messenger,* Christmas, pp. 2-4.
1967 *The Story of the Solomons.* Taroniara: Diocese of Melanesia Press.
1942-1959 Diary. Church of Melanesia Archives. Honiara.
n.d.a. A Missionary in Melanesia. Durrad Papers, MS Papers 1171: 3. Alexander Turnbull Library.
n.d.b. (1972) *The Melanesian Brotherhood.* 2nd ed. Revised by Brian Macdonald-Milne. London: Melanesian Mission.
n.d.c. (1956) Melanesian Memories (typescript), Bishop Patteson Theological Centre Library, Kohimarama, Solomon Islands.
n.d.d. History of the Melanesian Mission (typescript), Auckland.

Frater, A. S.
1947 "Depopulation in the New Hebrides." *Transactions, Fiji Society of Science and Industry,* pp. 166-185.

Frazer, James G.
1890 *The Golden Bough: A Study in Magic and Religion.* London: Macmillan. (An abridged form of Frazer's discussion on sympathetic magic is reprinted in Lessa and Vogt, 1972: 415-430.)

Freeman, John F.
1965 "The Indian Convert: Theme and Variation." *Ethnohistory* 12: 113-128.

Freeth, Robert E.
1916 "Christian Influence on a Dying Race. *The East and the West* 14: 382-394.

Frerichs, Albert and Sylvia
1969 *Anutu Conquers In New Guinea.* Minneapolis: Augsburg Publishing House.

Garanger, Jose
1971 "Incised and Applied-relief Pottery, Its Chronology and Development in Southeastern Melanesia and Extra Comparisons." In R. C. Green and M. Kelly (eds.) *Studies in Oceanic Culture History,* Vol. 2, pp. 53-66. Honolulu: Bishop Museum, Pacific Anthropological Records No. 12.
1972 *Archaeologie des Nouvelles-Hebrides.* Publications de la Societe des Oceanistes No. 30. Paris: Musee de l'Homme.

Garrett, John
1982 *To Live Among the Stars: Christian Origins in Oceania.* Geneva: World Council of Churches Publications.

Geddes, W. R.
1948 An Analysis of Culture Change in Fiji. Unpublished Ph.D. thesis, London School of Economics and Political Science.

Gibbs, Philip
1977 "Blood and Life in a Melanesian Context." In Knight (ed.), *Christ in Melanesia: Exploring Theological Issues,* pp. 166-177. Goroka: The Melanesian Institute.

Gibellini, Rosino (ed.)
1979 *Frontiers of Theology in Latin America.* Maryknoll, NY: Orbis Books.

Gifford, E. W.
1924 "Euro-American Acculturation in Tonga." *Journal of the Polynesian Society* 33: 281-292.

Giles, W. E.
1968 *A Cruize in a Queensland Labour Vessel to the South Seas.* Deryck Scarr (ed.). Canberra: Australian National University Press.

Gillin, John
1948 *The Ways of Men.* New York: Appleton-Century-Crofts.

Gladstone, W. E.
1879 *Gleanings of Past Years, Personal and Literary*, 2 vols. London: John Murray.

Gluckman, Max
1958 "Analysis of a Social Situation in Modern Zululand." *Rhodes-Livingston Papers,* No. 28. Manchester.
1963 *Order and Rebellion in Tribal Africa.* London: Cohen and West.

Goldie, John F.
1908 "The People of New Georgia, Their Manners and Customs and Religious Beliefs." *Proceedings of the Royal Society of Queensland* 22: 23-30.

Goldman, Irving
1970 *Ancient Polynesian Society.* Chicago: University of Chicago Press.

Goldschmidt, Walter
1956 "Culture and Behavior." Proceedings of the International Congress of Ethnological and Anthropological Sciences. Philadelphia.
1966 *Comparative Functionalism.* Berkeley: University of California Press.

Golson, J.
1968 "Archaeological Prospects for Melanesia." In I. Yawata and Y. H. Sinoto (eds.), *Prehistoric Culture in Oceania.* A Symposium Presented at the Eleventh Pacific Congress. Honolulu: Bishop Museum Press.
1971 "Lapita Ware and its Transformations." In Green and Kelly (eds.), pp. 67-76.
1972 "Both Sides of the Wallace Line: New Guinea, Australia, Island Melanesia and Asian Prehistory." In N. Barnard (ed.), *Early Chinese Art and Its Possible Influence in the Pacific Basin.* New York: Interarts Cultural Press.

Goodenough, J. G.
1876 *Journal of Commodore Goodenough, R.N., C.B., C.M.G., During His Last Command as Senior Officer on the Australian Station, 1873-1875,* edited with a memoir by his widow. London.

Goodenough, Ward H.
1963 *Cooperation in Change.* New York: Russell Sage Foundation.

Godschalk, J. A.
1977 Where the Twain Shall Meet. A Study of the Autochthonous Character of Some Movements in New Guinea. Doctoraal scriptie, Faculteit der Godgeleerdheid, Rijksuniversiteit te Utrecht.

Gottschalk, Louis
1969 *Understanding History.* New York: Alfred Knopf.

Grace, George
1961 "Austronesian Linguistics and Culture History." *American Anthropologist* 63: 359-368.
1964 "Movements of the Malayo-Polynesians, 1500 B.C. - 500 A.D.: The Linguistic Evidence." *Current Anthropology* 5: 361-368, 403-404.
1968 "Classification of the Languages of the Pacific." In A. P. Vayda (ed.) *Peoples and Cultures of the Pacific*, pp. 63-79. Garden City, NY: The Natural History Press.

Graebner, Fritz

1911 *Methode der Ethnologie.* Heidelberg: C. Winter.

Grattan, C. Hartley

1963a *The Southwest Pacific to 1900.* Ann Arbor: University of Michigan Press.

1963b *The Southwest Pacific Since 1900.* Ann Arbor: University of Michigan Press.

Great Britain

1872a *Hansard's Parliamentary Debates,* 3rd Series, Vol. 211.

1872b *Parliamentary Papers.* Vol. 43 (C. 496): Report of the Proceedings of H. M. Ship *Rosario*, during Her Cruise among the South Sea Islands, between 1st November 1871 and 12th February 1872.

1873a *Parliamentary Papers.* Vol. 50 (244): Communications Respecting Outrages Committed upon Natives of the South Seas Islands.

1873b *South Sea Islands.* Return to an Address of the House of Lords dated 10th February 1873, For Copies of Extracts of any Communications of Importance Respecting Outrages Committed Upon Natives of the South Sea Islands which may have been received from the Governors of any of the Australian Colonies. London: Colonial Office.

Green, Kaye C.

1974 Historical Outline of European Contacts and Bibliography for Use of Project Collaborators and Researchers in the Eastern District, B.S.I. Working Paper Archaeology No. 34, Department of Anthropology, University of Auckland (mimeograph).

Green, Roger C.

1963 "A Suggested Revision of the Fijian Sequence." *Journal of the Polynesian Society* 72: 235-253.

1973 "Conquest of the Conquistadors." *World Archaeology* 5: 14-31.

1976 "Languages of the Southeast Solomons and Their Historical Relationships." In R. C. Green and M. M. Creswell (eds.), pp. 47-60.

1977 *A First Culture History of the Solomon Islands.* Auckland: University of Auckland Bindery.

Green, Roger C. and M. Kelly (eds.)

1971 *Studies in Oceanic Culture History, Vol. 2.* Honolulu: Bishop Museum, Pacific Anthropological Records No. 12.

Green, Roger C. and M. M. Creswell (eds.)

1976 *Southeast Solomon Islands Cultural History: A Preliminary Survey.* Wellington: The Royal Society of New Zealand, Bulletin No. 11.

Greenberg, J. H.
1971 "The Indo-Pacific Hypothesis." In J. D. Bowen, et al. (eds.), *Linguistics in Oceania, Vol. 8.* Current Trends in Linguistics, T. Sebeok, general editor. The Hague: Mouton.

Grimes, Barbara F. (ed.)
1978 *Ethnologue* 9th ed. Huntington Beach, CA: Wycliffe Bible Translators.

Grover, John
1973 "San Jorge's Ghosts and Things That Go Bump in the Night." *Pacific Islands Monthly*, January, pp. 61-65.

Groves, W. C.
1936 *Native Education and Culture-contact in New Guinea.* Melbourne.
1940 Report on a Survey of Education in the British Solomon Islands Protectorate. Tulagi: n.p. (WPHC MP2736/1939).

Guiart, Jean
1951 "Forerunners of Melanesian Nationalism." *Oceania* 22: 81-90.
1952 "John Frum Movement in Tanna." *Oceania* 22: 165-177.
1956 "Culture Contact and the 'John Frum' Movement on Tanna." *Southwestern Journal of Anthropology* 12: 105-116.
1962 *Les Religione de l'Oceanie.* Paris: Presses Universitaires.
1970 "The Millenarian Aspect of Conversion to Christianity in the South Pacific." In S. Thrupp (ed.) *Millennial Dreams in Action,* pp. 122-138. New York: Schocken Books.

Gunson, Niel
1965 "Missionary Interest in British Expansion in the South Pacific in the Nineteenth Century." *Journal of Religious History* 3: 296-313.
1969 "The Theology of Imperialism and the Missionary History of the Pacific." *Journal of Religious History* 5: 255-265.
1978 *Messengers of Grace: Evangelical Missionaries in the South Seas 1797-1860.* Melbourne: Oxford University Press.

Guppy, H. B.
1887 *The Solomon Islands and Their Natives.* London: Swan Sonnenschein, Lowrey and Company.

Gutch, John
1971 *Martyr of the Islands: The Life and Death of John Coleridge Patteson.* London: Hodder and Stoughton.

Gutierrez, Gustavo
1973 *A Theology of Liberation.* Maryknoll, NY: Orbis Books.

Habel, Norman C. (ed.)
1979 *Powers, Plumes and Piglets: Phenomena of Melanesian Religion.* Bedford Park, South Australia: The Australian Association for the Study of Religions.

Hackman, Brian D.
1968 *A Guide to the Spelling and Pronounciation of Place Names in the British Solomon Islands Protectorate.* Honiara: Government Printer.

Haddon, A. C. and James Hornell
1936-1938 *Canoes of Oceania.* 3 vols. Bernice P. Bishop Museum Special Publications 27-29. Honolulu: Bishop Museum Press.

Hagesi, Robert
1972 Towards Localization of Anglican Worship in the Solomon Islands. Unpublished B.D. thesis, Pacific Theological College, Suva, Fiji.

Hall, Edward T.
1959 *The Silent Language.* Garden City, NY: Doubleday.
1966 *The Hidden Dimension.* Garden City, NY: Doubleday.
1976 *Beyond Culture.* Garden City, NY: Anchor Press/Doubleday.
1979 "Learning the Arabs' Silent Language." *Psychology Today,* August, pp. 45-54.

Hamlin, H.
1932 "The Problem of Depopulation in Melanesia." *Yale Journal of Biology and Medicine,* Vol. 4.

Hanke, Louis
1970 *Aristotle and the American Indian: A Study in Race Prejudice in the Modern World.* Bloomington: Indiana University Press.

Harding, Thomas G.
1967 *Voyagers of the Vitiaz Strait.* Seattle: University of Washington Press.

Harding, Thomas G. and Ben J. Wallace (eds.)
1970 *Cultures of the Pacific.* New York: The Free Press.

Harris, George L.
1967 The Mission of Matteo Ricci, S.J. Unpublished Ph.D. dissertation, the Catholic University of America, Washington, D.C.

Harwood, Frances H.
1971 The Christian Fellowship Church: A Revitalization Movement in Melanesia. Unpublished Ph.D. dissertation, University of Chicago.

1978 "Intercultural Communication in the Western Solomons: The Methodist Mission and the Emergence of the Christian Fellowship Church." In James. A. Boutilier, et al. (eds.), *Mission, Church, and Sect in Oceania,* pp. 231-250. Ann Arbor: University of Michigan Press.

Hays, H. R.
1958 *From Ape to Angel: An Informal History of Social Anthropology.* New York: Alfred Knopf.

Hayward, Victor (ed.)
1966 *The Church as Christian Community: Three Studies of North India Churches.* London: Lutterworth.

Heath, Ian
1980 Land Policy in the Solomon Islands. Unpublished Ph.D. thesis, La Trobe University, Bundoora, Australia.

Heine-Geldern, R.
1964 "One Hundred Years of Ethnological Theory in the German Speaking Countries: Some Milestones." *Current Anthropology* 5: 407-418, with commentary by Paul Lesser, pp. 416-417.

Henderson, John R.
1974 "Missionary Influence on Haida Settlement and Subsistence Patterns, 1876-1920." *Ethnohistory* 21: 303-316.

Herskovits, Melville J.
1937a "The Significance of the Study of Acculturation for Anthropology." *American Anthropologist* 39: 259-264.
1937b *Life in a Haitian Valley.* New York: Knopf.
1937c "African Gods and Catholic Saints in New World Negro Belief." *American Anthropologist* 39: 635-643.
1938 *Acculturation: The Study of Culture Contact.* New York: J. J. Augustin.
1943 "The Negro in Bahia, Brazil: A Problem in Method." *American Sociological Review* 8: 394-402.
1945 "The Processes of Cultural Change." In Ralph Linton (ed.), *The Science of Man in the World Crisis,* pp. 144-170. New York: Columbia University Press.
1955 *Cultural Anthropology.* New York: Alfred A. Knopf.
1967 *Cultural Dynamics.* New York: Alfred A. Knopf.

Herlihy, J. M.
1977 Distance, Decay and Development Effectiveness: Steps Toward a Hypothesis. Work-in-progress seminar paper, Department of Human Geography, Australian National University, Canberra.

Hesselgrave, David J.
1978 *Communicating Christ Cross-Culturally.* Grand Rapids: Zondervan.

Hezel, Francis X.
1978 "Indigenization as a Missionary Goal in the Caroline and Marshall Islands." In James A. Boutilier et al. (eds.), *Mission, Church, and Sect in Oceania* pp. 251-273. Ann Arbor: University of Michigan Press.

Hiebert, Paul G.
1978a "Conversion, Culture and Cognitive Categories." *Gospel in Context* 1 (4): 24-29.
1978b "Missions and Anthropology: A Love/Hate Relationship." *Missiology* 6: 165-180.

Higgins, John Seville
1958 *One Faith and Fellowship.* Greenwich, CT: Seabury.

Hilliard, David L.
1966 Protestant Missions in the Solomon Islands, 1849-1942. Unpublished Ph.D. thesis, Australian National University, Canberra.
1969 "The South Sea Evangelical Mission of the Solomon Islands: The Foundation Years." *The Journal of Pacific History* 4: 41-64.
1970a "Bishop G. A. Selwyn and the Melanesian Mission." *New Zealand Journal of History* 4: 120-137.
1970b "John Coleridge Patteson, Missionary Bishop of Melanesia." In J. W. Davidson and Deryck Scarr (eds.), *Pacific Island Portraits*, pp. 177-200. Canberra: Australian National University Press.
1974 "Colonialism and Christianity: The Melanesian Mission in the Solomon Islands." *The Journal of Pacific History* 9: 93-116.
1978 *God's Gentlemen: A History of the Melanesian Mission, 1849-1942.* St. Lucia: University of Queensland Press.

Hobhouse, L. T.
1906 *Morals in Evolution: A Study in Comparative Ethics.* New York: Holt, Rinehart and Winston (reprinted 1925).

Hocart, A. M.
1914 "Mana." *Man* 14 (46): 97-101.
1922a "The Cult of the Dead in Eddystone of the Solomons." *Journal of the Royal Anthropological Institute* 52: 71-112, 259-305.
1922b "Mana Again." *Man* 22 (79): 139-141.

1925 "Medicine and Witchcraft in Eddystone of the Solomons." *Journal of the Royal Anthropological Institute* 55: 229-270.

1931 "Warfare in Eddystone of the Solomons." *Journal of the Royal Anthropological Institute* 61: 301-332.

1932 "Natural and Supernatural." *Man* 32 (78): 59-61.

Hoebel, E. A.

1972 *Anthropology: The Study of Man.* 4th ed. New York: McGraw-Hill.

Hogbin, H. Ian

1934 "Culture Change in the Solomon Islands: Report on Fieldwork in Guadalcanal and Malaita." *Oceania* 4: 233-267.

1935 "Sorcery and Administration." *Oceania* 6: 1-32.

1936 "Mana." *Oceania 6: 241-274.*

1939 *Experiments in Civilization: The Effects of European Culture on a Native Community of the Solomon Islands.* London: George Routledge and Sons.

1958 *Social Change.* London: Watts.

Hogbin, H. Ian (ed.)

1973 *Anthropology in Papua New Guinea: Readings from the Encyclopedia of Papua and New Guinea.* Melbourne: Melbourne University Press.

Hogbin, H. Ian and Camilla Wedgewood

1952-1953 "Local Grouping in Melanesia." *Oceania* 23: 241-276; 24: 58-76.

Holth, Sverre

1968 "Towards an Indigenous Theology." *Ching Feng* 11 (4): 5-26.

Hopkins, A. I.

1927 *Melanesia Today: A Study Circle Book.* London: SPCK.

1928a *In the Isles of King Solomon: Twenty-five Years Among the Primitive Solomon Islanders.* London: Seeley, Service and Company.

1928b "Native Life in the South-West Pacific: Two Points of View." *International Review of Missions* 17: 543-549.

1936 "The White Corks and the Black Net." In Stuart Artless (ed.), *The Church of Melanesia,* pp. 29-37. London: Melanesian Mission.

n.d. (1934) Autobiography (typescript). Church of Melanesia Archives, Honiara, Solomon Islands.

Horton, Robin

1971 "African Conversion." *Africa* 41: 85-108.

Hughes, Daniel T.
1978 "Mutual Biases of Anthropologists and Missionaries." In James A. Boutilier, et al. (eds.), *Mission, Church, and Sect in Oceania*, pp. 65-82. Ann Arbor: University of Michigan Press.

Hughes, E. C.
1949 "Social Change and Status Protest: An Essay on the Marginal Man." *Phylon* 19.

Hunter, Monica (Wilson)
1934 "Methods of Study of Culture Contact." *Africa* 7: 335-350.
1936 *Reaction to Conquest: Effects of Contact with Europeans on the Pondo of South Africa.* London: Oxford University Press.

Im Thurn, Sir Everad and Leonard C. Warton (eds.)
1925 *Journal of William Lockerby, Sandalwood Trader, in the Fiji Islands, 1808-1809, with other papers.* London: Hakluyt Society.

Inglis, John (ed.)
1872 *The Slave Trade in the New Hebrides.* Edinburgh: Edmonson and Douglas.

Inglis, Judy
1957 "Cargo Cults: The Problem of Explanation." *Oceania* 27: 249-263.

Ivens, Walter G.
1907 *Hints to Missionaries to Melanesia.* London: Melanesian Mission.
1918 *Dictionary and Grammar of the Language of the Sa'a and Ulawa, Solomon Islands.* Washington: Carnegie Institute of Washington.
1926 "Notes on the Spanish Account of the Solomon Islands, 1568." *The Geographical Journal of the Royal Geographical Society* 67: 342-351.
1927 *Melanesians of the Southeast Solomon Islands.* London: Kegan Paul, Trench, Trubner and Company.
1930 *The Island Builders of the Pacific.* London: Seeley, Service and Company.
1936 "Religion and Customs of the Melanesians." In Stuart Artless, (ed.), *The Church in Melanesia*, pp. 17-26. London: Melanesian Mission.

Jack-Hinton, Colin
1969 *The Search for the Islands of Solomon, 1567-1838.* Oxford: Clarendon Press.

Jackson, K. B.
1972 Head-hunting and Santa Ysabel, Solomon Islands, 1568-1901. Unpublished BA. Honors thesis, Department of History, Australian National University, Canberra.

1975 "Head-hunting in the Christianization of Bugotu, 1861-1900." *The Journal of Pacific History* 10: 65-78.

Jacomb, Edward

n.d. (1914) *France and England in the New Hebrides: The Anglo-French Condominium.* Melbourne.

Jarvie, I. C.

1963 "Theories of Cargo Cults: A Critical Analysis." *Oceania* 34: 1-32, 108-136.

1964 *The Revolution in Anthropology.* New York: Humanities Press.

1966 "On the Explanation of Cargo Cults." *European Journal of Sociology* 7: 299-312.

1972 "Cargo Cults." In *Encyclopedia of Papua and New Guinea* Vol. 1: 133-136. Melbourne: Melbourne University Press.

Johnson, Howard A.

1963 *Global Odyssey: An Episcopalian's Encounter with the Anglican Communion in Eighty Countries.* New York: Harper and Row.

Kamma, Freerk C.

1972 *Koreri: Messianic Movements in the Biak-Numfor Culture Area.* The Hague: M. Nijhoff.

Keesing, Felix M.

1934 "The Changing Life of Native Peoples in the Pacific Area." *American Journal of Sociology* 39: 443-458.

1939 *The Menomini Indians of Wisconsin: A Study of Three Centuries of Culture Change.* Philadelphia: American Philosophical Society.

1941 *The South Seas and the Modern World.* New York: John Day and Company.

1953 *Culture Change: An Analysis and Bibliography of Anthropological Sources to 1952.* Stanford Anthropological Series Number 1. Stanford: Stanford University Press.

Keesing, Roger M.

1968 "Chiefs in a Chiefless Society: The Ideology of Modern Kwaio Politics." *Oceania* 38: 278-280.

1978a *'Elota's Story: The Life and Times of a Solomon Island Big Man.* St. Lucia: Queensland University Press.

1978b "Politico-Religious Movements and Anticolonialism on Malaita: Maasina Rule in Historical Perspective." *Oceania* 48: 241-261; 49: 46-73.

1982 *Kwaio Religion: The Living and the Dead in a Solomon Island Society.* New York: Columbia University Press.

Keesing, Roger M. and Peter Corris

1980 *Lightning Meets the West Wind: The Malaita Massacre.* New York: Oxford University Press.

Kennedy, D. G.

1967 Marching Rule in the British Solomon Islands Protectorate: A Memorandum on the Origin of the Term. n.p. (Copy presented to Dr. C. E. Fox by the writer, housed in the Bishop Patteson Theological Centre Library, Kohimarama, Solomon Islands.)

Kerchoff, A. C. and T. C. McCormick

1955 "Marginal Status and Marginal Personality." *Social Forces* 34: 48-55.

Keysser, Christian

1980 *A People Reborn* (translation of *Eine Papuagemeinde*). Pasadena: William Carey Library.

Kluckhohn, Clyde

1936 "Some Reflections on the Method and Theory of the Kulturkreislehre." *American Anthropologist* 38: 157-196.

Knight, James

n.d. The Mission of the Local Church and the Religious Traditions of Melanesia. MS. prepared for the Sedos Research Seminar.

Knight, James (ed.)

1977 *Christ in Melanesia: Exploring Theological Issues.* Goroka: The Melanesian Institute.

1978 *Challenges and Possibilities for the Study of Religion in Melanesia. Point* No. 2, Goroka: The Melanesian Institute.

Knoebel, J.

n.d. (1973) Lessons From Traditional Melanesian Leadership Patterns for Ministereal Training Today. Prepared for Study Institute M.A.T.S. (mimeograph).

Knox, W. L.

1923 *The Catholic Movement in the Church of England.* London: P. Allan and Company.

Koskinen, Aarne A.

1953 *Missionary Influence as a Political Factor in the Pacific Islands.* Helsinki: Suomalaisen Kirjallisuuden Seuran Kirjapainon Oy.

1957 "On the South Sea Islanders' View of Christianity." *Studia Missiologica Fennica* (Helsinki) 1: 7-16.

Koyama, Kosuke

1974 *Waterbuffalo Theology.* Maryknoll, NY: Orbis Books.

Kraemer, Hendrick

1938 *The Christian Message in a Non-Christian World.* London: The Edinburgh House Press.

1956 *Religion and the Christian Faith.* London: Beccles.

1960 "Synkretismus." In F. Little and H. Walz (eds.), *Weltkirchenlexikon*, pp. 1416-1419. Stuttgart.

1962 "Synkretismus." *Religion in Geschichte und Gegenwart* 6: 563-568.

Kraft, Charles H.

1973 "Dynamic Equivalence Churches." *Missiology* 1: 39-57.

1977 "Can Anthropological Insight Assist Evangelical Theology?" *Christian Scholar's Review* 7: 165-202.

1979 *Christianity in Culture: A Study in Dynamic Biblical Theologizing in Cross-Cultural Perspective.* Maryknoll, NY: Orbis Books.

Kraft, Charles H. and Tom H. Wisley (eds.)

1979 *Readings in Dynamic Indigeneity.* Pasadena: William Carey Library.

Kraft, Marguerite G.

1978 *Worldview and the Communication of the Gospel.* Pasadena: William Carey Library.

Krass, A. C.

1974 *Go . . . And Make Disciples.* London: SPCK.

Kroeber, A. L.

1948 *Anthropology.* New York: Harcourt, Brace and World.

Kuper, Henry

1924 "A Solomon Islands Historical Drama." *Journal of the Polynesian Society* 33: 162-165.

La Barre, Weston

1971 "Materials for a History of Studies of Crisis Cults: A Bibliographic Essay." *Current Anthropology* 12:3-44.

Lacey, Roderic

1973 "The Egna World View." *Catalyst* 3 (2): 37-47.

Lacey, Thomas A.

1927 *The Anglo-Catholic Faith.* New York: Doran.

Lalive d'Epiney, Christian

1969 *Haven of the Masses: Pentecostal Movements in Chile.* London: Lutterworth.

Lambert, S. M.

1934 *The Depopulation of Pacific Races.* B. P. Bishop Museum, Special Publication No. 23. Honolulu: Bishop Museum Press.

Landecker, Werner S.

1951 "Types of Integration and their Measurement." *American Journal of Sociology* 56: 332-340.

Lane, Robert B.

1965 "The Melanesians of South Pentecost, New Hebrides." In Lawrence and Meggitt (eds.), *Gods, Ghosts, and Men in Melanesia*, pp. 250-279. Melbourne: Oxford University Press.

1975 "Review of R. H. Codrington's 'The Melanesians.' " *Journal of the Polynesian Society* 84: 95-96.

Langenkamp, B. and J. Knoebel

1971 The Religious Life of Indigenous Catholic Religious. (Mimeograph.)

Lanternari, Vittorio

1963 *The Religions of the Oppressed: A Study of Modern Messianic Cults.* New York: Knopf.

Laracy, Hugh M.

1969 Catholic Missions in the Solomon Islands, 1845-1966. Unpublished Ph.D. thesis, Australian National University, Canberra.

1971 "Marching Rule and the Missions." *The Journal of Pacific History* 6: 96-114.

1976 *Marists and Melanesians: A History of Catholic Missions in the Solomon Islands.* Canberra: Australian National University Press.

Latham, R. T. E.

1927 The New Hebrides Condominium. Unpublished MA. thesis, University of Melbourne.

Latukefu, Sione

1974 "From Mission to Church in the Pacific." *Catalyst* 4 (2): 18-30.

Laurentin, Rene

1972 *Liberation, Development and Salvation.* Maryknoll, NY: Orbis Books.

Law, Howard W.

1968 *Winning a Hearing: An Introduction to Missionary Anthropology and Linguistics.* Grand Rapids: Wm. B. Eerdmans.

Lawrence, Peter

1973 "Religion and Magic." In Hogbin (ed.), *Anthropology in Papua and New Guinea: Readings from the Encyclopedia of Papua and New Guinea,* pp. 201-226. Melbourne: Melbourne University Press.

Lawrence, Peter and Mervyn J. Meggitt (eds.)

1965 *Gods, Ghosts, and Men in Melanesia.* Melbourne: Oxford University Press.

Layard, John

1942 *Stone Men of Malekula.* London: Chatto and Windus.

Lee, Jung Young
1979 *The Theology of Change: A Christian Concept of God in an Eastern Perspective.* Maryknoll, NY: Orbis Books.

Lee, Peter H. K.
1974 "Indigenous Theology — Over-cropped Land or Underdeveloped Field?" *Ching Feng* 17 (1): 5-17.

Lee, Robert
1967 *Stranger in the Land: A Study of Church in Japan.* London: Lutterworth.

Leenhardt, Maurice
1979 *Do Kamo: Person and Myth in the Melanesian World.* Chicago: University of Chicago Press.

Leeson, Ida
1952 *Bibliography of Cargo Cults and Other Nativistic Movements in the South Pacific.* Sydney: South Pacific Technical Paper No. 30.

Lessa, William A. and Evon Z. Vogt
1965 *Reader in Comparative Religion: An Anthropological Approach, 2nd ed.* (3rd ed. 1972). New York: Harper and Row.

Levine, Donald N.
1968 "Cultural Integration." *International Encyclopedia of the Social Sciences,* Vol. 7, pp. 372-380. New York: Macmillan and Free Press.

Lewis, Albert B.
1932 *Ethnology of Melanesia.* Chicago: Field Museum of Natural History.

Lewis, Oscar
1942 *The Effects of White Contact upon Blackfoot Culture with Special Reference to the Role of the Fur Trade.* American Ethnological Society Monograph No. 6.

Lincoln, Peter
1975 *Maps of Austronesian Languages: Melanesia and South Melanesia.* Honolulu: Department of Linguistics, University of Hawaii.

Linker, Ruth Tunipe
1959 The Possibility of Assessing the Effect of the Queensland Labour Trade on Acculturation in Melanesia. Unpublished MA. thesis, University of Pennsylvania, Philadelphia.

Linton, Ralph
1936 *The Study of Man.* New York: Appleton-Century-Crofts.
1943 "Nativistic Movements." *American Anthropologist* 45: 230-240.

Linton, Ralph (ed.)

1940 *Acculturation in Seven American Indian Tribes.* New York: Appleton-Century-Crofts.

Little, F. and H. Walz (eds.)

1960 *Weltkirchenlexikon.* Stuttgart.

Lloyd, Peter

1966 *The Church of England 1900-1965.* London: SCM Press.

Loeliger, Carl

1980 "Christianity and Culture." *Catalyst* 10: 75-85.

1981 Christianity and Culture. Pre-publication draft prepared for a forthcoming book on Christian Missions and Development in Papua New Guinea and the Solomon Islands. (Mimeograph.)

Loewen, Jacob

1975 *Culture and Human Values.* South Pasadena: William Carey Library.

Lowie, Robert H.

1916 "Plains Indian Age Societies: Historical Summary." American Museum of Natural History, *Anthropological Papers,* Vol. 11: 877-984.

1937 *The History of Ethnological Theory.* New York: Rinehart and Company.

Lubbock, Sir John

1865 *Prehistoric Times, as Illustrated by Ancient Remains and the Manners and Customs of Modern Savages.* London: Williams and Norgate.

1870 *The Origin of Civilization and the Primitive Condition of Men.* London: Longmans, Green.

Luke, P. Y., and J. B. Carman

1968 *Village Christians and Hindu Culture: A Study of a Rural Church in Andhra Pradesh, South India.* London: Lutterworth.

Luxton, C. T. J.

1955 *Isles of Solomon: A Tale of Missionary Adventure.* Auckland: Methodist Foreign Missionary Society of New Zealand.

Luzbetak, Louis

1963 *The Church and Cultures.* Techny, IL: Divine Word.

Lycett, Margaret

1935 *Brothers: The Story of the Native Brotherhood of Melanesia.* London: SPCK.

Macdonald, D.

1878 *The Labour Traffic versus Christianity in the South Sea Islands.* Melbourne: Hutchinson.

MacDonald, Mary

1981 "Sorcery and Society." *Catalyst* 11: 168-181.

Macdonald-Milne, Brian

n.d. (ca. 1981) *Spearhead: The Story of the Melanesian Brotherhood.* Watford, England: The Melanesian Mission.

MacQuarrie, Hector

1948 *Vouza and the Solomon Islands.* New York: Macmillan.

Madariaga, Salvador de

1955 *Hernan Cortes: Conqueror of Mexico.* 2nd ed. Chicago: Henry Regnery Company.

Madsen, William

1957 *Christopaganism: A Study of Mexican Religious Syncretism.* New Orleans: Middle American Research Institute, Tulane University.

Maher, Robert F.

1958 "Tommy Kabu Movement of the Purari Delta." *Oceania* 29: 75-90.

1961 *New Men of Papua: A Study in Culture Change.* Madison: University of Wisconsin Press.

Maine, Sir Henry

1861 *Ancient Law: Its Connection with the Early History of Society and Its Relation to Modern Ideas.* London.

Mair, Lucy P.

1934 "The Study of Culture Contact as a Practical Problem." *Africa* 7: 415-422.

1938 "The Place of History in the Study of Culture Contact." In L. Mair (ed.), *Methods of Study of Culture Contact in Africa.*

1971 "Cargo Cults Today." *New Society*, No. 433.

Mair, Lucy P. (ed.)

1938 *Methods of Study of Culture Contact in Africa.* International Institute of African Languages and Cultures, Memorandum 15.

Malinowski, Bronislaw

1922 *Argonauts of the Western Pacific.* London: Routledge and Kegan Paul.

1938 "Anthropology of Changing African Cultures." In Lucy P. Mair, (ed.), *Methods of Study of Culture Contact in Africa.*

1939 "The Present State of Studies in Culture Contact." *Africa* 12: 27-47.

1945 *Dynamics of Culture Change: An Inquiry into Race Relations in Africa.* P. M. Kayberry (ed.). New Haven: Yale University Press.

1949 (Orig. 1923) "The Problem of Meaning in Primitive Languages." Supplement I in C. K. Ogden and I. A. Richards, *The Meaning of Meaning* 10th ed., pp. 296-336. London: Routledge and Kegan Paul.

Maloat, Paliau

1970 "The Story of My Life from the Day I Was Born until the Present Day." In Marion W. Ward, (ed.), *The Politics of Melanesia,* Fourth Waigani Seminar, pp. 145-161. Canberra: Australian National University Press.

Mandelbaum, David (ed.)

1963 *Selected Writings of Edward Sapir in Language, Culture and Personality.* Berkeley: University of California Press.

Mander, Linden A.

1954 *Some Dependent Peoples of the South Pacific.* New York: Macmillan.

Mantovani, Ennio

1977 "A Fundamental Melanesian Religion." In James Knight (ed.), *Christ in Melanesia: Exploring Theological Issues,* pp. 154-165. Goroka: The Melanesian Institute.

Marau, Clement

1894 *Story of a Melanesian Deacon: Clement Marau.* Translated with an introduction by R. H. Codrington. London: SPCK.

Marett, R. R.

1914 *The Threshold of Religion.* 3rd ed. London: Methuen and Company.

Markham, Albert Hastings

1873 *The Cruise of the "Rosario" amongst the New Hebrides and Santa Cruz Islands, Exposing the Recent Atrocities with the Kidnapping of Natives of the South Seas.* 2nd ed. London: S. Low, Marston, Low and Searle, Dawsons, Folkstone.

Markham, C. R. (ed.)

1904 *The Voyages of Pedro Fernandez de Quiros, 1595 to 1606.* 2 vols. London: Hakluyt Society.

Martin, K. L. P.

1924 *Missionaries and Annexation in the Pacific.* London.

Marwick, C. G. (compiler)

1935 *The Adventures of John Renton.* Kirkwall.

Maude, H. E.

1968 *Of Islands and Men: Studies in Pacific History.* Melbourne: Oxford University Press.

Mayers, Marvin K.
1974 *Christianity Confronts Culture.* Grand Rapids: Zondervan.

Mbiti, John S.
1970 "Christianity and Traditional Religions in Africa." *International Review of Missions* 59 (236): 430-440.
1971 *New Testament Eschatology in an African Background: A Study of the Encounter between New Testament Theology and African Traditional Concepts.* London: Oxford University Press.
1972 "Some African Concepts of Christology." In *Christ and the African Revolution: Theological Contributions from Asia, Africa and Latin America,* pp. 51-62. London: SPCK.
1979 "The Gospel in the African Cultural Context." *Toward Theology in an Australian Context,* pp. 18-26. Adelaide: The Australian Association for the Study of Religions.

McGregor, Donald E.
1982 (Orig. 1975) *The Fish and the Cross.* Goroka: The Melanesian Institute.

McIntosh, A. D.
1961 New Zealand Interest and Participation in the Labour Traffic Prior to Bishop Patteson's Death, 20 September 1871. Unpublished M.A. thesis, University of Otago, Dunedin.

McKinnon, John M.
1972 Bilua Changes: Culture Contact and its Consequences, A Study of the Bilua of Vella Lavella in the British Solomon Islands. Unpublishd Ph.D. thesis, Victoria University, Wellington.
1975 "Tomahawks, Turtles and Traders." *Oceania* 45: 290-307.

McLennan, J. F.
1865 *Primitive Marriage: An Inquiry into the Origin of the Form of Capture in Marriage Ceremonies.* Edinburgh: Black.

McLintock, A. H. (ed.)
1966 *An Encyclopedia of New Zealand,* Vol. 3. Wellington: R. E. Owen, Government Printer.

Mead, Margaret
1928 *An Inquiry into Cultural Stability in Polynesia.* Columbia University Contributions to Anthropology No. 9. New York: Columbia University Press.
1932 *The Changing Culture of an Indian Tribe.* Columbia University Contributions to Anthropology No. 15. New York: Columbia University Press.
1956 *New Lives for Old.* New York: William Morrow.

Mead, S. M.

1973a *Material Culture and Art in the Star Harbour Region, Eastern Solomon Islands.* Toronto: Ethnographic Monograph of the Royal Ontario Museum.

1973b "Folklore and Place Names in Santa Ana, Solomon Islands." *Oceania* 43: 215-237.

Meggitt, Mervyn

1977 *Blood is Their Argument.* Palo Alto: Mayfield.

Melanesian Mission

1861 *Isles of the Pacific: Account of the Melanesian Mission and of the Wreck of the Mission Vessel. Also the Bishop of New Zealand's Sermon on the Consecration of the Rev. J. C. Patteson, M.A., in St. Paul's Church, Auckland, N.Z., with a Letter from the Missionary Bishop.* Melbourne: Samuel Mullen.

1866 *Journal of the Mission Voyage to the Melanesian Islands of the Schooner "Southern Cross:" Made in May - October, 1866.* Auckland.

1873 *Melanesian Mission Report of the English Committee for 1873.* Ludlow: Edward J. Partridge.

1903 *The Island Voyage and Report, 1902.*

1904 *Melanesian Mission Report Issued by the English Committee 1903.* London.

1919 Memorandum on the Future of the Melanesian Mission. London: English Committee (for private circulation only).

1924 *The Constitutions, Canons and Regulations of the Missionary Diocese of Melanesia together with such Canons and other Proceedings of the General Synod of the Church of New Zealand as Affect the Missionary Diocese of Melanesia.* Auckland.

1949 *The Faith of the Church: Lessons in the Faith for Junior Schools in the Diocese of Melanesia.* Summer Hill, N.S.W.

1965 *Proceedings of the Diocesan Synod Held at St. Mary's School, Maravovo, July 5th to July 15th, 1962, together with Reports and Other Documents Presented to Synod.* Taroniara: Melanesian Mission Press.

1970 *Melanesian Mission Broadsheet* No. 18, August 1970. Christ-Church.

n.d. (ca. 1899) *The Melanesian Mission: Some Testimony to the Efficacy of its Work in Humanizing, Civilizing and Christianizing the Natives of the Islands of the S. W. Pacific Ocean.* London.

n.d. (1926) *Melanesia: Historical and Geographical.* Southern Cross Booklet No. 1. London.

n.d. (1949) *Pacific Progress 1849-1949, Being the Illustrated Centenary Book of the Diocese of Melanesia.* Chatham: Parrett and Neves (pages unnumbered).

n.d. *About Melanesia, No. 4: Medical Work in Melanesia* (n.p.).

n.d. *About Melanesia No. 6: "Lady Missionaries and One of the Empire's Best." Being an Extract from "A Trader in the Savage Solomons"* (n.p.).

n.d. *About Melanesia No. 7: Native Women of the Solomons, "Mothers' Union Work."* Sydney.

n.d. *About Melanesia No. 8: Training Young Melanesians.* Being an Address to the Annual Meeting of the English Committee, Church House, Westminister, London, May 29th, 1936 by the Reverend George Warren, Melanesian Mission. Sydney.

1857-1910 *Annual Reports.* Auckland or Sydney.

1875-1890 *The Island Voyage.* Ludlow: Edward J. Partridge.

1895-1946 *Southern Cross Log* (Australian and New Zealand edition). Sydney and Auckland.

1907-1966 *Southern Cross Log* (English edition). London.

1954-1955 *O Sala Ususur.* Taroniara, Solomon Islands.

1958-1967 *Melanesian Messenger.* Taroniara and Honiara.

Mennell, Philip

1892 *The Dictionary of Australasian Bibliography, 1855-1892.* London: Hutchinson and Company.

Merton, Robert K.

1957 *Social Theory and Social Structure.* New York: Free Press.

Messenger, John C.

1959 "The Christian Concept of Forgiveness and Anang Morality." *Practical Anthropology* 6: 97-103.

1960 "Reinterpretations of Christian and Indigenous Beliefs in a Nigerian Nativist Church." *American Anthropologist* 62: 268-278.

Michener, James A.

1959 *Hawaii.* New York: Random House.

Miller, Elmer

1973 "The Christian Missionary: Agent of Secularization." *Missiology* 1: 99-107.

Miller, J. Graham

1948 "Naked Cult in Central West Santo." *Journal of the Polynesian Society* 57: 330-351.

Mitchell, R. C. and H. W. Turner

1966 *A Bibliography of Modern African Religious Movements.* Evanston: Northwestern University Press.

Molesworth, B. H.

1917 The History of Kanaka Labour in Queensland. Unpublished M.A. thesis, University of Queensland.

Montgomery, H. H.

1896 *The Light of Melanesia: A Record of Fifty Years' Mission Work in the South Seas.* 3rd ed, 1908. London: SPCK.

Moorhouse, H. C.

1929 Report of the Commissioner Appointed by the Secretary of State for the Colonies to Enquire into the Circumstances in which Murderous Attacks Took Place in 1927 on Government Officials on Guadalcanal and Malaita. London: HMSO, Cmd. 3249.

Moresby, John

1876 *Discoveries and Surveys in New Guinea and Polynesia.* London: J. Murray.

Morgan, Lewis Henry

1877 *Ancient Society.* New York: Henry Holt.

Morison, Samuel Eliot

1949 "The Struggle for Guadalcanal August 1942 - February 1943." *History of U.S. Naval Operations in World War II,* Vol. V. Boston: Little, Brown and Company.

Morrell, Benjamin

1832 *A Narrative of Four Voyages to the South Sea, North and South Pacific Ocean, Chinese Sea, Ethiopic and Southern Atlantic Ocean, Indian and Antarctic Ocean from the Year 1822 to 1831.* New York: J. and J. Harper.

Morrell, W. P.

1960 *Britain in the Pacific Islands.* Oxford: Clarendon.

Moses, J. A.

1969 "The German Empire in Melanesia, 1884-1914: A German Self-analysis." Second Waigani Seminar, *The History of Melanesia.* Canberra: Australian National University Press.

Murdock, George Peter

1964 "Genetic Classification of the Austronesian Languages: A Key to Oceanic Culture History." *Ethnology* 3: 117-126.

Murphree, Marshall W.

1969 *Christianity and the Shona.* London School of Economics Monographs on Social Anthropology No. 36. London: Athone Press.

Murphy, Kevin (ed.)

1974 *The Church and Adjustment Movements.* Goroka: The Melanesian Insititute.

Mushete, Ngindu
1978 "Authenticity and Christianity in Zaire." In Edward Fashole-Luke, et al. (eds.), *Christianity in Independent Africa*, pp. 228-241. Bloomington: Indiana University Press.

Mylene, Louis George
1908 *Missions to Hindus.* London: Longmans, Green.

Naban, Johnson
1976 The History of the Work of the Anglican Church in the Solomons. Unpublished B.D. thesis, Pacific Theological College, Suva, Fiji.

Nadel, S. F.
1951 *The Foundations of Social Anthropology.* London: Cohen and West.

Nash, Philleo
1937 "The Place of Religious Revivalism in the Formulation of the Intercultural Community of the Klamath Reservation." In Fred Eggan (ed.), *Essays on the Social Anthropology of North American Tribes.* Chicago: University of Chicago Press.

Naylor, Larry L.
1974 Culture Change and Development in the Balim Valley, Irian Jaya, Indonesia. Unpublished Ph.D. dissertation, Southern Illinois University, Carbondale.

Neill, Stephen
1958 *Anglicanism.* London: Penguin Books.
1966 *Colonialism and Christian Missions.* London: Lutterworth.

Nerdrum, J. G. B.
1902 "Impressions and Adventures under Seven Years Stay on the Solomon Islands." (Translation of an article from the *Norwegian Geographical Society Yearbook 1901-1902*, pp. 22-55, by P. Stenbo.)

Nettl, Peter
1969 "Power and the Intellectuals." In C. C. O'Brien and W. D. Vanech (eds.), *Power and Consciousness*, pp. 15-32. London.

Newbolt, M. R. (ed.)
1939 *John Steward's Memories: Papers Written by the Late Bishop Steward of Melanesia.* Chester: Phillipson and Golder.

New Guinea Research Unit
1972 *Bibliography of Cargo and Nativistic Movements in New Guinea.* Port Moresby and Canberra: New Guinea Research Unit.

Newman, Philip L.
1961 Cargo Cults and Melanesian Revitalization Movements. Unpublished MA. thesis, University of Pennsylvania, Philadelphia.

Nida, Eugene A.

1954 *Customs and Cultures: Anthropology for Christian Missions.* New York: Harper and Row.

1960 *Message and Mission: The Communication of the Christian Faith.* New York: Harper and Row.

1966 "Missionaries and Anthropologists." *Practical Anthropology* 13: 273-277, 287.

1968 *Religion Across Cultures.* New York: Harper and Row.

Nida, Eugene A. and William D. Reyburn

1981 *Meaning Across Cultures.* Maryknoll, NY: Orbis Books.

Niebuhr, H. Richard

1951 *Christ and Culture.* New York: Harper and Row.

Niehoff, Arthur (ed.)

1966 *A Casebook of Social Change.* Chicago: Aldine.

Nyamiti, Charles

1973 *The Scope of African Theology.* Kampala: GABA Publications.

O'Brien, C. C. and W. D. Vanech (eds.)

1969 *Power and Consciousness.* London.

O'Brien, Denise and Anton Ploeg

1964 "Acculturation Movements Among the Western Dani." *American Anthropologist* 66 (4) part 2: 281-292.

O'Connor, Gulbun Coker

1973 The Moro Movement of Guadalcanal. Unpublished Ph.D. dissertation, University of Pennsylvania, Philadelphia.

O'Reilly, P.

1948 "Malaita (Iles Solomons), un exemple de revendications indigenes." *Missions Maristes d'Oceanie,* 2nd yr. No. 15: 149-152.

Ofori, Patrick E.

1977 *Christianity in Tropical Africa.* A Selective Annotated Bibliography. Nendeln: KTO Press.

Oliver, Douglas L.

1955 *A Solomon Island Society.* Cambridge: Harvard University Press.

1961 *The Pacific Islands.* 2nd ed. Cambridge: Harvard University Press.

Oliver, Roland

1952 *The Missionary Factor in East Africa.* London: Longmans.

Olland, S. L.
1925 *The Anglo-Catholic Revival.* London: A. R. Mowbray.
1963 *A Short History of the Oxford Movement.* London: Faith Press Reprints (1st ed. 1915).

Oosterwal, Gottfried
1967 "Cargo Cults as a Missionary Challenge." *International Review of Missions* 56: 469-477.
1973 *Modern Messianic Movements: As a Theological and Missionary Challenge.* Elkhart: Institute of Mennonite Studies.

Oosthuizen, G. C.
1968 *Post-Christianity in Africa: A Theological and Anthropological Study.* London: C. Hurst and Company.

Osborne, Ken
1982 "Counselling in Sorcery Cases." *Catalyst* 12: 181-191.

Palmer, Bruce Stewart
1977 Options for the Development of Education in the Solomon Islands: A Critical Analysis. Unpublished Ph.D. thesis, University of New England, Australia.

Palmer, George
1871 *Kidnapping in the South Seas: Being a Narrative of a Three Month's Cruise of H. M. Ship "Rosario."* Edinburgh.

Park, Robert E.
1928 "Human Migration and Marginal Man." *American Journal of Sociology* 33: 881-893.

Parkenham, Walsh W.
1892 *Modern Heroes of the Mission Field.* 3rd ed. London: Hodder and Stroughton.

Parnaby, O. W.
1964 *Britain and the Labor Trade in the Southwest Pacific.* Durham, NC: Duke University Press.

Parrat, J. K.
1969 "Religious Change in Yoruba Society—A Test Case." *Journal of Religion in Africa* 2 (2).

Parratt, John
1976 *Papuan Belief and Ritual.* New York: Vantage Press.

Parsons, Elsie Clews
1936 *Mitla: Town of Souls.* Chicago: University of Chicago Press.

Parsons, Talcott and Edward A. Shils (eds.)
1951 *Toward a General Theory of Action.* Cambridge: Harvard University Press.

Parsonson, G. S.

1949 Early Protestant Missions in the New Hebrides 1839-1861. Unpublished M.A. thesis, University of Otago, Dunedin, New Zealand.

1964 The Evangelization of the Pacific Islands. Third Address Delivered to the Historical Association (Canterbury) on 17 March 1964. Dunedin: Hocken Library, ms.

1967 "The Literate Revolution in Polynesia." *The Journal of Pacific History* 2: 39-57.

Paton, Frank H. L.

1913 *Slavery under the British Flag.* Melbourne: Brown Prior.

Patterson, Mary

1974-1975 "Sorcery and Witchcraft in Melanesia. *Oceania* 45: 132-160, 212-234.

Patteson, John Coleridge

n.d.a. *A Letter from the Right Reverend John Coleridge Patteson, D.D. to* *** (11 November 1862). Auckland.

n.d.b. *The Melanesian Mission.* (Address delivered at St. Mary's Schoolroom, Balmain, Sydney, 2 April 1864; published with a lecture by R. H. Codrington.) Torquay.

n.d.c. "Ysabel Island" (A Story for Children). Enclosed in a letter to Lady Stephen, October 31, 1866. Stephen Family Papers MSS 777/111. Mitchell Library, Sydney.

1855-1871 Patteson Papers. Letters from John Coleridge Patteson to his father and sisters. United Society for the Propagation of the Gospel, London: U.S.P.G. Archives (Microfilm, Department of Pacific and Southeast Asian History, Australian National University, Canberra).

Patton, J. V.

1931 *Soldiers and Servants under the Southern Cross.* Melbourne: Board of Education, Diocese of Melbourne.

Paul, Benjamin D. (ed.)

1955 *Health, Culture, and Community.* New York: Russell Sage Foundation.

Pauw, B. A.

1960 *Religion in a Tswana Chiefdom.* London: Oxford University Press for the International African Institute.

1975 "Universalism and Particularism in the Beliefs of Xhosa-speaking Christians." In Michael G. Whisson and Martin West (eds.), *Religion and Social Change in Southern Africa: Anthropological Essays in Honour of Monica Wilson,* pp. 153-163. Cape Town: David Philip.

Pawley, Andrew
1972 "On the Internal Relationships of Eastern Oceanic Languages." In R. C. Green and M. Kelly (eds.), *Studies in Oceanic Culture History,* Vol. 3. Honolulu: Bishop Museum, Pacific Anthropological Records No. 13.

Peel, J. D. Y.
1968a *Aladura: A Religious Movement Among the Yoruba.* London: Oxford University Press for the International African Institute.
1968b "Syncretism and Religious Change." *Comparative Studies in Society and History* 10: 121-141.

Penny, Alfred
1887 *Ten Years in Melanesia.* London: Wells Gardner, Darton.
1876-1886 Diaries, 11 Vols. B 807-817, Mitchell Library, Sydney.

Perry, W. J.
1923 *The Children of the Sun: A Study in the Early History of Civilization.* London: Methuen.

Peterson, Nicholas
1966 "The Church Council of South Mala: A Legitimized form of Masinga Rule." *Oceania* 36: 214-230.

Pickett, J. Waskom
1933 *Christian Mass Movements in India.* New York: Abingdon Press.

Piddington, Ralph
1932 "Psychological Aspects of Culture-contact." *Oceania* 3: 312-324.

Pike, Eunice and Florence Cowan
1959 "Mushroom Ritual versus Christianity." *Practical Anthropology* 6: 145-150.

Pilhofer, Georg
1962 *Werdende Kirche in Neuguinea — Kopie oder Original? Geschichtliches und Grundsatzliches zur Frage des Verhaltnisses von alten und Jungen Kirchen.* 3 vol. Neuendettelsau: Freimund-Verlag. (Vol. 3 has been translated by F. E. Pietz with an introduction by Joel M. Maring, but to date is an unpublished manuscript in possession of the author.)

Pitt-Rivers, George L. F.
1927 *The Clash of Cultures and the Contact of Races.* London: George Routledge and Sons.

Pozas, Ricardo
1962 *Juan the Chamula: An Ethnological Re-creation of the Life of a Mexican Indian.* Berkeley: University of California Press.

Prebble, A. C.

1931 George Augustus Selwyn, The Apostle of Melanesia. Unpublished M.A. thesis, University of Auckland.

Queensland Legislative Assembly

1906 "Sugar Industry Labour Commission . . . together with the minutes of proceedings, minutes of evidence taken before the Commission, and appendices." *Votes and Proceedings*. Vol. 2.

Radin, Paul

1913 "The Influence of the Whites on Winnebago Culture." *Proceedings of the State Historical Society of Wisconsin,* pp. 137-145.

Ralston, Caroline

1970 "The Beach Communities." In J. W. Davidson and Deryck Scarr (eds.), *Pacific Island Portraits,* pp. 79-93. Canberra: Australian National University Press.

Rannie, Douglas

1912 *My Adventures among South Sea Cannibals.* London: Seeley, Service and Company.

Rapoport, Robert N.

1954 *Changing Navaho Religious Values: A Study of Christian Missions to the Rimrock Navahos.* Papers of the Peabody Museum of American Archaeology and Ethnology, Harvard University, Vol. XLI No. 2.

Raucaz, L. M.

1925 *Vingt-cing Annes d'Apostolat aux Iles Salomon Meridonales.* Lyons: Vitte.

1928 *In the Savage South Solomons: The Story of a Mission.* Lyon: Vitte.

Ray, S. H.

1922 "Obituary: Robert Henry Codrington, M.A., D.D., September 15, 1830 — September 11, 1922." *Man* 22: 169-171.

Read, Kenneth E.

1947 "Effects of the Pacific War in the Markham Valley, New Guinea." *Oceania* 18: 95-116.

Redfield, Robert

1930 *Tepostlan, A Mexican Village.* Chicago: University of Chicago Press.

Redfield, Robert, Ralph Linton and M. J. Herskovits

1936 "A Memorandum for the Study of Acculturation." *American Anthropologist* 38: 149-152.

Rice, Edward
1974 *John Frum He Come.* Garden City, NY: Doubleday.

Richards, A. I.
1935 "The Village Census in the Study of Culture Contact." *Africa* 8: 121-144.

Richardson, Don
1974 *Peace Child.* Glendale: Regal Books, G/L Publications.
1981 *Eternity in Their Hearts.* Ventura, CA: Regal Books.

Rimoldi, M.
1971 Hahalis Welfare Society of Buka. Unpublished Ph.D. thesis, Australian National University, Canberra.

Rivers, W. H. R.
1914 *The History of Melanesian Society.* 2 vols. Cambridge: Cambridge University Press.

Rivers, W. H. R. (ed.)
1922 *Essays on the Depopulation of Melanesia.* Cambridge: Cambridge University Press.

Roberts, Stephen H.
1927 *Population Problems of the Pacific.* (Reprinted in 1969, New York: AMS Press, Inc.)

Robertson, William
1777 *The History of America.* 2 vols. (Reprinted in 1822, Philadelphia: Robert and Thomas Desilver.)

Rodman, Margaret and Matthew Cooper (eds.)
1979 *The Pacification of Melanesia.* ASAO Monograph No. 7. Ann Arbor: University of Michigan press.

Rohorua, L.
1898 "Tales of Ulawa in Heathen Days before the Schools Began There." *Southern Cross Log,* September, pp. 6-7.

Romilly, Hugh Hastings
1887 *The Western Pacific and New Guinea: Notes on the Natives, Christian and Cannibal, with some Account of the Old Labour Trade.* 2nd ed. London.

Rosensteil, Annette
1959 "Anthropology and the Missionary." *Journal of the Royal Anthropological Institute* 89: 107-116.

Ross, Angus
1964 *New Zealand Aspirations in the Pacific in the Nineteenth Century.* Oxford: Clarendon Press.

Ross, Harold M.

1973 *Baegu: Social and Ecological Organization in Malaita, Solomon Islands.* Urbana: University of Illinois Press.

1978 "Competition for Baegu Souls: Mission Rivalry on Malaita, Solomon Islands." In James Boutilier, et al. (eds.), *Mission, Church, and Sect in Oceania,* pp. 163-200. Ann Arbor: University of Michigan Press.

Rutherford, Noel

1971 *Shirley Baker and the King of Tonga.* Melbourne: Oxford University Press.

Sahay, Keshari

1968 "Impact of Christianity on the Urdon of the Chaupur Belt in Chotangpur: An Analysis of its Cultural Process." *American Anthropologist* 70: 923-942.

Sahlins, Marshall D.

1958 *Social Stratification in Polynesia.* Seattle: University of Washington Press.

1970 (Orig. 1963) "Poor Man, Rich Man, Big Man, Chief: Political Types in Melanesia and Polynesia." In T. Harding and B. Wallace (eds.), *Cultures of the Pacific*, pp. 203-215. New York: The Free Press.

Salamone, Frank A.

1972 "Structural Factors in Dukawa Conversion." *Practical Anthropology* 19: 219-225.

1975 "Continuity of Igbo Values After Conversion: A Study in Purity and Prestige." *Missiology* 3: 33-43.

1976 "Learning to be Christian: A Comparative Study." *Missiology* 4: 53-64.

1977 "Anthropologists and Missionaries: Competition or Reciprocity?" *Human Organization* 36: 407-412.

1978 "Early Expatriate Society in Northern Nigeria: Contributions Toward a Refinement of a Theory of Pluralism." *The African Studies Review* 21 (2): 39-54.

1979 "Epistemological Implications of Fieldwork and Their Consequences." *American Anthropologist* 81: 46-60.

Sapir, Edward

1916 "Time Perspective in Aboriginal American Culture: A Study in Method." Reprinted in D. G. Mandelbaum (ed.), *Selected Writings of Edward Sapir in Language Culture and Personality.* Berkeley: University of California Press.

1924 "Culture, Genuine and Spurious." *American Journal of Sociology* 29: 401-429.

Sarawia, George

1968 *They Came to My Island: The Beginnings of the Mission in the Banks' Islands.* Translated by D. A. Rawcliffe. Taroniara: Diocese of Melanesia Press.

Sayes, Shelley

1976 The Ethnohistory of Arosi, San Cristobal. Unpublished M.A. thesis, University of Auckland.

Scarr, Deryck

1967 *Fragments of Empire: A Study of the Western Pacific High Commission, 1877-1914.* Canberra: Australian National University Press.

1970 "Recruits and Recruiters: A Portrait of the Labour Trade." In J. W. Davidson and Deryck Scarr (eds.), *Pacific Islands Portraits,* pp. 225-251. Canberra: Australian National University Press.

Schapera, I.

1935 "Field Methods in the Study of Modern Culture Contacts." *Africa* 8: 315-328.

1936 "The Contribution of Western Civilization to Modern Kxatla Culture." *Transactions of the Royal Society of South Africa* 24 (3): 221-251.

1938 "Contact between European and Native in South Africa." In Lucy P. Mair (ed.), *Methods of Study of Culture Contact in Africa.*

Scheffler, Harold W.

1963 "Choiseul Island Descent Groups." *Journal of the Polynesian Society* 72: 177-187.

1964a "The Genesis and Repression of Conflict: Choiseul Island." *American Anthropologist* 66: 789-804.

1964b "Political Finance in Melanesia: Big Men and Discs of Shell." *Natural History* 74: (10): 20-25.

1964c "The Social Consequences of Peace on Choiseul Island." *Ethnology* 3: 398-403.

1965 *Choiseul Island Social Structure.* Berkeley: University of California Press.

Schmidt, Wilhelm

1931 *The Origin and Growth of Religion.* London: Methuen.

1939 *The Culture Historical Method of Ethnology.* New York: Fortuny's Publishers.

Scholefield, G. H. (ed.)

1940 *A Dictionary of New Zealand Biography.* Vol. 2. Wellington: Department of Internal Affairs.

Schwartz, Theodore

1962 *The Paliau Movement in the Admiralty Islands, 1946-1954.* Anthropological Papers of the American Museum of Natural History, Part 2, pp. 211-421.

Schwarz, Brian

1980 "Seeking to Understand Cargo as Symbol." *Catalyst* 10: 14-27.

Segundo, Juan Luis

1973-1974 *A Theology for Artisans of a New Humanity.* 5 vols. Maryknoll, NY: Orbis Books.

1976 *The Liberation of Theology.* Maryknoll, NY: Orbis Books.

Selwyn Papers

"Letters from the Bishop of New Zealand and Others, 1842-1867" and "Papers by or Concerned with Bishop G. A. Selwyn." Selwyn College Library, Cambridge University. (Typescript in the Auckland Institute and Museum Library, MS 273.)

Selwyn, George A.

1850 *Two Letters from Bishop Selwyn.* Eton: E. P. Williams.

1857 Letter to His Sons Written from the *Southern Cross* at Sea, dated 17 October 1857. Auckland Institute and Museum Library, MS 273 Vol. 1: 298-391.

Selwyn, George A., et al.

1853 *Extracts from New Zealand Letters During the Years 1851-1852.* Eton: E. P. Williams.

Shevill, Ian

1949 *Pacific Conquest: The History of 150 Years of Missionary Progress in the South Pacific.* Sydney: The National Missionary Council of Australia.

Shineberg, Dorothy

1966 "The Sandalwood Trade in Melanesian Economics, 1841-1865." *The Journal of Pacific History* 1: 129-146.

1967 *They Came for Sandalwood: A Study of the Sandalwood Trade in the South-West Pacific, 1830-1865.* Melbourne: Melbourne University Press.

1971 "Guns and Men in Melanesia." *The Journal of Pacific History* 6: 61-82.

Shineberg, Dorothy (ed.)

1971 *The Trading Voyages of Andrew Cheyne, 1841-1844.* Pacific History Series No. 3. Canberra: Australian National University Press.

Shorter, Aylward
1973 *African Culture and the Christian Church: An Introduction to Social and Pastoral Anthropology.* London: Chapman.
1977 *African Christian Theology: Adaptation or Incarnation?* Maryknoll, NY: Orbis Books.

Shutler, Mary Elizabeth and Richard Shutler Jr.
1967 "Origins of the Melanesians." *Archaeology and Physical Anthropology in Oceania* 2: 91-99.

Shutler, Richard Jr. and Mary Elizabeth Shutler
1975 *Oceanic Prehistory.* Menlo Park, CA: Cummings.

Siegel, B. J. (ed.)
1955 *Acculturation: Critical Abstracts, North America.* Stanford: Stanford University Press.

Simcox, Carroll E.
1968 *The Historical Road of Anglicanism.* Chicago: Henry Regnery Company.

Simons, Gary F.
1976 *Bibliography of Solomon Island Linguistics.* Ukarumpa, Papua New Guinea: Summer Institute of Linguistics.
1978 Language Variation and Limits to Communication. Unpublished Ph.D. dissertation, Cornell University, Ithaca, New York.

Simons, Linda
1977 *A Listing of Publications in Solomon Island Languages.* Workpapers in Solomon Island Languages No. 1. Honiara: Summer Institute of Linguistics.

Skinner, Elliott P.
1958 "Christianity and Islam among the Mossi." *American Anthropologist* 60: 1102-1119.

Smalley, William A. (ed.)
1967 *Readings in Missionary Anthropology.* Tarrytown, NY: Practical Anthropology.
1978 *Readings in Missionary Anthropology II.* South Pasadena: William Carey Library.

Smith, G. Barnett
1893 *Eminent Christian Workers of the Nineteenth Century.* London: SPCK.

Smith, G. Elliot
1928 *In the Beginning: The Origin of Civilization.* New York.
1929 *Human History.* New York: Norton.
1933 *The Diffusion of Culture.* London: Watts.

Smith, M. G.

1960 *Government in Zazzau, 1800-1950.* London: Oxford University Press.

1962 "History and Social Anthropology." *Journal of the Royal Anthropological Institute* 92: 73-85.

Solomon Islands

1932 *Annual Report 1932.* Office of District Officer, Auki, 25 January 1933.

1948-1954 *Annual Report of the British Solomon Islands.* London: HMSO.

1962 *White Paper No. 3: Educational Policy.* Honiara: Government Printer.

1977 *Annual Report 1976.* Honiara: Government Printer.

Somerville, Boyle T.

1897 "Ethnographical Notes in New Georgia, Solomon Islands." *Journal of the Royal Anthropological Institute* 26: 357-412.

1928 *The Chart-Makers.* London: W. Blackwood.

Song, Choan-Seng

1977 *Christian Mission in Reconstruction: An Asian Analysis.* Maryknoll, NY: Orbis Books.

1979 *Third-Eye Theology: Theology in Formation in Asian Settings.* Maryknoll, NY: Orbis Books.

1982 *The Compassionate God.* Maryknoll, NY: Orbis Books.

Southall, Aidan

1965 "A Critique of Typology of States and Political Systems." In M. Banton (ed.), *Political Systems and the Distribution of Power,* pp. 113-140. ASA Monographs No. 2. New York: Praeger.

Specht, James

1969 Prehistoric and Modern Pottery Traditions of Buka Island. Unpublished Ph.D. thesis, Australian National University, Canberra.

Spicer, Edward H. (ed.)

1952 *Human Problems in Technological Change.* New York: Russell Sage Foundation.

1961 *Perspectives in American Indian Culture Change.* Chicago: University of Chicago Press.

Spier, L.

1921 "The Sun Dance of the Plains Indians." American Museum of Natural History, *Anthropological Papers*, Vol. 16, part 1.

Stanner, W. E. H.

1958 "On the Interpretation of Cargo Cults." *Oceania* 29: 1-25.

Steel, Robert

1880 *The New Hebrides and Christian Missions, with a Sketch of the Labour Trade.* London: Nisbet.

Steinbauer, Friedrich

1974 "Cargo Cults: Challenge to the Churches?" *Lutheran World* XXI (2): 160-172.

1979 *Melanesian Cargo Cults: New Salvation Movements in the South Pacific.* St. Lucia, Queensland: University of Queensland Press.

Steward, John M.

1928 *The Brothers, Melanesian Mission.* Auckland: Melanesian Mission.

1936 "The Native Evangelistic Brotherhood." In Stuart Artless (ed.), *The Church in Melanesia,* pp. 53-61. London: Melanesian Mission.

Stewart, H. L.

1929 *A Century of Anglo-Catholicism.* London: J. M. Dent and Sons.

Stipe, Claude

1968 Eastern Dakota Acculturation: The Role of Agents of Culture Change. Unpublished Ph.D. dissertation, University of Minnesota.

1980 "Anthropologists versus Missionaries: The Influence of Presuppositions. *Current Anthropology* 21: 165-168, 176-179.

Stonequist, E. V.

1937 *The Marginal Man: A Study in Personality and Culture Conflict.* New York: C. Scribner's Sons.

Stott, John and Robert T. Coote (eds.)

1979 *Gospel and Culture.* Pasadena: William Carey Library.

Strelan, John G.

1975 "Our Common Ancestor: Toward a Theological Interpretation of Cargo Cults." *Catalyst* 5 (2): 33-40.

1977a "Eschatology, Myth and History in Melanesia." In James Knight (ed.), *Christ in Melanesia: Exploring Theological Issues.* Goroka: The Melanesian Institute.

1977b *Search for Salvation: Studies in the History and Theology of Cargo Cults.* Adelaide: Lutheran Publishing House.

Sturtevant, William C.

1966 "Anthropology, History and Ethnohistory." *Ethnohistory* 13: 1-51.

Sundkler, Bengt Gustaf M.
1948 *Bantu Prophets in South Africa.* London: Lutterworth Press (2nd ed. 1961, London: Oxford Universtiy Press).

Suri, Ellison
1976 Music in Pacific Island Worship with Special Reference to the Anglican Church in Lau Malaita Solomon Islands. Unpublished B.D. thesis, Pacific Theological College, Suva, Fiji.

Swadling, Pamela
1981 *Papua New Guinea's Prehistory: An Introduction.* Port Moresby: National Museum and Art Gallery.

Swan, K. J.
1958 Early Australasian Contact with the New Hebrides. Unpublished M.A. thesis, University of Sydney.

Swindler, Doris R.
1968 "Problems of Melanesian Racial History." In Andrew P. Vayda (ed.), *Peoples and Cultures of the Pacific,* pp. 27-44. New York: Natural History Press.

Taber, Charles R.
1978 "The Limits of Indigenization in Theology." *Missiology* 6: 53-79.

Tavoa, Michael H.
1977 Towards Melanesian Theology with Special Reference to Belief in Spirit in Islands of North Pentecost. B.D. thesis, Pacific Theological College, Suva, Fiji.

Taylor, Brian
1974 Towards a Sociology of Religious Conversion: A Critique and Some Proposals. Paper presented at the University of Aberdeen Sociology of Religion Conference, February 15-16, 1974.

Taylor, John V.
1958 *The Growth of the Church in Buganda: An Attempt at Understanding.* London: SCM Press.

Taylor, John V., and Dorothea A. Lehmann
1961 *Christians of the Copperbelt: The Growth of the Church in Northern Rhodesia.* London: SCM Press.

Teggart, Frederick J.
1925 *Theory of History.* New Haven: Yale University Press.

Thomas, Richard M.
1964 The Mission Indians: A Study of Leadership and Cultural Change. Unpublished Ed.D. dissertation, University of California, Los Angeles.

Thomas, William L.
1968 "The Pacific Basin: An Introduction." In Andrew P. Vayda (ed.), *Peoples and Cultures of the Pacific,* pp. 3-26. New York: Natural History Press.

Thompson, Roger C.
1971 "Commerce, Chrisianity and Colonialism: The Australian New Hebrides Company 1883-1897." *The Journal of Pacific History* 6: 25-38.

Threlfall, Neville
1975 *One Hundred Years in the Islands: The Methodist/United Church in the New Guinea Islands Region 1875-1975.* Rabaul: Toksave na Buk Dipatmen.

Thrupp, Sylvia L. (ed.)
1970 *Millennial Dreams in Action: Studies in Revolutionary Religious Movements.* New York: Schocken Books.

Thurnwald, Richard
1935 *Black and White in East Africa.* London: Routledge.

Tiffany, Sharon
1978 "Introduction: Indigenous Response." In James Boutilier, et al. (eds.), *Mission, Church, and Sect in Oceania*, pp. 301-305. Ann Arbor: University of Michigan Press.

Tillich, Paul
1959 *Theology of Culture.* New York: Oxford University Press.

Tippett, Alan R.
1954 "The Nature and Social Function of Fijian War." *Transactions and Proceedings of the Fijian Society* 5 (4): 137-155.
1956 The Nineteenth Century Labour Trade in the South West Pacific: A Study of Slavery and Indenture as the Origin of Present-Day Racial Problems. Unpublished M.A. thesis, American University, Washington, D.C.
1967 *Solomon Islands Christianity: A Study in Growth and Obstruction.* London: Lutterworth.
1968 *Fijian Material Culture: A Study of Culture Context, Function and Change.* Honolulu: Bishop Museum Bulletin No. 232.
1971 *People Movements in Southern Polynesia.* Chicago: Moody Press.
1973a *Aspects of Pacific Ethnohistory.* South Pasadena: William Carey Library.
1973b "The Phenomenology of Worship, Conversion and Brotherhood: An Anthropologist's Point of View." In Walter Houston Clark, et. al. (eds.), *Religious Experience: Its Nature and Function in the Human Psyche,* pp. 92-109. Springfield, IL: Charles Thomas Publisher.

1973c The Structure and Analysis of an Event: An Exercise in Ethnohistorical Reconstruction. Pasadena: School of World Mission, Fuller Theological Seminary (mimeograph).

1973d *Verdict Theology in Missionary Theory.* South Pasadena: William Carey Library.

1975a "Christopaganism or Indigenous Christianity." In T. Yamamori and C. Taber (eds.), *Christopaganism or Indigenous Christianity,* pp. 13-34. South Pasadena: William Carey Library.

1975b "Formal Transformation and Faith Distortion." In T. Yamamori and C. Taber (eds.), *Christopaganism or Indigenous Christianity,* pp. 97-118.

1975c "The Meaning of Meaning." In T. Yamamori and C. Taber (eds.), *Christopaganism or Indigenous Christianity,* pp. 169-195.

1976 The Phenomenology of Cross-Cultural Conversion in Oceania. (Collection of "Research in Progress Pamphlets," essays written from 1967 to 1976.) Pasadena: School of World Mission, Fuller Theological Seminary (mimeograph).

1977 The Ways of the People: Reader in Anthropology, Selections from the writings of Christian Missionaries. Unpublished manuscript. Pasadena: School of World Mission, Fuller Theological Seminary.

n.d.a. Functional Substitutes in Fijian Christianity. Unpublished manuscript. Pasadena: School of World Mission, Fuller Theological Seminary.

n.d.b. Patterns of Religious Change in Communal Society. Unpublished manuscript. Pasadena: School of World Mission, Fuller Theological Seminary.

n.d.c. Contemporary Departures from Traditional Christianity in Cross-Cultural Situations. Paper presented to the Religious Research Association Symposium on "The Impact of Non-Traditional Forms of Religiosity on Religious Organizations."

Trompf, G. F., C. E. Loeliger and J. Kadiba (eds.)

1980 *Religion in Melanesia.* Part A and B. Port Moresby: The University of Papua New Guinea.

Tryon, Darrell T.

1972 *The Languages of the New Hebrides: A Checklist and General Survey.* Pacific Linguistics, Series A No. 35. Papers in Linguistics of Melanesia No. 3: 43-84.

Tucker, H. W.

1872 *Under His Banner: Papers on the Missionary Work of Modern Times.* London: SPCK.

1879 *Memoir of the Life and Episcopate of George Augustus Selwyn, D.D.: Bishop of New Zealand, 1841-1869, Bishop of Lichfield, 1867-1878.* 2 vols. London: William Wells Gardner.

Turner, H. W.

1967 *African Independent Church.* Vol. I — History of an African Independent Church, the Church of the Lord (Aladura). Vol. II — The Life and Faith of the Church of the Lord (Aladura). Oxford: Clarendon Press.

1981 "Religious Movements in Primal (or Tribal) Societies." *Mission Focus* 9: 45-55.

Tuza, Esau

1970 Towards Indigenization of Christian Worship in the Western Solomons. Unpublished B.D. thesis, Pacific Theological College, Suva, Fiji.

Tylor, Edward B.

1865 *Researches into the Early History of Mankind and the Development of Civilization.* London.

1871 *Primitive Culture: Researches in the Development of Mythology, Religion, Language, Art and Customs.* 2 vols. Boston: Estes and Lauriat.

Ubanowicz, Charles

1972 Tonga Culture: The Methodology of an Ethnohistoric Reconstruction. Unpublished Ph.D. dissertation, University of Oregon, Eugene.

United Nations

1953 *Report of United Nations Visiting Mission to Trust Territories in the Pacific, Reports on New Guinea.* 12th Session. New York.

Uthwatt, W. A.

1910-1911 "The Melanesian Mission in the Solomons." *Australian Church Quarterly Review* 1: 234-243.

Valentine, Charles A.

1958 Introduction to the History of Changing Ways of Life on the Island of New Britain. Unpublished Ph.D. dissertation, University of Pennsylvania, Philadelphia.

1960 "Uses of Ethnohistory in an Acculturation Study." *Ethnohistory* 7: 1-27.

1970 (Orig. 1963) "Social Status, Political Power, and Native Response to European Influence in Oceania." *Anthropological Forum* 1: 3-55. Reprinted in T. Harding and B. Wallace (eds.), *Cultures of the Pacific*, pp. 337-384. New York: The Free Press.

Van Akkern, Philip

1970 *Sri and Christ: Indigenous Church in East Java.* London: Lutterworth.

Van Dusen, Henry P.

1945 *They Found the Church There: The Armed Forces Discover Christian Missions.* New York: Charles Scribner's Sons.

Van Gennep, Arnold

1960 *The Rites of Passage.* Chicago: The University of Chicago Press.

Vayda, Andrew P. (ed.)

1968 *Peoples and Cultures of the Pacific.* Garden City, NY: The Natural History Press.

Visser't Hooft, W. A.

1967 "Accomodation — True and False." *South East Asia Journal of Theology* 8 (3): 5-18.

Voegelin, C. F. and F. M. Voegelin

1977 *Classification and Index of the World's Languages.* New York: Elsevier.

Von Allmen, Daniel

1975 "The Birth of Theology." *International Review of Missions* 64 (253): 37-52.

Waddy, P. Stacy

1903 *Visit to Norfolk Island.* Newcastle: Federal Printing and Bookbinding Works.

Wagner, Gunter

1936 "The Study of Culture Contact and the Determination of Policy." *Africa* 9: 317-331.

Waite, Deborah B.

1969 Solomon Islands Sculpture. Unpublished Ph.D. dissertation, Columbia University, New York.

Wallace, Alfred R.

1869 *The Maylay Archipelago* 2 vols. London: Macmillan.

Wallace, Anthony F. C.

1956 "Revitalization Movements." *American Anthropologist* 58: 264-281.

1961 *Culture and Personality.* New York: Random House.

1969 *Death and Rebirth of the Seneca.* New York: Knopf.

Wallis, Wilson D.

1943 *Messiahs: The Role in Civilization.* Washington: American Council on Public Affairs.

Wand, J. W. C.

1948 *The Anglican Communion.* New York: Morehouse-Gorham.

1961 *Anglicanism in History and Today.* London: Weidenfield and Nicolson.

Ward, Marion W. (ed.)

1970 *The Politics of Melanesia.* Fourth Waigani Seminar. Canberra: The Research School of Pacific Studies, Australian National University.

Waterman, T. T.

1927 "The Architecture of the American Indians." *American Anthropologist* 29: 210-230.

Watson, James B.

1965 "From Hunting to Horticulture in the New Guinea Highlands." *Ethnology* 4: 295-309.

Watt, Agnes C. P.

1896 *Twenty-five Years' Mission Life on Tanna.* London.

Watters, R. F.

1960 "Cargo Cults and Social Change in Melanesia." *Pacific Viewpoint* 1: 104-107.

Wawn, William T.

1973 (Orig. 1893) *The South Sea Islanders and the Queensland Labour Trade.* Edited with an Introduction by Peter Corris. Pacific History Series No. 5. Canberra: Australian National University Press.

Welbourn, F. B.

1961 *East African Rebels: A Study of Some Independent Churches.* London: SCM Press.

1971 "Missionary Stimulus and African Responses." In Victor Turner (ed.), *Colonialism in Africa.* Cambridge: Cambridge University Press.

Welbourn, F. B. and B. A. Ogot

1966 *A Place to Feel at Home: A Study of Two Independent Churches in Western Kenya.* London: Oxford University Press.

Welchman, Henry

1889-1908 Missionary Life in the Melanesian Islands. Diaries, 12 vols. London: Melanesian Mission. (Also on microfilm, A.J.C.P. M728, 805, 806, National Library of Australia, Canberra.)

Westermann, Diedrich

1934 *The African Today.* London: Oxford University Press.

1937 *Africa and Christianity.* London: Oxford University Press.

Westermarch, E. A.

1906-1908 *The Origin of Moral Ideas.* 2 vols. London: Macmillan.

Western Pacific High Commission, Inwards Correspondence (WPHC,IC). (Files located in the Western Pacific Archives, Suva, Fiji.)

1930 F. Ashley to M. Fletcher, 29 October. WPHC,IC 3561/1930.

1932 Malaita District Report 1931. WPHC,IC 1214/1932.

1932 J. Barley to M. Fletcher, 9 December. WPHC,IC 2594/1931.

1940 Sir Harry Luke to C.O., 27 November 1939. WPHC,IC 2195/1940.

Whisson, Michael G. and Martin West (eds.)

1975 *Religion and Social Change in Southern Africa: Anthropological Essays in Honour of Monica Wilson.* Cape Town: David Philip.

White, Geoffrey M.

1978 Big Men and Church Men: Social Images in Santa Isabel, Solomon Islands. Unpublished Ph.D. dissertation, University of California, San Diego.

1979 "War, Peace, and Piety in Santa Isabel, Solomon Islands." In Margaret Rodman and Matthew Cooper (eds.), *The Pacification of Melanesia,* pp. 109-139. Ann Arbor: University of Michigan Press.

White, J. Peter

1971 "New Guinea: The First Phase in Oceanic Settlement." In R. Green and M. Kelly (eds.), *Studies in Oceanic Culture History,* Vol. 2, pp. 45-52. Honolulu: Bishop Museum, Pacific Anthropological Records No. 12.

Whiteman, Darrell L.

1974 "The Christian Mission and Culture Change in New Guinea." *Missiology* 2: 17-33.

1975 "Marching Rule Reconsidered: An Ethnohistorical Evaluation." *Ethnohistory* 22: 345-374.

1976 Agents of Change and Schismogenesis: The Courtesy of Culture Contact. Paper presented at the Annual Meeting of the Southwestern Anthropological Association, April 15, 1976, San Francisco.

1977 Missionaries and Socio-religious Change: An Analysis of the Melanesian Mission in the Solomon Islands, 1849-1974. Paper presented at the 75th Annual Meeting of the American Anthropological Association, December 1977, Houston.

1979 Communication of the Gospel Amidst Cultural Diversity: An Anthropological Perspective on Christian Missions. Paper presented at the 16th Graduate Student Theological Seminar, September 15, 1979, Winona Lake, Indiana.

1981a "From Foreign Mission to Independent Church: The Anglicans in the Solomon Islands." *Catalyst* 11: 73-91.

1981b "Some Relevant Anthropological Concepts for Effective Cross-Cultural Ministry." *Missiology* 9:223-239.

1982 "Development without Destruction: The Case of Holokama Plantation on Santa Isabel Solomon Islands." *Catalyst* 12: 15-36.

Whiteman, Darrell L. and Gary F. Simons

1978 *The Languages of Santa Isabel: A Sociolinguistic Survey.* (In press.)

Whorf, Benjamin Lee

1956 *Language, Thought and Reality: Selected Writings of Benjamin Lee Whorf.* Edited and with an introduction by John B. Carroll. New York: The Technology Press of MIT and John Wiley and Sons.

Widjaja, Albert

1973 "Beggarly Theology: A Search for a Perspective Toward Indigenous Theology." *South East Asia Journal of Theology* 14 (2): 39-45.

Williams, F. E.

1935 *The Blending of Cultures: An Essay on the Aims of Native Education.* Territory of Papua, Anthropological Reports No. 16.

Williams, H. W.

1935 "The Reaction of the Maori to the Impact of Civilization." *Journal of the Polynesian Society* 44: 216-243.

Williams, Ronald G.

1972 *The United Church in Papua New Guinea and the Solomon Islands: The Story of the Development of an Indigenous Church on the Occasion of the Centenary of the LMS in Papua 1872-1972.* Rabaul: Trinity Press.

Williams, Thomas

1858 *Fiji and the Fijians, Vol. I: The Islands and Their Inhabitants.* London: Alexander Heylin.

Williamson, Robert W.

1914 *The Ways of the South Sea Savage.* London: Seeley, Service and Company.

Williamson, Sidney George

1965 *Akan Religion and the Christian Faith.* Accra: Ghana Universities Press.

Wilson, Cecil

1900-1909 Extracts from Letters to His Wife, 1900, 1903, 1904, 1909. In the possession of Rev. John C. J. Wilson, Otane, New Zealand (typescript).

n.d. (1904) *Women of Melanesia.* Melanesian Mission. Reprinted from *Southern Cross Log*, October 1904, pp. 6-10.
1932 *The Wake of the Southern Cross.* London: John Murray.

Wilson, Ellen
1915 *The Isles that Wait: By a Member of the Melanesian Mission.* London: SPCK.
1935 *Dr. Welchman of Bugotu.* London: SPCK.
1936 "Healing the Sick." In Stuart Artless (ed.), *The Church in Melanesia,* pp. 63-73. London: Melanesian Mission.

Wilson, Monica
1971 *Religion and the Transformation of Society: A Study in Social Change in Africa.* Cambridge: Cambridge University Press.

Winter, Ralph D. and Steven C. Hawthorne (eds.)
1981 *Perspectives on the World Christian Movement.* Pasadena: William Carey Library.

Wissler, Clark
1914 "The Influence of the Horse in the Development of Plains Culture." *American Anthropologist* 16: 1-25.
1917 *The American Indian.* New York: Oxford University Press.
1923 *Man and Culture.* New York: Crowell.

Woodford, Charles M.
1888 "Exploration of the Solomon Islands." *Proceedings of the Royal Geographic Society* 10: 351-376.
1890a *A Naturalist Among the Head-Hunters: Being an Account of Three Visits to the Solomon Islands: 1886, 1887, 1888.* London: George Philip and Son.
1890b "Further Exploration of the Solomon Islands." *Proceedings of the Royal Geographic Society* 12: 393-418.
1908 "Notes on the Manufacture of the Malaita Shell Bead Money of the Solomon Group." *Man* 8: 81-84.
1909 "The Canoes of the British Solomon Islands Protectorate." *Journal of the Royal Anthropolgical Institute* 39: 506-516.

Worsley, Peter
1957 *The Trumpet Shall Sound: A Study of "Cargo" Cults in Melanesia.* London: MacGibbon and Kee. (2nd ed. 1968, New York: Shocken Books.)

Wright, Cliff (compiler)
1978 *Melanesian Culture and Christian Faith.* Honiara: Solomon Islands Christian Association.
1979 *New Hebridean Culture and Christian Faith: Two Heads and Two Hearts.* Vila: Pacific Churches Research Centre.

Wurm, S. A.

1967 "Linguistics and the Pre-history of the South-western Pacific." *The Journal of Pacific History* 2: 25-38.

1970 "Austronesian and the Vocabulary of Languages of the Reef and Santa Cruz Islands: A Preliminary Approach." In S. A. Wurm and Laycock (eds.), *Pacific Linguistic Studies in Honor of Arthur Capell*, pp. 468-553. Pacific Linguistics, Series C, No. 13.

1971 "A Thousand Languages." In Peter Hastings (ed.), *Papua New Guinea: Prospero's Other Island.* Sydney: Angus and Robertson.

Yamamori, T. and C. Taber (eds.)

1975 *Christopaganism or Indigenous Christianity?* South Pasadena: William Carey Library.

Yen, Douglas E.

1963 "Sweet Potato Variation and Its Relation to Human Migration in the Pacific." In J. Barrau (ed.), *Plants and Migration of Pacific Peoples.* Honolulu: Bishop Museum Press.

1971 "The Development of Agriculture in Oceania." In R. Green and M. Kelly (eds.), *Studies in Oceanic Culture History,* Vol. 2, pp. 1-12. Honolulu: Bishop Museum, Pacific Anthropological Records No. 12.

1973 "The Ethnobotany of the Voyages of Mendana and Quiros in the Pacific." *World Archaeology* 5: 32-43.

1974 *The Sweet Potato and Oceania: An Essay in Ethnobotany.* Bishop Museum Bulletin No. 236. Honolulu: Bishop Museum Press.

Yonge, C. M.

1872 *In Memoriam John Coleridge Patteson.* London: James Parker and Company.

1874 *Life of John Coleridge Patteson: Missionary Bishop of the Melanesian Islands.* 2 vols. London: Macmillan.

Young, Florence S. H.

n.d. (1925) *Pearls from the Pacific.* London: Marshall Brothers, Ltd.

Young, Hugh

1977 "The Living Legend." *The Solomons News Drum,* July 1, 1977, p. 3. Honiara.

Zeleneitz, Martin

1979 "The End of Headhunting in New Georgia." In M. Rodman and M. Cooper (eds.), *The Pacification of Melanesia,* pp. 91-108. Ann Arbor: University of Michigan Press.

Index